PIETER DE HOOCH

PETER C. SUTTON

PIETER
DE HOOCH

Complete Edition
with a catalogue raisonné

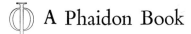 A Phaidon Book

 CORNELL UNIVERSITY PRESS
ITHACA, NEW YORK

© 1980 by Phaidon Press Limited, Oxford

First published 1980 by Cornell University Press.

International Standard Book Number 0–8014–1339–7
Library of Congress Catalog Card Number 80–7667

Printed in Great Britain
Text printed by Aberdeen University Press
Monochrome plates printed at The University Press, Oxford
Colour plates printed by Charles Woodward Ltd, Devizes

Contents

Acknowledgements

The publishers are grateful to all museums, institutions and private collectors who have given permission for the works of art in their possession to be reproduced.

The following plates are reproduced by gracious permission of Her Majesty Queen Elizabeth II: Plates VI, 39, 80.

The Royal Bank of Scotland as trustees of a family settlement have generously given permission for the reproduction of Plate VIII.

Photographs have been kindly supplied by the following: A.C.L. (Brussels): Plates 97, 189; Archives Photographiques (Paris): Plate 41; Derek Balmer (Bristol): Plate 95; Bullaty Lomeo Photographers (New York): Plate 28; A. C. Cooper Ltd (London): Plates 100, 133, 148, 166, 167, 186; Dienst Verspreide Rijkskollekties (The Hague): Plate 187, Fig. 63; A. Dingjan (The Hague): Plates 26, 35, 37, 154, Figs. 5, 10; Lily Eijsten (Amsterdam): Fig. 2; Gabinetto Fotografico Nazionale (Rome): Plate 184; Giraudon (Paris): Plate 146; Jaap Hiller Fotografie (Haarlem): Plate 3; Ralph Kleintempel (Hamburg): Plate 87, Fig. 40; Landesbildstelle Rheinland (Düsseldorf): Plate 51; Sydney W. Newbery (London): Plates 24, 25, 99; Rheinisches Bildarchiv (Cologne): Plates 125, 176.

Preface

Pieter de Hooch's fame rests today primarily on the series of superbly tranquil interior and courtyard scenes which he began in the late 1650s. Peopled by only a few middle class figures, these works depict quiet episodes from everyday life. Orderly space predominates and the effects of light and atmosphere are acutely observed. As the author of these pictures, De Hooch has come to be regarded, along with his contemporary, Johannes Vermeer, as one of the outstanding artists who were active in Delft in the mid-seventeenth century.

The purpose of the present text is to discuss De Hooch's works and the formation and changes of his style, and to assess the significance of his pictorial achievement. An effort has been made to characterize his relation and contribution to the art and ideals of his age. The plates illustrating his paintings are arranged roughly chronologically in order to provide an overview of the stylistic vicissitudes of his art. Readers with more specialized interests in questions of attribution, chronology, and documentation are directed to the catalogue. All the accepted works as well as borderline pictures, rejected works, and paintings for which no visual records are known, are discussed or listed there. A list of documents pertaining to the artist's life, a complete bibliography, and a concordance complete the volume.

In undertaking such a study one invariably owes a great debt to writers who have gone before. Fifty years have passed since the appearance of W. R. Valentiner's insightful and sensitively written monograph, the last major study of De Hooch's art. Serious examination of the artist's work had begun about one century earlier with the publication of J. Smith's *catalogue raisonné* (1833 & 1842). Much of the little that is known of De Hooch's life emerged in the last quarter of the nineteenth century through the archival work of H. Havard (1877), F. D. O. Obreen (1877), A. Bredius (1881a–b & 1889), and P. Haverkorn van Rijsewijk (1880 & 1892). Appearing in 1907, Hofstede de Groot's invaluable *catalogue raisonné* sought to unravel the duplications and false attributions of Smith's catalogue and to list all of the artist's existing and recorded works. Five larger studies of De Hooch have appeared in this century; those of A. de Rudder (1913), C. E. Collins Baker (1925), C. Brière-Misme (1927), Valentiner, and F. van Thienen (1945). Students of the literature will recognize that the present author is not in agreement with many of the views expressed by earlier writers. Nonetheless, the debt owed to them is considerable.

A more personal debt is owed to the many private collectors, museum curators, and dealers who graciously received me, extended every courtesy in the interest of my research, and generously granted permission to illustrate works in their possession or charge. Heartfelt thanks for assistance in archival investigations are extended to P. J. M. de Baar, S. A. C. Dudok van Heel, H. W. van Leeuwen, J. M. Montias, and R. A. D. Renting. The staffs of the Rijksbureau voor Kunsthistorische Documentatie in The Hague, the Witt Library in London, and the Frick Art Reference Library in New York were tireless in aiding my research. The technical departments of the National Gallery in London, the National Gallery in Washington, the Rijksmuseum in Amsterdam, and the Germanisches Museum in Nuremberg have provided insights into De Hooch's working methods. Well considered advice on iconographic topics was offered by E. de Jongh and J. Becker.

The present monograph was based on a dissertation presented to the faculty of Yale University in 1978. A number of informed readers, including Albert Blankert, Christopher Brown, James Burke, Walter Liedtke, J. M. Montias, Otto Naumann, Eric Jan Sluyter, Charles Talbot, and Arthur Wheelock read the dissertation and offered discerning suggestions for revisions. Many of these appear in the present text. Mary

Jane Pagan and her associates typed the final manuscript with admirable fastidiousness. For moral support Mary Lynn Riesmeyer and Francis and Jacqueline Sutton are gratefully acknowledged.

A special debt of gratitude is owed to the Board of Trustees of the National Gallery in Washington, without whose support in the form of a David E. Finley Fellowship (1976–9) the completion of this project would have been immeasurably more difficult. Keith Roberts (who unfortunately passed away before the book's publication), Dr. I. Grafe and Simon Haviland of the Phaidon Press are acknowledged for their various contributions to the realization of this work.

Lastly, for his patience in the supervision of the dissertation and his keen interest in the project at all stages, this book is dedicated to my friend and teacher, Egbert Haverkamp Begemann.

The Life of the Artist

Despite new discoveries, knowledge of Pieter de Hooch's life remains scanty.[1] No mention of the artist appeared in seventeenth-century literature and, apart from an occasional signature on notarial documents, his only personal legacy was his art. From the scattered archival references a skeletal biography may be fashioned.

De Hooch was baptized in the Reformed Church in Rotterdam on 20 December 1629 (Doc. 4). His father, Hendrick Hendricksz. de Hooch, was a master bricklayer, and his mother, Annetge Pieters, was a midwife.[2] Nothing is known of his youth. Writing in 1721, Houbraken was the first author to mention the artist, but referred to him only, in passing, as a pupil of the Haarlem painter Nicolaes Berchem at the same time as Jacob Ochtervelt.[3] Presumably this period of study took place in Haarlem some time prior to De Hooch's first appearance as a resident of Delft in August 1652 (Doc. 14). By this date he had established contact with the Delft painter Hendrick van der Burch.[4] In the following year he was recorded as a painter and servant (dienaar) to a linen merchant named Justus de la Grange (Doc. 15). This was probably a commercial arrangement whereby the artist agreed to hand over all or part of his production in return for his keep or other benefits. Such agreements were not uncommon during the period; Berchem and Emanuel de Witte worked for periods under similar arrangements.[5] An inventory of paintings owned by the merchant in 1655 (Doc. 23) included eleven undescribed paintings by De Hooch, supporting the presumption of such a relationship. Although De la Grange was the heir to a considerable inheritance, he seems to have been perennially debt-ridden.[6] Whether his financial irresponsibility hastened the end of his association with the painter is unknown. At any rate, there is no proof De Hooch ever resided with him and their relationship appears to have been short-lived. In 1653, the year of the painter's documented contact with the merchant, De Hooch and his future wife appeared in Leiden at the baptism of the first child of Barent Gast, a silversmith and the brother-in-law of Hendrick van der Burch (Doc. 17).[7]

The following year De Hooch was recorded as living on the Lombertstraat in Rotterdam, no doubt in his father's house (see Docs. 12–13), when he was betrothed to Jannetge van der Burch, then living on the Binnenwatersloot in Delft (Docs. 18 & 19). With no basis in fact, many writers have assumed that Jannetge was the daughter of the faiencer Hendrick Beuckelsz. van der Burch.[8] Although her baptismal record has not been found, it is far more likely that she was the daughter of Rochus Hendricksz. van der Burch, a candlemaker and the father of the painter Hendrick van der Burch.[9] Rochus owned a house on the Binnenwatersloot, and Hendrick and various members of the Van der Burch family are repeatedly linked with Jannetge and De Hooch through various baptismal records.[10] De Hooch and Van der Burch signed three documents together in Delft in 1652, 1654 and 1655 (Docs. 14, 20 & 24)[11] and De Hooch travelled to Leiden in 1656 to witness the baptism of the latter's first child (Doc. 28).

On 20 September 1655 De Hooch was inscribed in the Delft guild (Doc. 25). At this time he paid only three of the twelve guilders required as an entrance fee for artists born outside the city. The practice was not unusual; two years earlier Johannes Vermeer had at first paid only part of his entrance fee. De Hooch subsequently made two additional payments against his debt (Docs. 27 & 30), but the 2 fl 17 st which remained outstanding in 1657 were never paid. Several explanations for this unsettled debt are possible: the guild may have grown lax in the enforcement of its laws (we note that Carel Fabritius evidently painted 'illegally' in the city for at least two years before joining the guild); De Hooch may simply have been careless about his finances; or even this modest sum may have been beyond the artist's ability to pay.

While no documentary references to the artist are known from 1657 to 1661, when he first appeared in Amsterdam at the baptism of his daughter Diewertje (Doc. 36),[12] De Hooch's earliest dated pictures are of 1658. Among the six works bearing this date are two courtyards (Cat. 35 & 36) with motifs derived from Delft monuments. The exact date of the painter's move to Amsterdam is unknown. MacLaren observed that a courtyard scene in London dated 166[?] (Cat. 44) seems to represent a section of the old Town Wall in Delft, suggesting that De Hooch remained in Delft until at least 1660.[13] However, he probably left the city by May of that year when his wife attended the baptism of Van der Burch's son in the Westerkerk in Amsterdam (Doc. 33). In 1663 De Hooch again appeared in Delft (Doc. 39), presumably only as a visitor, and could conceivably have executed the painting now in London at that time. In any event, the burial records of the artists' children who died in 1663 and 1665 state that he was living in Amsterdam on the Regulierspad and Engelspad respectively. These 'paths' were located outside the old walls of the city and the dwellings there housed some of the most impoverished residents of Amsterdam. It is probable, therefore, that De Hooch lived in very modest circumstances when he first came to the city.

By May 1668 the artist evidently had moved to the Konijnenstraat near the Lauriergracht where he remained for at least the next two years (Docs. 46 & 47).[14] This change of address may signal a slight improvement in his financial situation. The majority of his patrons in Amsterdam seem to have been middle and upper middle class merchants.[15] We know, furthermore, that around 1670 De Hooch was commissioned to paint the portrait of the prosperous Jacott-Hoppesack family of Amsterdam (Cat. 92). Nevertheless, there is no record of his ever having owned a house in the Konijnenstraat or elsewhere and he remained poor enough to escape the tax registers of 1674.

In 1670 De Hooch testified twice in the law suit brought by Adriana van Heusden, the widow of the Amsterdam notary Joris de Wijs, against the painter Emanuel de Witte.[16] Two years later the last of the artist's seven children was baptized. From this point until his death twelve years later we have no documentary information about him. This final hiatus is particularly unfortunate in the light of what we now know about his death. He was buried in the Sint Anthonis Kerkhof in Amsterdam on 24 March 1684 coming from the 'Dolhuys' (bedlam) (Doc. 50). The date and circumstances of his entry into the insane asylum are unknown. All we may safely surmise is that De Hooch's family were not in the financial position to spare the artist his grim final surroundings.[17]

Briefly recapitulated, the archival data indicate that De Hooch was born in Rotterdam in 1629, had moved to Delft by 1652, was employed by a linen merchant and joined the guild in Delft in September 1655. Contact with the painter Hendrick van der Burch was established in these years and after settling in Amsterdam in 1660–1 De Hooch is known to have encountered works by De Witte. He evidently remained a resident of Amsterdam until his death in the madhouse in 1684. Throughout his life De Hooch seems to have been relatively poor.

The Early Years

In tracing De Hooch's early career we are hampered by several factors. Although most of his paintings are signed, none are dated, or datable, before 1658. Furthermore, as with many young painters whose personal styles are still in the process of formation, De Hooch's early works can easily be confused with those of other artists who painted in related manners. Long unrecognized, De Hooch's youthful production only began to be identified around the turn of this century, principally through the efforts of W. Bode.[1] In the initial excitement of the rediscovery, the authentic oeuvre was obscured by erroneous attributions. Although borderline pictures remain, several falsely assigned works can now be removed from the oeuvre and a few newly discovered paintings added, with the result that the true artist emerges more clearly.

De la Grange's inventory (Doc. 23) proves that De Hooch had begun his artistic activity by 1655 and he was described as a painter as early as 1653 (Doc. 15). Moreover, it seems safe to presume that an artist who was twenty years old in 1649–50 would have tried his hand at painting by the late 1640s. Ordinarily a trustworthy reporter of such matters, Houbraken informs us that De Hooch studied alongside his fellow Rotterdamer, Jacob Ochtervelt (1634–82), under the tuition of the Haarlem landscapist Nicolaes Berchem (1620–83). Although this period of study cannot be precisely dated, it probably occurred in Haarlem in the latter half of the 1640s. Berchem had entered the Haarlem guild in 1642, and reappeared in the city in 1646, 1649, and 1657.[2] The late 1640s were a period of rapid change in his art, which culminated around 1649 in the realization of his mature Italianate manner (see Fig. 1). While comparable sunny, bucolic scenes appear among Ochtervelt's earliest paintings,[3] virtually nothing in De Hooch's youthful production suggests contact with Berchem. The works which have been attributed to De Hooch and cited as evidence of Berchem's influence cannot be accepted (see Cat. D 33–4, Plate 187). We should not, however, reject Houbraken's statement out of hand; its very unlikeliness lends it a certain plausibility. Furthermore, comments offered by Descamps in 1753[4] and listings in eighteenth-century sales catalogues (Cat. C 255–7)[5] suggest unidentified paintings might still prove that De Hooch began his career as a painter of Italianate landscapes. It also should be borne in mind that while all Dutch artists learned the practical skills from their teachers, few (Rembrandt's students excepted) remained stylistically dependent long after the conclusion of their training. Indeed, Ochtervelt is a case in point.

In place of landscapes, the majority of De Hooch's earliest known works represent tavern and stable scenes peopled by peasants and soldiers (see Cat. 2, 4–14, Plates 2, 4–12, 14, Col. Plate I). Unlike in his later and better known paintings, the figures in these pictures tend to dominate their shadowed and only summarily defined surroundings. A restricted palette is employed and the youthful painter's touch is broad and liquid. Strong chiaroscuro effects appear in some scenes, while elsewhere a milder light gently dispels the darkness. Although their sources are varied, many of the early works naturally reflect influences the painter would have encountered in his youth in Rotterdam and Delft.

Rotterdam, the city of De Hooch's birth, was of only limited importance as an artistic centre in seventeenth-century Holland. It, nevertheless, supported a small community of artists whose works may have first attracted him to the profession. The city's proximity to Flanders, and particularly to Antwerp, often was reflected in her painters' work and was especially significant for artists specializing in low-life genre. The boisterous peasant scenes of Cornelis Saftleven (1607–81), Pieter de Bloot (1601–58), H. M. Sorgh (1611–70), and his pupil A. Diepraem (1622–70) clearly are indebted to the Flemish painters Adriaen Brouwer and David Teniers the Younger.

Not surprisingly, De Hooch's early scene of a *Merry Drinker* and his rather boorish companions (Cat. 4, Col. Plate I) seems to owe more to Flemish than to Dutch sources. When Bode first published it he correctly observed that its composition and figure types were derived from Brouwer's pictures.[6] The jocular fellow with raised glass is a first cousin to the Flemish artist's coarser drinkers and, as Bode observed, the bearded man recalls counterparts in the paintings of Brouwer's follower, David Ryckaert III. While De Hooch could have absorbed Brouwer's legacy in Haarlem, where the Flemish artist had worked and De Hooch presumably studied, it seems more probable that he learned these lessons in Rotterdam. The design and execution of De Hooch's *Merry Drinker*, in fact, bear a close resemblance to H. M. Sorgh's approximately contemporaneous translations of the Flemish tavern scene type. As in the latter's *Two Smokers* (Fig. 2), the figures are seated in the light and grouped around a crude table, which a partition separates from the shadowed space in the distance. A similar technique is employed, which rises to an impasto in the execution of the figures while leaving the remainder of the scene thinly brushed in translucent greys and browns. Connections such as these raise the possibility that De Hooch could have spent an initial, although undocumented, period of study in his native city.

The artist's early paintings of bivouacking soldiers, eight of which bear his signature, align themselves with a different tradition. During the long war with Spain the pervasive presence of the military provided the artists of the Lowlands with ample opportunities to observe the life of soldiers. Some painters, like Sebastian Vrancx and Philips Wouwerman, chose to depict battles and plundering, while others turned to the easeful interludes of war. In the 1630s and 40s guardroom scenes became a specialized category of painting in Holland. The principal practitioners of this genre were Pieter Codde, Willem Duyster, and Simon Kick in Amsterdam, Jacob Duck in Utrecht and The Hague, and Anthonie Palamedesz in Delft. Action was usually minimized in their works and themes simple: soldiers playing cards or tric-trac, or merely smoking and drinking. The only contests were played out over the gaming board or between the sexes.

De Hooch's early soldier paintings treat many of the same themes. In the stable interior in Cologne (Cat. 11, Plate 9A), an officer flirts with a serving woman while a card game unfolds; and in the related picture in the Borghese Gallery (Cat. 10, Plate 8) quartering soldiers relax with clay pipes and tankards as they listen to a fluteplayer. Both works employ dark horizontal designs of a type encountered in earlier guardroom scenes. Yet, while the previous generation had often employed diffuse compositions of numerous figures De Hooch focuses upon a few brightly illuminated figures in the foreground. Even in such early works he already exhibits a special fascination with the effects of light. From the outset of his career, De Hooch displayed a subtle command of the adjustments of tonal values and a taste for silhouette and vivid local colouration. The dominant browns and tans of his shadows are accompanied in the lighted passages by white, reddish-orange, yellow, and an occasional blue and green.

In a stable scene in Leningrad (Cat. 6, Plate 5) a soldier doffs his hat as he offers a glass of wine to a rather demure young peasant woman. The design resembles that of a painting in Zurich (Cat. 7, Plate 6), where carousing soldiers drink up as a trumpeter sounds the call for their departure. The figures in these early works often appear independently conceived and do not always fully relate to one another. Slender in proportion, the soldiers and hostesses have rather narrow faces, long noses, and slightly pinched extremities. Their movements frequently are abrupt and angular; arms are extended to hold glasses aloft, or cocked and jauntily placed akimbo (see Cat. 8, 12–13, Plates 7, 11–12). In comparison to his later works, De Hooch's early paintings reveal a greater concern for anecdotal narration and correspondingly less interest in the expressive use of space. Yet details like the view to a distant doorway in the painting in Zurich already anticipate aspects of his later designs.

De Hooch's interest in guardroom themes may have initially been stimulated by the versatile Rotterdam painter Ludolf de Jongh (1616–76).[7] Thirteen years De Hooch's senior, De Jongh distinguished himself as a painter of portraits, historical subjects, and hunting and genre scenes. His activity in the last field is still little understood, because we suffer from a paucity of signed and dated works. A painting of *A Man Reading a Letter* dated 1657 (Fig. 3) illustrates his mature genre style. Its smooth execution and relatively amply proportioned figure types reappear in two soldier paintings (Cat. D 20, D 21, Plates 181, 182) which were attributed to De Hooch until Fleischer correctly assigned them to De Jongh.[8] As the author observed, these supplements to De Jongh's oeuvre increase the likelihood that he played a role in the formation of De Hooch's early style. With its abruptly foreshortened doorway at the left and triangular grouping of central figures, De Jongh's *Paying the Hostess* (Cat. D 20, Plate 182) resembles the designs of De Hooch's paintings in Leningrad and Zurich (Cat. 6, 7, Plates 5, 6). Moreover, the theme of the officer settling accounts with the hostess was treated on two later occasions by De Hooch, in a painting of 1658 in the Marquis of Bute's Collection (Cat. 27, Plates 24, 25) and in a late work in New York (Cat. 111, Plate 114). As Fleischer observed, the central figures in the former painting may have been based on their counterparts in the De Jongh. De Jongh's art evidently attracted other Rotterdamers in these years. Ochtervelt's early hunting and historical scenes clearly reflect his influence and the figure types of his youthful guardroom scenes also resemble those of De Jongh.[9] While De Hooch's figures tend to be slimmer and his brushwork—true to his interest in Flemish genre—broader, he probably was drawn to the art of De Jongh, who, after all, was the principal painter of guardroom scenes in Rotterdam during his youth.

De Hooch was recorded as a resident of his native city in 1654, but had been living in Delft as much as two years earlier (Doc. 14). As we have seen, his contact with the local painter Hendrick van der Burch (1627–after 1666) is documented repeatedly in the early and mid-1650s. In the past the facts of Van der Burch's life have been misconstrued and his oeuvre obscured with numerous misattributions.[10] Long assumed to be a forerunner of De Hooch, he was, in fact, a contemporary. Although no certain dates have been discovered in his paintings, his rare signed guardroom scenes (see Fig. 54) and those which can be confidently attributed to him (see Fig. 4)[11] were probably executed during his early years of association with De Hooch. These works closely resemble the latter's in choice of subject, design, and attention to the effects of light (compare Cat. 10, 11, Plates 8, 9A).[12] Yet Van der Burch was clearly a technically less accomplished painter. His compositions suffer from a lack of clarity and his spatial constructions are often awkwardly exaggerated. Employing a painterly technique recognized by flickering, rather disembodied highlights, the artist frequently compromises the tactility of his figures. Since none of the shared features of the works of De Hooch and Van der Burch are found solely in the latter's art, it seems likely that the two painters were exposed to common influences and that their contact most profited the less innovative artist, namely Van der Burch.

Probably of greater significance for De Hooch in these years was the art of Gerard Terborch (1617–81).[13] Recent archival discoveries have revealed that Terborch was in Delft in 1653 and signed a document with the young Johannes Vermeer.[14] In the same year he dated the painting known as *Unwelcome News* (Fig. 5), which undoubtedly served as the model for a signed painting by De Hooch now in Barcelona (Cat. 16, Plate 15). In addition, early sales catalogues suggest that De Hooch made at least one other picture after or in the manner of guardroom scenes by Terborch (see Cat. C 234), who was to have a significant impact on De Hooch on several later occasions. The painting in Barcelona represents an ambitious, if not altogether successful, early attempt at the construction of more clearly defined interior space. In imitation of his model, De Hooch adopts a tighter mode of execution, while Terborch's psychological refinement is sacrificed to a more comical interpretation of the arrival of what no doubt are marching orders. As the officer frowns glumly, his lady companion sheds melodramatic tears and the courier seems to make a rhetorical gesture of sorrow.[15]

Terborch was one of the first artists to exchange the horizontal format, which had dominated the earlier genre tradition, for upright compositions. In the process of this adaptation the number of figures was reduced and their scale increased, while a new effort was made to unify figures and space through a more consistent treatment of light.[16] In addition to Terborch, several Amsterdam painters, including Jacob van Loo (1621–70), Gerard van Zijl (c. 1607–65), and the Rembrandt pupil Gerbrand van den Eeckhout (1621–74), also changed over to the new compositional type around 1650. While it is unknown whether De Hooch had contact with the art of these painters, his *Tric-Trac Players* in Dublin (Cat. 12, Plate 11) is reminiscent of works like Van den Eeckhout's painting of this theme dated 1651 (Fig. 6).[17] Both works adopt the newly simplified compositional format and similarities appear in the grouping of the players and the attention to tonal gradations, which contribute to a more cogent relationship between figures and space. A handsome little panel depicting a *Soldier in a Cuirass with a Serving Woman* (Cat. 13, Plate 12), which is probably the pendant to the picture in Dublin, is again conceived and designed in a manner resembling works like Van den Eeckhout's *Card Players* of 1652.[18] De Hooch's technique is less pasty and his shadows, because of the lighter overall tonality, less impenetrable. Yet if he knew Van den Eeckhout's work, as he undoubtedly did Terborch's, it could have been a factor in the formation of his first manner. As Blankert recently observed, the same can also be said of the rarer genre scenes by Jacob van Loo.[19]

Thus two artistic traditions formed the primary influences on De Hooch's early work: Flemish low life genre, particularly as interpreted by Sorgh; and the guardroom painting tradition, as transformed by its later practitioners, such as De Jongh, Terborch, Van den Eeckhout, and Van Loo. As we have seen, these artistic currents were accessible to the artist in the principal cities in which he resided in his early years, namely Rotterdam and Delft. In general, De Hooch's early works break little ground in the sense of creating a new style or broaching new subjects. One exception is the theme of the *Wounded Soldier*, which Fleischer has perceptively observed was the subject of the altered stable scene in London (Cat. 14, Plate 14).[20] In its treatment of a potentially tragic event, the work is virtually unique in the guardroom tradition.

Less unconventional, but no less remarkable as a departure from De Hooch's customary thematic repertoire, is a little panel depicting the *Liberation of St. Peter from Prison* (Cat. 3, Plate 3).[21] Fully signed, the picture is the artist's only known treatment of a religious theme. The technique of paint application and the treatment of light and figures (notably the soldiers and the angel) closely parallel De Hooch's early manner (cf. Cat. 7, 10, Plates 6, 8). Additive in appearance, the overall composition seems to reflect the thinking of a young artist working from multiple and only partially absorbed sources. With the darkened form of one of the guards serving as a *repoussoir* in the foreground, the design recalls earlier representations of the theme by Utrecht painters like Gerrit van Honthorst (see Fig. 7) and Abraham Bloemaert. The Saint's facial type and diminutive feet and hands call to mind the types employed by Barent Fabritius, who, it has been conjectured, could have worked in Delft in or before 1652.[22] Surprising as it may initially seem, De Hooch was not the only Dutch genre painter of his time to experiment with religious painting. Some of his most outstanding contemporaries, including Metsu and Vermeer, depicted religious subjects in their youth. The prevailing theory, borrowed from the Italians, which proclaimed history painting to be the highest pursuit to which an artist could aspire, may well have been a factor in the decisions to treat such themes. In specifically choosing the subject of the Liberation—affording as it did yet another opportunity to depict soldiers—De Hooch did not, in fact, venture so very far from the preferred themes of his youth. Yet within his own oeuvre De Hooch's painting remains an isolated statement, which he evidently chose not to repeat.

De Hooch's pictures of the mid-1650s testify to his acquaintance with the most recent trends in Dutch genre painting and anticipate aspects of the masterpieces he was to execute at the end of the decade. The lightened tonality of the painting in Zurich (Cat. 7, Plate 6), the primary colour scheme of the costumes in the picture in Leningrad (Cat. 6, Plate 5), the geometry of the design and the view through a series of interconnected spaces in the painting in London (Cat. 14, Plate 14), and the effort at a more orderly space construction in the painting in Barcelona (Cat. 16, Plate 15) are some of the elements which the artist was to combine so successfully in the next stage of his career.

[After the manuscript had gone to the printer a signed example of De Hooch's early work representing *Soldiers Playing Cards, with a Woman and Two Children* (Cat. 11 bis) appeared on the Amsterdam art market. In design and colouring it resembles the paintings in the Borghese Gallery and Cologne (Cat. 10, 11) and in execution may be likened to the pictures in Leningrad and Zurich (Cat. 6, 7). The memory of Flemish genre painting (Teniers, Ryckaert, etc.) is again evident in the figure types. Especially noteworthy is the combination of soldiers and domestic genre motifs, which forms a link between the artist's youthful themes and those of his mature Delft period.]

III

The Years in Delft 1652–60/61

When the 22-year-old De Hooch first appeared in Delft in 1652 he did so at an auspicious moment. The city, which had nurtured few innovative artists in the first half of the century, was being transformed into a vital centre of artistic creativity. Amidst the rapid generation and exchange of ideas taking place in Delft in the 1650s De Hooch fashioned his own style. By 1658, the year in which his first dated pictures appear (see Cat. 26–8, 30, 33, 34, Plates 23–6, 28, 32, 33, Col. Plates VI, VIII, IX), he displays a masterly command of the techniques of space construction, the use of perspective, and the treatment of light and atmosphere. The dark, ill-defined barns and taverns of his early career are replaced by orderly, light-filled interiors and courtyards. Where the figures formerly dominated their surroundings, a new balance is struck with the spatial environment. In some instances the old soldiering themes persist, while elsewhere a new interest in middle-class domestic subjects appears. An easeful sense of well-being and an unapologetic delight in bourgeois comfort are conveyed by the new pictures. To grasp De Hooch's relation and contribution to Delft painting it is necessary to examine the complex circumstances under which he came of age as a painter.

LIFE AND ART IN DELFT

At the outset of the Eighty Years War, Delft was the focal point of activities which shaped the fate of all the United Provinces.[1] As the seat of the Prinsenhof, the headquarters of William the Silent (1533–84) and the meeting place of the States General, the town enjoyed military and political significance disproportionate to its small size. Many of the nation's proudest figures had been born in Delft: the admirals Piet Hein and Marten Harpertsz. Tromp; Prince Frederick Henry, the son of William and one of the war's military heroes; Hugo Grotius, the jurist and statesman; and the scientist Anton van Leeuwenhoek, one of the first microbiologists. The town was rich. Before the devastating fire of 1536 it paid the highest taxes of any city in the province of Holland. In the following century the revenues filling the municipal coffers from the leasing of Delft's surrounding 'common lands' were equal to those generated by Dordrecht, Schiedam, and Rotterdam collectively. Although the city's older industries—cloth manufacturing and brewing—enriched the few, the general citizenry also knew relative prosperity.

Over the course of the seventeenth century, Delft drew inward. While occasionally still serving as a theatre for political events, the city gradually surrendered its active role in the nation's affairs. A small group of families espousing aristocratic ideals and orthodox Calvinism came to dominate the civic administration. Wealth remained but was used more and more conservatively. The entrepreneurs were increasingly replaced by more cautious *rentiers*; while capital could readily be found for high-yield ventures such as those of the Dutch East and West Indies Companies, little money was reinvested in local business. At a time when trade and industry were expanding briskly throughout Holland—and nowhere so dramatically as in Amsterdam—Delft's economic base was shrinking. Its crafts—porcelain manufacture and tapestry weaving—remained strong, but many businesses languished. The textile industries, suffering from competition with the English, curtailed their activities or moved elsewhere and by 1667 the city's breweries had fallen in number from more than 100 to 15. Land reclamation and the damming of rivers had transformed Delft from an open port to a virtually landlocked city. Commercial shipping at Delfshaven was increasingly rerouted through the burgeoning port of Rotterdam.

In contrast to more progressive cities in Holland, religious intolerance was practised openly in Delft. Not only Catholics and Remonstrants, but all non-Calvinist sects, like Lutherans and Mennonites, were barred from holding public office. While the house of Orange enjoyed considerable popular support in Delft, the patrician oligarchy accepted centralist government only reluctantly and in the interest of defence. When the threat of war had subsided, they remained fiercely committed to local autonomy and the preservation of their unrestricted economic liberties. Prince William II's sudden and early death in 1650 enabled the city fathers to reaffirm their domination of the city's politics and essentially pre-mercantile economy. The once vigorous city went into a decline, which left it virtually dormant until the nineteenth century.

The conservative spirit seemed to be reflected in the layout of the city itself. Whereas most seventeenth-century Dutch towns were a tangle of narrow streets and alleyways, Delft had had a clearly organized ground plan since the Middle Ages. A regular system of canals and streets, meeting at right angles and forming a grid, culminated in the large rectangular marketplace, where the Nieuwe Kerk and Town Hall still stand. The dominant impression of the city, then as now, was of long vistas bordered by low brick dwellings. In his *Journal de Voyages* of 1665, Balthasar de Monconys observed, 'Les rues sont toutes si droictes et si regulières, qu'on sçait d'abord tous les endroits.' Delft's chronicler, Dirck van Bleyswijk, also claimed that Delft was the cleanest of all Dutch cities. The town's neat and orderly appearance, so suited to the mentality of the inhabitants, found its clearest expression in the works of De Hooch and his colleagues.

The preeminence of a few privileged families in Delft society affected many aspects of life in the city. After *c.* 1635 members of the ruling families often possessed degrees in law and prided themselves on their intellectual and aesthetic interests. These were expressed in a taste for classical learning, natural science 'rariteitenkabineten', and the collecting of fine works of Asian art culled from ships returning from the East. Improvements in public education resulted from the interest in learning. Delft's excellent crafts in part may be seen as an expression of the aristocratic society's love of rare and well-wrought objects. Among the master craftsmen active in the city were the tapestry designer Frans Spierings and the renowned ceramics makers Frederik van Frijtom and the Hoppesteyns. Similarly, the quiet and precious art of De Hooch and Vermeer was appropriate to this conservative environment. Although their identity remains unknown, the proud and soberly attired family who posed for De Hooch's painting in Vienna (Cat. 24, Col. Plate III) capture the seignorial spirit of the local bourgeoisie. Sheltered within the intimate confines of their little courtyard, the sitters seem an embodiment of the prosperous and insular society of Delft.

In the quarter-century prior to De Hooch's arrival, Delft had a heterogeneous community of artists who, for the most part, worked in imported styles or perpetuated established artistic traditions. 'High life' merry company scenes, the invention of the early genre painters from Haarlem and Amsterdam, were popularized in Delft by Anthonie Palamedesz (1601–73) (see Fig. 8). Jacob Jansz. van Velsen (d. 1656) became his follower. 'Low' genre was represented by the scenes of barns and kitchens which Egbert van der Poel (1612–64) painted.[2] With their rustic still-life details, these works align themselves with the southern (Rotterdam and Middelburg) peasant painting tradition of artists like Cornelis Saftleven and Frans Ryckhals. Still-life painting in the, by then, outdated manner of Bosschaert was practised by Balthasar van der Ast (1593/4–1657), while Harmen van Steenwyck (1616–after 1655) produced still lifes of a more current type based on the art of the Haarlem painters Pieter Claesz and G. W. Heda. The gifted sea and landscape painter Simon de Vlieger settled briefly in Delft in the 1630s, but his inventive art seems to have had little impact on local painting. Pieter van Asch (1603–78), virtually the only other Delft landscapist of the period, produced indifferent works in the tonal manner perfected by Van Goyen and Salomon van Ruysdael. The distinguished history painter Jacob Pynas (d. after 1656) was active in Delft in the 1630s. By this time, however, he was content to repeat the forms he and his Pre-Rembrandtist colleagues had invented early in the century. Christiaen van Couwenbergh (1604–64) executed history paintings in a style derived from the Utrecht Caravaggisti. Lastly, and perhaps most typically, artists from the Delff and Van Vliet families carried on a highly formalized portraiture tradition descended from the art of that favourite of the Stadholder's court, Michiel van Miereveld (1567–1641).

I. The Merry Drinker (Cat. 4). *c.* 1650. Staatliche Museen, East Berlin

II. Tric-Trac Players (Cat. 12). *c.* 1652–5. National Gallery of Ireland, Dublin. See also Plate 11

As a centre of artistic creativity, therefore, Delft had been of only limited importance. There were, however, two independent-minded painters who proved the exceptions to the rule. The first, Leonaert Bramer (1596–1674),[3] would have rightly been acknowledged by his contemporaries as the most important Delft painter of his generation. Repeatedly named a 'hoofdman' of the guild, Bramer produced cabinet-sized paintings of history and occasional genre subjects in a highly personal manner. Many were nocturnal scenes with bold lighting effects. The artist was acquainted with the young Vermeer and it has been suggested, perhaps correctly, that he was the latter's teacher.[4] Bramer was also active as a painter of murals and worked in fresco, a rare practice in Northern Europe in the seventeenth century. In this capacity he may have attracted and influenced Carel Fabritius, who is also known to have executed murals. Yet, beyond their general concern with problems of lighting, Bramer's easel paintings seem to have held little interest for the Delft painters of De Hooch's generation.

Of greater significance was Paulus Potter (1625–54)[5] who, like De Vlieger, was only connected with the city for a brief period. Potter joined the Delft guild in 1646 but was at The Hague by 1649. The intervening years saw the fruition of his art and the production of his most ambitious work, the *Young Bull* of 1647 (Mauritshuis, The Hague, no. 136). Potter is best remembered for his uncompromisingly naturalistic animal paintings. Yet the uniqueness to Delft art of his subject matter has probably obscured the perception of his role in the formation of the new painting style of the 1650s.[6] Many of the characteristics we associate with 'classical' Delft painting—the informal naturalism, monumental repose, and vertical painting format—are already evident in a work like the *Two Cows and a Bull* of 1647 (Fig. 9). The way in which Potter places his animals against the brilliant blankness of a summer sky differs little from the practices of later Delft genre painters who set their figures against light-coloured walls. Much as in De Hooch's works of the following decade, the morning light in the *Cows Driven to Pasture*, also of 1647 (Czernin Collection, Residenzgalerie, Salzburg, no. 187), streams from the distance toward the viewer, passing along the sides of objects (in this case animals) and silhouetting forms in the foreground. Above all, it is Potter's sensitivity to the workings of natural light, to its silvery tonality and *contre-jour* effects, which marks him as an important precursor of De Hooch and his Delft colleagues. The sunny Italianate landscapes of Adam Pynacker, who appeared in Delft in 1649, may also have contributed to the lightening of Delft palettes. Yet it was Potter who, more than any other artist active in Delft before 1650, anticipated the designs and lighting systems subsequently perfected by the city's painters.

As we have suggested, the artistic fortunes of Delft changed suddenly and quite dramatically around 1650. The reasons for these changes and their rapidity are difficult to pinpoint. In part they reflect general trends in Dutch painting, while in other respects they signal a new indigenous spirit of innovation. Aside from Potter's art, the earliest evidence of these new attitudes appears in the work of two architectural painters, Gerard Houckgeest (c. 1600–61)[7] and Emanuel de Witte (1617–92).[8] Many of the most significant later achievements of Delft painters involved new approaches to spatial construction and the expressive application of perspective. Viewed with historical hindsight, therefore, it seems logical that the new ideas should first manifest themselves in paintings of architecture.

Houckgeest evidently initiated the new experiments in 1650 and was followed almost immediately by De Witte.[9] While the latter had concentrated mainly on historical and religious subjects prior to this date, Houckgeest had worked as a painter of fantastic church interiors in the tradition of the sixteenth-century Antwerp artist and author of perspective manuals, Jan Vredeman de Vries. Bartholomeus van Bassen, one of Vredeman de Vries's later followers and a member of the guilds in Delft and The Hague, probably was Houckgeest's teacher. At the age of about fifty, Houckgeest suddenly broke with the earlier tradition and began executing scenes of specific churches with intricately angled views and multipoint perspectives. His *Interior of the Nieuwe Kerk* (Fig. 10) and De Witte's *Interior of the Oude Kerk* (Wallace Collection, London, no. P254), both dated 1651, illustrate the new type. They depict a few large unembellished architectural motifs lit by strong sunlight and seen obliquely in the apse of an identifiable church. While views of actual architecture had appeared earlier, notably among the paintings of Pieter Saenredam, the degree to which these new church interiors achieved an impression of informal naturalism is unprecedented.

The name of the abundantly talented painter Carel Fabritius (1622–54) has been invoked to account for the sudden appearance of these ideas in Delft.[10] A student of Rembrandt at the same time as the Dordrecht painter, Samuel van Hoogstraten (1627–78), Fabritius was said to be living in Delft in 1650 and joined the guild two years later. At least for a brief period, his stay in the city coincided with those of Houckgeest and De Witte; the latter was in Amsterdam by 1651 and the former was recorded in Bergen-op-Zoom in the following year. According to various writers, including Van Bleyswijk, Van Hoogstraten, and Arnold Houbraken, the artist was renowned for his mastery of perspective.[11] Judging from his few surviving paintings, he also possessed an acute sense of the spatial functions of tone and texture. As in certain works by Terbrugghen and other Caravaggisti, his paintings often employ a dark figure against a light field. Unlike the Utrecht painters, however, Fabritius favoured a broad and richly layered technique, which testifies to Rembrandt's legacy.

Fabritius died as a result of injuries he suffered when the powder magazine in Delft exploded in 1654.[12] The task of assessing his pictorial achievement has been sorely complicated by this calamity. Beginning with Van Bleyswijk's detailed account of the artist's death and the appended poetic eulogy by the author's publisher, Arnold Bon, an air of romance has grown up around him, with the result that it is now difficult to distinguish the man from the myth. The probable loss of part of the artist's oeuvre in the explosion has further encouraged writers to speculate about the extent of his influence. In a large measure, Fabritius's reputation as the fountainhead of the Delft School rests upon the presumed qualities of unknown paintings. If his existing and documented oeuvre is considered within the context of Delft painting of the period it becomes clear that the view of Fabritius as the sole initiator of perspectival and illusionistic experiments is exaggerated. In fact, none of his surviving works of this type predate his Delft colleagues' new architectural paintings.[13] Brilliant as his achievements were, they were not isolated.

Fabritius's *View in Delft* of 1652 (Fig. 12) is the only surviving work unquestionably by the artist's hand to demonstrate his skill in the use of perspective for illusionistic effects.[14] As in the new architectural paintings, an identifiable site is depicted. Perspectival distortions in the scene—the Nieuwe Kerk in the distance, for example, appears disproportionately small—seem to reflect the canvas's original function: it was probably initially mounted on a curved (hemicylindrical) surface at the back of a perspective box.[15] Documents mention perspective boxes by Fabritius[16] and modern reconstructions of the original structure seem to confirm the efficacy of its illusion. The Dutch evidently were the first to construct such devices and built them in various shapes and sizes. Van Hoogstraten's *Perspective Box* in the National Gallery of London (no. 3832) is the best preserved example in a rectangular format and still charms visitors daily with its deceptively illusionistic views of a tiny domestic interior.

An early inventory reference to 'een raempge door Fabritius' (a little window by Fabritius) suggests that he also painted views through windows.[17] None has survived, but they probably shared characteristics with the illusionistic windows and doorways painted by Van Hoogstraten[18] and a picture entitled the *Terrace* in Chicago (Fig. 11). Although the attribution of the latter work remains problematic, its style has been associated with Fabritius's in the past.[19] The picture represents a view through an open window to a sunny courtyard, where a couple share a glass of wine. Like Van Hoogstraten's window paintings it is executed on a life-size scale (measuring more than 100 cm in height) and seems designed to create the impression that the canvas is an actual window. Fabritius and Van Hoogstraten also shared an interest in *trompe-l'oeil* still lifes.[20] The former's *Goldfinch* (Mauritshuis, The Hague, no. 605) typically employs a shallow space in order to minimize the need for pictorial, and hence 'artificial', relief. An interest in illusionism captured the imaginations of many Dutch painters in these years. According to Houbraken and a document of 1664, another Dordrecht artist, Cornelis Bisschop, painted illusionistic panels in which the deception was enhanced by carved outlines.[21] The distinguished cityscape painter, Jan van der Heyden, visited Delft in these years (see *View of the Oude Kerk*, The Detroit Institute of Arts, Detroit) and occasionally introduced anamorphic details into his works.[22] These illusionistic paintings—or, as they were known in seventeenth-century Holland, 'bedriegertjes' (little deceits)—often achieved compelling effects. Yet none probably surpassed the standard of illusionism set by Fabritius's *View in Delft*. The architectural painter's desire for naturalistic fidelity in the representations of actual scenes had been realized. The perspective box had demonstrated the limits of mimetic reproduction.

In 1652, the year when De Hooch was first recorded as a resident of Delft, Houckgeest appeared in Bergen-op-Zoom and Fabritius executed his *View in Delft*. There is little reason to suppose that the young painter was prepared to respond immediately to the achievements of these masters. Despite the absence of dated works, he probably continued to execute guardroom scenes during his early years in the city. By 1658, however, his art had undergone substantial changes. His paintings now display a highly rationalized spatial order and a heightened awareness of the effects of aerated light and shade. Undoubtedly the interest that Fabritius and the architectural painters demonstrated in perspective provided important inspiration for De Hooch's new spatial concerns. His sharpened sensitivity to the effects of natural light also certainly owes much to these artists, as well as, and perhaps more fundamentally, to Potter. Yet the achievement of De Hooch's works of *c.* 1658 amounted to more than a mere sum or synthesis of parts. At once ordered and informal, his serene images of Dutch homes and courtyards were unprecedented. No earlier works had so successfully applied a cogent perspective system to the naturalistic representation of genre themes in secular spaces. To many of the artistic problems Dutch painters had posed themselves in these years, De Hooch's new paintings afforded innovative solutions.

The only artist to surpass De Hooch's achievements was Johannes Vermeer, Delft's greatest painter.[23] De Hooch and Vermeer must have maintained close ties in these years. While the exact nature of their relationship is unclear, there is little support for the theory that Vermeer anticipated the changes that occurred in De Hooch's art.[24] None of the luminous small-scale genre works for which he is so admired can be shown to predate 1658, the year signalling De Hooch's full artistic maturity. Moreover, Vermeer's only dated picture from the 1650s, the *Procuress* of 1656 (Staatliche Gemäldegalerie, Dresden), is a large animated genre scene in the tradition of the Utrecht Caravaggisti. With its dark and shallow composition, the picture bears little resemblance to the art he subsequently produced. Although De Hooch joined the guild almost two years after Vermeer, he was three years older and could reasonably be expected to arrive at his mature style earlier. To the essential question of the two artist's relation, we must return. At this point, though, we should take a closer look at De Hooch's art and its historical context.

INTERIOR GENRE SCENES

The *Card Players* of 1658 in Buckingham Palace (Cat. 28, Col. Plate VI, Plate 26) illustrates the full flowering of the naturalistic impulse in De Hooch's art. The subject is familiar enough, soldiers gaming with a female companion at a table (cf. Cat. 11, 12, Plates 9A, 11). Yet now we are only aware of these activities secondarily. The remarkably compelling rendering of space is the work's principal interest. In place of the rustic settings of the early paintings, the corner of a brightly lit and clearly defined middle-class interior is depicted. A consistent spatial recession is established by the regular pattern of the tiled floor and the geometry of the walls and ceiling. Tall windows in the rear wall and a backlighted doorway illuminate the room. With few exceptions (see Cat. 41, 44, Plates 45, 48), it is always summertime in De Hooch's pictures and the doors and windows open wide to admit the moist Dutch air and silvery light. The view, or 'doorkijkje', through the doorway in the present work offers a glimpse of a sunny inner court where a serving woman is seen bringing wine to the players. No other artist has ever equalled De Hooch's achievement in the evocation of the contiguity of indoor and outdoor space. Despite their rigorous order, his interiors are never confining. As the walls promise shelter, so the doors and 'doorkijkjes' connote release.

The space and its occupants in this work are presented in perfect accord. Less animated than their earlier counterparts, the figures in De Hooch's works of the late 1650s retain a slender angularity, which now complements the architecture. Emphatic gestures are avoided and figure motifs often appear framed by architectural members. Although De Hooch is often criticized as a figure painter, his slow-moving and straight-silhouetted people were ideally suited to these newly ordered surroundings. More facile or energetic figures would disrupt the essential quiet. Mindful of these effects, De Hooch now took up the old soldiering themes with a new restraint, rejecting garrulous display and minimizing anecdote. At least to the modern viewer, his figures seem at times to function only to insure that his spaces are inhabited. In the painting of a *Woman and Two Men Drinking* in the National Gallery in London (Cat. 29, Plate 27) a white-bearded man, who initially appeared by the serving girl near the fireplace, evidently was thought expendable by the artist and was painted out. Reducing the population of the room to four relatively still figures has subtly enhanced the impression of uncluttered spatial order. A cool daylight filters into the room, whetting the rich colours of the costumes and tempering the rectilinear design. Enveloped in the luminous atmosphere and firmly situated in space, the figures are again at one with their environment. As in the related picture in the Queen's collection, the naturalistic effect of the whole is entirely convincing.

The achievements of these pictures brought to fruition certain ideas which had first appeared in Dutch genre around the turn of the decade. During the first half of the century genre interiors were usually defined in only the most cursory of terms.[25] In Palamedesz's *Merry Company* of 1633 (Fig. 8), for example, the suggestion of a corner and a few foreshortened furnishings suffice to give spatial definition to the room. Occasionally tiled floors and doorways were introduced to enhance recession, yet genre spaces were more often implied than fully described. An alternative and decidedly minor trend appeared in the works of the later followers of Jan Vredeman de Vries, notably Dirck van Delen (1604/5–71) and Bartholomeus van Bassen (1613–52).[26] Founded on the author's perspective designs (see Fig. 13), these interiors were fully bounded by five planes (three walls, ceiling, and floor) and took the form of large, imaginary halls richly decorated in a Renaissance style (see Fig. 14). Their elegant genre figures frequently were added by other hands. Derived as these interiors were from perspective models, their organization deliberately stressed orthogonal recession and a prominent vanishing point. Space was defined linearly; little or no concern was shown for atmospheric perspective.[27] In both of these types of interiors numerous figures were usually arranged laterally across the space. As we have noted, around 1650 artists like Terborch and Van den Eeckhout began painting genre scenes with upright compositions and fewer and proportionately larger figures and motifs. Despite the greater unity of their designs, the illusion of space was still largely dependent upon the arrangement and disposition of the figures. In Terborch's works the uniformly dark backgrounds are never broken by a visible light-source and serve to focus attention on the principal actions in the foreground.

Some of the earliest efforts to combine the new compositions with more rigorous spatial order appear in the paintings of Isaak Koedijk (1616/17–68).[28] The sources for Koedijk's art and its full significance are still only partially understood. His methods of spatial construction in a painting like *The Empty Beaker* of 1648 (Fig. 15)[29] are not inherently different from those of the De Vriesian painters. Here, however, the elaborate architectural fantasies are replaced by a simple bourgeois interior. The organization of the plain box-like space bears a strong resemblance to paintings by De Hooch of a decade later, like the *Girl Drinking with Soldiers* of 1658 in the Louvre (Cat. 26, Plate 23). The foreshortened windows, the receding ceiling beams and bare floor, the view to an adjoining space at the right, even the position of the table and wall-hanging, are surprisingly similar. Koedijk's painting would not be mistaken for a product of the Delft School; its slick execution and airless space reflect the painter's Leiden origins. However, this and other contemporary works by the artist[30] testify to a growing interest among Dutch genre painters in perspectival effects and more orderly spatial arrangements.[31]

We do not know whether De Hooch knew the art of Koedijk.[32] It is quite possible, though, that the Dordrecht painter Nicolaes Maes (1634–93)[33] encountered the latter's work in Amsterdam when he was Rembrandt's pupil around 1650.[34] Maes returned to his birthplace in 1653. Although it again cannot be proven that he and De Hooch established personal contact,[35] the similarities many writers have observed in their art suggest that the two men were probably aware of one another's work. Without knowledge of the fact that Maes was four years De Hooch's junior, Thoré-Bürger even suggested he might have been the latter's teacher.[36] Around 1654 Maes began executing domestic genre scenes with more complex spatial designs. The resemblance between these works and De Hooch's interiors of *c.* 1658 serves to reaffirm the common interest in perspective and illusionism uniting artists from Delft and Dordrecht in these years.

De Hooch's painting of a *Woman with a Baby on her Lap, and a Small Child* of 1658 (Cat. 30, Plate 28) presents a superbly understated image of maternal life in the home. The same clean and orderly room seems to reappear in the famous picture in the Rijksmuseum, Amsterdam (Cat. 31, Plate 29). There the door to a storage space is opened, a painting on the wall eliminated, and a chair resting on a 'soldertien' (a wooden platform used to stave off the chill of the stone floor) is introduced into the far room. The major features of these two related paintings—the upright frontal composition, tiled foreground, and view to a back-lighted secondary space—appeared earlier in Maes's *Idle Servant* of 1655 (Fig. 16). Yet whereas Maes casts part of his room in shadow to de-emphasize areas of difficult spatial transition, De Hooch floods his scenes with light, confident of their spatial coherence. His command of perspective is clearly more sophisticated than the Dordrecht painter's and his rendering of the subtle gradations of light and shade far more assured.

Maes's painting has also often been compared with Vermeer's *Sleeping Girl* (Fig. 17), essentially a transitional work in the latter's oeuvre and not to be dated earlier than c. 1657.[37] Similarities appear in both theme and design. Like Maes, Vermeer employs an additive approach to spatial construction. For the same reason that Maes casts the small staircase at the left of his picture in shadow, Vermeer disguises the threshold to the hallway and adjoining room: transitions between interconnected spaces were still a problem.[38] It was only with De Hooch's painting of c. 1658 that continuous and perspectively coherent space was fully realized. Within the tradition of interior genre the degree of naturalistic probity in these scenes was unprecedented.

De Hooch's move to more orderly spatial designs coincided with the initial appearance of maternal and domestic themes in his work. In or shortly before 1658, he began painting scenes of women attending to household chores (Cat. 18, 20, 36, 37, 40A–C, Plates 17, 39, 40, 43, 44, Col. Plate IV) or silently ministering to children (Cat. 17, 30–2, 42, Plates 16, 28–31, 46, Col. Plate VII), subjects that occupied him throughout the remainder of his career. The Delft period interiors depict uneventful episodes from the daily life of women in a particularly disarming and unsentimental fashion. Typical is a composition of which there are at least two versions, in Karlsruhe and in Washington (Cat. 40A & B, Plates 43, 44). Here the narrative is restricted to the simple act of a woman making a small enclosed bed while looking to a child who stands silhouetted in the doorway. As the firm geometric foundations of the design reinforce the impression of a secure and well-ordered household, so the lighting effects vividly enliven the scene. Streaming in from the garden and through a tiny 'voorhuys', the warm morning light plays upon the tiled floor and gently intermingles with a second light filtering through the window in the left wall. In the related picture in the Rijksmuseum, the so-called *Mother's Duty* (Cat. 42, Plate 46), the housework has been completed and the child nuzzles into its mother's lap to have lice removed from its hair, a common requirement in times less concerned with personal hygiene. Here again, De Hooch finds a special beauty in the most prosaic aspects of life.

Domestic subjects had appeared with some frequency in earlier Dutch art and were enjoying a noticeable increase in popularity around 1650.[39] Maes, once more, could have provided inspiration for De Hooch's adoption of these themes. The *Woman Nursing an Infant* in San Francisco (Cat. 32, Col. Plate VII) is descended from a series of near views of women at work which Maes painted about 1655 (see *Woman Making Lace*, Fig. 18; and *Woman Scraping Parsnips*, National Gallery, London, no. 159; both dated 1655). Like Maes, De Hooch employs a bare frontal composition which complements the simple wordless serenity of his mother and child. The scene in Berlin of a woman who, having suckled the child, threads her bodice (Cat. 51; see detail Plate 55), once was attributed to Maes and may also be indebted to pictures like the latter's so-called *Tired Nurse* of 1655.[40] Despite these resemblances, we encounter a more highly ordered vision of domesticity in De Hooch's art. While the boundaries of Maes's spaces are often merely hinted at, the walls of De Hooch's rooms and courtyards—those perimeters of private life—are maintained as a firmly visible, yet comfortable framework for the workaday activities of his middle-class women.

The degree of spatial unity and order De Hooch realized in his interiors of c. 1658 was not achieved immediately. The painting in Barcelona (Cat. 16, Plate 15) documents his first uncertain steps in this direction. *Mother, Child, and a Serving Woman* (Cat. 17, Plate 16), testifies to an early effort at the construction of more complex spaces. Here not only the composition, but also the warm colour scheme of reds and browns as well as the domestic subject are reminiscent of Maes. The system of backlighting resembles the mode of illumination employed in *Woman Preparing Vegetables* (Cat. 18, Plate 17), in the Louvre, where further advances can be observed in the consistent representation of interrelated interior and exterior space. De Hooch had a genius for seeing the expressive possibilities of spaces which were at once compartmentalized and contiguous. Even in the enclosed interiors he sought out ways to cleverly subdivide the room, as in the Marquis of Bute's picture (Cat. 27, Plates 24–5), where the soldiers in the corner are separated from the haggling in the foreground by curtains forming a discrete space within the space.

The treatment of the light and elements of the design in the *Woman Preparing Vegetables* are reminiscent of domestic scenes by the enigmatic Jacobus Vrel.[41] Vrel painted a series of vertical panels depicting dark rooms inhabited by a woman viewed from the rear and illuminated by tall windows in the back wall.[42] While he is usually considered to be only a follower of De Hooch, the certain date of 1654 appearing on his painting of a *Woman at a Window* (Fig. 19) proves that he anticipated aspects of the Delft interior type.[43] Despite their charming simplicity, Vrel's interiors display only a rudimentary knowledge of spatial construction. His limited production and rather naive manner suggest that he may only have been an amateur painter who shared common sources with the Delft painters. Maes has been suggested as a possible source,[44] and, given the propensity of 'naive' artists for the adoption of forms from other media, we would add the potential inspiration of Geertruyt Roghman's earlier prints (see Fig. 44).

As we have seen, De Hooch's *Card Players* of 1658 (Cat. 28, Col. Plate VI) and the contemporary painting in the National Gallery in London (Cat. 29, Plate 27) reveal the artist's fully matured command of the technique of perspective construction. A check of the orthogonals in the former work confirms that they meet in a precise vanishing point to the left of the head of the seated officer in the foreground. The artist evidently took considerable pains with the construction of his spaces in these years. Infra-red photographs of the National Gallery's painting reveal traces of underdrawing in the beams overhead and the windows at the left, indicating that the perspective scheme and the outlines of the architectural environment were drawn directly on the painted ground. The figures, as clearly revealed in the thin passages, were only added after the spatial environment had been completed. If, as seems likely, De Hooch's working method after c. 1658 involved an initial drawing on the painting's ground, it would in part explain the curious fact that no drawings by his hand have been identified.[45] We would hasten to add, however, that De Hooch's art is hardly unique in this regard; the oeuvres of many of the greatest painters of the age, including Frans Hals and Vermeer, are also devoid of drawings.

In constructing the linear foundations of his spaces, De Hooch may simply have placed a pin at the vanishing point to facilitate the sighting of his orthogonals; Vermeer seems to have employed this technique in his *Art of Painting* (Kunsthistorisches Museum, Vienna, no. 9128).[46] Of greater concern than an artist's actual method of spatial construction is his overall concept of perspective. Inasmuch as De Hooch's perspectives were constructed with orthogonals, they reflect orthodox perspective practices. This is to say, the laws governing his single-point perspective systems were derived from the writings of Leon Battista Alberti and their foundation in the assumptions of Euclidean optics. Perspective treatises readily available to the artist provided recipes for the application of linear perspective, as well as theoretical support for these techniques.[47] It is unlikely, though, that these manuals would have satisfied all of De Hooch's artistic demands.

Traditional orthogonal perspective addressed only one factor in the problem of pictorial space construction. Light, colour, and atmosphere are also determinants of perspective. De Hooch and his Delft colleagues were acutely aware of the space-defining properties of these phenomena and, in a large measure, their sensitivity to these factors marks their departure from conventional perspective practices. The spirit of empirical observation which brought advances in many fields of learning in these years—notably navigation, cartography, astronomy, and medicine—also inspired optical research. Wheelock has persuasively demonstrated that debates then current regarding the nature of optics and their implied invalidation of traditional perspective laws created an experimental atmosphere in which artists took a more flexible approach to perspective.[48] One reflection of this new attitude was the artists' willingness to utilize visual phenomena which were observed with the aid of optical instruments, such as mirrors, lenses, and the camera obscura. Seventeenth-century writers described and recommended the use of such devices and Van Hoogstraten observed that their consultation enhanced the natural appearance of a painting.[49]

By the 1650s lenses of relatively high quality were being manufactured in Delft. The microscopist Van Leeuwenhoek was active in the city after 1654 and later served as a trustee of Vermeer's estate. His presence could have stimulated local painters' interests in optics. Yet the Delft artists' concern with the nature of vision undoubtedly was more practical than scientific. Optical instruments were probably consulted only insofar as the insights provided were applicable to immediate artistic problems. While there is some inconclusive evidence to suggest that Vermeer employed the camera obscura,[50] no specific characteristics of De Hooch's art are necessarily dependent upon the use of optical devices. Nevertheless, the unrivalled visual fidelity of the camera obscura surely would have been of interest to an artist with De Hooch's concern for naturalistic appearances. Optical devices provided information about the very properties of light, atmosphere, and colour which distinguish De Hooch's approach to perspective from that of the De Vriesian painters. It seems likely, therefore, that he would have availed himself of these lessons.

De Hooch's contemporaries quickly recognized the significance of his interiors of *c.* 1658. The rectilinear spatial designs of Vermeer's paintings in Berlin–Dahlem (Fig. 21) and Braunschweig (Herzog Anton Ulrich-Museum) were probably inspired by De Hooch works (compare Cat. 28, 29, Col. Plate VI, Plate 27) and must have been executed shortly thereafter.[51] The compositions of other approximately contemporary paintings by the two artists also testify to their close ties. In De Hooch's *Soldiers Playing Cards* (Cat. 25, Plate 22) and Vermeer's *Soldier with a Laughing Girl* (Fig. 20) three-quarter-length figures seated at a table by a window are set in relief by the darkened form of a soldier on the near side of the table. Although the proximity of the figures to the viewer and the resulting formal concentration of the images seem more typical of Vermeer's art, De Hooch may again have been the design's creator.[52]

De Hooch and Vermeer shared an acute sense of the workings of natural light. In their ability to render the subtle modulations of sunshine cast obliquely on a bare plaster wall the two men have known no equals. Although both illuminated their scenes with daylight, De Hooch's light is somewhat clearer and more intense. Accordingly, his shadows are darker and contribute to bolder contrasts. Like his spatial designs, his lighting systems are often more complex than those of Vermeer. While the latter usually employed a single fixed source of light, De Hooch often enlivened his compositions with several (see Cat. 40A–C, 42, 51, Plates 43, 44, 46, 54). The two artists are united, however, by their uncommon sensitivity to certain optical effects, such as secondary reflections. This perception accounts for the luminous glow on the lateral wall beneath the window in the two compositionally related paintings mentioned above (Cat. 25, Plate 22 and Fig. 20) and in the Louvre's painting of 1658 (Cat. 26, Plate 23). The girl pouring wine in De Hooch's scene in New York (Cat. 19, Plate 18) is reflected in the window and resembles the mirrored detail in Vermeer's *Girl Reading a Letter* (Staatliche Gemäldegalerie, Dresden, no. 1336).

Intimately related to the two artists' sensitivity to light was their perception of colour. Around 1658 De Hooch's palette became increasingly composed of pure unmixed hues.[53] In his brilliant painting in San Francisco (Cat. 32, Col. Plate VII, Plates 30, 31) this trend is brought to fruition in the costume of the nursing mother, which is composed of the triad of primary colours, red, yellow, and blue. The simplicity of this scheme is the colouristic correlative of a superbly unembellished composition. In works of this period one can legitimately speak of a form of 'classical' sublimation both in terms of the design and of the optical values of light and colour. Vermeer's famous *Kitchen Maid* (Rijksmuseum, Amsterdam, no. A 2344) is one of the finest expressions of the classical impulse of Delft painting and, perhaps in response to De Hooch's palette, also employs a restricted colour scheme of primary hues.

Clearly De Hooch and Vermeer worked in close contact in the late 1650s. Some of the shared features of their art reflect common sources and it would beggar the case to suggest that De Hooch remained unaffected by Vermeer's art. Suffice it to say, however, that De Hooch had discovered his own style by 1658 and seems to have been the more innovative artist at this stage. The artistic dialogue established between the two painters in these years continued even after De Hooch's move to Amsterdam. As we shall see, though, in subsequent exchanges Vermeer increasingly assumed the more creative role in their relationship.

COURTYARDS, GARDENS, AND A STREET SCENE

In addition to interiors, De Hooch also painted a series of outdoor genre scenes in the late 1650s and early 60s. Most of these are situated in small brick courtyards, the likes of which may still be seen at the back of old Delft homes. Such courtyards were particularly common in the area around the Binnenwatersloot, where De Hooch's wife was living at the time of the couple's marriage. Removed from the public thorough-fares, these intimately scaled enclosures constitute an extension of the domestic environment. The women in De Hooch's pictures step out into these spaces to carry on their chores in the open air (see Cat. 20–1, 34, 36–7, 44–6, Col. Plates IV, V, IX, XI, Plates 33, 39, 40, 48, 49) or to share a brief drink with their more leisurely male companions (Cat. 23, 33, 35A–B, Col. Plate VIII, Plates 20, 32, 34–6). Rarely is the 'huisvrouw' encountered outside her little walled enclave, and then only on purposeful errands, fetching water or spreading linen in the bleaching yard (Cat. 21, Col. Plate V). Just as in the actual locale in Delft, De Hooch's tidy courtyards and gardens reiterate the geometry of his interiors. The overriding impression is of order and human proportion. Although the horizons studded with church spires and gabled roofs are a constant reminder that the city is close at hand, these are private places imbued with a special calm.

The felicitous year 1658 once again signalled De Hooch's full mastery of the courtyard theme. Two compositionally related pictures bearing this date (Cat. 33, 34, Col. Plates VIII, IX) reveal the same harmonious combination of informal naturalism and rectilinear order witnessed in his contemporary interiors. The quietly disposed figures strike a perfect balance with the comfortably habitable architecture. Brickwork in the foregrounds acts like the tiled floors of his rooms to facilitate perspectival recession. In both pictures a portal, surmounted by a tablet which once hung over the entrance to the Sint Hierony-musdael Cloister in Delft, offers a view through the adjoining house and out once more into the open air. The 'doorkijkje' again serves to relieve the impression of closure, both pictorially and psychologically. In the picture in London this breezeway shelters the still figure of a woman viewed *à contre-jour*, a motif which is recognized as a hallmark of De Hooch's art. All of the courtyard scenes from this period are upright in format and the majority are frontally disposed, although the point (or, in most cases, area) of focus of the lines of sight is usually pulled to one side. A mild and pervasive summer sunlight illuminates most of these works and the colour schemes are dominated by the warm reds and tans of brick. Occasionally, however, the artist enlivened his designs with a slanting late afternoon sun, creating bolder patterns of light and shade (see Cat. 36, 37, Plates 39, 40).

De Hooch's first courtyard scenes contributed to the emergence after *c*. 1650 of the cityscape as a fully independent genre in painting.[54] Together with paintings by Saenredam and Beerstraten of the Old Town Hall in Amsterdam, which burned down in 1652,[55] Fabritius's *View in Delft* (Fig. 12) marks the advent of the new type. Strictly speaking, the latter's painting and De Hooch's courtyards cannot be classified as cityscapes proper since genre elements predominate over the urban environment as major, if not principal, themes. Yet the study of the rise of the cityscape would only be obscured by the exclusion of these works. No doubt as a product of the new architectural painting and local artists' interest in perspective, Delft became one of the original centres of cityscape painting. Many early town views had a commemorative purpose in recording either a past situation or an event, like the fire at the Town Hall. Two Delft painters, Egbert van der Poel and Daniel Vosmaer (active 1650–66)[56] made a speciality of depicting the explosion in Delft and its aftermath. They usually present expansive vistas of the city from distant points of view. Consequently their paintings have more in common with the tradition of topographical city profiles, to which Vermeer's *View of Delft* (Mauritshuis, The Hague) also belongs, than with De Hooch's more intimately conceived urban genre scenes.[57]

The *Portrait of a Man with a Young Girl and Beggars* (the so-called 'Burgomaster of Delft and his Daughter') of 1655 (Fig. 22) by Jan Steen (1625/6–79) is far closer in conception to De Hooch's outdoor scenes. From 1654 to 1657 Steen's father leased a brewery for his son in Delft.[58] No documentary evidence suggests Steen ever remained long in the city but this painting proves that he painted in Delft and suggests that he may have contributed to the changes which occurred in cityscapes and genre scenes produced there.[59] The setting is the front of a house facing the Oude Delft Canal, on which Steen's brewery was situated. In the distance the tower of the Nieuwe Kerk and the Prinsenhof appear. As in Houckgeest's and Fabritius's recent works, a topographically accurate view is depicted. The orderly design and the tonal and structural clarity anticipate characteristics of De Hooch's courtyards. Some of the shared features of the two painter's works may reflect common sources. Genre scenes situated before the doorways of houses or in loosely defined courtyards had appeared earlier in the works of Isaak van Ostade, (possibly) Terborch, and Maes.[60] None of their pictures, however, displayed the degree of spatial order and coherence which Steen attempted in his portrait and which was ultimately realized in De Hooch's courtyards of *c.* 1658.

As a family portrait with genre elements in an exterior urban setting, Steen's painting also may be cited as a forerunner of De Hooch's *Family in a Courtyard* in Vienna (Cat. 24, Col. Plate III, Plate 21). The latter work is De Hooch's largest and most ambitious picture from these years. The 'sitters' are disposed with deliberate informality in a courtyard with a white-pilastered arbour, which abuts the old Town Wall of Delft. A brick walkway leads the eye through a gate to an adjoining court and beyond to the tower of the Nieuwe Kerk. While earlier Dutch and Flemish artists had portrayed couples and family groups in outdoor settings, most commonly in imaginary landscapes and gardens,[61] De Hooch seems to have been the first to represent a family in a simple middle-class courtyard.

The naturalistic appearance of De Hooch's setting belies the fact that the composition is actually a translation of traditional De Vriesian designs. Dirck van Delen's *Palace Courtyard with Figures* dated 1635 (Fig. 23) is typical of the architectural fantasies Vredeman de Vries's followers confected from the perspectivist's models for palatial courtyards (see Fig. 24). When De Hooch's composition is compared with the Van Delen we note a similar juxtaposition of a near view of figures and architecture and a deep centralized view to distant architectural apertures. Yet in De Hooch's picture the memory of the perspective models has been eliminated by the substitution of common Delft motifs for the elements of architectural fantasy. The heavy-columned porch with staircase in De Vries's prototype has become a simple arbour and stairs; the grand building with central archway and cupola has been transformed into a succession of garden gates concluding with the familiar Delft church spire. While the prominent orthogonals of De Vries's model dominate Van Delen's composition, the perspectival system in the De Hooch is subordinated to the primary goal of a natural appearance.

The naturalistic transformation which De Hooch performed on De Vriesian palace court designs resembles the changes which Houckgeest and De Witte had wrought earlier on the church interiors. As Wheelock has observed, Houckgeest's *Interior of the Nieuwe Kerk* (Fig. 10) reinterprets motifs found in De Vries's *Perspective*,[62] applying the designs to a naturalistic view of an actual church rather than to a contrived *retardataire* architectural fantasy. The spatial formulae of Steen's portrait of 1655 also have precedents in earlier paintings by the De Vriesian painters.[63] In each of these cases, the artist's adaptation of his sources moderates the abstract rigidity of the designs without forsaking the expressive potential of the perspective system.

Where De Hooch and his older colleagues part company is in the degree of fidelity to what they saw before them. Although De Hooch's pictures appear to record actual sites, they are largely the products of his imagination. Glimpses of Delft monuments, including the Oude Kerk (Cat. 20–2, Col. Plates IV, V, Plate 19), the Nieuwe Kerk (Cat. 21, 24, 35A–B, 36, Col. Plates III, V, Plates 34–7, 39), the Town Hall (Cat. 36, Plates 37, 39), and the old Town Wall (Cat. 24, 39, 44, Col. Plate III, Plates 42, 48), regularly appear in his outdoor scenes. Yet the recurrence of altered and relocated details confirms that these paintings include fictitious assemblages of naturalistic motifs. The same arbour appears in different positions in the courtyard scenes in Vienna, Washington, and London (Cat. 24, 39, 44, Col. Plate III, Plates 21, 42, 48); and in the latter two works, the same waterpump is discreetly resituated. While the two brilliant courtyards of 1658 in Edinburgh (Cat. 33, Col. Plate VIII) and London (Cat. 34, Col. Plate IX) are variants of a single design, close comparison reveals that they differ in virtually all details. Similarly, although the same room often seems to reappear in the interior scenes of this period (compare Cat. 30, 31, Plates 28, 29) one cannot assume that the naturalistic appearance arises from literal reportage. The interior of the *Bedroom* (Cat. 40A–C, Plates 43, 44) reappears with only minor adjustments of viewpoint and furnishings in the Rijksmuseum's painting (Cat. 42, Plate 46), only to undergo major architectural alterations in the picture in New York (Cat. 43, Plate 47). Clearly De Hooch's intentions differed from those shared by Fabritius and the architectural painters in the early years of the decade. Fidelity to the actual site was replaced in his work by a more subjective form of naturalism. While the illusion of reality was no less plausible, the goal of mimetic exactitude had been abandoned.[64]

From around 1658 De Hooch painted not only variations of designs, but also replicas of his own works, a practice which seems to have survived into his later career (see Cat. 60A & B and 112A & B). Over-painting in the courtyard scene in the Mauritshuis (Cat. 35B, Plate 35) has obscured the fact that the work is a faithful repetition of a painting in Washington which is probably the original (Cat. 35A, Plate 34). The *Bedroom* scene also exists in several autograph versions (Cat. 40A–C). De Hooch's willingness to repeat himself in this manner may seem odd to the modern viewer, who values invention above what may seem here to be mere execution. Nevertheless, this was a common, and indeed quite practical, solution to which Dutch painters resorted when faced with the happy situation that a work proved attractive to more than one buyer. On one occasion De Hooch painted a scene (see Cat. 41, Plate 45) which closely resembles a detail of a larger composition (see Cat. 40A–C, Plates 43, 44), a case which, to the present author's know-ledge, is unique in the history of Dutch genre.

Although we cannot say with certainty when De Hooch first turned to outdoor scenes, the superbly tranquil painting of women laundering clothes (Cat. 20, Col. Plate IV) is doubtless one of the earliest and probably slightly predates 1658. Several large pentimenti in the background seem to testify to a more intuitive approach to composition than one encounters in the rigorously ordered courtyards dated 1658 (Cat. 33–4, Col. Plates VIII, IX).[65] Subtle adjustments of light and atmosphere enhance the space, and the artist's perception of textures is particularly fine in the renderings of the bare and lime-covered masonry. Set off from the surroundings by their brightly coloured costumes of red, lemon-yellow, and blue, the women go about their work in an unhurried but efficient manner. Brickwork showing through their garments again indicates that the figures were painted into the scene after the architecture had been completed.

The tower of the Oude Kerk and the gabled house appearing in the distance of this work reappear in altered relation to one another in the scene of a *Woman with a Child in a Bleaching Ground* (Cat. 21, Col. Plate V) and a lost picture of a child buying an apple from a woman (Cat. 22, Plate 19), known today through a drawing after the picture. The latter seems to have been De Hooch's only street scene and is also his only known treatment of an outdoor peddling theme. Maes had painted scenes of pedlars at the doors of houses by *c.* 1655, but he placed far greater emphasis on the figures than on their surroundings.[66] De Hooch's *Street Scene* and *Bleaching Ground* tip the balance in favour of the urban environment and come as close as he ever would to pure cityscape. Vermeer's famous *View in Delft* (Rijksmuseum, Amsterdam, no. A 2860) is a logical extension of these ideas and must count De Hooch's works among its sources. The scene of a *Woman Drinking with Two Soldiers* (Cat. 35A, Plate 34), like the courtyards dated 1658 (Cat. 33, 34, Col. Plates VIII, IX), establishes a more equitable relationship between figures and architecture. In such works the seemingly divergent goals of the cityscape and the genre painter are met and resolved. Never before in painting had people and highly rationalized urban spaces coexisted quite so naturally.

Garden scenes are less common than courtyards in De Hooch's oeuvre and draw on an older tradition in Dutch painting. In the early decades of the century artists like David Vinkboons, Dirck Hals, and Esaias van de Velde had depicted fashionably dressed young people in parks and gardens. Predictably, the occasional formal garden scenes by the De Vriesian painters employed more elaborately contrived spatial designs.[67] Van Hoogstraten's *Portrait of a Couple in the Garden of a Country House* of 1647 (Fig. 25) aligns itself with the time-honoured garden-portrait tradition, and, in formal terms, represents an intermediate stage between the garden scenes of the De Vriesian painters and De Hooch. While a new concern with the effects of light in the open air is evident, the perspective system still exhibits an abstract prominence. De Hooch's *Woman and Child in a Garden* (Cat. 38, Plate 41) moderates perspectival recession by disrupting orthogonals at irregular intervals and lowering the horizon. Modestly scaled domestic buildings bordering the view replace the palaces and imposing country villas of earlier garden scenes. As in the artist's court-yards, the effect is at once intimate and compellingly true to life.

De Hooch must be credited with being the first artist to realize the full expressive potential of orderly, middle-class courtyard and garden spaces. To all intents and purposes, the naturalistic courtyard theme was his invention. His paintings successfully combine perspectival techniques translated from earlier art with the new empirical naturalism of his immediate predecessors in Delft. The principal historical significance of his achievement is the unprecedented standard of truth he brought to fictitious compositions of exterior urban space. His courtyard scenes are at once artificially contrived and wholly credible. With these works and related interior genre scenes, De Hooch played a central role in the formation of the mature Delft School style.

The Early Years in Amsterdam 1660/61—70

De Hooch had settled in Amsterdam by April 1661 (see Doc. 36) and may have moved there as much as one year earlier (Doc. 33). During the preceding century the great merchant city had experienced unprecedented growth.[1] Between 1575 and 1675 the land area had increased sixfold and from 1590 to 1640 the population nearly quadrupled.[2] By 1640 the city had about 140,000 inhabitants, while Delft probably had only 25–30,000. The increases in Amsterdam's population were primarily the result of immigration; at mid-century more than 50 per cent of the bridegrooms married in the city were born elsewhere. One in four residents came from abroad and the tone was distinctly cosmopolitan.

Part of Amsterdam's attraction stemmed from her extraordinary prosperity. With the closing of the Scheldt River in 1585 the forces of the United Provinces effectively put an end to Antwerp's preeminence among the North European trading centres and the stage was set for Amsterdam's rapid succession. It became the capital of the far-flung Dutch colonial empire and a centre of world banking and of the lucrative European grain trade. War with Spain had not hampered Amsterdam's enrichment nor even prevented her pragmatic merchants from doing business with their enemies. Indeed, the country's war for freedom was financed in a large measure by the city's burgeoning trade. Amsterdam paid fully one half of the province of Holland's contributions to the States General; Holland, in turn, paid 56 per cent of the total revenues.

The city fathers were no less jealous of their economic sovereignty than their counterparts in Delft and by mid-century the regent oligarchy had also begun to resemble an urban aristocracy. Yet the civic administration remained relatively more progressive in its attitudes and institutions. Unlike in Delft, the tone of the city was still set by the enterprising merchant and professional classes. The regents were committed to a milder form of Calvinism (although still in many respects doctrinaire) and to relative freedom of thought and religion. Amsterdam's reputation for tolerance drew the oppressed—Jews from Spain and Portugal, Huguenots from France, refugees from the Thirty Years War in Germany, and large numbers of skilled workers from the Spanish Netherlands—as well as less disenfranchised folk. The city fathers rightly looked upon the new arrivals as a source of strength.

With its rich potential clients and large and innovative artistic community, Amsterdam also presented a powerful attraction to artists. From around 1640—indeed, even before the establishment of an indigenous Delft painting style—a pattern emerged of artists emigrating from Delft to Amsterdam. Over the next thirty years this exodus contributed to a marked decline in the number of artists in the southern city.[3] Like her other trading institutions, Amsterdam's art market was highly competitive. Our knowledge of how De Hooch fared in this new marketplace is limited, but there is little reason to suppose that his fortunes were substantially improved by the move.[4] The addresses given in his childrens' burial records of 1663 and 1665 (Docs. 40 & 43) indicate that he was living on the outskirts of the city in a very poor area. In this, the city's golden age, many citizens knew only dross and disease. No less than one fifth of the population was killed by plague in 1663–4.

The large *Family Portrait* in Cleveland (Cat. 53, Col. Plate XII, Plate 57), dated 1663, proves that De Hooch had some success in securing commissions during his early years in Amsterdam. With this picture we are introduced to a world of greater elegance than has previously been encountered in the artist's works. Whereas the well-to-do Delft family who sat for the portrait in Vienna (Cat. 24, Col. Plate III) had been depicted in a modest courtyard setting, the new clientele is portrayed making music in a richly decorated interior with a marble floor and fireplace. Spacious by Dutch standards, the room is elaborately decorated with an expensive and well-crafted oak wardrobe, a tapestry, an oriental carpet, and (possibly) imported vases and lacquer boxes of East Asian design. Clearly the family wished to be portrayed amidst the symbols of its worldly success. By comparison, the Delft family seems conspicuously reserved and perhaps a trifle provincial.

Although the identity of the sitters in the Cleveland portrait has eluded us, in all likelihood they were members of an Amsterdam merchant's family. De Hooch painted portraits of several such families. An inventory of 1707 of the estate of Petronella de la Court, widow of the owner of the Zwaan brewery, Adam Oortmans, included a family portrait by De Hooch (Cat. C 261) and the same family owned other paintings by him (Cat. C 20–1, C 143).[5] Around 1670 he also portrayed the family of the wealthy Amsterdam cloth merchant Jan Jacott (Cat. 92, Plate 95). Thus, the artist knew the patronage of that element of Amsterdam society which most vividly reflected her prosperity, the rich and socially ambitious merchants.[6] Amsterdam's upper-class merchants took their notions of refinement and cultivation from the elite circles of the regents and the landed aristocracy. While the likes of Oortmans and Jacott retained their ties with industry and trade, they increasingly aspired to the elegant lifestyles of the reigning families of Amsterdam. De Hooch became one of the artists who satisfied these men's desires for likenesses of themselves and their families which seemed to affirm the success and propriety of their ambitions.

The portrait type to which the Cleveland painting belongs had, in fact, been employed several years earlier in the representation of an actual regent's family by the gifted Leiden painter, Gabriel Metsu (1629–67).[7] Metsu had moved to Amsterdam by 1657 and in that year painted *The Family of the Amsterdam Burgomaster Dr. Gilles Valckenier* (Fig. 26).[8] Here, as in De Hooch's portrait, an elegant family group is depicted in a moment of leisure in a dark and spacious horizontal interior with a lighted doorway. While De Hooch places greater emphasis on clear spatial definition and local lighting, the two painters share a painstaking technique. The detailed rendering of stuffs and surfaces functions as the stylistic correlative to the refined aspirations of the sitters. The history of elegant family portraits with genre elements in orderly interiors deserves further study. Flemish precedents appear in the art of Gonzales Coques and Gillis van Tilborgh. Working in Holland, Nicolaes Knupfer executed a similar *Portrait of a Family Singing* around 1646 (Staatliche Kunstsammlungen, Dresden). The portrait type enjoyed increased popularity toward the end of the century and its formulae helped to shape the eighteenth century's 'conversation piece'.

It is fortunate that the scarcity of dated works which characterized De Hooch's Delft production is somewhat relieved in his Amsterdam years. Between 1663 and 1670 he dated paintings in all years except 1666. Some of these dates have been overlooked or misread in the past. Lord Barnard's painting (Cat. 69, Plate 72) is dated 1665; the date on the picture at Hampton Court (Cat. 77, Plate 80) should read 1667, not 1677; and the portrait in the Duc de Trévise Sale (Cat. 75, Plate 78) was said in the nineteenth century to be signed and dated in the same year. These dates facilitate a fairly precise assessment of the artist's style until the end of the decade.

The stylistic changes witnessed in the portrait in Cleveland are consistent with those which appeared in De Hooch's genre paintings shortly after his arrival in Amsterdam. His other painting of 1663 (Cat. 52, Plate 56) represents two women in satin and fur-trimmed costumes storing linen in a handsome chest of oak and inlaid ebony. Fluted pilaster mouldings decorate the door and windows. Once more, the surroundings are richer than those of the comparable domestic scenes of the Delft period (cf. Cat. 40A, 42, Plates 43, 46). As in the *Family Portrait*, a tighter mode of execution and a shadowed, but rigorously ordered, horizontal composition is employed. The lighting effects, contrasting the subdued half light of the room with the brilliant daylight of the doorway, have become more exaggerated and the colour scheme has shifted to a cooler register. A certain rigidity in the design arising from the repeated vertical accents of the chest, standing women, and pilasters, serves almost as a formal parallel to the rectitude of the household. More luxurious settings also appear in a series of merry company scenes from this period (Cat. 55–8, Plates 58–61), which exchange the frugal Delft interiors with their whitewashed walls for rooms hung with richly gilt leather.

De Hooch's conversion to the more elegant variety of genre scene could in part have been inspired by Metsu and Jan Steen. The former's *Visit to the Nursery* of 1661 (Fig. 27) and Steen's two versions of *Soo Gewonen, Soo Verteert* (*Easy Come, Easy Go*) in the Boymans Museum in Rotterdam and formerly in the Earl of Lonsdale's Collection, of 1661 and 1660 respectively, anticipate his rich and ample interiors of *c.* 1663.[9] De Hooch's figure groups of this period are among the liveliest in his oeuvre and also reveal points of resemblance with those of the two Leiden painters. As Waagen observed,[10] the officer and the girl in the painting in Nuremberg (Cat. 55, Plate 58) partake of the 'character and humour' of Steen's art and the same could be said of the animated revellers in the painting in Lisbon (Cat. 57, Plate 60). A picture from these years in the Wellington Museum represents a woman at her toilet surprised by a male visitor (Cat. 70, Plate 73) recalling the theme of Metsu's playful *Intruder* in the National Gallery in Washington.

Despite these resemblances, De Hooch's early Amsterdam works display a greater geometric order than the contemporary works of either Metsu or Steen. In the *Family Portrait* and the *Linen Closet* all five planes of the interior are indicated. The resulting increase in the emphasis on cubic orthogonal space is typical of De Hooch's paintings from his first years in Amsterdam (see Cat. 54–8, Col. Plate XIII, Plates 58–61) and calls to mind the very De Vriesian tradition which the master's works of the late 1650s had done so much to supplant. No doubt the memory of the older spatial formulae was invoked with full knowledge of its associations with the grand and luxurious interiors of an earlier era. Although a number of Dutch genre painters, including Ludolf de Jongh, Hendrick van der Burch, and Vermeer,[11] experimented with more rigidly cubic interiors in the 1660s, De Hooch sustained the greatest interest in these designs and most successfully realized their compatibility with elegant 'high life' themes.

Some stylistic features of De Hooch's paintings of 1663 had appeared in several paintings which are probably earlier. It cannot always be determined with certainty whether these works were executed in Delft or Amsterdam. While the views to a narrow street in the Bentinck–Thyssen Collection's painting (Cat. 48, Plate 51) and to a little 'hofje' in the Wallace Collection's picture (Cat. 49, Plate 52) suggest Delft origins, the subdued tonality and the pronounced lighting contrasts are more appropriate to the artist's first years in Amsterdam. The close resemblance in execution of the *Mother Beside a Cradle* in Berlin (Cat. 51) to the Cleveland portrait also points to the early Amsterdam years. On several occasions in the early 1660s (see Cat. 45, 46, 59, 60A, Plates 49, 62–4, Col. Plate XI) De Hooch again took up the courtyard and garden themes first treated in his Delft period. The organization of the brilliant painting of a *Woman and Her Maid in a Courtyard* in the Hermitage (Cat. 46, Col. Plate XI) recalls the compositions of *c.* 1658–60, but its crisp linear clarity, bright cool tones, and view to a relatively wide canal, again suggest origins in the early Amsterdam years.

Subtle stylistic changes distinguishing the Delft and Amsterdam periods also seem evident in the compositionally related paintings of maternal subjects in San Francisco (Cat. 32, Col. Plate VII) and the Wallace Collection (Cat. 61, Plate 65). While the designs are basically identical, the picture in London increases the geometric rigidity of the composition by altering the pattern of the floor, reducing the number of accessories and adjusting the disposition of the figures. The colour scheme has become more intense and the light chillier and less evenly modulated. The result is an image of greater formality and restraint. Like the picture of a *Young Couple with a Dog* in New York (Cat. 43, Plate 47), which replaces the simple vestibule of its Delft period prototype (see Cat. 40A–C, Plates 43, 44) with a view to a room hung with gilt leather, the Wallace Collection's painting is probably based on a design first conceived in Delft and altered after the artist's move to Amsterdam.

The precision and refinement of De Hooch's new style may in part have been a response to Leiden 'fijnschilder' genre painting. One of the earliest writers to mention De Hooch, J. B. Descamps, writing in 1753, apparently was better acquainted with the painter's Amsterdam period paintings than with those of his Delft years.[12] He felt that De Hooch's paintings most resembled those of Metsu and Frans van Mieris.[13] Frans van Mieris the Elder (1635–81) was Gerard Dou's most gifted pupil and perfected a highly refined mode of execution which coupled minute detail and highly finished modelling of surfaces. Van Mieris's influence on Dutch genre painters after *c.* 1660 was considerable. Yet, while one can point to specific

instances of his impact on artists like Vermeer and Ochtervelt,[14] his importance for De Hooch was limited to his general role as a predecessor in the adoption of more refined painting techniques. As Descamps perceptively observed, De Hooch retained a broader touch and less precise manner than either Metsu or Van Mieris. When we speak, therefore, of a greater refinement in De Hooch's Amsterdam manner, it is a matter of degree relative to the works of his Delft period.

The influence Descamps believed Van Mieris had exerted on De Hooch was probably more a matter of shared sources in the art of Gerard Terborch. To a lesser extent, the same may also be true of the author's comments regarding Metsu's influence. As early as the mid-1650s Terborch had begun painting elegantly conceived genre scenes of great technical and psychological sophistication (see Fig. 28; the so-called 'Parental Admonition' of c. 1654–5). Unrivalled in rendering the sheen of silk garments, Terborch invented a repertoire of figure motifs which were freely quoted by many later Dutch genre painters. The most famous motif—the silk-clad woman standing in lost profile—proved irresistible to De Hooch, particularly after 1670 (see Cat. 77, 93, 114–17, 121, 158, Plates 80, 97, 117–20, 124, 161). Other figures in De Hooch's paintings of the early Amsterdam years also owe much to Terborch. The woman seated at her dressing table (Cat. 70, Plate 73)[15] or quietly reading a letter (Cat. 63, 85, Plates 67, 88);[16] the man exchanging ceremonious greetings with a woman at a doorway (Cat. 84, Plate 87);[17] or the couple who casually share a lemon drink at a table (Cat. 59; see detail Plate 63);[18] all recall Terborch's art. His influence is also easily recognized in Metsu's *Visit to the Nursery* (Fig. 27). Yet the older master's spaces never possess the amplitude and definition which mark the latter work as an important precursor of De Hooch's first Amsterdam interiors.

The only artist whose work we are certain De Hooch knew during his early years in Amsterdam is Emanuel de Witte. In 1670 (cf. Doc. 47) De Hooch testified to having seen a portrait by De Witte of *Adriana van Heusden at the New Fishmarket in Amsterdam* (two existing versions[19]) in the home of Joris de Wijs, where the older painter lived and painted under contract to the owner. This would have occurred before 1663, by which time De Witte had left the house, taking the picture and three others with him. The version of the Adriana van Heusden portrait in London was attributed to De Hooch several times in the nineteenth century and carried a false signature.[20] Although De Hooch evidently did not execute either market scenes or church interiors, contact between the two artists seems to be reflected in their secular interiors. De Witte's *Woman Playing the Harpsichord* (Fig. 29)[21] resembles works by De Hooch from the early 1660s like the *Woman Reading with a Child* (Cat. 50, Plate 53), last seen in the Arenberg Collection. The two interiors employ a similar horizontal composition with a deep centralized view through a series of spaces. While both artists alternate passages of light and shade in their receding vistas, De Witte distributes his light in bands, a technique foreign to De Hooch. Neither work is dated; however, De Witte's picture is an isolated statement within his oeuvre, and thus probably was painted in response to the elegant new interior type perfected by De Hooch.[22] On the other hand, De Hooch may have consulted De Witte's church interiors when, in the mid-1660s, he turned to the depiction of still grander architectural spaces in a series of pictures with settings derived from the new Amsterdam Town Hall.

The most conspicuous expression of Amsterdam's prosperity and of the shift in official taste to classicism was the new Town Hall (today the Royal Palace) designed by Jacob van Campen (1595–1657).[23] Begun in 1648—the year of the formal recognition of the Republic's independence—the monumental structure was the grandest public building of its kind yet erected in Europe. It exemplified the artistic ideals of the urban aristocracy and, having been financed through taxes, was a source of great pride for the general citizenry. Four of De Hooch's paintings from the mid 1660s include references to the building (see Cat. 66–8, 76, Plates 69–71, 79).

The painting in the Thyssen-Bornemisza Collection in Lugano (Cat. 66, Plate 71) depicts the *Council Chamber of the Burgomasters* (today Van Speyk Hall), which was in the part of the Town Hall opened in 1655. As in the compositionally related painting of approximately the same date in Copenhagen (Cat. 65, Plate 68), an illusionistic curtain has been painted into the picture. Curtains often were hung over pictures in seventeenth-century Dutch households—probably for protective purposes—and many artists included such *trompe-l'oeil* devices in their works after *c.* 1650.[24] The painting in Lugano presents a view down the length of the lofty chamber to the northern wall, where a large fireplace is surmounted by a painting finished by Ferdinand Bol in 1656 and still hanging today *in situ*. The citizens of Amsterdam evidently were free to visit the Town Hall;[25] Jacob Vennekool's illustrations (Fig. 30) depict people promenading about the galleries with their children and dogs. No doubt, the figures who stand and gesture in De Hooch's painting are some of these admiring visitors. Oddly enough, though, the architecture they peruse does not correspond in all details to that which they would have encountered in the new building on the Dam. De Hooch has redesigned the pattern of the tile floor and opened an entirely fictitious view to a backlighted room at the left. In the actual structure this doorway has always opened on a blind hallway.

Paintings in Leipzig (Cat. 68, Plate 69) and Strasbourg (Cat. 67, Plate 70) also derive their surroundings from the Town Hall. In both of these cases the settings are based on the galleries adjoining the Burgerzaal on the first floor. The Strasbourg painting has been marred by nineteenth-century overpainting, which eliminated an additional male figure and added a view to a room through the archway at the left. While it is difficult, therefore, to assess the degree of fidelity of the artist's original conception, it appears to correspond to the actual structure in most details. As in the Lugano painting, the figures are quite plausible as members of the sightseeing citizenry. The painting in Leipzig, on the other hand, makes quite a different impression. Here fact and fancy mix more freely. A view to a room hung with gilt leather (in this case by the artist's own hand) replaces a stairway beneath the right arch at the end of the gallery and numerous minor changes appear in the pattern of the tiled floor and the architectural decorations. The most startling intrusion of fiction, though, is the appearance of Raphael's *School of Athens* in place of one of the episodes from the Revolt of the Batavians which decorated the lunettes of the galleries. In selecting this detail De Hooch no doubt wished to underscore the parallel between the classicism of High Renaissance painting and the ideals embodied in the architecture of the new Town Hall.

It was not De Hooch's intention here to give an accurate account of the building or even of activities, like the sightseeing in the Lugano and Strasbourg paintings, which were appropriate to it. Rather it seems the architectural quotations were designed to enhance the impression of social merrymaking in a lavish and fashionably styled setting. In the context of the music and drinking, the interior is transformed into a palatial private dwelling, the likes of which were nowhere to be found in Amsterdam. An exterior view of the Town Hall was employed for similar effects somewhat later in a painting of a *Man and Woman Playing Music on a Terrace* (Cat. 76, Plate 79). The building appears silhouetted against the sky and irrationally detached from the Amsterdam skyline. Like the curtain hung from the porch overhead and the suggestion of a formal garden beyond, the structure functions as a luxurious accessory. By its association with the most current and elevated aesthetic ideals, the reference ensured a resonance of refinement in the scene.

The blending of actual architecture and invention in De Hooch's Town Hall series resembles aspects of De Witte's approach to architectural painting in these years. Although De Witte was inspired by various ecclesiastical buildings in Amsterdam, he rarely depicted them faithfully. The actual architecture often was altered for compositional purposes and even motifs from churches in different towns were occasionally recombined to form new and grander imaginary structures.[26] The organization of De Hooch's views of the galleries of the Town Hall (Cat. 67, 68, Plates 69, 70) may be compared with the naves of De Witte's imaginary churches, and the sequential alteration of light and shade which articulates the space in the picture in Strasbourg recalls the older artist's designs. The mixture of actual and imaginary elements in these pictures again emphasizes the subjective nature of the 'realism' so often celebrated in Dutch painting. The fact, furthermore, that the imaginary elements in so many of the architectural painters' compositions have only recently been recognized and De Hooch's alterations of the Town Hall's architecture previously overlooked,[27] is a testimony to the extraordinary efficacy of the artists' inventive powers.

In the painting of *Skittles Players* at Waddesdon Manor (Cat. 60A, Plate 64) the fashionable young people who populate the artist's contemporary interiors are transported to a suitably grandiose outdoor setting. Casually engaged in their sport, they are arranged along a pathway in a formal garden decorated with

III. A Family in a Courtyard (Cat. 24). *c.* 1657–60. Akademie der bildenden Künste, Vienna. See also Plate 21

IV. Two Women with a Child in a Courtyard (Cat. 20). *c.* 1657. Toledo Museum of Art, Toledo

topiary and statues. In the background a country house appears. With its monumentally ordered façade the building might be a fanciful reduction of one of the recent architectural projects in a classical idiom, such as Van Campen's Mauritshuis or Justus Vingboon's Trippenhuis. During these years many wealthy Amsterdam families—again, no doubt, in emulation of the landed aristocracy—built summer homes.[28] The preferred sites were along the Amstel and Vecht rivers. Following the rise of the cityscape, artists like Van der Heyden made a speciality of depicting the more famous country houses and their surrounding gardens.[29] Imaginary country villas were also a standard feature of the idealized garden party tradition in genre painting.[30] De Hooch's painting and the later works of De Jongh (see Fig. 61)[31] form a link in the chain of this tradition, which extends from the medieval love garden to the eighteenth century's *fêtes champêtres*. As with De Hooch's interiors of the early 1660s, aspects of the Waddesdon Manor composition are reminiscent of earlier spatial designs; note, for example, the resemblance to Van Hoogstraten's portrait of 1647 (Fig. 25). Yet the work in no way succumbs to the unworldly abstraction of the De Vriesian painters' renditions of this theme.[32]

In the late 1660s De Hooch's simple courtyard scenes were followed by paintings, like those in the Duc de Trévise and Huldschinsky sales (Cat. 75, 76, Plates 78, 79), depicting elegant ladies and gentlemen on marble terraces with heavy-columned porches. These two pictures are similar in size and design and have been considered, perhaps correctly, to be pendants; while the former picture is clearly a family portrait, it is questionable whether the figures in the latter painting bear portrait features.[33] We know very little about the nature of pendants in Dutch art and virtually nothing about genre paintings designed as companion pieces. Nevertheless, it is clear that the execution of pendants was more common in seventeenth-century Holland than elsewhere in Europe. Entries in sales catalogues suggest that De Hooch not only designed genre scenes as pendants (see Cat. 12, 13; 150, 151, Plates 11, 12; 153, 154), but also, as in the present and a somewhat later case (see Cat. 92, 93, Plates 95, 97), may have painted portraits and genre pieces as companions. Undoubtedly the linking of these works affects their meanings. In the terrace scenes, the theme of music in the companion piece may, as in certain portraits (cf. Cat. 53), allude to the harmonious nature of the family group with which it was paired.

Elegant family portraits on porches had been executed about a decade earlier in Amsterdam by De Hooch's contemporary Barent Graat (1628–1709). The latter's *Portrait of a Family* of 1658 (Fig. 31) represents the type of portrait after which De Hooch's painting in the Duc de Trévise Sale (Cat. 75, Plate 78) is modelled. This type probably has Flemish origins in the art of Van Dyck and Gonzales Coques (1614–84). Although De Hooch is more likely to have encountered Graat's works, Coques' small-scale family portraits on terraces may also have been known to him.[34] Descamps, again, was the first to observe Coques' precedents for De Hooch, a perception which has been neglected in the modern literature.[35]

Genre scenes on terraces or porches opening on gardens, like De Hooch's pictures in the Huldschinsky Sale (Cat. 76, Plate 79) and a Private Collection (Cat. 91, Plate 94), reflect an older tradition in Dutch painting. Artists like Esaias van de Velde had painted such scenes early in the century.[36] More recently these themes had been treated by a number of Amsterdam painters, including Van den Eeckhout, Van Loo, Graat, and G. P. van Zijl.[37] Together with the *Skittles Players* (Cat. 60A, Plate 64), De Hooch's terrace scenes align themselves with the idealized garden scene tradition and partake of its potential for amorous (love garden) associations.

Maternal and domestic themes continued to appear in De Hooch's art. The lady of the household now is mistress of a richer domain and attended more frequently by a serving woman. The painting in Vienna (Cat. 54, Col. Plate XIII) offers a particularly fine example of the artist's elegantly spare new domestic interior type. While the physical chores are increasingly relegated to servants, the mistress continues to care for the infants herself. Maternal subjects are taken up in a series of extremely dark horizontal interiors with strong patterns of light on the back wall (see Cat. 71-4, Plates 74-7). While this group has been dated in the 1670s the resemblance in design to Lord Barnard's painting of 1665 (Cat. 69, Plate 72) and in lighting to the picture of 1664 in Budapest (Cat. 63, Plate 67) suggests a date toward the middle of the preceding decade. Here as elsewhere in De Hooch's dark later works, the virtual illegibility of many details in the

c

shadows suggests that these paintings have probably darkened considerably with time. While the lower range of tones in most seventeenth-century Dutch pictures has quite naturally shifted downward, the darkening effect in De Hooch's later works has almost certainly been more dramatic than usual. This may be the result of the particular chemistry of his medium or of the effects on the painting's ground of the wax used in relinings. Thus, while his dramatic chiaroscuro—so much admired by eighteenth-century writers—was an intentional effect, we no doubt observe it today in an exaggerated state.

Certain works from De Hooch's production of the 1660s are thematically and formally more isolated than others. The scene of a *Wounded Man Being Treated in a Stable* (Cat. 80, Plate 83) returns to a subject he had treated in his early altered painting in London (Cat. 14, Plate 14). Its style, however, suggests origins in the late 1660s, or even possibly later. Single-figure compositions, like the *Woman Weighing Coins* in Berlin (Cat. 64, Col. Plate XIV) are quite rare in De Hooch's work. In several early sales this picture was evidently sold as a Vermeer and it is clearly related to the latter's painting of a *Woman Holding Scales* in Washington (Fig. 32).[38] Neither work is dated; however, whereas the De Hooch appears as a virtually unique statement within his oeuvre, Vermeer's picture is only one of a series of quiet single-figure compositions he painted at the height of his career. Undoubtedly De Hooch knew the Vermeer and adopted its composition shortly after it was executed. Conceivably he first encountered it when he visited Delft in 1663. The main features of Vermeer's design—the three-quarter-length profile view of a woman holding scales over a table before a window—are taken over in De Hooch's painting. Yet De Hooch has opened the window, introduced a view through a doorway at the right, and eliminated the painting on the wall. Small as these changes may seem, they result in quite dissimilar effects, which clarify the differences between the two artists. The picture which frames the woman's head in the Vermeer is equal to exactly one quarter of the surface of the canvas and reflects the precise underpinnings of a thoroughly rationalized design. In the De Hooch we witness greater formal diffusion. The geometry of the architecture operates more independently from the placement and disposition of the figure. The result is an impression of greater spaciousness and a commensurate sacrifice of the monumental concentration of his model. The omission of the picture of the Last Judgement appearing in Vermeer's painting also strips the work of its 'clavis interpretandi'. To this important point we shall return. At this juncture, however, it is clear that in the dialogue between the two great artists, the direction of the primary influence was reversed shortly after De Hooch's move to Amsterdam.

Briefly reviewed, De Hooch's production in the first decade of his activity in Amsterdam parallels a general trend in Dutch art toward greater elegance. His subject matter became richer and more pretentious and his style correspondingly more highly refined. Adopting a tighter mode of execution, the artist turned to progressively darker tonalities and cooler and deeper local colour schemes. His spatial designs became more rigidly ordered and his figures less pliant. The cosy bourgeois settings of the Delft period were increasingly exchanged for the luxurious apartments and gardens of the very rich. Occasionally the artist also repeated his own and other artists' successful earlier designs and themes. This practice increased through the seventies and the trend towards a more mannered refinement, perceptible by 1665, was brought to fruition.

The Late Years in Amsterdam c. 1670–84

In 1670 De Hooch was residing in the Konijnenstraat (Doc. 47). For the remaining 14 years of his life the paintings are virtually the only record we possess of his activities. Save for the records of the baptism of a third son in 1672 (Doc. 49) and of the artist's burial (Doc. 50), no documentary information pertaining to De Hooch's last years has been discovered. We know, however, that these were difficult times for the Dutch people. The war with the English (1665–7) had strained the economy and in 1672—the calamitous 'Rampjaar'—the French, succeeding where the Spanish had failed, occupied large parts of the United Provinces.

A full study of the economic repercussions of these events on the artistic community and the art market has yet to be written. However, scattered information suggests that the fortunes of many Dutch painters—who had previously relied on relatively low profit margins—were seriously affected. In extreme cases artists and art dealers went bankrupt or left the country,[1] while others sought to supplement their incomes with extra-artistic ventures. Steen took to innkeeping and Vermeer let his house 'Mechelen' and moved in with his mother-in-law. De Hooch's financial situation was, if anything, probably worse. In 1674 his income was sufficiently meager to entirely escape the Amsterdam tax registers.

Like Steen and others,[2] De Hooch seems to have increased his rate of production in his later years. Although some earlier writers have been overgenerous in their attributions to the late career,[3] the trend was significant. Approximately 75 pictures, or about 45 per cent of the oeuvre, survive from the last 14 years of his activity. By c. 1675 there is also evidence of some unevenness in the quality of execution. At present, only conjectural explanations can be offered for these developments. Too little is known about De Hooch's prices to confirm the theory, but his increased production and attendant lapses in quality may have been a response to reduced profits in a depressed marketplace. It is also conceivable that his final mental illness affected the quality of his work. Here, though, we are on highly speculative ground.

The prevailing view of the artist's later career offers still another explanation. Modern writers have repeatedly cast De Hooch in the role of the archetypal representative of the 'decline' of Dutch art. His later works have been characterized as the products of a society grown complacent and of an artist whose creative faculties had been exhausted. The most recent survey of Dutch painting puts it bluntly, '. . . after [De Hooch] moved to Amsterdam, he quickly lost his inspiration and charm, and sank to the role of a second-rate painter.'[4] For Valentiner, the late production seemed to confirm the narrow limitations of his talent and intellect.[5] Such criticism seems, at least in part, based on the false presumption that the late works should be judged by the same aesthetic criteria as the Delft pictures. A fairer and more accurate appraisal is obtained when the pictures are assessed within the context of Dutch art after c. 1670. In short, the late production must be judged on its own terms.

By 1670 the goal of a 'natural appearance of the whole'—the phrase we have used to characterize the aims of De Hooch and the other leading Delft painters in the 1650s—no longer seemed an adequate objective. The emphasis increasingly fell on stylistic refinement and artifice. These changes are illustrated by a comparison of De Hooch's *Jacott-Hoppesack Family Portrait* of c. 1670 (Cat. 92, Plate 95) and the earlier *Family Portrait* of 1663 (Cat. 53, Col. Plate XII). While both works depict the sitters in elegant, no doubt fictionalized, settings, there is a distinct difference in the approach to the factual record of the individual portraits. In the earlier work, as in the Delft period portrait (Cat. 24, Col. Plate III), the bourgeois reality of the sitters is presented with unflagging candour (see Plate 57). In the later picture the individual portrait character has been chastened and reformed; the family members display a mannered grace and a genteel detachment. Their slightly attenuated figure type—the embodiment of aristocratic slimness—appears elsewhere in De Hooch's works of this period (see Cat. 91, Plate 94) and had become a familiar ideal in Dutch portraiture and genre by *c.* 1670.[6] Ochtervelt developed it with great sophistication (see Fig. 33) and he and De Hooch often employed similar figure motifs and portrait formulae in these years.[7]

No doubt the cool and rather haughty civility expressed by the merchant Jacott and his family was meant to evoke the 'deftige' mentality of the regent class. The circles of the regents increasingly imitated the French aristocracy in these years. Even before the invasion of Louis XIV's troops, French styles and manners had made inroads in Holland. Late seventeenth-century Dutch architecture, literature, and fashion testify to these influences. On the other hand, the alleged impact of French painting on Dutch art has doubtless been overstressed. Far freer of foreign models than is usually supposed, the progressive refinement of later Dutch painting appears to have been largely an indigenous development. Indeed, it can be argued that the late Baroque period saw a much stronger influence pass from Holland to France than in the opposite direction.[8]

An interest in greater stylization infused all branches of Dutch painting after *c.* 1670. The growing complexity and superabundance of J. D. de Heem's 'pronkstilleven'; the sinewy and flapping forms of Adam Pynacker's landscapes; the grandly rhetorical gestures of Gerard de Lairesse's historical paintings; and the studied elegance of the later portraits by Maes are but a few expressions of this taste. Among genre painters, in addition to Ochtervelt, a more mannered and refined style was adopted by Van Hoogstraten, Eglon van der Neer (1634–1704), Caspar Netscher (1635/6–84), and other younger artists. As often as not, Terborch's quiet and superbly rarefied art provided the point of departure for later elegant company scenes. While Dutch artists had always borrowed freely, the increase in direct quotation from an established repertoire of motifs, such as Terborch's oeuvre, bespeaks a new attitude toward the process of picture-making. The emphasis had passed from invention to refinement and elaboration. The most vivid example of this trend is provided by the sons of Frans van Mieris, who continued to turn out works based on their father's prototypes well into the eighteenth century. A thorough command of a stylistic convention combined with technical facility were thus appreciated as positive and sufficient qualities in an artist.

Modern writers' low opinion of late seventeenth-century Dutch art seems to reflect a series of critical predispositions. The common view holds that the earlier naturalistic style of painting was a reflection of the middle-class virtues (practicality, forthrightness, etc.) believed to be embodied in the Dutch people at the height of their power as a nation. By the same token, it is reasoned, the later, refined manner must be equated with affluence and decadence. Yet it is at least arguable that the decline of the United Provinces after *c.* 1670 was not so much a matter of some failure of the national spirit as a change imposed from without by larger countries (especially France and England) which were able to reassert their power after long periods of internal disorder. Furthermore, it is not at all certain that such simple causal relationships exist between social factors and style in art. As we have seen, the naturalistic effects De Hooch achieved were deliberate artistry and not a 'naive' response to his environment.[9] Here again, we must beware of the nineteenth century's myth of naturalism as a 'styleless' style. Finally, the implied assumption in this view that one style of painting might be not only aesthetically but morally superior to another seems highly dubious.

The achievements of late Dutch painting can only be grasped through an understanding of the values of the age. These can best be described as manneristic.[10] In the late decades of the century stylization and rhetoric (both terms usually, and quite inappropriately, applied today in a pejorative sense) were seen as viable and desirable concerns. Sophistication and refinement were considered positive virtues to be actively cultivated. Clearly such priorities differed from the naturalistic ideals current during De Hooch's early career. A consciousness of these differences ensures a just assessment of the late career.

Accordingly, we should review De Hooch's late paintings objectively. While only nine of these works are dated, several others are datable and a general chronology can be constructed. Around 1670 he executed a series of paintings in which letters appear as central motifs. Epistolary activity—much of it inspired by the

French—enjoyed considerable popularity with the Dutch during these years and many genre painters chose themes involving letters. In one of De Hooch's less known works (Cat. 97, Plate 101), a man appears to be reading a letter aloud to a woman who has set her needlework aside to listen. Elsewhere (see Cat. 85, Plate 88), a woman silently reads a note while a young man, no doubt the courier, waits with a drink at the window. The psychological absorption of these figures is reminiscent of the art of Terborch, who played a central role in popularizing letter-themes. The delivery of a missive is the subject of the painting in the Rijksmuseum of 1670 (Cat. 94, Plate 96) and a compositionally related, but probably somewhat earlier, work in Hamburg (Cat. 84, Plate 87). When the former painting is compared with the Rijksmuseum's picture of 1663 (Cat. 52, Plate 56), we note a cooler tonality and a reduction in the intensity of local colouration. While the artist retained strong chiaroscuro effects, in the early and mid 1670s his palette was supplemented with pastel hues and his light took on the chilly shimmer of the white silks worn by his women.

The *Jacott-Hoppesack Family Portrait* (Cat. 92, Plate 95) of *c.* 1670 and the *Merry Company with Trumpeter* in Brussels (Cat. 93, Plate 97) are close in style and design and identical in size. Mentioned as pendants in an eighteenth-century sale, they may have been designed as companions. We recall that this possibility also arose in the case of an earlier portrait and genre scene (see Cat. 75, 76, Plates 78, 79). Here, however, the discrepancy between the themes is particularly striking. On the one hand we have a highly respectable family group and, on the other, a rather animated gathering of soldiers. If, as seems likely, these works were thought of as a pair, their meanings undoubtedly are interconnected. Were the two subjects perceived as in opposition, or did the trumpeter scene elicit positive associations (the reveille as a call to duty?) which reinforced those of the family portrait? As we shall see, there are no ready answers to such questions.

These two canvases are among the largest De Hooch ever painted. Although earlier works occasionally exhibited comparable dimensions (cf. Cat. 24, 51, 53, 66, Plates 21, 54, 71, Col. Plates III, XII), the large format was most typical of his musical and merry company scenes from the early and mid 1670s. Thirteen pictures from these years boast a measurement of 100 centimetres or more, providing additional evidence of an accelerated rate of work. Many artists of the period painted large pictures, no doubt partially in response to the increased scale of domestic architecture, particularly in Amsterdam, after *c.* 1640. The *Card Players* of *c.* 1670–4 (Cat. 96, Plate 99) adopts a design similar to that of a picture from the late 1660s (see Cat. 86, Plate 89), but is half as large again. With the increased scale we note a commensurate broadening in the execution and a somewhat greater animation in the figures. The woman at the left is of the new figure type of which we have spoken and again recalls Ochtervelt's elegantly vivacious ladies.

A series of three musical company scenes painted in the new, enlarged format (Cat. 108–10, Plates 110, 111, 112) can be dated around 1674 on the basis of the date on the picture in Honolulu (Cat. 108, Plate 110). All are multi-figure compositions grouped around a woman with a cello, who is reminiscent of Metsu's earlier works in a Terborchian vein.[11] The rooms are decorated with pilasters and murals and each is illuminated by a window at the left and a lighted doorway at the right. Compositions of more than three fashionably attired figures making music and arranged horizontally had been popular among genre painters of the generation of Dirck Hals and Codde, but had fallen out of favour in the 1640s and 50s. De Hooch's series follows a revival of such scenes, incorporating the motifs and techniques perfected by Terborch, which occurred in the mid 1660s.[12]

A related series, again employing the enlarged horizontal format and depicting numerous figures in grandly proportioned halls, was painted about this time or a year or two later (Cat. 114, 116, 117, Plates 117, 119, 120). The date 1675 formerly appeared on the picture in Philadelphia (Cat. 114, Plate 117) and seems appropriate to the style and costumes of this group. The courtly figures play music, embrace, and appear to dance. A standing woman in lost profile, candidly borrowed from Terborch's figural repertoire, appears prominently in the foreground of each of these works. In the picture in a German private collection (Cat. 115, Plate 118) this preferred motif (cf. Cat. 93, 121, Plates 97, 124) is all that survives of what probably was once a much larger picture similar in composition to the painting in Philadelphia. Extensive descriptions of two further pictures (Cat. C 135, C 136), now lost, suggest they too formed part of the original series. While the palatial settings of the paintings in this group link them to the Town Hall series of the previous decade, no quotations from known buildings have been identified.

In the painting in the Wellington Museum (Cat. 117, Plate 120) tall windows draped with red curtains cast a reddish glow on the revellers in the distance, which contrasts dramatically with the silvers, browns, and golds of the costumes of the figures in the foreground. A similar highly pronounced colour contrast appears in the picture in Philadelphia (Cat. 114, Plate 117). Like De Witte, De Hooch often accented his late deeply shadowed works with a brilliant and rather unnatural reddish-orange. The colour differs from the warm reds of his early works both in its intensity and in the degree to which it departs from pure unmixed hues. Strident colour schemes, often with acrid hues, were adopted by many painters in these years (see especially Van Mieris's later work) and may be seen as yet another expression of a mannerist aesthetic.

De Hooch's interest in domestic themes did not abate in his later years. Numerous paintings depict women attending to children, dispensing instructions to maidservants, and inspecting or partaking in the preparation of food. Occasionally ladies entertain themselves with household pets, feeding parrots (see Cat. 90, 102, Plates 93, 105) or, in the very late works, coaxing little dogs to dance giddily about on their hind legs (Cat. 151–2, Plates 154–5). Generally, though, in the home De Hooch's women remain an industrious breed and take the administration of the household very seriously. A group of four domestic scenes from these years (Cat. 87–90, Plates 90–93) represents the corner of a room with a fireplace on the back wall, recalling a design first employed by the artist in his Delft years (Cat. 32, Col. Plate VII). Now, however, a maidservant is added to the company and the general resemblance to the style and design of the painting of 1673 formerly in the Schloss Collection (Cat. 102, Plate 105) points to a date in the late sixties or early seventies. Contemporary works by the youthful Michiel van Musscher (1645–1705)[13] resemble the paintings of this group (compare the *Woman Handing a Coin to a Serving Woman*, Cat. 88, Plate 91, and Van Musscher's version of the theme, Fig. 34), suggesting that the two artists may have established contact in Amsterdam.

In the painting in Rotterdam (Cat. 101, Plate 104) and in a picture of which there are two versions, in Philadelphia and Copenhagen (Cat. 112A & B, Plate 115), a woman examines a fish brought by a maid-servant. In the latter composition, a third woman, presumably the fishmonger, waits in the doorway. The subject of the lady of the household scrutinizing food had been treated earlier in the courtyard scene in Leningrad (Cat. 46, Col. Plate XI) and in paintings by Quirin Brekelenkam and Hendrick Sorgh.[14] Similar themes appear repeatedly in De Hooch's later works (see Cat. 98, 99, 130, 136, Plates 100, 102, 135, 139). The time-honoured domestic image of a woman seated by a cradle had also figured in De Hooch's works of the 1660s (cf. Cat. 54, 71–2, 74, Col. Plate XIII, Plates 74, 75, 77), but in the following decade it became the most frequently repeated figure motif, appearing in compositions of both vertical (Cat. 101, 112A & B, Plates 104, 115) and horizontal formats (Cat. 98, 100, 125, 130–1, Plates 100, 103, 128, 135–6). The popularity of such images is confirmed by contemporary maternal scenes by Van Hoogstraten and Ochtervelt.[15] The motif is handled on a particularly monumental scale in the painting in Detroit (Cat. 113, Plate 116), pointing to origins roughly contemporary with the series of musical company scenes of c. 1674. A somewhat later date is proposed for the pictures in the P. Meyer Collection (as of 1950; Cat. 131, Plate 136) and Worcester (Cat. 130, Plate 135), which are similar in design to the very late domestic scenes in Boston (Cat. 140, Plate 143, dated 168[?]) and Aix-en-Provence (Cat. 141, Plate 144).

Most of De Hooch's domestic scenes of this period employ spatial designs developed earlier in his career. Two works (Cat. 123, 124, Plates 126–7), however, testify to a renewed experimentation with more elaborately subdivided interiors. The combination of decorative woodwork and complexly ordered spaces in these scenes calls to mind the art of De Hooch's former Delft colleague, Cornelis de Man. Another picture from this period, the *Sick Woman* (Cat. 132, Plate 133), has, in fact, been attributed to De Man. There, however, the similarity seems more a matter of superficial resemblance in costume, a voluminous robe being worn by both artists' male figures.

Particularly in the later years, De Hooch's figures often strike unusually rigid poses and move with oddly mechanical gestures; note, for examples, the figures in the doorways in Cat. 128 and 131 (Plates 131, 136), and the domestics in Cat. 124 (Plate 127). Since no drawings by the artist seem to have survived, one might assume that these traits arose from the practice of forgoing preparatory figure studies. There are, however, relatively few such studies by any Dutch genre painter. Another possible explanation could be the use of mannikins or lay figures.[16] Such devices were in use by the fifteenth century and frequently appeared in seventeenth-century Dutch painters' studios. Michael Sweerts, J. van Spreeuwen, and A. van Ostade depicted mannikins in paintings and Gerard Terborch is known to have owned a relatively large lay figure.[17] Typical examples of these devices appear in engravings by C. van de Passe (see Fig. 35). Mannikins, then as now, were employed for figure and drapery studies. Unfortunately, as in the case of optical instruments, there are no certain criteria for identifying pictures painted with the aid of these devices. The angularity and emotional containment of De Hooch's figures can just as readily be attributed to the prevailing ideals of human deportment. Indeed, contemporary works by Netscher and Eglon van der Neer confirm a taste for such manners. Thus, while the possibility should be borne in mind, it is virtually impossible, short of the discovery of an inventory mentioning such a device, to confirm De Hooch's use of mannikins.

Explicit quotations in De Hooch's later works were not restricted to borrowings from Terborch; Vermeer's art, once again, came into play. In the *Couple with a Parrot* in Cologne (Cat. 122, Plate 125) the scene is viewed through an open doorway serving as a sort of spatial diaphragm between the shadowed foreground and the brightly lit room beyond. The composition inverts the artists' customary hierarchy of design, transforming the secondary space into a principal stage of action; no longer an appurtenance, the 'doorkijkje' forms the whole of the design. In such compositional inversion there is again something of a mannerist sensibility. Architectural diaphragms had appeared in the earlier window paintings by Dou and Fabritius, and in the pictures of portals and doorways by Van Hoogstraten and Steen.[18] There can be little doubt, however, that De Hooch's primary source was Vermeer's *Letter* (Fig. 36). Where there once had been a dialogue between the two artists, there now existed a clear dependency. Scattered motifs in other late De Hooch's also may reflect Vermeer's influence. Valentiner likened the woman seated in the light in the Lehman Collection's painting (Cat. 120, Plate 123) to Vermeer (compare Fig. 21) and the memory of the latter's *Woman Holding Scales* (Fig. 32) may be reflected in the figure of the hostess in the painting in New York (Cat. 111, Plate 114). The suggestion is that De Hooch retained some contact with Delft even in his later years. We recall that as late as 1672 the Delft notary public Boogert and Jacobmine van der Burch (Hendrick van der Burch's sister and evidently a Delft resident until her death there in 1699) appeared as witnesses at the baptism of the artist's last child (Doc. 49).

De Hooch's late propensity for borrowed themes and motifs was also expressed in a return to the subjects of his youth. The handsome stable scene in New York (Cat. 111, Plate 114) adopts not only a setting reminiscent of his early works (compare Plate 6), but also the old theme of the disputed reckoning (cf. Plate 24). Drinking and gaming soldiers appear in rustic surroundings (see Cat. 126–7, Plates 129–30; compare Cat. 5, 12, Plates 4, 11), the likes of which had not been encountered in the artist's work for nearly twenty years. In the late tavern scene in Stockholm (Cat. 128, Plate 131) the central smoker returns full circle to De Hooch's first enthusiasm, the rowdy genre scenes of Brouwer and his followers. Finally, after a hiatus of more than a decade, the artist also readdressed himself to courtyard themes (Cat. 134–5, Plates 137-8). In these late works, the midday brilliance of the Delft paintings is exchanged for a subdued twilight shadow and the evening skies glow with the unworldly atmosphere of a Poussinesque landscape.

While several late works take up themes not previously encountered in De Hooch's repertoire, all seem to have been treated earlier by other genre painters. The sick woman and doctor (Cat. 132, Plate 133) was a long established theme handled by Dou, Steen, Van Mieris, and many others. In the painting of 1676 in Berlin (Cat. 133, Plate 134) a learned man surrounded by books addresses a seated woman holding a handkerchief. Although its subject is unclear, the picture, like the very weak thematically related painting of 1683 (Cat. 160, Plate 163), seems to derive from works like Metsu's *Usurer* of 1654 (Museum of Fine Arts, Boston).[19] Even the whimsical subject of a woman making dogs dance (Cat. 151–2, Plates 154–5) had been handled earlier by Van Mieris.[20] Once again, however, we should beware of assuming that the absence of new themes necessarily signals some drying up of creativity. Style, not thematic invention, was the standard of the new age.

Acknowledging these terms, however, does not account for the weak execution of many of the very last works. There are highly accomplished and technically refined pictures from the final seven years of the artist's activity, like the courtyard scene of 1677 in London (Cat. 134, Plate 137) and the *Woman with a Servant* in Lille, formerly dated 1680(?) (Cat. 143, Plate 146). Yet these are not so numerous as the works exhibiting crudely schematized designs and feeble or mechanical execution (see Cat. 136, 149, 151–2, 156, 157–8, 160, Plates 139, 152, 154–5, 159, 160–1, 163). It is tempting to speculate whether the poor quality of these last works was related in some way to the artist's mental illness. Yet we would hasten to point out that nothing is known of De Hooch's sickness nor of the circumstances which led to his death in the Dolhuys at the age of fifty-five. Furthermore, wide discrepancies of quality, the cause of some of the field's thorniest connoisseurship problems, were not exceptional in Dutch painting; Steen's art provides a case in point. If presently there can be no accounting for the weaknesses of De Hooch's last pictures, by the same token, too much remains unknown (not least the details of his illness) to countenance the traditional belief that his late production was a prime example of the 'decline' of Dutch art.

The artist dated at least one painting, of a *Sportsman and a Woman in a Landscape* (Cat. 161, Plate 164), in the last year of his life, perhaps an indication that he was not confined to the asylum until his final days. With its park-like surroundings, the work belongs to the elegantly formalized portraiture tradition practised by artists like Coques, Graat, and E. van der Neer.[21] In view of what we know of the events of the year of its completion, the doll-like figures and idyllic conceit of the setting have an unwanted poignancy.

Summarizing briefly, De Hooch's late career was filled with prodigious activity. His rate of production and often the scale of his works increased significantly. His manner became more stylized and his subjects proportionately more elegant and fanciful. These traits and the tendency to repeat or elaborate upon themes and motifs extracted from his own and other artists' earlier works make De Hooch's late paintings typical of their age. Where he parts company with his contemporaries is in his very last works, which display clear and unaccountable fluctuations in quality. Yet, as will be evident to the unbiased viewer, most of the late works display a tenebrous beauty needing no apologist.

De Hooch and the Tradition of Dutch Genre Painting: Iconographic Issues

We have referred repeatedly to De Hooch as a painter of 'genre' scenes. By this, in accordance with common modern usage, we have meant a painter of everyday life. The etymology of 'genre' leads to the French word meaning 'kind' or 'type' and its history would fill a long and interesting entry in an art-historical lexicon. While broader applications of the term remained in currency as they do today, the word genre seems not to have become synonymous with scenes of everyday life until the last quarter of the eighteenth century.[1] In the preceding century the Dutch had no generic equivalent.[2] Everyday themes were designated by neutral descriptive terms: 'geselschap' (usually translated as 'merry company'), 'conversatie' (conversation; not to be confused with the English 'conversation piece'), 'buitenpartij' (outdoor party), 'Een Juffrou met een meyt' (see Cat. C 19) or 'Een slapecamer' (see Cat. C 44).[3] Furthermore, while writers like Philip Angel and Samuel van Hoogstraten stressed that a painting should be an accurate record of the visual world, contemporary commentary on genre paintings is very scarce.[4]

Of all categories of Western painting, genre remains the least understood. In part this is because its meanings are so deeply rooted in the 'everyday' concerns and practices of the culture. Accepting for the moment that the basic subject of genre is the representation of daily events, these scenes conveyed to the artist and his public common associations elicited by the subject itself. Moreover, through his particular interpretation of a theme the artist could allude to certain concepts, by introducing, more or less overtly, a metaphoric dimension; in such cases one may speak of an allegorical aspect in the work of art. The artist may have intended thereby to teach his audience a lesson as the central message of his picture, as one of several meanings, or merely as a footnote to an otherwise uncharged representation of daily life. Additional variables must also be considered: the associations evoked by a certain subject in a given age could be lost or displaced over time; allegorical dimensions, with or without moral overtones, could be designed to be understood by all or only a small segment of the viewing public. Furthermore, certain genre themes owed their existence mainly to artistic traditions and only secondarily to representations of contemporary reality. It is hardly surprising, therefore, that the concept of Dutch genre has not remained fixed over the centuries.

In the nineteenth century Dutch art was assumed to be an ingenuous and literal transcription of visual reality, free of symbolic or literary allusions. Reviewing the Exposition Universelle of 1867, Thoré-Bürger found occasion to mention the earlier Dutch genre painters in the context of discussing a painting by Alfred Stevens, of which he wrote 'il s'agit de peinture simplement'. Concerning the subject matter of the genre scenes by De Hooch and his contemporaries, Thoré states, 'Toujours est-il que le sujet n'importe guère, pourvu que l'artiste ait bien rendu l'image qu'il a choisie.'[5] In the literature on De Hooch these 'art for art's sake' sentiments found their most enthusiastic expression with the publication of Eugène Fromentin's *Les Maîtres d'Autrefois* in 1876. Over the course of the last half century, the notion of Dutch art as *genre pur* has been discredited by various iconographic studies. Many paintings which had previously been perceived only on the level of literal reportage have been shown to have allegorical or emblematic meanings.[6] The insights provided by this research have forced us to reassess our ideas about the nature of realism in Dutch genre.[7] Until quite recently, though, little effort has been made to integrate these findings into a larger historical view of the changing concept of genre in Dutch painting.[8]

Genre painting originated in the sixteenth century in the works of Bosch, Massys, Lucas van Leyden, and their contemporaries. The earliest genre scenes shared characteristics with the contemporary allegory, in which the core of the meaning was embodied in subjects operating initially on a simple narrative or representative level. The naturalism and the quotidian appearance of these scenes rendered the allegorical content alternately more or less accessible and encouraged the curious informed viewer to seek out the didactic message. The characters, often peasants and beggars, were chosen from social strata different from those of the well-to-do citizens who owned the pictures. Scenes of incontinent or unethical behaviour were often depicted, at times with comic effects but not without an admonitory intent. In short, the first genre scenes were moralistic allegories concealed in images of everyday life.

From its inception the concept of genre began a process of change which continued through the seventeenth century to the present day. Many subjects which had first appeared in the sixteenth century—the kermesse, tavern and bordello scenes, 'high life' merry companies—were carried over into the following century. Yet the artists who treated these themes varied widely in the degree of their observance of genre's original aims. This tendency of iconographic conventions to be altered or displaced—a constant feature in the history of art—is not yet fully appreciated in writings on the meaning of Dutch genre.[9]

In the field of 'low life' or peasant painting, for example, the earlier practices survived into the first years of the seventeenth century in the works of artists like Adriaen van de Venne and David Vinckboons. The former's grisailles illustrate proverbs and sayings, and prints after Vinckboons's works were supplied with moralistic prescriptions.[10] By the mid-century, these meanings and, indeed, the ways of thinking which supported them, seem to have become less important. The paintings of Adriaen Brouwer and the later works of Adriaen van Ostade present very different images of the peasantry—the one brutish and uncivilized, the other prosperous and rather stupidly self-satisfied; however, both artists' meanings are openly expressed without resorting to metaphor or allegory. Jan Steen, on the other hand, reverted to the earlier practice, clothing moral adages (at times literally inscribed on the painting) in the comical guise of profligate merry-making.

Various usages of 'high' genre also appeared over the course of the century. Elegant merry-company scenes had first been popularized by Dirck Barendsz and other late sixteenth-century Dutch and Flemish mannerists.[11] The intent of these prototypes was clearly moral and cautionary; biblical narratives, such as the Last Judgement or the Prodigal Son, were introduced into the backgrounds of the scenes or alluded to in prints after the works (see Fig. 37).[12] The fashionably dressed young people represented by Buytewech and other early seventeenth-century genre painters were the subject of criticism in contemporary literature. In depicting the *jeunesse dorée*, these artists occasionally included emblematic details in their pictures for moralistic purposes.[13] E. de Jongh's studies have revealed the Dutchmen's propensity for erotic themes and many Dutch genre paintings include specific moral allusions to sexual conduct.[14] Yet while the outward forms of the merry company were repeated time and time again by Dirck Hals, Codde, Palamedesz, and their followers, its initial functions were often obscured or forsaken. As Gudlaugsson observed, Terborch—the most influential 'high life' painter after mid-century—was far more concerned with depicting the doings of well-heeled society than with conveying moral strictures.[15]

There were, to be sure, those who remained more traditional in their approach. The paintings of Dou, Van Mieris, Schalcken, and Van der Werff, testify to the survival of the allegorical-moral genre type until the end of the century. However, the increasing number of paintings which forgo the earlier practices reflects a growing diversification in the functions of genre. Gerard de Lairesse's discussion of 'Modern Painting' in 1707 still provided for the inclusion of 'vanitas' symbolism in genre, but his description of a hypothetical tea party proves that, for the eighteenth-century viewer, metaphoric dimensions were no longer a prerequisite of genre.[16] The implication is that by the time De Hooch began his career the introduction of referential meanings into genre had become optional and was left to the discretion of the artist.[17]

Residual elements from genre's original aims can be detected in some paintings by De Hooch and other Delft painters. Yet it was not De Hooch's practice to mix allegory and genre in the manner of the sixteenth century. For the most part, the meanings of his pictures are implicit in the associations evoked by the subjects themselves and only rarely have recourse to symbolism. Retrieving these associations is no simple matter. In his early guardroom scenes, for example, many activities are depicted which traditionally had been subjects of reproving comments in literature, prints, and emblems.[18] Drinking (see Cat. 4, 5, 7, 8, 13, Col. Plate I, Plates 4, 6, 7, 12),[19] smoking (Cat. 2, 4, 9, 10, Plates 2, 8, 10),[20] and the playing of cards (Cat. 5, 11, 13, Plates 4, 9A, 12),[21] and tric-trac (Cat. 12, Plate 11)[22] were all pastimes which had been found blameworthy. Furthermore, while membership in the local militia might be a source of pride, the presence of mercenary troops in the standing army had given the soldiering profession a rather checkered reputation. In early seventeenth-century literature soldiers were often portrayed as comic figures, the common foot-soldier as a drunken boor and the officers as affected and overdressed.[23] Something of this satirical spirit may be reflected in the picture in Rotterdam (Cat. 5, Plate 4), where a foppishly clad officer signals for another round with a pointedly graceless gesture. Upon first inspection, individuals in these scenes might also appear to be distant descendants of genre's original cast of 'disguised' characters: the drinker with raised glass (see Cat. 4, 7, 8, Col. Plate I, Plates 6, 7) strikes the time-honoured pose of the Prodigal Son squandering his inheritance;[24] and the trumpeter who blows reveille for the carousing soldiers (Cat. 7, Plate 6) could claim ancestry in the images of Gabriel announcing the Last Judgement which were appended to the earliest merry-company scenes (see Fig. 37).[25] By this time, however, the bloodlines had grown exceedingly thin and it seems unlikely that these oft repeated motifs still functioned on the level of symbol. Furthermore, it appears equally improbable that De Hooch designed these convivial scenes solely for the purpose of moral condemnation. In this the period of the First Anglo-Dutch War (1652–4) images of the military might also evoke favourable associations. Even in moments of leisure, soldiers remained the guardians of the country's freedom and, as evidenced by the wounded figure who once appeared in the painting in London (Cat. 14, Plate 14), De Hooch did not neglect the potential dangers of their service.

Nevertheless, vestigial forms of the moralizing tradition of genre probably survived in Delft painting. In early seventeenth-century genre scenes, religious attributes, often in the form of paintings within paintings, had been juxtaposed with secular merry making for admonitory purposes. In a painting of a *Party Group* (Cat. D 11, Plate 180) executed around 1660 and formerly attributed to De Hooch, potential allusions to the warnings of the Last Judgement are introduced by a painting of this subject on the back wall. Beside it hangs a clock, a traditional symbol of temperance.[26] The close conformity to the merry company's prototypes increases the likelihood that an admonitory meaning was intended.

Paintings within De Hooch's pictures from the late 1650s also suggest that a moralizing intent may have survived, albeit in a less programmatic form. In the Louvre's painting of 1658 (Cat. 26, Plate 23) a soldier pours a young girl a glass of wine while an older woman, reminiscent of the procuress types of earlier mercenary love scenes, looks on. The selection of Christ and the Adulteress for the subject of the picture on the wall hardly seems gratuitous and may be intended as a traditional 'clavis interpretandi'. The corner of the same picture appears in the upper right of the *Card Players* (Cat. 25, Plate 22). Here its potential message seems to be corroborated by other details. While a young serving woman looks on, the soldier with his back to the viewer plays an ace with a highly deliberate gesture. Cards, most commonly the ace of hearts, had long been used to allude to amorous themes in paintings.[27] Although the suit in this instance is spades, emblematic literature suggests that the card could be an allusion to fidelity to one love, a theme consistent with the implicit warning of the painting within the painting.[28]

In the picture of two officers and a girl of *c.* 1658 (Cat. 29, Plate 27) a painting over the mantelpiece of the Education of the Virgin, evidently based on the composition preserved in the Ering altarpiece (Fig. 38), may have been conceived in sacred opposition to the worldly diversions in the foreground. Although not immediately evident, a similar juxtaposition of sacred and profane elements is introduced into the painting in Leipzig (Cat. 68, Plate 69). As was noted, Raphael's *School of Athens* appears in the lunette. Bedaux observed that De Hooch probably knew the composition by way of Giorgio Ghisi's print, which identified the subject as Paul Preaching on the Areopagus in Athens.[29] Particularly in a later work such as this, however, it is not at all certain that the use of such details was motivated by a desire for moral instruction. The classicism of Raphael's composition, we recall, complemented the architecture of the Town Hall.

Formal considerations could just as readily have dictated the motif's inclusion as concern over its iconographic import.

One must be cautious, therefore, in seeking specific meaning in De Hooch's works even when the traditional device of a painting within a painting is employed. On several occasions in his later career the artist reintroduced the same painting, or parts thereof, into scenes with markedly different settings and activities. The painting in the background of the scene of people drinking and making music in Lord Barnard's Collection (Cat. 118, Plate 121) was based on Jan Saenredam's engraving after Goltzius's *Lot and his Daughters* (Fig. 39). The same source was employed for the picture over the mantelpiece in the domestic scene formerly in the Von Gutmann Collection (Cat. 89, Plate 92); and the right-hand side of the print served as the model for the embracing couple in the painting above the messenger delivering a letter to a woman in the painting in Hamburg (Cat. 84; detail, Fig. 40). In each of these works it would be possible to argue that a moral admonition was intended.[30] More to the point, however, is the fact that the artist felt at liberty to repeat the same potentially symbolic motif in a variety of different narrative contexts. In the process the specificity of the symbol is undermined and its potential moral content diminished.

The repetition of such sources appears elsewhere in De Hooch's art. Rembrandt's etching of the *Small Lion Hunt* served as the model not only for the painting over the mantelpiece in the large *Musical Party* in the Wellington Museum (Cat. 117, Plate 120), but also for murals in the *Merry Company with Trumpeter* (Cat. 107, Plate 113) and the *Jacott-Hoppesack Family Portrait* (Cat. 92, Plate 95). An unidentified representation of Venus and Cupid was repeated in the details of reliefs and paintings of various late musical (Cat. 105, 109, Plate 108, 111), merry-company (Cat. 107), and domestic scenes (Cat. 102-3, Plates 105-6). And, if we may belabour the point still further, another composition, also of a reclining Venus and Cupid, appears in both the candidly amorous painting from the Labia Collection (Cat. 106, Plate 109) and in the reserved scene of domestic economy in Los Angeles (Cat. 88, Plate 91). The multiple interpretability of emblematic motifs could no doubt, be invoked to partially explain the varied applications of these sources. Yet it seems far more likely that in such details De Hooch was in the habit of quoting convenient sources, usually prints, without much concern for their symbolic implications. The use, for example, of C. Bloemaert's print (Fig. 41) after Abraham Bloemaert's *Nativity* (Anton Ulrich-Museum, Braunschweig) for the picture over the fireplace in the painting of a *Man Reading a Letter to a Woman* (Cat. 97, Plate 101) probably only reflects the motif's general suitability to the calm and reverent atmosphere of the scene. De Hooch's repetition of such sources, once again, is symptomatic of the displacement of the traditional functions of genre.

Still another painting within a painting serves to illustrate the problems of interpreting De Hooch's imagery. Margarita Russell has recently observed that the picture of the Rape of Ganymede in the *Merry Company* in Lisbon (Cat. 57, Plate 60) was derived from a lost picture by Carel van Mander III, which in turn was based on Rembrandt's famous painting of this subject.[31] Given De Hooch's propensity for quoting from prints and the fact that the source is not reversed, the detail was probably based on Albert Haelwegh's print after Van Mander's work (Fig. 42).[32] Here again, we may only be dealing with a piquant and un-charged detail. In this particular instance, however, it is unlikely that the subject was selected at random. Other representations of the Ganymede theme had often included a barking dog, much like the one which appears in the lower right corner of the De Hooch.[33] Thus, the artist probably gave some consideration to the various ways in which the Ganymede theme had been treated, a concern which argues against its appearance as an incidental detail. The myth of Ganymede had been interpreted in a variety of ways.[34] While some commentaries noted the erotic implications, Neoplatonic texts interpreted the theme spiritually as the pure human soul lifted up to God. In addition, Ganymede could be the symbol of Aquarius. Noting the liberties which the seated gentleman takes with his lady companion in De Hooch's painting, one might conclude that the detail was designed to intensify, or alternatively, to spiritually oppose, the amorous and earthly associations of the scene. It is not clear, however, which, if any, of these meanings dictated the motif's inclusion. This lack of clarity again probably reflects the fact that the trans-mission of specific didactic and metaphoric allusions no longer was of paramount concern to the artist.[35]

Figurative references operate in De Hooch's art only as subordinate annotations to the central theme, which in this case is probably the elegant merry-making itself. The moralizing intentions of such scenes have, in my opinion, been greatly overstressed in recent iconographic investigations.

The freedom De Hooch exercised with regard to earlier iconographic conventions is perhaps most clearly demonstrated by the *Woman Weighing Coins* (Cat. 64, Col. Plate XIV).[36] As we have seen, the artist based his work on Vermeer's painting in Washington (Fig. 32). In taking over the composition he omitted the picture of the Last Judgement on the rear wall, thereby dispensing with Vermeer's 'clavis interpretandi'.[37] The effect of this omission is the elimination of the traditional mode of access to a metaphoric dimension in the painting. Although vestigial associations comparable to those evoked more explicitly by Vermeer could remain operative in the De Hooch,[38] the fact stands that De Hooch's treatment here is entirely consistent with his tendency to de-emphasize the allegorical and moral functions of genre.

More must be said of these ideas, but at this juncture it will be appropriate to return to the iconographic issues raised by De Hooch's works of the Delft years. We recall that about the time the artist first perfected his mature style in Delft he began to treat themes of the domestic life of women. Domestic subjects continued to concern him throughout his career, making up more than one-third of the oeuvre. Women and children, almost to the exclusion of husbands and fathers, are repeatedly represented in simple situations in the home. With these scenes De Hooch played an important role in that growth of interest in domestic subjects which occurred in Holland after mid-century. The fact is not yet sufficiently appreciated that domestic genre was only a minor strand in Dutch painting in the first half of the century. While the sixteenth-century tradition, initiated by Aertsen and Beuckelaer, of representing superabundant kitchen scenes was perpetuated by a few *retardataire* painters, like the Delft artists Pieter van Rijck and Cornelis Delff, domestic themes were almost exclusively the province of prints and drawings in the early decades of the century. Dutch mannerists, like Goltzius, occasionally designed allegorical prints in the guise of home life scenes (see Fig. 43). Working in a more naturalistic idiom, Jacob de Gheyn II drew scenes of women and children with a new intimacy, but again probably with a symbolic intent.[39] Although early seventeenth-century portraitists depicted women in domestic roles[40] the genre painters of Buytewech's generation rarely broached such themes; the Rotterdamer's superb drawing of *Two Women by a Hearth* of 1617 (Kunsthalle, Hamburg) seems not to have inspired comparable works in oils. Several Haarlem painters, including Dirck Hals and Judith Leyster, experimented with domestic genre as early as *c.* 1630, and the talented printmaker Geertruyt Roghman demonstrated a special interest in scenes of women engaged in housework during the 1640s (see Fig. 44).[41] Yet these works remained rather isolated statements. The guardroom painters, as their name implies, and the low life artists did little to alter this situation before *c.* 1650.[42]

One of the earliest painters to exhibit a sustained concern for domestic themes was Gerard Dou. The many scenes he executed after 1630 of women spinning, making lace, and labouring in the kitchen (see Fig. 46) undoubtedly served to kindle interest in these themes.[43] The works of Dou's Leiden School followers, notably Brekelenkam, were also probably influential in this regard. But it was not until around the time of the signing of the Treaty of Münster—the compact which brought an official end to the hostilities with Spain in 1648—that Dutch painters began to produce peaceful images of bourgeois home life in greater numbers. Paintings by Jan Baptist Weenix (see Fig. 45), Terborch, Van Loo, Maes (Figs. 16 and 18), and many others testify to the spread of the subject's popularity.[44]

The simplicity and repose of domestic themes suited the contemporary trend towards more 'classical' stylistic values. Yet if we are to understand the Dutch artists' increasing preoccupation with these themes we must examine the prevailing attitude toward the family and the individuals, particularly women, of which it was composed. Until quite recently little serious study has been undertaken into the social history of the Western European family.[45] It has become evident, though, that the family has not remained a static social unit over time but has undergone important changes in its make-up, functions, and internal emotional relationships. While the changes the seventeenth-century Dutch family underwent are still only partially understood, central to the ideals of the age seems to have been the notion that the maintenance of domestic virtue and order was of the highest social priority. With the abolition of monasticism and clerical celibacy in the new Republic a new emphasis was placed on the family and marriage. In this predominantly Protestant society, the family, not the church, became the principal forum for moral instruction and character development.

Iconographic investigations of domestic genre have only been undertaken in the last few years.[46] Art historians seem to have shared the social scientists' old assumptions about families being defined by certain constant needs and values which were either so self-evident or so personal as to be unworthy of serious examination. Part of this neglect also reflects a pattern of disregard for exemplary as opposed to admonitory themes in genre. Like Milton we have found it easier to write about vice than about virtue. For Dutch seventeenth-century moralists the presentation of models of virtuous conduct was not less important than the policing of unethical behaviour.

Jacob Cats (1577–1660) probably was the most influential of these writers. A reading of the prolific and highly popular Cats provides an introduction to the bourgeois ideals of the age. One of his major poetic treatises, *Houwelick* (Marriage),[47] presents his image of the model family in the course of characterizing the progression of a woman's life through six stages: Maecht, Vryster, Bruyt, Vrouwe, Moeder, and Weduwe (Maid, Sweetheart, Bride, Wife, Mother, and Widow). Prints by Adriaen van de Venne illustrated the text (see Fig. 47–8). The many servants who populate Cats's ideal household and the prosperous lifestyle of the master and mistress make it clear that his poem was addressed to the 'haute bourgeoisie'. Nevertheless, the numerous printings through which his works passed—a remarkable total of 50,000 copies of *Houwelick* were estimated to be in circulation by 1655[48]—prove that Cats was read by a much wider public. While many writers commented on women's roles and duties,[49] the pronouncements of 'Vader Cats' took on the weight of dogma for large sections of the middle classes.

The ideal woman who emerges is a rare creature of unquestionable virtue, modesty, and evenness of temper who lives a life wholly defined by her service to her husband, family, and home. Her youth is spent in preparation for marriage. When she is old enough to receive suitors she must guard her chastity, shunning liberal advances and gifts. Her spouse should be selected by her parents and an early marriage is preferable to a late one and the risk of spinsterhood. Once married, a woman's primary responsibility is obedience to her husband. Recalling Socrates, Cats states, 'De man betracht de wet des lants/ Het wijf den wille des mans' (Men should obey the laws and women their husbands).[50] In the author's ideal patriarchy a woman's skills and personal charms were considered worthless unless she pleased her husband.[51]

By far the largest section of the poem deals with the 'Vrouw' and begins with an account of the wife's duties:

> In early times on the first morning [of marriage],
> A key was given to the bride which admitted her to cares,
>> A key to the house and all the household duties,
>> And only then was a bride a complete wife.
> This we should follow here. There are various matters
> Which only concern the wife and her servants:
>> Above all her domain is the kitchen,
>> Linen, laundry and marketing belong to it.
> In addition, it is her responsibility to supervise the maids,
> And to divide up their chores reasonably,
>> The rearing of children also is a wife's concern,
>> At least until the child is seven years old.[52]

Cats makes it abundantly clear that a woman's place is in the home: '... *Huys-vrouw* is uwen naem. Een wort ... tot uwen pligt bequaem' (House-wife is your name. A word which [in itself] signifies your duty).[53] The wife undertakes her obligations silently, without complaint; quarrelsome and rebellious women were roundly criticized.[54] Although the mistress performs little physical housework herself, she must supervise the chores and administer the domestic economy.[55] Cats inventories the wife's duties in the kitchen and stresses that she should become an expert in all culinary matters so as to better guide her charges.[56] The servants who are entrusted with the marketing must be taught to seek out only the best and not the cheapest buys.[57] In Van de Venne's illustration (Fig. 47), much as in later works by De Hooch (Cat. 88, 124, Plates 91, 127), the lady of the household is shown dispensing money to a maid who holds a marketing basket.

Foreign observers also noted the premium the Dutch placed on a woman's domestic skills. In 1641 John Evelyn commented, upon visiting the Weeshuys, that the girls there were 'instructed so well in Housewifery, that men of good worth (who seek that chiefly in a Wife) frequently marry out of this Hospital'.[58] Of the Dutch housewife's penchant for tidiness, Parival wrote, 'Elles se piquent de propriété dans leurs maisons & dans leurs meubles au delà de tout ce qu'on peut s'imaginer. Elles font laver & frotter sans cesse . . .', adding the remark, 'On n'ozeroit cracher dans les chambres; ce n'est aussi la coutume de cracher dans les mouchoirs; de sorte qu'on peut juger que ceux qui sont flegmatiques se trouvent en grande peine . . .'.[59] Spring cleaning was described as a 'frightful operation' by a visiting Frenchman[60] and the English writer Brickman caustically observed that the Dutch kept 'their houses cleaner than their persons, and their persons [cleaner] than their souls . . .'.[61] Cognizant of their reputation for spotless homes, Dutchmen seem to have enjoyed telling stories at their own expense, some of which, according to Sir William Temple, were

> so extravagant that my sister took them for jest; when the Secretary for Amsterdam, that was of the company, desiring her to look out the window, said, Why Madame, there is the House where one of our magistrates going to visit the mistress of it, and knocking at the door, a strapping North Holland lass came and opened it; he asked, whether her mistress was at home, she said yes; and with that he offered to go in: but the wench marking his shoes were not very clean, took him by both arms, threw him upon her back, carried him across two rooms, set him down at the bottom of the stairs, pulled off his shoes, put him on a pair of slippers that stood there, all this without saying a word; but when she had done, told him, he might go up to see her mistress who was in her chamber.[62]

While it could, of course, lead to excess, this love of order and cleanliness was one source of the special beauty of De Hooch's paintings (see Cat. 31, 42, Plates 29, 46). Still another manifestation was the contemporary doll house. Hardly children's playthings, these minutely crafted structures were owned by the rich and displayed as 'kijkobjecten' (art objects). One of the few surviving examples (Fig. 49) actually was owned by Petronella de la Court, the wife of one of De Hooch's patrons.[63] Within its neat little confines the owner could admire a telescoped image of perfect 'haut bourgeois' domesticity complete from kitchen to 'kunstkamer'.

The elegant homes De Hooch depicted in his Amsterdam years bespeak similar ideals. With their added wealth, the women more closely approximate Cats's exemplary wife. Chores are increasingly relegated to servants while the mother continues to take an active part in rearing the children. In accordance with the contemporary prescriptions, she breast-feeds her infants (see Cat. 54, 98, 113, Col. Plate XIII, Plates 100, 116), rejecting the option to employ a wet-nurse, whose services she doubtless could afford.[64] The education and moral instruction of children were also important duties, but Cats discouraged harsh disciplinarians, acknowledging that even play might be an instructive pastime.[65] In De Hooch's works we encounter a particularly affectionate image of children (see Cat. 41, Plate 45). The mother lavishes attention on her offspring (see Cat. 30, 71–2, 87, Plates 28, 74–5, 90), sees that they are properly groomed (Cat. 42, Plate 46), clothed (Cat. 81, 104, Plates 84, 107), and refreshed (Cat. 31, Plate 29),[66] and, when the child is old enough, sends him off to school with a physically and spiritually nourishing breakfast (Cat. 48, Plate 51).[67]

Sympathetic and tolerant attitudes toward child-rearing were relatively new and far from universally accepted. The French retained considerably stricter views on the subject and in 1651 Parival wrote of the Dutch, 'Ils sont trop indulgens à leurs enfans, & ne les châtient pas assez.'[68] In the sixteenth century ties between Dutch parents and children probably were considerably looser than in the modern era or even in the later seventeenth century.[69] High infant mortality and the child's early departure from the home were but two reasons why parents would tend to become less emotionally involved with their children. In addition, the traditional view held that a woman's primary obligations were to her husband rather than to her children—an attitude still clearly expressed in *Houwelick*, where the discussion of the mother's responsibilities is very much shorter than that devoted to the wife's. The family, however, was undergoing changes in these years and attitudes toward pedagogy altered accordingly. With the rise of the wealthy entrepreneurial bourgeoisie the family became increasingly nuclear and private in its orientation. My impression is that the strictly patriarchal attitudes espoused by Cats were perpetuated as a literary tradition but gave way in actual Dutch society to greater personal autonomy for family members and closer affective relations in the home.[70]

Nonetheless, De Hooch probably knew the works of Cats. In the early *Family Portrait* (Cat. 24, Col. Plate III) an elderly woman—no doubt the grandmother—holds up a bunch of grapes by the stem. The source of this curious gesture has been identified by E. de Jongh in Cats's emblems.[71] The motif appears four times in the author's work and nowhere else in emblematic literature. Its rarity in earlier art increases the likelihood that De Hooch knew the motif, or at least its meaning, from Cats's publications.[72] In the author's *Maechden-plicht* (The Maid's duty, Middelburg, 1618) the emblem was used as a symbol of a maid's chastity. As he explained, however, in his comments on the 'Vryster-wapen' (Coat of Arms of the Spinster [or Sweetheart]; Fig. 50) in *Houwelick*, marriage and motherhood conferred a special status on a woman, which paradoxically also entitled a mother to be called maid. The notion of motherhood as a second form of virginity was supported by other writers.[73] Additional potentially symbolic elements in the painting seem to complement this theme. Enclosed gardens were traditional symbols of a woman's purity ('A garden enclosed is my sister, my spouse'; Song of Solomon, 4: 12)[74] and Cats frequently likened virtuous women to courtyards and gardens.[75] The vine growing on the side of the arbour at the right may also recall the biblical metaphors that Cats applied to the honourable wife.[76] Apples, like the one held by the woman at the left, could allude to the fruits of marriage or, in conjunction with the grapes, to the fall and redemption.[77] While it remains unclear whether these supplemental details would have activated symbolic associations for contemporary viewers, the conspicuousness of the grapes gesture leaves little doubt that the motif was intended to allude to the virtue of the family depicted.

Representations of the virtuous family constituted a long tradition in Dutch genre. One of the favourite themes was 'Het Gebed voor den Maaltijd' (Prayer before the Meal). The subject appears in a print by C. J. Visscher of 1607 with quotations from Psalms 127–8 alluding to familial virtue and enjoyed a considerable popularity among later genre painters, including De Hooch (see Cat. 48, Plate 51).[78] By the following century depictions of the good bourgeois family had become a standardized device for domestic propaganda, typified by the English 'conversation piece'. As we have noted, Gerard de Lairesse's comments of 1707 suggest that certain genre scenes were regarded as little more than an occasion for the depiction of social manners. But he goes on to say that 'If the artist find no Taste in representing Things in the antique Way, and yet think the Modern [i.e. genre of the writer's hypothetical tea party type] too mean, such an one may very commendably imploy himself in handling such subjects as the following'; whereupon he describes the 'Picture of Virtue':

> In a good Family, a prudent and respected Father; a careful and good-natured Mother; obedient Children; and humble and honest servants; The Father gives the law; the Mother enforces it to the children; and both they and the Servants obey; Again, the Father punishes; the Mother reconciles; the children love and fear; A good Father is also liberal in his Support of his Family; the careful Mother manages with Frugality, yet with Honour: All is in Peace and Order, and Virtue their aim.[79]

Clearly, Catsian moralistic thinking about the family could still be elicited by domestic scenes in the early eighteenth century. While elegant genre need no longer be interpreted morally, virtuous associations were still evoked by homey familial images.[80]

V. A Woman and a Child in a Bleaching Ground (Cat. 21). *c.* 1657–9. Private Collection, England

VI. Card Players (Cat. 28). 1658. Royal Collection. *Reproduced by gracious permission of Her Majesty Queen Elizabeth II.* See also
Plate 26

Emblem books also testify to the persistence of these ideas. For Roemer Visscher (see Fig. 51)[81] simple utensils were symbols in themselves of a thrifty and wisely run household. Certain activities, such as spinning (see Cat. 36, Plate 39) and sewing (Cat. 82–3, 97, Plates 85–6, 101) became virtually synonymous with domestic virtue.[82] Visscher interpreted a distaff as a symbol of moderation and a late seventeenth-century emblem of a spinner was provided with the motto, 'Huislykheid is 't vrouwen kroon cieraad' (Domesticity is a woman's crowning ornament).[83] In Jan Luiken's *Het Leerzaam Huisraad* (The Instructive Household Goods, Amsterdam, 1711) the full gamut of common domestic activities was illustrated and provided with pious Christian commentaries. Many of the chores the author depicted, such as making the bed, washing clothes, or storing linen (Figs. 52–3),[84] had been treated earlier in De Hooch's works (cf. Cat. 20, 40, 52, Col. Plate IV, Plates 43, 44, 56). Although specific religio-moralistic messages such as those encountered in Luiken's emblems are probably foreign to De Hooch's art, there can be little question that, at the level of common association, the contemporary viewer connected these images with the ideals of domestic virtue.

The search for 'deeper' meanings proves, on the whole, to be misplaced effort. Although potentially emblematic motifs occasionally appear in the artist's domestic scenes,[85] there is rarely sufficient congruence between the image and the symbol to confirm shared meanings. The grapes motif is a virtually unique case. De Hooch's approach may be contrasted in this regard to that of Dou, whose *Nature, Education, and Practice* (known today through a copy by W. J. Laquy, Rijksmuseum, Amsterdam, no. A 2320) provides an example of domestic genre which still employs the allegorical mode of representation descended from the previous century.[86] Dou's more traditional method is also illustrated in his *Apple Peeler* (Fig. 46), where a picture on the wall of Christ and the Samaritan Woman was probably included to underscore the virtue of the woman's activity in the preparation of a meal ('But whosoever drinketh of the water that I shall give him shall never thirst', John 4: 14).[87] When De Hooch treated the same theme (Cat. 61, Plate 65) he evidently felt that such referential reinforcement was no longer needed. In his paintings the virtuous associations of domestic themes arise directly from the images and rarely resort to metaphor or allusion.

Part of the difficulty in interpreting De Hooch's pictures arises from the diversity of possible associations his subjects could evoke. Scenes of music-making, for example, had long carried a wide variety of meanings.[88] The particular context in which the theme appears can sometimes clarify its function. In the painting in Cleveland (Cat. 53, Col. Plate XII) the fact that the music-makers have portrait features and are unquestionably members of a single family increases the likelihood that the music is an expression of familial harmony. No doubt as a result of these associations, music had become a traditional feature of family portraiture.[89] In the present work, the painting of the Sacrifice of Isaac over the fireplace may also have been designed to prompt thoughts on familial loyalty and obedience. On the other hand, the concord implied by a family group at music was not always of a virtuous kind; Steen's riotous representations of the saying, 'Soo voer gesongen, soo nagepepen' suffice to illustrate the theme's potentially negative associations. Here again the context clarifies the intent.

In most of De Hooch's genre scenes, however, the narrative context in no way encourages a symbolic or moral interpretation of the musical theme. The three large musical company scenes he painted around 1674 (Cat. 108–10, Plates 110, 111, 112) are all grouped around the figure of a woman with a cello. In Cesare Ripa's *Iconologia of Uytbeeldingen des Verstands* (Amsterdam, 1644) harmony is personified by a woman playing a cello. One of the expressions of harmony is love and Cats alluded to the amorous association of music in his emblem entitled, 'Amor docet Musicam', which depicts a cupid at a table surrounded by men and women making music.[90] Thus, in De Hooch's musical scenes there are potential allusions to both harmony and the related theme of love. Neither theme, however, was probably uppermost in the artist's mind when he executed these scenes. His principal concern seems rather to have been with the depiction of an exemplary image of elegant recreation. Nothing in these works implies a moral commentary and, given the fact that men play the cello just as prominently elsewhere in De Hooch's work (Cat. 68, 117, Plates 69, 120), we should not assume that their female counterparts have symbolic connotations. While

D

music could be a prelude to love, it was above all a genteel pastime which De Hooch and other con-temporary high genre painters perceived as appropriate to portrayals of a leisured class. In all likelihood, such images would have appealed to the artist's patrons. The rich Amsterdam merchants who owned paintings by De Hooch—men like Jan Jacott and Adam Oortmans—were probably more concerned with the maintenance of decorum than with the observance of a strict morality. Thus, new sociological condi-tions, although not necessarily causal in their effect, also probably contributed to the changes we have witnessed in the concept of genre.[91]

While the amorous associations of musical company scenes have often been overstressed,[92] De Hooch occasionally treated amorous themes quite explicitly. In the scene of *Two Embracing Couples* (Cat. 106, Plate 109) a cavalier reclining on a bench sidles up to a receptive young lady while a second couple share intimacies by the window.[93] A man and a woman in the painting in the Assheton Bennett Collection (Cat. 86, Plate 89) have been drinking. The painting over the mantelpiece reiterates the drinking theme, alluding to its potential excesses with an image of Silenus Supported by Satyrs loosely based on C. Jegher's print after Rubens.[94] The man has taken a hot coal from the hearth in order to light his pipe. He pauses momentarily to look at his female companion, who holds out her 'roemer' glass while speaking to a maid with a pewter decanter. The conjunction of the man's phallic tongs and the woman's open-mouthed glass is probably not accidental and could well have been designed as a sexual allusion.[95] Not uncommon in the art of the period, such 'naughty' gestures are employed by De Hooch in a more playful than condemnatory spirit and betoken a brand of coarse good humour typical of the age.

One amorous theme of particular interest, to which De Hooch addressed himself on several occasions, was that of lovers or quite possibly married couples (their status is unclear) rising at dawn. The early picture in Moscow depicts a man dressing while a woman makes the bed (Cat. 15, Plate 13). In a lamentably mutilated later painting in New York (Cat. 79, Plate 82) a woman brings a salver, ewer, and towel for the morning toilet.[96] The man seated at the right originally was speaking to a second woman in the bed, who disappeared when the right edge of the canvas was cut. In Lord Barnard's painting (Cat. 69, Plate 72) the couple have risen and the man in his night shirt offers a glass of wine to the woman threading her bodice. The gesture of the man pulling on his boot in the first painting and a stocking in the second may again be a sexual allusion.[97] It is noteworthy that in all of these scenes the artist has chosen to depict the dawn rather than the actual night of love. Themes of lovers meeting or parting at dawn continued to appeal to Dutch seventeenth-century popular song writers and poets like P. C. Hooft at a time when the traditional medieval dawn-theme had fallen out of literary favour in the rest of Europe.[98] Young married couples were also treated to this poetic convention; Cats's 'Vrouwe' opens with the new wife being roused at dawn to assume her duties. Thus, De Hooch's interest in dawn-themes may in part reflect their popularity in contemporary literature.

We have already noted that De Hooch's garden-scenes (see Cat. 60A, Plate 64) hark back to the earlier love garden tradition.[99] Some features of his courtyards, like the little arbours beneath which men and women sit drinking (see Cat. 23, 33, 38, 39, Col. Plate VIII, Plates 20, 41, 42), also have precedents in this tradition. One habitué of love gardens was the monkey, an animal who had acquired an unfavourable reputation as a lustful creature.[100] When a monkey draws the attention of the figures in one of De Hooch's elegant terrace scenes (Cat. 91, Plate 94) we are, as usual, sorely challenged to gauge the specificity of the motif's associations. Could recollections of its traditional admonitory uses still be brought into play or was the ape merely taken over with the rest of the exotic baggage of the elegant garden type?

Another preferred creature from De Hooch's domestic menagerie raises similar questions. On repeated occasions (see Cat. 122, 148, 150, Plates 125, 149, 153) he represented men and women feeding a parrot through the open door of its cage with titbits. The bird that escapes its cage was a traditional symbol of lost virginity.[101] One might conclude, therefore, that the ladies in these scenes were in danger from temptation and in need of warning. Yet if there was such a cautionary message, it would seem to have come somewhat belatedly in the painting formerly in Lord Northbrook's Collection (Cat. 90, Plate 93), where two women coax the bird from its cage in the company of a child. While the parrot could be associated with amorous dalliance, it was primarily a rare (imported) pet which, like the monkey, was suited to the idle diversions of rich households (see Cat. 75, Plate 78).

Clearly, both as a reflection of contemporary attitudes and as a matter of personal choice, De Hooch exercised his licence to draw on earlier iconographic traditions selectively. While emblematic details occasionally appear in his work, it would be incorrect to assume that each of his pictures had a symbolic or religio-moralistic intent. Inasmuch as he presented models of domesticity, his works reflect an ethical point of view. The Protestant exaltation of the family and married life is clearly reflected in his work. Yet his didactic goals should not be overstressed; particularly after his years in Delft, De Hooch was principally concerned with edifying representations of social ideals. The Calvinist imperative for instruction operates only as a secondary consideration in his work. Limited in its range of subject matter (guardrooms, domestic and merry company subjects), De Hooch's genre production is clearly rooted in artistic traditions and should not be construed as a literal record of reality or as pure genre. Nevertheless, in our considerations of his iconography, we should not lose sight of his obvious delight in the representation of the visual world. His paintings, after all, depict slices of life, but of a life of the artist's own making.

VII

De Hooch's Followers and Public

Although De Hooch is not known to have engaged students, a large body of work reflects the influence of his style and particularly of the manner that he perfected around 1658 in Delft. Over the course of the last century many paintings have been extracted from the master's oeuvre and assigned, more or less persuasively, to other artists. Collectively these artists have come to be known as the De Hooch School, a rather unfortunate misnomer. There remain, however, a goodly number of pictures, generally in the Delft manner, which continue to confound efforts at attribution. Some, like the *Woman Refusing a Glass of Wine* in the National Gallery in London, which has been assigned to no less than thirteen different artists,[1] are particularly intriguing because of their high quality and potential historical significance. In sorting out these questions we must also bear in mind that other artists, whose personal styles and even names might be unknown to us, could also have worked in the Delft style.[2] The complexity of the attribution problems should not, therefore, be underestimated.

Efforts to define the oeuvre of Hendrick van der Burch provide a case in point.[3] For Valentiner he was a convenient catch-all for near De Hooch paintings. Although the extent of his production remains unclear, his few signed pictures reflect his association with painters in both Leiden and Delft. Among De Hooch's followers he was the only artist to have documented contact with the master (see Docs. 14, 20, 22, 24, 28, 33). As we have seen, his early guardroom scenes seem to reflect this acquaintance (see Fig. 4) and testify to his interest in nocturnal lighting effects (see Fig. 54).[4] Although the similarities in these early works may in part reflect common sources, Van der Burch's debt to De Hooch's works of *c.* 1658 is clearly evident in his treatment of light and of the courtyard spaces in the *Woman with a Jug in a Courtyard* (Fig. 55) and in a small panel on loan to the Prinsenhof in Delft depicting a *Woman and a Child at a Window* (Dienst Verspreide Rijkskollekties, no. NK 2922). As with his early manner, his mature style can be distinguished from De Hooch's by his sketchier technique and flecked highlights. The painting in the Prinsenhof, long assigned to De Hooch, employs the window motif we have associated with Fabritius's late works and reconfirms the contemporary taste for illusionism. In his best works, such as these, Van der Burch demonstrates a considerable aptitude for the synthesis of current artistic ideas. By disposition, though, he was not a particularly creative painter and his tendency towards derivativeness is typically reflected in a certain stylistic eclecticism.

The works of Pieter Janssens Elinga (1623–before 1682) have also often been attributed to De Hooch.[5] His *Woman Reading* (Fig. 56) was once considered such a characteristic work by the master that the right side of the composition was employed by a deceitful nineteenth-century restorer as a model for the overpainted view to a backlighted chamber at the rear of the gallery in De Hooch's painting in Strasbourg (Cat. 67, Plate 70). Elinga's *Woman with a Pearl Necklace* (Bredius Museum, The Hague) is one of only two works to bear his signature and probably was based on De Hooch's *Woman Weighing Coins* (Cat. 64, Col. Plate XIV). In adapting his source he enlarged the interior space and increased its orthogonal rigidity. Much of Elinga's art is dominated by an overriding concern with simple perspectival order. In his *Woman Reading with a Maid Sweeping* (Fig. 58) the clearly bounded horizontal space recalls De Hooch's interiors of the early 1660s (Cat. 52–8, Col. Plates XII, XIII, Plates 56–61), but the overall effect barely disguises the reliance on perspective recipes.[6] Not only their inflexible spatial constructions, but also their formularized division of light and shade seem to betray a dependence upon artists' handbooks.[7] Yet certain preferred details of his lighting schemes probably stem directly from De Hooch. The shadow of a chair, which repeatedly appears in the right-hand corner of Elinga's interiors, strikes us as a caricature of De Hooch's carefully observed secondary reflections.

Like the art of Jacobus Vrel, the quiet domestic scenes by the Amsterdam artist Esaias Boursse (1631–72)[8] seem at times to anticipate qualities of De Hooch's late Delft period paintings. Nevertheless, his *Woman Beside an Unmade Bed* of 1656 (Wallace Collection, London) is closer in conception to works by Leiden painters, particularly Brekelenkam, than to those of the Delft artists. By 1661, the year of his *Spinner* (Fig. 57), Boursse had adopted more subtly illuminated and ordered interiors which, together with a small group of courtyard scenes, seem to reflect the impact of De Hooch's art. As we have seen, Vrel's interiors differ from De Hooch's in their rather simplistic spatial designs and in the absence of views to adjoining rooms. His lofty chambers tend to dwarf his figures and their curiously stunted or attenuated furnishings. Vrel also painted pictures of narrow streets bordered by brick and whitewashed houses. The bright daylight tonalities of these works often recall De Hooch's courtyards. Furthermore, the designs of a little-known painting in the Marquis of Bath's collection (Fig. 59) and a picture in Hamburg (Kunsthalle, no. 228) closely resemble that of De Hooch's lost *Street Scene* (Cat. 22, Plate 19). Although Vrel could conceivably have invented this design, it seems more probable that De Hooch was the originator. The latter was, after all, at the height of his creative powers in *c.* 1658.

Like Van der Burch and Elinga, the Delft painter Cornelis de Man (1621–1706) was older than De Hooch, but he too came under the younger artist's influence.[9] Serving repeatedly as a 'hoofdman' of the guild, De Man was a well respected member of the painters' community in Delft. His admiration for the carefully constructed interiors of De Hooch and Vermeer is evident in his *Chess Players* in Budapest (Fig. 60) and *The Letter* in the Musée des Beaux-Arts in Marseille. Unlike his more famous colleagues, De Man also experimented with oblique views of the corners of rooms. These designs probably were inspired by the dual-point perspectives of the Delft architectural painters and earlier genre scenes by Steen.[10] De Man's execution, at times resembling that of Eglon van der Neer (to whom *The Letter* was once attributed), tends to be tighter and more highly finished than De Hooch's.

Many of De Hooch's contemporaries responded to his art. Primarily dependent upon Maes for his domestic genre motifs, the Dordrecht painter Cornelis Bisschop (1630–74) was probably indebted to De Hooch for aspects of his spatial designs and lighting schemes.[11] The backlighted doorway, a time-honoured device for enhancing spatial relief, was employed with consummate skill by De Hooch. His influence probably may be detected in the motif's appearance in the works of De Witte (see Fig. 29), Metsu (see *Woman at a Spinet*, Stichting Willem van de Vorm, Boymans Museum, Rotterdam), and many others. When Ochtervelt transferred the theme of a vendor at a doorstep (first popularized by Maes) to the front halls of prosperous homes, his decision to silhouette the pedlars against the lighted doorway may have been inspired by De Hooch's examples.[12] We recall that Ludolf de Jongh seems to have had an impact on De Hooch in his youth. Although the resemblances between their approaches to interior space construction in the 1660s may only be a matter of parallel development, De Jongh's courtyard and later formal garden scenes (see Fig. 61; cf. Cat. 60A, Plate 64) doubtless owe much to De Hooch.[13] Mutual influences also seem to characterize the relationship between De Hooch and Barent Graat. While De Hooch's portraits on terraces of the late 1660s recall the typology of Graat's portraits of a decade earlier, the *Family Portrait* in Vienna (Cat. 24) probably predates Graat's *Company in a Garden* of 1661 (Rijksmuseum, Amsterdam, no. 3932) and could have inspired its design. At least in his own lifetime, the works of De Hooch's Amsterdam period influenced relatively fewer artists, but they too had their admirers. Paintings by Michiel van Musscher, Jan Verkolje, Eglon van der Neer, Job Berckheyde, and the Flemish artist Jan Siberechts seem to reflect interest in the painter's later interiors.[14]

De Hooch's art continued to exert an influence in the next century. Many of the best eighteenth-century Dutch artists copied, or executed works reminiscent of, his Delft and early Amsterdam period paintings. The small-scale portraits of Cornelis Troost (1697–1750) often exhibit the luminous tonality and orderly space one associates with Delft paintings (see *Jeronimus Tonneman and his Son*, 1736, National Gallery, Dublin). Troost seems to have owned at least one painting by De Hooch (see Cat. C 157) and his pupil

Jacobus Buys (1724–1801) and his daughter (who also studied under him) Sara Troost (1731–1803) made copies of De Hooch's paintings (cf. Cat. 73a, 34d, 39a, 51a). The Haarlem portraitist Frans Dekker (1684–1751) and his pupil Cornelis van Noorde (1731–95), the animal painter and decorator Aart Schouman (1710–92), and the most distinguished and prolific engraver in eighteenth-century Holland, Reinier Vinkeles (1741–1816), all made drawings after De Hooch (see Cat. 22a, 22d, 40h, 40i, 88b).[15] The master's *Woman with a Child in a Pantry* (Cat. 31) evidently was already a favourite among eighteenth-century artists, having been copied by Hermanns Numan (1744–1820) and Wybrand Hendriks (1753–1831) (cf. Cat. 31g & h) and clearly serving as a model for a painting by Abraham van Strij (1753–1826) (Fig. 63). Van Strij's domestic genre scenes often employ designs reminiscent of those of De Hooch and Ochtervelt and he is known to have copied the former's courtyard scene in Edinburgh (see Cat. 33a, b & d). Hendriks's copy of De Hooch's courtyard scene in Leningrad has survived (see Cat. 46a) and his own genre scenes and those of Jan Ekels the Younger (1759–93) are often reminiscent of Delft painting.

In no small measure, therefore, De Hooch's legacy remained an active force in eighteenth-century Dutch art. One would like to know more, however, about how his works were understood and valued both in his own time and by his posthumous public. Although, as we have noted, his name fails to appear in seventeenth-century literature, the silence of his contemporaries should not be construed as evidence of neglect. Dirck van Bleyswijck, whose *Beschryvinge der Stadt Delft* of 1667–8 was the primary source for later writers' information on Delft painters, confined his comments to artists who had been born in Delft, died there (e.g. Fabritius), or were working in the city at the time of his writing. Thus the timing of De Hooch's move to Amsterdam (c. 1660–1) probably was a major factor in the absence of early comment on his life and work.

De Hooch's works appear to have brought modest but not exceptionally low prices in his own lifetime and until the end of the century. The eleven early works which appeared in De la Grange's inventory of 1655 (Doc. 23) were valued between 6 and 20 fl, roughly on a par with the average valuation of the works listed.[16] The value of money at this time can be gauged by comparative wage levels. Around the middle of the century, a weaver in Leiden earned about 7 fl a week, a fisherman on a herring boat 5–6 fl, and a skilled worker in Amsterdam about 6–8 fl.[17] In 1678 two works by De Hooch (see Cat. C 19, C 44) were valued at 5 and 25 fl, and three years after his death three works (cf. Cat. C 232, C 1, C 84) attained 48, 50, and 70 fl respectively. It was not until 1707 (see Cat. C 143) that a painting by De Hooch commanded more than 100 fl and it was only in the third quarter of the eighteenth century that his works regularly sold for more than this amount.[18]

Our meagre sampling may not, of course, be representative; however, it would appear that De Hooch's highest seventeenth-century prices were lower than those commanded by Vermeer's paintings and amounted to only a small fraction of the prices paid for the much-sought-after works of Gerard Dou and Frans van Mieris.[19] The gap between the prices commanded, on the one hand, by De Hooch and the painters of the Delft School and, on the other, by Dou and the Leiden 'fijnschilders' was not closed until the first half of the nineteenth century.[20] Certain seemingly curious remarks in eighteenth-century sales catalogues, like the characterization in 1784 of De Hooch's painting in New York (Cat. 19, Plate 18) as 'in the manner of E. van der Neer', can probably be attributed to the prevailing taste for a more refined and polished manner of painting.[21]

The French dealer Paillet, in his unpublished notes on a trip to Holland in December 1784, wrote of De Hooch, 'nous ne plaçons pas les tableaux de ce maître au premier rang: à cause de Metzu et Terburg qui ont traité ce genre avec plus de supériorité.'[22] The very fact, though, that De Hooch's works were included in many of the most important private collections in Holland in the second half of the eighteenth century, including those of Gerrit Braamcamp, P. Locquet, H. Muilman, J. Gildemeester Jansz, J. Goll van Franckenstein, and J. Danser Nijman, is proof of the high regard in which his art was held. As we have seen, Descamps's comments of 1753 suggest that the author was more familiar with De Hooch's later works than with those of the Delft period. This reflects the fact that few of the earlier pictures had left Holland by that date. When the *Woman with a Baby on her Lap* (Cat. 30, Plate 28) appeared in the Comte de Vaudreuil Sale in Paris in 1784, J. B. P. Lebrun, who wrote the catalogue and purchased the painting at the sale, noted in the entry 'Ce maître, peu connu en France, est un des peintres qui a le mieux connu la magie des effets du soleil & des reflets ... Ses tableaux sont fort estimés en Hollande, c'est ce qui fait que l'on trouve peu d'occasions d'en apporter ici.' Eight years later Lebrun added the interesting comment, 'on a été long-tems sans connaître le mérite réel de cet habile artiste, parce qu'on substituait à son nom celui d'autres plus en vogue, pour vendre ses tableaux plus cher.'[23] The author's only criticism of the artist's works was that they sometimes exhibited 'trop d'un demi-teinte', perhaps indicating that the later pictures had already darkened considerably by the end of the eighteenth century.

Comments in early nineteenth-century sales catalogues suggest that interest in and knowledge of the artist's works was increasing. Writing in 1834, the dealer Nieuwenhuys observed that the turning point in connoisseurs' appreciation of De Hooch occurred in 1810 on the occasion of the P. de Smeth van Alphen Sale in Amsterdam (see Cat. 31, 34, both of which appeared in the sale).[24] English collectors, notably King George IV, Sir Robert Peel, and the Duke of Wellington, acquired important works by the artist in these years and in 1829 no less than six De Hoochs were exhibited at the British Institution. English artists of the period, like R. P. Bonington and Sir Edwin Landseer, made copies of his works (see Cat. 58e, 35a).

In 1833 John Smith made the first systematic attempt to list all of De Hooch's known works.[25] The fact that the artist was selected for this privileged study is proof in itself that the doubts Paillet had expressed about De Hooch's merits had been dispelled in the intervening half-century. In his introductory comments to the catalogue, Smith wrote of the 'genius of this excellent painter', celebrating his luminous and carefully considered effects of light. The steady rise in the prices paid for De Hooch's works during these years drew comments in sales catalogues and artists' lexicons.[26] By the 1860s a change in taste favouring De Hooch's Delft period works was an accomplished fact. In the Delessert Sale in 1869 the painting now in New York (Cat. 19) brought the highest price (150,000 frs), far outstripping sums paid for paintings by Metsu and Dou also owned by the collector.[27] The change in taste favouring Delft painting ran parallel with the rise of interest in 'realistic' landscape and peasant painting.[28]

The publications of Théophile Thoré, who used the pen name W. Bürger, and Charles Blanc also helped to focus interest on De Hooch's works in these years. Blanc exaggerated when he stated that De Hooch had been virtually unknown for more than a century, but correctly observed the changes in taste we have noted.[29] Like many nineteenth-century writers, Thoré viewed Rembrandt as the principal innovator of his age and consequently speculated that De Hooch could have learned his lighting techniques during a period of study under the master.[30] In his famous pioneering article on Vermeer, Thoré attributed several De Hoochs (Cat. 10, 19, 24, 25, 64) to Vermeer.[31] In addition, he argued that Vermeer had been forgotten in the eighteenth century and his oeuvre largely absorbed by that of De Hooch, a view commonly held until Blankert's recent study.[32] In point of fact, while several Vermeers were attributed to De Hooch in the latter half of the nineteenth century,[33] none seems to have been assigned to him in the preceding century. Remarks in eighteenth-century sales catalogues suggest that Vermeer was just as well known as De Hooch and perhaps even more admired; when the *Woman and Child in a Pantry* (Cat. 31) appeared in the Walraven Sale in 1765, it was described as 'zoo goet als de Delfze van der Meer' (as good as the Delft van der Meer).[34]

A radical democrat, Thoré was in part attracted to Dutch art because of his social and political ideals. In his conviction that Dutch art reflected what he took to be the egalitarian foundations of the Dutch nation he reflected new patterns of nineteenth-century thought.[35] Given the associations the author and many of his contemporaries attached to Dutch painting, Realist painters were making a potentially political statement when they borrowed from Dutch sources. This climate of thought must be borne in mind when we look, for example, at Millet's domestic interiors of the 1850s, which often recall those of Maes and De Hooch, or when we read Thoré's *Salon* reviews, which are filled with parallels drawn between his contemporaries' works and earlier Dutch painting.[36]

With the rise of Impressionism in the second half of the nineteenth century, interest in Delft painting increased dramatically. To many observers, the Impressionists' sensitivity to natural light and colour seemed to have been directly anticipated in the luminous works of Vermeer and De Hooch.[37] In truth, the myths of Impressionism—its spontaneity, optical fidelity, and 'l'art pour l'art' sensibilities—have probably hampered the modern understanding of Delft painting by encouraging the application of unhistorical values to the art. Indeed, all too often writers on De Hooch have failed to recognize the bias of their age. In 1882, Fromentin delivered a rhapsodic and wholly uncritical appreciation of De Hooch, praising his 'sincerity' (that most prized of all nineteenth-century values) in the conception of his subjects and his powers of execution, notably his control of 'les valeurs'. Yet the author concludes that it would be a miracle to be prayed for if a latter-day De Hooch could be found to displace the contemporary makers of 'mosaics'—a transparent reference to the Impressionists.

By 1906 Bode could state that De Hooch's Delft period works 'heute sind fast gesuchter als Gemälde Raffaels oder Rembrandts'.[38] One half dozen years later Hans Jantzen undertook an interesting and little known study entitled *Farbenwahl und Farbengebung in der holländischen Malerei des XVII. Jahrhunderts* (Parchim i. M., 1912). The purpose of the paper was to demonstrate the historical development of colour in Dutch painting, using De Hooch's oeuvre as primary example. Jantzen's conclusion was that this development culminated in a brief period around 1654–63 (corresponding roughly with De Hooch's Delft period) which was characterized by a highly rational approach to colour.[39] While the notion of analysing an artist's development strictly on the basis of colour may strike us today, somewhat regrettably, as unusual, it was typical of a certain species of highly formalistic art criticism which sprang from the era that also gave birth to abstract painting.[40]

A reading of the modern literature on the artist and of surveys of Dutch painting confirms that De Hooch has won a seat in the contemporary pantheon of the greatest Dutch painters. Yet writers have not granted the artist access without reservations. Criticizing De Hooch's pictorial draughtsmanship, Collins Baker noted, 'Without injustice we may regard him as the least professionally accomplished member in that remarkable constellation of the mid 17th century Dutch masters.'[41] In Valentiner's monograph on the artist we are repeatedly struck by the faintness of the author's praise; 'Pieter de Hooch war eine lyrische Natur mit feinen künstlerischen Instinkten, aber keinen überragenden geistigen Fähigkeiten.' In a large measure these mixed feelings reflect the inability of modern writers to reconcile the works of De Hooch's Delft period with those of his Amsterdam years. To the generations weaned on Impressionism, De Hooch's darkly elegant later works appeared as a betrayal of his earlier promise. The strength of these beliefs can be gauged by the remarkably hostile reactions which attended the acquisition in 1916 of the *Musical Party in a Courtyard* (Cat. 134) by the National Gallery in London. The action provoked a debate in the House of Commons, a censoring of the Gallery's Board of Trustees, and a hail of criticism in the press.[42] That such an excellent example of the artist's late style should provoke passionate objections may strike us now as irrational. However, the case serves to remind us of how difficult it is to escape the artistic preconceptions of one's time.

Thus, while De Hooch's works have been consistently admired, each new age has reassessed his art according to its own system of values. Of course, one would like to believe that the present study has been the most objective. Undoubtedly, though, it too is a product of its time; would our discussion of the domestic virtue genre tradition have appeared in an age less concerned with the social roles of women? One final case serves to re-emphasize these ideas. In 1939 Bredius published a picture (Fig. 64) which he identified as one of the finest specimens of De Hooch's Delft period and which was said to have been part of a Parisian private collection for many years.[43] The picture bore a strong compositional resemblance to the *Card Players* in Buckingham Palace (Cat. 28, Col. Plate VI) and, like that work, was signed and dated 1658. About this time a second picture (Fig. 65) resembling De Hooch's Delft period pictures (cf. Cat. 26, 29, Plates 23, 27) turned up and was acquired by the famous collector D. G. van Beuningen. Both works were hailed as important supplements to De Hooch's oeuvre. It seemed like a very fruitful period for the rediscovery of Delft School masterpieces; several years earlier the Boymans Museum had acquired a scene of the *Supper at Emmaus* which was celebrated as a hitherto unknown Vermeer. Only after the War was the truth of the matter revealed; all three works and a sizable group of paintings in the manner of other Dutch painters were forgeries by Han van Meegeren.[44] A third unfinished 'Pieter de Hooch' was discovered in the forger's studio in 1945. Examining these works closely from our temporal vantage point one initially wonders how the experts were fooled. The heavy-lidded figures remind one more of Marlene Dietrich and the fashion plates of the 1930s than of De Hooch's sitters. Even today, though, the honest viewer can admire (albeit somewhat perversely) the efficacy of Van Meegeren's deception. Rather than pride ourselves on our ability to identify latter-day fakes, we should try to recognize the inevitable distortions of our own vision, not merely to guard against forgeries, but to be better able to understand Dutch seventeenth-century pictures on their own terms.

Examples of De Hooch's signatures

Document 14 (see page 145)

Document 20 (see page 146)

Document 24 (see page 146)

Document 39 (see page 147)

Notes

CHAPTER I

The Life of the Artist

1. For a detailed account of the facts of the artist's life and their sources, see the chronologically arranged Documents. De Hooch was the usual spelling both on paintings and in documents during his early years and in the Delft period; after *c.* 1660 'de Hoogh' is more common. For examples of his signatures see page 57.

2. Annetge Pieters was the first of Hendrick de Hooch's three wives (see Docs. 1, 10 & 37). She was described as a widow and midwife as early as 1626 (testimonial concerning the identity of the father of a newborn child, Prot. Not. N. van Hagen, Rotterdam, O.N.A., 106/37; a similar document signed in the following year, Prot. Not. A. Hofflant, O.N.A., 255/17) and was said to be about 36 years old in 1632 (testimonial, together with Lammertge Daniëls and Mayken Bouwens, concerning an inheritance of the late Adriaentge Tijsz, Prot. Not. G. van der Houdt, Rotterdam, O.N.A., 286/33). Before her death in 1648 (Doc. 9) she bore her husband Hendrick five children (Docs. 4–8). Of these, only the eldest, Pieter, was alive in 1657 (see Doc. 31).

   Serving as a witness to documents drawn up in Rotterdam, Hendrick de Hooch was described as a 'bricklayer' in 1641 and 1644 (procuration by Pauwels Verschuyeren on behalf of Johan van Willigen, Prot. Not. V. Jacobsz, O.N.A., 429/28; and a building contract between Leendert de Jongh and Cornelis de Bruijn for a house on the south side of the Visserdijk, Prot. Not. A. van der Graaf, O.N.A., 332/209) and again as a 'master bricklayer' in 1660 (last will of Claes Denisz. Pael, Prot. Not. B. Roose, O.N.A., 678/852; communication R. A. D. Renting for this and all of the un-abbreviated archival references cited above). The latter title was given only to skilled artisans who were members of the guild. It required a period of apprenticeship, successful completion of a proficiency examination, and a certain amount of capital to set up one's own business. Two years after his marriage to Adrientge Philips de Wijmer in 1649, Hendrick purchased a house on the Lombertstraat in Rotterdam (Docs. 12–13) which he resold in 1663 (Doc. 41) after moving to Middelburg with his third wife. He attended the baptisms in Delft and Amsterdam of two of his son's children (Docs. 29 & 44). Although Pieter de Hooch was named in the will of his father's second wife (Doc. 31), she repudiated the document on her deathbed (Doc. 34) and it is unknown whether he ever received an inheritance.

3. Arnold Houbraken, *De groote schouburg der Nederlantsche konstschilders en schilderessen*, II, Amsterdam, 1721 (ed. P. T. A. Swillens; Maastricht, 3 vols., 1943–54, II, 27): 'Hem [Ludolf de Jongh] volgt, PIETER DE HOOGE, die uitmuntend is geweest in 't schilderen van Kamergezichten, en daar in Gezelschapjes van Haaeren en Juffrouwen. Hy heeft eenigen tyd by (den beruchten) *N. Berchem* geleert, te gelyk met *Jacob Ugtervelt . . .*' (Following Ludolf de Jongh [in sequence only], PIETER DE HOOGE, who was excellent in the painting of Interiors with Companies of Gentlemen and Ladies. He studied for a period with (the famous) *N. Berchem*, at the same time as *Jacob Ugtervelt . . .*).

4. Concerning Van der Burch, see P. C. Sutton, 'Hendrick van der Burch', *The Burlington Magazine* (forthcoming) (with earlier literature; hereafter 'Sutton').

5. Houbraken (II, 89) states that Berchem worked for a period for a man who paid him 10 fl per day. After 1660, De Witte placed himself at various times under contract to paint in return for his keep; see I. Manke, *Emanuel de Witte*, Amsterdam, 1963, 3 ff. (hereafter 'Manke').

6. Concerning De la Grange, see A. Bredius, 'Bijdragen tot de biographie van Pieter de Hoogh', *Oud-Holland*, 7 (1889), 162–5 (hereafter 'Bredius 1889'). Justus was baptized (Joost) in the Hooglandse Kerk, Leiden, 7 Dec. 1623, the son of Pieter de la Grange and Hester Bertens (or Berten) (communication P. J. M. de Baar). He completed his apprenticeship in the linen trade in 1641 (see *Gazette des Beaux-Arts*, 1927, 368, n. 1; from A. Bredius), was living in Delft in the following year (Delft, no. 1720, fol. 143) and again temporarily in 1650 when he made a will (Delft, no. 1674, fol. 856). On 21 Feb. 1651 he was residing at the Nieuwe Rijn when he was betrothed in Leiden to Margarieta Persijn, living at Rijn (commun. P. J. M. de Baar). The following June he claimed residence in Leiden (Prot. Not. J. van Caerdekamp, 23/6/1651, fol. 38) and, prior to his departure for North America in 1662, lived in and around villages in the vicinity of Leiden: Rijnsberg 1652, Koudekerk a.d. Rijn 1654, Noordwijk op Zee 1655–7, the vicinity of Oegstgeest 1658–9, Wassenaer 1659–60, and Warmond 1661 (see Bredius 1889 and unpub. notes at RKD; the merchant's movements have been confirmed by P. J. M. de Baar through various tax registers and notarial documents).

   De la Grange had an inheritance of 51,000 fl from his maternal grandmother Christina du Prée which in 1654 enabled him to purchase one-third ownership (the remaining two-thirds were bought by his relatives; total cost: 21,000 fl) of the 'De (gecroonde) Witte Eenhoorn', a brewery at the Stille Rijn (commun. P. J. M. de Baar). High taxes paid by the merchant and his ownership of a manor outside Noordwijk (Prot. Not. Outerman, Leiden, 10/10/1656) further testify to his wealth. His financial reversals began at the latest by 1655 when the inventory of his paintings (Doc. 23) was drawn up, presumably to cover a debt. In

1658 he empowered his wife to sell all his worldly goods (Prot. Not. Outerman, 18/11/1656, fol. 247) and in 1661 a document states that he 'tot soodanige decadentie geraect is, dat hij tegenwoordich met sijn huysvrouwe en drie cleyne kinderkens in seer groote extremiteit is comen te vervallen' (had succumbed to such decadence, that he and his wife and three small children had fallen into extreme hardship; Prot. Not. Outerman, 17/10/1661, fol. 374). Under pressure from his creditors, De la Grange initially planned to move to Tobago, but subsequently purchased the island of Tinicum (today in Delaware County, Pennsylvania). The transaction, involving a disputed bill of exchange, was the subject of lengthy litigation. Eight years after the merchant's death in the New Netherlands on 26 April 1664 his descendants lost the legal battle for the property; see G. Smith, *History of Delaware County*, Philadelphia, 1862, 84 & 145.

In addition to employing De Hooch, De la Grange was also in contact with the Leiden painter Hercules Patronus, who testified on the merchant's behalf in a matter concerning a painting by Porcellis (Prot. Not. Outerman, 19/6/1652, fol. 117), and with the ageing engraver and publisher Robert de Baudoux (b. 1574-5; see Thieme–Becker, III, 62), who was the stepfather of De la Grange's wife and evidently lived with the couple in Leiden and Rijnsberg in 1651-2 (commun. P. J. M. de Baar).

7. Concerning Gast, see Sutton, n. 7.

8. This theory, first advanced by H. Havard ('l'État civil des maîtres hollandais, Pieter de Hooch', *Gazette des Beaux-Arts*, 2 per., 15 [1877], 522), was repeated by W. R. Valentiner (*Pieter de Hooch*, Klassiker der Kunst, vol. 35, Stuttgart, 1929, xvi; hereafter 'Valentiner') and others. P. Haverkorn van Rijsewijk (*Nederlandsche Kunstbode*, 11 [1880], 164) was the only writer to question the theory, observing that the 'Heyndrick van der Burch' present at the baptism of De Hooch's son Pieter (Doc. 22), and who could be assumed to be related to the child's mother, did not sign his name with the patronymic 'Beuckelsz' used by the faiencer in official documents.

9. Jannetge doubtless is identical with the Jannetgen Rochus [dr. van der Burch] who appeared as a witness together with Rochus Hendricksz [van der Burch] and Jacomijntgen Rochus [dr. van der Burch] at the baptism of Barent Gast's first child in Delft in 1650 (see Sutton, n. 7). Rochus apparently married more than once (see Sutton 1979, n. 5). Thus, Jannetge probably was a sister, as Haverkorn van Rijsewijk surmised (1880, 164), or possibly a step-sister, of the painter Van der Burch.

10. Rochus was mentioned as the owner of a house on the Binnenwatersloot in a document of 1663 (Sutton 1979, doc. no. 31) and, without date, in the index to the Huizenprotocol (Delft, no. 3961, fol. 884v). Since the records of the early transfers of these houses have been destroyed, it cannot be determined when the family purchased the house.

Hendrick van der Burch's sister Jacquemyntyen (various spellings: Jacobmijntje, Jacobmine, etc.; 1629-99) attended the baptisms of De Hooch's first child in Delft (Doc. 22) and his last in Amsterdam (Doc. 49). She also joined De Hooch as a witness at the baptism of a child of the notary Francois Boogert in Delft in 1655 (Doc. 26). Van der Burch's mother, Divertge Jochemsdr. van Vliet, was present at the christening of De Hooch's daughter Anna in 1656 (Doc. 29) and two of the painter's children (the first having died) undoubtedly were named for her; 'Diewertje' in 1661

and 'Dieuwertien' in 1664 (Docs. 36 & 42). Heijndrick van der Burch, Dijwertgen Jochems van Vliet and Jannetgen van der Burch also appeared together in Delft at the baptism of the child of Boogert's sister in 1649 (see Sutton, doc. no. 5). Jannetge, and no doubt De Hooch himself, maintained contact with Van der Burch even after the latter's move to Amsterdam (cf. Doc. 33).

11. None of the documents the two painters signed together pertained to activities directly involving them. Rather it seems that they were simply personally acquainted with (and possibly even related by marriage to) the documents' author, the Delft notary Francois (Frans) Boogert; concerning Boogert, see Sutton, n. 14. Boogert purchased the house on the Binnenwatersloot owned by Van der Burch's parents. Furthermore, members of Van der Burch's family regularly attended baptisms in Delft of Boogert's children and De Hooch was present at the christening of Boogert's son in 1655 (Doc. 26). In the following year Boogert's wife, Susannetje Jans van Roon, attended the ceremony for De Hooch's daughter Anna (Doc. 29). The notary himself appeared at the baptisms of four of De Hooch's children in Amsterdam (Docs. 36, 38, 42 & 49), two of whom (again the first having died) were probably named Francois in his honour. In addition, De Hooch's wife and Boogert were witnesses at the baptism of a child of Barent Gast in Leiden in 1659 (Doc. 32; see note 7). Boogert's son, Johannes, later owned a painting by De Hooch (see Cat. C 86).

12. Although the painter's wife appeared in Leiden on one occasion in 1659 (Doc. 32), there is no evidence to suggest that the couple lived in Leiden at this or any other time.

13. N. MacLaren, *The Dutch School*, National Gallery Catalogues, London, 1960, 183-4; hereafter 'MacLaren'.

14. Bredius (1889, 165) deduced from a lost document (Doc. 45) dated 22 Nov. 1668 that De Hooch had been living at the address since May 1667. S. A. C. Dudok van Heel has called the author's attention to the fact that if the date on the missing document was correctly recorded we can only assume De Hooch had been a resident on the Konijnenstraat since May of 1668 because leases were renewed in May of each year.

15. The collectors documented as having owned De Hooch's paintings before c. 1720, and who, therefore, can be considered potential patrons, may (where their profession is known) be loosely divided into three occupational groups: merchants and businessmen (see Cat. C 1, C 20-1 & C 143 & C 261, C 85, C 89 & C 142, C 141, C 247, C 248, C 283); artists and art dealers (see Cat. C 269-70, C 272-4, C 276, C 281); and professionals and others (two doctors, an alderman, a tollkeeper, and a sexton) (see Cat. C 277-80, C 282, C 271, C 83, C 50). The largest group were the Amsterdam merchants. Concerning their relative prosperity, see Chap. IV, n. 6.

16. For a discussion of the case in point, see MacLaren, 458-9, and Manke, 4-5. In November 1670 (Doc. 48) De Hooch testified to having seen a painting by De Witte representing *Adriana van Heusden at the New Fishmarket in Amsterdam* at the home of Joris de Wijs in Amsterdam. This must have occurred before Sept. 1663, by which time De Witte had left the house taking the picture and three others with him. De Witte subsequently lodged with Laurens Mauritsz. Doucy (cf. Doc. 47), a hatmaker and art dealer, who counted De Hooch among the artists whose works he sold. According to Bredius's unpublished notes (see also Bredius, *Künstler-*

Inventare, II, 426), the painter Jan Looten claimed on 6 Sept. 1664 to owe Doucy 700 fl for seven pictures, including individual (undescribed) works by De Hooch (Cat. C 269), De Witte, Ruisdael, De Vlieger, Aert van der Neer, and two paintings by Kalf.

17. Families who enjoyed some financial security might avoid institutionalizing mentally ill relatives by providing for them privately. Such was the case with the disturbed children of the painter Claes Moyaert; see S. A. C. Dudok van Heel, 'De Schilder Claes Moyaert', *Jaarboek Amstelodamum*, 68, (1976) 31–2.

CHAPTER II
The Early Years

1. See W. Bode, *Rembrandt und seine Zeitgenossen*, Leipzig, 1906, 56ff.
2. On Berchem, see A. Blankert in exh. cat. *Nederlandse 17ᵉ eeuwse landschapschilders*, Centraal Museum, Utrecht, 1965, 147–9. Berchem and his wife Catharyna Claes (de Groot) made a will in Haarlem on 22 March 1649 (Prot. Not. Colterman, Haarlem, no. 230, fol. 314—previously unpublished; communication F. Tames, Haarlem Archives). Although no early sources mention a journey south, it has been assumed that the artist made a trip to Italy. Blankert's proposed date for this journey (*c.* 1653–5) correctly suggests that it probably postdated the period of the young Rotterdam painters' training under the master.
3. See Ochtervelt's *Hunting Party*, 1652, Städtische Museen, Karl Marx-Stadt (Chemnitz); repr. Valentiner, 190.
4. J. B. Descamps, *La vie des peintres . . .*, III, Paris, 1753, 162, 'Par sa manière de peindre, il paroît sûr qu'il fut un des meilleurs Élèves de *Nicolas Berchem*. Par ses premiers Tableaux on juge, avec raison, qu'il étudia ses principes dans cette grande École.'
5. While the first entry could refer to a work by Carel de Hooch (died 1628; no relation), the latter two clearly were attributed to Pieter.
6. W. Bode, 'Ein neu aufgefundenes Jugendwerk von Pieter de Hooch', *Zeitschrift für bildende Kunst*, N.F. 30 (1919), 305–8.
7. On De Jongh, see C. Hofstede de Groot, in Thieme & Becker, 19, Leipzig, 1926, 132–4; E. Plietzsch, *Holländische und flämische Maler des XVII. Jahrhunderts*, Leipzig [1960], 55ff.
8. R. E. Fleischer, 'Ludolf de Jongh and the Early Work of Pieter de Hooch', *Oud-Holland*, 92 (1978), 49–67. Additional stable and tavern scenes by De Jongh; signed, Sale Katz, Paris, 25 April 1951, no. 32; Private Collection, Brighton. *c.* 1929, (repr. Fleischer, figs. 18 & 19); Öffentliche Kunstsammlung, Basel; signed & dated 1658, Groninger Museum, Groningen (repr. Valentiner, 185 & 184 below).
9. See Ochtervelt's *Soldiers Drinking*, National Gallery, Prague, no. 0–8789; repr. Valentiner, 191 (left).
10. See P. Sutton, 'Hendrik van der Burch' (forthcoming).
11. Unsigned, but sold as a work by Van der Burch as early as 1809 (cf. Sutton, n. 27). At that time an attribution to the then little known artist was probably based on a signature or a trustworthy tradition.
12. As with De Jongh's genre scenes, Van der Burch's soldier paintings have at times been mistaken for those of De Hooch; see Cat. D 17–19.

13. On Terborch, see S. J. Gudlaugsson. *Gerard ter Borch*, 2 vols., The Hague, 1959–60 (hereafter 'Gudlaugsson').
14. See J. M. Montias, 'New Documents on Vermeer and his Family', *Oud-Holland*, 91 (1977), 267–87, doc. no. 46a, dated 22 Apr. 1653.
15. According to John Bulwer's contemporary guide to manual rhetoric, *Chirologia: or the Natural language of the hand . . .*, London, 1644, (also early Dutch eds.), 160–1, 'To put Finger in the eye, is their expression who crie, and would by that endeavour of nature ease themselves and give vent to their conceived headiness'.
16. See Gudlaugsson, I, 72–3.
17. Terborch also treated the tric-trac theme, albeit in a horizontal composition, in an early work in Bremen (Kunsthalle, cat. 1939, no. 135). Valentiner (xv, xxvii) first noted the resemblance between De Hooch's early guardroom scenes and those of Terborch and Van den Eeckhout.
18. Sale A. W. M. Mensing, Amsterdam, 15/11/1938, no. 30; repr. *The Burlington Magazine*, 69 (1954), 75, fig. 3.
19. A. Blankert, *Johannes Vermeer van Delft 1632–1675*, Utrecht-Antwerp, 1975, 46 (hereafter 'Blankert').
20. R. E. Fleischer, 'An Altered Painting by Pieter de Hooch', *Oud-Holland*, 90 (1976), 108–14.
21. See P. C. Sutton, 'A Newly Discovered Early Work by Pieter de Hooch', *The Burlington Magazine*, 121 (1979), 32–5.
22. See MacLaren, 123.

CHAPTER III
The Years in Delft 1652–60/61

1. The best general introduction to the history, culture, and art of Delft remains Max Eisler's *Alt-Delft Kultur und Kunst*, Amsterdam-Vienna, 1923; hereafter 'Eisler'.
2. See Rijksmuseum, Amsterdam, no. A 306, dated 1647.
3. See H. Wichmann, *Leonaert Bramer, sein Leben und seine Kunst*, Leipzig, 1923.
4. See Blankert, 12–13.
5. On Potter, see I. van Westrheene, *Paulus Potter*, The Hague, 1867; E. Michel, *Paul Potter*, Paris, 1907; C. Hofstede de Groot, *Catalogue Raisonné*, IV, 1912 (German ed. 1911).
6. Eisler (178–89) was the first to consider Potter's potential influence in this regard; see also A. B. de Vries, *Jan Vermeer van Delft*, Amsterdam, 1939.
7. On Houckgeest, see H. Wichmann, in Thieme & Becker, 17, 558 (with earlier lit.); W. Liedtke, 'Architectural Painting in Delft: 1650–1675', diss., Courtauld Institute, London, 1974; L. de Vries, 'Gerard Houckgeest', *Jahrbuch der Hamburger Kunstsammlungen*, 20 (1975), 25–56.
8. On De Witte, see I. Manke, *Emanuel de Witte 1617–1692*, Amsterdam, 1963; also Arthur K. Wheelock, Jr, 'Gerard Houckgeest and Emanuel de Witte: Architectural Painting in Delft, around 1650', *Simiolus*, 8 (1975–6), 167–85, hereafter 'Wheelock 1975–6'.
9. Houckgeest's earliest interior views of the Nieuwe Kerk are dated 1650: Kunsthalle, Hamburg, cat. 1966, no. 342; Sale, London, 26/11/1976, no. 80. Liedtke (diss.) correctly rejects Manke's view (Manke, 15–28) of the relationship between Houckgeest and De Witte, stressing the former's leadership in the turn to the painting of actual architecture and the creation of the Delft architectural painting type. Although a third Delft architectural painter, Hendrick van Vliet (1611–75), dated church interiors as early as 1652 (see *St.*

Pieterskerk in Leiden, Herzog Anton Ulrich-Museum, Braunschweig, no. 783) his style is clearly derived from Houckgeest and there is no evidence to suggest that he played an important role in the new discoveries.

10. See Manke, 26ff.; Wheelock (1975–6, 170) has correctly doubted this notion. On Fabritius, see H. F. Wijnman, 'De schilder Carel Fabritius. Een reconstructie van zijn leven en werken', *Oud-Holland*, 48 (1931), 100–41 (hereafter 'Wijnman'); and K. E. Schuurman, *Carel Fabritius*, (Palet Serie), Amsterdam, 1947 (hereafter 'Schuurman'). Christopher Brown is preparing a monograph on the artist.

11. Dirck van Bleyswijk, *Beschryvinge der Stadt Delft*, II, Delft, 1667, 852: 'CAREL FABRITIUS, a very fine and outstanding painter, who in matters of perspective and natural colouring or the placement of his colour was so skilful and powerful, that (according to the judgement of many connoisseurs) [he] never had his equal . . .'. In his *De Groote Schouburg* (III, Amsterdam, 1719, 337), Houbraken repeated Van Bleyswijk's comments, adding the observation: 'Karel Fabricius, an excellent painter of perspective, esteemed as the best in his time, was also a good portraitist.' Van Hoogstraten commended Fabritius's illusionistic mural paintings in the chapter on perspective ('Van de Deurzigtkunde') in his *Inleyding tot de Hooge Schoole der Schilderkonst*, Rotterdam, 1678, 274.

12. According to Van Bleyswijk (852f.), the artist was painting the portrait of Simon Decker (died 1657) at the time of the explosion. Decker was the 'koster' (sexton) of the Oude Kerk and his widow's inventory of 1669 included an undescribed painting by De Hooch (see Cat. C 271).

13. Two works by Fabritius are known to date from the late forties, the portrait of *Abraham de Potter*, datable to 1648 or 1649 (Rijksmuseum, Amsterdam, no. A 1591), and his lost *Family Portrait* of 1648 (formerly Boymans Museum, Rotterdam, cat. [1862], no. 94, destroyed by fire in 1864; see the catalogue entry and the imprecise watercolour copy made from memory by Victor de Stuers; repr. Schuurman, 43). Although the latter work can no longer be assessed accurately, neither picture suggests that Fabritius inspired the architectural painters' innovations.

14. In addition to the probable loss of works by the artist in the explosion, their scarcity may also be a result of the fact that Fabritius, like Bramer, worked in the perishable medium of fresco. None of his frescoes have survived, but several references seem to confirm his activity in this medium. Van Hoogstraten (*Inleyding*, 274) compared a mural painting by Fabritius in the house of Dr. Valentius in Delft to Giulio Romano's illusionistic frescoes at the Palazzo del Té in Mantua. The archives also record that a woman selling a brewery in Delft in 1660 requested permission to remove a section of wall painted by Fabritius. Clearly the mural in question was a fresco. The claim by Fabritius's widow that her husband had been a painter for the Prince of Orange (see *Oud-Holland*, 1890, 228) prompted W. R. Valentiner (*The Art Bulletin*, 14 [1932], 204) to suggest that the artist could have worked on murals at Rijswijk or Honselersdijk, as did Bramer and Couwenbergh. Liedtke has supported this theory (see note below); however, it seems to be contradicted by Van Hoogstraten's statement (ibid.) that the artist's works did not appear in permanent royal buildings or churches ('. . . maer't is te bejammeren dat zijn werken niet ergens in een vast Koninklijk gebouw of Kerke geplaetst zijn. . .').

15. The theory, first advanced by W. Martin, was reported by Schuurman (Schuurman, 53). Walter Liedtke's reconstruction of the box ('The "View of Delft" by Carel Fabritius', *The Burlington Magazine*, 117 [1976], 61–73) proposes, probably correctly, that the representation was continued on the structure's floor. Arthur Wheelock's theory (see 'Carel Fabritius: Perspective and Optics in Delft', *Nederlands Kunsthistorisch Jaarboek*, 24 [1973], 63–83) that Fabritius employed a tilted double-concave lens in painting the scene is ingenious but rather too elaborately contrived to command belief; see Liedtke's appraisal (ibid.) of Wheelock's theory, and the latter's response to Liedtke in his *Perspective, Optics, and Delft Artists around 1650*, (Harvard Univ. diss. 1973), Garland Series, New York, 1977, Preface (hereafter 'Wheelock diss.')—to be reviewed by Liedtke. Concerning perspective boxes, see also Susan Koslow, ' "De Wonderlijke Perspectyfkas": An Aspect of Seventeenth Century Dutch Painting', *Oud-Holland*, 82 (1967), 33–56.

16. See the four documents cited by Liedtke (176, 65).

17. Inventory of Willem Jansz. Cronenburch (d. 25 Oct. 1673), Prot. Not. T. van Hasselt, Delft, no. 2157; cf. Wijnman, 140.

18. See *Man at a Window*, dated 1653, Kunsthistorisches Museum, Vienna, no. 378; and *View Down a Corridor*, 1662, Durham Park, Gloucestershire, repr. *Apollo*, 81 (1965), 362, fig. 2.

19. Although the work is at present dubiously assigned to H. van der Burch, J. G. van Gelder (anonymously in commentary to cat. no. 39 [erroneously as by De Hooch] in exh. *Vermeer oorsprong en invloed*, Boymans Museum, Rotterdam, 1935) compared it to the late production of Fabritius and linked it to still another early inventory reference: 'een stuk van Fabritius daer Aelst zijn degen op geschildert heeft' (a painting by Fabritius in which [Willem (or Evert?) van] Aelst painted the sword); inv. of Aernout Eelbrecht, Leiden, 1683 (cf. Wijnman 1931, 140). The sword resting on the windowsill is the most highly finished detail of the picture and could be by another hand.

20. See Van Hoogstraten's *Trompe-l'Oeil*, 1652, Akademie der bildenden Künste, Vienna, no. 1406; repr. Blankert, fig. 13 (Engl. ed. fig. 14).

21. See C. Brière-Misme, 'Un petit maître hollandais: Cornelis Bisschop (1630–74)', *Oud-Holland*, 65 (1950), 31.

22. On Van der Heyden, see H. Wagner, *Jan van der Heyden*, Amsterdam–Haarlem, 1971. Regarding the artist's illusionistic experiments, see Wheelock diss., 166–9.

23. On Vermeer, see now Albert Blankert, *Johannes Vermeer van Delft 1632–1675*, Utrecht/Antwerp, 1975 (revised Engl. ed., Oxford, 1978), with documents compiled by Rob Ruurs and catalogue notes by Willem L. van de Watering.

24. The debate concerning the two artists' relationship has been argued at length. Thoré-Bürger (*Musées de la Hollande*, I, 1858, 272) first stated that Vermeer imitated De Hooch 'a little', but later avoided the issue in his pioneering article on Vermeer. Hofstede de Groot (*Catalogue Raisonné*, London, 1907, I, 471) found the question perplexing but implied that what he viewed as De Hooch's decline after he moved to Amsterdam was a result of the absence of Vermeer's 'refining effect'. Eduard Plietzsch (*Vermeer van Delft*, Leipzig, 1911, 25–8) was the first to propose that De Hooch's influence was critical for Vermeer's conversion from large figure compositions to smaller interior genre

scenes. W. R. Valentiner ('Pieter de Hooch, Part Two', *Art in America*, 15 (1927), 69) argued that Vermeer was the innovator in the relationship, a view which he restated in his monograph on De Hooch, and developed still further in his article 'Zum 300. Geburtstag Jan Vermeers, Oktober, 1933. Vermeer and die Meister der holländischen Genremalerei', *Pantheon*, 10 (1932), 305–24 (hereafter 'Valentiner 1932'). In the latter article Valentiner posited an accelerated development for Vermeer, dating several of his small genre scenes in the early 1650s and casting him in the creative role not only in his relationship with De Hooch, but also with Steen, Metsu, and Van Mieris. Most of his assumptions are untenable. In a review of Valentiner's book on De Hooch (*Zeitschrift für Kunstgeschichte*, 1 [1932], 85–6). Jakob Rosenberg recalled Plietzsch's observation and rejected Valentiner's view of the two artists' relationship. W. Martin (*De Hollandsche Schilderkunst in de 17de eeuw*, II, Amsterdam, 1936, 200) again saw Vermeer as the principal innovator. Recently Rosenberg and Slive (*Dutch Art and Architecture 1600 to 1800*, Baltimore, 1966, 124) have aptly stated 'The relationship between Vermeer and De Hooch is still a matter of conjecture. It seems that De Hooch anticipated certain elements of Vermeer's mature period, but later came under the influence of Vermeer's stronger personality.' Blankert (41–6, 78) expressed a similar view.

25. See E. Plietzsch, 'Randbemerkungen zur holländischen Interieurmalerei am Beginn des 17. Jahrhunderts', *Wallraf-Richartz-Jahrbuch*, 18 (1956), 174–96.

26. On Vredeman de Vries and his followers, see H. Jantzen, *Das Niederländische Architecturbild*, Leipzig, 1910, 19ff.; U. M. Schneede, 'Das repräsentative Gesellschaftsbild in der niederländischen Malerei des 17. Jahrhunderts und seine Grundlagen bei Hans Vredeman de Vries', dissertation, Christian-Albrechts-Universität, Kiel, 1965 (hereafter, 'Schneede diss.'); idem, 'Interieurs von Hans und Paul Vredeman', *Nederlands Kunsthistorisch Jaarboek*, 18 (1967), 125–68; H. Mielke, 'Hans Vredeman de Vries', dissertation, Freie Universität, Berlin, 1967.

27. After *c.* 1636 Van Delen occasionally executed more intimately conceived interior scenes. One of his paintings now in Rotterdam (dated 1636, Boymans-van Beuningen Museum, no. 1158) employs a shallower space, eliminates the view of the ceiling, and moves the viewer closer to the figures. As Jantzen (71) and Schneede (diss., 220–6) observed, such works constitute important steps toward De Hooch's later Delft interior type, but their pronounced linearity and elegant architectural details still betray an ancestry in De Vries's designs.

28. For biographical details see A. Bredius, 'Nieuwe bijzonderheden over Isaack Jansz. Koedyck', *Oud-Holland*, 27 (1909), 5–12; and C. Hofstede de Groot, in Thieme & Becker, 21, 1927, 111–13. A merchant as well as a painter, Koedijk was active in Leiden and Amsterdam. As Hofstede de Groot suggested, he was probably a follower of Gerard Dou. In 1650 he was appointed to the court of Shah Jehan in Batavia, where he remained from 1651 to 1659. Thus he was abroad during much of the crucial decade of change in Delft painting. On his art, see C. Hofstede de Groot, 'Die Koedijk-Rätsel und ihre Lösung', *Jahrbuch der königlich Preussischen Kunstsammlungen*, 24 (1903), 39–46; idem, 'Isaack Koedijk', in *Festschrift für Max J. Friedländer zum 60. Geburtstag*, Leipzig, 1927, 181–90.

29. Formerly Dr. L. J. K. van Aalst, Hoevelaken; another version: Sale Countess of Rosebery et al. (A. Faith), London, 24/3/1976, no. 66, ill.; the left hand side of the composition also exists in a third version: Sale Sedelmeyer, Paris, 25/5/1907, no. 108, ill. The design evidently was one of Koedijk's favourite compositions.

30. See *The Merry Drinker*, dated 1650, Hermitage, Leningrad, no. 1862.

31. The loss of important paintings by Koedijk has impaired our knowledge of his work. Two were in the famous Braamcamp Collection in the eighteenth century and were lost at sea after being purchased for Catherine II of Russia (see C. Bille, *De Tempel der Kunst of het Kabinet van der Heer Braamcamp*, 2 vols., Amsterdam, 1960). Copies (see note 34) and catalogue descriptions suggest that the lost painting would have provided additional evidence of the artist's knowledge of perspective techniques. The description, for example, of a picture of a *Woman Reading to a Man at a Table* (Braamcamp Sale, 31/7/1771, no. 45) mentions a view of figures conversing through an open door at the back of the room and adds the appreciative note 'owing to the astonishing skill the perspective shows an incomparable depth'.

32. Connections between Koedijk's art and Delft painting have been observed by several writers. Thoré-Bürger (1858, 101) speculated that De Hooch might have been Koedijk's teacher and A. von Wurzbach (*Niederländisches Künstler-Lexikon*, I, 1906, 312) believed that he imitated Vermeer and De Hooch. Hofstede de Groot (see note 28), on the other hand, stressed his connection with Dou and the Leiden School. L. Gowing (*Vermeer*, 1952, n. 60) saw Koedijk's art as a matter of 'parallel development' with Delft painting. Koedijk's precedents for the Delft School have only recently been considered. Wheelock (diss. 269–73) discussed the possibility of his influence on Vermeer, and F. W. Robinson (*Gabriel Metsu*, New York, 1974, 92, n. 9; hereafter 'Robinson') compared his spatial designs to those of Delft painters. The latter's theory, however, that Cornelis de Man could have provided the primary link between Koedijk and the Delft artists is untenable. Only one of De Man's genre scenes is dated (*The Sweeper* of 1666; repr. *Oud-Holland*, 52 [1935], 116, fig. 25) and none are likely to predate De Hooch's works of *c.* 1658.

33. For biographical details, see MacLaren, 227. On Maes, see W. R. Valentiner, *Nicolaes Maes*, Berlin–Leipzig, 1924. William Robinson is preparing a dissertation on the artist.

34. See Wheelock diss., 270–1. Koedijk's other lost work from the Braamcamp Sale (Amsterdam, 31/7/1771, no. 44), known today in copies by J. Laquy in watercolour (Museum Fodor, Amsterdam) and oils (Baron Mackay, Hilversum), represented a *Man Descending a Spiral Staircase* to surprise an amorous couple in the cellar and could have inspired Maes's several variations on the 'Eavesdropper' theme. The version in the Boston Museum is the closest in design and conception.

35. MacLaren (229) speculated that Maes might have visited Delft between 1650 and 1653. The timing of such a visit, however, would have placed him in the city before he executed the works which concern us here.

36. Thoré-Bürger 1858, 98. Although Thoré wished to see Rembrandt as De Hooch's primary influence he mentioned the latter's connection with Maes on several occasions (cf. 'Van der Meer de Delft', *Gazette des Beaux-Arts*, I^e per., 21 [1866], 315). Concerning Maes and De Hooch, see also

W. Bode, 1906, 59ff.; Valentiner, xxviii; MacLaren, 227 & 229; and Blankert, 46.

37. See Blankert, 44–6, cat. no. 4. The dating of Vermeer's works is highly problematic, but the present picture certainly must have been executed after the *Procuress* of 1656.

38. X-rays of the Vermeer (see J. Walsh & H. von Sonnenburg, in *The Metropolitan Museum of Art Bulletin*, 31, no. 4 [1973], pl. 95) indicate that he originally placed a dog in the passageway and a man in the far room, only to paint them out later. The decision to eliminate these details was probably made not only in the interest of psychological effect, but also for the sake of greater spatial continuity.

39. See Chap. VI, p. 45.

40. Formerly Dealer Katz, Dieren; repr. Robinson, fig. 197.

41. On Vrel, see C. Brière-Misme, 'Un "Intimiste" hollandais, Jacob Vrel', *Revue de l'Art ancien et moderne*, 67–8 (1935), 97–114, 157–72, hereafter 'Brière-Misme 1935'; E. Plietzsch, 'Jacobus Vrel und Esaias Boursse', *Zeitschrift für Kunstgeschichte*, 3 (1949); and G. Regnier, 'Jacob Vrel, un Vermeer du Pauvre', *Gazette des Beaux-Arts*, 110, (1968), 282ff. Nothing is known of the artist's life and the location of his activity is in dispute. Hofstede de Groot (1903; see note 28 above) suggested Gelderland while Valentiner (xxxii–xxxv) proposed Friesland or the Lower Rhine area. W. Martin (*De Hollandsche Schilderkunst*, II, 1936, 510, n. 289) preferred the eastern Netherlandish provinces or Westphalia because of the architecture in his paintings. Noting the Capuchin monks in Vrel's picture in Hartford (Wadsworth Atheneum, no. 167) Regnier suggested that he lived in a small town near the German or Flemish border, where such monks were more likely to be encountered than in the United Provinces. Most recently, L. de Vries ('Jan Steen', diss., Groningen, 1977) has proposed Dordrecht. Two of Vrel's works (see note 43) entered Archduke Leopold Wilhelm's collection soon after they were painted and could have been produced in the Southern Netherlands, where Leopold Wilhelm had been Governor. However, no record of the artist has been discovered in the Belgian archives.

42. See examples: Musées Royaux des Beaux-Arts, Brussels, inv. no. 2826; and Palais des Beaux-Arts, Lille.

43. See Brière-Misme 1935, 102. The picture appeared with a companion (ibid., fig. 12) in the inventory of the collection of Leopold Wilhelm drawn up in 1659 after the paintings had been transported from Brussels to Vienna. Since the picture was almost certainly acquired before 1656, when Leopold Wilhelm's governorship of the Spanish Netherlands ended, there is no reason to doubt the authenticity of the picture's date.

44. De Vries diss., 38.

45. While, rather surprisingly, no underdrawing is detectable in the early panel in London (Cat. 14), clear traces appear in the courtyard scenes of *c.* 1658–60 in Washington (Cat. 35A & 39) and in the interior in Nuremberg of *c.* 1664 (Cat. 55). For the wrongly attributed drawings see Cat. D 39–43.

Technical information about De Hooch's art is still limited, but he seems to have been less interested in the practical requirements that painting posed as a craft than the meticulous Vermeer. Irregular tensions in the paint film resulting from the stretching of the canvas can occasionally be detected along the edges of his paintings. Moreover, even in well preserved works, the upper layers of paint sometimes fail to cover underlying strata. Whereas Vermeer often employed the rare and costly pigment ultramarine, De Hooch

favoured common smalt (pulverized blue cobalt glass), which has often become transparent (as in the woman's dress in Cat. 29) or discoloured the medium (see J. Plesters's comments in exh. cat. London 1976, 5–7). To obtain certain greens, he employed the transient 'schietgeel' (literally 'fading yellow', a yellow lake pigment), which has often disappeared entirely, resulting in the curious blue foliage in some scenes (e.g. Cat. 34). On the other hand, not all De Hooch's pigments were inexpensive; both courtyard scenes in Washington (Cat. 35A & 39) contain vermilion. Examinations of several paintings from the late 1650s revealed light-coloured grounds made up primarily of lead white.

46. K. G. Hulten ('Zu Vermeers Atelierbild', *Konsthistorisk Tidskrift*, 17 [1948] 90–8) observed that remnants of what appears to be a pinhole (see his fig. no. 2) are visible at the vanishing point of Vermeer's painting.

47. In addition to Vredeman de Vries's publications, the *Institutio Artis Perspectivae* (The Hague, 1622; also Dutch eds.) by his pupil, Hendrick Hondius, also provided a repertoire of perspective models. Samuel Marolois's *Opera Mathematica ou Oeuvres Mathematicques traictions de Geometrie, Perspective, Architecture et Fortification* (The Hague, 1614; repub. nine times before 1662; in French, Dutch, Latin and German eds.) was the standard text for artists who sought a theoretical understanding of the laws of perspective.

48. See A. Wheelock, *Perspective, Optics, and Delft Artists around 1650*, New York, 1977, esp. Chap. 4, 132ff.

49. Van Hoogstraten (*Inleyding*, 263) wrote of the camera obscura: 'I am sure that the sight of these reflections in the dark can give no small light to the vision of young Artists; since besides gaining knowledge of nature, one sees here what main or general [characteristics] should belong to a truly natural painting (een recht natuerlijke Schildery)'. He goes on to say 'But the same is also to be seen in diminishing glasses and mirrors, which, although they distort the drawing somewhat, show clearly the main colouring and harmony.'

50. See Wheelock diss., chap. 7.3, with a critical review of the earlier literature. The visual effects associated with the camera obscura—principal planes of focus, 'circles of confusion', and highlight halation—do not appear in De Hooch's paintings.

51. Blankert (nos. 8 & 11) dates the pictures 1660–1 and 1662 respectively.

52. Valentiner (1932, 315) first noted the resemblance and assumed that the Vermeer was the prototype.

53. The best general discussion of De Hooch's development with respect to colour remains H. Jantzen's *Farbenwahl und Farbengebung in der Holländischen Malerei des XVII. Jahrhunderts*, Parchim i. M., 1912.

54. See Rolf Fritz, 'Das Stadt- und Strassenbild in der holländischen Malerei des 17. Jahrhunderts', diss. Berlin, 1932; W. Stechow, *Dutch Landscape Painting of the Seventeenth Century*, London, 1966, 124ff. (reviewed by A. Blankert, *Simiolus*, 2 [1967–8], 106); and *Opkomst en bloei van het Noordnederlandse Stadgezicht in de 17de eeuw*, exh., Historisch Museum, Amsterdam, & Art Gallery of Ontario, Toronto, 1977. Stechow correctly stressed the interrelatedness of landscape and cityscape painting, noting that the renewed emphasis around 1650 on structure and colour in landscape was a necessary precondition for the rise of the town view.

55. See J. Beerstraten's *The Old Town Hall of Amsterdam in Ruins* and P. Saenredam's *The Old Town Hall of Amsterdam*,

dated 1657, both in the Rijksmuseum, Amsterdam, nos. A 21 & C 1409 respectively. Saenredam's picture, like many of his painted compositions, was based on a detailed drawing made years earlier in 1641 (Municipal Archives, Amsterdam). He had begun making topographical drawings of exterior views by the 1620s and his works undoubtedly played an important role in the formation of the cityscape genre. Yet, as Stechow observed (see note 54), 'on the whole . . . town view painting was the result of stylistic change around 1650. Its origins lay, not in Haarlem, where Saenredam was working, but in Delft.'

56. On Vosmaer, see S. Donahue, 'Daniel Vosmaer', *Vassar Journal of Undergraduate Studies*, 19 (1964), 18–27.

57. Occasionally Vosmaer painted near views of the ruins with fewer motifs and upright designs (see Vassar College Art Gallery, Poughkeepsie, cat. 1967, 18, repr. 114). These, however, were probably inspired by De Hooch's courtyards of *c.* 1658, from which Vosmaer borrowed motifs on at least one occasion (see commentary, Cat. 24).

58. On Steen, see L. de Vries, 'Jan Steen "de Kluchtschilder"', diss., Groningen, 1977; biographical info.: 27–8. Steen's father, incidentally, served as the unfortunate guarantor for De Hooch's old patron, Justus de la Grange; see Bredius 1889, 164.

59. The painting's connection with the Delft School has long been recognized; see [note 19] exh. cat. Rotterdam 1935, no. 78a; also, De Vries diss., 39.

60. See Isaak van Ostade's *Rest at a Farm House* dated 1648, Frans Hals Museum, Haarlem; Terborch's *Family of the Stonegrinder in a Courtyard*, Staatliche Museen, Berlin–Dahlem, no. 793 (Gudlaugsson, no. 100, 'about 1653'); and Maes's *Woman Making Lace in a Courtyard*, dated 1654, Kunsthaus Heylshof, Worms, no. 41. L. de Vries (diss., 39) has argued that Maes's painting of *Two Women with a Beggar Boy* (formerly [?] W. G. Escher, Zurich; repr. Valentiner 1924, 48) was a source for Steen's portrait. However, Valentiner deciphered the former work's date as 1659, a reading more compatible with its style and confirmed by the date visible on a good photograph at the Witt Library.

61. Concerning portraits in imaginary gardens, see H. Kauffmann, 'Rubens und Isabella Brant in der Geisblattlaube', *Form und Inhalt, Kunstgeschichtliche Studien Otto Schmitt*, Stuttgart, 1950, 257–74; E. de Jongh & P. J. Vinken, 'Frans Hals als voorzetter van een emblematische traditie bij het Huwelijksportret van Isaac Massa en Beatrix van der Laen', *Oud-Holland*, 56 (1961), 117–52. Aspects of the figure arrangement of De Hooch's portrait recall earlier garden portraits; see Bartholomeus van der Helst's so-called *Presentation of the Bride in a Garden* of 1647 (Hermitage, Leningrad, no. 862), where the elders are seated at the right and the younger couple stands at the left. The portrait may also be compared to earlier representations of families on the terraces of elegant homes or country villas; see, for example, D. Teniers's *Portrait of the Artist and his Family* of *c.* 1645–6, Gemäldegalerie, Berlin–Dahlem, no. 857.

62. Wheelock 1975–6, 178; cf. *Perspective* (Dover reprint, 1968), pl. 23.

63. Compare D. van Delen's *Conversation Outside a Castle*, Royal Museum of Fine Arts, Copenhagen, cat. 1951, no. 163, ill. As De Vries observed (diss. 'Stellingen', no. 7), Job Berckheyde also performed naturalistic translations of De Vriesian designs in these years.

64. The subtlety with which De Hooch mixed fact and fiction is underscored by comparison with Vosmaer's oddly disjunctive *View of Delft with an Imaginary Portico* of 1665, Dienst Verspreide Rijkskollekties, The Hague; repr. Blankert, fig. 27.

65. Fabritius's *Sentinel* of 1654 (Staatliches Museum, Schwerin, no. G 2477), another potentially important precursor of De Hooch's courtyards, also exhibits a large pentimento beneath the archway.

66. See Maes's *Woman Selling Milk*, two similar versions: Rothschild Collection, HdG no. 31; & Wellington Museum, London, cat. no. 63. Compare also Cat. C 27.

67. See Van Delen's *Skittles Players*, Shipley Art Gallery, Gateshead, no. 419; cf. *Perspective*, pl. 43.

CHAPTER IV

The Early Years in Amsterdam 1660/61–70

1. On the growth of Amsterdam, see W. F. H. Oldewelt and A. E. d'Ailly, in *Zeven eeuwen Amsterdam*, 1, Amsterdam, (n.d.), 1–40, 37–63; H. Brugmans, *Opkomst en bloei van Amsterdam*, Amsterdam, 1911. Regarding the economy, see V. Barbour, *Capitalism in Amsterdam in the Seventeenth Century*, Ann Arbor, 1963.

2. P. Schraa, 'Onderzoekingen naar de bevolkingsomvang van Amsterdam tussen 1550 en 1650', *Jaarboek Amstelodamum*, 46 (1954), 1–33, espec. 27.

3. According to J. M. Montias's estimates (in the forthcoming sequel to his article, 'The Guild of St. Luke in 17th-century Delft and the economic status of artists and artisans', *Simiolus*, 4 [1977], 93–105; hereafter 'Montias 1977'), the total number of master-painters in Delft amounted to 47 in 1613, 58 in 1640, 51 in 1660, and 31 in 1680. During the thirty-year period between 1640 and 1670 the flow of artists between Delft and Amsterdam was virtually all in one direction. With the sole exception of Fabritius, who though coming from Midden Beemster was trained and probably made his livelihood in Amsterdam, no artists moved from Amsterdam to Delft. On the other hand, Montias cites numerous painters who made the opposite move. In addition to De Hooch, Jacob Pynas, Simon de Vlieger, Willem van Landen, Emanuel de Witte, Willem van Aelst, Paulus Potter, Isaak Junius, and Abraham van Beyeren all travelled from Delft to Amsterdam, either directly or *via* The Hague.

4. The scant information regarding De Hooch's prices is discussed in Chap. VII.

5. On the family and their collections, see I. H. van Eeghen, 'Het Poppenhuis van Petronella de la Court, huisvrouw van Adam Oortmans', *Jaarboek Amstelodamum*, 47 (1960), 159–67. Oortmans and his wife lived on the Achterburgwal in Amsterdam and had six surviving children, three daughters and three sons. A close correspondence exists between the ages of the four children represented in the painting in Cleveland and the ages of four of Oortmans's children in 1663; Nicolaes, age twelve; Maria, eleven; Anna Clara, five; and Adam, one year or less. The omission, however, of Willem (age seven) and Pieternella (age nine) prohibits identification with the portrait mentioned in the inventory. Another possible candidate is the *Family Portrait on a Terrace* (Cat. 77) which has been said to be signed and dated 1667 and may be the companion to the *Man and*

VII. A Woman Nursing an Infant, with a Child (Cat. 32). *c.* 1658–60.
M. H. de Young Memorial Museum, San Francisco. See also Plates 30 and 31

VIII. Figures Drinking in a Courtyard with an Arbour (Cat. 33). 1658.
On loan to the National Gallery of Scotland, Edinburgh. See also Plate 32

Three Women Playing Music on a Terrace (Cat. 78). Together these works could portray the Oortmans—De la Court family; the number and sex division of the sitters (the youngest child is probably male despite the dress) correspond to the members of the family. However, the ages of the sitters seem at variance with those of the family's children in 1667, and, what is more important, no mention of pendants is made in the inventory.

6. See Chap. 1, n. 15. Although middle- and upper middle-class merchants evidently constituted the majority of De Hooch's patrons in Amsterdam, a few exceptionally wealthy men owned his works. Nicolaes van der Perre (see Cat. C 141), for example, was descended from an influential family, worked for the Dutch East Indies Company, and left an estate worth 300,000 fl (see I. H. van Eeghen, in *Jaarboek Amstelodamum*, 68 [1975], 98). The registers of the tax of 1674 (amounting to one half of one percent of an eligible citizen's property) suggest that Henry Nieugart (see Cat. C 1; his mother was taxed 1000 fl) and Adolf Visscher (see Cat. C 85; taxed 700 fl) were considerably wealthier than their fellow merchants Oortmans and Jacott (taxed 210 and 300 fl respectively). On the other hand, the widow of Jan van Meurs (see Cat. C 19 & C 44), the widow of Willem van Beest's father (see Cat. C 283), Abel Horst (see Cat. C 282), and Anthony Daems (Cat. C 89 & C 142) were only taxed 125, 25, 5 and 5 fl, respectively. These figures, however, can be deceptive; Horst was taxed at his death in the 'first class' (a sign of wealth), Daems left a sizeable estate of 138,466 fl (estimated for the Collaterale Successie), and Van Beest's property was valued at 10,100 fl at his death (communication S. A. C. Dudok van Heel). These figures are given meaning if we recall that De Hooch's father could buy a house with a yard in Rotterdam in 1651 for only 1,700 fl (see Doc. 12). Furthermore, Montias (1977, 103) has determined that the median price for a house owned by a registered painter in Delft between 1620 and 1640 was 1,350 fl. Inflation probably had only a minor effect on the value of money in Holland in the seventeenth century.

7. On Metsu, see Franklin W. Robinson, *Gabriel Metsu (1629–1667). A Study of His Place in Dutch Genre Painting of the Golden Age*, New York, 1974 (reviewed by A. K. Wheelock, Jr. in *The Art Bulletin*, 63 [1976], 456–9); and S. J. Gudlaugsson, 'Kanttekeningen bij de ontwikkeling van Metsu', *Oud-Holland*, 83 (1968), 13–43.

8. See I. H. van Eeghen, 'De Familiestukken van Metsu van 1657 en van De Witte van 1678 met vier levengeschiedenissen (Gillis Valckenier, Nicolaas Listingh, Jan Zeeuw en Catharina van de Perre)', *Jaarboek Amstelodamum*, 68 (1975), 78–107. Valckenier became a member of the city council in 1652, later served repeatedly as reigning burgomaster, and, particularly after the fall of the Bicker and De Graeff families in 1672, exercised considerable power in the government. In 1674 he and his sister-in-law were taxed (together) 1,135 fl (for a total property of 227,000 fl), and he alone paid 155 fl and 25 fl (respectively) for his positions as the director of the East India Company and Burgomaster (communication S. A. C. Dudok van Heel). Thus, with the possible exception of Van der Perre, none of the recorded owners of De Hooch's works were as wealthy, or moved in as socially elevated circles, as Valckenier.

9. Noting the respective dates on the two artists' works, Wheelock (see note 7) correctly questioned Robinson's assumption (1974, 54) that Metsu's works of *c.* 1661–2 were inspired by De Hooch and the Delft School. A *Musical Company in an Elegant Interior* by Gerbrand van den Eeckhout employing the new compositional type has been said to be dated 1660 (Sale, Berlin, [Axel Kettner auction no. 282], 26–8/11/1969, no. 1053, ill.), but the costumes suggest a date toward the end of the decade.

10. G. F. Waagen, *Kunstwerke und Künstler in Deutschland*, Leipzig, I, 1843, 209.

11. See De Jongh's *Woman Receiving a Letter*, National Trust, Ascott House (repr. *Burlington Magazine*, 72 [1938], pl. VB); Van der Burch's *Officer and a Lady in an Interior*, W. L. Elkins Collection, Philadelphia Museum of Art (repr. Valentiner, 234); and Vermeer's *The Music Lesson*, Buckingham Palace, London (Blankert cat. no. 16: 'about 1664').

12. J. B. Descamps, *La vie des peintres flamands, allemands et hollandais*, III, Paris, 1753, 162–4. Descamps's comments formed the basis of most writers' accounts of De Hooch's life and art prior to Smith (1833) and thus deserve to be quoted at length: 'Les Ouvrages qu'il fit depuis (ses premiers tableaux) dans le goût de *Metzu* & de *Mieris*, prouvent que la prévention fondée des Amateurs pour ces illustres Artistes, détermina *de Hooge* à les imiter. Il réussit assez bien à marcher sur les traces de *Metzu*, de *Mieris*, de *Coques* & de *Slingelandt*, mais sans les atteindre; ses têtes & ses mains ont quelquefois la force de celles de *Vandyke*; sa touche est plus large que celles de *Mieris* & de *Metzu*, mais ses Tableaux n'en attrapent jamais le fini précieux: aussi nous gardons-nous bien de les placer sur la même ligne. *De Hooge* fut un imitateur qui n'est pas à dédaigner au dessous du degré éminent de *Metzu* & de *Mieris*, pour la finesse & la vérité du coloris: il est encore des places distinguées, & notre Artiste occupa une des premiers. Son dessein est correct & de bon goût; sa couleur est naturelle & même vigoureuse. Tout le faire, en général, de ses Tableaux est d'une grande facilité; ceux d'entre ses Ouvrages qui lui ont mérité plus de réputation, représentent des conversations: les habillements de ces personnages sont galants, & selon les modes de son temps; on y remarque même un choix conforme aux intérêts de le Peinture'.

13. On Van Mieris, see W. Martin *De Hollandsche Schilderkunst in de zeventiende eeuw*, II, Amsterdam, 220–4; E. Plietzsch, *Holländische und Flämische Maler des XVII. Jahrh.*, Leipzig, 1960, 49–55. Otto Naumann is now preparing a dissertation on the artist.

14. For Van Mieris's influence on Vermeer, see Blankert, 59ff.; on Ochtervelt, see Susan Donahue Kuretsky, *The Paintings of Jacob Ochtervelt*, Montclair, N.J., and Oxford, England, 1979, 15ff.

15. Compare Gudlaugsson, no. 127.

16. cf. Gudlaugsson, no. 111.

17. cf. Gudlaugsson, no. 139.

18. cf. Gudlaugsson, no. 192.

19. While MacLaren (458–60) believed that the work was identical with the version in the National Gallery in London (no. 2313), Manke (37, cat. no. 222) preferred seeing the version in the Blank Sale (New York, 16/11/1949, no. 26) as the original (cf. Manke, pl. 51). The former picture is generally considered to be superior in quality.

20. Manke cat. no. 222a (HdG no. 284); additional (unpub.) provenance: Sale Quatre-Solz de Lahante, Paris, 8/5/1838, no. 75 [as P.d.H.]—641 frs (without measurements).

21. The original (Manke, cat. no. 241) as well as a replica (Museum of Fine Arts, Montreal; Manke cat. no. 241a;

E

HdG [P.d.H.] no. 169) were sold repeatedly as works by De Hooch.

22. A date in the mid-1660s is preferable to Manke's date of *c.* 1660.

23. See R. van Luttervelt, *Het Raadhuis aan de Dam*, Amsterdam 1950; and C. Fremantle, *The Baroque Town Hall of Amsterdam*, Utrecht, 1959; hereafter 'Fremantle'.

24. See P. Reuterswärd, 'Tavelförhänget. Kring ett motiv i holländst 1600-talsmaleri', *Konsthistorisk Tidskrift*, 25 (1956), 97–113.

25. Fremantle, 42, n. 2.

26. See, for example, De Witte's *Imaginary Church Interior* of 1668 (Boymans–van Beuningen Museum, Rotterdam, no. 1993) with motifs derived from the Oude Kerk in Amsterdam and Sint Bavo in Haarlem.

27. Although the addition of the *School of Athens* has long been recognized as an imaginary element in the painting in Leipzig (see W. von Bode, *Die Galerie A. Thieme in Leipzig*, 1900, no. 45), Valentiner (xx) spoke of De Hooch's 'genaue Architekturstudien' of the Town Hall.

28. Antonie Rinck, who was probably an Amsterdam merchant, owned a painting of a *Flower Garden* by De Hooch in 1661 (see Cat. C 247) and rented a country house named 'Tulp en Burgh' near Ouderkerk (communication S. A. C. Dudok van Heel).

29. See H. Wagner, *Jan van der Heyden*, Amsterdam–Haarlem, 1971, 44–6.

30. cf. Dirck Hals's *Garden Party*, 1627, Rijksmuseum, Amsterdam, no. A 1796.

31. See also L. de Jongh's *Women in a Formal Garden*, Windsor Castle, repr. Valentiner, 189.

32. See Chap. III, n. 67.

33. See note 5 above.

34. See Coques's *Portrait of the Verbiest Family*, 1664, Buckingham Palace, London.

35. See note 12 above. The author's seemingly curious observation regarding the heads and hands of De Hooch's figures sometimes exhibiting the force of those of Van Dyck may also be an allusion to the influence of Coques, whose elegant portraits earned him the nickname 'little Van Dyck'.

36. See Staatliche Museen, Gemäldegalerie, Berlin–Dahlem, no. 1838.

37. See, for example, Gerbrand van den Eeckhout's *Party on a Terrace*, 1652, Worcester Art Museum, Worcester, acc. no. 1922, 208.

38. See W. von Bode, 'Jan Vermeer und Pieter de Hooch als Konkurrenten', *Jahrbuch der preussischen Kunstsammlungen*, 32 (1911), 1–2.

CHAPTER V

The Late Years in Amsterdam c. 1670–84

1. Blankert (10) notes the financial reversals suffered by the landscapist Jan Vermeer van Utrecht, the portraitist Bartholomeus van der Helst, and the Amsterdam art dealers Jacob van Neck and Gerard Uylenburgh. The marine painters Willem van de Velde the Elder and the Younger moved to England in 1672.

2. On Steen's late Leiden period, see De Vries diss., 67ff.

3. Valentiner, for example, attributed 83 works to the 'Second Amsterdam Period' (after *c.* 1670), as opposed to 28 for the 'First Delft Period' (1647–54), 36 for the 'Second Delft Period' (*c.* 1655–62) and 30 for the 'First Amsterdam Period' (*c.* 1662–70).

4. J. Rosenberg & S. Slive, *Dutch Art and Architecture 1600 to 1800*, Baltimore, 1966, 124.

5. Valentiner, xxiii. The theory of De Hooch's decline seems to have first been expressed by C. Hofstede de Groot, *Sammlung Schubart*, Munich, n.d. (*c.* 1895), 39–40. I. Q. van Regteren Altena ([review of Valentiner in] *Maandblad voor beeldende kunsten*, 7 [1930], 379–80) was virtually the only later writer to challenge this view.

6. See, for example, Steen's *Family Portrait* (the so-called 'Van Goyen Family') of *c.* 1665, Nelson Gallery–Atkins Museum, Kansas City, no. 67–8.

7. Compare, for example, the female musicians in Cat. 78 and Ochtervelt's *Woman Playing a Violin* (dated 1668, Royal Museum of Art, Copenhagen, cat. 1951, no. 518, ill.). The design of the latter's *Family Portrait* of 1670 (Museum of Fine Arts, Budapest, no. 4286) resembles (when reversed) that of De Hooch's contemporaneous *Jacott-Hoppesack Family Portrait* (Cat. 92).

8. See Oliver Banks, *Watteau and the North* (diss. Princeton, 1975), New York, 1977.

9. It is wrong, therefore, to speak of the late works as reflecting a 'loss of naïveté' (see M. J. Friedlaender, *Landscape, Portrait, Still-life*, New York, 1950 [trans. of *Essays über Landschaftmalerei und andere Bildgattungen*, The Hague, 1947], 188) or the 'limitations' of De Hooch's 'intellectual gifts' (cf. Valentiner, xx).

10. Blankert (74, 87) has written perceptively of the manneristic qualities of the late works of Vermeer and his contemporaries, but the negative associations implied in his use of the term are misleading. (On the concept of mannerism, see J. Shearman, *Mannerism*, London, 1967). Blankert conjectured that artists adopted the more stylized manner because they felt there was no possibility of 'improving' on the pictures produced in a naturalistic idiom between 1650 and 1670 ('"Verbetering" was niet meer mogelijk') and that this realization precipitated a 'crisis' in the artistic community. Yet there is little evidence of such a crisis and the move to greater stylization seems rather to have been looked upon as a logical and advantageous development. Given the artistic priorities of the age, artists like Ochtervelt and Pynacker undoubtedly believed they were 'improving' on their sources.

11. See Metsu's *Woman Playing the Viol da Gamba* of 1663, M. H. de Young Memorial Museum, San Francisco; repr. Robinson fig. 143.

12. See, for example, C. Netscher's *Musical Party* of 1665, Alte Pinakothek, Munich, no. 618.

13. On Van Musscher, see P. J. J. van Thiel, 'Michiel van Musscher's vroegste werk naar aanleiding van zijn portret van het echtpaar Comans', *Bulletin van het Rijksmuseum*, 17 (1969), 3–36.

14. See Brekelenkam's *Woman Inspecting Fish* of 1664, Assheton Bennett Collection, City Art Gallery, Manchester, cat. (1965) no. 11. One of Sorgh's paintings of this theme was erroneously attributed to De Hooch (Sale, London, 19/6/1931, no. 44).

15. See Van Hoogstraten's '*The First-Born*', 1670, Museum of Fine Arts, Springfield, no. 5202, and Ochtervelt's *The Nursery*, Natalie Labia Collection, repr. Susan Donahue Kuretsky, *The Paintings of Jacob Ochtervelt*, Montclair, N.J., and Oxford, England, 1979, fig. 84.

16. On mannikins, see P. T. A. Swillens, 'Beelden en lede-poppen in de Schilderkunst', *Maandblad voor beeldende kunsten*, 23 (1947), 247–58, 277–90; Arpad Weixlgartner, 'Von der Gliederpuppe', Göteborgs Kunstmuseum Årtstyck, 1953, 37–71; and E. F. van der Grinten, 'Le cachalot et le mannequin. Deux facettes de la réalité dans l'art hollandais du seizième et du dix-septième siècles', *Nederlands Kunsthistorisch Jaarboek*, 13 (1962), 149–79. Van der Grinten (n. 14) listed De Hooch among the artists who might have employed such aids.

17. cf. Gudlaugsson, II, 15–16.

18. See Van Hoogstraten's *View Down a Corridor*, 1662, Durham Park, Gloucestershire, and Steen's *Young Woman Pulling on her Stockings*, 1663, Buckingham Palace (exh. cat. London, 1971, no. 38).

19. Repr. Robinson, fig. 10.

20. Hermitage, Leningrad, no. 915.

21. See Coques's *Family Portrait in a Landscape*, 1647, Wallace Collection, London, no. P 92; and E. van der Neer's *Return from the Hunt*, 1677, Musée des Beaux-Arts, Lille, inv. 272 (repr. exh. cat. *Trésors des Musées du Nord*, Lille, 1972, no. 43).

CHAPTER VI

De Hooch and the Tradition of Dutch Genre Painting: Iconographic Issues

1. See W. Stechow & C. Comer, 'The History of the Term Genre', *Bulletin of the Allen Memorial Art Museum*, Oberlin College, 23, no. 2 (Spr. 1976), 89–94.

2. For discussion, see H. Miedema, 'Over het realisme in de Nederlandse schilderkunst van de zeventiende eeuw naar aanleiding van een tekening van Jacques de Gheyn II (1565–1632)', *Oud-Holland*, 89 (1975), 3–5 (hereafter 'Miedema 1975').

3. For further examples, see Lydia de Pauw-de Veen, *De begrippen 'schilder', 'schilderij', en 'schilderen' in de zeventiende eeuw*, Brussels, 1974, 167–89; and the numerous inventory entries in A. Bredius's *Künstler-Inventare*, 8 vols. The Hague, 1915–22.

4. P. Angel's *Lof der Schilder-konst*, Leiden, 1642, is addressed to his fellow 'na-bootsers van't leven'; concerning the author's brief remarks on a guardroom scene, see Miedema 1975, 4; regarding Angel's treatise, see idem, in *Proef*, Dec. 1973, 27–33. Van Hoogstraten wrote in his *Inleyding* (Rotterdam, 1678, 25), 'een volmaekte schildery is als een spiegel van de Natuer, die de dingen, die niet en zijn, doet schijnen te zijn, en op een geoorlofde vermakelijke en prijslijke wijze bedriegt' (a perfect painting is like a mirror of nature, in which non-existing things [in the painting] appear to exist and deceive in a pleasing and rewarding way).

5. Thoré–Bürger, *Salons de W. Bürger*, II, Paris, 1870, 380.

6. For a brief history of the iconographic study of Dutch paintings, see K. Renger, 'Zur Forschungsgeschichte der Bilddeutung in der holländischen Malerei', in exh. cat. *Die Sprache der Bilder*, Braunschweig, 1978, 34–8. See also the following pioneering studies: H. Kauffmann (review of Valentiner's *Pieter de Hooch*), in *Deutsche Literaturzeitung*, 17, 26 Apr. 1930, cols. 801–5 (hereafter 'Kauffmann 1930'); idem, 'Die Fünf Sinne in der niederländischen Malerei des 17. Jahrhunderts', in *Kunstgeschichtliche Studien. Festschrift für Dagobert Frey*, Breslau, 1943, 133–57; H. Rudolph,

' "Vanitas", die Bedeutung mittelalterlicher und humanistischer Bildinhalte in der niederländischen Malerei des 17. Jahrhunderts', in *Festschrift Wilhelm Pinder*, Leipzig, 1938, 405–33 (hereafter 'Rudolph 1938'); S. J. Gudlaugsson, 'Ikonographische Studien über die holländische Malerei und das Theater des 17. Jahrhunderts', diss., Würzburg, 1938; idem, *De Komedianten bij Jan Steen en zijn tijdgenooten*, The Hague, 1945.

7. See Seymour Slive, 'Realism and Symbolism in Seventeenth-Century Dutch Painting', *Daedalus*, 91 (1962), 469–500; E. de Jongh, 'Realisme en schijnrealisme in de Hollandse schilderkunst van de zeventiende eeuw', in *Rembrandt en zijn tijd*, exh. cat., Brussels, 1971, 143–94; and L. de Vries, 'Jan Steen en het Hollandse realisme', in diss., 102–10.

8. Books on the Dutch group portrait, still life, landscape, and marine painting exist, but a comprehensive study of genre painting has yet to be written. Concerning the tradition's stylistic development, see F. Würtenberger, *Das Holländische Gesellschaftsbild*, Schramberg, 1937; Plietzsch 1956 [see Chap. III, n. 25]; and S. J. Gudlaugsson's *Gerard Ter Borch*, 2 vols., The Hague, 1959–60. Concerning genre's conceptual changes, see L. de Vries 'Jan Steen en de traditie van de genreschilderkunst', in diss., 75–90. Although the author's view of the development of the concept of genre is excessively linear, his comments on the subject are the most perceptive to date.

9. Rudolph (1938) first observed evidence of these effects in Dutch genre, citing specific examples, as R. Keyszelitz later would ('Der "clavis interpretandi" in der holländischen Malerei des 17. Jahrhunderts', diss. Munich, 1956, 66–8; hereafter 'Keyszelitz'), in De Hooch's art. See also De Vries's discussion (diss. 84, 94–6) of 'iconographische slijtage' (roughly: iconographic erosion); and E. Haverkamp Begemann's comments, in *Willem Buytewech*, exh. cat., Rotterdam–Paris, 1974–5, Intro.

10. We should be aware, however, that messages formulated in the captions of prints after paintings do not always apply, or apply in the same degree, to the originals. There were intrinsic differences in the functions of seventeenth-century prints and paintings which affected their meanings. The probability that meanings in genre could be 'medium-bound' deserves further study.

11. See Würtenberger, 12–35; J. R. Judson, *Dirck Barendsz*, Amsterdam, 94–8; and F. C. Legrand, *Les peintres flamands de genre au XVIIᵉ siècle*, Paris–Brussels, 1963, 69–70.

12. See also K. Renger, 'Joos van Winghes *Nachtbancket met een Mascarade* und verwandte Darstellungen', *Jahrbuch der Berliner Museen*, 14 (1972), 161–93.

13. See E. de Jongh, *Zinne- en minnebeelden in de schilderkunst van de zeventiende eeuw*, Amsterdam, 1967, 24–5, (hereafter 'De Jongh 1967'); idem and others, *tot Lering en Vermaak*, exh. cat. Rijksmuseum, Amsterdam, 1976, no. 10 (hereafter, 'De Jongh et al. 1976').

14. See E. de Jongh, 'Erotica in vogel-perspectief. De dubbelzinnigheid van een reeks 17de eeuwse genre voorstellingen', *Simiolus*, 3 (1968–9), 22–74 (hereafter 'De Jongh 1968–9'). For further examples, see De Jongh et al. 1976, cat. nos. 13 & 18.

15. See Gudlaugsson, 117–8. The fact that the author cites potential literary and emblematic precedents in his catalogue entries but refrains from interpreting the artist's works according to these sources is consistent with his view of Terborch's freedom with respect to these traditions. The

subtle implications of this system unfortunately were abandoned in the exhibition catalogue *Gerard Ter Borch*, Munster–The Hague, 1974, where the pictures were often incorrectly interpreted as if they were direct illustrations of emblems.

16. *Het Groot Schilderboeck*, 2 vols., Amsterdam, 1714 (1st ed. 1707; Engl. ed. 1738), I, 167–201. For discussion see De Vries diss., 82–3.

17. Both Miedema (1975, 4) and De Vries (diss., 82) believe that changes in the concept of genre are evident by the mid-seventeenth century.

18. On emblems, see W. Heckscher & K. A. Wirth, 'Emblem, Emblembuch', in *Reallexikon zur deutschen Kunstgeschichte*, v, Stuttgart, 1959, 85–228; for the history of Dutch emblematic literature, see K. Porterman, *Inleiding tot de Nederlandse emblemata-literatuur*, Groningen, 1977; for a bibliography of Dutch emblem books, see J. Landwehr, *Dutch Emblem Books*, Utrecht, 1962 (Bibliotheca emblematica I); and for examples of the use of emblems in the interpretation of genre, see De Jongh's various publications (notes 7, 13, 14 & 71).

19. Excessive drinking was a major problem in seventeenth-century Holland. For literature and discussion, see De Jongh et al. 1976, 248, & n. 7; emblems: Gudlaugsson, II, 137.

20. Although various medicinal properties were attributed to tobacco, the relatively new habit of smoking was often criticized; see De Jongh et al. 1976, cat. no. 7. Above an emblem in R. Visscher's *Sinnepoppen*, Amsterdam, 1614: 'Veeltijds wat nieuws selden wat goets' (Often something new, seldom something good).

21. See De Jongh et al. 1976, cat. no. 35. Since the early fifteenth century games of chance had been associated with idleness and prodigality.

22. See De Jongh et al. 1976, cat. no. 22: in emblems alternately associated with idleness and human mortality.

23. See C. B. Playter, 'Willem Duyster and Pieter Codde', diss. Harvard Univ., 1972.

24. 'Gula' or intemperance was symbolized by a figure with a raised drinking glass; see I. Bergström, 'Rembrandt's Double Portrait of himself and Saskia at the Dresden Gallery: A Tradition Transformed', *Nederlands Kunsthistorisch Jaarboek*, 17 (1966), 163, n. 48.

25. E. Snoep-Reitsma ('De Waterzuchtige Vrouw van Gerard Dou en de betekenis van de lampetkan', in *Album Amicorum J. G. van Gelder*, The Hague, 1973, 285–92) and J. A. Emmens (see J. G. van Gelder, 'Jan Emmens als gesprekspartner', *Tirade*, 180 [1972], 472–80) both separately conjectured that Dou's *Trumpeter* in the Louvre could be a warning to the merry company in the background to remember the Last Judgement.

26. See De Jongh 1967, 60; De Jongh et al. 1976, 184 & n. 8.

27. See De Jongh et al. 1976, cat. no. 35. In the midst of the amorous scene in the Louvre (Cat. 58, Plate 61) (note the embracing couple in the shadows) a smiling girl reveals a hand containing a prominent ace of hearts to her male companion. The man seated on the far side of the table in the *Card Players* (Cat. 28, Col. Plate VI) holds out a card to the lady seated beside him, which one may also assume is an ace, the central marking being covered by the player's thumb.

28. An emblem in Otto van Veen's *Amorum Emblemata* (Antwerp, 1608) depicts a cupid holding aloft a small tablet inscribed with the number one while stepping on a second

bearing the numerals two to ten. The appended verses praise faithfulness to one love rather than many. The emblem has been used (see M. Praz, *Studies in Seventeenth-Century Imagery*, Rome, 1964, 54; De Jongh 1967, 49–50) to interpret a picture of a cupid (possibly the 'Cupido' in the inventory of the possessions of Vermeer's widow) holding up a playing card in Vermeer's paintings in London and the Frick Collection (Blankert, cat. nos. 25 & B2).

29. J. B. Bedaux, 'Minnekoorts-, zwangerschaps- en doodverschijnselen op zeventiende-eeuwse schilderijen', *Antiek*, 10 (1975–6), 27, n. 18; & De Jongh et al., 1976, 137.

30. Goltzius' print emphasized the explicit sexual aspects of the subject: the pose of the embracing couple, with the woman's leg thrown across the man's, traditionally signified sexual union (see L. Steinberg, 'Michelangelo's Florentine Pietà: the Missing Leg', *Art Bulletin*, 50 [1970], 343–53). Thus, a warning against amorous excess could be construed in both Lord Barnard's picture and the painting in Hamburg, where the message changing hands could be a love letter (concerning epistolary themes, cf. Gudlaugsson, II, 126–7; De Jongh 1971, 176–9; De Jongh et al. 1976, cat. nos. 2, 39 & 71). In the domestic scene, on the other hand, the motif would need to be interpreted in moral opposition to the virtuous activity in the foreground.

31. Margarita Russell, 'The Iconography of Rembrandt's *Rape of Ganymede*', *Simiolus*, 10 (1977), 18; hereafter 'Russell'.

32. Russell, fig. 19.

33. See De Jongh et al. 1976, cat. no. 29.

34. See Russell, 5–18.

35. De Jongh and his collaborators (De Jongh et al. 1976, 123 & cat. no. 29) have observed evidence of this trend. Recalling the theories of Kauffmann (1930), the authors raised the possibility that the merry-makers in the foreground of the present work might be an allusion to the Five Senses. Comparing the work to earlier representations of the theme, both in strictly allegorical form (Collaert) and in the guise of genre (I. Elyas and D. Hals), they concluded 'the theme of the senses in [De Hooch's] painting, as so often in the second half of the century, is deliberately sublimated (opzettelijk sterk gesublimeerd)'. The important implications of this observation for a historical view of the changing concept of genre unfortunately are not developed by the authors.

36. See Rudolph 1938, 405–11.

37. Rudolph's interpretation (ibid.) of Vermeer's picture as a 'vanitas' image is probably incorrect. S. Alpers' suggestion ('Describe or Narrate? A Problem in Realistic Representation', *New Literary History*, 8 [1976], 25) that an allusion to justice is intended probably comes closer to the truth and accords well with A. Wheelock's view of the picture (review of Blankert, *The Art Bulletin*, 59 [1977], 440) as a 'statement about the importance of temperance and moderation in the conduct of one's life'.

38. Consider C. Tümpel's theory (see 'Studien zur Ikonographie der Historien Rembrandts', *Nederlands Kunsthistorisch Jaarboek*, 20 [1969], 107–98) of the 'Herauslösung'—the practice of extracting a motif from its narrative context while retaining its original meaning.

39. See De Gheyn's drawing of *A Woman and Child at a Table*, Kupferstichkabinett, Staatliche Museen, Berlin-Dahlem; repr. and discussion, Miedema 1975.

40. See J. Wttewael's *Portrait of Eva Wttewael Making Lace*, Centraal Museum, Utrecht, no. 18022.

41. See, for example, D. Hals's *Woman Combing a Child's Hair* (Private Collection, London, 1956; repr. *Wallraf-Richartz Jahrb.*, 27 [1956], fig. 147), and Leyster's *The Rejected Offer* (Mauritshuis, The Hague, no. 564; for discussion, see F. F. Hofrichter, 'Judith Leyster's *Proposition*—between Vice and Virtue', *The Feminist Art Journal*, Fall 1975, 22–6), both of 1631, and the latter's *Woman Sewing* (National Gallery, Dublin, no. 468, and G. Stein Coll, Paris, 1937). It is noteworthy that two of the artists who first concentrated on domestic themes, Leyster and Roghman, were women.

42. Jacob Duck's *Woman Ironing* (Centraal Museum, Utrecht) probably dates from the 1650s; cf. De Jongh et al. 1976, cat. no. 19.

43. Rembrandt's domestic genre prints and drawings doubtless were an inspiration to Dou and his other pupils, but the master rarely treated such themes in paint and then usually in the guise of religious subjects, such as Tobias and Anna or the Holy Family.

44. See Gudlaugsson nos. 95 & 96; and Jacob van Loo's *Mother and Two Children*, Staatliche Museen, Berlin–Dahlem, no. 1588, *c.* 1655–60.

45. Lawrence Stone's *The Family, Sex and Marriage in England 1500–1800*, London, 1977 (hereafter 'Stone'), is the most important recent publication to spring from the new interest in the social history of the family. Unfortunately, no studies have concentrated so systematically upon the family in Dutch society. The basis for most discussions of domestic life in seventeenth-century Holland still remains the invaluable writings of G. D. J. Schotel: *Het Maatschappelijk Leven onzer Vaderen in de Zeventiende Eeuw*, Haarlem, 1868; *Het Oud-Hollandsch Huisgezin*, 2nd. ed., Haarlem, 1903. See also G. Kalff, 'Huiselijk en Maatschappelijk Leven in Amsterdam in de 17e Eeuw', in *Amsterdam in de zeventiende Eeuw*, 3 vols., 1901–4, II, Part II; A. L. J. de Vrankrijker, *Het Maatschappelijk Leven in Nederland in de Gouden Eeuw*, Amsterdam, 1937; A. W. Franken, *Het Leven onzer Voorouders*, The Hague, 1942; A. Staring, *De Hollanders Thuis, Gezelschapstukken uit drie eeuwen*, The Hague, 1957; Paul Zumthor, *Het Dagelijks Leven in de Gouden Eeuw*, Utrecht–Antwerp, 1962 (also in English and French eds.); J. L. Price, *Culture and Society in the Dutch Republic During the 17th Century*, New York, 1974; and A. Bailey, *Rembrandt's House*, Boston, 1978.

46. See E. Snoep-Reitsma, 'Chardin and the Bourgeois Ideals of his Time', *Nederlands Kunsthistorisch Jaarboek*, 24 (1973), 147–69, 170–243 (hereafter 'Snoep-Reitsma 1973'; although the author's principal focus is eighteenth-century French art, many perceptive observations are offered regarding the Dutch domestic genre tradition); M. G. A. Schipper-van Lottum, 'Een naijmantgen met een naijcussen', *Antiek*, 10 (1975), 137–63 (hereafter 'Schipper-van Lottum'); De Jongh et al. 1976, cat. nos. 3, 5, 19, 32 & 49 (and E. Reitsma's review of the exh., in *Vrij Nederland*, 37, 30/10/1976, 23).

47. Jacob Cats, *Houwelick, dat is de gantsche gelegentheyt des echten-staets*, Middelburg, 1625 (see *Alle de Wercken*, Amsterdam, 1712, 235–424).

48. Estimated by the Amsterdam publisher I. I. Schipper (foreword to 1st. ed. of *Alle de Wercken*, Amsterdam, 1655) who brought out the collected works no less than four times between 1655 and 1665 (cf. De Jongh [note 71 below], 173).

49. For more severely restrictive views on women's roles, see Petrus Wittewrongel, *Oeconomia Christiana ofte Christelicke huys-houdinge*, Amsterdam, 1655. See also Hippolytus de Vrye, *De Tien Vermakelijkheden des Houwelyks*, Amsterdam, 1678, a widower's comically bitter mockery of marriage and women.

50. Intro. to 'Vrouwe', 308.

51. cf. 'Vrouwe', 322.

52. Men gaf in ouden tijt, ontrent den eersten morgen, / Een sleutel aen de bruyt, tot ingang van de sorgen, / Een sleutel van het huys en al het huys—bedrief, / En dan was eerst de bruyt een gansch volkomen wijf. / Het dient hier nagevolgt. Daer sijn bescheyde saken / Die maer het wijf alleen, of hare boden raecken: / De keucken is voor al haer eygen heerschappy, / Het lywaet, met de wasch, en martgang dient'er by. / Noch staet tot haer besorgh de maeghden aen te leyden, / En, naer de reden eyscht, haer dienten afte scheyden, / Oock is de kinderqueeck de vrouwe toegepast, / Ten minsten eer de jeugt tot seven jaeren wast. 'Vrouwe', 309–10.

53. 'Vrouwe', 366; see also J. Cats, *Spiegel van den ouden ende nieuwen tijd*, The Hague, 1632, 32, no. xxii: 'Een goede vrouwe en een quaedt been/Dienen thuys en alleen' (A good wife and a bad leg serve at home and only there); J. de Brune, *Banket-werk van goede Gedachten*, Middelburg, 1657, 323: 'Een goede huys-moeder moet liever zien den rook van haer huys, als 't vuyr van een anders heyrt'. (A good 'house-mother' should prefer to see the smoke of her own house, than the fire of another's hearth).

54. 'Vrouwe', 310ff.; J. de Brune, *Nieuwe wyn in oude le'erzacken*, Middelburg, 1636, 273: 'Een boos wijf magh wel zijn bezucht. Het is een huys vol on-ghenucht'. (A wicked [or shrewish] wife shall be bemoaned. It is a house full of miseries); J. H. Krul, *Minne-spiegel ter deughden*, Amsterdam, 1639, 18; emblem entitled 'Een boose vrou, een quaet huwlijk' (A shrewish wife, a bad marriage); J. de Brune, *Banket-werk*, 1657, 206: under the heading 'Een vrouw moet weynigh spreken' (A wife should seldom speak); see also, *De Boosaardige en Bedriegelijke Huisvrou*, Amsterdam, 1682 (The Shrewish and Deceitful Housewife).

55. 'Vrouwe', 364.

56. 'Vrouwe', 252–3.

57. 'Vrouwe', 355.

58. E. S. de Beer ed., *The Diary of John Evelyn*, I, Oxford 1955, 32.

59. J. de Parival, *Les délices de la Hollande*, Leyden, 1651, 19.

60. C. Fraichot, *Remarques historiques et critiques faites dans un voyage d'Italie en Hollande dans l'Année 1704*, Cologne–Amsterdam, 1705; quoted in R. Murris, *La Hollande et les Hollandais au XVIIᵉ et au XVIIIᵉ siècle vus par les Français*, Paris, 1925, 113–4 (hereafter 'Murris').

61. J. Brickman, *Oprechte beschryving waer alle de Nederlanders, voornamentlijck de Hollanders haer aert, mannier en leven, als mede haer policy naecktelijck wert ontledet*, Delft, 1658, 6.

62. 'Memoirs 1672–9', *The Works of Sir William Temple, Bart.*, 4 vols., 1815 (Reprint, New York, 1968), II, 472–3.

63. See Chap. IV, n. 5.

64. 'Moeder', 395; J. van Beverwyck, *Schat der gesontheyt*, Utrecht, 1651, 605–15. Both writers warn of the neglect the child may suffer in the care of a wet-nurse.

65. 'Moeder', 397. Beverwyck (619) also felt play was important to increase a child's physical strength.

66. Beer, which doubtless is the beverage drawn from the keg in this scene, was commonly fed to children at this time. Beverwyck (617) even recommended that infants should be

weaned on a mixture of the drink, assuring his readers they need not fear that the child would become drunk.

67. The nutritional value of 'Boterham' (buttered bread) as a morning meal was commended by Beverwyck (442); compare Goltzius' *Allegory of Morning* (Fig. 43); for later examples, see Otto Naumann, 'The Lesson (Reattributed)', *The William A. Clark Collection* exh. cat. Corcoran Gallery, Washington, 1978, 69–71 (hereafter 'Naumann 1978').

68. *Les délices*, 20. Later French observers often noted the affectionate relationships between Dutch parents and children, cf. Murris, 95; for French views on child-rearing, cf. Stone, 478–80.

69. Snoep–Reitsma (1973, 199) sees a turning point in Dutch theoretical writing on child-rearing occurring towards the end of the seventeenth century.

70. According to Stone (4–9, 260), these trends were perceptible in the English family after 1640 and the latter's domestic values were probably partly derived from the Dutch.

71. E. de Jongh, 'Grape symbolism in painting of the 16th and 17th centuries', *Simiolus*, 7 (1974), 166–91; hereafter 'De Jongh 1974'. See also De Jongh et al. 1976, cat. no. 6.

72. De Jongh (1974, 174) cites earlier examples but notes that few predate the 1650s. See also Cat. C 82, an unknown painting of a *Family in an Interior*, ascribed to De Hooch in 1829, which included a grapes motif.

73. See De Jongh 1974, 175.

74. Concerning the Christian iconography of the 'hortus conclusus', see H. Aurenhammer, *Lexikon der christlichen Ikonographie*, I, 1959, 79; *Dictionnaire de théologie catholique*, VII, 1016; M. Levi D'Ancona, *The Iconography of the Immaculate Conception in the Middle Ages and Early Renaissance*, New York, 1957.

75. '... Het is een groote lof/Dat vrouwen zijn gelijck een toegesloten hof' ('Bruyt', 300); 'de weerde vrou ... / ... / Sy is gelijck een tuyn, die om den hof gevlochten, / Bewaert het edel fruyt van alle snoepgedrochten'. ('Vrouwe', 323).

76. See Psalms 128: 3; cf. 'Vrouwe', 323: 'Sy is een wijngaert-ranck ...'. The biblical text was paraphrased by many Dutch writers; see De Jongh 1974, 179, n. 34.

77. See De Jongh 1974, 179.

78. Additional examples by Dou, Brekelenkam, Van Mieris, Maes, Steen, and others; see Naumann 1978.

79. G. de Lairesse, *Het Groot Schilderboek*, Amsterdam, 1707, (Engl. ed. 1738, 143).

80. It was only later in the century that these associations became sentimentalized. See, for example, the journalist Bastide's rhapsodic poem on the virtues of maternal love which was prompted by De Hooch's painting now in the Rijksmuseum (Cat. 42, Plate 46); from *Le Temple des Arts, ou le Cabinet de M. Braamcamp*, Amsterdam, 1766 (quoted in full by A. Brookner, *Greuze*, London, 1972, 52–3).

81. Emblem entitled 'Sorght voor de koele wijn niet' (Care not for the cool wine), from R. Visscher's *Sinnepoppen*, Amsterdam, 1614, Part I, no. 32.

82. On spinning, see Gudlaugsson, II, 107; De Jongh 1967, 65; De Jongh et al. 1976, no. 3. From its biblical sources as one of the activities of a good wife (Proverbs 31: 19) spinning came to be a symbol of woman's virtue in historical subjects (e.g. Wise and Foolish Virgins; see also P. Galle's print after Goltzius of *Lucretia and her Women Spinning*), portraiture (see J. Bruyn Hzn, 'Vroege portretten van Maerten van Heemskerk', *Bulletin van het Rijksmuseum*, 3 [1955], 27–35)

and subsequently in genre. Concerning sewing, see Schipper-van Lottum, 137ff.

83. See *Sinnepoppen*, I, no. 38; and *Verzameling van uytgeleesene Sinne-Beelden*, Leiden, 1696, 4.

84. The commentary appended to the illustration of 'The Bed' (no. 3; Fig. 52) warns of the need to prepare oneself for the hereafter—sleep on a bed of virtue and awake refreshed (for eternity); 'The Wash Tub' (no. 24)—grace is obtained by working hard at the cleansing of the soul; and 'The Chest' (no. 7; Fig. 53)—a warning against corrupting the soul with earthly goods.

85. Combs and combing (see Cat. 42, Plate 46) were associated in emblems with the pursuit of a clean life (see Gudlaugsson, II, 106–7; De Jongh et al. 1976, cat. no. 49). The scene of a *Woman Carrying a Glass of Wine* (Cat. 38, Plate 41) may be compared to Cats's emblem (under the heading 'Eerlijke Vryagie [Honourable Courtship], *Spiegel van den voorleden en tegenwoordigen tijt*, in *Alle de Wercken*, 582) of a woman walking with a glass bottle, with the motto 'Il ne faut qu'un faux pas pour casser la bouteille'; the fact that the woman seems to be delivering the wine to a couple seated beneath an arbour may indicate that something of the emblem's meaning was recalled. In the *Courtyard Scene* in Basel (Cat. 45, Plate 49) a woman holds a basket of beans which she has evidently just picked from the tall plants behind her. On one of the shutters of the house the portrait of a man wearing a courtier's golden chain appears. In Cats's *Proteus ofte Minne-beelden verandert in Sinne-beelden* (Rotterdam, 1627, no. XXI) an emblem depicts a couple in a garden pointing to a beanstalk which has grown taller than its supporting stake. The appended verses warn against excessive ambition in the pursuit of rank. While, here again, it is conceivable a similar meaning was intended in the painting, De Hooch's general disregard for such 'disguised' references suggests the possibility is remote.

86. See J. A. Emmens, 'Natuur, Onderwijzing en Oefening. Bij een drieluik van Gerrit Dou', in *Album Discipulorum J. G. van Gelder*, Utrecht, 1963, 125–6; paraphrased in De Jongh et al. 1976, cat. no. 17.

87. See *Katalog*, Gemäldegalerie, Berlin–Dahlem, 1975, 132–3.

88. See P. Fischer, *Music in Painting of the Low Countries in the 16th and 17th Centuries* (Sonorum Speculum nos. 50–1), Amsterdam, 1972.

89. See De Jongh et al. 1976, cat. no. 45, with earlier examples.

90. *Spiegel van den Ouden en Nieuwen Tyt* (*Alle de Wercken*, 493); see also De Jongh et al. 1976, 59–60.

91. See De Vries's comments, diss. 85–7.

92. See, for example, A. P. de Mirimonde, 'Les sujets musicaux chez Vermeer de Delft', *Gazette de Beaux-Arts*, 6e per., 57 (1961), 29–52.

93. On erotic merry-company scenes, see De Jongh et al. 1976, no. 18. The motif of the man lying in the woman's lap may descend from the imagery of Samson and Delilah; on the theme, see M. Kahr, 'Delilah', *The Art Bulletin*, 55 (1973), 240–59.

94. F. G. Grossmann, *Paintings from the Assheton Bennett Collection*, Manchester, 1965, no. 27.

95. On the sexual associations of coals held by tongs, see De Jongh et al. 1976, cat. no. 28; on open vessels as vaginal symbols, see P. J. Vincken, 'Some Observations on the Symbolism of the Broken Pot in Art and Literature', *The American Imago*, 1958, 149ff.; & De Jongh 1968–9, 45, 47.

96. On these objects' traditional associations with moral purity, see Snoep-Reitsma (note 25), 287.

97. cf. De Jongh et al. 1976, cat. no. 68.

98. See A. T. Hatto ed., *Eos. An Inquiry into the Theme of Lovers' Meetings and Partings at Dawn in Poetry*, The Hague, 1963; P. K. King, *Dawn Poetry in the Netherlands*, Amsterdam, 1971, esp. Chap. 3.

99. On the tradition, see De Jongh et al. 1976, cat. no. 27; and O. Banks, *Watteau and the North*, New York, 1977, 151ff.

100. See H. W. Janson, *Apes and Ape Lore in the Middle Ages and the Renaissance*, London, 1952; De Jongh et al. 1976, cat. nos. 27 & 55.

101. See De Jongh 1968-9, 49-52; De Jongh et al. 1976, cat. no. 50.

CHAPTER VII
De Hooch's Followers and Public

1. Its earliest recorded attribution was to De Hooch (see HdG no. 189); for subsequent attributions, see MacLaren, no. 2552 (as 'Delft School', but tentatively assigned to C. Fabritius in the commentary); I. Q. van Regteren-Altena (*Oud-Holland*, 75 [1960], 175ff.) as Vermeer; and Blankert (see De Jongh et al. 1976, 63, n. 2) as an early work by E. van der Neer. The large-scale, the halated highlights and reflections, and the motif of the *trompe-l'oeil* door at the left edge call to mind Van Hoogstraten's art, but the high quality of the execution is difficult to reconcile with the Dordrecht painter's uneven manner.

2. Consider, for example, the case of Adam Pick; see Blankert, 50.

3. See P. Sutton, 'Henrick van der Burch' (forthcoming).

4. The youthful artists' close ties are reflected in the difficulty we encounter in separating their hands. *The Nocturnal Scene in an Inn* in the Henle Collection, for example, could be by either painter. Nocturnal subjects are rare, but not unheard of, in De Hooch's oeuvre (see Cat. 127; and Cat. B 2, C 230, C 235, C 281, C 284).

5. On Elinga, see C. Brière-Misme, 'A Dutch Intimist: Pieter Janssens Elinga', (a series of four articles) in *Gazette des Beaux-Arts*, 31 (1947), 89-102; 151-64; 32 (1948), 159-76; 347-66 (with earlier literature; hereafter 'Brière-Misme 1947-8, I-IV').

6. Elinga's other signed painting, the *Room without Figures* (Brockhaus Collection, Lugano; repr. Brière-Misme 1947-8, III, fig. 3), moves still closer to perspective book illustrations. Figureless interiors were painted in these years by other artists from the Delft circle: see *The Slippers*, Louvre, RF 3722 (probably correctly attributed to Van Hoogstraten by Plietzsch and Foucart; cf. *Hollandse Schilderijen uit Franse Musea*, exh. cat., Rijksmuseum, Amsterdam, 1971, no. 44, ill.) and *Interior with Woman's Jacket on a Chair*, Staatliche Museen, Berlin–Dahlem, no. 912 D (a firm attribution is difficult, but Plietzsch's assignment [see Berlin–Dahlem, cat. 1975, 72-3] to C. Bisschop may be correct if one does not share his belief that the work is a study).

7. Compare the lighting systems prescribed in Salomon de Caus, *La Perspective avec la raison des ombres et miroirs*, London, 1612, II, chap. 8 (repr. in P. Descargues, *Perspective*, New York, 1977, 84-5, pl. 59).

8. On Boursse, see C. Brière-Misme, 'Un "Intimiste" hollandais: Esaias Boursse 1631-1672', (a series of four articles in) *Oud-Holland*, 69 (1954), 18-30; 72-91; 150-66; 213-21 (with earlier literature).

9. On De Man, see C. Brière-Misme, 'Un émule de Vermeer et de Pieter de Hooch: Cornélis de Man', *Oud-Holland*, 52 (1935), 1-26; 97-120.

10. See De Man's *Gold Weigher* (on loan Centraal Museum, Utrecht), repr. Brière-Misme 1935, II, fig. 17; compare Steen's *Driekonigenavond*, H.M. The Queen, Buckingham Palace, repr. L. de Vries, *Jan Steen*, 1976, pl. 14.

11. On Bisschop, see C. Brière-Misme, 'Un petit maître hollandais: Cornélis Bisschop (1630-1674)', (a series of five articles in) *Oud-Holland*, 65 (1950), 24-40; 104-16; 139-51; 178-92; 227-39. Bisschop's two versions of the *Woman Sewing* (signed, with dealer L. Koetser, London, 1957, repr. Brière-Misme, 189, fig. 9; and Valentiner, no. 246, erroneously as H. van der Burch, formerly assigned to De Hooch, HdG no. 96a) seem to reflect De Hooch's influence.

12. See, for example, *The Fishmonger*, Mauritshuis, The Hague, no. 195; compare Cat. 49.

13. See *Woman with a Serving Girl in a Courtyard*, Metropolitan Museum, New York, no. 20.155.5, repr. Valentiner, no. 252 [erroneously as H. van der Burch]; compare Cat. 44.

14. See, respectively, Fig. 34; Verkolje's *Musical Company* dated 1673, Rijksmuseum, Amsterdam, no. A721; Van der Neer's *A Dutch Interior* (Fig. 62), Museum of Fine Arts, Boston, inv. no. 41.935; Berckheyde's *Woman Reading a Letter*, signed, dealer Hoogsteder, The Hague, (repr. Valentiner, 205); and Siberecht's *Domestic Interior*, dated 1671, Royal Museum, Copenhagen, no. 661.

15. On many of the artists mentioned here and below, see E. R. Mandle, *Dutch Masterpieces from the Eighteenth Century*, exh. cat., Minneapolis–Toledo–Philadelphia, 1971.

16. While a Van Beyeren was valued at 100 fl and a Lievens and a (Carel?) Fabritius at 40 fl, a 'trony van Rembrant' was set at 20 fl and a pair of Van Goyens brought only 3 fl. De Hooch's works received valuations comparable to those of the other genre painters in the inventory: Droochsloot, two valued at 26 fl and F. Ryjkhals (the genre painter from Middelburg), 10 and 6 fl.

17. See J. G. van Dillen, *Van rijkdom en regenten. Handboek tot de economische en sociale geschiedenis van Nederland tijdens de Republiek*, The Hague, 1970, 182, 244, 295 (as cited in J. L. Price, *Culture and Society in the Dutch Republic during the 17th Century*, New York, 1974, 122ff).

18. A rise in De Hooch's prices is signalled by the I. Walraven Sale (Amsterdam, 14/10/1763) in which two works (Cat. 31 & 28) sold for 450 and 480 fl respectively.

19. Compare the prices brought by Vermeer's works in the Sale in Amsterdam in 1696 (Blankert, nos. 5, 7, 9-11, 13, 15, 16, 20 & 26). A Dou (cf. HdG no. 85) sold for 605 fl as early as 1663; his triptych brought 4025 fl in 1701, and 6000 fl in 1719. Otto Naumann informs the author that Van Mieris's small-scale single-figure works sold in his own lifetime for 600-1000 fl, and his larger multi-figure paintings (often sold to foreign nobility) fetched between 1500 and 3000 fl.

20. In the Braamcamp Sale of 1771, superior paintings by De Hooch (Cat. 26, 27 & 42) brought 420, 500 and 610 fl; Dou's triptych attained the highest price in the sale (14,000 fl); two works by Van Mieris brought 1206 and 3610 fl; and an Ary de Vois fetched no less than 1210 fl.

21. The eighteenth century's high regard for the carefully finished works of Eglon Van der Neer is reflected in the fact that Smith included the artist in his *Catalogue Raisonné*

of 1833. Other remarks in sales catalogues also reflect contemporary tastes: a *Sick Woman* by De Hooch (possibly Cat. 132) was likened in 1789 to 'des bonnes productions de Nescher'; the detail and execution of the Rijksmuseum's painting (Cat. 71) was compared in 1815 to Dou's technique; and the brushwork of the painting in Indianapolis (Cat. 116) was complimented by the author of a 1779 catalogue as being equal in finish to the works of Terborch.

22. National Archives, Paris, no. o¹ 1918²/136. The dealer acquired the painting now in Los Angeles (Cat. 88) on this trip.

23. J. B. P. Lebrun, *Galerie des peintres flamands, hollandais et allemands*, I, Paris–Amsterdam, 52.

24. C. J. Nieuwenhuys, *A Review of the Lives and Works of Some of the Most Eminent Painters*, London, 1834, 154.

25. John Smith, *A Catalogue Raisonné of the Works of the Most Eminent Dutch, Flemish and French Painters*, IV, London, 1833, 217–42; *Supplement*, 1842, 563–74.

26. The author of the Le Roy Sale catalogue (Paris, 1843; see Cat. 95) wrote, 'Marchant de pair avec Metzu et Terburg, les tableaux de P. de Hoog sont également recherchés et atteignent, ici commes en Hollande, de très hauts prix'. See also, C. Kramm, *De Levens en Werken der Hollandsche en Vlaamsche Kunstschilders*, III, Amsterdam, 1859, 734, where the author notes the exceptionally high price (100,000 frs) reported as having been paid for a De Hooch (possibly Cat. 111) in Russia.

27. HdG (Metsu) no. 104 & HdG (Dou) no. 175; both in the Delessert sale, 15/3/1869, for 8400 and 7500 frs respectively.

28. These trends seem to be reflected in the prices brought at the Scarisbrick Sale (London, 10/5/1861): De Hooch (Cat. 40B)—£441; E. van der Neer—£90 & £162; A. van Ostade—£493; Ruisdael—£1312; Pynacker—£42. The sale also illustrates the limited understanding of De Hooch's art at this time; both Vermeer's *Laughing Girl* (Fig. 20) and De Witte's *Portrait of Adriana van Heusden* (Nat. Gal., London, no. 3682) were assigned to De Hooch (cat. nos. 89 and 21).

29. Charles Blanc, *Histoire des peintres de toutes les écoles*, vol. II, 'École Hollandaise', II, Paris, 1863, 1–8; idem,' Galerie Delessert', *Gazette des Beaux-Arts*, 2e per., I (1869), 201ff.

30. See W. Bürger, *Galerie d'Arenberg*, 1854, 37; idem, *Musées de la Hollande*, I, 1858, 98; idem, *Trésors d'art en Angleterre*, Brussels, 1860, 317.

31. W. Bürger, 'Van der Meer de Delft', *Gazette des Beaux-Arts*, 21 (1866), 292–330, 458–70, 542–75.

32. See Blankert, 92ff.

33. See Blankert cat. nos. 5 (and note 28 above), 6, 12 & 19.

34. Similarly, when the painting now in Birmingham (Cat. 62) appeared in the Van de Velde Sale in 1774, the author noted, 'Alles is zeer uitvoerig behandelt, hebbende dit Stukje veel gelykenis in deszelfs houding en kleur naar de schilderyn van de Delfsche van der Meer' (Everything is amply finished, in design and colour the picture bears much resemblance to the paintings by Van der Meer of Delft). Note, on the other hand, that the *Woman Weighing Coins* (Cat. 64) seems to have been repeatedly sold as a Vermeer in these years.

35. In 1825 Comte asserted in his *Considérations philosophiques sur les sciences et sur les savans* that a man's thinking process and modes of expression were a function of the period in which he lived. Hegel's *Vorlesungen über die Aesthetik* (1832) then made the first attempt to draw specific connections between the qualities of Dutch paintings and social, economic and religious conditions in seventeenth-century Holland.

Subsequently, Dutch painting has served as the classic example for the thesis that a causal relationship exists between social and environmental factors and style in art.

36. For Thoré's remarks on De Hooch, see W. Bürger, *Salons de T. Thoré, 1844–1848*, Paris, 1870, 336; T. Thoré, *Salons de W. Bürger 1861 à 1868*, Paris, 1870, I, 115, 130–1, 149, 225, 331; II, 50, 134, 140, 169, 377, 380. The author correctly observed similarities between De Hooch's paintings and those of the Dutch and Belgian nineteenth-century artists, Josef Israëls, Hendrick de Braekeleer, Jan August Hendrick Baron Leys, and Christoffel Bisschop. In discussing a work by the French painter François Bonvin he notes, 'Le meilleur maître à étudier pour M. Bonvin serait Pieter de Hooch, qu'il connait à peu près sans doute par les tableaux du Louvre'; see now G. P. Weisberg, 'François Bonvin and an Interest in Several Painters of the Seventeenth and Eighteenth Centuries', *Gazette des Beaux-Arts*, 6e per., 76 (1970), 359ff., esp. 363.

37. W. Bode (*Die Gemäldegalerie des Herrn A. de Ridder*, Berlin, 1910, 11) likened a painting long attributed to De Hooch (Cat. D 27) to Manet's art. The exhibition *Five Centuries of Painting in the Light of Vermeer*, The Hague–Paris, 1966, testified to the persistence of such ideas.

38. W. Bode, *Rembrandt und seine Zeitgenossen*, Leipzig, 1906, 58.

39. cf. H. Jantzen, 7: 'Diese Phase wird charakterisiert durch die Wahl der primären Trias Rot, Gelb, Blau in grösster Dichtigkeit und Sättigung der Qualitäten bei strengster kompositioneller Gebundenheit, wobei die positiven warmen Farben eine entscheidende Führung erhalten'.

40. Catalogues of collections made at this time often went to great lengths to provide minute colour descriptions; cf. H. Posse's catalogue of the Kaiser–Friedrich–Museum, Berlin I (1911); II (1913). The complex formal analyses in the literature on De Hooch in these years also seem to reflect a mode of perception conditioned by modern painting; see, for example, W. Rothes, 'Terborch und das holländische Gesellschaftsbild', *Die Kunst dem Volke*, 1921, nrs. 41/42, 44ff.

41. C. H. Collins Baker, *Masters of Painting: Pieter De Hooch*, London, 1925, 2.

42. Although the critics argued that the purchase was unwise because De Hooch was already represented in the Museum, and untimely because acquisition funds were low, the principal objection was to the presumed quality of the work. An anonymous writer in *The Connoisseur* (44, [1916], 235–6) quoted Bode's remarks on late De Hooch (he 'sacrifices his individuality to the taste of the time') and called the purchase 'an act of folly on the part of the Trustees'. D. S. Macoll ('The New De Hooch at the National Gallery', *The Burlington Magazine*, 29 [1916], 25–6) reviewed the arguments over the acquisition and wrote of the picture: 'This discouraging record will surprise no one who sees it. Not to mince matters, it is a poor picture, a work of the painter's late and bad period'.

43. A. Bredius, 'Een Prachtige Pieter de Hooch', *Oud-Holland* 56, (1939), 126–7.

44. See P. B. Coremans, *Van Meegeren's Vermeers and De Hooghs*, Amsterdam, 1947; for technical analyses, see R. Breek & W. Froentjes, 'Application of Pyrolysis Gas Chromatography on some of Van Meegeren's Fake Vermeers and Pieter de Hoochs', *Studies in Conservation*, 20 (1975), 183–9.

Catalogue

INTRODUCTION

The catalogue is divided into four sections. The first includes all those works which, in my opinion, are authentic. The material in this section is organized approximately chronologically, as are the corresponding plates. The advantages of this system, which clarifies the changes in style and content, in my judgement outweighs its disadvantage—the false impression that each work has a precise place in a chronological sequence. Most works have been personally examined. Those known only through photographs or reproductions are designated by an asterisk following the title. In the instances where there was only a marginal degree of doubt regarding a picture known only through photographs it has seemed best to include it among the accepted works, with a note characterizing its inconsistencies.

The second section, 'Tentatively Accepted and Questionable Works (catalogue numbers prefixed by a 'B'), lists a small group of works which, at this time, as a result of either their problematic style or condition, defy a decision on authenticity. It seemed wiser to admit grey areas where they exist than to deny them. The material in this section, as in the remaining two sections, is organized by subject matter according to the Classified Summary of Contents on page 120.

Works known solely through descriptions are included in the third section (catalogue number prefixed by a 'C'). Only those cited by Hofstede de Groot and those which, unknown to him, appeared in sales or literature prior to 1830 have been included. During the nineteenth century the number of works wrongly assigned to the artist increased dramatically. Later references have, therefore, been excluded to avoid overloading this section with spurious attributions.

The final section, 'Works Wrongly Attributed to De Hooch' (catalogue numbers prefixed by a 'D'), comprises paintings and drawings which are at present incorrectly attributed to the artist in public collections or have wrongly entered the literature on De Hooch as originals and still retain their false attributions. Alternative names have been proposed for some works, while others remain authorless. In the absence of a signed or documented drawing by the artist, or of one which can be related to a painting, none of the drawings which have been assigned to De Hooch can be accepted. An annotated concordance completes the catalogue.

Autograph replicas, copies in all media, and reproductive prints are listed under their models or prototypes.

Titles of paintings have frequently been changed and rendered generally descriptive rather than specifically interpretative. This, in my opinion, enhances consistency with the titles the Dutch applied to their pictures in the seventeenth century and eliminates misconceptions arising from latter-day anecdotal titles. Measurements are recorded in centimetres. Signatures have been newly transcribed wherever possible. The provenance entries provided by Smith (1833 & 1842), Hofstede de Groot (1907), and later writers have all been checked and many corrected or amended. New provenance references, some of which were discovered in C. Brière-Misme's unpublished papers, are designated with an asterisk before the citation. Most references to literature and exhibitions have been abbreviated; for their full titles, consult the Bibliography.

The following abbreviations appear:

a.c. (anonymous collection)
b.i. (bought in)
Dlr. (dealer)
P.C. (private collection)
Prov. (Provenance)
prob. (probable)
poss. (possible)
attr. (attributed)
w/o m. (without measurements)
drwg. (drawing)

RKD (Rijksbureau voor Kunsthistorische Documentatie, The Hague)
FARL (Frick Art Reference Library, New York)
Witt (Witt Library, London)
HdGf (C. Hofstede de Groot's 'fiches': transcriptions of sales catalogue entries and personal notes on paintings by Hofstede de Groot, his collaborators and successors, at the RKD)
HdG Handex (C. Hofstede de Groot's personal annotated copy of his *Catalogue Raisonné*, RKD)
BMf (C. Brière-Misme's unpublished papers, RKD)

Abbreviations employed in citations of exhibitions:

B.I. (British Institution, London)
R.A. (Royal Academy, London)

The following periodicals are abbreviated in the Literature entries:

A. (*Apollo*)
A.B. (*Art Bulletin*)
A.Q. (*Art Quarterly*)
A.N. (*Art News*)
B.K.N.O.B. (*Bulletin van de koninklijke Nederlandsche Oudheidkundige Bond*)
Burl. M. (*The Burlington Magazine*)
C. (*Connoisseur*)
G.B.A. (*Gazette des Beaux-Arts*)
I.S. (*International Studio*)
J.d.K.p.K. (*Jahrbuch der Königlich preussischen Kunstsammlungen*)

J.S.K. (*Jahrbuch der kunsthistorischen Sammlungen des allerhöchsten Kaiserhauses*)
M.B.K. (*Maandblad voor Beeldende Kunsten*)
M.f.K. (*Monatshefte für Kunstwissenschaft*)
N.K.J. (*Nederlands Kunsthistorisch Jaarboek*)
O.H. (*Oud-Holland*)
O.K. (*Openbaar Kunstbezit*)
P. (*Pantheon*)
R.d.A. (*La Revue de l'art ancien et moderne*)
R.f.K. (*Repertorium für Kunstwissenschaft*)
Z.f.b.K. (*Zeitschrift für bildende Kunst*)

A. Accepted Works

1. **Self-Portrait** (?) (Plate 1)   1648–9 (?)
Rijksmuseum, Amsterdam, no. A 181.

Panel 32.5× 34 cm. (fragment). Signed lower right: P.D.H. (and inscribed) Aetatis 19.

PROV.: Sale J.F. Sigault & J.J. van Limbeck, Amsterdam, 12/5/1834, no. 121—De Vries, 29 fl.

LIT.: Balkema 1844, 143; Thoré-Bürger 1858–60, I, 99; Kramm 1859, 734; Blanc 1863, 8, ill.; Thoré-Bürger, 1866, 315; Van Vloten 1874, 297; Lemcke 1878, 6–7; Gower 1880, 69, 72, ill.; Havard 1880, 133:2; Wedmore 1880, 51; A. Bredius, *Catalogue des peintures du Musée de l'Etat à Amsterdam*, Amsterdam, 1887, no. 158; HdG 1892, no. 8 [not by P.d.H.]; Wurzbach, I, 716 [not by P.d.H.]; HdG, 569, n. 3 [not by P.d.H.]; R, 9; F. Schmidt-Degener, *Verslagen omtrent 's Rijks verzamelingen van geschiedenis en kunst*, 49 (1926), 12, ill.; BM, 363, ill.; Val. 265 [1649], ill. frontispiece; Martin 1935–6, II, 207; Goldscheider, *Five Hundred Self-Portraits*, 1936, 38, fig. 234; T, 3, ill.; Van Hall 1963, 143, no. 960:1; Amsterdam, R., cat. 1976, 288, no. A 181 [attr. to P.d.H.].

The panel formerly had a strip added at the bottom edge which made the sitter appear to be holding a painter's palette. Bredius recognized in 1887 that this strip was a later addition[1] and when the picture was cleaned in 1926 it was removed. The lower edge of the panel has been cut; it reveals no bevelling and the composition has obviously been cropped at the bottom. The cutting probably occurred at the time the strip was added. Despite these changes, as Schmidt-Degener observed, the inscription appears to be genuine.[2] The work was described as a self-portrait as early as the 1834 sale and the identification may reflect a trustworthy tradition. Schmidt-Degener's suggestion that the sitter could be De Hooch's patron, Justus de la Grange, is pure speculation. Moreover, De Hooch was only thirteen years old when De la Grange turned nineteen in 1642. If the work is a self-portrait, it must have been executed in December of 1648 or the following year. The date finds some support in the picture's resemblance in execution to the early signed painting of a *Soldier Smoking* (Cat. 2).

NOTES: [1] Bredius, *Catalogue*, 1887, no. 158. [2] Schmidt-Degener, in *Verslagen*, 1926, 12.

2. **A Soldier Smoking** (Plate 2)   c. 1650
John G. Johnson Collection, Philadelphia, no. 499.

Panel 34.7× 27 cm. Signed lower left on table edge: P D HOOCH

PROV.: Sale M. Wolf, Berlin, 25/5/1857, no. 386; Sale J.J. Merlo et al., Cologne, 9/12/1891, no. 80—410 mks; Von Bock Collection, Quedlinburg, 1892;[1] Sale Wyl von Wymetal et al., Cologne, 14–15/6/1895, no. 115; date and circumstances of picture's entry into Johnson Coll. unknown.[2]

LIT.: HdG 1892, no. 79; Wurzbach, I, 717; HdG no. 282; Val. 1913, no. 499 [P.d.H.; mid 1650s]; R, 102; BM, 284; Val. 1927, 76, no. 2 [1647–57]; Val. no. 9 [c. 1650]; Phila., J.C., cat. 1972, 19, no. 499 [H. van der Burgh].

Although previously doubted,[3] the signature appeared to be sound when the picture was cleaned in 1970 and is probably genuine. The present attribution to Van der Burch cannot be supported. The colour scheme of red and yellow in the costume and the thin execution are typical of De Hooch's earliest works.

NOTES: [1] HdG 1892, no. 79. Not in the Bock Sale, London, 5/2/1895. [2] Phila, J.C., cat. 1972, 19, no. 499. [3] Wurzbach, I, 717, & J.C. cat.

3. **Liberation of St. Peter** (Plate 3)   c. 1650–5
Ch. de Roy van Zuydewijn, Amsterdam.

Panel 30.5× 37.5 cm. Signed right on pedestal: P. [d]. hooch.

PROV.: (Prob.) Sale L. Coben, Malines, 8/11/1808, no. 84 (w/o m.);[1] P. C., Belgium.[2]

LIT.: Sutton 1979, 32–5, fig. 50.

A recent cleaning revealed the artist's signature and the picture was probably sold as a De Hooch as early as 1808.[3] The panel has been cut along the left edge and, probably to a lesser extent, along the bottom. The number '179' is stencilled on the reverse.

NOTES: [1] Cat. entry transcribed in Sutton 1979, 35, n. 5. [2] Communication Ch. de Roy van Zuydewijn. [3] cf. note 1.

4. **The Merry Drinker** (Col. Plate I)   c. 1650
Staatliche Museen, Gemäldegalerie, East Berlin, cat. no. B 33.

Panel 50× 42 cm. Signed lower left: P · D · hooch

PROV.: *Sale J. van Zurendaal, Leyden, 25/6/1785, no. 32—Coclers, 25 fl; Sale Earl of Camperdown, London, 11/4/1919, no. 104—Agnew, £357;[1] P. C., Germany (M. Hollitscher, Berlin ?[2]); Sale Major Forbes Fraser, London, 22/1/1931, no. 46, ill.;[3] dlr. Haberstock, Berlin, c. 1935;[4] acq. from the Dresdener Bank, 1936 (1946–58 in the U.S.S.R.).[5]

LIT.: Bode 1919, 307, ill. 305; BM, 378, n. 1; Val. no 13 [after 1650].

First published by Bode, the picture was rejected by Brière-Misme. Judging only from a photograph, Valentiner questioned the signature and found the picture uncharacteristic of De Hooch. The Flemish influences which Bode noted in the composition and figure types are in fact typical of, and appropriate to, De Hooch's first manner. The signature is authentic.

NOTES: [1] Bode 1919, 307. [2] Sale cat. 1931. [3] RKD notes. [4] ibid. [5] Correspondence Frau Dr. I. Geismeier.

5. *A Soldier with an Empty Glass and a Serving Woman*
(Plate 4)   *c.* 1650–5
Museum Boymans-van Beuningen, Rotterdam, no. 2499.
D.G. van Beuningen Collection.
Panel 44×35 cm.
PROV.: Hendrick Verschuuring, The Hague, 1754;[1] Sale
Verschuuring, The Hague, 17/9/1770, no. 106 [Metsu]; Sale
C. van Heemskerk, The Hague, 18/11/1783, no. 5 [Metsu or in
his manner]—82 fl; ★Sale 'Deux Amateurs', Leyden, 26/8/1788,
no. 56 [P. de Hoge in the style of Metsu]—Wubbels, 82 fl;[2] dlr.
H.M. Clark, Amsterdam, 1919;[3] sold to A.F. Rulps; sold to
D.G. van Beuningen, Rotterdam,[4] cat. (1949) no. 50; acq.
1958.
EXH.: (a) On loan to Boymans Museum, Rotterdam, 1920;[5]
(b) Rotterdam 1935, no. 31, fig. 35; (c) Paris 1952, no. 100.
LIT.: Descamps, II, 1754, 245 [Metsu]; HdG (Metsu), no.
204b; CB, 3; BM, 370, ill.; Bredius 1928, 66, ill.; Val. no. 16
[*c.* 1653]; CB 1930, 198; Hannema 1949, no. 50, ill. no. 93;
Rotterdam, B.M., cat. 1962, no. 2499, ill.; Fleischer 1978, n. 18.

Attributed to Metsu by Descamps, the picture appeared in
two eighteenth-century sales under that name, but was sold
as the work of 'P de Hoge in the style of Metsu' in 1788. Listed
by Hofstede de Groot among Metsu's works in his *Catalogue
Raisonné*, the picture was reassigned to De Hooch when it
was exhibited in Rotterdam in 1920. With its animated interchange between a soldier and a serving woman in the foreground and group of sketchily painted card players in the
distance, the composition resembles that of Cat. 13 (Plate 12).
The lightened tonality, painterly execution, and colour scheme
may be compared to Cat. 7 (Plate 6).
NOTES: [1] Descamps, II, 1754, 245. [2] Incorrectly listed under
HdG no. 279; cf. Cat. 126. [3] HdGf. [4] ibid. [5] BM, 370.

6. *A Soldier Offering a Glass of Wine to a Seated Woman*
(Plate 5)   *c.* 1650–5
Hermitage, Leningrad, no. 6316.
Panel 71×59 cm. Signed lower left: P · De · hooch
PROV.: ★Sale L. ten Kate, Amsterdam, 29/5/1776, no. 55—J.
Spaan, 113 fl; Sale P. Calkoen, Amsterdam, 10/9/1781, no. 65—
Nijman, 130 fl; Duke of Leuchtenberg Coll., St Petersburg,[1]
until 1912;[2] art market, later Pushkin Museum, Moscow.[3]
LIT.: Néoustroieff 1904, 13; HdG no. 271 [an early work];
R, 18, 104 [1653–7]; BM, 370–1, ill. 369; Val. no. 184 [Metsu];
E. Plietzsch, in *P.*, 17 (1936), 11, n. 1 [P.d.H.]; Leningrad,
Hermitage, cat. 1958, no. 6316 [*c.* 1653]; Robinson 1974, 55,
n. 97 [Metsu; late 1650s].

Plietzsch,[4] Valentiner, and most recently, Robinson have
all incorrectly attributed the work to Metsu. Plietzsch later
assigned it to De Hooch.[5] It is signed in a characteristic manner
by the artist and bears all the marks of an early work by De
Hooch. A similar composition appears in the following scene
(Cat. 7, Plate 6). Some lack of clarity in the design, noticeable,
for instance, in the unhappily upstaged smoker on the far side
of the table, seems to testify to the youthful origins of the work.
NOTES: [1] Néoustroieff 1904, 13. [2] BM, 317. [3] ibid. [4] cf. Val.
no. 184. [5] *P.*, 1936.

**7. *Two Soldiers and a Serving Woman with a Trumpeter
in a Stable*** (Plate 6)   *c.* 1650–5
David M. Koetser, Zurich.
Panel 76×66 cm. Signed lower right: P · de · hooch.
PROV.: Sale H.A. Bauer, Amsterdam, 11/9/1820, no. 55—

Meusardt, 61 fl; Sale P.J. de Marneffe, Brussels, 24/5/1830, no.
148—De Schrijver, 160 fl; (prob.) Sale Dunford, London,
28/4/1855, no. 87 (w/o m.); Sale Lord Blackford et al. (a.c.),
London, 24/5/1954, no. 113—Sabin; Hare Coll., Woking,
Surrey,[1] from which it was acquired by D.M. Koetser, Zurich.
LIT.: HdG no. 278.

Without knowledge of the picture, Brière-Misme and
Valentiner accepted and discussed a copy (see 'a' below) as the
original. The superior quality and numerous pentimenti of
the present work prove it is the original. The subject of
soldiers drinking up before a departure heralded by a trumpeter
appears in two later works by De Hooch (see Cat. 93 & 107,
Plates 97, 113). Trumpeters rousing merry companies also
appear in the works of Terborch (see Gudlaugsson, nos. 38 &
123), De Jongh (Cat. D 20 & D 21, Plates 181, 182), H. van der
Burch (Val. nos. 222 & 223) and Dou (Martin, no. 86 left).
NOTES: [1] Correspondence D.M. Koetser.

7A. Version or copy? 48×38 cm. Sale Paris, 5/3/1793, no. 42:
the description corresponds in all details except for the mention
of a goblet held in the woman's left hand.

(a) Copy. Panel 74.5×59.5 cm. PROV.: Dlr. G. Douwes, exh.
Noordwijk, 7–8/1925, no. 23, ill.; Sale Cologne, 14/12/1926,
no. 50, pl. 9. LIT.: BM, 370; Val. no. 15 [*c.* 1653]; CB 1930, 198.

**8. *Two Soldiers with a Serving Woman and a Boy in a
Tavern*** ★ (Plate 7)   *c.* 1650–5
Present location unknown.
Panel 49×50 cm.
PROV.: Dlr., Frankfurt a. M., 1924;[1] dlr. Van Diemen,
Berlin, 1924;[2] A.M. Hackenbroch, Frankfurt a. M., Jan.
1925;[3] W. Heilgendorff, Berlin, 1929.[4]
EXH.: Berlin (Schäffer) 1929, no. 32.
LIT.: Lilienfeld 1924–5, 184, ill. 183; Val. no. 11 [*c.* 1652];
Wichmann 1929, 10.

The motif of the figure with a raised glass appears frequently in De Hooch's early works (see Cat. 4, 7, & 13, Col.
Plate I, Plates 6, 12). The figure types, particularly that of the
central soldier, and the colours (as described by Valentiner)
seem appropriate to the youthful artist.
NOTES: [1] Lilienfeld 1924–5, 184. [2] RKD notes. [3] HdGf.
[4] Exh. and HdGf.

9. *Two Soldiers Drinking with a Serving Woman* ★ (Plate 10)
                                                   c. 1650–5
Private Collection.
Panel 52×46 cm. Signed lower left on barrel.[1]
PROV.: Sale [Nathan Katz], Paris, 7/12/1950, no. 34, pl. XXII
[*c.* 1653–5]; Sale Paris, 20/6/1961, no. 75, pl. XI; Victor Lyon,
Paris; Sale Paris, 28/3/1979, no. 171, ill.

According to the Katz sale the picture was authenticated
by Valentiner in 1948. The present author knows the work
only in poor reproductions.
NOTES: [1] Katz Sale cat.

10. *Soldiers with a Serving Woman and a Flute Player*
(Plate 8)   *c.* 1650–5
Borghese Gallery, Rome, inv. no. 269.
Panel 60×73 cm.
PROV.: Acq. in 1783 by Marcantonio Borghese.[1]
LIT.: 'Bibl. gen. Documenti', 1783, no. 94 [P.d.H.];
'Inventario Fidecommisso', 1833, 13 ['Giovanni Le Ducq'];

C. de Ris, *Moniteur*, 1862 [Vermeer]; Thoré-Bürger 1866, 549–50, no. II [Vermeer]; Lemcke 1878, 20 [Vermeer]; Havard 1888, 36, no. 12 [Vermeer]; A. Venturi, *Il Museo e la Galleria Borghese*, Rome, 1893, 141 [P.d.H.]; Bode 1906, 57 [P.d.H.]; Wurzbach, I, 717 [P.d.H.]; HdG no. 272; Jantzen 1912, 9–10; R, 18, 28, 103 [1653–7]; Lilienfeld 1924, 453; CB, 3; BM, 372; Val. no. 20 [*c.* 1654]; Würtenberger 1937, 81; Della Pergola, II, 1959, no. 240, ill.; Fleischer 1978, n. 10; Sutton 1979, 35, fig. 51.

Described when acquired in 1783 as 'una Bambocciata più grande di P. de Hage', the work did not appear in the Borghese Inventory of 1790 and was attributed to Johan le Ducq (no doubt confused with Jacob Duck) in the inventory of 1833. Clement de Ris, Thoré, Lemcke and Havard all attributed it to Vermeer. Venturi assigned it to De Hooch and the attribution has been accepted in recent literature. The horizontal composition with figures assembled around a table at the left resembles that of the signed picture in Cologne (Cat. 11, Plate 9A). The dog at the lower right does not appear in copy 'a' below and may be a later addition.

NOTES: [1] Della Pergola, II, 1959, no. 240.

(a) Copy. (Photo RKD). Sale Shirlaw, London, 11/6/1925, no. 117 (as G. Terburg; w/o m.).

(b) Copy. (Photo RKD). A. Gola, Rome. Canvas 58×72 cm.

(c) Copy (damaged). (Photo RKD). Associazione Pro-Palombara-Sabina, Palombara-Sabina near Rome, 1961.

(d) Copy (left hand side of composition only). (Photo RKD). Spiridon Coll., Rome, Jan. 1925. 60×49 cm.

11. *A Soldier and a Serving Girl with Cardplayers* (Plate 9A)   *c.* 1655

Wallraf-Richartz-Museum, Cologne, no. 2841.
Canvas 58×71 cm. Signed lower left: P de hoogh
PROV.: Sale F.D. Bugge, Copenhagen, 21/8/1837, no. 355; Sale Foster, London, 25/5/1892, no. 118 or 127;[1] Rev. Allen and later H. Ward, London (n. d.);[2] dlr. Sedelmeyer, Paris, *c.* 1910, sold to R. Koeber, Hamburg,[3] before 1925;[4] L. Vogel, Schmöckwitz near Berlin, by 1927;[5] acq. 1950.
EXH.: Berlin 1925, no. 183, ill.
LIT.: HdG no. 261; BM 372, 376, 371 ill.; Val. xvi, no. 12 [*c.* 1652]; *Jahrbuch*, W-R.M., 15 (1953), 245; Vey-Kesting 1967, 56–7, no. 2841, ill. no. 73.
The work is signed in the lower left, not on the cart as reported by Brière-Misme.[6] It and Cat. 11 bis are the only signed early works on canvas and horizontal in format.
NOTES: [1] Vey-Kesting 1967, 57 (from Valentiner). [2] BM, 372. [3] ibid. [4] Exh. [5] BM, 372. [6] ibid.

11 bis. *Soldiers Playing Cards, with a Woman and Two Children*★ (Plate 9B)   *c.* 1655

Dealer P. de Boer, Amsterdam.
Canvas 62×77 cm. Signed lower right: P · d · hoogh ·
PROV.: ★Sale Marquis of Salamanca, Paris, 3–6/3/1867, no. 93—380 frs; Serafin Martinez Collection;[1] Sale Van Bauchau et al., Brussels, 3/2/1874, no. 34.[2]
LIT.: Havard 1880, 131:2; HdG no. 263.
Identical with Cat. C 231, the picture only appeared after the book went to print. Like the picture in Cologne (Cat. 11), it is horizontal in format, on canvas, and signed with a 'g' in

the last name—a rare practice in the early years. For further discussion, see Addendum to chapter 11.
NOTES: [1] Havard 1880, 131:2. [2] HdG no. 263.

12. *Tric-Trac Players* (Col. Plate II, Plate 11)   *c.* 1652–5

National Gallery of Ireland, Dublin, no. 322.
Panel 46×33 cm. Signed upper right on partition: P · de · hooch ·
PROV.: Sale H. Twent, Leyden, 11/8/1789, no. 27—Delfos (together with its pendant) 101 fl; Sale Baron van Coehoorn, Amsterdam, 19/10/1801, no. 28—Coclers (together with its pendant) 102 fl; dlr., England, 1879;[1] dlr. Haines Bros., London, from whom it was acquired in 1892.
EXH.: Dublin 1964, no. 114.
LIT.: Bode 1906, 57; HdG no. 253; R, 18, 100 [1653–7]; Lilienfeld 1924, 453–4; Lilienfeld 1924–5, 188, no. I; CB, 3; BM, 362, 372; Val. xvi, no. 17 [*c.* 1653]; CB 1930, 198; Rosenberg-Slive-TerKuile, 124, pl. 99B; Dublin, N.G., cat. 1971, 78, no. 322; Fleischer 1976, 108, fig. 2; 1978, 55, fig. 13.
The painting appeared in two early sales with a companion piece which Hofstede de Groot incorrectly identified with his no. 279, the picture now in Saltram House (Cat. 126, Plate 129). The companion was, in fact, the picture now in an English Private Collection (Cat. 13, Plate 12). The two works bear a strong stylistic resemblance, are close in size and could well have been designed as pendants. The centrally lit group of figures around a table is typical of De Hooch's early works as is the colour scheme of white, yellow, and greyish brown with accents of red and orange.
NOTES: [1] Bode 1919, 306.

13. *A Seated Soldier with a Standing Serving Woman* (Plate 12)   *c.* 1652–5

Private Collection, England.
Panel 43.5×37 cm. Signed upper right: P · de · hooch·
PROV.: ★Sale H. Twent, Leyden, 11/8/1789, no. 26—Delfos (together with its pendant) 101 fl;[1] ★Sale Baron van Coehoorn, Amsterdam, 19/10/1801, no 29—Coclers (together with its pendant) 102 fl; Private Collection, U.S.A., mid-nineteenth cent.;[2] dlr. E. Speelman, London.
Previously unpublished, the picture appeared in two early sales as the pendant to our Cat. 12 (Plate 11).
NOTES: [1] This and the following entry were incorrectly listed under HdG no. 279; cf. Cat. 126. [2] Correspondence E. Speelman.

14. *A Soldier with Dead Birds and Other Figures in a Stable* (Plate 14)   *c.* 1655–7

National Gallery, London, no. 3881.
Panel 53.5×49.7 cm.
PROV.: Sale O.W.J. Berg, Amsterdam, 7–8/7/1825, no. 51—Regemorter, 38 fl;[1] Sale Madame de Falbe, London, 19/5/1900, no. 141 [Jan Baptist Weenix]—A.H. Buttery, 85 gns; sold by Buttery, June 1900, to C. Fleischmann[2] (name later changed to Ashcroft); presented to the National Gallery by F.N. & O.S. Ashcroft, 1924.
EXH.: (a) Leiden 1906, no. 21; (b) Anon. [Ashcroft] Coll. exh., London (Agnew's), 6/1915, no. 45.
LIT.: A. Bredius, *De Leidsche tentoonstelling in 1906*, Haarlem, 1907, n. 19; HdG no. 269; R, 101; *Burl. M.*, 27 (1915), 171; CB, 3, 5, pl. 1; BM, 374–5, 377; Val. 1927, 69; Val. xvi, xxii, no. 27 [*c.* 1653–5]; CB 1930, 198; Von Weiher 1937, 114; T,

15, 32, ill. 12; MacLaren, 190–1, no. 3881; London, N.G., pls., I, no. 153; Gerson 1966, 310; Fleischer 1976, 108–14, figs. 1, 3, 4, 5 [mid-1650s]; Fleischer 1978, 55, fig. 12.

Fleischer has recently observed that the picture was overpainted sometime after it was sold in 1825 and before it appeared as a J.B. Weenix in a sale in 1900. It originally depicted a wounded soldier in the right foreground who is still visible in X-rays.[3] The subject of a wounded soldier was treated later by the artist (Cat. 80, Plate 83).[4] While the figure types and the execution of the present work are close to Cat. 12 & 13 (Plates 11, 12), the greater interest in the geometric division of space may indicate a slightly later date.

NOTES: [1] Fleischer 1976, 110–11. [2] MacLaren, 191, ns. 5 & 6. [3] cf. Fleischer 1976, fig. 4. [4] The theme also appears in a weak picture wrongly attributed to De Hooch; Sale London, 22/4/1929, no. 101.

15. *A Soldier Dressing and a Woman Making a Bed* (Plate 13)
c. 1655–7

Pushkin Museum of Fine Arts, Moscow, no. 2621.
Panel 40 × 53 cm.
PROV.: (Prob.) Sale L. de Moni, Leyden, 13/4/1772, no. 31 [P.d.H. or in his manner]—Van der Vinne, 20 fl;[1] presented to Czar Alexander I by Prince W.S. Troubetzkoy in 1818; Hermitage, Leningrad.
LIT.: Leningrad, Hermitage, cat. (1838) [Martin van Veen]; Waagen 1864, 165 [J. van Craesbeeck]; Leningrad, Hermitage, cat. 1895, no. 943 [P.d.H.]; Bode 1906, 57; Wurzbach, I, 717; HdG no. 75 & prob. 79 [earliest period]; R, 104; Rothes 1921, 44, fig. 72; Lilienfeld 1924–5, 184; CB, 3; BM, 375, 378, ill. 377; Val. 1927, 68, n. 1; Val. no. 24 [*c.* 1653–5]; T, ill. 11; Moscow, P.M., cat. 1951, no. 2621.

When the picture was presented to Czar Alexander I in 1818 it was thought to be a portrait of Peter the Great painted during his stay in Holland by Adriaen van de Venne. It was first attributed to De Hooch by Bode. Its resemblance to the signed painting in Barcelona (Cat. 18, Plate 17) provides support for the assignment. A similar blond light and rather crude perspective appear in both interiors and the treatment of the gilt leather decorations is the same. The present work may have been cut down on the top and bottom edges; but as the panel has been shaved and cradled, this question remains open. As Valentiner noted,[2] the theme of a soldier dressing reappears in Cat. 79 (Plate 82).

NOTES: [1] HdG no. 79. [2] Val. no. 24.

(a) Copy. Panel 16.2 × 15.1 cm. Sale Pohl, Hamburg, 25–27/1/1921, no. 180, pl. 4 [Style of A. van der Werff].

16. *The Bearer of Ill Tidings* (Plate 15)   *c.* 1654–7
Museo de Arte de Cataluña, Barcelona, no. 65005. (Cambó Collection).
Panel 68 × 56 cm. Signed lower left: P. d · hooch
PROV.: *Sale Dr. Goldschmidt of Frankfurt, Paris, 5–6/3/ 1869, no. 79 [attr. to P.d.H.];[1] Baron Eduard van Niesewand, Brussels, cat. (1886), 34; Sale Van Niesewand, London, 9/6/1886, no. 34; Sale Wyl von Wymetal et al., Cologne, 14–15/6/1895, no. 116; dlr. Berlin, 1926;[2] acquired for the Cambó Collection in Berlin in 1927 from an aide to Prince Hohenzollern-Sigmaringen.[3]
LIT.: J. de Brauwere, *Collection Niesewand Catalogue*, Brussels, 1886, 34; HdG no. 246a; BM, 374; Val. no. 23 [*c.* 1653–5]; Sánchez Cantón 1955, 98–9, no. 42, pl. 52;

Gudlaugsson, II, 109, pl. x; Valdivieso 1973, 116–7, 223, no. 158 [H. van der Burch], fig. 153.

De Brauwere first observed the resemblance to the painting by Terborch in the Mauritshuis (Fig. 5). Gudlaugsson noted the precedent of a composition by Palamedesz (ill. Gudlaugsson, II, pl. x, fig. 3) for the Terborch, but the seated woman and other details of the present picture clearly derive from the latter work. Without having seen the picture, Hofstede de Groot initially conjectured that it might be a reversed copy of the Terborch, but upon examining it in 1926 accepted the attribution to De Hooch.[4] While Valentiner felt that the attribution was 'not entirely certain', Gudlaugsson accepted it, adding that the picture also resembled a painting ascribed to H. van der Burch.[5] The steep perspective of the present work is the principal feature recalling Van der Burch; however, exaggerated spatial designs also occur in early signed De Hoochs (compare Cat. 7, Plate 6). The signature appears to be genuine. Executed after the Terborch of 1653, the work probably predates the technically more accomplished works of 1658 by several years.

NOTES: [1] BMf. [2] BM, 374. [3] Sánchez Cantón 1955, 98. [4] BM, 374. [5] Ill. *Beeldende Kunst*, xx, nr. 50; with dlr. Douwes, 1934.

17. *Mother and Child with a Serving Woman* (Plate 16)
c. 1657

Private Collection, Switzerland.
Panel 43 × 32 cm. Monogrammed on barrel.
Although the provenance of this previously unpublished work remains unknown, a clipping from an unidentified early English sale catalogue appears on the back of the panel. It reads, 'De Hooge. no. 30 Interior with a Lady and Child'. The backlighted design and the subdued but warm tonality most resemble Cat. 18 (Plate 17). Together with Cat. 11 bis (Plate 9B), these two works probably constitute the artist's earliest paintings of domestic themes.

18. *A Woman Preparing Vegetables, with a Child* (Plate 17)
c. 1657

Louvre, Paris, inv. no. 1372.
Panel 60 × 27 cm. Signed lower left: P D Hooch (the 'D' and 'H' intertwined).
PROV.: Acq. by Denon from the dlr. La Fontaine, who had brought it from Holland; entered the Musée Napoléon 1802–8.
LIT.: S no. 62; Nagler 1838, 291; Waagen 1839, 600; Kugler 1847, II, 512; Kramm 1859, 733; Waagen 1862, 113; Blanc 1863, 4, 8, ill. 3; Villot 1865, II, no. 223; Havard 1880, 108:2; Gower 1880, 70, 112; Wedmore 1880, 54, ill.; Havard 1881, 187, fig. 54; HdG 1892, no. 68; Rooses 1894, 179, 180, ill.; Wurzbach, I, 717; HdG no. 36; Jantzen 1912, 11–12; R, 27, 37, 75, 97, ill. 54; Demonts 1922, no 2414; CB, 4; BM, 58 [*c.* 1658], 64; Val. no. 42 [*c.* 1656]; Foucart 1976, 31.

The signature is unusual but the picture is undoubtedly authentic. Its rather dark tonality and panel support link it to Cat. 17 and 19 (Plates 16, 18). All three works display a new interest in more complex spatial arrangements. The subject appears in earlier paintings by Dou (cf. Martin, 122, l. & r.).

PRINTS: J.A. Classens (H. no. 1); J.J. Oortman (H. no. 9); C. Jacques (cf. Blanc 1863, 3); C. Courtry (cf. Wedmore 1880, 54).

(a) Copy, with changes. Virginia Museum of Fine Arts,

Richmond. Panel 59.5×46.7 cm. PROV.: *(Prob.) Sale J. Danser Nijman, Amsterdam, 16/8/1797, no. 115—Roos, 15 fl; *(prob.) Sale H. ten Kate, Amsterdam, 10/6/1801, no. 89—Josy, 21 fl;[1] Sale Countess of Chichester et al. (Marquess of Dufferin and Ava), London, 22/2/1929, no. 81—G. Douwes; dlr. Douwes, Amsterdam, 1934;[2] dlr. Duits, 1944;[3] dlr. Hallsborough, London, 1950;[4] A.D. & W.C. Williams, 1951; bequeathed 1951. EXH.: Amsterdam (Douwes) 1934, no. 33 ill. LIT.: (Prob.) HdG no. 300; Val. no. 262 [c. 1656]; Bull., V.M.F.A., 11 (1951), no. 5; Virginia Museum cat. 1966, no. 97 [school of P.d.H.].

NOTES: [1] This and the previous entry appear under HdG no. 300. Hofstede de Groot's transcription of the catalogue entry omits the mention of the child who is noted in the Nijman sale catalogue. No doubt the tub in which the woman chops vegetables was mistaken for a wash tub in the ten Kate sale catalogue. [2] Exh. cat. [3] Burl. M., 84 (1944), ii. [4] RKD notes.

(b) Copy, (Photo RKD). H. Michels Coll., Düsseldorf.

(c) Copy with changes. Canvas 60×49 cm. Sale Paris, 28/6/1934, no. 14 [School of P.d.H.; '. . . variante à demi-inversée de l'Intérieur conservé au Musée du Louvre'.]

19. A Merry Company with Two Men and Two Women (Plate 18) c. 1657

Metropolitan Museum of Art, New York, no. 29.100.7. Bequest of Mrs. H.O. Havemeyer, 1929.

Panel 67.9×58.5 cm.

PROV.: *(Prob.) J. Odon, Amsterdam, 6/9/1704, no. 10;[1] Baron Delessert, Paris, 1833–69;[2] Sale F. Delessert, Paris, 15–18/3/1869, no. 36, ill.—Narischkine, 150,000 frs; Sale B. Narischkine, Paris, 5/4/1883, no. 16—Cedron, 160,000 frs; Sale E. Secrétan, Paris, 1/7/1889, no. 128, ill.—Durand Ruel, 276,000 frs; Mrs. H.O. Havemeyer, New York, by 1895.[3]

EXH.: (a) New York 1909, xxvi, no. 53, ill. [c. 1658]; (b) New York (Knoedler) 1915, no. 5 [c. 1658]; (c) New York 1930, no. 71, ill.; (d) Little Rock 1963, 28.

LIT.: S no. 34; Delessert Coll. cats., 1844, 1846, 1848, 1850 & 1860; Thoré-Bürger, in G.B.A., 1e per., 16 (1864), 313 [Vermeer]; Thoré-Bürger 1866, 316–17, 551, no. 14 [Vermeer]; C. Blanc, in G.B.A., 2e per., 1 (1869), 202–3, ill.; Havard 1880, 104:3; Havard 1888, 36, no. 15 [Vermeer]; Bredius 1889, 161, n. 2; Bode 1895, 72; Wurzbach, 1, 716, 717; HdG no. 192; Val. 1910a, 9; Jantzen 1912, 24; R, 105; Val. 1926, 47, 61, fig. 2; BM, 60, 57 ill.; Val. 1927, 74, 76, no. 7; Bredius 1928, 65; Val. xiii, xvii, no. 62 [c. 1661]; New York, M.M.A., cat. 1931, no. A76-4; Val. 1932, 317; Würtenberger 1937, 82.

Despite earlier attributions to De Hooch, Thoré-Bürger assigned the work to Vermeer. The composition and lighting system resemble those of Cat. 26 and 29 (Plates 23, 27), which also depict the corner of a room with figures grouped around a table by a window. In the present picture, though, the darker tonality and panel support recall the artist's early paintings, suggesting it may slightly predate 1658. The somewhat exaggerated perspective (note the unusually small bed at the right) might also point to earlier origins (cf. Cat. 16, Plate 15); however, compare Cat. 26 (Plate 23), dated 1658. The hanging on the wall appears to represent a harbour scene and is inscribed: POTLN PIMA(S?) CAP (EAT ?) III IIA . . . URBIUM (or COMPLURIUM) DOMINA (III) IX.

NOTES: [1] Description and measurements correspond, however, as on canvas. [2] S no. 34; and Delessert cats. [3] Bode 1895, 7.

PRINTS: C. Courtry (cf. Delessert sale cat.); D. Mordant (H. no. 8).

20. Two Women with a Child in a Courtyard (Col. Plate IV) c. 1657

Toledo Museum of Art, Toledo, acc. no. 49.27. Gift of Edward Drummond Libbey, 1949.

Panel 68×57.5 cm. Signed lower left on step: P d · hooch ·

PROV.: Dlr. J. van der Kellen, Rotterdam, sold to Cottier, London, c. 1889;[1] Inglis Collection, 1895;[2] W.B. Thomas, Boston, 1907;[3] J. Pierpont Morgan, New York, by 1909;[4] dlr. Rosenberg & Stiebel, New York, 1948.[5]

EXH.: (a) New York 1909, without cat. no.;[6] (b) on loan to Metropolitan Museum, New York, 1909–14;[7] (c) Rotterdam 1935, no. 36 [1656], fig. 39.

LIT.: Bode 1895, 72; HdG no. 287; Val. 1910a, 9, fig. 10; R, 105; Val. 1926, 61; BM, 65, ill.; Val. 1927, 77, no. 18; Val. no. 40 [1656]; CB 1930, 198 [1656]; Val. 1932, 319 [1656]; Martin 1935–6, II, 202 [1656]; MacLaren, 185, n. 15; Gerson 1966, 308, ill.; Stechow 1966, 125, fig. 252; O. Wittman, in A., 86 (1967), 472, fig. 13; Toledo, M.A., cat. 1976, 80, pl. 131 [late 1650s].

MacLaren corrected Valentiner's assertion, repeated several times by later writers, that the picture was dated 1656.[8] Although signed, it reveals no trace of a date. The painting is darker in tonality than the courtyards dated 1658 and less highly ordered. As in Cat. 21 and 22 (Col. Plate V, Plate 19), the Oude Kerk in Delft appears in the distance. The work is probably one of the artist's earliest treatments of a courtyard space.

NOTES: [1] HdG no. 287. [2] Bode 1895, 73. [3] HdG no. 287. [4] BM, 65, [5] Toledo, M.A., Cat. 1976, 80. [6] Val. 1910a, 9. [7] BM, 65. [8] Val. no. 40.

21. A Woman and a Child in a Bleaching Ground (Col. Plate V) c. 1657–9

Private Collection, England.

Canvas 73.5×63 cm. Signed lower left: P · D · Hooge (last four letters added later?).

PROV.: Dlr. Farrer, London, before 1842:[1] Baron Edouard de Rothschild, Paris, by 1907;[2] Baron Edmond de Rothschild, Paris, by 1927.[3]

LIT.: S s no. 24; Blanc 1863, 6; Havard 1880, III:2; HdG 1892, no. 72; Wurzbach, 1, 717; HdG no. 298; BM, 65–6, ill.; Bredius 1928, 65; Val. no. 41 [c. 1656]; CB 1930, 198; Val. 1932, 319; Martin 1935–6, II, 202 [c. 1656]; T, 26, 29, ill. 15 [1657].

The diagonal composition with an expansive bleaching yard resembles the design of Cat. 38 (Plate 41). The gabled building at the left and the tower of the Oude Kerk beyond also appear in Cat. 20 and 22 (Colour Plate IV, Plate 19). Valentiner's suggestion[4] that the doorway at the left leads to De Hooch's own courtyard is unfounded speculation. The fictitious nature of De Hooch's composition is demonstrated by the fact that, when the Oude Kerk is viewed from the same angle as in the painting, the tower of the Nieuwe Kerk should appear to the right of its present position.

NOTES: [1] S s no. 24. [2] HdG no. 298. [3] BM, 65. [4] Val. no. 40.

22. Woman and Child in a Street (Plate 19) c. 1657–9

Formerly Lord Ashburton, The Grange; destroyed by fire. Canvas 76.2×62.2 cm.

PROV.: Sale Helsleuter, Paris, 25/1/1802, no. 71—Paillet, 3440 frs; Sale G. Müller, Amsterdam, 2/4/1827, no. 29—Brondgeest, 6000 fl;[1] Alexander Baring, 1833;[2] Lord Ashburton, The Grange, by 1837,[3] destroyed by fire in Bath House, London, before 1907.[4]

EXH.: London, R.A., 1871, no. 175.

LIT.: S no. 15; Waagen 1837–8, II, 89; Nagler 1838, 287; Immerzeel 1842, II, 52; Waagen 1854, II, 105; Blanc 1857–8, II, 208; Waagen 1862, 113; Blanc 1863, 8; Gower 1880, 112; Havard 1880, 110:2; HdG 1892, no. 39; Wurzbach, I, 717; HdG no. 293; R. 99.

The painting was destroyed by fire in the last century, but its design has been preserved in a drawing (see 'b' below) which is illustrated here. Frequently mentioned in nineteenth-century literature, the picture brought unusually high prices and was accorded special praise in the Helsleuter sale catalogue for its atmospheric perspective and plein-air naturalism. The diagonal composition with the receding wall and converging skyline of Delft monuments resembles Cat. 21 and 36 (Col. Plate V, Plates 37, 39). Like these works it probably dates from the late 1650s. According to sales descriptions the child in the picture was offering the woman a coin for one of the apples she sells.

NOTES: [1] According to the copy of the catalogue in the Leyden Print Room to Emmerson, 6450 fl; or according to S no. 15, £550. [2] S no. 15. [3] Waagen 1837–8, II, 89. [4] HdG no. 293.

(a) Copy. By C. van Noorde (1731–95). Drwg. w/o m. PROV.: Sale J. Lauwers, Amsterdam, 3/12/1802, C no. 3; Sale J.E. Graves, Amsterdam, 5/5/1806, A no. 6; (prob.) Sale Haarlem, 9/5/1807, no. 27.

(b) Copy. (Same as the above?) Drwg.: 31.7×21.6 cm. PROV.: J.L. Field, London, 1930–46, loaned to *Winter Exh.* Burlington Fine Arts Club, London 1930–1, no. 59, [P.d.H.?; signed lower right 'P de Hoge fct']; Sale Murray et al. (Field), London, 16/10/1946, no. 107 [attr. P.d.H.].

(c) Copy (weak; photo RKD). Painting, w/o m. Formerly D.G. van Beuningen, Rotterdam.

(d) Poss. copy. By F. Dekker (1684–1774). Drwg. w/o m. PROV.: Sale F. van der Schaft, Amsterdam, 19/4/1814, G no. 36: 'A Street Scene, after P. de Hooge . . .'.

23. *A Woman and Two Men in an Arbour* (Plate 21)
c. 1657–60

Metropolitan Museum of Art, New York, acc. no. 1976.100.25. Bequest of Harry G. Sperling.

Panel 43×36.5 cm. Signed lower left: P. d hoo[ch]

PROV.: (Prob.) Sale D. Sellar, London, 17/3/1894, no. III (w/o m.)—Smith £100; dlr. Van Slochem, New York, 1912;[1] M. van Gelder, Uccle, *c.* 1929.[2]

LIT.: HdG no. 306; Val. no. 37 [*c.* 1656].

The picture has been overpainted but is surely genuine. While arbours appear in several De Hoochs of the late 1650s, none dominates the scene as in this work.

NOTES: [1] Val. no. 27. [2] ibid.

24. *A Family in a Courtyard* (Col. Plate III, Plate 21)
c. 1657–60

Akademie der bildenden Künste, Vienna, inv. no. 715.
Canvas 114×97 cm.

PROV.: Presented by Graf Lamberg [as a Terborch] to the Akademie in 1821.

EXH.: (a) Brussels 1947, no. 55, pl. 93 [*c.* 1665]; (b) Amsterdam 1947, no. 78; (c) Paris, Petit Palais, 11/1947–3/1948; (d) Stockholm, N.G., 5–8/1948; (e) Copenhagen, R.M., 12/1948–2/1949; (f) London 1949, no. 80; (g) Washington–New York–San Francisco, 1949–50, no. 46; (h) St. Louis, C.A.M., 3–4/1951; (i) Toledo, M.A., 5–6/1951; (j) Toronto, A.G., 8–9/1951; (k) Boston, M.F.A., 10–12/1951; (l) Oslo 1952, no. 70, pl. 24; (m) Innsbruck, 1952; (n) Vienna 1953, no. 181; (o) Zurich 1953, no. 63; (p) Rome–Milan 1954, no. 62; (q) Brussels 1977–8, 46–47.

LIT.: 'Übergabeinventar der Sammlung Lamberg-Sprinzenstein', 1822 [Terborch]; Waagen 1862, 110 [Vermeer]; H. Schwemminger, *Verzeichnis der Gemälde-Sammlung*, Vienna, 1866, no. 435 [Vermeer]; Thoré-Bürger 1866, 550, no. 13 [Vermeer]; Vosmaer 1874, 145–6 [P.d.H.]; Lemcke 1878, 20, ill. 17 [Vermeer]; Havard 1888, 36, no. 14; C. von Lützow, *Kat. der Gemäldegalerie*, Vienna, 1889, inv. no. 715; HdG 1892, no. 87; T. von Frimmel, *Geschichte der Wiener Gemäldesammlungen*, Leipzig–Berlin, I, 1901, 174, no. 715 [P.d.H. or Vermeer]; Bode 1906, 59; Wurzbach, I, 718; HdG no. 321; R, 33, 103; M. Eisler, in *J.S.K.*, 33 (1916), 253, fig. 23; Bode 1919, 306; Eisler 1923, 255, ill. 27; Petrovics 1924, ill. 64; CB, 5; BM, 57; R. Eigenberger, *Die Gemäldegalerie der Akademie*, Vienna–Leipzig, 1927, I, 209, II, pl. 130; Val. no. 31 [*c.* 1655]; Val. 1932, 319 [*c.* 1654]; Martin 1935–6, II, 202; J.G. van Gelder, 'Carolus Fabritius exit aut redivivus', *Festschrift für Max Friedländer*, The Hague, 1942, 62–3 [C. Fabritius]; T, 19–22, ill. 13 [*c.* 1655]; Plietzsch 1956, 182; Pelinck 1958, n. 6; Gerson 1966, 308; Praz 1971, 121, fig. 82; Vienna, A.d.b.K., cat. 1972, no. 78, fig. 17 [*c.* 1662]; De Jongh 1974, 168, figs. 9 & 10.

Acquired as a Terborch in 1821, the painting was attributed to 'Vermeer in the manner of De Hooch' by Waagen and to Vermeer by Thoré-Bürger and others.[1] Vosmaer first assigned it to De Hooch and the attribution has gained general acceptance. Van Gelder's dissenting opinion that the work could be by Carel Fabritius cannot be accepted. Frimmel's identification of the sitters as members of the Helm family is pure speculation. The date of around 1662 proposed in the most recent catalogue of the collection is probably slightly too late. The execution and silvery tonality link the picture to the courtyard scene of 1658 in London (Cat. 34, Colour Plate IX). At the same time, however, the deep view through a series of courtyards resembles motifs in the other courtyard in London of 1660–1 (Cat. 44, Plate 48), suggesting the date may only need to be adjusted by a year or two. The pilastered arbour at the right reappears in Cat. 39 and 44 (Plates 42, 48). D. Vosmaer borrowed the couple at the left in one of his views of Delft after the explosion of 1654.[2]

NOTES: [1] According to Thoré-Bürger (1866), Suermondt and Mündler also attributed the work to Vermeer. Lemcke (1878) and Frimmel (1901)—the latter tentatively—also later lent their support to the attribution. [2] Johnson Coll., Phila., cat. 1972, no. 500.

PRINTS: W. Unger (cf. Vosmaer 1874).

(a) Copy (modern). G. Hirth, Munich, *c.* 1901 (cf. Frimmel 1901, 175).

(b) Copy. By Penther. Count Lanckoronski, Vienna, *c.* 1901 (cf. Frimmel 1901, 175).

IX. The Courtyard of a House in Delft, with a Woman and a Child (Cat. 34). 1658.
National Gallery, London. See also Plate 33

X. Detail from Plate 48: A Woman and a Maid in a Courtyard (Cat. 44). 1660–1 or 1663. National Gallery, London

25. **Two Soldiers Playing Cards and a Girl Filling a Pipe**
(Plate 22)   *c.* 1657–8
Private Collection, Switzerland.

Panel 50.5×45.7 cm. Signed left on back of the chair:
P.D.H.

PROV.: (Prob.) Sale Amsterdam, 24/11/1806, no. 30 (w/o m.)
—Roos, 300 fl; Sale London, 1819—Woodburn, £115 10 s;[1]
Sale P. van Cuyck, Paris, 17/2/1866, no. 47—Auguiot, 1060
frs; Sale Auguiot, Paris, 1/3/1875, no. 12—9400 frs; Pereire
Coll., Paris, by Apr. 1911[2]–1929;[3] dlr. Wildenstein, New
York, 1933–41;[4] acq. by E. Bührle from a French dlr., 1953.[5]

EXH.: (a) Los Angeles 1933, no. 16 [1655]; (b) Hartford 1934,
no. 25; (c) Rotterdam 1935, no. 34; (d) Amsterdam 1935, no.
152a [*c.* 1658]; (e) Kansas City 1940–1, no. 28 [1655]; (f)
Zurich, Kunsthaus, 1953; (g) 1958, no. 80; (h) Munich, Haus
der Kunst, 1958, no. 86.

LIT.: S no. 26; Thoré-Bürger 1866, 550, no. 12 [Vermeer];
Havard 1880, 131:3; HdG no. 264; BM, 372–4, ill. 373; Val.
no. 32 [*c.* 1655]; CB 1930, 198; Val. 1932, 318, 198; Gowing
1952, 108–9, n. 59, ill. 107; Fleischer 1978, 56, fig. 15.

In tone and colour the picture most resembles the painting
of 1658 in the Louvre (Cat. 26, Plate 23). The more angular
gestures may indicate a slightly earlier date. Thoré-Bürger
assigned the work to Vermeer and Valentiner noted its
resemblance to that artist's painting in the Frick Collection
(Fig. 20)[6] which he felt was the source for its composition.
It is unclear, however, which artist invented the design.

NOTES: [1] S no. 26. [2] HdGf. [3] Val. no. 32. [4] Exh. a–e. [5] Exh. g.
[6] Val. 1932, 318.

26. **A Girl Drinking with Two Soldiers** (Plate 23)   1658
Louvre, Paris, inv. no. RF 1974-29. Gift of Mme Gregor
Piatigorsky.

Canvas 68.8×60 cm. Signed and dated lower left on bench:
P.D.H./1658

PROV.: Sale G. Braamcamp, Amsterdam, 31/7/1771, no. 87—
Jan Hope, 420 fl; H.P. Hope, 1818[1] & 1833;[2] by descent to
H.T. Hope, by 1837[3] until after 1859;[4] by descent to Mrs.
Hope, by 1881;[5] by descent to Lord F. Pelham Clinton-Hope,
by 1891[6] (collection purchased as a whole by Colnaghi and
Wertheimer in 1898); Baron Alphonse de Rothschild, Paris;[7]
by descent to Baron Edouard de Rothschild, Paris, by 1921;[8]
H. Goering, *c.* 1944 (restituted to the Rothschilds, 1947);[9]
Mme Gregor Piatigorsky (daughter of Baroness Edouard de
Rothschild).

EXH.: (a) London, B.I., 1818, no. 101; (b) 1864, no. 85;
(c) London, R.A., 1881, no. 126; (d) London, S.K.M., 1891,
no. 34; (e) Paris 1946, no. 85.

LIT.: S no. 2; Waagen 1837–8, II, 145; Waagen 1854, II, 119;
Kramm 1859, 733; Havard 1880, 128:3; HdG 1892, no. 46;
Wurzbach, I, 717; HdG no. 195; Jantzen 1912, 24; R, 98;
BM 1921, 343; BM, 58, 60, 61, ill. 55 [1658]; Val. no. 33
[*c.* 1655–61]; CB 1930, 198; Würtenberger 1937, 82; Bille
1961, I, fig. 87, II, no. 87, 21–21a, 99; Foucart 1976, 31–4, ill. 30.

In 1837 Waagen reported that the picture had suffered
from overcleaning. While some passages, particularly in the
background, show wear, a recent cleaning has revealed much
of the central group's original condition. Brière-Misme first
noted that the picture was dated—a fact overlooked by
Valentiner. Two other interiors with soldiers are dated 1658
(see Cat. 27 & 28, Col. Plate VI, Plate 24) and an undated
but contemporary picture of a similar subject in London (Cat.

29, Plate 27) has a related design. Hofstede de Groot identified
the subject of the picture on the wall as Christ and the
Adulteress. A large engraved view of Amsterdam also appears
on the wall and a small figure of Mercury is visible on the
armoire seen through the doorway.

NOTES: [1] Exh. a. [2] S no. 2. [3] Waagen 1837–8, II, 145.
[4] Kramm 1859, 733. [5] Exh. c. [6] Exh. d. [7] HdG no. 195.
[8] BM 1921, 343. [9] Exh. e.

PRINT: cf. J. Burnet, *Treatise on Painting*, London, 1825 &
later eds., pl. 8.

27. **A Soldier Paying a Hostess** (Plates 24–5)   1658
Marquis of Bute Collection, Scotland.

Canvas 71×63.5 cm. Signed right: P · D · H · / 1658

PROV.: Sale G. Braamcamp, Amsterdam, 31/7/1771, no. 86—
Fouquet, 500 fl; 1st Marquis of Bute, Luton Park, by 1800.[1]

EXH.: (a) London, B.I., 1822, no. 116; (b) 1847, no. 93;
(c) 1854, no. 103; (d) London, R.A., 1870, no. 13; (e) London,
Bethnal Green Museum, 1883 (cf. Richter 1884); (f) Glasgow
1884 (ibid.) (g) London, R.A., 1929, no. 309, pl. 30; (h) Berlin
1929, no. 36, pl. 13; (i) Amsterdam 1935, no. 156, ill.; (j)
Rotterdam 1935, no. 42, fig. 45; (k) Edinburgh 1949, no. 17;
(l) London, R.A., 1952–3, no. 508; (m) London (Agnew)
1978, no. 22.

LIT.: 'Pictures at Luton', 1800, no. 291; 'Luton Hoo.
Catalogue Raisonné', 1822, no. 279; S no. 1; Waagen 1837–8,
II, 570; Waagen 1854, III, 477; Kramm 1859, 733; Blanc 1863,
2, 8; Havard 1880, 132:2; J.P. Richter, *Cat. of the Coll. . . .* [of]
the Marquess of Bute, London, 1884, no. 84; HdG no. 1892,
no. 43; Wurzbach, I, 717; HdG no. 268; R, 35, 100; CB, 5;
Val. 1926, 58; BM, 60; Val. xvii, no. 48; R. Fry, in *Burl. M.*,
54 (1929), 57, pl. IIIB; Wichmann 1929, 10; T, ill. 23; Bille
1961, ill. no. 86, II, 20–20a, 99; Fleischer 1978, 64, fig. 22.

The theme of a soldier paying a hostess was treated by
Ludolf de Jongh (Cat. D 20, Plate 182), H. van der Burch,
and later by De Hooch himself in Cat. 111 (Plate 114).

NOTES: [1] Unpub. cat., 1800, no. 291. Although the work
did not appear in the incomplete unpub. cat. of 1799, it may
have already entered the collection by this date; communication C. Armet, Archivist to the Marquis of Bute.

(a) Copy. (Compare Copy 'd'.) Canvas 70×60 cm. PROV.:
Sale Crosnier, Paris, 22/5/1855, no. 19 [P.d.H.]; Sale François,
Paris, 7/11/1860, no. 33 [attr. P.d.H.]; Sale Destournières &
Vautier, Paris, 20/2/1862, no. 21 [Sch. of P.d.H.]; Sale Paris,
10/3/1864, no. 72 [attr. P.d.H.].

(b) Copy. Dlr. London, 1894 (cf. HdG no. 268).

(c) Copy (same?). Mrs. Hobson, Washington, *c.* 1929 (cf. Val.
no. 48).

(d) Copy. (Same as Copy 'a'?) Canvas 75×63 cm. PROV.:
Sale R.A., Paris, 17/6/1931, no. 70. [P. Janssens]; Major W.H.
Trapp, 1942 (ill. in *A.*, 35 [2/1942], 48); Sir William Rook,
Wimbledon Common, 1951.

28. **Card Players** (Col. Plate VI, Plate 26)   1658
Royal Collection, Buckingham Palace, London.

Canvas 76.2×66 cm. Signed right on bench: P · D · H · /
1658

PROV.: Sale I. Walraven, Amsterdam, 14/10/1763, no. 16—
Van der Lande, 450 fl; Sale N. Doekscheer, Amsterdam,
9/9/1789, no. 17—Van der Schley, 500 fl; Sale Quarles van

F

Ufford & Hoofman, Amsterdam, 19/10/1818, no. 18—Roos, 2270 fl; sold by J. Hulswit to C.J. Nieuwenhuys in 1823 for 2,500 fl;[1] sold by Nieuwenhuys to Baron von Mecklenberg,[2] who in turn sold it to J. Smith in 1825 for 15,000 frs;[3] Smith sold it to Lord Farnborough for George IV.[4]

EXH.: (a) London, B.I., 1826, no. 8; (b) 1827, no. 73; (c) 1837, no. 101; (d) London, R.A., 1881, no. 113; (e) 1891, no. 85; (f) 1929, no. 303, pl. 29; (g) Bristol 1946, no. 1, ill.; (h) London, R.A., 1946-7, no. 307; (i) The Hague 1948, no. 3; (j) London, R.A., 1952-3, no. 382; (k) London 1971, no. 11, pl. 12.

LIT.: Terwesten 1770, 504; S no. 48; Nieuwenhuys 1834, 154-5, n. 1; Waagen 1837-8, II, 167; Jameson 1844, 26, no. 48; Waagen 1854, II, 10-11; Kramm 1859, 733; Waagen 1862, 113; Blanc 1863, 8; Gower 1880, 112; Havard 1880, 130:1; HdG 1892, no. 41; HdG c. 1895, n.p., ill.; Wurzbach, I, 717; HdG no. 254; R, 17, 21, 28, 35, 99, ill. op. 44; London, B.P., cat. 1920, no. 48; Rothes 1921, 40, fig. 71; Eisler 1923, 251; Lilienfeld 1924, 453; CB, 5; Val. 1926, 47, 58; BM, 58; Val. xiii, xvii, no. 51; R. Fry, in *Burl. M.*, 54 (1929), 64, pl. 111A; *A.*, 9 (1929), 139; CB 1930, 198; Cust 1931, no. 10, ill.; *Burl. M.*, 66 (1935), 219; Martin 1935-6, II, 202, fig. 103; Würtenberger 1937, 82; T, 32; Rosenberg-Slive-TerKuile, 124, pl. 99A.

Valentiner incorrectly asserted that the painting was the companion piece to our Cat. 29 (Plate 27).[5] Despite a close compositional resemblance and comparable style and size, there is no reason to assume the two works were designed as pendants.

NOTES: [1] Nieuwenhuys 1834, 155, n. 1. The picture did not appear in the Hulswit Sale (Amsterdam, 28/10/1822) as reported in HdG no. 254. Nieuwenhuys also contradicts the price of 4500 fl reported by Smith to have been paid Hulswit. [2] ibid. [3] S no. 48. [4] Nieuwenhuys 1834, 155, n. 1. Seguier (see cat. 1885, no. 22) evidently confused the picture with our Cat. 29 when he stated it had been in the Pourtalès Collection. [5] Val. no. 51.

PRINT: P.J. Arendzen (cf. HdG c. 1895).

(a) Copy. 75×66 cm. Sale London, 19/6/1922, no. 117.

(b) Copy (with changes). By J. Andriessen (1742-1819). Drwg. Private Collection, Amsterdam (see I.H. van Eeghen, *Bull. v. het Rijksmuseum*, 29 [1971], 173-82, figs. 5-6). Part of a sheet of studies containing copies of six paintings in the Doekscheer Collection. The copy reveals several variations in detail: the man drinking at the left wears a hat, an additional window appears over the door and the two windows at the left have been omitted.

29. *A Woman Drinking with Two Men, and a Serving Woman* (Plate 27) c. 1658

National Gallery, London, no. 834.

Canvas 73.7×64.6 cm. Signed lower left on table: P D H

PROV.: (Poss.) Sale D. Ietswaart, Amsterdam, 22/4/1749, no. 197—70 fl;[1] Sale Van Leyden, Paris, 10/9/1804, no. 43—Paillet, 5500 frs; in 1826 bought with other pictures from the Comte de Pourtalès, Paris, by Emmerson and Smith, who sold it to Sir Robert Peel, Bart.;[2] purchased with the Peel Collection, 1871.

EXH.: London 1976, no. 60, ill. 54.

LIT.: (Poss.) Hoet 1752, II, 251; S no. 49; Waagen 1837-8, I, 287; Jameson 1844, 354, no. 14; Kugler 1847, II, 512; Waagen 1854, I, 403; Blanc 1857-8, II, 220: Blanc 1863, 6, 8;

Gower 1880, III; Havard 1880, 62, 87, 126:2; Wedmore 1880, 53; Havard 1881, 183, fig. 53; HdG 1892, no. 37; Armstrong 1904, 21, 42; Wurzbach, I, 717; HdG no. 183; Jantzen 1912, 24, 25; R, 28, 50, 98, ill. op. 64; Eisler 1923, 251, ill. 252; CB 5, 6 [c. 1658-9], pl. IV; Val. 1926, 61; BM, 58 [c. 1658], 62; Val. xiii, xvii, no. 52 [c. 1658]; T, 32, 35, 44, 46-7, ill. 24; Plietzsch 1956, 182; London, N.G., pls., I, no. 150; MacLaren, 186-8, no. 834; Blankert 1975, 32, 33, 45 [c. 1658], 48, fig. 23; Welu 1975, 535, n. 35; Foucart 1976, 31-2, fig. 2.

MacLaren noted the many pentimenti. The artist painted out the figure of a white-bearded man who had appeared to the left of the girl on the right; the man in profile initially wore a broad hat and perhaps held a flute glass in his right hand; other details of the figures and architecture also reveal changes. As noted in the Van Leyden sale catalogue, the male figure with two pipes on the far side of the table may be pretending to play the violin. In 1881 Havard titled the painting 'La Chanson Joyeuse'—evidently assuming the girl with her back to the viewer was singing. MacLaren identified the subject of the painting above the fireplace (attributed to Ferdinand Bol in the Van Leyden sale catalogue) as The Education of the Virgin. A. Laing noticed the possible source for this detail in an (early seventeenth-century Flemish?) altarpiece in the Eszterhazy Chapel at Ering, South Bavaria (Fig. 38).[3] The map on the far wall has been tentatively identified by Welu as an early state of a map of the Seventeen Provinces of the Netherlands published by Huyck Allart (active c. 1650-75). The painting's resemblance in style and design to Cat. 28 (Col. Plate VI) support a date of c. 1658.

NOTES: [1] Insufficient description; cf. MacLaren, 188, n. 2. [2] S no. 49. [3] Communication C. Brown.

(a) Copy. By J.H. Muntz (1727-98). Drwg. w/o m. Sale Maarseveen, Amsterdam, 28/10/1793, B no. 19; Sale Ploos van Amstel, Amsterdam, 3/3/1800, W no. 3; Sale Van der Schley & Du Pré, Amsterdam, 22/12/1817, N no. 7.

30. *A Woman with a Baby on her Lap, and a Small Child* (Plate 28) 1658

Private Collection.

Panel 60×47 cm. Signed and dated lower left: P · D · H · / A 1658[1]

PROV.: (Poss.) Sale P. van der Lip, Amsterdam, 14/6/1712, no. 25 or 26 (w/o m.)—90 or 66 fl;[2] Sale Comte de Vaudreuil, Paris, 24-5/11/1784, no. 76—Lebrun, 2600 frs; Earl of Mulgrave, London, by 1815;[3] Sale Earl of Mulgrave, London, 7/4/1838, no. 56 (w/o m.); Sale Baron de Mecklenberg, Paris, 11/12/1854, no. 4[4]—Nieuwenhuys, 5450 frs; *Sale Vicomte de M[ontaut], Paris, 14/5/1858, no. 30—10,800 frs;[5] P. van Cuyck, 1858;[6] Isaac Péreire, Paris, by 1864;[7] Sale Péreire, Paris, 6-9/3/1872, no. 127, ill.[8]—20,200 frs; Roxard de la Salle, Nancy, by 1875;[9] Sale De la Salle, Paris, 28/3/1881, no. 19—Brame, 30,000 frs; Baron Albert Oppenheim, Cologne, cat. (1904), no. 21; Sale Oppenheim, Berlin, 27/10/1914 [delayed to 19/3/1918], I, no. 20, ill.; Dr. Walter von Pannwitz, Berlin, by 1918,[10] cat. (1926), no. 53.

EXH.: (a) London, B.I., no. 80; (b) Paris 1866, no. 88; (c) Nancy 1875,[11] no. 115; (d) Rotterdam 1935, no. 40, fig. 43; (e) New York-Toledo-Toronto 1954-5, 44, ill.

LIT.: (Poss., cf. n. 2) Hoet 1752, I, 147; S no. 16; Blanc 1857-8, II, 503; Blanc 1863, 8; Thoré-Bürger, in *G.B.A.*, 16 (1864), 308, ill.; Thoré-Bürger 1866, 316; A. Bray, *La peinture à l'exposition rétrospective de Nancy*, Nancy, 1875, 119; Havard 1880, 91:1, 95:2; HdG 1892, no. 30; *Collection de Baron Albert Oppenheim*, Paris, 1904, no. 21, pl. XVIII; Wurzbach, I, 717; HdG no. 6; R, 21, 28, 35, 73, 82, ill. op. 16; Bode 1919, 308; Lilienfeld 1924, 453; CB, 4–5; Friedländer 1926, I, 42, no. 53, ill.; Val. 1926, 58, n. 2; BM, 58; Val. xvii, no. 49; Martin 1935–6, II, 202; T, 32–4, 43, 44, ill. 27.

Although the room appears to be the same as that in Cat. 31 (Plate 29), Hofstede de Groot's assumption that the two works were designed as companion pieces seems unlikely.[12]

NOTES: [1] The date appears to have been strengthened. [2] Insufficient catalogue description: '25. Een Vrouwtje, in een Portaal, met een kindje, van P. de Hooge, seer natuurlyck geschildert. 90–0. 26. Een Weerga, van dezelve. 66–0'. See commentary Cat. 31. [3] Exh. a & S no. 16. [4] As dated 1698. [5] BMf. [6] Péreire Sale cat. [7] Thoré-Bürger 1864, 308. Friedländer's statement (1926) that the work appeared in the Paturle Sale in 1872 could not be substantiated; the Paturle Sale (Paris, 28/2/1872) was composed of modern paintings. [8] As dated 1698. [9] Exh. c. [10] HdGf. [11] See Bray 1875, 119. [12] HdG 1892, no. 30; see commentary, Cat. 31.

PRINT: E. Hédouin (cf. Péreire Sale cat. 1872).

31. *A Woman with a Child in a Pantry* (Plate 29)   c. 1658
Rijksmuseum, Amsterdam, no. A 182.

Canvas 65×60.5 cm. Signed lower left: P·D·H·

PROV.: (Poss.) Sale P. van der Lip, Amsterdam, 14/6/1712, no. 25 or 26 (w/o m.)—90 or 66 fl;[1] Sale I. Walraven, Amsterdam, 14/10/1765, no. 15—J.J. de Bruyn, 450 fl; Sale J.J. de Bruyn, Amsterdam, 12/9/1798, no. 25—De Vos, 2600 fl; (prob.) Sale P. de Smeth van Alphen, Amsterdam, 1–2/8/1810, no. 45—Schmidt, 3025 fl;[2] Sale Widow Hogguer, née Ebeling, Amsterdam, 18–21/8/1817, no. 19—J. de Vries, 4010 fl; in the Museum in Amsterdam by 1833.[3]

EXH.: (a) Paris 1921, no. 23, ill.; (b) London 1929, no. 346, pl. 32; (c) Amsterdam 1935, no. 153 [c. 1657]. (d) Rotterdam 1935, no. 41, fig. 44; (e) Brussels 1946, no. 54, pl. II; (f) Zurich 1953, no. 65, pl. 31 [c. 1658]; (g) Rome 1954, no. 64, pl. 34; (h) San Francisco–Toledo–Boston 1966–7, no. 86, ill.

LIT.: (Poss.) Hoet 1752, I, 147; Terwesten 1770, 504; S no. 25; Nieuwenhuys 1834, 154; Immerzeel 1843, II, 52; Blanc 1857–8, II, 267; Thoré-Bürger 1858, 100; Waagen 1862, 113; Blanc 1863, 8; Van Vloten 1874, 298; Lemcke 1878, 8–9; Gower 1880, 72, ill.; Havard 1880, 85, 98:2; Havard 1881, 187, fig. 55; HdG 1892, no. 3; Wurzbach, I, 716; HdG nos. 1 & 14; Geoffroy 1908, 53, ill.; Jantzen 1912, 11; R, 16, 21, 35, 72, 82, 95, ill. op. 14; Steenhoff 1920, 165; BM 1921, 342; Rothes 1921, 52, fig. 76; Eisler 1923, 252, ill.; CB, 4–5; Val. 1926, 58, n. 2; BM, 58 [c. 1658]; Val. xiii, no. 50 [c. 1658]; Martin 1935–6, II, 202, fig. 102; T, 32–3, 36, 43, 44, ill. 25; BM 1947–8, IV, 363, fig. 7; Oosterloo 1948, 172, fig. 52; Gerson 1952, 38, fig. 105; Baard in O.K., 1959, 26a–26, ill.; Rosenberg-Slive-TerKuile, 125, pl. 100A; Amsterdam, R, Cat. 1976, no. A 182.

The same room viewed from a point slightly farther to the right appears in Cat. 30 (Plate 28). In that work a painting hangs on the wall which was painted out by the artist in the present painting, and there are also other changes in the furnishings. Hofstede de Groot's assumption that the two works were pendants was based on a notation in the Walraven Sale catalogue (copy in the Leiden Print Room) which stated that the picture had been sold in 1712 for 66 fl.[4] The writer

assumed that the reference was to no. 26, the companion to no. 25, in the Van der Lip sale.[5] No measurements were recorded for either entry and the description of no. 25 (which mentions only one child) would better apply to this painting than to its putative companion. The two pictures differ in size and are painted on different supports. Thus, while they are undoubtedly contemporaneous, they are unlikely to be pendants. The present work displays a warmer tonality and less intense colouration than the picture dated 1658. However, this is probably in part a result of the fact that the latter work is on panel.

NOTES: [1] See the commentary and note 2 to Cat. 30. [2] The description corresponds, but (incorrectly ?) with the measurements 23×24" (58.4×60.9). [3] S no. 25. [4] HdG 1892, no. 3. [5] See Cat. 30, n. 2.

PRINTS: W. Unger (H. no. 12); Cramer (H. no. 3).

(a) Copy. W/o m. Sale Stevens, Paris, 4/3/1847, no. 152 (BMf).

(b) Copy. By Hansen (L.J. Hansen 1803–54?). Canvas 65×58 cm. Sale J. Slagregen, Amsterdam, 19/8/1856, no. 26.

(c) Poss. copy (see HdG no. 24a). 50.8×43.2 cm. Sale W. Clouwes et al., London, 4/2/1901, no. 117.

(d) Copy with changes (same?). (See HdG no. 24c). Signed lower right: P.D.H. Panel 54×46 cm. Sale Gleitsman et al., Munich, 7/12/1903, no. 45, ill.; Sale Munich, 1/5/1905, no. 185. (The woman in the picture is based on Metsu's painting in Dresden; cf. Robinson, fig. 128).

(e) Copy. (According to HdG no. 1.) Sir A. Haytor, London, c. 1907.

(f) Copy. Canvas 74×61 cm. Sale Poulett et al. (a.c.), London, 11/6/1969, no. 204.

(g) Copy. By W. Hendriks (1749–1831). Drwg. w/o m. Sale W. Hendricks. Amsterdam, 27/2/1832, A no. 20; Sale Amsterdam, 14/2/1835, A no. 20.

(h) Copy. By H. Numan (1744–1820). Drwg. w/o m. Sale Amsterdam, 17/3/1857, H. no. 153.

(i) Copy. By D.C. Pareira. Watercolour. Sale Gruyter, Amsterdam, 24/10/1882, no. 86; Sale M. van Swyndreyt, Amsterdam, 25/11/1903, no. 1418.

32. *A Woman Nursing an Infant, with a Child*
(Col. Plate VII, Plates 30, 31)   c. 1658–60
M.H. de Young Memorial Museum, San Francisco, inv. no. 61-44-37. Gift of the Samuel H. Kress Foundation, 1961. (Kress Coll. no. K2120).

Canvas 67.8×55.6 cm. Remnants of a signature on the footwarmer.[1]

PROV.: (Prob.) Van Loon Collection, Amsterdam, 1825;[2] the collection acq. by the Rothschilds of Paris by 1880;[3] Ronald Brakespeare, Henley;[4] dlr. Knoedler, New York, 1916;[5] Private Collection, New York, by 1926;[6] Sale, The late K.D. Butterworth, New York, 20/10/1954, no. 29; Frederick Mont, New York; Samuel H. Kress Collection, at M.H. de Young Memorial Museum, since 1955.

EXH.: (a) New York (Knoedler's) 1925, no. 6;[7] (b) Washington 1961–2, no. 45; (c) Kansas City 1967–8, no. 6.

LIT.: S no. 43; Havard 1880, 91:2; HdG 1892, no. 73; HdG

no. 11; Val. 1926, 61, fig. 6; BM, 72, ill. 70; Val. 1927, 76, no. 15; Val. xviii, no. 71 [*c.* 1663]; T, 41, 46, ill. 40; A. Frankfurter, in *A.N.*, 54 (4/1955), 58; A. Neumeyer, *A.Q.*, 18 (1955), 279, fig. 5; R. Rosenblum, *Art Digest*, 29 (1955), 23; Suida 1955, 26, ill. 27; *Art Treasures for America* (Kress Coll.), London, 1961, 154, 212, no. 146; San Francisco D.Y. Mus. cat. 1966, 133 [about 1663]; Eisler 1977, 153, no. K2120 [the later 1660s or the early 1670s], fig. 139.

Smith stated that the picture was the companion to our Cat. 38. While the two works date from roughly the same period and differ only slightly in size, their considerable differences in design suggest it is unlikely the artist designed them as a pair.

Brière-Misme first noted the compositional resemblance to the painting in the Wallace Collection (Cat. 61). While the latter work probably dates from the early years in Amsterdam (*c.* 1663), the lighter palette of primary hues and slightly broader execution of the present work suggest origins in the later years of the Delft period. Eisler's dating is certainly too late but he correctly observed small changes in the work which suggest evidence of overpainting; the jug at the right formerly revealed a handle and the birdcage was surmounted with straw or a vine.[8]

NOTES: [1] According to Eisler 1977, 'P. d Hooch'; cf. n. 7. [2] According to Havard (1880, 91:2) identical with S no. 43. [3] Havard 1880, 91:2 (see also 117:2). [4] Ref. exh. a. [5] BM, 72. [6] Val. 1926, 61. [7] As signed 'P. de Hooch'. [8] cf. Val., no. 71.

33. *Figures Drinking in a Courtyard with an Arbour*
(Col. Plate VIII, Plate 32)   1658
National Gallery of Scotland, Edinburgh. On loan from the Royal Bank of Scotland as Trustees of a Family Settlement.
Canvas on panel 66.5×56.5 cm. Signed and dated left centre on pier: P · D · H · / 1658

PROV.: *Empress Josephine, Château Malmaison, Rueil, cat. (1811), no. 67, inv. (1814), no. 1012, valued at 300 frs;[1] Walscott [Wolschott?] Collection, Antwerp;[2] bought in Berlin, a few years before 1833, by Edward Solly;[3] Sale E. Solly, London, 31/5/1837, no. 90—G. Byng, £535; George Byng, London, 1839[4] & 1842;[5] Viscount Enfield, by 1856;[6] by descent to the Earl of Stafford, Wrotham Park, Enfield; on loan to the National Gallery, London, 1952.[7]

EXH.: (a) London, B.I., 1839, no. 8; (b) 1842, no. 187; (c) 1856, no. 56; (d) London, R.A., 1881, no. 101; (e) 1893, no. 64; (f) 1929, no. 311; (g) 1938, no. 240; (h) 1952-3, no. 376.

LIT.: Malmaison cat. 1811, no. 67; S no. 47; S s no. 15; Waagen 1857, 323; Kramm 1859, 733; Lescure 1867, 274; Havard 1880, 95:3 [confused with replica mentioned in S s]; HdG 1892, no. 53; Wurzbach, I, 717; HdG no. 299; R, 17, 21, 35, 101; CB, 4-5, pl. II; Val. 1926, 57, 58; BM, 62, ill. 59; W. Martin, in *C.*, 83 (1929), 137, pl. X; Val. xvi, xvii, no. 54; T, 34, 35, ill. 28; Gerson 1952, 38, fig. 106; M. Brockwell, in *C.*, 131 (1953), 36, ill.; *A.N.*, 5 (1/1953), ill. 32; MacLaren, 188-9; Grandjean 1964, 145, no. 1012; Blankert 1975, 55-7, fig. 29.

The tablet above the archway is the same as that in the variant of the same date in London (Cat. 34, Col. Plate IX). As Hofstede de Groot first observed,[8] the tablet originally hung over the entrance to the Hieronymusdael Cloister in Delft. It has survived and is presently set in the wall of the garden behind Oude Delft no. 157. The inscription reads: 'dit is in sint hieronimus daelle/ wildt v tot pacientie en lijdt-/ saem-

heijt begeeven/ wandt wij muetten eerst daelle/ willen wij worden verheeuen 1614' (This is St. Jerome's vale, if you wish to repair to patience and meekness. For we must first descend if we wish to be raised.) While the tablet in the painting is partially obscured by vines and does not follow the original's legend exactly, as MacLaren observed, it is closer to its source, especially in the division of the lines, than its counterpart in the painting in London. This fact, taken together with the improved grouping of the figures in the picture in London, suggests that the painting in Edinburgh is the earlier of the two variants. The present work also displays a more intense colour scheme than the London version.

NOTES: [1] According to the catalogue of the Solly Sale of 1837 (see below) the picture was in the Malmaison Collection; for the 1811 cat., see Lescure 1867, 270 ff.; for the 1814 inventory, see Grandjean 1964, 145. The picture did not appear in the various Malmaison sales. [2] S no. 47 & Solly Sale cat. The picture did not appear in the Wolschot Sale (Antwerp, 1/9/1817) as stated in HdG no. 299. [3] S no. 47. [4] Exh. a. [5] Exh. b & S s no. 15. [6] Exh. c. [7] Gerson 1952, 38. [8] HdG no. 291.

(33A) Version or copy. According to Smith (S s no. 15): 'a duplicate . . . somewhat clearer in tone, with some trifling variations in the details [which] was imported from Holland by Mr. Chaplin in 1839. Formerly in the collection of Mr. Koopman at Utrecht'. Hofstede de Groot incorrectly identified the work as the painting in Washington (Cat. 35A).

(a) Copy. By A. van Strij (1753–1826). Panel 67.3×55.8 cm. Sale P.v.d. Santheuvel & J. van Strij, Dordrecht, 24/4/1816, no. 56.

(b) Copy. By A. van Strij. Drwg. w/o m. (for the above?). Sale J. van Strij, Dordrecht, 24/4/1839, A no. 1—J. Schmidt.

(c) Copy. C.B. Smith, Paisley, 11/1928 (HdGf.)

(d) Copy. (Photo RKD; neg. no. L5844). Signed and dated 1658. Canvas 69×58 cm. With dlr. G. Stein, before 1946. (Possibly identical with 'a' above, however, the supports are said to be different.)

(e) Copy. 70×57 cm. H. Ker Cokburne; Sale, London, 19/3/1954, no. 104.

(f) Poss. Copy. Panel 67.3×55.9 cm. Sale London, 5/11/1954, no. 84: 'P. de Hooch (after). The Courtyard of a Dutch House with an Arbour.'

(g) Poss. Copy (see also Cat. 34). By J. Stolker (1729–85). Drwg. w/o m. Sale De Jongh, Rotterdam, 26/3/1810, T. no.4: 'naar P. de Hooge. Hironymus Dale, een oud gestigt te Delft, breeder op de achterzijde van de teekening omschreven.'; Sale Rotterdam, 4/6/1828, A no. 7.

34. *The Courtyard of a House in Delft, with a Woman and Child* (Col. Plate IX, Plate 33)   1658
National Gallery, London, no. 835.
Canvas 73.5×60 cm. Signed and dated left on base of arch: P · D · H ·/An° 1658

PROV.: Sale P. de Smeth van Alphen, Amsterdam, 1-2/8/ 1810, no. 46—prob. Yperen for Backer,[1] 2075 fl; bought in 1825 for 10,750 fl from Backer's widow, Mevr. J.W. Backer of Amsterdam, by W. Brondgeest for W. Emmerson,[2] who sold it to Sir Robert Peel before 1833;[3] purchased in 1871 with the Peel Collection.

LIT.: S nos. 50 & prob. 18; Nieuwenhuys 1834, 156; Waagen 1837–8, I, 287; Nagler 1838, 291; Jameson 1844, 355, no. 14; Kugler 1847, II, 512; Waagen 1854, I, 403; Kramm 1859, 734; Blanc 1863, 6, 8; Thoré-Bürger 1866, 315 [1653]; Van Vloten 1874, 297; Gower 1880, 71, III; Havard 1880, 95:2, 112:1; Wedmore 1880, 51, 53; HdG 1892, no. 38; Bode 1906, 58; Wurzbach, I, 717; HdG no. 291; Jantzen 1912, 20, 23; R, 17, 21, 28, 35, 62, 99, ill. 48; Rothes 1921, 52, fig. 87; Eisler 1923, 248, ill. 254; Lilienfeld 1924, 453; CB, 5, 7, pl. III; Val. 1926, 57, 58; BM, 58, 62; Val. 1927, 74; Val. xvi, no. 55; Martin 1935–6, II, 202, fig. 104; T, 34; London N.G., pls., I, 151; MacLaren, 188–9, no. 835; Gerson 1966, 310–12; Blankert 1975, 56, fig. 30.

A close variant of the composition, also signed and dated 1658, is in Edinburgh (Cat. 33, Col. Plate VIII). MacLaren correctly observed that the present work is probably the later of the two. Its overall tonality is lighter and the colours are somewhat more evenly modulated.

NOTES: [1] See MacLaren, n. 8. [2] MacLaren, n. 9. [3] S no. 50.
PRINT: Rajon (H. no. 11).

(a) Copy. (Photo RKD). Canvas 72×57 cm. Sale, London, 12/5/1961, no. 183.

(b) Copy. (Photo RKD). Private Collection, Holland, 1939.

(c) Copy. Sale Van den Eeckhout, Paris, 9/3/1861, no. 47 (BMf.).

(d) Copy. By J. Buys (1724–1801). Drwg. w/o m. Sale Ploos van Amstel, Amsterdam, 3/3/1800, Y no. 30—De Graat, 61 fl.

(e) Copy. By C. Buys (1745–1826). Drwg. w/o m. Sale Engleberts, Amsterdam, 14/12/1807, G. no. 3—De Vries.

(f) Poss. copy. (See Cat. 33g).

35A. *Two Soldiers and a Woman Drinking in a Courtyard* (Plates 34, 36, 38)   c. 1658–60

National Gallery of Art, Washington, D.C., no. 56. Andrew Mellon Collection, 1937.

Canvas 68×59 cm.

PROV.: Sale C.S. Roos, Amsterdam, 28/8/1820, no. 51—Van Eyck, 750 fl; Baron Lionel de Rothschild, by 1842,[1] until after 1873;[2] by descent to Baron Alfred de Rothschild, Halton Manor, cat. (1884), no. 19; at the Baron's death, passed to Lord Carnarvon,[3] Newbury, England; Andrew W. Mellon, Washington, by 1926.[4]

EXH.: (a) London, R.A., 1873, no. 187; (b) San Francisco 1939, no. 81a, ill.; (c) New York 1939, no. 201.

LIT.: S s no. 30; Waagen 1854, II, 130; Havard 1880, 128:1; C. Davis, *A Description of the Works of Art forming the Collection of Alfred de Rothschild*, I, London, 1884, no. 15, ill.; HdG no. 295; R, 61, 65; CB, 6–7 [c. 1663]; Val. 1926, 47, 58, 61, fig. 4; BM, 63, ill. 61; Val. 1927, 76, no. 10; Val. xiii, xvii, no. 44 [c. 1656]; Gerson 1966, 312; Washington, N.G., cat. 1975, 178, no. 56 [c. 1660], ill. 179; Walker 1976, 288, no. 384 [c. 1660], ill. 289.

Brière-Misme incorrectly assumed that the Rothschild and Mellon provenances referred to two different pictures. An autograph replica (Cat. 35B, Plate 35) is in the Mauritshuis in The Hague. In that work the soldier on the far side of the table has been overpainted. The probability that the present work is the first version and not the replica, as suggested by Valentiner,[5] is supported by its superior quality and a number

of minor pentimenti. The wall at the back of the courtyard may be a section of the Old Town Wall in Delft and the tower of the Nieuwe Kerk is seen in the distance.

NOTES: [1] S s no. 30. The reference to the S.A. Koopman Sale (cf. HdG no. 295) is incorrect; the only De Hooch in this sale was our Cat. 84. [2] Exh. a. [3] BM, 63. [4] Val. 1926. [5] See notes to Val. nos. 43 & 44.

35B. *A Man Smoking and a Woman Drinking in a Courtyard* (Plate 35)   c. 1658–60

Mauritshuis, The Hague, no. 835. Gift of Heer & Mevr. Ten Cate-Van Wulfften Palthe, 1947.

Canvas 78×65 cm.

PROV.: J. Smith, sold 1822;[1] William Wells of Redleaf, by 1828;[2] Sale W. Wells, London, 12/5/1848, no. 95—Farrer, £590 15s;[3] Lord Overstone, by 1851,[4] until after 1871;[5] Lord and Lady Wantage, London, by 1888,[6] cat. 1905, no. 108; Earl of Crawford and Balcarres, London, by 1921,[7] until after 1929;[8] dlr. Katz, Dieren, cat. 1935, no. 27;[9] H.E. ten Cate, Almelo, by 1938.[10]

EXH.: (a) London, B.I., 1828, no. 93; (b) 1851, no. 69; (c) London, R.A., 1871, no. 208; (d) 1888, no. 95; (e) London, Guildhall, 1894, no. 50; (f) London, B.F.A.C., 1900, no. 8A; (g) Paris, 1921, no. 25; (h) London, R.A., 1929, no. 319; (i) Rotterdam 1935, no. 37, fig. 40; (j) Amsterdam 1935, no. 154 [c. 1658], ill.; (k) Rotterdam 1938, no. 91, fig. 134; (l) Providence 1938, no. 22; (m) New York (Schaeffer) 1939, no. 6; (n) New York 1939, no. 201 [c. 1656]; (o) Detroit 1939, no. 24; (p) Pittsburgh–St. Louis 1940, no. 15; (q) Newark 1940, no. 21; (r) Cincinnati 1941, no. 37; (s) Detroit 1941, no. 32, ill.; (t) New York (Duveen) 1942, no. 29, ill.; (u) Chicago 1942, no. 20, ill.; (v) Montreal 1944, no. 76, ill.; (w) Delft 1950–1, no. 10; (x) Cape Town 1952, no. 23, ill.; (y) Tel Aviv 1954; (z) Stockholm 1959, no. 225; (aa) Montreal 1967, no. 98 [c. 1656], ill.; (bb) Tokyo–Kyoto 1968–9, no. 30, ill. det. (cover).

LIT.: S no. 30; Waagen 1857, 130; Havard 1880, 133:1; *A Catalogue of Pictures forming the Collection of Lord and Lady Wantage*, London, 1905, no. 108, ill.; Wurzbach, I, 717; HdG no. 297; R, 61, 65, 101; Val. 1926, 61; BM 63; Val., xvii, no. 43 [c. 1656]; CB 1930, 198 [after 1656]; Gerson 1966, 310; The Hague, M., cat. 1977, no. 835.

The picture is an autograph replica of the painting in Washington (Cat. 35A, Plate 34) and probably was executed shortly after that work. The soldier who appears on the far side of the table in the painting in Washington is visible in X-rays of the present picture and was overpainted by a later hand. When this overpainting was applied the far edge of the table was extended to support the jug which the soldier formerly held aloft in his hand.

NOTES: [1] S no. 30. [2] Exh. a. [3] According to the Wantage cat. (p. vi) acquired by Jones Loyd (later Lord Overstone). [4] Exh. b. [5] Exh. c. [6] Exh. d. [7] Exh. g. [8] Exh. h. [9] Exh. i & j. [10] Exh. k.

(a) Copy (of Cat. 35B). By Sir Edwin Landseer (1802–73). Oil sketch, millboard, 31.5×26.5. (Executed while picture was in the Wells Coll.; cf. Wantage cat. 1905, no. 125).

(b) Copy (of Cat. 35A [or B?]). Dutch dlr., 1903 (according to HdG no. 295, copy of our Cat. 35A; however, possibly copied from 35B before it was overpainted).

(c) Copy (of Cat. no. 35A [or B?]). By W.J. Laquy. (1738–98).

Drwg. w/o m. (Poss.) Sale Van Hall, Amsterdam, 21/2/1814, I, no. 23; Sale Amsterdam, 13/4/1829, D no. 1; Sale Rotterdam, 22/11/1841, A no. 7.

36. *Two Women in a Courtyard* (Plates 39, 37)   *c.* 1657–60
Royal Collection, Buckingham Palace, London.

Canvas 69.2×54 cm. Signed lower left: P · D · HOOCH

PROV.: Sale, Amsterdam, 18/10/1819, no. 27—Hulswit, 506 fl; Sale R. Bernal, London, 8/5/1824, no. 33—Peacock, £150 ;[1] Sale T. Emmerson, London, 2/5/1829, no. 152—bought for George IV, 426 £.

EXH.: (a) London, B.I., 1829, no. 108; (b) London, R.A., 1886, no. 98; (c) 1946–7, no. 347; (d) The Hague 1948, no. 2, ill. 13; (e) London, R.A., 1952–3, no. 408; (f) London, Q.G., 1971, no. 14, pl. 13.

LIT.: S no. 27; Waagen 1837–8, II, 167; Jameson 1844, 27, no. 49; Waagen 1854, II, 11; Kramm 1859, 733; Blanc 1863, 8; Gower 1880, 112; Havard 1880, 110:1; HdG 1892, no. 40; Bode 1906, 58; Wurzbach, I, 717; HdG no. 292; R, 61, 99, 56, ill.; London, B.P., cat. 1920, no. 47; Rothes 1921, 47, fig. 85; CB, 6, 7 [*c.* 1664–5]; BM, 58 [*c.* 1658], 65, 66; Val. no. 45 [*c.* 1656]; Cust 1931, no. 19, ill.

The steeple of the Nieuwe Kerk and the tower of the Delft Town Hall appear in the distance at the right. The light tonality and the colour scheme of primary hues are typical of the artist's works of *c.* 1658. A date of 1657 appears on a copy (see 'c' below) and could document a lost date on the original.

NOTES: [1] Full description and measurements provided in S no. 27.

(a) Copy. Panel 53×45 cm. Sale R.W. Hacker, Frankfurt, 26/4/1901, no. 146; Sale Zürbach, Frankfurt, 30/10/1901, no. 79.

(b) Copy. Canvas 68×53 cm. Sale A. Paris et al. (Krentzlin), Frankfurt, 13/5/1897, no. 98; Sale Von Huene, Cologne, 25/4/1898, no. 53, ill.; Sale Berlin, 20/1/1899, no. 161, ill.

(c) Copy. (Photo RKD.) Signed and dated: '. . . ooch 1657'. Baron Lohr von Schell, Starnberger See, June 1929.

(d) Copy. Canvas 67.3×52 cm. Sale Lord Carrington, London, 9/5/1930, no. 29.

(e) Copy. (Photo Witt.) 25.3×19 cm. T.G.S. Binnie, London.

37. *A Woman Carrying a Bucket in a Courtyard**
(Plate 40)   *c.* 1658–60
Private Collection, England.

Canvas 49.4×41 cm. Signed lower right: P.D.H.

PROV.: Sale Jonkheer J.G. van Franckenstein, Amsterdam, 1/7/1833, no. 36—J.N. Hulswit, 2025 fl; Lionel de Rothschild, London, by 1878;[1] Alfred de Rothschild, London;[2] Sale Victor de Rothschild, London, 19/4/1937, no. 5, pl. IV—Agnew, £17,500.

EXH.: (a) London, R.A., 1878, no. 106; (b) Liverpool 1944, no. 6, ill.; (c) London, A.C., 1945, no. 13, pl. I; (d) London, R.A., 1952–3, no. 413.

LIT.: S no. 53; S s no. 23; Havard 1880, 108:1; HdG nos. 296 & 303; *Burl. M.*, 70 (1937), vii, ill.; *A.N.*, 35 (4/24/1937), 8, ill.; *A.*, 40 (1944), 139 [1656 or 7], ill. on cover.

When Smith described the work he mentioned 'two busts [which] decorate the fence of a garden on the left, the gate of which is open'. The design most resembles Cat. 36 (Plate 39),

where a woman is also depicted crossing a courtyard. Certain details, like the fence at the right and the pastoral view through the gateway, call to mind the artist's courtyard scenes of the early 1660s (cf. Cat. 46 & 59).

NOTES: [1] Exh. a. [2] HdGf.

38. *A Woman with a Glass of Wine and a Child in a Garden* (Plate 41)   *c.* 1658–60
Private Collection.

Canvas 62×58 cm. Signed left on windowsill: P. D hooch

PROV.: Van Loon Collection, Amsterdam, by 1842;[1] the collection was acquired by the Rothschilds, by 1880;[2] Baron Edouard de Rothschild, Paris, 1907;[3] Baron Edmond de Rothschild, Paris, 1927[4] & 1929;[5] H. Goering, *c.* 1944[6] (restituted to the Rothschilds, 1947).

EXH.: Paris 1946, no. 86.

LIT.: S no. 42; S s no. 14; Thoré-Bürger 1858–60, I, 99, II, 61, n. 1; Havard 1880, 117:2; HdG 1892, no. 73; Wurzbach, I, 717; HdG no. 309; R, 97; BM 69, ill.; Bredius 1928, 65; Val. no. 35 [*c.* 1656]; Val. 1932, 319.

Smith cited the picture as the companion piece to our Cat. 32 (Col. Plate VII),[7] but it is unlikely the two works were designed as pendants.

NOTES: [1] S s no. 14. [2] Havard 1880, 117:2. [3] HdG no. 309. [4] BM, 69. [5] Val. no. 35. [6] Exh. [7] S no. 42.

39. *A Woman and a Child in a Courtyard* (Plate 42)
   c. 1658–60
National Gallery of Art, Washington, D.C., no. 630. Widener Collection, 1942.

Canvas 73.5×66 cm. Signed lower left: P D HOOCH

PROV.: Dlr. Lawrie, London, 1903;[1] dlr. Sully, London;[2] dlr. Knoedler, Paris, who sold it to P.A.B. Widener, 1905;[3] Joseph E. Widener, Philadelphia.

EXH.: New York 1909, no. 54, ill.

LIT.: Armstrong 1904, 43, n. 1; HdG no. 294 [*c.* 1660]; R, 100; HdG & Val. 1913, n.p.; CB, 4–5; Val. 1926, 57, 61, fig. 3; BM, 70; Val. 1927, 76, no. 13; Val. no. 39 [*c.* 1656]; T, 20, 29–30 [*c.* 1658], ill. 17; Washington, N.G., cat. 1975, 178, no. 630 [*c.* 1660], ill. 179.

The same arbour appears in the painting in Vienna (Cat. 24, Col. Plate III) and, in the distance, in the picture in London probably dated 1660 or 1661 (Cat. 44, Plate 48). In the latter work the same pump also appears. As usual, these motifs have been rearranged, doubtless with disregard of their actual location. The wall in the distance is probably based on the old Town Wall in Delft; however, pentimenti at the right suggest it, too, was altered substantially.

NOTES: [1] HdG no. 294. [2] BMf. [3] ibid.

(a) Copy. By J. Buys (1724–1801). M. van Berg, New York (HdGf).

40A. *The Bedroom* (Plate 43)   *c.* 1658–60
Staatliche Kunsthalle, Karlsruhe, inv. no. 259.

Canvas 51.8×60.6 cm. Monogrammed on table crosspiece.

PROV.: Acq. 1831 from dlr. Noë, Stuttgart.[1]

EXH.: Rotterdam 1935, no. 43, fig. 46.

LIT.: Parthey 1863–4, I, 622, no. 12; L. Viardot, in *G.B.A.*, 17 (1864), 127; W. Lübke, *R.f.K.*, 10 (1887), 375; HdG no. 72; R, 28, 61, 64, 102, ill. op. 28; Rothes 1921, 48, 50, fig. 82; Lilienfeld 1924, 454; CB, 6 [*c.* 1660]; Val. 1926, 61 [before

1663]; BM 58, 64; Val. xvii, no. 58 [*c.* 1660]; Martin 1935–6 II, 203, fig. 105; T, 26, 36, 43, ill. 34; Lauts 1960, no. 25, ill. det. on cover; Lauts 1966, I, 152, no. 259 [*c.* 1658–60].

The composition exists in several versions, of which this has been rightly considered to be the best. While the present work is the clearest in tone and particularly fresh in execution, the question of which of the existing versions was the first remains unresolved. Neither this nor the painting in Washington (Cat. 40B) exhibits significant pentimenti or other features which would allow its identification as an original version. W. Stechow suggested, perhaps correctly, that all versions might be replicas of a lost original.[2] The design proved to be one of De Hooch's favourite compositions in these years (cf. Cat. 42 & 43, Plates 46, 47).

NOTES: [1] Lauts, I, no. 259. The picture did not appear in the collection of the House of Baden in the eighteenth century as stated in Hofstede de Groot. [2] Correspondence, 1960; see Lauts 1966.

40B. *The Bedroom* (Plate 44)   *c.* 1658–60
National Gallery of Art, Washington, D.C., no. 629. Widener Collection, 1942.

Canvas 51 × 60 cm.

PROV.: Sale Lord Radstock, London, 12–13/5/1826, no. 14— 70 gns;[1] * (prob.) Sale J. Smith, London, 2–3/5/1828, no. 40 (w/o m.)—Stafford;[2] Duke of Sutherland, Gower or York House, 1833,[3] Stafford House, London, by 1837;[4] sold in 1846, through dlr. E. Rutley in London to Morant;[5] Sale R. Field, London, 6/6/1856, no. 520 (w/o m.)—£43;[7] Sale C. Scarisbrick, London, 10/5/1861, no. 119 (w/o m.)—Nieuwenhuys, £441;[8] Sale A. Hope, London, 30/6/1894, no. 32, ill.— C. Wertheimer, £2257;[9] P.A.B. Widener, by 1894;[10] Joseph E. Widener, Philadelphia.

EXH.: (a) Paris (Sedelmeyer) 1898, no. 70, ill. op. 86; (b) New York 1909, xxvi, no. 55 [*c.* 1660], ill.; (c) San Francisco 1939, no. 81a [*c.* 1656], ill.

LIT.: S no. 29 (& 55?); J.D. Passavant, *Kunstreise durch England und Belgien*, Frankfurt a.M., 1833, 63; Waagen 1837–8, II, 67; Jameson 1844, 205, no. 124; Waagen 1854, II, 71; Thoré-Bürger 1857, 319; Blanc 1863, 8; Havard 1880, 107:2; Bode 1906, 59; Wurzbach, I, 717; HdG no. 78; Val. 1910a, 9; HdG & Val. 1913, n.p.; R, 105; CB, 6 [*c.* 1660]; Val. 1926, 59, 61 [before 1663]; BM, 58; Val. 1927, 75, 76, no. 12; Val xvii, no. 59 [*c.* 1660], ill. 179; Walker 1976, 291, no. 388 [*c.* 1660], ill.

Valentiner[11] assumed that this picture was a replica of the version in Karlsruhe (Cat. 40A, Plate 43), but neither can be identified as the original. Only slightly less finely executed, the present work is unquestionably autographed and of the highest quality. It and the version formerly in Philadelphia (Cat. 40C) differ from the Karlsruhe painting in minor details: the decorations on the top and the bottom of the mirror frame have been omitted; a checked pattern (like that of the tablecloths in Cat. 19, 25 & 26) appears on the bedspread lying on the chair; and a wisp of straw now appears at the feet of the woman.

NOTES: [1] See S no. 29. Smith no. 55 refers to a similar picture (described in reverse) which was bought in at Christie's in 1827 for £150. While it was stated in HdG no. 78 that the two works were identical, the latter may be another version. [2] The pencilled annotation 'Stafford' appears in the copy of the catalogue of the sale in the RKD. The sale is perhaps identical with that referred to in S no. 55, if the date

recorded there is incorrect. [3] Passavant 1833, 63; S no. 29. [4] Waagen 1837–8, II, 67; Jameson 1844, 204, no. 124. [5] Smith's unpublished notes (according to HdGf). The painting in the sale in Amsterdam in 1838 (cf. HdG no. 78) was our Cat. 42. The 1847 Cremer sale reference, also cited in HdG, is incorrect. [6] As 'from the Sutherland Collection'. [7] HdG no. 78. [8] cf. n. 9. [9] With the provenance: Radstock, Stafford & Scarisbrick colls. [10] Widener inv. 1894, no. 138. [11] Val. 1910a & Val. no. 59.

40C. *The Bedroom**   *c.* 1658–60
Present location unknown.

Canvas 53 × 61 cm. Signed lower left on table crosspiece: P.D.H.

PROV.: (Poss.) Six van Hillegom, Amsterdam, brought to England before 1833 by Chaplin;[1] Edmund Lloyd, Manchester, by 1842, by descent to Capt. E.N.F. Lloyd; Sale Lloyd, London, 30/4/1937, no. 108, ill.—Knoedler, £3045; dlr. Knoedler & Co., New York, 1937—after 1945; Sale Philadelphia Museum of Art, New York, 29/2/1956, no. 17, ill.

EXH.: (a) Manchester 1857, no. 1060; (b) Baltimore 1943, 23, ill. 22; (c) New York (Knoedler's) 1945, no. 5.

LIT.: (Poss.) S no. 36; S s no. 11; Thoré-Bürger 1860, 319; (poss.) Havard 1880, 107:3 [= S no. 36]; HdG no. 84; 'The Lloyd Collection', *Country Life*, 17/4/1937, cvii.

Judging only from photographs, the present version appears weaker than Cats. 40A & 40B. The chamber pot which figures in the other versions apparently was overpainted when the picture appeared in the Lloyd sale but had reappeared by the time the picture was sold in 1956.

NOTES: [1] Although both Thoré-Bürger (1860, 319) and Hofstede de Groot (no. 84) stated that the picture formerly in the Six van Hillegom collection (S no. 36) was probably identical with the painting later in the Lloyd collection (S s no. 11), the identification cannot be substantiated. Furthermore, Smith's approximate measurements for the Six picture suggest it was slightly larger (56 × 71 cm.) than the other versions.

Possible Additional Versions (known only from descriptions)

40D. *The Bedroom.* Canvas 51 × 60 cm. Sale S.J. Stinstra, Amsterdam, 22/5/1827, no. 86—De Vries, 25 fl. (The identification [see HdG no. 78] with Cat. 40B. cannot be substantiated.)

40E. *The Bedroom.* Canvas approx. 56 × 71 cm. Six van Hillegom coll. before 1833 (cf. S no. 36). (The identification [see HdG no. 84] with Cat. 40C cannot be substantiated.)

40F. *The Bedroom* (see HdG no. 86). 28 × 33 cm. Sale E.W. Lake, London 11/7/1845, no. 27—Evans, £25. (According to HdG no. 86, also Sale H.A.J. Munro of Novar, London, 1/6/1878, no. 314; however, no work of this description appeared in the sale.)

40G. *The Bedroom* (cf. Cat. C 44). Inv. widow of J. Meurs, Amsterdam, 1678.

(a) Copy. Toledo Museum of Art, Toledo, acc. no. 29.79. Gift of Edward Drummond Libbey, 1925. Canvas 52.3 × 67 cm. Signed lower right (falsely): P D Hoog. PROV.: H. Reinhardt, New York; E.D. Libbey, 1913–25.[1] EXH.: St. Louis 1947, no. 25 [*c.* 1660], ill. LIT.: O. Wittman, in *A.*, 86 (12/1967), 466, pl. xiii; Toledo, M.A. cat. 1976, 81, pl. 132 [P.d.H.]. The picture corresponds in the smallest details with Cat. 40B. It is, however, clearly inferior in quality and is probably a copy by another hand. A copy (see 'b' below) appeared with the Washington painting in the Scarisbrick Collection and may be identical with this work.

NOTES: [1] Toledo, M.A., cat. 1976, 81.

(b) Copy (same?). Sale C. Scarisbrick, London 24/5/1861, no. 567.

(c) Copy. With London dlr., *c.* 1900 (ref. HdG no. 78).

(d) Copy. Panel 48×61 cm. Sale M.L.S., Brussels, 26/5/1930, no. 53; Sale L. Spiegels, Brussels, 7/12/1931, no. 57.

(e) Copy. (Photo RKD.) Dlr. Katz, Dieren, 1938.

(f) Copy (with changes). (Photo RKD.) Dr. S. Schweitzer, Basel.

(g) Copy (left hand side only). M. Bormal, Paris, 1926 (BMf).

(h) Copy. By C. van Noorde (1731-95). Drwg. w/o m. Sale Ploos van Amstel, Amsterdam, 3/3/1800, PP no. 47; (prob.) Sale Schepens, Amsterdam, 21/1/1811, C no. 4 [N. van Noorde].

(i) Copy. By R. Vinkeles (1744-1816). Drwg. w/o m. (Poss.) Sale De Vos, Amsterdam, 30/10/1833, O no. 7; Sale Amsterdam 11/11/1845, J. no. 242; Sale Elzer, Amsterdam, 20/11/1866, no. 134; Sale Amsterdam, 27/10/1874, no. 648.

41. *'Kolf' Players* (Plate 45)   *c.* 1658-60

National Trust, Polesden Lacey, no. 44. Hon. Mrs. Ronald Greville Bequest, 1942.

Panel 63.5×45.7 cm. Signed lower left on door: P d hooch

PROV.: Count von Fries, Vienna;[1] Sale H. Héris, Brussels, 19-20/6/1846, no. 27—Piérard de Valenciennes, 2400 frs; Sale Piérard de Valenciennes, Paris, 20-1/3/1860, no. 29—2500 frs; Sir H.H. Campbell, Bart., by 1861;[2] Sale Campbell, London, 25/5/1867, no. 77 (b. i.); Sale Campbell, London, 16/6/1894, no. 37—Lesser; Rt. Hon. William McEwan, by descent to Hon. Mrs. Ronald Greville, by 1913.[3]

EXH.: (a) London, B.I., 1861, no. 108; (b) London, G.G., 1913-14, no. 63, ill.; (c) London, R.A., 1929, no. 324, ill.; (d) London (Slatter), 1945, no. 1; (e) London, R.A., 1952-3, no. 443; (f) London, A.C., 1956, no. 20; (g) London et al., A.C., 1960, no. 13, pl. vii.

LIT.: HdG no. 305; Cust 1914, 206; BM, 64-5, ill. 63; Val. no. 57 [*c.* 1660]; J.G. van Gelder, in *Burl. M.*, 45 (1953), 34, n. 2; Zumthor 1962, 167; Polesden Lacey, Nat. Trust, cat. 1976, no. 44.

The motif of a small child standing in an open doorway closely resembles a detail appearing on the left side of the composition entitled 'The Bedroom' (see Cat. 40A–C, Plates 43, 44). While the picture differs from those works in being on panel and upright in format, Van Gelder's belief that the work is a fragment seems unconvincing. Considering its substantial size and the completeness of its design, it is improbable that the work was ever appreciably larger. The quality of execution in the various versions of the Bedroom theme is particularly fine in the passages corresponding to this work. It is possible, therefore, that the panel preceded and inspired these works. Nothing, however, in the handling of the present work suggests that it was painted merely as a preparatory study. It is less likely, although conceivable, that the artist recognized the special beauty of the detail of the larger design and extracted it as a model for an independent picture. In either case, the practice seems unique.

As Zumthor noted, the children have been playing 'kolf', a game analogous to modern hockey which was played on ice in the winter and on level ground in the summer. Several of the tiles on the wall seem to depict children's games and acrobats and may be intended to reinforce the central theme. The signature, which was doubted in the collection's catalogue, is typical for the period and probably genuine.

NOTES: [1] See Héris sale cat. 1846. [2] Exh. a. [3] Exh. b.

42. *A Woman Delousing a Child's Hair* (Plate 46)

c. 1658-60

Rijksmuseum, Amsterdam, no. C 149. On loan from the City of Amsterdam (A. van der Hoop Bequest) since 1885.

Canvas 52.5×61 cm. Signed lower right on child's chair: P · d · hooch

PROV.: Gerard Braamcamp, Amsterdam, prob. by 1753,[1] and certainly by 1766;[2] Sale Braamcamp, Amsterdam, 31/7/1771, no. 88—Van der Dussen, 610 fl;[3] Sale J.L. van der Dussen, Amsterdam, 31/10/1774, no. 7—Yver, 750 fl;[4] J. Faesch, Basel, by 1779;[5] Sale J.J. de Faesch, Amsterdam, 3-4/7/1833, no. 20—3500 fl+7½% (b. i.; or Jansen for Moget, 2590 fl[6]); Sale Amsterdam, 24/4/1838, no. 18—Brondgeest, 3311 fl; sold by Brondgeest, for 3724 fl. to A. van der Hoop, 1838; gift to the City of Amsterdam, 1854.

EXH.: (a) Rotterdam 1935, no. 45, fig. 48; (b) Amsterdam 1935, no. 157 [*c.* 1660], ill.; (c) Antwerp 1956, no. 85; (d) Rome 1956-7, no. 138.

LIT.: (Poss.) Descamps, III, 1753, 164; Bastide, *Le Temple des Arts, ou le Cabinet de M. Braamcamp*, Amsterdam, 1766, 79; J.G. van Meusel, *Miscellaneen Artistischen Inhalts*, Erfurt, I, 1779, Part 2, 27; S nos. 3, 4, 67; S s no. 1; Thoré-Bürger 1858-60, 57-8, no. 54; Waagen 1862, 113; Blanc 1863, 2, 8; Amsterdam, V.d.H. Mus., cat. 1872, no. 52; Van Vloten 1874, 298; Lemcke 1878, 10; Gower 1880, III, ill. op. 71; Havard 1880, 74, 89:2, 90:1, 90:2, 93:3; Wedmore 1880, 55; A. Bredius, *Die Meisterwerke des Rijksmuseums zu Amsterdam*, Munich, n.d. (1887-8), 78 [Boursse], ill.; HdG 1892, no. 5; Wurzbach, I, 717; HdG no. 71; Jantzen 1912, 3; R, 64, 96, ill. op. 32; Steenhoff 1920, 165; Rothes 1921, 47, 48, fig. 81; Eisler 1923, 247-8, ill. 249; Val. 1926, 61; BM, 58 [*c.* 1658], 267; Val. 1927, 73; BM 1935, 162; Val. xiii, xvii, xxiv, no. 60 [*c.* 1660]; T, 36, 43, ill. 35; Oosterloo 1948, 172, fig. 51; BM 1954, 1, 24; R.C. Hekker & W.J. Berghuis, *B.K.N.O.B.*, 12 (1959), 81; Bille 1961, I, 34, 76, II, 21, 100; E. van Uitert, in *O.K.*, 12 (1968), 6-7, ill.; Amsterdam, R., cat. 1976, 317, no. C 149, ill.

The same room, with small changes, appears in the various versions of the Bedroom theme (see Cat. 40A-C, Plates 43, 44) and, with more significant architectural alterations, in Cat. 43 (Plate 47). The theme of a woman delousing a child's hair had been treated earlier by D. Hals, Terborch, Brekelenkam, and others.[7] Although the warm brown tonality resembles the subdued palette of paintings by Boursse, Bredius' attribution (which he later recanted) to that artist cannot be supported.

NOTES: [1] Descamps, III, 1753, 164; 'Chez M. Braamcamp... il y a un joli tableau qui représente le dedans de deux appartements, où sont deux figures'; compare Cat. 27 which also was in this collection. [2] Bastide 1766. [3] S no . 3 (with incorrect measurements). [4] Measurements reversed; S no. 4 mentions additional figures in the adjoining room (?). [5] Meusel, I, 1779, Part 2, 27. [6] S s no. 1 and the copy of the sale cat. at the RKD. [7] See Gudlaugsson, II, no. 95.

PRINT: C.L. van Kesteren (H. no. 7).

(a) Copy. By A. de Vries (1841–72). 50×57.5 cm. G. Koper Coll., Haarlem, 1968 (cf. *O.H.*, 69 [1968], 229).

(b) Copy. By W. J. Laquy (1738–98). Drwg. w/o m. Sale Van der Dussen, Amsterdam, 31/10/1774, A. no. 21. (With the original; see above.)

43. *A Young Couple with a Dog* (Plate 47)   *c.* 1660–5
Metropolitan Museum of Art, New York, inv. no. 14.40.613. Benjamin Altman Bequest, 1913.

Canvas 54.8×62.8 cm.

PROV.: (Poss.) Sale H.A.J. Munro, London, 1/6/1878, no. 313;[1] Rodolphe Kann, Paris, by 1892,[2] cats. (1900), no. 14, (1907), I, no. 52; dlr. Duveen, Paris, 1907.[3]

LIT.: HdG 1892, no. 71; W. Bode, *Gemäldesammlung des Herrn Rudolf Kann in Paris*, Vienna, 1900, no. 14, ill; Wurzbach, I, 717; *Catalogue de la collection Rodolphe Kann* (Sedelmeyer), Paris, I, 1907, no. 52, pl. 52; HdG nos. 74 [*c.* 1665] & (poss.) 241; F. Monod, in *G.B.A.*, 5e per., 8 (1923), 310 [*c.* 1665]; CB, 8; BM, 267 [*c.* 1670 or slightly earlier]; Val. 1927, 76, no. 8; Val. xvii, no. 61 [around 1660–2]; New York, M.M.A., cat. 1931, no. H 762.

The room resembles those in Cat. 42 (Plate 46) and the various versions of the Bedroom theme (Cat. 40A–C, Plates 43, 44). Here, however, the design of the tiled floor has become more complex (compare the floor pattern in Cat. 52, Plate 56, dated 1663) and the view of a garden has been exchanged for an adjoining room hung with gilt leather. Thus, while the design stems from De Hooch's later years in Delft, the new richness of the interior decoration may indicate origins in the early years of the artist's period in Amsterdam. The picture is in a poor state of preservation.

NOTES: [1] HdG no. 241: according to the catalogue description, the man is stroking the dog (?). [2] HdG 1892, no. 71, [3] HdG no. 74.

44. *A Woman and a Maid in a Courtyard* (Col. Plate X, Plate 48)   1660–1 or 1663
National Gallery, London, no. 794.

Canvas 73.7×62.6 cm. Signed and dated lower right: P · D · H · / 166 (?).

PROV.: On sale in Amsterdam, 1833;[1] Sale Comte de Perregaux, Paris, 8–9/12/1841, no. 14—Paillet (for Delessert[2]), 12,700 frs; Baron Delessert, Paris, 1841–69;[3] Sale Delessert, Paris, 15–18/3/1869, no. 31—Baxall (for the National Gallery), 43,000 frs.

EXH.: London 1976, no. 61, ill.

LIT.: S no. 37; S s no. 29; *Notices sur la collection de tableaux de MM. Delessert*, Paris, 1844, no. 57; 1846, no. 79; 1850, no. 82; 1860, no. 82; Blanc 1857–8, II, 447; Blanc 1863, 8; C. Blanc, in *G.B.A.*, 2e per., I (1869), 205; Vosmaer 1874, 146; Gower 1880, III.; Havard 1880, 99:2; Wedmore 1880, 53; HdG 1892, no. 36; HdG *c.* 1895, n.p., ill.; Armstrong 1904, 43; Wurzbach, I, 717; HdG no. 290 [1665]; Jantzen 1912, 25, 28; R, 17, 22, 28, 36, 49, 55, 99, ill. 18; Rothes 1921, 52, fig. 86; CB, 6–7 [1665]; Val. 1926, 62 [1665]; BM, 69 [1665]; Val. 1927, 69; Val. no. 38 [prob. 1655]; CB 1930, 198; London, N.G., pls. I, 149; MacLaren, 185–6, no. 794; Gerson 1966, 308 [1660].

The date formerly appeared as 1665. Valentiner[4] believed that it had been altered and should read 1655 or 6. When the picture was cleaned and the repaint removed the date was revealed to be 166(?). The courtyard space and the wall at the end of the garden are reminiscent of Delft scenery. Thus, the picture was probably executed just prior to De Hooch's move to Amsterdam in 1660–1, or perhaps on his return visit to the city in 1663. As MacLaren noted, the work closely resembles the courtyards of 1658. Thus, a date of *c.* 1660–1 seems most plausible.

NOTES: [1] S no. 37. [2] S s no. 29. [3] See the various cats. of the collection. [4] Val. no. 38.

PRINT: P.J. Arendzen (cf. HdG *c.* 1895).

45. *A Girl with a Basket in a Garden* (Plate 49)   1661?
Kunstmuseum, Basel, acc. no. G.1958.22. Gift of Max Geldner, 1958.

Canvas 69.5×59 cm. Signed left on windowsill: P D hoo[c]h 1651 (altered)

PROV.: Private Collection, England, sold to dlr. Sully, before 1912;[1] dlr. Duveen, Paris, 1912;[2] dlr. Sedelmeyer, Paris, cat. 1913, no. 13, ill.; dlr. Duveen, 1925;[3] Sir Alfred Mond, London, 1927;[4] Lord Melchett, London, 1929;[5] P.C., Holland, 1934;[6] dlr. D. Katz, Dieren, 1934–6;[7] Schaeffer Gallery, New York, by 1936;[8] dlr. M. Sterner 4/1942;[9] Max Geldner.

EXH.: (a) Paris (Sedelmeyer) 1913, no. 13, ill. [s. & d. 1661]; (b) Detroit 1925, no. 12. [1651]; (c) London, R.A., 1929, no. 344 [1651]; (d) Arnhem 1934, no. 62 [1651]; (e) Haarlem (Katz) 1934, no. 1 [1651]; (f) Rotterdam 1935, no. 38, fig. 41 [1651]; (g) Amsterdam 1935, no. 152 [165(4?)]; (h) Amsterdam 1936, no. 78 [1651].

LIT.: W.R. Valentiner, in *American Magazine of Art*, 3/1925, 126; F. Freund, in *Cicerone*, 17 (5/1925), 463 [1651], ill. 462; Val. 1926, 52, 57 [1651], fig. 1; BM, 66–8, 67 [1661?]; Val. 1927, 73; Bredius 1928, 65; Val. xvii, no 46 [s. & d. 'in white' (?) 1651 or 1657]; I.Q. van Regteren Altena, *M.B.K.*, 7, 1930, 380; T, 30–1 [1657?], 47, ill. 19; *Das Vermächtnis Max Geldner*, Öffentliche Kunstsammlung, Basel, 1958, 13, ill.; Basel, Kunstm., cat. 1966, 150 [1651], ill.; Gerson 1966, 310.

The date on the work now reads 1651; the '5' is the most heavily drawn of the numerals. This date, however, is clearly too early. While it has been read variously (see references above), it was first deciphered as 1661 when the work was with Sedelmeyer in 1913. Such a reading is consistent with the style which may be compared with that of Cat. 44 (Plate 48) of 1660–1 or 1663. The date may have been altered when the picture was cleaned sometime after 1913 and before 1927.[10] The cleaning revealed a man's portrait on the shutter of the window.[11] The gabled building in the distance appears (with minor architectural alterations) in the background of Cat. 46.

NOTES: [1] HdGf. [2] BM, 68. [3] Exh. b. [4] BM, 68. [5] Exh. c. [6] Exh. d. [7] Exh. e, f, g, h. [8] *Parnassus*, 8 (12/1936), 24. [9] FARL photo. [10] BM, 67–8; Brière-Misme was the only writer who argued for a dating of 1661. [11] Compare the old state of the picture, Val. no. 46.

46. *A Woman and a Maid with a Pail in a Courtyard* (Col. Plate XI)   1660–5
Hermitage, Leningrad, no. 943.

Canvas 53 × 42 cm.

PROV.: Sale Langeac, Paris, 14–15/12/1808, no. 36—La Fontaine, 1100 frs; acq. soon thereafter by Czar Alexander I; in the Hermitage since 1810.

EXH.: The Hague–Paris 1966, no. 24, ill.

LIT.: S s no. 3; Waagen 1862, 114; Blanc 1863, 8; Waagen 1864, 140, no. 860; Lemcke 1878, 8; Gower 1880, 112; Havard

1880, 100:1; HdG 1892, no. 75; Wurzbach, I, 717; HdG no. 41 [1658–60]; Jantzen 1912, 23; R, 44, 45, 104, ill. op. 46; Rothes 1921, 52, fig. 88; CB, 6–7 [c. 1664–5]; BM, 68 [c. 1661]; Val. 1927, 69 [earlier than 1665]; Val. xiii, xvii, no. 47 [c. 1657]; T, 28, 30–1; Leningrad, Hermitage, cat. 1958, no. 943, fig. 179; S.J. Gudlaugsson in O.H., 83 (1968), 31.

Brière-Misme correctly recognized the painting's resemblance to Cat. 45 (Plate 49), which probably was once dated 1661. The cooler tonality and slicker execution (Waagen somewhat exaggeratedly likened it to Dou's manner) of the present work may indicate a slightly later date. At any rate, the broad canal visible through the gate at the left is more appropriate to settings in Amsterdam than in Delft and one may probably assume, therefore, that the work postdates April 1660. Highly individualized, the seated woman may be a portrait. The picture has recently been cleaned and appears in superb condition.

(a) Copy. By W. Hendriks. Watercolour 29×22.5 cm. PROV.: Sale Heemskerk, Haarlem, 26/5/1809, no. 62; Sale J. Goll van Frankenstein, Amsterdam, 1/7/1833, FF no. 11; Sale Amsterdam, 20/11/1843, T no. 3; Sale Amsterdam, 14/2/1855, C. no. 82—Engelbertz, 11 fl; Sale Amsterdam, 17/10/1874, no. 547; Sale H.M. Montauban van Swyndregt et al., Amsterdam, 5/4/1906, no. 87; Sale Jhr. A. Boreel et al., Amsterdam, 15/6/1908, no. 267—Hofstede de Groot; now RKD.

47. *A Soldier Smoking, with a Woman by a Hearth*★
(Plate 50)   *c.* 1660–3
Baron van der Feltz, Holland.

Canvas 71.5×54 cm.

PROV.: Private Collection, Wiesbaden;[1] Mr. Weid, Amsterdam; Sale Dr. L.D. van Hengel, Dieren, 19/5/1953, no. 357, ill. [H. van der Burch]—Baron van der Feltz; Sale London, 21/6/1968, no. 36, ill. (bought in).

LIT.: *Connaissance des Arts*, 1969, no. 1.

Several writers discussed a copy (with minor changes; see 'a' below) as the original. Gudlaugsson astutely observed the resemblance in style of the present work to the painting in Cleveland of 1663 (Cat. 53, Col. Plate XII).[2] Discussing the copy, which he attributed to Van der Burch, Valentiner compared the seated smoker to his counterpart in our Cat. 23 and other details to elements of a painting probably correctly attributed to Van der Burch in the Frick Collection (cat. 1968 II, 147).[3] The latter picture is undoubtedly by a different hand and probably postdates the present work. A serving boy who appears at the open door in the copy probably also originally figured in this picture. On the back wall hangs a large map of the Seventeen Provinces.

NOTES: [1] For this and the following entry, communication A.C.A.W. Baron van der Feltz. [2] Letter (15/6/1957) to Baron van der Feltz. [3] Val. no. 231 (below).

(a) Copy with changes. Present location unknown. Panel 68.5×52 cm. PROV.: Sale J.L. Menke, Antwerp, 1/6/1904, no. 54, ill. [Ochtervelt]; E. van Gutmann, Vienna;[1] Max Freiherr von Goldschmidt-Rothschild, Frankfurt a.M., 1925;[2] G. Oberlaender, Reading, Pa., by 1929;[3] Sale G. Oberlaender, New York, 25/5/1939, no. 230 [H. van der Burch].[4] EXH.: Frankfurt am Main 1925, no. 110 (no. 104, pl. 97 in enlarged cat. of 1926). LIT.: HdG no. 251 ['poss. by P.d.H.']; R, 97; BM, 72, n. 3 [P.d.H.]; Val. no. 232 [H. van der Burch]. Several different states of the picture are documented in

photographs. The three-legged table, the landscape on the rear wall, the serving boy at the door, and other details do not appear in the original.

NOTES: [1] Exh. [2] Exh. [3] Val. no. 232.

48. *A Woman Preparing Bread and Butter for a Boy*
(Plate 51)   *c.* 1660–3
Kunstmuseum, Düsseldorf, inv. no. D–16/70. On loan from the Bentinck–Thyssen Collection.

Canvas 65×52 cm. Signed lower right on footwarmer: P. d hooch

PROV.: Sale Amsterdam, 16/4/1750, no. 4—57 fl; Sale J. Gildemeester Jansz., Amsterdam, 11–13/6/1800, no. 74[1]—Yver, 415 fl; Sale A. Meynts, Amsterdam, 15/7/1823, no. 44—Brondgeest, 1450 fl; Baron J.G. Verstolk van Soelen, The Hague, 1833;[2] sold to M.H. Bingham Mildmay, 29/6/1846;[3] Sale H. Bingham Mildmay, London, 24/6/1843, no. 30, ill.—Colnaghi & Lawrie, £2625; Sir George Drummond, Montreal, by 1907;[4] Sale Drummond, London, 26/6/1919, no. 185, ill.—Knoedler's, 7600 gns; Andrew W. Mellon, Washington, before 1927;[5] Schloss Rohoncz Collection, Recnitz, Hungary, later Baron Thyssen-Bornemisza, Lugano-Castagnola, cat. (1937), no. 200.

EXH.: (a) London, R.A., 1876, no. 205; (b) Munich 1930, no. 158, pl. 56; (c) Munich, Alte Pinakothek, 1931; (d) Paris, I.N., 1965, no. 28, pl. IX; (e) Paris 1970, no. 28, pl. 9; (f) Bielefeld 1973, no. 9, ill. 16.

LIT.: Hoet 1752, II, 288; S no. 54; Waagen 1857, 342; Havard 1880, 96:1; HdG 1892, no. 48; Roberts 1897, II, 220; Bode 1906, 59; Wurzbach, I, 717; HdG no. 10; Val. 1910a, 5, no. 1; R, 105; BM, 72, ill. 71; Val. 1927, 76, no. 9; *A.N.*, 27 (2/1929), 5, ill.; 28 (8/1930) 16, ill.; Val. no. 64 [c. 1662]; T, 36, ill. 37.

With its darkened foreground, backlighted view to a street, and upright format, the design resembles aspects of Cat. 49. Both works must have been executed toward the end of the artist's years in Delft or soon after his arrival in Amsterdam. The boy, who appears to be saying grace while his mother prepares his breakfast, is undoubtedly on his way to the school (identified by the sign inscribed 'Schole') which can be seen through the doorway. A woman buttering bread also appears in a very late work (Cat. 142).

NOTES: [1] As on panel (?). [2] S no. 10, valued at 200 gns. [3] See W.H.J. Weale, *A Descriptive Catalogue of the Collection of the Earl of Northbrook*, London, 1889, in which a list of works which were in the Verstolk van Soelen collection is appended. The picture appears as no. 13. [4] HdG no. 10. [5] BM, 72; Val. no. 64.

49. *A Boy Handing a Woman a Basket in a Doorway*
(Plate 52)   *c.* 1660–3
Wallace Collection, London, P 27.

Canvas 74×60 cm. Signed lower right: P D [H]

PROV.: Sale M.T. Andrioli, widow of J. Cliquet, Amsterdam, 18/7/1803, no. 19—C.S. Roos, 800 fl; Baron van Brienen van de Grootelindt, Amsterdam, by 1833;[1] Sale Van Brienen, Paris, 8–9/5/1865, no. 14—Lord Hertford, 50,000 frs; Sir Richard and Lady Wallace, London.

EXH.: (a) Bethnal Green 1872–5, no. 99; (b) London, R.A., 1893, no. 60.

LIT.: S no. 45; Inventory of the Van Brienen Collection, 1854 (Municipal Archives, Amsterdam, Prot. Not. J.P. van

Etten, N.A.A., 21684, 28/12/1854); Vosmaer 1874, 146; Havard 1880, 103:1, 104:1, HdG 1892, no. 52; Wurzbach, I, 717; HdG no. 34 [1664]; R, 16, 28, 100, ill. 22; Rothes 1921, 51, fig. 80; CB, 6–7 [c. 1664], pl. VII; BM, 71–2, Val. xiii, xvii, no. 63 [c. 1662]; London, Wallace Coll., cat. 1968, no. P 27 [c. 1664–5], ill.

The view, which extends through a small courtyard and hallway into the street and ultimately to the doorway of a building on the opposite side of a canal, resembles the view through the doorway in Cat. 51 (Plate 54). The coats of arms in the window no doubt were those of the owners or previous inhabitants of the house. At the left, beneath the mono-grammed dexter shield, the name 'Cornelis Jansz' or 'Jac' appears; on the right, beneath the sinister shield, the name 'Marnie' or 'Maerti'. The commonness of these names and the absence of a system for identifying such monograms has so far frustrated efforts to identify the bearers of the coats of arms. The shield above the archway in the courtyard, with a dark-blue or black band on a yellow or gold field, is un-usually simple and may be the artist's invention.

NOTES: [1] S no. 45; see also Van Brienen inv. 1854, valuation: 8000 fl.

50. *A Woman Reading, with a Child*★ (Plate 53) c. 1662–6
Present location unknown.
Canvas 58× 76 cm.
PROV.: (Poss.) Sale Maystre of Geneva, Paris, 17/4/1809, no. 35—500 frs;[1] (prob.) Sale J.L. La Neuville, Paris, 6/11/1811, no. 54 (w/o m.)—332 frs; The Duke of Arenberg, Brussels, by 1855[2] until after 1936.[3]
EXH.: (a) Arenberg Ducal Palace, 1855;[4] (b) Düsseldorf 1904, no. 326.
LIT.: Blanc 1857–8, II, 285; W. Bürger (T. Thoré), *Galerie d'Arenberg à Bruxelles*, Brussels, 1859, 37–8; Lafenestre-Richtenberger 1896, 141, ill. 140; Bode 1906, 60; Wurzbach, I, 717; HdG nos. 5 & poss. 18; W. Martin, in *M.f.K.*, I (1908), 742, fig. 9; R, 28, 29, 96, ill. op. 60; Rothes 1921, 51, fig. 77; Eisler 1923, 256; CB, 5, 6, [c. 1659]; BM, 72; Val. no. 66 [c. 1662]; Martin 1935–6, I, fig. 10, II, 203; T, 38–9, ill.

According to Hofstede de Groot the painting was slightly overcleaned and beneath the retouching on the table the original drawing was somewhat different. This retouching was said to extend under the edge of the frame. Thoré-Bürger identified the subject of the painting at the left as Perseus and Andromeda and according to the author of the Habich Sale (Cologne, 9/5/1892) the original picture appeared there as no. 149 (as attributed to an unknown artist of the School of Rubens).[5] While the deep view through a doorway resembles that in Cat. 49 (Plate 52), the breadth and spaciousness of the horizontal composition and the somewhat squatter figure types may indicate a slightly later date.

NOTES: [1] cf. HdG no. 18; the dimensions are correct, but the figure crossing the courtyard is said to be a woman. [2] Exh. a. [3] Martin 1935–6, II, 203. [4] Thoré-Bürger, *Gal. Arenberg*, 1859, no. 27. [5] The same theme is also treated in a painting in one of C. van der Lamen's genre scenes, repr. Bernt, II, no. 657.

Possible Versions (known only from descriptions):

50A. (See above, Maystre Sale, 1809; HdG no. 18).

50B. Version or copy? Panel 25.5× 30.4 cm. Sale A. Miron of Orleans, Paris, 17/3/1823, no. 44 (HdG no. 21).

(a) Copy. (Photo Witt.) By F. du Mesnil, 1777. 63.5× 81.3 cm. Sale Sadler et al. (a.c.), London, 16/6/1950, no. 151.

(b) Copy. Canvas 57× 73 cm. Sale V. Guibert, Paris, 8/12/1964, no. 36, ill.

(c) Copy (with minor changes). Panel 55× 63 cm. PROV.: Marcell de Nemes, Budapest; Fearson Gallery, New York, 1923; E.W. Edwards, Cincinnati, 1929; Sale London, 29/11/1974, no. 56. (Wrongly attributed by Valentiner [Val. no. 194 (above)] to P. Janssens Elinga and incorrectly identified as HdG no. 21).

(d) Copy (right side only). Canvas 54× 47.5 cm. Sale Van den Schriek of Louvain, Brussels, 8/4/1861, no. 160 [after P.d.H.]; Sale B[oitelle], Paris, 10/1/1867, no. 112 [attr. to P.d.H.].

(e) Copy (right side only). (Same as the above?) Sale, Paris, 14–25/1/1825, no. 46 [w/o m.; style of P.d.H.].

(f) Copy (right side only). (Same as copy (d)?) Canvas 60× 40 cm. Signed: 'P. de Hoogh'. Musée des Beaux-Arts, Lyon.

(g) Copy (right side only). (Photo RKD.) Present location unknown.

(h) Copy (right side only; without woman). Canvas 60× 51 cm. Sale Brussels, 8–9/12/1959, no. 408, ill. [attr. to P.d.H.]; Sale Scarsdale et al. (a.c.), London, 16/11/1960, no. 138.

51. *A Woman Lacing her Bodice beside a Cradle*
(Plates 54, 55)   c. 1661–3
Staatliche Museen, Gemäldegalerie, Berlin–Dahlem, no. 820B.
Canvas 92× 100 cm.
PROV.: Sale Marin, Paris, 22/3/1790, no. 102—Saubert, 1500 frs; Madame Hoffman, Haarlem, 1827;[1] bought in 1846 by Nieuwenhuys from the executors of the Hoffman estate;[2] Sale Schneider, 6–7/4/1876, no. 13—Berlin Museum, 135,000 frs.
EXH.: (a) Washington 1948, no. 99; (b) New York et al. 1948–9, no. 63; (c) Brussels 1950, no. 57, pl. 82 [c. 1659–60]; (d) Amsterdam 1950, no. 57, fig. 97; (e) Paris 1951, no. 91, pl. 118.
LIT.: S nos. 9 & 52 [description reversed]; S s no. 26; L. Wronski, in *R.d.A.*, 5 (1876), 16 [N. Maes]; L. Gonse, in *R.d.A.*, 5 (1876), 72; Gower 1880, 90:3, 93:2; HdG 1892, no. 16; Bode 1906, 59; Wurzbach, I, 716; HdG no. 3; Jantzen 1912, 13–18; R, 16, 27, 39, 43, 101, ill. op. 26; Bode 1919, 308; Lilienfeld 1924, 453; CB, 6, 7 [c. 1665]; Val. 1926, 61 [before 1663]; BM, 58, 62; Val. xvii, no. 56 [c. 1659–60]; T, 35–6, ill. 31; BM 1954, 78–9, fig. 6; Gerson 1966, 310; Rosenberg-Slive-TerKuile, 125, pl. 100B; Robinson 1974, 62, 83, n. 93; Berlin–Dahlem, St.M., cat. 1975, 206, no. 820B [c. 1659–60].

The palette, figural types and strong tonal contrasts relate the picture to Cat. 48 and 49 (Plates 51, 52). In scale, design and execution it most resembles the *Family Portrait* of 1663 (Cat. 53, Col. Plate XII). The two pictures share a relatively finer touch than has previously been encountered in De Hooch's work. The canvas is one of the largest of the artist's paintings of domestic themes.

NOTES: [1] S no. 52. [2] Annotation in Smith's personal copy of his *catalogue raisonné* (HdGf).
PRINT: A. Lalauze (cf. Schneider sale cat.)

(a) Copy. By Sara Troost (1731–1803). Drwg. w/o m. Sale C. Ploos van Amstel, Amsterdam, 3/3/1800, W no. 16.

52. *Two Women Beside a Linen Chest, with a Child*
(Plate 56)   1663

Rijksmuseum, Amsterdam, no. C 1191. On loan from the City of Amsterdam since 1928.

Canvas 72×77.5 cm. Signed and dated lower right: P d HOOCH / 1663

PROV.: Baron Lockhorst, Rotterdam, 1726;[1] *Sale Amsterdam, 8/6/1763, no. 138—Rendorp, 215 fl; Sale J. Rendorp, Amsterdam, 16/10/1793 (delayed to 9-10/7/1794), no. 25[2]—Coclers, 295 fl; bought in Scotland by J. Smith, £500;[3] Six van Hillegom, Amsterdam, by 1833;[4] Sale Six, Amsterdam, 16/10/1928, no. 15, ill.—Vereeniging Rembrandt.

EXH.: (a) Amsterdam 1872, no. 110 [1667]; (b) 1900, no. 46; (c) 1935, no. 158; (d) New York 1939, no. 202, pl. 75; (e) Detroit 1939, no. 25, ill.; (f) Pittsburgh–St. Louis 1940, no. 34, pl. 10; (g) Newark 1940, no. 22; (h) Cincinnati 1941, no. 39, pl. 9; (i) Detroit 1941, no. 33; (j) Montreal 1942, no. 17, ill.; (k) New York (Duveen) 1942, no. 10, ill.; (l) Chicago 1942, no. 21, ill.; (m) Rome 1956-7, no. 137, pl. 33; (n) Stockholm 1959, no. 226.

LIT.: S no. 38 [1663]; Thoré-Bürger 1858-60, I, 99; H. Havard, in *G.B.A.*, 2e per., 6 (1872), 380-1; H. Havard, *Les merveilles de l'art hollandais exposées à Amsterdam en 1872*, 1873, 57-8; Gower 1880, 111.; Havard 1880, 87, 109:2 [1667]; HdG 1892, no. 13; Wurzbach, I, 716; HdG no. 25; Jantzen 1912, 27; R, 16, 21, 35, 54, 96, ill. op. 10; Rothes 1921, 47, 50, fig. 73; Eisler 1923, 256; CB, 6; Val. 1926, 58 n. 2, 61; BM 71, 72; Val. 1927, 69; Val. xiii, xvii, xxii, no. 69; Martin 1935-6, II, 107; Von Weiher 1937, 114; T, 42-3, 50, ill. 42; E. Moses, in *The Pacific Art Review*, I (1941), 33-6, fig. 1; Keyszelitz 1956, 66; MacLaren, 184; Gerson 1966, 310; Slive-Rosenberg-TerKuile, 126, fig. 103; F.F. Mendels, *Spiegel Hist.*, 4 (1969), 543, fig. 2; Robinson, in exh. cat. St. Petersburg-Atlanta, 1975, 44, n. 1; Amsterdam, R., cat. 1976, 316, no. C 191, ill; Eisler 1977, 153.

Although the date has sometimes been read as 1667, Smith deciphered it as 1663 in the first published reference to the picture. Thus, together with Cat. 53 (Col. Plate XII) the work bears the earliest certain date among the paintings from the artist's years in Amsterdam. The small statue of Perseus with the head of Medusa perched above the doorway appeared when the picture was cleaned in 1928.

NOTES: [1] S no. 38: according to the author the picture was sold with the Lockhorst collection and then was taken to Scotland, from whence Smith purchased the picture. However, it was sold twice in Amsterdam later in the eighteenth century and presumably did not reach the Scottish collection until after 1794. [2] As on panel (?). [3] See note 1. [4] S no. 38.

53. *Family Portrait Group Making Music* (Col. Plate XII, Plate 57)   1663

The Cleveland Museum of Art, Cleveland, acc. no. 51.355. Gift of the Hanna Fund, 1951.

Canvas 100×119 cm. Signed lower left P D HOOCH [16]63

PROV.: Lord Wharncliffe, by 1829;[1] bought by Smith between 1833 & 1842;[2] W. Theobald, by 1842;[3] Sale Theobald, London, 10/5/1851, no. 76—£115; Private Collection, Yorkshire;[4] E.E. Cook, Bath;[5] dlr. Scott & Fowles, New York.[6]

EXH.: (a) London, B.I., 1929, no. 165; (b) Newark, Museum, 1955 (no cat.); (c) Omaha, Joslyn Art Mus., 1957 (no cat.); (d) Cleveland 1958, no. 58, ill. [c. 1668-70]; (e) Kansas City 1967-8, no. 5, ill. 13; (f) Cleveland, C.M.A., 1973 (no cat.).

LIT.: S no. 63; S s no. 27; Havard 1880, 122:1; HdG no. 157; R, 101; L.H. Burchfield, in *Bull.*, C.M.A., 39 (1952), 121-3, ill.; Staring 1956, 86, pl. x; Cleveland, M.A., *Handbook*, 1958, no. 447; Gerson 1966, 310; Cleveland, M.A., *Handbook*, 1969, 126, ill.; Praz 1971, 184, 190, fig. 151; P. Eikemeier, in *P.*, 32 (1974), 260 n. 6; S. Sherrill, in *Antiques*, 109 (1976), 163-5, pl. XXI.

The signature and date were discovered by the present author. The picture above the fireplace probably represents the Sacrifice of Isaac;[7] its subject was first identified by W.H. Gerdts Jr.[8] The carpet on the table resembles so-called Transylvanian church carpets.[9] The two vases on top of the oak wardrobe were identified by W. Stechow as of the Kang-hsi type.[10] While the lacquer boxes may be of East Asian origin, Stechow noted that such work was also done in Amsterdam from c. 1600 onward. Three musicians play an alto recorder, a small citern, and a violin while the fourth beats time. A viola da gamba stands on the left.

NOTES: [1] Exh. a. [2] S no. 63 & S s no. 27. [3] S s no. 27. [4] Exh. d. [5] Exh. d. [6] C.M.A. files. [7] Not the Descent from the Cross as suggested by Burchfield, 1952. [8] Letter to C.M.A., 22/11/1955. [9] See Sherrill, 1976, [10] C.M.A. files.

54. *A Woman with an Infant and a Serving Woman with a Child* (Col. Plate XIII)   c. 1663-5

Kunsthistorisches Museum, Vienna, inv. no. 5976. Bequeathed by Karl and Rosalie Goldschmidt, 1903.

Canvas 64×76 cm.

PROV.: Sale Helsleuter (Van Eyl Sluyter?), Paris, 25/1/1802, no. 72—Constantin, 1500 frs; Sale E.M. Engelberts et al., Amsterdam, 25/8/1817, no. 90—De Vries, 770 fl; Sale Widow of J.H. Molkenboer, née Schenkhuizen, Amsterdam, 6/9/1853, no. 11—Derksen or Meffre, 1575 fl; *Sale La Comtesse Lehan, Paris, 2-3/4/1861, no. 14;[1] *Sale Marquis de la Rochebousseau, Paris, 5-8/5/1873, no. 175—5550 frs; Sale J. Wilson, Paris, 14/3/1881, no. 63—Malinet, 12,000 frs; Sale [Brame], Paris, 20/3/1883, no. 26; Sale A.J. Bösch, Vienna, 28/4/1885, no. 25, ill.—Grünwald, 2520 fl; Karl and Rosalie Goldschmidt, Vienna.

EXH.: (a) Zurich 1946-7, no. 318 [c. 1670-5]; (b) 1953, no. 68 [c. 1670-5]; (c) Rome 1954, no. 67, pl. 35.

LIT.: S no. 12; Blanc 1863, 8; H. Perrier, in *G.B.A.*, 2e per., 7 (1873), 362; Havard 1880, 115:1; HdG no. 66; Wurzbach, II, 102; R, 16, 56, 61, 86, 102, ill. op. 34; M. Eisler in *J.S.K.*, 33 (1916), 280, pl. 32; CB, 6, 7, [c. 1663?]; BM, 264; Val. no. 118 [c. 1670-5]; BM 1947-48, IV, 365, fig. 9.

A date of 1663-5 (Collins Baker suggested 'c. 1663') is preferable to the date of c. 1670-5 proposed by Valentiner. The refined execution, strong local colouration and elegantly restrained horizontal composition recall the works of the early to mid-1660s. The motif of a child urging a serving woman to depart on her errands reappears in Cat. 88 (Plate 91) and striped wall-hangings also figure in Cat. 66, 77 and 78 (Plates 71, 80, 81).

55. *An Officer and a Woman Conversing, and a Soldier at a Window* (Plate 58)   c. 1663-5

Germanisches Museum, Nuremberg, no. 406.

Canvas 60×63 cm. Signed left on chairback: P D HOOCH

PROV.: (Poss.) Private Collection, Regensburg, 1833;[1] Landauerbrüderhaus, Nuremberg, 1840;[2] Germanisches Museum, cat. (1886), no. 320.

LIT.: S no. 68; Waagen 1843–5, I, 209; Parthey 1863–4, I, 622; Gower 1880, 112; Havard 1880, 115:2, 129:1; HdG 1892, no. 67; Bode 1906, 58 [*c.* 1658]; Wurzbach, I, 717; HdG no. 194; Nuremberg, G.M., cat. 1909, no. 406; R, 102; BM, 74; Val. no. 72 [*c.* 1663]; Würtenberger 1937, 84.

The picture is probably roughly contemporary with the painting in the Rijksmuseum of 1663 (Cat. 52, Plate 56). With its horizontal composition and gilt leather wall-hanging it may be compared with the other merry company scenes of this period (Cat. 56–8, Plates 59–61).

NOTES: [1] S no. 68; Hofstede de Groot (see HdG no. 194) believed Smith was in error and incorrectly stated that the picture was identical with the painting appearing in the De Groot Sale of 1804; this was the painting in Philadelphia by H. van der Burch (Val. no. 234). [2] *Verzeichnis der Königlichen und städtischen Gemälde, die in der königlichen Gemäldegalerie in Nürnberg im Landauerbrüderhaus aufgestellt sind*, Nuremberg, 1840, no. 63.

(a) Copy. Canvas on panel 58×66 cm. Sale Denant et al., Berlin, 27/10/1903, no. 42.

56. *A Party of Four Figures at a Table* (Plate 59) *c.* 1663–5
Metropolitan Museum of Art, New York, no. P 100. Robert Lehman Collection, 1975.

Signed lower left on crosspiece of chair: P · D · HOOCH

PROV.: Everill collection (?);[1] Samuel S. Joseph, London, by 1892;[2] later Mrs. Joseph, who sold it to dlr. Knoedler, who sold it to Philip Lehman.[3]

EXH.: (a) London, R.A., 1894, no. 78; (b) Colorado Springs 1951–2, n.p., ill.; (c) Paris 1957, no. 26, pl. 30; (d) Cincinnati 1959, no. 136, ill.

LIT.: HdG 1892, no. 47; C. Hofstede de Groot, in *R.f.K.*, 17 (1894), 172; Wurzbach, I, 717; HdG no. 187; R, 100; BM 1921, 343; BM, 72–3; Val. 1927, 77, no. 23, ill. op. 70; Val. no. 78 [*c.* 1665]; CB 1930, 198; A.L. Mayer, in *P.*, 5 (1930), 118, ill.; T.A. Heinrich, in *Bull.*, M.M.A., 12 (1954), 202, ill. 229; Szabo 1975, 75, ill. no. 80; W.H. Vroom, in *Bull. v. h. Rijksmuseum*, 27 (1979), 10, ill.

The picture was enlarged by about 2 cm. on all sides during a relining which took place sometime before the picture was cleaned by W. Suhr in 1953. In design and execution it most resembles Cat. 57 (Plate 60); compare also Cat. 55 and 58 (Plates 58, 61). At the right a young man saunters down a passageway to meet an old man leaning on a stick at the door. The motif may be designed to recall themes such as Lazarus at the Rich Man's Door, or Rich Children, Poor Elders (see Cat. B13, Plate 177),[4] in which wealth and poverty are juxtaposed for admonitory purposes. The picture of Adam and Eve embracing after the Fall may also be intended as a cautionary note to the scene of merry-making in the foreground.

NOTES: [1] HdG no. 187. [2] Exh. a. [3] BM, 72, n. 5. [4] Compare D. Hals's treatment of the theme, Landesmuseum, Oldenburg, repr. *Die Sprache der Bilder*, exh., Braunschweig, 1978, cat. no. 13,

57. *A Party of Five Figures, with a Man Entering from a Doorway* (Plate 60) *c.* 1663–5
Museu Nacional de Arte Antiga, Lisbon, inv. no. 1620–P. Palácio Nacional da Ajuda, 1920.

Signed lower left on crosspiece of chair: P D Hooch

PROV.: Royal Collections (since early eighteenth century?[1]).

EXH.: (a) Rotterdam 1935, no. 47, fig. 50; (b) Amsterdam 1976, no. 29, ill. 130.

LIT.: BM 1921, 340–4 [*c.* 1670]; Lilienfeld 1924, 454; BM, 73 [*c.* 1670]; Val. no. 79 [*c.* 1665]; CB 1930, 198; Lisbon, Mus., cat. 1956, no. 198.

Pentimenti appear around the heads of the man pulling the bell-cord and the fiddler seated beside him. Both figures probably initially wore broad-brimmed hats. In design the work is closest to Cat. 56 (Plate 59), and in paint application to Cat. 58 (Plate 61). The colouration is highly varied and intense, in a fashion similar to the paintings of 1663 in the Rijksmuseum (Cat. 52, Plate 56) and of 1665 in Lord Barnard's collection (Cat. 69, Plate 72). Although somewhat dirty, the picture appears to be in a fine state of preservation.

NOTES: [1] Brière-Misme speculated that the picture could have been acquired by Mariette with Count Fraula's collection for King Juan V between 1725 and 1727. However, there is no proof that the King acquired the collection or this picture.

58. *Card Players beside a Fireplace, with an Embracing Couple and a Serving Boy* (Plate 61) *c.* 1663–5
Louvre, Paris, inv. no. 1373.

Canvas 67×77 cm. Signed lower left on base of column: P · D · HOOCH

PROV.: (Poss.) Wassenaar van Obdam, The Hague, 1750;[1] Sale Comte du Barry, Paris, 15/12/1777, no. 175—680 frs; Sale C. Tolozan, Paris, 28/2/1801, no. 54—St. Martin [for the Musée Napoleon[2]], 1350 frs; Musée Napoleon, Paris, cat. (1801), no. 330.

LIT.: S no. 5; Nagler 1838, 291; Waagen 1839, 600; Kramm 1859, 733; Thoré-Bürger 1860, 317; Waagen 1862, 13; Blanc 1863, 6, 8, ill. 5; Villot 1865, II, 224; Thoré-Bürger 1866, 316; Vosmaer 1874, 146; Fromentin 1876, 328–9; Gower 1880, 70–1, 112; Havard 1880, 54–5; HdG 1892, no. 69; Wurzbach, I, 717; HdG no. 255; Jantzen 1912, 30–1; R, 27, 87, 97, ill. op. 42; BM 1921, 341; Demonts 1922, 118, no. 2415; CB, 6–7 [*c.* 1664], pl. VI; BM, 73 [*c.* 1668], 74; Val. no. 77 [*c.* 1665]; CB 1930, 198; Martin 1935–6, II, 206 [*c.* 1665], fig. 106; Würtenberger 1937, 84, pl. XXI; BM 1947–8, III, 163, fig. 4; T. Lunsingh Scheurleer, in *Bull.*, Rijksmuseum, 2 (1954), 86 ff.; Gerson 1966, 308, ill. 312; Foucart 1976, 31; De Jongh et al., in exh. cat. Amsterdam 1976, 153, n. 4.

In composition the picture recalls the painting of 1663 in Cleveland (Cat. 53, Col. Plate XII). Like the stylistically related painting in Lisbon (Cat. 57, Plate 60), however, it probably slightly postdates the Cleveland painting. T. Lunsingh Scheurleer has noted that a fragment of gilt leather preserved in the Rijksmuseum has a similar pattern to that of the wall-hangings in the painting. The motifs of cupids and roses in this pattern, like the ace of hearts shown by the seated woman to her standing companion, probably are intended to reinforce the painting's amorous associations.

NOTES: [1] The author of the Tolozan sale catalogue incorrectly stated that the picture was in the W. van Obdam sale (The Hague, 19/8/1750; Hoet 1752, II, 290). Whether it was ever part of the latter collection is unknown. [2] Villot 1865, II, no. 224.

PRINT: Sargent (cf. Blanc 1863, 5).

(a) Copy. Canvas 65×77 cm. Sale Festetics, Amsterdam, 22/1/1834, no. 69; Sale Reston, London, 21/5/1898, no. 75.

(b) Copy. Panel 45×59 cm. Sale Minnigerode–Allerburg et al., Berlin 16/10/1917, no. 62, pl. 5.

(c) Copy. W/o m. Sale Roqueplan, Paris, 14/12/1855, no. 98— Rousseau, 17 frs.

(d) Copy. (Photo RKD.) By H. Poterlet.

(e) Copy (of woman playing cards only). By R.P. Bonington (1802–28). Drwg. 13.5×7.5 cm. Castle Museum & Art Gallery, Nottingham.

59. *Three Figures at a Table in a Garden*   (Plates 62, 63)
                                                 c. 1663–5
Rijksmuseum, Amsterdam, no. C 150. On loan from the City of Amsterdam since 1885.

Canvas 61×47 cm. Signed lower left on bench: P D HOOCH

PROV.: Brought to England by Chaplin;[1] O'Neil Collection, 1832;[2] Van der Hoop Collection, by 1842;[3] gift to the city in 1854.

EXH.: (a) Paris 1921, no. 24; (b) Rotterdam 1935, no. 48, fig. 51; (c) Amsterdam 1935, no. 155; ill.; (d) Brussels 1946, no. 55, pl. 88; (e) Paris 1950–1, no. 45 [*c.* 1665], pl. 32; (f) Zurich 1953, no. 67 [*c.* 1665]; (g) Rome 1954, no. 66.

LIT.: S no. 61; S s no. 25; Thoré-Bürger 1858–60, II, 61–2, no. 57; Waagen 1862, 113; Amsterdam, V.d.H. Mus., cat. 1872, no. 53; Van Vloten 1874, 298; Vosmaer 1874, 146; Van der Kellen 1876, 152, ill.; Lemcke 1878, 10, ill. 9; Havard 1880, 62, 124:3; Havard 1881, 187; HdG 1892, no. 6; Wurzbach, I, 716; HdG no. 286 [1660–5]; Jantzen 1912, 20, 22, 27; R, 71, 96, ill. op. 50; Steenhoff 1920, 165–6; Rothes 1921, 40, fig. 84; Eisler 1923, 254–5, ill.; CB, 6, 7 [*c.* 1664–5]; BM, 70; Val. 1927, 73, 74; Val. xxiv, no. 80 [*c.* 1665]; CB 1930, 198; Martin 1935–6, II, 207; T, 46, ill. 43; Osterloo 1948, 177, fig. 54; Gerson 1966, 310; Amsterdam, R., cat. 1976, 317, no. C 150, ill.

The architecture of the brick house with white pilasters resembles that of the buildings in Cat. 45 and 46 (Col. Plate XI, Plate 49); all three works may be variations on a single structure. The fence at the left also reappears in an altered form in the other pictures. The relatively fine execution and vivid colouration are most like the treatment of Cat. 46.

NOTES: [1] S no. 61. [2] ibid. [3] S s no. 25.

PRINTS: C.L. Faivre (H. no. 6); Barbere (cf. Van der Kellen 1876).

60A. *Skittles Players in a Garden* (Plate 64)   *c.* 1663–6
The James A. de Rothschild Collection, Waddesdon Manor, cat. no. 62.

Canvas 69.8×62.2 cm. Signed lower right on vase: P. D. H[OOCH][1]

PROV.: Sale G. Morant, London 19/5/1832, no. 113 (w/o m.)— £220;[2] (poss.) Private Collection, Amsterdam;[3] John Walter at Bearwood, by 1857,[4] until after 1894;[5] acquired by Baron Ferdinand de Rothschild;[6] by descent to present collection.

EXH.: (a) Manchester 1857, no. 953; (b) London, B.I., 1861, no. 77; (c) London, R.A., 1894, no. 80; (d) 1938, no. 279 [*c.* 1665].

LIT.: S no. 59; Blanc 1857, 181, 187; Waagen 1857, 294; Thoré-Bürger 1860, 318; Havard 1880, 132; HdG 1892, no. 15; C. Hofstede de Groot, in *R.f.K.*, 17 (1894), 172 [1658–60]; Wurzbach, I, 717; HdG no. 308 [an early work]; R, 101; BM, 77–8; Val. 278 (without ill.); Martin 1935–6, II, 206 [*c.* 1665];

E. Waterhouse, *The James A. de Rothschild Collection at Waddesdon Manor, Paintings*, London, no. 62 [about 1665], ill. 149, detail, 151; Wagner 1971, 44.

The provenance has been confused with those of copies and/or versions. Waterhouse stated the certain facts of the pedigree. Of the existing versions this is clearly the highest in quality and execution and the best preserved. The vase of poppies at the right and the lily and tulip beside it only appear in this work and in a weak copy (Cat. 60b). The head of the statue which appears in the copy in Cincinnati (Cat. 60a) and which is overpainted in the picture in St. Louis (Cat. 60B) may also have once figured in this work, but does not appear in infra-red photographs. A date contemporaneous with, or a year or two after, the small courtyard scene in the Rijksmuseum (Cat. 59) seems most plausible.

NOTES: [1] The last four letters of the signature are later additions. [2] S no. 59; this was the only version mentioned by Smith with the pot of poppies (see commentary) and it was said to be 'more elaborate in finishing'. [3] Thoré-Bürger (1860, 318) believed he had seen the work in a private collection in Amsterdam before 1857. [4] Waagen 1857, 294; see also Exh. 'a', the sticker of which is on the back of the canvas. [5] Exh. c. [6] Waterhouse 1967, no 62.

60B. *Skittles Players in a Garden*   *c.* 1663–6
City Art Museum, St. Louis, acc. no. 20:1929.
Canvas 67.9×73.7 cm.

PROV.: Marquis de Colbert-Chabannais, by 1866;[1] by descent to the Duchess de Doudenville; by descent to the Comtesse de l'Aigle, Paris, by 1927;[2] acq. from dlr. Wildenstein, New York, 1929.

EXH.: (a) Paris 1866 (not in cat.);[3] (b) Detroit 1929, Suppl. no. 39a; (c) Chicago 1933, no. 67; (d) Toronto 1950 no. 20; (e) Philadelphia 1950–1, ill. no. 43; (f) Pittsburgh 1954, no. 42, ill.; (g) New York (Wildenstein) 1958, no. 21, ill. 39.

LIT.: HdG no. 313; BM, 76–9, ill.; W.R. Valentiner, in *P.*, I (1928), I [*c.* 1665–8], ill.; Val. no. 82 [*c.* 1665]; Martin 1935–6, II, 206 [*c.* 1665]; *Handbook*, C.A.M. St. Louis, 1953, 104, ill.

The provenance as reported by Brière-Misme and Valentiner was probably confused with that of the copy in Cincinnati (Cat. 60a). In its present condition this is the only version of the composition with a horizontal format. The picture, however, has suffered considerably from later restorations and could, prior to 1866, have been cut down at the top and perhaps added to on both sides. Apparently when the picture was cleaned and relined in 1958[4] a monogram in the lower left[5] and two additional skittles balls disappeared. The position of the legs of the man at the left was also altered.[6] The head of the statue which appears above the hedge on the right in the copy in Cincinnati (Cat. 60a) and an old woman visible in the distance beyond the house in all other versions are still overpainted in the present picture. Scattered overpainting appears throughout the work. While the painting is difficult to assess in its present condition, it appears to be a much reworked replica of Cat. 60A.

NOTES: [1] Citing a notation made by Thoré-Bürger (see note 3), Brière-Misme claimed that the picture had appeared in the Emmerson (London, 1829) and Perrier (Paris, 1843) sales. These references, however, probably apply to the copy in Cincinnati (Cat. 60a); the painting(s) in the sales was upright in format and measured about 70×65 cm. If the picture was cut down (see commentary) the Emmerson sale might apply, but the picture in the Perrier sale undoubtedly was the copy (see note 3, cat. 60a). [2] BM, 79.[3] No. 262 in the supplementary list compiled by Thoré-Bürger and appended to the copy of the catalogue in the Bibliothèque d'art et d'archéologie de l'Université de Paris. [4] No documentation available. [5] Still mentioned in Exh. g. [6] Compare Val. no. 82.

Possible Versions (known only from descriptions):

60C. Version or Copy. Canvas 81.3×72.4 cm. Sale Amsterdam, 26/4/1769, no. 51. (Incorrectly stated in HdG no. 308 as being probably identical with our Cat. 60A).

60D. Version or copy. W/o m. Sale London, 15/4/1791, no. 68.

60E. Version or copy. W/o m. Exh. London, B.I., 1847, no. 127 (lent by J. Stuart, Esq.).

(a) Copy. Cincinnati Art Museum, Cincinnati, acc. no. 1950.19. Gift of Mary Hanna. Canvas 74×66.3 cm. PROV.: Sale T. Emmerson, London, 1/5/1829, no. 61—170 gns;[1] *(prob.) Duke of Marlborough;[2] *(prob.) Paul Perrier, Paris, 16/3/1843, no. 19—Artaria of London, 4800 frs;[3] dlr. Knoedler, New York, 1925.[4] EXH.: (a) New York (Knoedler) 1925, no. 11; (b) Rotterdam 1935, no. 49, fig. 52; (c) Amsterdam 1935, no. 159 [c. 1665], ill.; (d) Cleveland 1936, no. 224; (e) Cincinnati 1941, no. 38, pl. 9; (f) New York–Toledo–Toronto 1954–5, no. 45, ill.; (g) Seattle 1962, 13, 74, ill. op. 74; (h) Columbus 1967, ill. frontispiece. LIT.: S no. 58; (prob.) Balkema 1844, 143; (prob.) Thoré-Bürger 1860, 318; Havard 1880, 131:4; Val. 1926, fig. 7; BM, 76; Val. 1927, 76, no. 14 [incorrectly as HdG no. 308]; Val. no. 81; Martin 1935–6, II, 206 [c. 1665]; Plietzsch 1960, 57–8, fig. 80 [Ludolf de Jongh?]; Gerson 1966, 310. Balkema and Thoré-Bürger referred to a work in the Perrier collection which was probably this painting. The present work is clearly the weakest of the three versions presently attributed to the artist. Its laboured execution and unmodulated colours suggest the hand of a copyist. Plietzsch's tentative attribution to Ludolf de Jongh is untenable. The picture has suffered horizontal losses and some inpainting is evident.

NOTES: [1] S no. 48; canvas 71.1×64.8. According to Smith the work was less highly finished than the picture now at Waddesdon Manor (S. no. 59). [2] Perrier Sale cat. [3] The monogram H.A. (intertwined) and the date 1843 appear on the back of the canvas; these undoubtedly are the dealer Henry Artaria's markings. [4] Exh. a.

(b) Copy. Canvas 67.3×61 cm. Bought by E. Breffit from a dlr. in Bristol, c. 1880; Harold Weber; presented to Pembroke College, Cambridge, 1956.

(c) Copy. Canvas 82.5×67.3 cm. Signed. Sale J. Gooch, London, 6/5/1908, no. 135 [P.d.H.]. (BMf.)

61. *A Woman Peeling Apples, with a Small Child* (Plate 65)
c. 1663

Wallace Collection, London, no. P 23.
Canvas 70×54 cm.
PROV.: Sale C. Perier, London, 5/4/1848, no. 6—Lord Hertford, £283 10 s; Lord Hertford, Manchester House, London; Sir Richard and Lady Wallace, London.
EXH.: (a) Bethnal Green 1872–5, no. 105; (b) London, R.A., 1893, no. 55.

LIT.: Waagen 1857, 88; Thoré-Bürger 1866, 551, no. 16 [Vermeer]; Harvard 1888, 36, no. 19 [Vermeer]; HdG 1892, no. 55; HdG c. 1895, no. 55 Roberts 1897, I, 152; Wurzbach, I, 717; HdG no. 33; Jantzen 1912, 26–7; R, 21–2, 36, 99, ill. 58; Rothes 1921, 44, fig. 75; Lilienfeld 1924, 453; CB, 6–7 [c. 1664–5]; Val. 1926, 58, n. 2, 61 [approx. 1663]; BM, 71 [1663], 72; Val. xvii, no. 70 [c. 1663]; Suida 1955, 26 [1663]; Rosenberg-Slive-TerKuile, 126, pl. 102A; London, Wallace Coll. cat. 1968, no. P23, ill; Eisler 1977, 153.

Hofstede de Groot correctly observed that the picture is probably of the same period as the painting dated 1663 in the Rijksmuseum (Cat. 52, Plate 56). The design closely resembles that of Cat. 32 (Col. Plate VII). A similar fireplace with a woman seated before it appears in the adjoining room in Cat. 55 (Plate 58).

PRINT: P.J. Arendzen (cf. HdG c. 1895).

61A. Version or copy. Canvas 61×45.7 cm. Sale Paris, 29/1/1816, no. 12—Perignon, 1800 frs. (The picture was the subject of special praise in the introduction to the catalogue and brought a good price.)

(a) Copy. (Photo RKD.) Canvas 66×54 cm. EXH.: Kleykamp, The Hague, 1930, no. 15 [P.d.H.]

(b) Copy. (Same?) With dlr. E. Bolton, London, 10/1926 (HdGf).

(c) (Poss.) copy. W/o m. Sale Paris, 23–4/11/1829, no. 55: 'After Pieter de Hooge. A charming copy representing a woman peeling some apples for her child.'

62. *A Woman Placing a Child in a Cradle* (Plate 66)
c. 1663–7

Museum and Art Gallery, Birmingham. On loan from Mrs. Oscar Ashcroft.
Panel 45×37 cm. Monogrammed & dated 164[?] (both false).
PROV.: (Poss.) D. Ietswaart, Amsterdam, 22/4/1749, no. 199 (w/o m.)—De Kommer 16 fl 10s;[1] *Sale J. de Kommer, Amsterdam, 15/4/1767, no. 61—Van de Velde, 210 fl; Sale F. van de Velde, Amsterdam, 7/9/1774, no. 43—Brouwer, 287 fl; Sale Duval, Paris, 28/11/1904, no. 6—Kleinberger, 19,000 frs; F. Fleischmann, London, by 1907[2] (name later changed to Ashcroft).
EXH.: (a) Birmingham 1950, no. 28; (b) London, R.A., 1952–3, no. 409; (c) London 1958, no. 5.
LIT.: HdG nos. 8 & (poss.) 13b; R, 99; BM, 263, ill. 261; Val. no. 89 [c. 1668–73]; J.G. van Gelder, *Burl. M.*, 95 (1953), 34.

The dress was previously overpainted[3] and the whole surface has been abraded through overcleaning. Hofstede de Groot correctly doubted the monogram and date 1643 which were visible when the work was sold in 1904. The design may be compared with that of Cat. 61 and the squat, fully rounded figure type with those of Cat. 63 (Plate 67), dated 1664, and 77 (Plate 80), dated 1667. Van Gelder felt that the work was nearer the style of S. van Hoogstraten, but the forms and what (prior to the overcleaning) must have been a relatively fine touch in the work are appropriate to De Hooch's production in these years. The panel support is rare in the period, but not unique (cf. Cat. 71).

NOTES: [1] HdG 13b; although no measurements were reported, the picture was probably identical with the work later sold by De Kommer. [2] HdG no. 8. [3] Compare old state, Val. no. 89.

63. *A Woman Reading a Letter by a Window* (Plate 67)
1664

Museum of Fine Arts, Budapest, no. 5933.

Canvas 55×55 cm. Signed and dated lower right on cross-piece of table: ·P. d · hoogh 1664

PROV.: (Poss.) bought by P.J. Thys for 31 fl in Haarlem in 1800 and sold in July of that year to G. van der Pot van Groeneveldt for 60 fl;[1] Sale G. van der Pot van Groeneveldt, Rotterdam, 6/6/1808—Allard of Paris, 155 fl; Count Eszterhazy, Papa, Hungary, *c.* 1850;[2] Count Pálffy, Budapest, by 1888,[3] acq. in 1923.

EXH.: (a) Budapest 1888, no. 295; (b) Bordeaux 1972, no. 40.

LIT.: Havard 1880, 114:2; HdG nos. 177 & 90; R, 103; Lilienfeld 1924, 454; Petrovics 1924, 62-4, ill. op. 62; CB, 6; BM, 270; Val. no. 74; Kauffmann 1930, col. 805; Val. 1932, 317; Pigler 1968, I, 323, no. 5933, II, pl. 304.

The square format is highly unusual and probably indicates that the canvas has been altered. Through the open window the tower of Amsterdam's Westerkerk is visible.

NOTES: [1] HdGf.: reference to a letter of 18/6/1800 from P.J. Thys to G.v.d. Pot mentioning an undescribed De Hooch the former had recently acquired. According to the notation (without source) this probably was the picture sold to Van der Pot in July 1800. [2] Pigler 1968, I, 323. [3] Exh. a.

64. *A Woman Weighing Gold Coins against Silver Coins* (Col. Plate XIV)
c. 1664 or later.

Staatliche Museen, Gemäldegalerie, Berlin-Dahlem, no. 1041B.

Canvas 61×53 cm.

PROV.: (Prob.) Sale The Hague, 1780 (?), no. 97 [Vermeer]—180 fl;[1] Sale G.H. Trochel et al., Amsterdam, 11/5/1801, no. 48 [Vermeer]—Van der Schley, 60 fl;[2] (prob.) Sale Amsterdam, 16/6/1802, no. 99 [Vermeer]—Gruyter, 140 fl;[3] (prob.) Sale Amsterdam, 13/6/1809, no. 100 [Vermeer]—146 fl;[4] (poss.) Sale W. Beckford, Fonthill Abbey, 11/10/1823, no. 191 (w/o m.)—£30 9s;[5] Sale Brun of Geneva, Paris, 30/11/1841, no. 20—865 frs; *Sale M.H.D., Paris, 30/1/1845, no. 27—684 frs;[6] *(prob.) Sale Prince de Talleyrand, Paris, 9-10/3/1847, no. 33 (w/o m.);[7] acq. from a Parisian dlr. in 1910.

EXH.: (a) Schaffhausen 1949, no. 60; (b) Brussels 1950, no. 58, pl. 81 [*c.* 1664]; (c) Amsterdam 1950, no. 58, fig. 99; (d) Paris, 1951, no. 92, pl. 119; (e) Oslo 1959, no. 32 [*c.* 1664], ill.

LIT.: (Prob.) Thoré-Bürger 1866, 554, no. 26;[8] HdG no. 96; W. Bode 1911, 1-2a [*c.* 1656-8], ill.; Cust 1914, 205; R, 13, 14, 101, ill. op. 6; Rothes 1921, 44, fig. 74; Lilienfeld 1924, 453-4; CB, 3; BM, 72 [after 1660]; Val. 1927, 74; Val. xviii, no. 75 [*c.* 1664]; Val. 1932, 317; Martin 1935-6, II, 200; Rudolph 1938, 406-13; T, 18, 39-41, 50, ill.; BM 1947-8, III, 160, fig. 2; Gowing 1952, 135-6, no. 10; Berlin-Dahlem, St.M. cat. 1975, 207, no. 1041B, ill.; Blankert, 96, 118, n. 9; C. Harbison, in *Print Review*, 5 (Spr. 1976), 83, no. 10, ill.; S. Alpers, *New Literary Hist.*, 8 (1976), 25, fig. 13.

The picture appeared several times in early sales as a Vermeer and undoubtedly was inspired by the latter's picture in Washington (Fig. 32). Most writers have dated the Vermeer in the early 1660s.[9] The woman in De Hooch's picture wears a jacket similar to those worn by the women in Cat. 63 and 69 (Plates 67, 72), which are dated 1664 and 1665 respectively. On the other hand, the pervasive *demi-teinte* also resembles the tonality of works from the early 1670s (cf. Cat. 94, Plate 96). Thus, while the costume would suggest that the picture

was executed shortly after its model, elements of the style leave the possibility open for a later date.

Figures weighing gold had appeared in sixteenth-century genre paintings,[10] and were treated by Bramer,[11] Willem de Poorter,[12] Metsu,[13] and others. It has not hitherto been noticed that the woman in De Hooch's picture weighs silver coins against gold coins, a detail which may have a bearing on the picture's meaning.

NOTES: [1] HdG [Vermeer] no. 9a. The measurements and description correspond in all details except for the mention of a black cap worn by the woman. The headgear, which was also mentioned in the sales in 1802 and 1809, may have been overpainted. [2] Discovered by W.L. van de Watering; see Blankert, 118, n. 9. [3] ibid. and BMf. [4] HdG (Vermeer) no. 9a. [5] The picture brought a considerably lower price than the £167 commanded by the other De Hooch in the sale (our Cat. B 7A). [6] BMf. [7] ibid. [8] Ref. sale 1780(?). [9] Blankert, cat. no. 15 [1662-5]. [10] See Berlin, St.M., cat. 1975, no. 656A, as by A. Hemessen (?). [11] See Wichmann, cat. nos. 267-71. [12] See Blankert, fig. 32. [13] HdG (Metsu) no. 55.

64A. Possible Version or Copy. W/o m. Sale W. Beckford, Fonthill Abbey, 11/10/1823, no. 191—£30 9s: 'The Interior of a Room with a Woman Weighing Gold.' (HdG 96; see Prov. above and note 5).

65. *A Couple with Musicians in a Hall* (Plate 68)   *c.* 1664-6
Royal Museum of Fine Arts, Copenhagen, no. Sp. 615.

Canvas 72×67 cm. Signed lower left: P. d · hooch ·

PROV.: Sale Amsterdam, 7-8/5/1804, no. 73—Pruissenaar, 181 fl; Consul West, Copenhagen, cat. (1807), no. 54; acq. with the West Collection in 1809 for the Danish Royal Collection; on display in the Christianberg Palace, Copenhagen, 1842.[1]

EXH.: Rotterdam 1935, no. 50, fig. 53.

LIT.: *Raisonneret Catalog over Consul West's Samling of Malerier*, Copenhagen, 1807, no. 54; S s no. 31; Gower 1880, III; Havard 1880, 127:3; HdG 1892, no. 31; Wurzbach, I, 717; HdG no. 124 [an early work]; Jantzen 1912, 32; R, 31, 32, 103, ill. op. 82; BM 1921, 343; CB 6, 7 [*c.* 1666]; BM 74; Val. xiii, xx, xxii, no. 84 [*c.* 1666-8]; Würtenberger 1937, 85; Copenhagen, R.M., cat. 1951, 136, no. 327, ill.; Reuterswärd 1956, 107, n. 23; Robinson 1974, 99, n. 8.

The present title of the work, 'The Minuet', is almost certainly incorrect. Although the dance was first introduced at the French Court around 1650 and its popularity spread rapidly, it cannot be established that this is the step that the couple are performing, nor is it certain that they are dancing at all. Neither Smith nor the author of the 1804 sale catalogue described any such activity. Dancing subjects had, however, appeared in earlier genre paintings.[2]

Hofstede de Groot noted that the picture had been over-cleaned. Some abrasion is visible in the shadow beneath the curtain, where an early restorer became overzealous in his attempt to reveal more of the painting on the wall which probably depicts the Adoration of the Shepherds. The picture is not so badly preserved as Valentiner suggested. In style and execution it resembles the series of paintings De Hooch executed in the mid-1660s employing motifs from the Town Hall in Amsterdam (see especially Cat. 66); however, no certain architectural quotations appear in this work. X-rays (see Fig. 66) reveal the half-length portrait of a man beneath

XI. A Woman and a Maid with a Pail in a Courtyard (Cat. 46). 1660–5. Hermitage, Leningrad

XII. Family Portrait Group Making Music (Cat. 53). 1663. The Cleveland Museum of Art, Cleveland. See also Plate 57

the paint surface.[3] Although De Hooch executed a small *Self Portrait* (?) (Cat. 1), no large-scale single-figure portraits can be attributed to him and none were mentioned in early sales or inventories. It seems probable, therefore, that the picture was painted over another artist's work.

NOTES: [1] S s no. 31. [2] cf. D. Hals' *The Ball*, s. & d. 1643, Royal Museum, Copenhagen, cat. 1951, no. 288. [3] I am grateful to Mr. Hendrik Bjerre of the Museum's Conservation Department for sharing this information, and to Mr. Rubow, the Museum's Director, for granting permission to publish the X-ray.

66. *The Council Chamber of the Burgomasters in the Town Hall in Amsterdam, with Figures* (Plate 71)   *c.* 1664–6

The Thyssen-Bornemisza Collection, Lugano–Castagnola, cat. no. 139.

Canvas 112.5×99 cm. Signed lower left: P D HOOCH (in perspective)

PROV.: Count von Stackelberg, Faehna Castle, Estonia, by 1907;[1] dlr. Van Diemen, Berlin, 1925;[2] dlr. Boehler & Steinmeyer, Munich, 1929;[3] Reinhardt Gallery, New York, 1931;[4] dlr. Katz. Dieren. 1934[5]—after 1937;[6] W.J.R. Dreesmann, Amsterdam, cat. (1942), I, 8; Sale Dreesmann, Amsterdam, 22–5/3/1960, no. 4, ill.; acq. 1960.

EXH.: (a) Dorpat, Estonia, 1918; (b) Amsterdam 1925 (no cat. no.); (c) London, R.A., 1929, no. 308; (d) Pittsburgh 1930, no. 4; (e) New York (Anderson Gall.) 1931, no. 96; (f) Haarlem 1934, no. 2; (g) Amsterdam 1935, no. 161 [*c.* 1670] ill.; (h) Rotterdam 1935, no. 51, fig. 54; (i) Amsterdam 1936, no. 77; (j) Amsterdam (Waaggebouw) 1937; (k) Eindhoven (Katz) 1937, no. 30; (l) Cologne 1937, no. 263; (m) Rotterdam 1955, no. 78, fig. 142; (n) Amsterdam 1975, 13, fig. 6.

LIT.: HdG no. 180; R, 104; H. Schneider, in *J.d.K.p.K.*, 47 (1926), 85; BM, 74, ill. 75; *I.S.*, 6/1927, 49; Val. xii, xx, no. 85 [*c.* 1666–8]; Würtenberger 1937, 85; *Verzameling Amsterdam W.J.R. Dreesmann*, I, 1942, 8, ill. op. 43; Plietzsch 1956, 182; Fremantle 1959, 71, n. 4, fig. 73; Gerson 1966, 308; Rosenberg-Slive-TerKuile, 126, pl. 102B [*c.* 1666–8]; Gudlaugsson 1968, n. 56; Ebbinga–Wubben 1969, 159–60, no. 139, pl. 160; Bernt, II, fig. 552.

The painting is the only known visual document recording certain aspects of the original Council Chamber. The walls were hung with striped material (paid for in 1658) and the lower sections of the windows had red shutters opening inwards. The burgomasters sat around the table before the fireplace. Above the mantelpiece hangs Ferdinand Bol's painting representing the constancy and incorruptibility of the Roman consul Caius Fabricius Luscinus in the army camp of King Pyrrhus of Epirus. Beneath it are four verses by J. van den Vondel, which can be translated: 'Fabricius holds out in Pyrrhus' army shelter, / Overcome neither by gold nor ignominious cravings, / Nor elephants' loud roaring, nor fiercest threatenings. / Thus yields no Man of State to rumours nor to gifts.' Like the painter's other works with motifs derived from the Town Hall, it probably dates from the mid-1660s. The dog in the foreground, as evident from a pentimento, first was placed farther to the left. The signature is perspectively foreshortened as in Cat. 74 and 83 (Plates 77, 86).

NOTES: [1] HdG no. 80. [2] BM, 74. [3] Exh. c. [4] Exh. e. [5] Exh. f. [6] Exh. l.

67. *A Couple Walking in the Gallery of the Town Hall* (Plate 70)   *c.* 1663–5

Musée des Beaux-Arts, Strasbourg, inv. no. 213.

Canvas 72×85 cm. Monogrammed lower left on base of pilaster.

PROV.: Sale H. Reydon, Amsterdam, 5–6/4/1827, suppl. no. 54—Hans, 70 fl; Howard Galton, Hadzor House, by 1854,[1] until after 1857;[2] Sale J. Strutt, London, 22/6/1889, no. 34—Colnaghi, £399; acq. in 1890 by W. Bode from dlr. Warneck, Paris, for the Museum.

EXH.: (a) Manchester 1857, no. 950; (b) Amsterdam 1925, II, no. 422; (c) Rotterdam 1935, no. 52; (d) Amsterdam 1935, no. 160 [*c.* 1670], ill.; (e) Basel 1947, no. 167; (f) Bordeaux 1959, no. 80 [*c.* 1670]; (g) Paris 1970–1, no. 115, ill. 109; (h) Amsterdam 1971, no. 57 [*c.* 1668–70], ill. 141, det. 24.

LIT.: Waagen 1854, III, 222; Thoré-Bürger 1860, 317–18; T. von Frimmel, in *R.f.K.*, 1891, 244; HdG 1892, no. 86; Terey, in *Z.f.b.K.*, 28 (1893), 176; Wurzbach, I, 718; A. Girodie, in *R.d.A.*, 22 (1907), 181–2; HdG no. 199; R, 27, 102; Lilienfeld 1924–5, 187; Val. 1926, 63; BM, 75; Val. xiii, xx, no. 86 [*c.* 1666–8]; Strasbourg, Mus. cat., 1938, no. 173 [*c.* 1670]; T, 56, ill. 46 [before 1665]; BM 1947–8, IV, 360, fig. 3.

When the picture was sold in 1827, another man in a black cloak was visible in the middle distance at the left. Sometime after this sale and probably before 1854—when Waagen described the work without referring to an additional figure—the man was painted out and a view into a room was painted in beneath the archway at the left. Brière-Misme[3] correctly observed that this view was derived by the restorer from a picture by P. Janssens Elinga in Munich (Fig. 56), which at the time was attributed to De Hooch. As in the painting in Leipzig (Cat. 68), the architecture is derived from the galleries on the first floor of the Town Hall in Amsterdam. In this case we have a view down the east Gallery to the statue of Mercury which is situated between the two entranceways to the public stairs. Van Thienen—a reliable authority on such matters—dated the picture before 1665 on the basis of the costumes. The detailed handling of the paint resembles the execution of De Hooch's works of *c.* 1663–5 (compare Cat. 52, Plate 56).

NOTES: [1] Waagen 1854, III, 222. [2] Exh. a; Thoré-Bürger 1860, 317–8. [3] Brière-Misme 1947–8, IV. 360.

68. *A Musical Party in a Hall* (Plate 69)   *c.* 1664–6

Museum der bildenden Künste, Leipzig, inv. no. 1031.

Canvas 81×68.3 cm.

PROV.: *Sale Amsterdam, 17/4/1783, no. 122—Cats, 72 fl;[1] *Sale Jacques Bergeon, The Hague, 4/11/1789, no. 13—80 fl;[2] Sale P. de Grand, Paris, 16/2/1809, no. 102—Paillet, 2620 frs; acq. from James Collection, London, in 1892 by Alfred Thieme, Leipzig, cat. (1900), no 45; bequeathed by Alfred Thieme, 1916.

EXH.: (a) Leipzig 1914, no. 67; (b) Berlin (Schäffer) 1929, no. 34.

LIT.: S no. 20; Blanc 1857–8, II, 262; Havard 1880, 118:3; HdG 1892, no. 34; W. von Bode & U. Thieme, *Die Galerie A. Thieme in Leipzig*, 1900, 32 [1662–5], no. 45, pl. II; Wurzbach, I, 717; HdG no. 126 & 141; Lilienfeld 1924, 454; Val. 1926, 62; BM, 75–6, ill; Val. 1927, 70; Val. xiii, xix, xx, xxii, no. 83 [*c.* 1666–8]; Wichmann 1929, II; Martin 1935–6, II, 206; Würtenberger 1937, 84; Gerson 1966, 310; Leipzig, Mus. Cat. 1967, no. 1031, ill. no. 33; J.B. Bedaux in *Antiek*, 10 (1975–6),

27, n. 18; E. de Jongh et al. in exh. cat. Amsterdam 1976, 137, fig. 30c.

An overpainted passage appears immediately behind the seated couple in the foreground and undoubtedly hides the figure of a black servant who, according to sales descriptions of 1783 and 1789, handed the bass viol player a glass of wine. Numerous pentimenti are also visible. The canvas has been enlarged by about 4–5 cm at the top and slightly (approx. 2 cm) on both sides. The architectural setting is probably derived from the northeast Gallery of the Town Hall (compare Fig. 30). However, the pattern of the tiled floor and the view to a room through the right archway are the artist's inventions. In place of the painting in the lunette De Hooch has included Raphael's fresco of the *School of Athens* (Stanza della Segnatura, Vatican, 1508–10).

NOTES: [1] cf. note 2. [2] Sale of HdG no. 141: '*The Duet.* In an [elegant] interior a lady sits with a music book on her lap. Beside her a man sits playing a bass viol. A moor offers him a glass of wine. A gentleman sits [and a child stands] by a table [which is covered with a carpet on which a dish of oranges rests; further back a couple are seen in conversation; on the right side another couple stroll in another room. Very natural in sunlight as in construction and perspective, the picture is outstanding in execution].' Canvas 77 × 64 cm. (The additions in brackets from the 1783 sale catalogue.) See commentary.

69. *A Man with a Glass of Wine and a Woman Lacing Her Bodice* (Plate 72)   1665

Lord Barnard, Raby Castle, Darlington, no. 146.

Canvas 53.5 × 64 cm. Signed and dated lower left on crosspiece of table: P d [H]ooch 1665

PROV.: Lord Barnard, Raby Castle, by 1907;[1] Sale Lord Barnard, London, 30/3/1922, no. 56, ill. (b. i.).

EXH.: (a) London, R.A., 1912, no. 74; (b) London (Slatter's) 1949, no. 16 [1675], ill.; (c) Wales Arts Council Touring Exh. 1959, no. 27; (d) Hull 1961, no. 48 [1685].

LIT.: HdG no. 179; CB, 6–8 [dated 1665]; BM, 267; Val. no. 159 [c. 1675–80]; CB 1930, 198.

Collins Baker was the only writer to correctly decipher the date 1665. The painting apparently represents lovers or a married couple at their morning toilet and should be compared to the fragmentary picture of several years later (Cat. 79, Plate 82). The partly curtained painting of a nude woman above the door may be designed to reinforce the picture's potentially amorous theme.

NOTES: [1] HdG no. 179.

70. *A Woman at Her Toilet, with an Officer* (Plate 73)   c. 1665

Wellington Museum, Apsley House, London, inv. no. 1571-1948.

Canvas 52 × 62 cm. Signed lower left on crosspiece of table: P d Hooch

PROV.: Sale H. Muilman, Amsterdam, 12/4/1813, no. 68—Ryers, 201 fl;[1] Sale W. Ryers, Amsterdam, 21/9/1814, no. 61—Nieuwenhuys, 205 fl; *Sale [Le Rouge], Paris, 16/1/1816, no. 7; Duke of Wellington, by 1821.[2]

EXH.: (a) London, B.I., 1821, no. 138; (b) 1852, no. 10; (c) London, Guildhall, 1892, no. 77.

LIT.: Gower 1880, 112; HdG 1892, no. 57; London, Apsley Hse. cat. 1900, I, no. 9, ill.; Wurzbach, I, 717; HdG no. 73

[a late work]; R, 100; CB, 6, 8 [c. 1672], pl. XII; BM, 267; Val. no. 73 [after 1664]; Kauffmann 1930, col. 805; J.A. Gaya Nuño, *Pintura europea perdida por España*, Madrid, 1964, 57; Valdivieso 1973, 289.

The design and toilet theme may be compared to Cat. 69 (dated 1665). A similar pastoral view appears through the central doorway in both works. The animated interchange between the woman and the soldier recalls the central couple in Cat. 55.

NOTES: [1] Repeatedly reported incorrectly to have been taken as booty at the battle of Vitoria in 1813; see: Apsley Hse. cat. 1901, I, 31, no. 9; Gaya Nuño 1964, and Valdivieso 1973. The later sales in which the picture appeared dispute this statement. [2] Exh. a.

71. *Mother and Child by a Cradle* (Plate 74)   c. 1665–8

Rijksmuseum, Amsterdam, no. C 148. On loan from the City of Amsterdam since 1885.

Panel 36.5 × 42 cm. Signed lower left on crosspiece of table: P D HOOCH

PROV.: Sale P. Loquet, Amsterdam, 22/9/1783, no. 139—Delfos, 355 fl; Sale Van Leyden, Paris, 10/9/1804, no. 44—Noer de Bruil, 1930 frs;[1] *Sale Perignon, Paris, 17/4/1815, no. 30;[2] Sale Juriaans, Amsterdam, 28/8/1817, no. 26—De Vries, 990 fl; Sale G. Schimmelpennick, Amsterdam, 12/7/1819, no. 40—De Vries, 799 fl; Sale A. Saportas, Amsterdam, 14/5/1832, no. 37—De Vries, 925 fl; A. van der Hoop, Amsterdam, by 1842,[3] bequeathed to the City of Amsterdam, 1854.

EXH.: Bucharest 1972.

LIT.: S nos. 19 & 21; S s no. 12; Thoré-Bürger 1858–60, II, 60–1, no. 56; Amsterdam, V.d.H. Mus., cat. 1872, no. 51; Lemcke 1878, 10; Havard 1880, 74, 89:1, 92:3; Havard 1881, 187; HdG 1892, no. 4; Wurzbach, I, 716; HdG nos. 2 & 17; W. Martin, in *M.f.K.*, I (1908), 742; R, 95, ill. op. 38; Steenhoff 1920, 169; Rothes 1921, 50, fig. 83; CB, 6, 7, [c. 1663?]; BM, 265; Val. no. 124 [c. 1670–5]; Martin 1935–6, II, 207; Bille 1961, I, 121; Amsterdam, R., cat. 1976, 318, no. C 148.

The 'replica' mentioned by Hofstede de Groot as being in the Stockholm Museum is a contemporary work with a similar but different design (Cat. 72, Plate 75). Collins Baker incorrectly suggested that Cat. 54 (Col. Plate XIII) could be a pendant. The panel support is rare in the artist's later years.

NOTES: [1] HdG no. 17. [2] BMf. [3] S s no. 12 (erroneously as on canvas).

(a) Copy (of left hand side, with changes). Present location unknown. Canvas 37.5 × 30 cm. PROV.: Lord St. Leonards;[1] Sale A. Seymour, London, 4/7/1896, no. 34—Colnaghi, 135 gns; dlr. Kleinberger, Paris, 1907;[2] dlr. J. Boehler, Munich, 1924;[3] Leonard Mendelsohn, Detroit, 1929.[4] EXH.: Detroit 1929, no. 38. LIT.: HdG no. 7 [genuine but late]; BM, 266; Val. 1927, 77, no. 27; Val. no. 125 [c. 1670–5]. Although accepted in the literature, the picture is almost certainly the work of a copyist.

NOTES: [1] Cat. 1896 sale. [2] HdG no. 7. [3] BM, 266, n. 4. [4] Exh.; Val. no. 125.

72. *Mother and Child by a Cradle* (Plate 75)   c. 1665–8

Nationalmuseum, Stockholm, no. 473.

Canvas 54 × 65 cm. Formerly remnants of a signature.[1]

PROV.: Royal Museum, inv. 1816, no. 1021.

EXH.: Stockholm 1967, no. 76.

LIT.: Wurzbach, I, 717 [as signed, 'I. v. hoo . . .']; HdG no. 13 [s.: 'P.D. HOO . . .']; R,103; BM, 265; Val. no. 126 [c. 1670–5]; Stockholm, N.M., cat. 1958, no. 473.

Valentiner's dating is surely too late. The work is closely related in design and execution to Cat. 71 (Plate 74) and both probably date roughly from the period of Lord Barnard's painting of 1665 (Cat. 69, Plate 72) or shortly thereafter. On the wall appears a portrait of an Oriental in the manner of the Rembrandt School.

NOTES: [1] According to Stockholm cat. and earlier writers; no signature could be deciphered by the present author.

73. *A Woman Plucking a Duck, with a Woman by a Fireplace*★ (Plate 76) c. 1665–8
National Museum, Danzig, no. MNG/SD/360/M
Canvas 54×64.5 cm. Signed left on windowsill.

PROV.: ★(Prob.) Sale, Haarlem, 9/8/1774, no. 24 (w/o m.), Sale P. Fouquet, Amsterdam, 13/4/1801, no. 31—La Fontaine, 63 fl; acq. collection 1872.

LIT.: S s no. 2; Danzig, Mus. cat. 1902, no. 79; HdG no. 27; R, 28, 102; BM, 265; Val. no. 128 [c. 1670–5]; Tomkiewicz 1950, no. 154, pl. 147; Danzig, Mus. cat. 1969, no. 65, ill.

Smith described the work from a drawing which may have been identical with the one by Buys later owned by Hofstede de Groot (see copy 'a' below). With a woman seated to the side of a room beside a lighted window while a serving woman attends to chores in the shadows, the composition resembles those of Cat. 71 & 72.

(a) Copy. By J. Buys. Drwg. 26.9×31.8 cm. Signed and dated 1779. Sale van Dyck, Amsterdam, 14/3/1791, E no. 6; C. Hofstede de Groot; RKD, The Hague.

74. *Mother and Child by a Window, with a Woman Sweeping* (Plate 77) c. 1665–8
The Wernher Collection, Luton Hoo, Bedfordshire, no. 37.
Canvas 65×80 cm. Signed lower left: P D HO[OC]H (in perspective).

PROV.: Prince Woronzow Collection;[1] dlr. T. Lawrie & Co., London, 1848;[2] dlr. Dowdeswell, London;[3] acq. by Sir Julius Wernher.

LIT.: HdG no. 87; R, 100; BM, 265; Val. no. 129 [c. 1670–5].

As in Cat. 66 and 83 (Plates 71, 86) the signature is perspectively foreshortened. The woman seated in the light by a window recalls the central motif of Cat. 63 (Plate 67), dated 1664. A woman sweeping also appears in an early and a later picture (Cat. 17 & 124, Plates 16, 127) as well as in the contemporary picture in the Rijksmuseum (Cat. 71, Plate 74). The design inverts one of the artist's favourite compositions of these years (see Cat. 71–3, Plates 74–6) by bringing the figure in shadow to the foreground and moving the woman silhouetted by the light to the back of the room.

NOTES: [1] BM, 265. [2] HdG no. 87. [3] The sticker of the Paris dlr. Momper also appears on the back without date.

75. *Family Portrait on a Terrace*★ (Plate 78) 1667 (?)
Present location unknown.
Canvas 67×77 cm. Signed and dated: P. d'Hoog. 1667 (?)[1]
PROV.: Sale Leroy d'Etoilles, Paris, 21–2/2/1861, no. 53 [S. van Hoogstraten]—580 frs; Sale Baron de Beurnonville,

Paris, 6/5/1881, no. 336 (b. i.?); ★Sale Baron de Beurnonville, Paris, 24/3/1883, no. 24—Féral, 3500 frs;[2] dlr. Durand Ruel, New York and Paris, by 1917,[3] sold by 1929;[4] Sale Duc de Trévise, Paris, 19/5/1938, no. 43—55,000 frs.

LIT.: HdG nos. 242 & 243a; Val. 1927, 77; BM, 272, ill. 274; Val. no. 149; Pelinck 1958, no. 6.

Valentiner's proposed date of c. 1675–80 is certainly too late. The figure types and the small scale are more consistent with the artist's works of the late 1660s and the date 1667 which appeared on the picture when it was sold in 1861 probably was authentic. Brière-Misme noted the resemblance to Cat. 76 (Plate 79). Given the similarity in size and design, the two works may, as she suggested, have been designed as pendants. The sitters have not been identified.

NOTES: [1] According to the d'Etoilles sale catalogue the picture bore an 'apocryphal' signature and date to this effect. [2] HdG 243a; cf. full description in sale cat. [3] BM, 272. [4] Val. no. 149.

76. *A Musical Party on a Terrace*★ (Plate 79) c. 1667
Present location unknown.
Canvas 67×79 cm. Monogrammed lower right.[1]

PROV.: Sale C.J. Nieuwenhuys, London, 10/5/1833, no. 34—(b. i.), 85 gns;[2] Sale R. de Cornelissen, Brussels, 11/5/1857, no. 30; Sale Gilkinet, Paris, 18/4/1863, no. 27—Vicomte de Buisseret, 2900 frs; Sale Vicomte de Buisseret, Brussels, 29–30/4/1891, no. 51—4500 frs; dlr. Sedelmeyer, Paris, 1891,[3] sold to Baron Königswarter, Vienna, 1891;[4] resold to Sedelmeyer, 1892;[5] sold to C.D. Borden, New York, in 1894,[6] cat. (1911), no. 4; Sale C.D. Borden, New York, 13–14/2/1913, no. 25, ill.—Knoedler, $5100; O. Huldschinsky, Berlin, by 1914;[7] Sale O. Huldschinsky, Berlin, 10/5/1928, no. 15—Fischer; Klingenstein Collection, New York.[8]

EXH.: (a) Paris (Sedelmeyer) 1894, no. 19, ill.; (b) New York 1909, no. 57, ill. [c. 1665–70]; (c) Berlin 1914, no. 70.

LIT.: Nieuwenhuys 1834, 153–6; S s no. 13; Havard 1880, 122:2; HdG no. 136; Val. 1910a, 9; W.R. Valentiner & A.F. Jaccaci, *Old and Modern Masters in the Collection of Mr. C.D. Borden*, New York, 1911, 14–15, 37, no. 4, ill. op. 37; Cust 1914, 205; pl. IIB; Plietzsch, in *Z.f.b.K.*, 6/1914, 231; R, 83, ill. op. 80; CB, 6, 7 [c. 1667]; Val. 1926, 47, 63; BM, 272; Val. 1927, 70; Val. xiii, xx, xxiii, no. 148 [c. 1675–80]; Würtenberger 1937, 86.

Collins Baker correctly dated the work c. 1667. In composition and style it closely resembles the *Family Portrait on a Terrace* (Cat. 75, Plate 78), which formerly was dated in that year and could be a pendant.

NOTES: [1] Exh. a & b; and Borden Sale cat. [2] S s no. 13. [3] Sedelmeyer's records (BMf). [4] ibid. [5] ibid. [6] ibid. [7] Exh. c. [8] FARL.

77. *Two Women and a Man Making Music* (Plate 80) 1667
Picture Gallery, Royal Collection, Hampton Court, inv. no. 659.
Canvas 52×62 cm. Signed lower left: P D Hooch / 16[6]7

PROV.: Buckingham Palace, by 1854(?);[1] Hampton Court, by 1898.[2]

LIT.: (Poss.) Waagen 1854, II, 11;[3] Wurzbach, I, 717; HdG no. 129 [1647 or 1667]; Cust 1914, 205–6, pl. 2C; R, 99 [1647 or 1667]; CB, 6–7 [c. 1667], pl. VIII; BM, 276; C.H. Collins Baker, *Catalogue of the Pictures at Hampton Court*, Glasgow, 1929, 79, no. 669 [1667]; Val. no. 136 [1667 (1677?)].

Although the third digit of the date is difficult to decipher, the only reasonable date for the work is 1667.

NOTES: [1] Waagen (1854) mentioned a painting by De Hooch of a *Lady at a Harpsichord* which was hung high and 'treated almost entirely in half light'. If the author mistook the table at the right for an instrument he might have been referring to this picture. [2] Cat. 1898, no. 669. [3] See note 1.

78. *A Woman with a Mandolin and a Couple at a Table Singing* (Plate 81)   *c.* 1667–70

Taft Museum, Cincinnati, acc. no. 1931.395.

Canvas 70×58 cm. Signed lower right on footstool: P. de Ho . . .

PROV.: Dlr. Arthur Ruck, London, Oct. 1920;[1] dlr. Scott & Fowles, New York; sold to Charles P. Taft of Cincinnati in 1924.

LIT.: BM, 276; Val. no. 135; Cincinnati, Taft Mus. cat., n.d., no. 130.

The date of *c.* 1675 proposed by Valentiner is probably too late. The relatively tight execution and boldly contrasted colour scheme (the woman's skirt is red, her top orange; the carpet is orange, blue, red, and black) are more typical of the works of the preceding decade. The figure types point to the late 1660s.

NOTES: [1] HdGf.

79. *A Woman with a Basin and a Flagon, and a Man Dressing* (Plate 82)   *c.* 1667–70

Metropolitan Museum of Art, New York, acc. no. 32.100.15. The Michael Friedsam Collection, 1931.

Canvas 61.5× 52 cm.

PROV.: Sale A. de J. de Pinto, Amsterdam, 11/4/1785, no. 2[1]—Van der Schley, 45 fl; Van Helsleuter Collection;[2] sold by Héris of Brussels to Colonel de Biré, 1839;[3] Sale Biré, Paris, 25–6/3/1841, no. 12—5950 frs; Sale Mawson, Paris, 22/2/1850, no. 31—1950 frs; Arnold Collection, New York, 1851;[4] Michael Friedsam, New York, by 1917.[5]

EXH.: (a) Montreal 1944, no. 75, ill. 83; (b) Hartford 1950–1, no. 51; (c) New York 1971, no. 14; (d) St. Petersburg–Atlanta 1975, no. 30, ill.

LIT.: Blanc 1857–8, II, 441; Blanc 1863, 8; HdG nos. 95 & 80; G. Pene du Bois, in *Arts and Decoration*, Ju. 1917, 397; BM, 268, ill. 270; Val. 1927, 77, no. 22; Val. no. 127 [*c.* 1670–5]; B. Burroughs & H.B. Wehle, *Bull.*, M.M.A., 27 (1932), 48, no. 84, ill.

Brière-Misme was the first to note that the picture was identical with the painting in the De Pinto Sale of 1785. According to the catalogue description the canvas was originally horizontal and included a woman in the bed at the extreme right conversing with the seated man. Approximately 18 cm were cut from the right side and about 5 cm added at the top edge before the canvas appeared in the Biré Sale in 1841. In addition, the man and the chair may have been overpainted at the time the canvas was cut since no mention of them was made in the detailed descriptions in either the Biré or the Mawson sale catalogue. De Hooch first treated the theme of lovers at their morning toilet in Cat. 15 (Plate 13) and then again in Cat. 69 (Plate 72). Valentiner's dating of the work is probably too late.

NOTES: [1] 56.6×96.5 cm. See commentary. [2] cf. Biré cat.; the work did not appear in the Helsleuter Sale (Paris, 25/1/1802).

as stated by Hofstede de Groot. [3] Note from H.A. Hammond-Smith in M.M.A. files. [4] ibid. [5] Pene du Bois 1917.

80. *A Wounded Man Being Treated in a Stable*★ (Plate 83)   *c.* 1667

Present location unknown.

Canvas 41×49 cm.

PROV.: ★Sale Amsterdam, 20/5/1799, no. 49—Van de Vinne, 18 fl. ;[1] dlr. Sully, London, 1913;[2] London art market, 1915–25;[3] Sale R.H. St. Maur et al., London, 10/7/1925, no. 145; Sale S.M. Samuel et al. (a.c.), London, 25/3/1927, no. 150; dlr. Asscher & Welker, London, *c.* 1928;[4] dlr. F. Kleinberger, Paris. *c.* 1928;[5] Sale London, 4/8/1950, no. 130; Sale Williams-Wynn et al. (J.H. Linnart), London, 30/6/1965, no. 102.

LIT.: BM, 374, ill.; Val. no. 106 [*c.* 1671–4]; Kauffmann 1930, col. 805; Fleischer 1976, 111–4, fig. 6; Fleischer 1978, 55 [early or mid-1650s], fig. 12.

About 8 cm were cut from the right edge of the canvas some time after 1799, when the picture was sold with the measurements 42.5× 57 cm. Another figure, whose hand holding a sword or a stick is still visible, originally appeared at the right. This may well have been the wounded man's assailant. The attention of the seated woman evidently was directed toward the missing figure. The same subject was treated in the early work in London (Cat. 14, Plate 14), where the victim has been overpainted. Both Brière-Misme and Fleischer believed that the present picture could also be an early work. However, Valentiner was probably correct to date it later in the artist's career; compare the type of the seated woman to that of the ladies in the painting of 1667 at Hampton Court (Cat. 77, Plate 80).

NOTES: [1] With the description: 'A soldier, whose wound is being treated; nearby two women and a child'. [2] HdGf. [3] BM, 374. [4] RKD photo. [5] ibid.

81. *Mother and Child with a Boy Descending a Stair* (Plate 84)   1668

H. Bischoff, Bremen. On loan to the Kunsthalle, Bremen. Canvas 65× 55 cm. Signed lower left: P · d · hoogh · / 1668

PROV.: ★Sale, Amsterdam, 23/8/1808, no. 69—Van der Schley, 100 fl; Duc de Broglie, Paris;[1] dlr. Kleinberger, Paris,[2] (sold to) A. de Ridder, Schönberg near Cronberg im Taunus, cats. (1910), no. 35 (1913), 9–10; Sale A. de Ridder, Paris, 2/6/1924, no. 30, pl. 24—Kleinberger, 80,000 frs; dlr. F. Kleinberger, Paris, until after 1929;[3] C.J.K. van Aalst, Hoevelaken, cat. (1939), 170, until after 1962;[4] dlr. Cramer, The Hague, 1966–7, cat. no. 13; dlr. Brod., London, 1969;[5] Sale Lady Vansittart et al. (a.c.), London, 10/7/1974, no. 42, ill.

EXH.: (a) New York (Kleinberger) 1913, no. 34; (b) Berlin (Schäffer) 1929, no. 35; (c) IJzendijke 1955, no. 26; (d) Delft 1962, no. 20, ill.; (e) Antikbeurs exh., Delft, Prinsenhof, 1966; (f) Laren 1969, no. 22, ill.

LIT.: Bode 1910, no. 25; Bode 1913, 9–10, pl. 34; CB, 1925, 6, 7; BM, 267; Val. no. 87; Wichmann 1929, 11; J.W. von Moltke (ed.), *Dutch and Flemish Old Masters in the Collection of Dr. C.J.K. van Aalst*, Huis-te-Hoevelaken, 1939, 170, pl. XI; T, 44, 57–8, ill. 47.

The motif of the woman ministering to her child recalls Cat. 42 (Plate 46) and the theme of the schoolboy appeared earlier in Cat. 48 (Plate 51). The design may be compared to that of a painting by Metsu at Buckingham Palace.[6]

NOTES: [1] Bode 1910, no. 25. [2] ibid. [3] Exh. b. [4] Exh. d. [5] Exh. f. [6] Robinson, fig. 69.

82. *A Woman Sewing, with a Child* (Plate 85)   *c.* 1668
The Thyssen-Bornemisza Collection, Lugano–Castagnola, no. 200.

Canvas 55×45 cm.

PROV.: Sale Mej. C.M. Schouten, Gouda, 22/5/1792, no. 14; Sale, Amsterdam, 11/7/1798, no. 46—Royens, 13 fl; Sale F. Meazza, Milan, 15/4/1884, no. 76, ill.;[1] Sale Prince Troubetskoy, Paris, 3/5/1892, no. 15, ill.[2]—1600 frs; Sale Lefèvre-Bougon of Amiens, Paris, 1–2/4/1895, no. 24, ill.—Sedelmeyer, 3150 frs; dlr. C. Sedelmeyer, 1895;[3] Wernher Weissbach, Berlin, by 1907,[4] until after 1915;[5] H. Reinhardt Galleries, New York (sold to) Art Institute, Minneapolis,[6] (sold to) I. Weitzner, (sold to) dlr. Rosenberg & Steibel, New York, 1958;[7] acq. 1958.

EXH.: (a) Paris (Sedelmeyer) 1895, no. 15, pl. 15; (b) Berlin 1915, no. 62.[8]

LIT.: HdG no. 4; R, 101; *Bull.*, Minneapolis Art Institute, 13 (12/1924), 66–7, ill. (cover); *Handbook*, M.A.I., 1926, 36, ill.; Val. 1926, 47, 61, fig. 5; BM, 266; Val. 1927, 77, no. 21; Val. xiii, no. 65 [*c.* 1662]; T, 44, 50, ill. 41; Keyszelitz 1956, 67; Ebbinge-Wubben 1969, 158–9, no. 138 [1662 or 1663], II. pl. 160; Eisler 1977, 153.

Late nineteenth-century sales and exhibition catalogues and Valentiner mention traces of a signature.[9] The picture, particularly its right half, was repeatedly overpainted in the nineteenth century.[10] In 1958 the overpaintings were removed. Ebbinge-Wubben mentioned that the picture had been attributed to Cornelis Bisschop and correctly rejected the proposal as untenable. However, his proposed dating (1662 or 1663) is probably somewhat too early. Although the design recalls earlier domestic scenes (cf. Cat. 32 & 61, Col. Plate VII, Plate 65) the figures and execution point to origins in the later 1660s (compare Cat. 77 & 81, Plates 80, 84). An interesting technical feature observed by W. Suhr is the use of silver foil glazed with green and brown in the wall-hanging behind the woman.[11]

NOTES: [1] Signed. [2] Monogrammed lower left. [3] Exh. a. [4] HdG no. 4. [5] Exh. b. [6] *Bull.* M.A.I., 13 (1924), 66–7; [7] Communication W. Suhr. [8] Signed. [9] See notes 1, 2 and 8. [10] Compare the various states illustrated in the sales catalogues and literature; see also Ebbinge-Wubben's comments. [11] Correspondence, 1976.

83. *A Woman Sewing and a Man Drinking** (Plate 86)   *c.* 1668
Michaelis Collection, The Old Town House, Cape Town. Donated by Lady Michaelis, 1933.

Canvas 56.5×47.6 cm. Signed lower right: P D HOOCH (in perspective)

PROV.: Sale Schimmelpenninck, Amsterdam, 12/7/1819, no. 41—Roos, 200 fl; Sale C.S. Roos, Amsterdam, 28/8/1820, no. 50—Brondgeest, 470 fl; Sale King of Bavaria, Munich, 5/12/1826, no. 72;[1] Sale Chevalier de Solirène, Paris, 22–4/4/1829, no. 48; Sale Sir W. Knighton, London, 21–3/5/1885, no. 473—£105; J.P. Heseltine, London, by 1886,[2] until *c.* 1920;[3] dlr. T. Agnew, London;[4] Sir Max Michaelis, Tandridge Court, Surrey.

EXH.: (a) London, R.A., 1886, no. 69; (b) London, Guildhall, 1892, no. 71; (c) On loan Dulwich Picture Gallery, 1917.

LIT.: S no. 46; Havard 1880, 94:2; HdG 1892, no. 45; Wurzbach, I, 717; HdG nos. 186 & 227; BM, 266; Val. no. 142 [*c.* 1675–80]; T, 36, 44, 48, 56, ill. 49; D. Bax, *Catalogue of the*

Michaelis Collection, Cape Town, 1967, no. 13, ill.; W.H. Gravett, in *A.*, 102 (1975), 273, pl. 10.

While the composition resembles that of the painting of 1670 in the Rijksmuseum (Cat. 94, Plate 96) the figure types and smaller format suggest a somewhat earlier date. The signature is perspectively foreshortened as in Cat. 66 and 74 (Plates 71, 77). The stern of a ship, whose masts and rigging are visible through the mullioned windows, is seen through the open doorway.

NOTES: [1] S no. 46; HdG no. 227 (with an erroneous transcription of the catalogue description which states that the man sits rather than stands). [2] Exh. a. [3] BM, 266. [4] Val. no. 192.

84. *A Woman Receiving a Letter from a Man* (Plate 87)   *c.* 1668–70
Kunsthalle, Hamburg, inv. no. 184.

Canvas on panel 57×53 cm.[1] Signed right on door frame: P · d · hooch

PROV.: *Sale Amsterdam, 19/12/1770, no. 100—Van der Bogaard, 67 fl; Sale J. Caudri, Amsterdam, 6–7/9/1809, no. 24—Dupré, 31 fl;[2] Sale S.A. Koopman, Utrecht, 9/4/1847, no. 8—Gruyter, 561 fl; (poss.) M.T. Schwelling of Aix-la-Chapelle, Brussels, 10/4/1850, no. 23—Coclers, 38 fl;[3] J. Hudtwalker-Wesselhoeft, Hamburg, cat. (1886), 22; acq. from the collection, 1888.

LIT.: S s no. 10; Havard 1880, 116:2; W. Bode, *Die Gemäldesammlung des Herrn Johannes Wesselhoeft in Hamburg*, Vienna, 1886, 22–3; HdG 1892, no. 26; Wurzbach, I, 717; HdG no. 182; Jantzen 1912, 32; R, 27, 102; Mellaart 1923, 269; Val. 1926, 62; BM, 79, ill. 78; Val. xix, no. 93 [*c.* 1670]; Hamburg, Kunsthalle, cat. 1956, no. 184 [*c.* 1670].

Although thematically related to the painting in the Rijksmuseum of 1670 (Cat. 94, Plate 96), the present work displays a slightly finer touch and a bolder colour scheme which may point to earlier origins.

NOTES: [1] Incorrect measurements (71×64) recorded by Hofstede de Groot and Valentiner resulted in several errors in the provenance; see note 2. [2] Erroneously included by Hofstede de Groot as a possible entry for our Cat. 94. The references to the Reynders Sale of 1821 and the Lapeyrière Sale of 1825 listed under HdG no. 182 are also incorrect and refer in fact to Cat. B 7A. [3] In the copy of the catalogue at the RKD the annotation 'copie' appears and the picture brought an unusually low price.

(a) Possible copy. (cf. Schwelling Sale 1850 in prov. above and note 3).

85. *A Woman Reading a Letter and a Man at a Window* (Plate 88)   *c.* 1668–70
Nationalmuseum, Stockholm, inv. no. 471.

Panel 57×49 cm.

PROV.: Queen Louisa Ulrica, Sweden, inv. 1760, no. 277; Royal Museum, inv. 1795, no. 205.

EXH.: Stockholm 1967, no. 77.

LIT.: HdG 1892, no. 84; Wurzbach, I, 717; HdG no. 198; R, 103; CB, 6, 8 [*c.* 1672]; BM, 270, ill. 271; Val. no. 94 [*c.* 1670]; Stockholm, N.M., cat. 1958, no. 47, ill. 97.

The motif of the woman reading a letter by a window appeared in the painting of 1664 in Budapest (Cat. 63). Like Cat. 84, to which the present work is related in colour, tone and execution, it probably dates from the end of the decade. It was transferred from canvas in 1866.

86. *A Man and Two Women Conversing* (Plate 89)

c. 1668–70

City Art Museum, Manchester. The Assheton Bennett Collection.

Canvas 70×61.8 cm. Signed lower left on base of column: p d · hooch

PROV.: *(Prob.) Sale J. van Buren, The Hague, 7–12/11/1808, no. 21 (w/o m.); Edward Cave;[1] Assheton Bennett, by 1952.[2]

EXH.: (a) London, R.A., 1952–3, no. 369; (b) 1965, no. 94.

LIT.: Grossmann 1965, no. 27, pl. III.

The design is very close to Cat. 96, but the smaller scale and tighter handling suggest a date in the late 1660s.

NOTES: [1] Grossmann 1965, no. 27. [2] Exh. a.

87. *Two Women Teaching a Child to Walk* (Plate 90)

c. 1668–72

Museum der bildenden Künste, Leipzig, inv. no. 1558.

Canvas 67.5×59 cm. Signed on window: P d · Hoo [. . .]

PROV.: *Sale Amsterdam, 19–20/8/1801, no. 37—Vinkeles, 200 fl;[1] acquired by Baron Speck von Sternberg, Lützschena, in 1811;[2] cats. (1827), no. 128 (1889), no. 204; acq. from Speck von Sternberg Collection, 1945.

EXH.: (a) Leipzig 1914, no. 195; (b) 1937, no. 35.

LIT.: *Verzeichnis der von Speck'schen Gemälde-Sammlung*, 1827, no. 128; *Verzeichnis von Ölgemälden . . . in der Freiherrlich Speck v. Sternberg'schen Sammlung*, 1889, no. 204; HdG 1892, no. 62; Wurzbach, I, 717; HdG no. 35 [later years of his best period]; R, 102; E. Plietzsch, in *M.f.K.*, 8 (1915), 48; Lilienfeld 1924, 453; CB, 6 [*c.* 1672]; BM, 263, ill. 262; Val. no. 90 [*c.* 1668–72]; Leipzig Mus. cat. 1967, 84, no. 1558.

The interior most resembles that of Cat. 88 (Plate 91). Compositionally the work is also related to Cat. 89 and 90 (Plates 92, 93). As Valentiner noted, these four works form a group connected with, and probably slightly predating, the painting of 1673 formerly in the Schloss Collection (Cat. 102, Plate 105). The child wears a 'valhoed' (literally, 'falling hat'), which had a protective cushion around the brim (see also Cat. 89, 90, 102 & 145, (Plates 92, 93, 105, 148).

NOTES: [1] HdG handex, and BMf. [2] According to the catalogue of the collection of 1889; no acquisition date appeared in the 1827 catalogue. Assuming the date is correct the painting of similar description which appeared in the S[éréville] Sale (Paris, 1824) must have been a slightly smaller version or copy.

87A. Version or copy? Canvas 61×50.7 cm. Sale C.J. de S[éréville], Paris, 22/1/1824, no. 65 (b.i.; 2000 frs). LIT.: S no. 22; Blanc 1863, 8; Havard 1880, 103:3.

(a) (Prob.) copy. (Same as the above?) Sale Bruslé, Paris, 1–2/3/1839, no. 112 (w/o m.): 'After P. de Hoogh. A Dutch woman presents a pear to a child supported by leading strings which aid the child in walking.'

88. *A Woman Handing a Coin to a Serving Woman with a Child* (Plate 91)

c. 1668–72

Los Angeles County Museum of Art, Los Angeles, no. M.44.2.8. Mr. and Mrs. Allan C. Balch Collection, 1944.

Canvas 73×66 cm. Signed right on fireplace: P D HOOCH

PROV.: Sale J.C. Symonsz., Amsterdam, 25/11/1778, no. 12—Nijman, 520 fl;[1] (poss.) with dlr. Paillet, who brought it to France and offered it unsuccessfully to the Comte d'Angivillers for Louis XVI, 10/5/1785;[2] Sale J. Danser Nijman, Amsterdam, 16/9/1797, no. 114—Roos, 400 fl; Sale B. Ocke, Leyden,

21–2/4/1817, no. 54—Van der Berg, 370 fl; Sale [A.B. Roothaan], Amsterdam, 29/3/1826, no. 39—Brondgeest, 1185 fl; Sir Charles Bagot, by 1833;[3] Sale Bagot, London, 18/6/1836, no. 37—Nieuwenhuys, £68; Sale D. van der Schrieck, Brussels, 8–10/4/1861, no. 34—Schollaert (son-in-law of V.d. Schrieck), 6000 frs; Schollaert Collection, Louvain, until 1899; G. Helleputte (formerly Schollaert), Louvain, 1899 until his death in 1925;[4] art market, New York;[5] dlr. Kleykamp, The Hague, 1927;[6] dlr. Knoedler, New York, 1927;[7] Allan C. Balch, Los Angeles, 1927–44.

EXH.: (a) London, B.I., 1834, no. 107; (b) The Hague (Kleykamp) 1927, no. 19, ill.

LIT.: S no. 11; Havard 1880, 102:2; HdG nos. 30, 31 & 51; R, 32, 97; BM, 264, ill. 268; Val. 1927, 76, no. 16; Val no. 91 [*c.* 1668–73]; *Quarterly*, L.A.C.M., 4 (Spr. & Sum., 1944), 10, ill. 7; R. Mckinney, in *A.N.*, 11 (1945), ill. 12; Los Angeles, C.M.A., cat. 1954, II, 67, pl. 73.

The interior most resembles that of Cat. 87 (Plate 90) and the composition is related to Cat. 89 and 90 (Plates 92, 93). The motif of the child urging the serving woman to depart on her errands had appeared earlier in Cat. 54 (Col. Plate XIII).

NOTES: [1] As on panel (?). According to HdG no. 30 it was sold to Nijman, in whose collection it later appeared; however, it, or a very similar work, was in Paillet's possession in the intervening years. [2] BM, 264 & BMf. See the notes on the pictures bought by Paillet on his trip to Holland, French National Archives, O¹1918².136: 'A picture with three figures in an interior. A young woman gives a servant money to go marketing.' [3] S no. 11. [4] BM, 265; cf. HdG no. 31. [5] BM, 265. [6] Exh. b. [7] Val. 1927, 76.

(a) Copy. By W.J. Laquy (1738–98). Drwg. 38.7×33 cm. PROV.: Sale J.D. Nijman, Amsterdam, 19/3/1798, K no. 9—Pruissenaar, 52 fl; Sale J. Gildemeester Jansz., Amsterdam, 24/11/1800, BB. no. 6; Sale F. Munnikhuyzen et al., Amsterdam, 27/11/1820, no. 18—Singendonk, 32 fl; Sale P.M. Kesler, C. Apostool et al., Amsterdam, 13/5/1844, B no. 11—Brondgeest, 19 fl; (poss.) Sale Amsterdam, 14/2/1855, A no. 35—Arnold, 7 fl; (poss.) Sale D. van Lankeren, Amsterdam, 22/1/1856, no. 196—Steffelaar, 10 fl; (poss.) Sale Amsterdam, 27/10/1874, no. 581; Sale Mrs. A. James, London, 15/10/1948, no. 41. (Probably executed when original was with Nijman.)

(b) Copy. By A. Schouman (1710–92). Drwg. w/o m. PROV.: Sale J. Lauwers et al., Amsterdam, 13/12/1802, G no. 15; Sale J. Valette, Amsterdam, 26/10/1807, A no. 11.

89. *A Woman with a Child and a Serving Woman** (Plate 92)

c. 1668–72

Present location unknown.

Canvas 70×63.5 cm. Signed left on windowsill: P de Hooch[1]

PROV.: *Sale Amsterdam, 6/7/1768, no. 29—166 fl;[2] Sale P. Locquet, Amsterdam, 22/9/1783, no. 138—Gildemeester, 220 fl;[3] Sale Gildemeester Jansz., Amsterdam, 11–13/6/1800, no. 78—Roos, 185 fl; *Sale H.W. Campe, Leipzig, 24/9/1827, no. 151—Reimer of Berlin, 100 mks; Sale E.W. Lake, London, 11/7/1845, no. 16—Nieuwenhuys, £66; Sale Paley et al. (Berger), London, 16/6/1900, no. 107—Dowdeswell, £1102; bought from Dowdeswell in 1900 by dlr. C. Sedelmeyer, Paris, cat. (1901), no. 20; (sold to) C.T. Yerkes, New York, in Sept. 1900,[4] cat. (1904), no. 51; Sale Yerkes, New York, 5/4/1910, no. 132—Dowdeswell, $12,800; dlr. F. Kleinberger, Paris, before 1911;[5] Max von Gutmann, Vienna, by 1911.[6]

EXH.: Paris 1911, no. 74.

LIT.: S. no. 14; Havard 1880, 103:2; *Catalogue of . . . the Collection of Charles T. Yerkes*, New York, 1904, no. 51; W. Martin, *M.f.K.*, 1911, 439, pl. 92; HdG no. 38; Dayot 1911, no. 77, ill. 80; BM, 263; Val. no. 88 [*c.* 1668–73].

The work is related in composition to Cats. 87, 88 and 90 (Plates 90, 91, 93).

NOTES: [1] HdG no. 38. [2] HdG handex. [3] C. 28″×15″; presumably a misprint for 28″×25″; (71.1×63.5 cm). [4] BM, 263; [5] Exh. [6] Exh.

89A. Replica or copy. Canvas 69×60 cm. Sale Colby et al., London, 18/3/1960, no. 8—Hallsborough, 800 gns. Judging from photographs the work looks inferior to the picture formerly with Von Gutmann and may be a copy. Among other small changes, the curtain on the window has been deleted. The provenance may be confused with the original, which is of approximately the same dimensions.

90. **Women with a Child Feeding a Parrot**★ (Plate 93)
c. 1668–72

Private Collection, England.

Canvas 79.5×66 cm.

PROV.: ★(Poss.) Sale, Paris, 9/12/1811, no. 54—560 frs;[1] (poss.) Sale C. Perrier, Paris, 18–21/4/1838, no. 17 (w/o m.)—3000 frs; Duc de Berri Collection;[2] imported to England by Hume, 1840;[3] dlr. Chaplin, London, by 1854; (sold to) Thomas Baring by 1857,[4] who died in 1873 leaving his collection to his nephew, The Earl of Northbrook, London, cat. (1889), no. 48; Northbrook collection until after 1930;[5] Clive Cookson, Nether Warden, Hexham, by 1951;[6] Sale Mme A. de Rothschild et al. (a.c.), London, 30/6/1971, no. 12, ill.; dlr. L. Koetser, London, cat. (1972), no. 1, ill.

EXH.: (a) Newcastle 1951, no. 23; (b) London, R.A., 1952–3, no. 390.

LIT.: S s no. 6; Waagen 1857, 99; Blanc 1857–8, II, 433; Blanc 1863, 8; Havard 1880, 97:1; R. Gower, *The Northbrook Gallery*, London, 1885, 32; W.H.J. Weale, *A Descriptive Catalogue of the Collection of . . . the Earl of Northbrook*, London, 1889, no. 48; HdG 1892, no. 50; Wurzbach, I, 717; HdG no. 113; R, 99; Rothes 1921, 44, fig. 69; Lilienfeld 1924, 453; CB, 6, 8 [1672], pl. XI; BM, 263; Val. no. 111 [*c.* 1673]; CB 1930, 198 [1672]; Bernt, II, no. 550.

Compositionally related to Cat. 87–9 (Plates 90–2), the work probably slightly predates the picture of a similar theme formerly in the Schloss Collection (Cat. 102, Plate 105). Collins Baker dated the work 1672, but did not state whether this was based on an inscription. Figures feeding parrots appear in several later pictures (Cat. 122, 148–50, Plates 125, 149, 152–3).

NOTES: [1] Possibly a smaller version. The reference to the Croese Sale (Amsterdam, 1811), listed by Havard (1880, 97:1) and repeated in the Rothschild sale cat. of 1971, is incorrect; the sale refers instead to our Cat. 102. [2] S s no. 6. [3] ibid. [4] Waagen 1857, 99. [5] CB 1930, 198. [6] Exh. a.

90A. Poss. version or copy. 70×51 cm. (See Sale Paris, 1811 in PROV. above.)

91. **Three Women and a Man with a Monkey on a Terrace** (Plate 94)
1669

Private Collection, England.

Canvas 70×85.5 cm. Signed left on stool: P. de Hooch An 1669

PROV.: Dlr. Colnaghi, London, 1935;[1] Mrs. G. Hart, Forest Row, Sussex, 1952[2]—after 1956;[3] dlr. Koetser, London, 1959;[4] dlr. J. Mitchell, London, 1962–4.[5]

EXH.: (a) Rotterdam 1935, no. 54, fig. 57; (b) Worthing 1952, no. 19; (c) London, R.A., 1952–3, no. 446; (d) Brighton 1956, no. 85 [late 1650s]; (e) London (Koetser) 1959, no. 3, ill.

LIT.: *C.*, 144 (12/1959), vii; 151 (10/1962), v; *Burl. M.*, 105 (3/1963), pl. LIX; *C.*, 155 (3/1964), 182, ill.

Figure groups on terraces had appeared about two years earlier in the artist's work (see Cat. 75 & 76).

NOTES: [1] Rotterdam 1935, no. 54. [2] Exh. b. [3] Exh. d. [4] Exh. e. [5] Adv. in *C.*, 151 (10/1962), v, & 155 (3/1964), 182.

92. *Portrait of the Jacott-Hoppesack Family* (Plate 95)
c. 1670

Private Collection, England.

Canvas 97×114.5 cm.

PROV.: Sale Dundas, London, 29/5/1794, no. 8—Williamson, £6 6 s;[1] ★Sale Viscount Haberton, London, 15/4/1864, no. 70—Smith £210; T.A. Poynder;[2] Lady Islington, 1952–3.[3]

EXH.: London, R.A., 1952–3, no. 462.

LIT.: HdG no. 322a; J.G. van Gelder, in *Burl. M.*, 95 (1953), 34 [manner of E. van der Neer]; Pelinck 1958, cols. 308–11, ill.

Pelinck identified the coats of arms on the side of the fireplace as those of the Jacott and Hoppesack families. Jan Jacott (*c.* 1631–after 1683) was a cloth merchant who lived on the Warmoesstraat in Amsterdam with his wife Elisabeth Hoppesack (*c.* 1632/3–70). Their three children are depicted in the picture; Balthasar (born *c.* 1658/9), Magdalena (born *c.* 1659/60) and a daughter (born after 4/10/1667 and buried 9/7/1672). On the basis of the children's ages and costumes, the picture can be dated *c.* 1670. Since the mother died in July of that year, one would assume that the work was executed in the first half of 1670. It is possible, though, that her likeness was executed posthumously. The decorations of the room, with murals separated by pilasters, resemble those of a series of musical company scenes the artist painted about 1674 (see Cat. 108–10, Plates 110, 111, 112) and of the painting in Berlin (Cat. 107, Plate 113). As in the last-mentioned work, Rembrandt's etching *Small Lion Hunt* (Hind no. 180) provided the source for the mural on the right. Over the mantel a painting seems to represent a Venus and Cupid subject. The view to a country home seen through the open doorway indicates that the setting is not a record of the family's home in Amsterdam but a product of the artist's imagination. In 1864, and probably also in 1794, the picture was sold with a companion piece, now in Brussels (Cat. 93). Despite doubts which have been expressed about De Hooch's authorship (Van Gelder preferred to ascribe the work to the 'manner of Eglon van der Neer' and it is presently filed at the RKD under the name of S. van Hoogstraten), the picture is undoubtedly by the artist's hand.

NOTES: [1] HdG 322a; entitled 'The Ancient Family of the Williamsdorps of Holland'. A granddaughter of the Jacott-Hoppesack marriage was the wife of J.L.P. van Wilmsdorff (1703–57). [2] Exh. [3] Exh.

93. *A Merry Company with a Trumpeter* (Plate 97)
c. 1670

Musées Royaux des Beaux-Arts, Brussels, inv. no. 7018. Fernand Houget Bequest, 1963.

Canvas 99×113 cm. Signed right above door: P. D'. Hoogh · f

PROV.: *(Prob.) Sale Sir L. Dundas, London, 29/5/1794, no. 9—£12;[1] *Sale Lord Haberton, London, 19/4/1864, no. 69—Eckford, £81;[2] Jules Porgès, Paris;[3] Sale Vicomte J. de la L . . ., Brussels, 3/7/1919, no. 97, ill.;[4] Sale D.G. Déry, New York, 19–20/4/1923, no. 150, ill.—A. Seligman, Rey & Co.; dlr. F. Kleinberger, Paris, 1924;[5] purchased by F. Houget of Verviers from dlr. Davies, Paris, 1925.

EXH.: Verviers, Musées Communals, 10/1956.

LIT.: BM, 278; Val. no. 133 [*c.* 1675]; *Bull.,* M.R.d.B.A., 1963, 5–6, 14, 16, 103; Brussels, M.R.d.B.A., cat. 1973, no. 96, ill.

The picture was sold in 1864 and probably in 1794 as the companion piece to the portrait of the *Jacott–Hoppesack Family* (Cat. 92, Plate 95), which is datable *c.* 1670. Nearly identical in size, the two works are close in style and composition and may have been designed as pendants. The theme of the trumpeter amidst a merry company gathering also appears in an early painting (Cat. 7, Plate 6) and in a somewhat later work in Berlin (Cat. 107, Plate 113).

NOTES: [1] Described only as 'Conversation—The Companion' (to our Cat. 92); the identification, however, is supported by the fact that the two works were later sold again as companions in 1864. Presumably the purchaser of the work in the 1794 sale was Williamson, who was listed as the buyer of the portrait. [2] As the companion piece to our Cat. 92. [3] Sale cat. 1919. [4] The picture did not appear in the Yerkes Sale of 1910 as stated by Valentiner; that work was our Cat. 147. [5] BM, 278, n. 2.

94. *A Woman and a Young Man with a Letter* (Plate 96)
1670

Rijksmuseum, Amsterdam, no. C 147. On loan from the City of Amsterdam since 1885.

Canvas 68×59 cm. Signed and dated on windowsill: P. d' hooch. f. 1670

PROV.: Madame Kemper, Leyden, 1827;[1] J. Meijnders, Amsterdam, 1838; A. van der Hoop, Amsterdam, by 1842;[2] bequeathed to the city in 1854.

EXH.: (a) Amsterdam 1925, II, no. 421; (b) Schaffhausen 1949, no. 62; (c) Cape Town 1952, no. 24; (d) Oslo 1959, no. 33, ill.; (e) Brussels 1971, no. 56, ill. 72.

LIT.: S no. 51; S s no. 22; Thoré–Bürger 1958–60, II, 55–60, no. 55; Amsterdam, V.d.H. Mus. cat. 1872, no. 50; Van Vloten 1874, 297–8; Lemcke 1878, 9; Havard 1880, 75, 114:3; Havard 1881, 187; HdG 1892, no. 7; Wurzbach, I, 716; HdG no. 173; Jantzen 1912, 32, 33; R, 23, 36, 84, 96, ill. op. 84; Steenhoff 1920, 169; BM 1921, 344; Rothes 1921, 51, fig. 79; Mellaart 1923, 269, pl. B; Lilienfeld 1924, 453; idem. 1924–5, 186; CB, 6, 8, pl. IX; Val. 1926, 62; BM, 79; Val. xix, no. 92; Martin 1935–6, II, 207; T, 42, 44, 58, ill. op. 54; Oosterloo 1948, fig. 53; Amsterdam, R., cat. 1976, 316–7, no. C 147, ill.

The theme of the woman and a letter-carrier also appears in Cat. 84 (Plate 87). As Hofstede de Groot noted, the doorway appears to open onto the Kloveniersburgwal in Amsterdam.

NOTES: [1] S no. 51. The reference to the Caudri sale as a possible provenance entry in HdG no. 173 is in error; this was our Cat. 84. [2] S s no. 22.

95. *A Man Playing a Lute and a Woman Singing**
(Plate 98)   Prob. 1670

Present location unknown.

Canvas 73.5×62.2 cm. Signed and dated on windowsill: P d . . . oo. A. 1670 (?)[1]

PROV.: Bought in The Hague by Mr. Enthoven in 1841;[2] Sale Le Roy de Bruxelles, Paris, 3–4/4/1843, no. 18—1300 frs; Sale D. van der Schrieck of Louvain, Brussels, 8–11/4/1861, no. 35—A. Lamme, 2550 frs; Sale H. de Kat of Dordrecht, Paris, 2–3, 7–8/5/1866, no. 38—2300 frs; Sale C. de Boissere, Paris, 19/2/1883, no. 23; *Sale Baron de Beurnonville, Paris, 3/6/1884, no. 254—7700 frs; Marquis de Blaisel, Paris;[3] Emile Vautier (the painter), Brussels, (sold to) P. Errera of Brussels in 1893;[4] by descent to Alfred Errera (in 1952, on consignment to dlr. Knoedler, New York, later returned to the owner[5]); Wildenstein & Co., London, 1960.[6]

EXH.: London (Wildenstein) 1960, no. 19 [signed and dated: P. d . . oo . . 65].

LIT.: S s no. 7; Havard 1880, 119:1 & 2; HdG no. 121; R, 30, 31, 32, 36, 97, ill. op. 72; CB, 6 [1670]; Val. 1926, 62; BM, 276; Val. no. 95 [1670].

Although the last two digits of the date were read as '65' when the picture was exhibited in 1960, the date 1670 appeared on the work as early as 1866 and was confirmed by several later writers. The latter date is supported by the close stylistic connection with Cat. 94 of that year. Fragments of an inscription, obscured by the figure of the man and the chair, are visible on the open harpsichord: '. . . ET SOLEMEN/ . . . . BORUM/ . . . . . LORIA . . . XCEL.' According to Valentiner, Brière-Misme was the first to notice that the view through the open door at the right is the same as that in a painting in the Frick Collection which is probably correctly attributed to Van der Burch.[7] It is uncertain which of the two artists invented the motif; conceivably a common source inspired both painters. The glass ball overhead reccurs in Cat. 109.

NOTES: [1] Transcribed in HdG no. 121. [2] S s no. 7. [3] HdG no. 121. [4] ibid. [5] ibid. [6] Exh. [7] See Frick Collection, cat., I, 1968, 147–9, ill.

96. *Card Players at a Table* (Plate 99)   *c.* 1670–4
Private Collection.

Canvas 107.3×93.3 cm. Signed upper left on the mantel: P · d · Hoogh · f ·

PROV.: Sale H. van Maarseveen, Amsterdam, 28/10/1793, no. 1—165 fl; Thomas Mansel Talbot, Penrice House, Glamorgan, Wales; by descent to C. Methuen-Campbell; dlr. Agnew, London; dlr. Wildenstein, New York.

LIT.: HdG no. 258.

Close in design to Cat. 86 (Plate 89), the work probably postdates that picture by several years. The larger format and the figure types (particularly the soldier in the foreground) link the picture to De Hooch's works of the early 1670s. Card-playing had been the subject of several earlier paintings (cf. Cat. 25, 28 & 58, Col. Plate VI, Plates 22, 61).

97. *A Man Reading a Letter to a Woman* (Plate 101)
c. 1670–4

Private Collection, France.

Canvas 77×69 cm. Signed on the footwarmer: P. d. Hoogh

PROV.: Baron van Brienen van de Grootelindt, Amsterdam, by 1833;[1] Sale Van Brienen van de Grootelindt, Paris, 8–9/5/1865, no. 15—12,000 frs.

EXH.: Paris, I.N., 1965, no. 27, pl. viii.

LIT.: S no. 44; Inv. of the Van Brienen Collection, Prot.

Not. J.P. van Etten, Amsterdam Municipal Archives, N.A.A. 21684, 28/12/1854; Havard 1880, 113:2; HdG no. 240; R, 98.

The theme of a man reading to a woman who interrupts her needlework to listen had appeared in an earlier work which has been attributed to De Hooch (Cat. B 5, Plate 170). Compositionally the work resembles a series of domestic scenes the artist painted in the late 1660s or early '70s (see Cat. 87–90, Plates 90–3). The man wears a costume similar to that worn by the lute-player in the painting of 1670 formerly in the Errera Collection (Cat. 95, Plate 98). Over the fireplace a picture of a Nativity appears which is based on Cornelis Bloemart's print of 1625 after Abraham Bloemart's painting in Braunschweig (Anton Ulrich-Museum, cat. 1976, no. 171; see Fig. 41).

NOTES: [1] S no. 44.

98. *Woman and Child, with a Serving Woman Holding Asparagus** (Plate 100)   *c.* 1670–4

Present location unknown.

Canvas 71 × 82 cm. Signed left on fireplace: P d Hooch[1]

PROV.: *Sale Jonkheer Frans van Harencarspel Eckhardt, Amsterdam, 15/8/1842, no. 54; Sale P.J. & B., van der Muelen of Coblenz, Amsterdam, 22/8/1850, no. 32—De Vries, 1750 fl; Sale Dr. Van Cleef of Utrecht, Paris, 4/4/1864, no. 47—Meffre, 9000 frs; Sale Paris, 4/3/1889, no. 23; dlr. Durand Ruel, Paris, 1907;[2] Lord Swathling, London, by 1910;[3] Sale Lord Swathling, London, 12/7/1946, no. 26, ill.

EXH.: (a) London, R.A., 1910, no. 69; (b) 1938, no. 246; (c) London (Slatter) 1945, no. 19.

LIT.: HdG no. 64; BM, 265; Val. no. 119 [*c.* 1670–5]; Slive 1974, 108, n. 3.

The design, when reversed, closely resembles that of Cat. 99 (Plate 102). Scenes of serving women presenting food to their mistresses for inspection appeared frequently in these years (see Cat. 99, 101, 112A & B, Plates 102, 104, 115). Valentiner's proposed date of *c.* 1670–5 is acceptable.

NOTES: [1] Transcribed from photograph. [2] HdG no.64. [3] Exh. a.

99. *Two Women and a Child by a Fireplace* (Plate 102)   *c.* 1670–4

North Carolina Museum of Art, Raleigh, acc. no. 52.9.45.

Canvas 64 × 77 cm. Signed right on fireplace: P. d Hooch

PROV.: *Sale F.W. Greebe, Amsterdam, 8/12/1788, no. 3—Yver, 185 fl; Sale J. Pekstok, Amsterdam, 17/12/1792, no. 38—Van der Schley, 231 fl; Sale Jonkheer F. van Harencarspel Eckhardt, Amsterdam, 15/8/1842, no. 53—Hoffmann's executors, 810 fl; Sale P. Voüte, Amsterdam, 12–13/11/1845, no. 32—Burton, 800 fl; dlr. Dowdeswell, London, 1920;[1] acquired by Martin A. Ryerson, Chicago, 1921;[2] Silberman Galleries, New York, 1950;[3] purchased by the State of North Carolina, 1952.

EXH.: Atlanta 1950, no. 21 [*c.* 1670–5].

LIT.: HdG no. 60; Val. 1926, 61 [mid-1660s]; BM, 265; Val. 1927, 77, no. 25; Val. no. 123 [*c.* 1670–5]; Val. 1956, no. 54 [*c.* 1670–5].

Similar in style and design to Cat. 98 (Plate 100), the picture also shares motifs, like the figure silhouetted in the stairway, with Cat. 101 (Plate 104).

NOTES: [1] BM, 265. [2] ibid. [3] Exh.

100. *A Woman Seated beside a Cradle, with an Older Woman* (Plate 103)   *c.* 1670–4

Pushkin Museum of Fine Arts, Moscow, no. 2030.

Canvas 52 × 61 cm. Signed left on windowsill: P d Hoogh

PROV.: (Prob.) Sale Juda van Benjamin, Amsterdam, 4/11/1782, no. 20;[1] *Sale D. Mansveld, Amsterdam, 13/8/1806, no. 68—149 fl;[2] Prince Youssoupoff, St. Petersburg, by 1864.[3]

EXH.: St. Petersburg 1909, no. 372.

LIT.: Waagen 1864, 414; HdG no. 12; Wurzbach, II, 102; R, 104; BM, 263; Val. no. 156 [*c.* 1675–80]; CB 1930, 198; Moscow, P.M., cat. 1961, no. 2030.

The horizontal composition with a woman seated in the shadowed foreground and silhouetted against reflected light recalls designs from the mid to later 1660s (compare Cat. 71 & 72, Plates 74, 75); however, the figure types point to later origins.

NOTES: [1] See HdG no. 12: the window was said to be open. [2] Compare also Cat. C 31, a similar but slightly larger work. [3] Waagen 1864, 414.

101. *A Woman and a Serving Girl with a Fish* (Plate 104)   *c.* 1670–4

Museum Boymans-van Beuningen, Rotterdam, inv. no. 2500.

Canvas 83 × 72 cm.

PROV.: *Sale J.M. Quinkhardt, Amsterdam, 15/3/1773, no. 13—Pothoven, 320 fl;[1] Sale Piet Calkoen Willemsz., Amsterdam, 10/9/1781, no. 64—A. Calkoen, 208 fl; (prob.) P.C. Amsterdam, 1833;[2] Sale P. van Romondt et al., Amsterdam, 11/5/1835, no. 10—Roos; Sale J.G. Voigt, Amsterdam, 19/10/1837, no. 38—Brondgeest, 1350 frs; *(prob.) Sale [Tardieu], Paris. 31/3–3/4/1841, no. 45 (w/o m.)—Simonet, 7900 frs;[3] *(poss.) Sale [Tardieu], Paris, 9/5/1843, no. 34, (w/o m.)—3000 frs;[4] Sale [Tardieu], Paris, 4/2/1851, no. 10—Berville, 1500 frs; Chaplin Collection, London;[5] Sale J.A. Tardieu, Paris, 10/5/1867, no. 24—Nieuwenhuys, 1500 frs; Sale Leboeuf de Montgermont, Paris, 16/6/1919, no. 194—Sedelmeyer (for Preyer), 175,000 frs; dlr. A. Preyer, The Hague, 1923;[6] dlr. Knoedler, New York, 1925;[7] dlr. Kleykamp, The Hague, 1926–9;[8] dlr. Knoedler, 1931;[9] ten Bos Collection, Almelo;[10] D.G. van Beuningen Collection, by 1952;[11] acq. 1958.

EXH.: (a) New York (Knoedler) 1925, no. 7; (b) The Hague (Kleykamp) 1926, no. 24, ill.; (c) 1928, no. 16; (d) 1929, no. 28; (e) New York (Kleinberger) 1931, (w/o cat. no.); (f) Paris 1952, no. 101; (g) Rotterdam 1955, no. 79, fig. 143.

LIT.: S no 65; Havard 1880, 102:3; HdG no. 61; O. Hirschmann, 'Die Sammlung A. Preyer im Haag', *Cicerone*, 15 (2/1923), 125, ill. 133; Val. 1926, 61 [mid-1660s]; BM, 265; Val. 1927, 77, no. 17; Val. no. 120 [*c.* 1670–5]; Rotterdam, B.M. cat. 1962, 68, no. 2500 [*c.* 1670–5], ill.

According to the Montgermont Sale catalogue, the picture was said to be signed in the upper left 'P. de Hoogh. f'. When it was exhibited in 1955 a signature was reported as appearing on the fireplace. No signature is now visible on the work. The figure types and motifs, such as the maid showing food to the seated woman, recall Cat. 98 and 99. Here, however, the composition is adapted to an upright format as in Cat. 112A & B (Plate 115). Valentiner's dating of the work is probably approximately correct.

NOTES: [1] The work did not appear in the Quinkhardt Sale of 1798 as reported in HdG no. 61. [2] S. no. 65 with approximate

measurements of 28″×23″ (71×58.4 cm). ³ BMf. ⁴ ibid.:
'Une servante montrant du poisson à sa maîtresse'. The picture
is not to be identified with S s no. 18 as suggested in Hofstede
de Groot; this was probably a copy or version of the painting
in Aix (cf. Cat. 141a). Consequently the work was not in
the De Reus collection in The Hague in 1842. ⁵ Ref. Tardieu
Sale cat. 1867. ⁶ *Cicerone*, 1923. ⁷ Exh. a. ⁸ Exh. b, c, d.
⁹ Exh. e. ¹⁰ Exh. f. ¹¹ Exh. f.

102. *Woman and Child with a Parrot* (Plate 105)   1673
Present location unknown (disappeared in the last war).
Canvas 76×67 cm. Signed and dated 1673.
    PROV.: Sale, Rotterdam, 3/8/1811, no. 22—Van der Haar,
385 fl; Sale H. Croese, Amsterdam, 18/9/1811, no. 117—Van
Raven, 725 fl; Sale [Croese], Amsterdam, 20/7/1812, no. 21—
Van der Werf, 507 fl; Sale J. Hulswit, Amsterdam, 28/10/1822,
no. 42—Hopman, 1000 fl; (prob.) Sale Comte de Pourtalès,
London, 19/5/1826, no. 103 (w/o m.)—(poss.) sold by M. de la
Hante, 15,000 frs;¹ (poss.) Sale F. Kalkbrenner, Paris,
14/1/1850, no. 11—Castaing, 3650 frs;² (poss.) J. Caroyon-
Talpayrac Collection; ³ *(poss.) Sale A. Seymour, London,
4/4/1896, no. 35;⁴ dlr. F. Kleinberger, Paris;⁵ A. Schloss, Paris,
by 1906.⁶
    EXH.: Leiden 1906, no. 22 (s. & d. 1673).
    LIT.: (Poss.) Blanc 1857–8, II, 470;⁷ A. Bredius, *De leidsche
tentoonstelling in 1906*, Haarlem, 1907, n. 20, pl. 20; HdG nos.
114 & 236a; Jantzen, 1912, 31; R, 98; C. Misme, 'Catalogue
Collection Schloss', (unpub.), n.d., no. 119; BM, 263; Val.
no. 108; Kauffmann 1930, col. 805.
    The theme of a woman feeding a parrot had appeared in a
slightly earlier painting (Cat. 90, Plate 93) and seems to have
been the invention of Frans van Mieris. Over the door a relief
of Venus and Cupid appears which also figures in Cat. 107
(Plate 113) and in several other works from this period.
    NOTES: ¹ Ref. Kalkbrenner Sale cat. 1850. ² Identical
according to HdG [English ed.] no. 114; however, described
only as 'Scène d'intérieur', Canvas 75×66 cm.³ HdG no. 114;
contrary to the author's statement, the picture was not in the
sale of this collection (Paris, 27/3/1893). ⁴ 'Interior, with ladies
and children with a parrot'; 29″×26″ (73.7×66 cm). ⁵ HdG
no. 114. ⁶ Exh. ⁷ Ref. Kalkbrenner Sale.

(a) Copy. Panel 49×41.2 cm. Sale Goudstikker et al., Cologne,
5/2/1941, no. 69 [P.d.H.], pl. 29.

**103. *A Woman Knitting, with a Serving Woman and a
Child*** (Plate 106)   c. 1673
Private Collection, England.
Canvas 72.4×62.7 cm.
    PROV.: Acquired by the Duke of Montagu c. 1770;¹ Duke
of Buccleuch, Montagu House, cat. 1820;² sold in 1965 by the
late Duke to Marlborough Fine Art Ltd., London.
    EXH.: (a) London, B.I., 1829, no. 134; (b) National Gallery,
London, 1917; (c) London, R.A., 1929, no. 334.
    LIT.: Montagu House, cat. 1820; S no. 57; Havard 1880,
III:3; *Catalogue of the Pictures in Montagu House*, London,
1898, no. 35; HdG no. 112; R, 100; CB, 6 [c. 1672]; BM, 263,
ill. 267; Val. no. 109 [c. 1673]; CB 1930, 198.
    In design and figure types the picture most resembles the
painting dated 1673 formerly in the Schloss Collection (Cat.
102, Plate 105). The source for the partially curtained painting
of Venus and Cupid on the wall also served for the reliefs in

the overdoors in Cat. 102 and 107 (Plates 105, 113). The child
is holding a marzipan with a carnation in the centre.
    NOTES: ¹ Communication, the Duke of Buccleuch. ² ibid.

104. *Two Women and a Child Preparing to Depart*
(Plate 107)   c. 1673
Pushkin Museum of Fine Arts, Moscow, no. 1679.
Canvas 75×61 cm. Signed left on table: P d hooch
    PROV.: (Prob.) acquired by Lafontaine in Holland, 1797;¹
(prob.) Sale Lafontaine, Paris, 12/12/1798, no. 11 (w/o m.);
Prince Youssoupoff, by 1864;² formerly, The Hermitage,
Leningrad.
    EXH.: St. Petersburg 1909, no. 276.
    LIT.: Waagen 1864, 415; HdG no. 76; R, 104; CB, 8 [after
1675]; Val. 1926, 61 [mid-1660s]; BM, 263; Val. xix, no. 112
[c. 1673]; Moscow, P.M., cat. 1961, no. 1679.
    Valentiner correctly observed that the connection with Cat.
102 (Plate 105) suggests a date of c. 1673. The theme of a
woman preparing to go shopping also appears in a work
which has been attributed to De Hooch (Cat. B 1, Plate 167).
    NOTES: ¹ Ref. Sale cat. 1798. ² Waagen 1864.

104A. Possible version or copy. Canvas 86.3×53.3 cm. Sale
(without date) 1800, no. 33 (German cat. at RKD; not in
Lugt); Sale M . . ., Scheckgraben, Vienna (?), May 10 (without
year; Lugt no. 11061), no. 29.

**105. *A Couple Playing Music at a Table, with a Serving
Woman and a Couple Embracing*** (Plate 108)   c. 1673–5
Private Collection, England.
Canvas 57×65 cm. Signed right over door: P d Hooghe¹
    PROV.: G. Cornwall Legh, Eaton Place, London, (prob.) by
1867;² Henry Cornwall Legh, High Legh Hall, London, cat.
(c. 1893), no. 14; Sir Joseph Robinson, London; Sale Robinson,
London, 6/7/1923, no. 67 (bought in); by descent to Princess
Labia, Cape Town.³
    EXH.: (a) (Prob.) London, B.I., 1867, no. 103;⁴ (b) London,
R.A., 1958, no. 55, ill.; (c) Cape Town 1959, no. 43; (d)
Zurich 1963, no. 25 [c. 1675–80], fig. 8.
    LIT.: *Catalogue of the Collection of Paintings at High Legh Hall*,
Birmingham, n. d. (c. 1893), no. 14, ill.; BM, 277, 278, 281
ill.; Val. no. 150 (above), [c. 1675–80]; A. Scharf, in *Burl. M.*,
100 (1958), 304.
    The amorous theme and horizontal composition with a
view to a garden relate the work to Cat. 106 (Plate 109). The
same male model with long curly hair seems to reappear
elsewhere in works of the early 1670s (cf. Cat. 95 & 111,
Plates 98, 114) as does the relief of Venus and Cupid over the
door (see Cat. 102, 103, 107 & 109, Plates 105, 106, 111, 113).
    NOTES: ¹ Transcribed from a photograph. ² Exh. a. Accord-
ing to the P. de Boer exh. cat. Amsterdam 1937, no. 20, the
painting with G. Cornwall Legh at this time was our Cat. 154.
Unlike the present picture, though, the latter work did not
appear in the High Legh cat. of c. 1893, suggesting the De
Boer catalogue was probably in error. ³ Exh. c. ⁴ See note 2.

105A. Possible version or copy. Panel 66×77 cm. Sale
Amsterdam, 15/7/1772, no. 30—30 fl. (See Cat. C 101.)

**106. *Two Embracing Couples, with a Man Smoking and a
Serving Boy*** (Plate 109)   c. 1673–5
Private Collection.
Canvas 63.5×80 cm. Signed on bench: P d · Hooch¹

PROV.: *(Prob.) Sale Amsterdam, 20/3/1764, no. 31—the broker Ottens, 14 fl;[2] *Sale Ploos van Amstel, Amsterdam, 30/10/1780, no. 26—Wubbens, 42 fl; Admiral Radstock;[3] Marquis of Stafford;[4] dlr. F. Kleinberger, Paris;[5] Sir George Donaldson, London, 1902;[6] (sold to) Sir Joseph Robinson of South Africa; Sale Robinson, London, 6/7/1923, no. 66, ill. (bought in); by descent to Princess Labia; Sale The late Princess Labia, London, 27/11/1963, no. 15, ill.—Hallsborough Galleries; Hallsborough Gall., 1965.[7]

EXH.: (a) London, R.A., 1958, no. 51, ill.; (b) Cape Town 1959, no. 42, pl. 33; (c) Zurich 1962, no. 26; (d) London (Hallsborough) 1965, no. 18, ill.

LIT.: HdG no. 184 [a late work]; R, 100; BM 1921, 342; BM, 278–80, ill 283; Val. no. 150 (below), [c. 1675–80]; A. Scharf, in *Burl. M.*, 100 (1958), 304.

Prior to Hofstede de Groot's writing, and until the picture was cleaned in c. 1964, the man lying on the bench held a glass aloft in his left hand.[8] The removal of the overpaint revealed that the man's hand originally rested in the woman's lap. The amorous theme and the design relate the work to Cat. 105 (Plate 108). The same source for the Venus and Cupid painting over the fireplace was employed in Cat. 88 (Plate 91).

NOTES: [1] Transcribed from photograph. [2] 'An interior, with a woman in a satin dress; beside her an officer who caresses her; with additional elements', 27″×33″ (68.5×83.7 cm). [3] Princess Labia Sale cat. 1963. [4] ibid. No supporting evidence for this or the above entry has been found. [5] HdG no. 184. [6] ibid. [7] Exh. c. [8] cf. Val. no. 150 (below).

107. *A Merry Company with a Trumpeter* (Plate 113)
c. 1673–5

Staatliche Museen, Gemäldegalerie, Berlin-Dahlem, no. 1401.
Canvas 85×92 cm. Signed left on door: Pieter de Hoo[g]h

PROV.: Sale A. Stevens, Paris, 1–2/5/1867, no. 19—Berlin Museum, 3200 frs; on loan to Städt. Museum, Magdeburg, 1889, returned 1904; on loan Münster Museum, 1931–45.

EXH.: (a) Washington 1948, no. 100 [as P.d.H?]; (b) New York et al., 1948–9, no. 64.

LIT.: Havard 1880, 116:1; HdG 1892, no. 63; Wurzbach, I, 716 [as signed falsely]; HdG no. 176 ['about 1660, or may be later']; R, 101, ill. op. 76; CB, 8; BM, 274; Val. no. 107 [c. 1671–4]; Kauffmann 1930, col. 805; Pelinck 1958, n. 3.

While the signature with the unabbreviated first name is unusual, it does not seem, as Wurzbach suggested, false. The trumpeter theme was treated in an early painting (Cat. 7, Plate 6) and in the picture of c. 1670 in Brussels (Cat. 93, Plate 97). In the latter work a man with a flute glass toasts in a similar fashion. Architectural resemblances appear in an approximately contemporaneous series of musical company scenes (Cat. 108–10, Plates 110–12).

108. *A Musical Party with Four Figures** (Plate 110) 1674
Academy of Arts, Honolulu, acc. no. 3798.1.
Canvas 98×115 cm. Signed and dated over door: P. d' Hoogh 1674

PROV.: *(poss.) Sale Fiseau, Wildeman et al., Amsterdam, 12/10/1768, no. 22 (bought in);[1] *(poss.) Sale, Amsterdam, 12/2/1770, no. 39;[2] Von Peucker Collection, Berlin, by 1856;[3] *S.E.M. Openheim, Cologne, 14/10/1878, no. 29; dlr. Schall, Baden-Baden;[4] Charles T. Yerkes, Chicago, cats. (1893), no. 28

and (1904), no. 50; Sale C.T. Yerkes, New York, 5–8/4/1910, no. 133; Sale Haworth et al. (Gerald Stanley), London, 21/11/1952, no. 22, ill.—Frost & Reed; dlr. Frost & Reed Ltd., London, 1953;[5] purchased in 1971 from Hirschl & Adler Gall., New York.

LIT.: M. Schasler, *Berlins Kunstschätze*, Berlin, 1856, 414, no. 19; Parthey 1863–4, I, 622; Yerkes Coll. cat. 1893, no. 28, ill.; 1904, no. 50, ill.; HdG nos. 130, 161a, and poss. 138; BM, 1921, 344; CB, 6 [1670]; BM, 276; Val. no. 103 [c. 1671–4]; Würtenberger 1937, 85; T, 59, ill. 57.

The date 1674, which appears on the painting, has often been overlooked. The work is closely related in style and composition to cat. 109 and 110 (Plates 111, 112). According to Valentiner, Hofstede de Groot first noted that the view through the doorway recalls the courtyard of the Exchange in Amsterdam.

NOTES: [1] 'A musical company in a handsome interior with a sunny view through the door', Canvas 92.6×118.3 cm. (not in HdG); see note 2. [2] HdG no. 138 (91.4×111.8 cm); this and the preceding sale, however, may apply to Cat. 109. [3] Schasler 1856, no. 19; Parthey 1863–4, I, 622. Reference to the Von Peucker collection is made in the Oppenheim sale catalogue. Compare also the painting offered as a Vermeer to the Brussels Museum in 1861 (Cat. C 130). [4] Yerkes Sale cat. [5] C. 123 (11/1953).

109. *A Music Party with Five Figures* (Col. Plate XV, Plate 111)
c. 1674

Royal Museum of Fine Arts, Copenhagen, no. Sp. 613.
Canvas 92×105.5 cm. Signed right above door: P · d · Hoogh ·

PROV.: (Poss.) Sale Amsterdam, 9/4/1687, no. 19—70 fl;[1] *(poss.) Sale Fiseau et al., Amsterdam, 12/10/1768, no. 22 (bought in);[2] *(poss.) Sale, Amsterdam, 12/2/1770, no. 39;[3] Fredensborg Castle, by 1792;[4] entered the Royal Collection of Paintings, 1827.[5]

LIT.: (Poss.) Hoet 1752, I, 5, no. 19; F.W.B. von Ramdohr, *Studien auf einer Reise nach Dänemark*, I, Hannover, 1792, 237; Gower 1880, 111; HdG 1892, no. 32; Wurzbach, I, 717; HdG no. 125, and poss. 136b & 138; BM, 276; Val. 1927, 70; Val. xxii, no. 101 [c. 1671–4]; Würtenberger 1937, 85; BM 1947–8, IV, 364–5, fig. 8; Copenhagen, R.M., cat. 1951, no. 328, ill.; Gerson, 1966, 310.

A date of about 1674 is supported by the strong resemblance in style and design to the painting dated in that year in Honolulu (Cat. 108, Plate 110). Similar architecture appears in Cat. 107 and 110 (Plates 112, 113). The motif of the woman seated by the window at the left resembles that of the painting of 1670 formerly in the Errera Collection (Cat. 95, Plate 98), where a glass sphere also appears suspended from the ceiling.[6]

NOTES: [1] Identical according to J.C. Spengler, *Catalog over Det Kongelige Billedgalleri paa Christiansborg*, Copenhagen, 1827, no. 613; see Hoet 1752, I, 5, no. 19 & HdG no. 136b. K. Madsen repeated the reference (Royal Museum, cat. 1904, no. 151), adding a question mark. No documentary support or recorded explanation for Spengler's identification appears in the records of the Museum. [2] Also possibly identical with Cat. 108. [3] HdG 138; also poss. ident. with Cat. 108. [4] Von Ramdohr 1792. [5] Kunstkammerets Inventarius, IV, 10, no. 1042. [6] Concerning the possible associations of such objects, see E. de Jongh, 'Pearls of Virtue and Pearls of Vice', *Simiolus*, 8 (1975–6), no. 2, 69 ff.

110. *A Musical Company with Five Figures* (Plate 112)
                                                  c. 1674
Deder Collection.
Canvas 90×108 cm. Signed right above door: P d Hoogh f
PROV.: *Sale D. Mansveld, Amsterdam, 13/8/1806, no. 67—
40 fl; Count Fries, Vienna;[1] Sale H. Héris, Brussels, 19–20/6/
1846 no. 28—Le Roy, 2300 frs; acquired in 1872 from J.C.
Robinson[2] by Sir Francis Cook, Doughty House, Richmond,
cats. (1914), II, no. 268, and (1932), no. 268; dlr. Agnew,
London, 1944–6; R.P. Silcock, Preston, Lancashire, 1946–Oct.
1953; dlr. Duits, London, 1953–4; Hallsborough Gall.,
London, 11/1954–2/1955; dlr. Sabin, London, 3/1955–3/1959;
St. James Gall., London, 1959; dlr. D. Koetser, Zurich,
1959–68; Brod Gall., London, 1969.[3]
EXH.: (a) London (Hallsborough) 1955, no. 13; (b) Tokyo
1969; (c) Münster 1975, fig. 26.
LIT.: HdG 1892, no. 61; Wurzbach, I, 717; HdG no. 135;
R, 100; J.O. Kronig, *A Catalogue of . . . the Collection of Sir
Frederick Cook Bt.*, II, *Dutch and Flemish Schools*, 1914, 46, no.
268; CB, 6, 8; BM, 276; Val. no. 102 [*c.* 1671–4].

The picture is related in style and composition to Cat. 108
(dated 1674) and 109 (Plates 110, 111).

NOTES: [1] Héris Sale cat. 1846. Compare also the painting attr.
to Vermeer in 1861 (Cat. C 130). [2] Cook Coll. cat. (1914), no.
268. [3] Prov. from 1944 to 1969 provided by Brod Gallery,
London.

111. *An Officer Paying a Woman in a Stable* (Plate 114)
                                                  c. 1674
Metropolitan Museum of Art, New York, acc. no. 58.144.
Gift of Stuart Borchard and Evelyn B. Metzger, 1958.
Canvas 94.5×111.1 cm. Signed upper right on beam:
P · d · Hoogh ·
PROV.: Sale J.G. Cramer, Amsterdam, 13/11/1769; Sale
Amsterdam, 30/11/1772, no. 15; Duc de Morny, by 1863;[1]
Sale Duc de Morny, Paris, 31/5/1865, no. 53—P. Demidoff;
P. Demidoff, St. Petersburg; acquired in Russia in 1922 by
dlr. Satinover of New York;[2] acquired in 1923 by Samuel
Borchard, New York.[3]
EXH.: New York (Duveen) 1942, no. 31, ill.
LIT.: (Prob.) Kramm 1859; 734;[4] H. Havard, in *G.B.A.*,
1863, 297–8; Havard 1880, 132:1; HdG nos. 276 & 281;
Val. 1926, 58; BM, 260–1, ill. 259; Val. 1927, 76, no. 6; Val.
XVII, no. 105 [*c.* 1671–4]; C. Gilbert, in exh. cat. Waltham
1966, 44; Fleischer 1978, ns. 10 & 17.

The theme of the disputed reckoning was treated earlier
in the painting of 1658 in the Marquis of Bute's collection
(Cat. 27, Plate 24). The scale and execution link the work to
the musical company series of *c.* 1674 (Cat. 108–10, Plates
110–12).

NOTES: [1] Havard, in *G.B.A.*, 1863. Also possibly identical
with the painting mentioned in a Parisian news report of
12/1/1857 (cf. Kramm 1859, 734) as having been acquired by
the Duc de Morny for 100,000 frs while on a mission for
Napoleon III to St. Petersburg. [2] BM, 260–1. [3] ibid. [4] See note 1.
PRINT: L. Lagrange (cf. Havard 1863, 297).

112A. *Mother and Child with a Serving Girl* (Plate 115)
                                                  c. 1674–6
John G. Johnson Collection, Philadelphia, no. 501.
Canvas 85.8×79 cm.
PROV.: Sale E. Hooft (widow of W. Valckenier), Amsterdam,

31/8/1796, no. 14—Roos, 200 fl;[1] *Sale, Amsterdam, 20/5/
1799, no. 48—Pruissenaar, 130 fl; *Sale, Amsterdam,
16/6/1800, no. 10—Stork, 112 fl; Artis Collection, 1833;[2] *(prob.)
Sale, London, 23/4/1836, no. 63 (w/o m.)—57 gns; *Sale Rev.
W. Jones Thanes, London, 10/7/1886, no. 137—£131;[3] J.G.
Johnson, Philadelphia, by 1913.[4]
LIT.: S no. 39; Havard 1880, 102:1 [erroneously as S. no.
40]; HdG no. 28; Val. 1913, no. 501 [*c.* 1665]; BM, 265; Val.
285, under no. 114; Johnson Coll. cat. 1941, 29, no. 501 [as
copy after P.d.H.; early eighteenth century]; Copenhagen,
R.M. cat. 1951, 137; Phila., J.C., cat. 1972, 47, no. 501 [copy
after P.d.H.]; Slive 1974, 108, n. 3.

Valentiner noted that the provenance had been confused
with that of the version in Copenhagen (Cat. 112B).[5] Although
no pentimenti or other internal evidence prove that the present
work was the original, Valentiner probably was correct in
suggesting that this was the earlier of the two. Despite doubts
expressed in the catalogues of the collection, the work is
probably genuine and is typical of the artist's products of the
mid-1670s.

NOTES.: [1] Erroneously listed under HdG no. 28; see Cat.
112B. Contrary to the statement in the most recent catalogue
of the collection, the work did not appear in this sale. [2] S. no. 39
(with measurements reversed). [3] BMf. [4] Val. 1913, 96. [5] ibid.

112B. *Mother and Child with a Serving Girl*   *c.* 1674–6
Royal Museum of Fine Arts, Copenhagen, no. Sp. 614.
Canvas 91.5×83 cm. Formerly remnants of a signature on
the footwarmer.[1]
PROV.: Purchased in Holland in 1759 by dlrs. Wahls and
Morrells and sold to King Frederick V of Denmark.[2]
EXH.: Berlin 1929, no. 38.
LIT.: Wahl's *Manuel*, 1737–65, no. 80 ['copie']; Wurzbach,
I, 717; HdG no. 28; Val. 1913 (under no. 501); Val. 1926, 61
[mid-1660s]; BM, 52 [Ochtervelt], 265 [P.d.H.; the first
reference a typographical error?]; Val. no. 114 [*c.* 1670–5];
Copenhagen, R.M., cat. 1951, 137, no. 329, ill.; Slive 1974,
108, n. 3.

When the picture was inventoried in 1760 it was listed as a
copy. It is not so freely executed as the version in Philadelphia
(Cat. 112A), but its relatively good quality and the fact that
the artist repeated his own compositions raise the possibility
that the painting may be an autograph replica.

NOTES: [1] See K. Madsen, R.M., cat. 1904, no. 152. [2] Inventory Manuel 1737–65, no. 80. The early date of acquisition
proves that the Philadelphia version was the work which
figured in the later sales.

113. *Mother and Child by a Cradle* (Plate 116)   *c.* 1674–6
The Detroit Institute of Arts, Detroit, acc. no. 89.39. Gift
of James E. Scripps.
Canvas 79.4×58.1 cm. Signed lower right on cradle: P [d]
Hoogh
PROV.: Count de Montgermont.[1]
EXH.: (a) Detroit 1925, no. 13; (b) 1929, no. 37; (c)
Indianapolis 1937, no. 33.
LIT.: BM, 226; Val. 1927, 77, no. 26; Val. no. 113 [*c.* 1671–4]
W. Heil, in *P.*, 5 (1930), 34; Detroit, I.A., cat. 1930, no. 104
[*c.* 1671–3]; Detroit, I.A., *Checklist*, 1970, no. 70; Slive 1974,
108, n. 3.

The relatively large scale of the figures and the subdued
tonality suggest a date in the mid-1670s. The concentration

upon the single motif of the mother and child is unusual in this period. A picture with similar vertical measurements and fitting this work's description except for the reference to a woman by a fire appeared in two early sales (see Cat. C 26). Conceivably, the present work could have been cut down.

NOTES: [1] *Catalogue of the Scripps Collection*, Detroit Museum, 1889.

114. *A Party of Six Figures* (Plate 117)   prob. 1675
Philadelphia Museum of Art, Philadelphia, acc. no. W' 12-1-17. The Wilstach Collection.

Canvas 82× 100 cm. Formerly signed and dated 1675.

PROV.: Dlr. Lesser, London, 1889;[1] Sir Charles Robinson, London, 1892;[2] R. Wanamaker, Philadelphia, by 1898,[3] cat. (1904), no. 22; W.P. Wilstach, Philadelphia.

EXH.: Paris (Sedelmeyer) 1898, no. 71, ill. [s. & d. 1653].

LIT.: Bredius 1889, 167, n. 2; HdG 1892, no. 51; E.C. Siter, *Catalogue of the R. Wanamaker Collection*, Philadelphia, 1904, no. 22; Wurzbach, I, 717 [1653]; HdG no. 197 [1675]; Jantzen 1912, 13; R, 105; BM, 1921, 342; M.W. Brockwell, *Catalogue of the W.P. Wilstach Collection*, Philadelphia, 1922, no. 153; CB, 3, 8 [1675]; BM, 276 [1675]; Val. no. 138 [1675]; Kauffmann 1930, col. 805; Phila. Mus. cat. 1965, 33.

The picture formerly bore a signature and a date, which was initially read as 1653[4] and later probably correctly deciphered by Hofstede de Groot as 1675. During a restoration in *c.* 1940 the inscription disappeared and the overpainting on the standing woman's headgear was removed.[5] In theme and composition the picture seems to have resembled a smaller, lost work by the artist (see Cat. C 135). Infra-red photographs reveal another figure, or perhaps a bust on a pedestal, beneath the archway at the right. The picture has been overcleaned.

NOTES: [1] HdG no. 197. [2] HdG 1892, no. 51. [3] Exh. [4] Exh. [5] Compare old state, Val. no. 138.

115. *A Standing Woman with a Woman Playing the Cello* (Plate 118)   *c.* 1675
Private Collection, West Germany.

Canvas 67× 52 cm.

PROV.: *(Prob.) Sale Deux Amateurs, Leiden, 26/8/1788, no. 57—De Marré, 30 fl;[1] A.J. Cliffe, London, 1892;[2] Alfred Beit, London, cats. (1904), II, and (1913), no. 29; Sale Mrs. Arthur Bull, London, 25/10/1946, no. 21—Slatter; dlr. Slatter, London, 1947;[3] Sale Château de Steenokkerzeel et al. (F. Kuranda of Vienna), Brussels, 13–14/10/1953, no. 326, pl. IV; Dr. G. Henle, Duisburg;[4] dlr. X. Scheidwimmer, Munich, 1975.[5]

EXH.: London (Slatter) 1947, no. 4, ill.

LIT.: W. Bode, *Die Kunstsammlungen des Herrn Alfred Beit*, Berlin, 1904, 57; HdG nos. 127 & prob. 140; W. Bode, *Catalogue of the Collection of Pictures . . . of Mr. Otto Beit*, London, 1913, 8, 76–7, no. 29 [*c.* 1675]; R., 99; *Burl. M.*, 89 (1947), ill. 162B; 117 (1975), ill. suppl. 3.

The picture probably was once horizontal in format, having been cut substantially at the left and to a lesser extent on the right and upper edges.[6] This dismemberment probably took place between 1788 and 1892. It eliminated a male figure at the left, who originally faced the woman with her back to the viewer (compare the composition of Cat. 114). Prior to the picture's entrance into the Beit collection and until 1946–7, a table with a Turkish carpet was painted in at the left.[7] No

doubt this addition was designed to compensate for the vacant passage left by the severing of the canvas. The date *c.* 1675, proposed in the Beit Collection catalogue, is acceptable.

NOTES: [1] HdG no. 140: 'In an interior, a gentleman and a lady dressed in white satin are dancing beside a young woman who plays a bass viol; other accessories . . .', C. 30″× 35″ (76.2 × 88.9 cm). [2] Beit Coll. cat. [3] Exh. [4] Communication Dr. Henle. [5] *Burl. M.*, 117 (12/1975), suppl. 13. [6] See probable original measurements, note 1. [7] The table was still visible when the picture was sold in 1946 but had disappeared when Slatter exhibited it in the following year.

116. *A Musical Party* (Plate 119)   *c.* 1675
Indianapolis Museum of Art, Indianapolis, acc. no. 67.21. Gift of Mr. & Mrs. Miklos Sperling.

Canvas 92.7× 109.8 cm. Remnants of a signature over the door.

PROV.: Sale Abbé de Gevigney, Paris, 1–29/12/1779, no. 400—Langlier, 697 frs; Sale Marquis de Salamanca, Paris, 3–6/6/1867, no. 92—(bought in?) 10,200 frs; *(prob.) Sale Marquis de Salamanca et al., Paris, 25/1/1875, no. 58 [attr. to P.d.H.]—6000 frs;[1] Dowager Duchess of Richelieu, Princess of Monaco;[2] Edward Jones, New York, 1927;[3] purchased from Parisian dlr. in 1927 by J.D. Levy of New York;[4] Sale Mrs. J. Heine (formerly Mrs. J.D. Levy), New York, 24–5/11/1944, no. 254, ill; Acquavella Gall., New York; L.S. Kaplan, New York; Sale Earl of Elgin et al. (L.S. Kaplan), London, 27/6/1958, no. 46—J. Mitchell; Miklos Sperling, Indianapolis, 1958.

EXH.: Indianapolis 1972.

LIT.: S no. 7; Havard 1880, 120:1, 121:1; HdG 1892, 188, no. 7; HdG no. 166; BM, 277, 279, ill.; Val. no. 152 [*c.* 1677–80]; Indianapolis, I.A.M., cat. 1970, no. 101, ill; Valdivieso 1973, 289.

The signature, now illegible, read 'P.D. Hoog fecit' in 1867,[5] and 'P D HOOCH fecit' as recently as 1944.[6] Overpainting, formerly visible on the wall behind the music-makers and in the face of the woman seated on the far side of the table,[7] was removed prior to 1958.[8] A date of *c.* 1675 is proposed on the basis of the resemblance in style to Cat. 114 (Plate 117), which was formerly dated in that year.

NOTES: [1] 'Cavaliers et Amazones. Scene d'intérieur', Canvas 93× 110 cm. [2] Heine Sale cat. 1944. [3] ibid. [4] BM, 277. [5] Salamanca Sale cat. 1867. [6] Heine Sale cat. 1944. [7] cf. repr. Heine Sale cat. 1944. [8] cf. repr. Kaplan Sale cat. 1958.

117. *A Musical Party with Twelve Figures* (Plate 120)   *c.* 1675-7
Wellington Museum, Apsley House, London, inv. no. 1487–1948.

Canvas 103× 133 cm. Remnants of a signature on the fireplace.[1]

PROV.: Sale J. van der Linden van Slingeland, Dordrecht, 22/9/1785, no. 189—Beekman, 70 fl;[2] purchased in 1818 in Paris by Ferol de Bonnemaison for the first Duke of Wellington.[3]

EXH.: (a) London, B.I., 1821, no. 86; (b) 1829, no. 181; (c) 1847, no. 118; (d) 1856, no. 87; (e) London, R.A., 1888, no. 53; (f) 1929, no. 328; (g) Delft 1962, no. 22, ill. 8.

LIT.: *Athenaeum*, 14/6/1856, & 11/2/1888; HdG 1892, no. 58; London, Apsley Hse., cat. 1901, II, no. 36; Wurzbach, I, 717;

HdG nos. 128 [towards 1670] & 139; BM, 277; Val. no. 143 [c. 1675–80]; Pelinck 1958, ns. 3 & 7; Kauffmann 1965, no. 38, ill.; Gerson 1966, 310.

While the work is thematically related to the series of musical companies of c. 1674 (Cat. 108–10, Plates 110, 111, 112), its broader execution suggests a slightly later date. Efforts to identify the heraldry shields on the fireplace have been unsuccessful. The male shield has a yellow or gold horizontal band on a reddish orange field, while the female shield has three-pointed silver stars on a blue field. The extreme simplicity of the designs suggests that they may have been invented by the artist. Pelinck incorrectly suggested that the picture could be the companion piece mentioned in sales to the *Jacott–Hoppesack Portrait* (Cat. 92, Plate 95). The design on the marble floor, with a central circular pattern, appears elsewhere in works of this period (see Cat. 108, 114 & 156 (Plates 110, 117, 159).

NOTES: [1] According to HdG no. 128, signed 'P. De Hooge'. [2] HdG no. 139, with incorrect measurements; the sale catalogue records 40″×50″ (101.5×129.5 cm). [3] Apsley Hse. cat. 1901.

118. *Three Figures at a Table, and a Couple at a Harpsichord*
(Plate 121)   c. 1675–7
Lord Barnard, Raby Castle, Darlington, no. 128.
Canvas 92.5×115 cm. Signed over door: P · d · Hooghe
PROV.: *Sale, Amsterdam, 10/9/1800, no. 59—Gruyter, 71 fl; *Sale, Paris, 18/4/1803, no. 106—Paillet, 300 frs;[1] Sale L.B. Coclers, Amsterdam, 8/4/1816, no. 50—Roos, 180 fl;[2] Lord Barnard, by 1912.[3]
EXH.: (a) London, R.A., 1912, no. 87; (b) 1929, no. 333; (c) Leeds 1936, no. 16; (d) London, R.A., 1952–3, no. 471.
LIT.: Havard 1880, 126:1, HdG nos. 178, 145 & 151; CB, 8; BM, 277; Val. no. 132 [c. 1675].

The compositional scheme, with a group of figures gathered in the left foreground and a second group situated in the rear of the room, recalls the design of Cat. 117 (Plate 120). Fragments of an inscription are visible on the harpsichord: 'SOL D . . ./ GL . . ./ ANS. . .'.

NOTES: [1] Havard (1880, 126:1) transcribed the entry from this sale but recorded the date 11/7/1803 (another sale organized by Paillet and Delaroche in which no De Hoochs appeared). HdG no. 145 repeats this error. [2] HdG no. 151. [3] Exh. a. The picture was not in the sale of Lord Barnard's collection as stated by Brière-Misme and Valentiner.

119. *A Man and a Serving Woman behind a Screen, with Card Players*★ (Plate 122)   c. 1675–80
Present location unknown.
Canvas 88×81 cm. Signed upper left: P · d · Hoogh ·[1]
PROV.: Sale J. Fokker, Amsterdam, 29/6/1814, no. 25—Peters, 150 fl; Sale Comte F. de Robiano, Brussels, 1/5/1837, no. 280—1760 frs; Sale Georg Stange of Lübeck, Cologne, 20–1/3/1879, no. 45; Sale G. Habich, Kassel, 9–10/5/1892, no. 79, ill.—Consul Weber, 3120 mks; Consul Weber, Hamburg; purchased in 1913 by dlr. Sedelmeyer, Paris, for 80,000 frs;[2] Sale R. Visscher-Burckhardt, Sevogelstr. 11, Basel, 8/1919.
LIT.: Woltman-Woermann, *Geschichte der Malerei*, III, v. 2, 735; O. Eisenmann, 'Die Sammlung Habich', in *Z.f.b.K.*, 1892, 166; HdG 1892, no. 29; Wurzbach, I, 716; HdG no. 266 [a late work of inferior quality]; R, 98; BM, 273, n. 4; Val. no. 104 [c. 1671–4].

The palatial proportions of the architecture recall the picture of 1675 in Philadelphia (Cat. 114, Plate 117), but the squatter and rounder figure types may indicate a later date.
NOTES: [1] Facsimile in Habich Sale cat. 1892. [2] R, 98.

120. *A Couple Playing Cards, with a Serving Woman*
(Plate 123)   c. 1675–80
Metropolitan Museum of Art, New York, inv. no. P257. Robert Lehman Collection, 1975.
Canvas 68×58.5 cm. Signed (falsely) at foot of back wall: P D H
PROV.: (Prob.) Pastor, Geneva;[1] Sale Comte de M[orny], Paris, 24/5/1852, no. 10 (w/o m.; bought in); Sale Duc de Morny, Paris, 31/5/1865, no. 54—Baron Seillière, 12,700 frs;[2] Baron de Beurnonville, Paris;[3] George d'Epernay; Boesch, Vienna; Sale [Exeter], London, 14/6/1888, no. 166;[4] purchased in 1896 from dlr. Durand Ruel by Charles H. Senff, New York;[5] Sale Senff, New York, 28/3/1928, no. 21, ill.—Scott & Fowles, $34,000; Joseph Kerrigan, New York, 1929;[6] Sale E.S. Kerrigan, New York, 8–10/1/1942, no. 279; Sale Scott & Fowles, New York, 20/3/1946, no. 73, ill.; Robert Lehman, New York, by 1959.[7]
EXH.: (a) Detroit 1929, no. 39; (b) Cincinnati 1959, no. 135; (c) New Haven 1960, no. 15.
LIT.: Blanc 1857–8, II, 493; Kramm 1859, 754; L. Lagrange, 'La galerie de M. le Duc de Morny', *G.B.A.*, 1863, 298; Havard 1880, 131:1; HdG no. 262; BM, 273; Val. 1927, 77, no. 20, ill. 71; Val. no. 131 [c. 1670–5 or somewhat earlier]; Val. 1932, 318, n. 1.

The figure types suggest a date in the late 1670s. Evidence of overpainting appears in the women and in the screen at the right. The signature is false.
NOTES: [1] Sale cat. 1852. [2] BMf. [3] This and the following two references were listed in the Senff Sale cat. 1928; no confirmation could be found for any of them. [4] BMf. [5] Senff Sale cat. 1928. [6] Exh. a. [7] Exh. b.

121. *A Party of Four Figures at a Table* (Plate 124)
    c. 1675–7
Corcoran Gallery of Art, Washington, D.C., inv. no. 26.103. William Andrews Clark Collection.
Canvas 86.3×69.8 cm. Signed upper centre on cartouche: P d HOO . . .
PROV.: R. von Kauffmann, Berlin, 1892;[1] Gottfried von Preyer, Vienna;[2] W.A. Clark, New York, by 1907;[3] acq. 1926.
EXH.: (a) Berlin 1890, no. 137; (b) Washington, Corcoran Gall. of Art, 1908–9.
LIT.: HdG 1892, no. 17; Wurzbach, I, 716; HdG no. 191 [after 1670]; Jantzen 1912, 31; R, 105; BM, 278; Val. 1927, 77, no. 31, ill.; Val. no. 134 [c. 1675]; J.D. Breckenridge, *Dutch and Flemish Paintings in the W.A. Clark Collection*, Washington, 1955, 29, ill. 28.

The execution most resembles that of Cat. 117 (Plate 120).
NOTES: [1] Exh. a. [2] HdG. [3] ibid.

122. *A Couple with a Parrot* (Plate 125)   c. 1675–7
Wallraf-Richartz-Museum, Cologne, no. Dep. 239.
Canvas 73×62 cm.
PROV.: Sale Bicker & Watersloot, Amsterdam, 19/7/1809, no. 21—Teengs, 145 fl; Sale D. Teengs, Amsterdam, 24/4/1811, no. 57—Gruyter, 76 fl; (poss.) Sale La Neuville, Paris,

14/11/1813, no. 34 (w/o m.)—601 frs;[1] bought by dlr. D.M. Koetser at Dowell's Auction Rooms, Edinburgh;[2] dlr., London, 1932;[3] dlr. Katz, 1934[4] & 1935;[5] Ten Bos Collection, Almelo;[6] acq. by the Wallraf-Richartz-Kuratorium, 1960.

EXH.: (a) Arnhem 1934, no. 63 [signed]; (b) The Hague (Katz) 1934, no. 66 [signed]; (c) Rotterdam 1935, no. 53, fig. 56 [s. & d. 'P.d. Hooch f 1668'].

LIT.: HdG no. 118 & poss. 118a; Val. 1932, 317 [1668], ill. 307; O.H. Förster, in *Jahrbuch*, W-R-M, 23 (1961), 379, ill. 268; Vey-Kesting 1967, 57, ill. no. 76; A. Kagner, in *Die Künste*, 3 (3/1972), 139, ill.; Blankert 1975, 78, fig. 39.

The picture formerly bore a signature and the date 1668,[7] which, judging from an old photograph at the RKD, appeared above the doorway at the level of the man's head. The costumes, however, suggest a later date. As Gudlaugsson noted,[8] the picture probably was executed in the late 1670s. Valentiner first observed that the composition was derived from Vermeer's picture in the Rijksmuseum (Fig. 36).

NOTES: [1] See Cat. C 81 (= HdG no. 118a; not identical with the picture in the Gildemeester Jansz. Sale; see Cat. 150). [2] Communication D.M. Koetser. [3] Val. 1932, 307. [4] Exh. a & b. [5] Exh. c. [6] Vey-Kesting 1967, 57. [7] cf. Val. 1932 & Exh. c. [8] Reported by Vey-Kesting 1967.

123. An Asparagus Vendor, with Two Women and a Man* (Plate 126) c. 1675–80

Private Collection, Minneapolis.
Canvas 76.2×104 cm. Signed left on windowsill: Pr. d · Hooch ·

PROV.: *Sale S. Stinstra, Amsterdam, 26/3/1783, no. 61—Fouquet, 30 fl; *(prob.) Sale Isabella Stinstra (widow of Pieter de Clercq, jr.), Amsterdam, 30/6/1829, no. 5—Brondgeest, 1800 fl;[1] (poss.) Gott Heirlooms, London, 1/12/1894, no. 31 (w/o m.)—Steinmeyer, £378;[2] Sale J.S.W.S. Erle Drax, London, 19/2/1910, no. 80—Lesser, 920 gns; dlr. Klienberger, Paris, 1911[3] & 1922;[4] dlr. Böhler, Munich, 1924;[5] Sale Marczell de Nemes, Amsterdam, 13/11/1928, no. 60, ill. (bought in?); Sale M. von Nemes, Munich, 16/6/1931, no. 50, ill.; dlr. W. Paech, Amsterdam, 1936;[6] Sale Mrs. S.H. Lebur et al. (a.c.), London, 11/2/1944, no. 28; Sale W.J. Sterling of Keir et al. (Wyndam Birch), London, 26/6/1946, no. 30—Beattie; Sale Davies et al. (Lady of Title), London, 4/7/1951, no. 45, ill.—Newhouse Gallery; W.P. Chrysler, New York, by 1957.[7]

EXH.: (a) Paris 1911, no. 74b; (b) Paris (Kleinberger) 1911, no. 36, ill.; (c) Amsterdam (Paech) 1936, no. 31; (d) Birmingham et al., 1957–8, 18, ill.

LIT.: (Prob.) HdG no. 228; Dayot 1911, no. 78; W. Martin, in *M.f.K.*, 1911, 433; Lilienfeld 1924, 453; BM, 284; Val. no. 145 [c. 1675–80]; T, 42, 44, 50, 54, ill.

The figure types suggest a date in the latter half of the 1670s and the greater complexity of the architecture and wainscoting connect the work with Cat. 124 (Plate 127). A woman offering asparagus also appears in Cat. 98 (Plate 100).

NOTES: [1] cf. HdG no. 228: 'Interior with four figures. The light falls from above at the back and produces a good effect', 29½"×40" (75×102 cm). While the cursory description would not by itself allow identification with the work, the correspondence in the measurements and the reappearance of the Stinstra family ownership lend support to the connection. [2] 'Woman buying Asparagus'. [3] Exh. a & b. [4] BM, 284, n. 6. [5] ibid. [6] Exh. c. [7] Exh. d.

124. A Woman giving Money to a Girl with a Marketing Basket, with a Woman Sweeping* (Plate 127) c. 1675–80

Present location unknown.
Canvas 59×66 cm. Signed over doorway: P d Hoogh

PROV.: Sale Bugge, Copenhagen, 21/8/1837, no. 354; Berthold Richter, Berlin, 1890;[1] collection as a whole passed to Joseph Block, Berlin, by 1928;[2] dlr. Katz, The Hague, 1934.[3]

EXH.: (a) Berlin 1890, no. 136; (b) 1906, no. 66, ill.; (c) exh. of Block Coll., Dr. A. Gold's Gallery, Berlin, 1928, no. 4; (d) The Hague (Katz) 1934, no. 67.

LIT.: A. Bredius, in *J.d.K.p.K.*, 9 (1890), 221; Wurzbach, I, 716; HdG no. 26; R, 102; BM, 284 [erroneously as HdG no. 37]; Val. no. 155 [c. 1675–80].

With its relatively elaborate domestic architecture, the painting may be compared to Cat. 123 (Plate 126). The marketing money theme appeared earlier in Cat. 88 (Plate 91). The short and rather stocky proportions of the figures suggest origins in the later 1670s.

NOTES: [1] Exh. a. [2] Exh. c. [3] Exh. d.

125. A Mother with Two Children and a Serving Woman* (Plate 128) c. 1675–80

Present location unknown.
Canvas 83×82 cm.

PROV.: In 1804 transferred from the Prince Bishop's Castle, Würzburg, to Schleissheim Castle; Schleissheim Picture Gallery, cats. (1885), no. 459, (1919), no. 3812; given in exchange to dlr. E. Plietzsch, Berlin, 1936;[1] Dr. Bolzani, Berlin, 1936.[2]

LIT.: Parthey 1863–4, I, 632, no. 13; HdG 1892, no. 82; Wurzbach, I, 717; HdG no. 42; Schleissheim, Royal Picture Gallery, cat. 1914, no. 3812; BM, 284; Val. no. 157 [c. 1675–80].

The nearly square format is unusual and the work may once have been slightly wider.

NOTES: [1] Communication, Direktion der Bayerischen Staatsgemäldesammlungen. [2] RKD photo.

(a) Copy. (Photo RKD.) Canvas 59.5×91 cm. Signed lower right: Pietro D. Hoog. Sale R. Piloty, Munich 14/11/1911, no. 674, ill.; dlr. Van Diemen, Berlin, 1920 (HdGf).

(b) Copy. (Photo RKD.) Canvas 55×67 cm. U. Suits, Wittmund.

126. A Serving Woman and an Officer, with Card Players (Plate 129) c. 1675–80

The Saltram Collection, National Trust, Plympton, no. 58T.
Canvas 54.5×64.7 cm.

PROV.: Norton, London, before 1842;[1] Saltram House, after 1844.[2]

EXH.: London, A.C., 1960, no. 16.

LIT.: S s no. 5; Havard 1880, 127:1, HdG no. 279; *The Saltram Collection*, Nat. Trust, London, 1977, 31, no. 58T.

According to the catalogue of the collection, the picture was formerly ascribed to S. van Hoogstraten and was (re)attributed to De Hooch in 1960 by H. Buttery. While the theme recalls the master's youthful works (compare Cat. 5, Plate 4), its style suggests a date no earlier than c. 1675.

NOTES: [1] S s no. 5 & HdG no. 279. The provenance listed by Hofstede de Groot is in error. The picture in the Leyden

Sale of 1788 was our Cat. 5; and the painting in the Van Coehoorn Sale of 1801 was our Cat. 13. The transcription of Smith's description in HdG no. 279 is also incorrect.[2] It is not known when the picture entered the collection, but it does not appear in the catalogue of 1844.

127. *A Woman Seated by a Fire with Two Gaming Soldiers** (Plate 130)   *c.* 1675–80

Present location unknown.

Canvas 40×50.2 cm. Signed upper left on fireplace: P·D HOOGH[1]

PROV.: Sale Heydeman et al. (E.H. Gwilt), London, 4/5/1945, no. 36—Agnew, £735; Sale Duke of Norfolk et al. (G. H. Edgar), London, 14/12/1962, no. 128—Nicholls, 750 gns; dlr. P. de Boer, Amsterdam; Brod Gallery, London.

EXH.: London (Agnew), 6–7/1948, no. 20.

A rare nocturnal scene (cf. Cat. C 230, C 235, C 281 & C 284), the picture appears to be a late work which, like Cat. 111, 126 and 128 (Plates 114, 129, 131), returns to the artist's earlier themes. The model who served for the mustachioed soldier on the far side of the table also appears in Cat. 111 and 126 (Plate 114, 129).

NOTES: [1] Transcribed from photograph.

128. *Tavern Scene with a Smoker* (Plate 131)   *c.* 1675–80

Nationalmuseum, Stockholm, no. 472.

Canvas 51×64 cm.

PROV.: In the possession of the Swedish Crown by 1816.[1]

LIT.: Stockholm, N.M., cat. 1900, no. 472 [copy after]; HdG no. 275; R, 103; BM, 284; Val. no. 263 [*c.* 1670–5]; Stockholm, N.M., cat. 1958, no. 472 [attr. to P.d.H.].

The picture is in problematic condition, but, as Hofstede de Groot stated, it is undoubtedly authentic.

NOTES: [1] Inv. 1816, no. 1017.

129. *A Woman Holding a Wineglass in a Doorway* (Plate 132)   *c.* 1675–80

Dr. John C. Weber, U.S.A.

Panel 40×31.6 cm. Signed left on windowsill: P d. hooch

PROV.: (Prob.) Sale D. Teengs, Amsterdam, 24/4/1811, no. 59 (w/o m.)—Van Yperen, 11 fl; Sale H. Reydon et al., Amsterdam, 5–6/4/1827, no. 54—Roos, 95 fl; Sale, Amsterdam, 5/7/1833, no. 13—Gykema, 38 fl 50; Mrs. E. Piercy Taylor-Smith, Colepike Hall, Lanchester;[1] J.D. Klassen, Rotterdam, 1935;[2] dlr. Katz, Dieren, 1937;[3] dlr. Asscher & Welker, London, 1937;[4] Sale, New York, 17/12/1969, no. 45A, ill.; dlr. L. Koetser, London, 1970.[5]

EXH.: (a) Rotterdam 1935, no. 44, fig. 47; (b) Eindhoven (Katz) 1937; (c) Toronto 1937, no. 20; (d) London (L. Koetser), Spr. 1970, no. 7, ill.

LIT.: HdG no. 94; Gowing 1952, 112, n. 64.

While the closely focused view of a single figure and the panel support are unusual, the work is not unprecedented in the artist's oeuvre. The panel at Polesden Lacey (Cat. 41, Plate 45) also depicts a relatively large-scale figure framed in a doorway. Like that work, the picture may also be related to details from other multifigure compositions; compare, for example, the woman holding a glass in the doorway at the right of Cat. 137 (Plate 140). The large and simple forms of the figure suggest a date in the mid to late 1670s. Compare also Cat. C67.

NOTES: 1 Exh. a & b. [2] Exh. a. [3] Exh. b. [4] Exh. c. [5] Exh. d.

130. *Mother and Child with a Serving Woman Holding a Duck* (Plate 135)   *c.* 1675–80

Worcester Art Museum, Worcester, Mass., acc. no. 1925.117.

Canvas 56.2×65.8 cm. Signed right on step: P · d Hoogh·

PROV.: *Sale J.M. Quinkhard, Amsterdam, 15/3/1773, no. 14—J. Spaan, 156 fl; *Sale [Fiseau], Amsterdam, 30/8/1797, no. 97—I. Smit, 200 fl; Sale Mvr. A.M. Hogguer, née Ebeling, Amsterdam, 18/8/1817, no. 21—I. Smit, 310 fl;[1] Comtesse de Miranda (née Nilson), Paris;[2] Duc de Morny, Paris;[3] A. de Ridder, Schönberg near Cronberg, Taunus, cat. (1913), no. 35; Sale A. de Ridder, Paris, 2/6/1924, no. 31—160,000 frs; purchased from John Levy Gall., New York, 1925.

EXH.: New York (Kleinberger) 1913, no. 35.

LIT.: S no. 23;[4] Havard 1880, 94:1;[5] HdG no. 52; E.A. Benkard, 'Die Sammlung de Ridder', *Kunst und Künstler*, 1912, 607–8, ill.; Bode 1913, 10, no. 35 [before 1665], pl. 35; BM, 265; Val. no. 116 [*c.* 1670–5]; Slive 1974, 107–9 [after 1670], ill. 557.

Bode suggested that the work was executed in Delft before 1665 because of the church spire in the distance. As Slive observed, however, the tower is closer to that of the Westerkerk in Amsterdam, than to any church in Delft. Similar interiors appear in Cat. 131, 141 and 140 (Plates 136, 144, 143). The date 168(?) on the last mentioned suggests this group probably dates toward 1680. While Slive left the possibility open that the picture might be a copy or the work of a follower, it is certainly by De Hooch. The signature has perhaps been strengthened, but is not untypical for the period.

NOTES: [1] As Slive noted (1974, n. 4), Smith (no. 33) and Hofstede de Groot (no. 52) were in error in suggesting that the picture in the Muilman Sale of 1813 could be identical with the present work. That work, as Slive tentatively suggests, was the picture last seen in the P. Meyer collection (Cat. 131). [2] Bode 1913, no. 35. [3] ibid. [4] Ref. Hogguer Sale. [5] ibid.

131. *Mother and Child by a Fireplace** (Plate 136)   *c.* 1675–80

Present location unknown.

Canvas 50.8×61 cm. Signed left on fireplace.[1]

PROV.: Sale H. Muilman, Amsterdam, 12/4/1813, no. 67—Hulswit, 426 fl;[2] offered unsuccessfully by a dlr. to Museum in Rotterdam in 1895 or 6;[3] Private Collection, Amsterdam, 1906;[4] Sale J. Camberlyn et al. (Beckeringh Collection), Amsterdam, 13/7/1926, no. 725, ill.; dlr. Van Diemen, Amsterdam, 1929;[5] dlr. Slatter, London, 1946;[6] Percy B. Meyer, 1950.[7]

EXH.: (a) Amsterdam 1906, no. 66; (b) Amsterdam 1929, no. 75, pl. 75; (c) London (Slatter) 1946, no. 1, ill.; (d) Birmingham 1950, no. 30.

LIT.: S no. 23; Havard 1880, 94:1; HdG nos. 19 & 24; BM, 265; Val. no. 115 [*c.* 1670–5]; T, 58, ill. 53; Slive 1974, 108, 109, ns. 3 & 4.

Similar compositions and interiors, with minor architectural alterations, appear in Cat. 130, 140 and 141 (Plates 135, 143, 144).

NOTES: [1] According to HdG no. 24, 'dubiously, "P. d. Hoog"'; on a photograph taken *c.* 1945; 'P d Hoogh'. [2] HdG no. 19; incorrectly listed as a possible entry for Cat. 130. On the other hand, the reference to the Hogguer sale of 1817

XIII. A Woman with an Infant and a Serving Woman with a Child (Cat. 54). *c.* 1663–5. Kunsthistorisches Museum, Vienna

XIV. A Woman Weighing Gold Coins against Silver Coins (Cat. 64). *c.* 1664. Staatliche Museen, Berlin-Dahlem (listed erroneously as a possible entry under S no. 23 and HdG no. 19) does not apply to Cat. 131. [3] HdG no. 24. [4] Exh. a. [5] Exh. b. [6] Exh. c. [7] Exh. d.

132. *A Doctor and a Sick Woman*★ (Plate 133)   *c.* 1675–80
Present location unknown.

Canvas 65×56 cm. Signed right on fireplace: P d Hooch[1]

PROV.: ★Sale [Lenglier], Paris, 6/4/1789, no. 60—Marin, 270 frs; (prob.) Sale, Amsterdam, 16/6/1800, no. 12—Rijers, 12 fl;[2] Semenov Collection, St. Petersburg, cat. (1906), no. 227; acquired in 1910, by Czar Nicolas II, at whose death it entered the Hermitage;[3] dlr. Katz, 1934;[4] dlr. Van Diemen, 1935;[5] dlr. Katz, 1937;[6] Sale French et al. (Dr. A. Feldman), London, 26/11/1958, no. 149—Vanderkar; dlr. A. Brod, London, 1959.[7]

EXH.: (a) The Hague (Katz) 1934, no. 68; (b) Eindhoven (Katz) 1937, no. 29; (c) London (Brod) 1959, no. 25.

LIT.: *Études sur les peintures* [...] *qu'on trouve dans la collection Semenov* . . ., St. Petersburg, 1906, 95, no. 227; HdG no. 77; R, 104; BM, 52 [C. de Man]; Val. no. 146 [*c.* 1675–80]; BM 1935, II, 113 [C. de Man], fig. 23; Robinson 1974, 81, n. 68.

Brière-Misme's attribution to Cornelis de Man is based only on a superficial resemblance to that artist's work and cannot be accepted. While the man's costume appears in De Man's work, it also figures in De Hooch's art (cf. Cat. 123, Plate 126). He may be identified as a doctor by the presence of a basket used to hold the urinalysis glass on the table. As in earlier representations of this theme by Dou, Steen, and others, the woman's ailment no doubt will be diagnosed as lovesickness or pregnancy.

NOTES: [1] Transcribed from photo; according to Semenov cat.: 'P de hooch'; Exh. c: 'P. de HOOCH'. [2] As on panel (?). [3] BM 1935, 113, n. 1. [4] Exh. a. [5] BM 1935, 113. [6] Exh. b. [7] Exh. c.

133. *A Man with a Book, and Two Women* (Plate 134)   1676
Staatliche Museum, Gemäldegalerie, East Berlin, cat. no. B 102.

Canvas 63.5×75 cm. Signed and dated left on step: P. d · Hoogh f · 1676 ·

PROV.: (Prob.) Sale, Haarlem, 23/9/1811, no. 4 (w/o m.); ★(poss.) Sale D. van Dijl, Amsterdam, 22/11/1813 (postponed to 10/1/1814), no. 71;[1] Sale J.W.G.D. of London, Paris, 25/2/1869, no. 35—1000 frs;[2] Sale Pommersfelden Collection, Paris, 21/2/1880, no. 21—1105 frs; Sale Baron de Beurnonville, Paris, 6/5/1881, no. 338—Hecht, 3300 frs; dlr. Sully, London, 1905;[3] Sale Vte. J. de La L . . . et al. (Sainte-Gudule), Brussels, 3/7/1919, no. 96; dlr. Paris, 1920, who later sold the picture in Germany;[4] M. von Nemes, Munich, 1927;[5] dlr. Berlin, 1929;[6] acq. from Dresdener Bank in 1936.

LIT.: HdG no. 104 and poss. 219; CB, 8; BM, 271; Val. no. 144.

Entitled 'The Notary' in the modern literature, the subject is unclear. The books and other accessories near the man at the left identify him as a man of learning. The standing woman holds an hourglass and the seated woman a handkerchief. Perhaps, as the modern title implies, the woman in black is seeking professional advice or assistance. The picture is in poor condition.

NOTES: [1] See HdG no. 219. [2] BMf. [3] HdGf. [4] BM, 271. [5] HdGf. [6] Val. no. 144.

134. *A Musical Party in a Courtyard* (Col. Plate XVI, Plate 137)   1677
National Gallery, London, no. 3047.

Canvas 83.5×68.5 cm. Signed right above the arch: P. d Hoogh · 1677 ·

PROV.: Jonkheer Johan Steengracht van Oostkappelle, The Hague, by 1833;[1] Sale H.A. Steengracht, Paris, 9/6/1913, no. 33 (bought in; 84,000 frs); sold by order of the executors of the Steengracht estate in Sale R. Peltzer, Amsterdam, 26/3/1914, no. 323, ill.—Goudstikker; acq. from dlr. Goudstikker, 1916, for 75,000 frs.

EXH.: (a) The Hague (Goudstikker) 1915, no. 20; (b) London 1976, no. 62, ill.

LIT.: S. no. 35; Gower 1875, 58; Gower 1880, III; Havard 1880, 119:3; Bredius 1889, 167; HdG 1892, no. 25; C. von Lützow, in *Z.f.b.K.*, 3 (1892), 166; C.G. 't Hooft, *Verzameling Steengracht*, 1899; Wurzbach, I, 717; HdG no. 122; Jantzen 1912, 33; C. 34 (1914), 144; R, 36, 96; Maccoll 1916, 25–6, ill.; C., 44 (1916), 235–6; BM, 1921, 344; Eisler 1923, 256; Lilienfeld 1924, 453; Lilienfeld 1924–5, 186; CB, 3, 8; Val. 1926, 63; BM, 259, 277, 281; Val. xx, no. 147; Martin 1935–6, II, 206; T, 58, ill. 55; London, N.G., pls., 152; MacLaren, 190, no. 3047; Gerson 1966, 312; J. Mills, 'Carpets in Pictures'; *Themes and Painters in the National Gallery*, ser. 2, no. 1, N.G., London, 1975, 34, pl. 26.

MacLaren correctly noted that the houses across the canal are probably not accurate renderings of actual buildings, and observed that the one dated 1620 is in the style of Hendrick de Keyser and reminiscent of the 'Huis met de Hoofden' of 1622 on the Keizersgracht in Amsterdam. Mills identified the Persian carpet as of the Herat variety.

NOTES: [1] S no. 35.

(a) Copy. Sale London, 22/1/1954, no. 127.

135. *Two Men and a Serving Woman in a Courtyard* (Plate 138)   *c.* 1677–80
Royal Museum of Fine Arts, Copenhagen, inv. no. 1641.

Canvas 84.5×69.5 cm. Signed upper right over door: · P d Hoogh ·

PROV.: Royal Cabinet of Curiosities, 1761;[1] at Fredensborg Castle, cat. 1848, no. 309.

EXH.: Berlin 1929, no. 39.

LIT.: HdG no. 288 ['attribution . . . is uncertain; . . . may be by Ochtervelt']; R, 104; Val. no. 163 [*c.* 1680; erroneously as Panel 50×36.5 cm]; Kauffmann 1930, col. 805; Copenhagen, R.M., cat. 1951, 137, no. 330.

The theme recalls the artist's works of the late 1650s (compare, for example, Cat. 35A, Plate 34), but the figure types, colouration and dramatic lighting suggest a date close to that of Cat. 134 (Plate 137), dated 1677. The attribution to Ochtervelt, tentatively proposed by Hofstede de Groot, is unacceptable.

NOTES: [1] Copenhagen, R.M., cat. 1951, no. 330.

136. *A Woman with a Duck, and a Woman with a Cabbage*★ (Plate 139)   After 1677
Present location unknown.

Canvas 63×75 cm.

PROV.: Sale, Amsterdam, 16/7/1819, no. 17—De Vries, 125 fl; dlr. E. Bolton, London, 1929;[1] Violet Lady Melchett, by 1945;[2] Sale Lady Melchett, London, 6/3/1946, no. 113—Sir

H

Alexander Korda; Sale Countess of Rosebery et al. (Mrs. A.I. Metcalf), London, 24/3/1976, no. 45, ill.

EXH.: London (Slatter) 1945, no. 11.

LIT.: HdG no. 53; Val. no. 154 [*c.* 1675–80].

Valentiner believed that this was the better of the two versions of the composition and probably correctly judged the other to be a copy. The present work, nevertheless, looks very laboured in photographs and both pictures may be based on a lost original. The woman in the doorway evidently was overpainted in 1929.[3]

NOTES: [1] Val. no. 154. [2] Exh. [3] Compare Val. no. 154.

a) Probable copy. Present location unknown. Canvas 63×75 cm. PROV.: Dlr. Langton Douglas, London, 1924;[1] dlr. Sackville, London.[2] LIT.: BM, 265; Val., 286, under no. 154.

Valentiner identified the work as a copy. It differs from Cat. 136 in small details: the woman in the doorway holds a plate; a jug appears by the step on which she stands; and the boy by the fire wears a different hat.

NOTES: [1] BM, 265, n. 7 (probably the dealer referred to in Val. no. 154). [2] RKD photo.

137. *A Musical Party with Three Figures and a Serving Woman*★ (Plate 140)   *c.* 1677–80
Present location unknown.

Canvas 64.5×73.6 cm. Signed left on windowsill: P d Hoogh

PROV.: (Poss.) Sale Servad, Amsterdam, 25/6/1778, no. 43—Ploos van Amstel, 51 fl;[1] Sale Engelberts & Tersteeg, Amsterdam, 13–14/6/1808, no. 73—Van Yperen, 121 fl; (poss.) Sale, Amsterdam, 20/6/1810, no. 32—Hulswit, 26 fl;[2] Sale Jolles, Amsterdam, 30/11/1812, no. 42—Van Yperen, 86 fl; Burton Collection, Brussels;[3] ★Sale Leroy d'Etoilles, Paris, 22/2/1861, no. 52—2000 frs; Baron de Beurnonville, Paris;[4] Desmotte de Lille;[5] 'Cabinet L.L.';[6] Sale Mr. X of Cambrai, Paris, 25/11/1889, no. 9—Durand Ruel, 8200 frs; Sale J.F. Talmadge, New York, 20/2/1913, no. 17—P. Mersch, $8600; dlr. Sedelmeyer, Paris, 1917;[7] Jules S. Bache, New York, *c.* 1927;[8] dlr. Kleinberger, Paris, 1929 & 1931;[9] Sale F. Kleinberger, New York, 18/11/1932, no. 51, ill.; Andre de Coppet, New York, 1940;[10] Sale The Late Morris I. Kaplan of Chicago, London, 12/6/1968, no. 50, ill.—Brod Gallery, London, 1969.[11]

EXH.: (a) Berlin 1929, no. 33; (b) New York (Anderson) 1931, no. 63; (c) New York (Kleinberger) 1931, no cat. no.; (d) New York 1940, no. 103, ill.

LIT.: HdG nos. 149 & poss. 147a; BM, 276; Val. no. 153 [*c.* 1677–80].

On the harpsichord lid is the inscription (vertically) 'SOL DEO . . .' and (horizontally) 'SIC/ TRAN . . ./ . . . RIA'. Valentiner's date of *c.* 1677–80 is acceptable.

NOTES: [1] The measurements correspond; however, the description mentions a garden through the doorway rather than a canal. Compare also Cat. C 95. [2] See HdG no. 147a. [3] Sale cat. 1861. [4] Sale cat. 1913. [5] ibid. [6] ibid. [7] BMf. [8] BM, 276. [9] Exh. a, b & c. [10] Exh. d. [11] *A.*, 2/1969, xxi.

138. *A Woman with a Lute and a Man with a Violin*★ (Plate 141)   After 1677
Present location unknown.

Canvas 66×59 cm.

PROV.: Sale 'In Holland, 1788, no. 12—20 fl';[1] ★(prob.) Sale, Amsterdam, 10/6/1789, no. 12—Bogaard, 20 fl;[2] Sale

J.C. Werther, Amsterdam, 25/4/1792, no. 76; ★Marquis of Stafford;[3] Count Fesch, Rome (?);[4] ★Sale Goldsmith, London, 26/2/1856, no. 60; dlr. P. & D. Colnaghi, London, 1888;[5] Dr. M. Schubart, Dresden, 1889;[6] Sale Schubart, Munich, 23/10/1899, no. 32, ill.—Bovery, 9100 mks.

EXH.: (a) Leipzig 1889, no. 18; (b) Munich, Königl. Kunstausstellungspalast, 6–7/1895, no. 26.

LIT.: A. Bredius, in *Z.f.b.K.*, 1890, 132; Schlie, in *R.f.K.*, 13 (1890), 159; HdG 1892, no. 65; C. Hofstede de Groot. *Sammlung Schubart*, Munich, n.d. (*c.* 1895), 39–40, 52, ill.; T. Frimmel, in *Z.f.b.K.*, 1894, 218; HdG no. 171 [late period]; R, 100; BM, 276; Val. no. 137 [*c.* 1675].

The architecture abruptly opens at the left onto a river with a boat, marking this as one of the artist's most fanciful compositions. The woman leaning against a table as she plays recalls the central figure in Cat. 78 (Plate 81).

NOTES: [1] See HdG no. 171; the incomplete reference probably applies to the following sale. [2] The catalogue description corresponds to the picture in all details except for the mention of a woman (later painted out?) seated beside the man who tunes his violin. [3] See Goldsmith Sale cat. 1856. [4] ibid. The picture did not appear in any of the Fesch sales. [5] HdG no. 171. [6] Exh. a.

139. *A Woman Playing a Lute, with other Figures*★ (Plate 142)   After 1677.
Present location unknown.

Canvas 67×57 cm. Signed: P · d Hoogh ·[1]

PROV.: ★Sale J. de Kommer, 15/4/1767, no. 20—De Winter, 41 fl; Sale, F. van de Velde, Amsterdam, 7/9/1774, no. 44—Bogaard, 48 fl; ★Sale S. van der Stel, Amsterdam, 25/9/1781, no. 66—Werther, 20 fl; Sale J.C. Werther, Amsterdam, 25/4/1792, no. 78—Yver, 36 fl; Sale A. Schuster et al., Cologne, 14/11/1892, no. 74, ill.

LIT.: Wurzbach, I, 717; HdG nos. 143 & 168; BM, 277; Val. no. 167 (left), [after 1680].

While the backlighted design still recalls compositional schemes the artist first employed in the late 1650s (compare Cat. 27, Plate 24), the work must date from very late in his career.

NOTES: [1] Transcription from HdGf.

140. *A Woman Kneeling by a Fire and a Woman with a Basket* (Plate 143)   168 (?)
Museum of Fine Arts, Boston, acc. no. 03.607.

Canvas 57.7×69.5 cm. Signed and dated lower left: P · d · Hoogh/ A. 168(?).

PROV.: ★Sale, Amsterdam, 23/5/1764, no. 179—Van der Schley; Sale Meffre, Paris, 9–10/3/1863, no. 43—4950 frs; ★Sale Comte de Bearnetz, Paris, 12/2/1869, no. 17—1200 frs;[1] ★Sale [Bernier de Passy], Paris, 5/5/1874, no. 23—2500 frs;[2] Sale Ritter Lippmann von Lissingen of Vienna, Paris, 16/5/1876, no. 25—4000 frs; Sale Baron de Beurnonville, Paris, 9/5/1881, no. 337—Walchen of Moltheim, 7200 frs; ★Sale [Prince of Liechtenstein], Paris, 16/5/1882, no. 23—Sedelmeyer, 4800 frs;[3] bought by Colnaghi from Sedelmeyer 26/1/1886;[4] Sale D.P. Sellar, Paris, 6/6/1889, no. 42—Sedelmeyer, 6000 frs; bought by Durand Ruel from Sedelmeyer 6/1889;[5] dlr. Sedelmeyer, 1898;[6] Mrs. Samuel D. Warren, Boston; acq. at Sale S.D. Warren, New York, 8/1/1903, no. 97, with funds provided by Mrs. S.D. Warren.

EXH.: Paris (Sedelmeyer) 1898, no. 73 [s. & d. 1656].

LIT.: A. de Lostalot, 'Collection de M.J. de Lissingen', *G.B.A.*, 2e per., 13 (1876), 492 [1656]; E.E., 'Die Galerie Lippmann-Lissingen', *Z.f.b.K.*, 11 (1876), 217–8 [1656]; Havard 1880, 105:3 [1656]; Wurzbach, I, 717; HdG no. 40; R, 98; Boston, M.F.A., cat. 1921, no. 121 [with note that Bredius dates it 'about 1670']; CB, 4 [1656]; BM, 266; Val. 1927, 77, no. 30; Val. no. 122; Slive 1974, 109, n. 3 [1688].

The date on the picture was first reported in the Meffre sale of 1863 as reading 1656. All later sales reported the same date, which Hofstede de Groot correctly rejected as too early. Without knowledge of the year of the artist's death, Slive deciphered the date as 1688. The last numeral is virtually illegible but the first three are almost certainly 168(?). Thus the work is probably a product of the last four years of the artist's activity. In execution it most resembles Cat. 141 (Plate 144), and the design of both works may be compared to Cat. 130 and 131 (Plates 135, 136).

NOTES: [1] BMf. [2] ibid. [3] ibid. [4] ibid. [5] ibid. [6] Exh. a.
PRINT: Billy (cf. Sellar Sale cat. 1889).

141. *Two Women by a Fireplace* (Plate 144)   c. 1680–4
Musée Granet, Aix-en-Provence, inv. no. 849.1.224.
Canvas 74 × 84 cm. Signed lower left: P · d · Hoogh
PROV.: *(Poss.) Sale, Amsterdam, 20/6/1803, no. 67 [by or in the manner of P.d.H.]—Gruyter, 107 fl;[1] *(poss.) Sale D. Teengs, Amsterdam, 24/4/1811, no. 58—Coclers, 80 fl;[2] F.M. Granet bequest, 1849, no. 71.
LIT.: Aix-en-Provence M.G., cat. 1900, no. 359; Wurzbach, I, 716; HdG no. 172a; BM, 264; Val. no. 121 [c. 1670–5].

The extremely dark palette and the compositional scheme are very similar to Cat. 140 (Plate 143). As in the latter work, the almost wholly illegible details in the shadows suggest that the work has darkened considerably with time.

NOTES: [1] Possibly identical with the copy 'a' below. [2] 'In an interior two women sit [?] by a burning fire; through an open door a man is seen reading . . .'; Canvas 29″ × 31″ (73.6 × 78.7 cm). Possibly identical with the copy.

(a) Copy. Canvas 71.5 × 85 cm. Museum, Poznan, inv. no. MO 822; cat. (1958), no. 72. PROV.: De Reus, The Hague, 1842;[1] *Sale G. Stange of Lübeck, Cologne, 20/3/1879, no. 46; Czarnecki Collection, Dobrzyca, Poland. LIT.: S s no. 18; Havard 1880, 100:2.

NOTES: [1] S s no. 18. The entry cannot apply to the Aix painting because Granet, who bequeathed the picture to the Museum, died in 1841. However, the Amsterdam Sale of 1803 and the Teengs Sale listed as possible entries for the original may apply to this work.

(b) Probably copy. (HdG no. 67). Canvas 34 × 39 cm. Sale Krupp, jun. et al., Cologne, 29/10/1894, no. 93.

142. *A Woman Taking Butter from a Plate Held by a Little Girl** (Plate 145)   c. 1680 or later
Present location unknown.
Canvas 93 × 82 cm.
PROV.: Cornelissen Coll., Brussels, 1842 (sold, 1010 fl);[1] *Sale Leroy, Paris, 18/4/1842, no. 24;[2] *Sale Leroy, Paris, 3/4/1843, no. 19;[3] *Sale Cousin, Paris, 3/4/1846, no. 44;[4] Sale, Paris, 1/4/1882, no. 20—6100 frs; *Van de Veen Coll., Holland, 1889; *Sale I. Scott of San Francisco, New York, 9/2/1906, no. 36, ill.;[5] *Sale, New York, 10/1/1907, no. 107.
LIT.: Havard 1880, 104:2; HdG no. 65.

The work is known to the author only through a poor reproduction in the Scott Sale catalogue, but it appears to be genuine. The subject recalls that of Cat. 48 (Plate 51) and features of the design and interior resemble Cat. 113 (Plate 116). The figure types point to a very late date.

NOTES: [1] Havard 1880, 104:2. [2] BMf. [3] ibid. [4] ibid. [5] Sale cat. 1906.

143. *A Woman with a Serving Girl* (Plate 146)   1680?
Palais des Beaux-Arts, Lille, inv. no. P304.
Canvas 65 × 55 cm. Remnants of a signature and date below window.[1]
PROV.: Sale S.J. Stinstra, Amsterdam, 22/5/1822, no. 85—De Vries, 60 fl; bequeathed by Alexander Leleux, 1873.
EXH.: (a) Valenciennes 1918, no. 168; (b) Berlin 1964, no. 23; (c) Paris 1970–1, no. 116 [c. 1675–80], ill. 107.
LIT.: Gower 1880, 111; HdG 1892, no. 35; Wurzbach, I, 717; HdG no. 29; F. Benoit, *La Peinture au Musée de Lille*, II, Paris, 1909, no. 121 [c. 1670], ill.; R, 27, 97; CB, 6 [1670?]; BM, 264; Val. no. 140 [c. 1675–80]; A. Chatelet, *Cents chefs-d'oeuvre du Musée de Lille*, 1970, 116, no. 50.

In 1909 Benoit could decipher the remnants of a date ending in 'o', and speculated, as Collins Baker later would, that the picture could have been dated 1670. The style, however, clearly suggests a later date (compare the works of 1670: Cat. 92, 94 & 95, Plates 95, 96, 98). Although Cat. 140 (dated 168?) and 141 (Plates 143, 144) are not so well preserved, they exhibit a comparable technique. It is quite possible, therefore, that the present work was once dated 1680.

NOTES: [1] According to Benoit, cat. 1909, no. 121: 'Pr d hoog . . . . . o' (see commentary). According to Exh. a: 'P. de hoog'; Exh. c: 'P. de . . .'; only the 'P' still remains clear.

144. *A Woman Seated by a Window with a Child in a Doorway* (Plate 147)   c. 1680
Metropolitan Museum of Art, New York, acc. no. 93.22.2. Gift of George A. Hearn, 1893.
Canvas 54.1 × 66.7 cm.
PROV.: (Prob.) Sale M. Zachary, 31/5/1828, no. 24—£96;[1] (Prob.) M. Zachary, London, 1832;[2] *(prob.) Sale Zachary, London, 30/3/1838, no. 42 (w/o m.)—£52; *(prob.) Sale J.A. Beaver, London, 20/6/1840, no. 100 (w/o m.)—Nieuwenhuys, £94;[3] (prob.) Sale Tardieu, Paris, 31/3–3/4/1841, no. 46 (w/o m.)—3000 frs;[4] *Sale J.A. Tardieu, Paris, 10/5/1867, no. 25—620 frs;[5] Sale [Max Kahn], Paris, 3/3/1879, no. 31; dlr. Sedelmeyer, Paris, 1888 & 1892.[6]
EXH.: (a) (Prob.) London, B.I., 1832, no. 104; (b) Vancouver 1957, fig. 10.
LIT.: (Prob.) S no. 56; Havard 1880, 98; HdG nos. 39 & prob. 55; BM, 265; Val. no. 141 [c. 1675–80]; New York, M.M.A., cat. 1931, no. H76–1.

The heads of both figures, the feet of the girl, and details of the scene through the doorway were previously over-painted.[7] These alterations were still visible in 1929 and a subsequent cleaning left some passages abraded.[8] The general execution and specifically the treatment of the light falling on the woman seated before the gilded wall-hanging resemble the painting in Lille of 1680(?) (Cat. 143, Plate 146).

NOTES: [1] See S no. 56 & HdG no. 55. The description corresponds but the measurements are recorded (incorrectly?) as 23″ × 33″ (58.4 × 83.8 cm); probably bought in; see following entry. [2] Exh. a. [3] With reference to the Zachary Coll. [4] BMf. [5] ibid. [6] HdG no. 39. [7] The Tardieu Sale cat. of 1867 mentions 'clumsy restorations'. [8] Compare Val. no 141.

145. *A Woman Sewing, with a Serving Girl and a Child* (Plate 148)   *c.* 1680

Dlrs. G. Douwes, Amsterdam, & D.M. Koetser, Zurich (owned jointly).

Canvas 67.5×58 cm.[1] Signed on windowsill: P d Hooch

PROV.: *(Poss.) Sale M. d'Herbouville, Paris, 26/5/1829, no. 19;[2] Marquis de Crillon; Princess de Polignac;[3] *Sale, London, 6/2/1897, no. 78—Colnaghi, £70;[4] dlr. P. & D. Colnaghi, London, 1897 & 1901;[5] William McKay, 1902;[6] Sale Tollemache Estates et al. (Mrs. E.S. Borthwick-Norton), London, 15/5/1953, no. 82, ill.—Mensing; B. de Geus van den Heuvel, by 1955;[7] Sale B. de Geus van den Heuvel, Amsterdam, 26/4/1976, no. 26, ill.

EXH.: (a) London (Colnaghi) 1897; (b) 1901; (c) London, R.A., 1902, no. 179; (d) IJzendijke 1955, no. 27; (e) Laren 1958, no. 104; (f) Arnhem 1960-1, no. 26, ill. no 55; (g) Delft 1962, no. 21.

LIT.: HdG nos. 32 & 68; R, 97; Val. no. 110 [*c.* 1670-3].

In theme, design and figure types the work resembles Cat. 143 (Plate 146).

NOTES: [1] Enlarged by about 2 cm on all sides. [2] BMf. with smaller dimensions; cf. Cat. 145A. [3] HdG no. 32. [4] HdG no. 68. [5] Exh. a & b. [6] Exh. c. [7] Exh. d.

145A. Poss. version or copy. Canvas 54×51 cm. Sale M. d'Herbouville, Paris, 26/5/1829, no. 19.

146. *A Couple Making Music at a Table, with a Serving Girl* (Plate 150)   *c.* 1680

Hermitage, Leningrad, inv. no. 815.

Canvas 65×53 cm. Signed left on windowsill: P d Hooch

PROV.: *Sale, Amsterdam, 19/12/1770, no. 101; entered collection between 1774 and 1783.

LIT.: Waagen 1864, 190, no. 861; Gower 1880, 112; Havard 1880, 123:2; HdG 1892, no. 76; Wurzbach, I, 717; HdG no. 133 [1670-5]; R, 82, 84, 104, ill. 92 [*c.* 1670-5]; Lilienfeld 1924, 453; Lilienfeld 1924-5, 187; CB, 8 [after 1675]; BM, 259, 276; Val. no. 165 [*c.* 1680]; CB 1930, 198.

Valentiner dated the picture, probably correctly, *c.* 1680. The type of the woman at the table recalls the lady of the household in Cat. 143 (Plate 146) and the serving woman may be compared with the woman kneeling in Cat. 140 (Plate 143). A painting on the wall depicts a bearded man with a fur hat in the manner of the Rembrandt School.

147. *A Man with a Serving Woman at a Table*★ (Plate 151)   *c.* 1680

Present location unknown.

Panel 51×47 cm.

PROV.: Charles T. Yerkes, cat. (1893), no. 27; Sale C.T. Yerkes, New York, 5/4/1910, no. 131—Preyer, $4000; lent by A. Preyer to the Mauritshuis in 1910;[1] (Preyer died in 1927 and the picture had been sold by 1929).[2]

LIT.: Yerkes Coll. cat. 1893, no. 27, ill.; 1904, I, no. 49, ill.; HdG no. 193; W. Martin, in *B.K.N.O.B.*, 3 (1910), 173, ill.; K. Erasmus, in *Cicerone*, 3 (1911), 84, ill.; Jantzen 1912, 32; R. Bangel, in *Cicerone*, 6 (1914), 49, fig. 6; BM, 261; Val. no. 162 [*c.* 1680].

Aspects of the design and figures recall Cat. 146. According to the Yerkes collection catalogues and Valentiner, the picture is on panel, an unusual support for a late work.

NOTES: [1] Martin 1910. [2] Val. no. 162.

148. *A Woman Feeding a Parrot, with a Man and a Serving Woman* (Plate 149)   *c.* 1680

Present location unknown.

Canvas 50.8×43.8 cm. Signed left on windowsill: P d Hooghe[1]

PROV.: *Sale Constantin, Paris, 18/3/1816, no. 44—Perignon, 380 frs; Sale Perignon, Paris, 10/12/1817, no. 25—300 frs; bought (4/11/1904) from T. Ward by dlr. Sedelmeyer;[2] dlr. Sedelmeyer cat. 1905, no. 16; sold (7/11/1905) to Vischer Boetger;[3] H.B. Jacobs, Baltimore, by 1927;[4] Sale Clark et al. (H.B. Jacobs), New York, 23/10/1941, no. 54, ill.

EXH.: (a) Paris (Sedelmeyer) 1905, no. 16. ill.; (b) Grand Rapids 1940, no. 16.

LIT.: HdG no. 115; BM, 273; Val. no. 166 (left) [incorrectly as on panel; after 1680].

The figures resemble those of Cat. 143 and 146 (Plates 146, 150), suggesting a date of *c.* 1680. Scenes of a couple coaxing a parrot from its cage also appear in Cat. 122 and 150 (Plates 125, 153).

NOTES: [1] Transcribed from photograph. [2] F. Lugt's annotated copy of the Sedelmeyer cat. 1907. [3] ibid. [4] BM, 273.

149. *A Man Offering a Letter to a Lady Feeding a Parrot* (Plate 152)   After 1680

Leger Galleries, London.

Canvas 57.1×50.8 cm.

PROV.: *Sale H. Rottermondt, Amsterdam, 18/7/1786, no. 128;[1] (poss.) Sale P. Oets et al., Amsterdam, 31/1/1791, no. 48—Fouquet, 14 fl;[2] *(prob.) Sale, London, 15/4/1791, no. 12 (w/o m.);[3] Sale Baron de Beurnonville, Paris, 3/6/1884, no. 255 [attr. to P.d.H.]—1780 frs; Sale [Baron de Beurnonville], Paris, 29/1/1885, no. 39 [attr. to P.d.H.]; R. Pelzer, Cologne, 1887;[4] Sale Von Mengerhausen et al., Bonn, 2-3/7/1889, no. 34, ill.; Freiherr von Mansberg, Dresden, by 1892[5] (collection dispersed by 1917[6]); dlr. Van Dieman, Berlin, 1922;[7] dlrs. Asscher, Koetser & Welker, London, 1926;[8] A. van Welie, The Hague, by 1929;[9] Sale N. Katz et al., Brussels, 9/3/1953, no. 27, pl. 6; Sale, Brussels, 18/11/1969, no. 81, pl. 6; Sale, London, 24/3/1971, no. 85, ill.

EXH.: (a) Deventer, Stadhuis, 1948, no. 12; (b) London (Leger) 1972, no. 3, ill.

LIT.: HdG 1892, no. 23; Wurzbach, I, 717 [doubtful]; HdG no. 110 [late] and poss. 116; R, 102; BM, 284; Val. no. 175 (right) [after 1680]; CB 1930, 198.

Illustrations in sales catalogues indicate that the picture has been overpainted, perhaps on several occasions. While the attribution to the artist was doubted in the two Beurnonville Sale catalogues and by Wurzbach, the picture was sold as a De Hooch in the eighteenth century and is probably correctly ascribed to his last years of activity.

NOTES: [1] Sold with our Cat. C 106 for 22 fl. [2] See Cat. No. C 80 (= HdG no. 116), as on panel; sold with our Cat. C 107 (same as C 106?). [3] 'A Lady feeds a parrot; a servant brings a letter.' [4] HdG 1892, no. 23. [5] ibid. [6] BM, 284, n. 9. [7] ibid. [8] Witt photo. [9] Val. no. 175, rt.

150. *Figures with a Parrot at a Table* (Plate 153)   After 1680
Private Collection, Holland.

Canvas 67× 56 cm. Signed lower left on crosspiece of table:
P. D. HOOCH

PROV.: *Sale F. W. Greebe, Amsterdam, 8/12/1788, no. 13—
Foucquet, 20 fl; (prob.) Sale J. Gildemeester Jansz., Amsterdam,
11/6/1800, no. 81—Josi, 50 fl;[1] (prob.) Sale Amsterdam,
7–8/5/1804, no. 74—Van Yperen, 92 fl;[2] Sale A. Meynts,
Amsterdam, 15/7/1823, no. 45—Hopman, 105 fl; purchased
in England in 1884 by Consul Weber, Hamburg, cat. (1892),
no. 255; Sale E.F. Weber, Berlin, 20/2/1912, no. 303—
Sedelmeyer, 22,000 mks; Sale E. Fischhof, Paris, 14/6/1913, no.
55; dlr. Sedelmeyer, Paris, cat. (1913), no. 12; purchased in
1917 from dlr. F. Muller by Jonkheer H. Loudon, Wassenaar.

EXH.: Paris (Sedelmeyer) 1913, no. 12, ill.

LIT.: J. von Pflugk-Hartung, 'Die Weberische Gemälde-
sammlung', *R.f.K.*, 8 (1885), 80–94; F. Schlie, *Hervorragende
Gemälde niederländischer Meister der Galerie Weber*, Vienna,
1891, 8; K. Woermann, *Wissenschaftl. Verzeichnis der älteren
Gemälde der Galerie Weber*, Hamburg, 1892, no. 255; HdG
1892, no. 28; K. Woermann, in *Graphische Künste*, 14 (1891),
30; Wurzbach, I, 717; HdG nos. 111 & prob. 117; G. Mourey,
'La collection Eugene Fischof', *Les Arts*, 137 (5/1913), 2; R, 102;
Lilienfeld 1924, 453; CB, 8; BM, 273; Val. no. 166 (right)
[after 1680].

The painting was sold in 1788 and almost certainly in 1800
as the companion piece to the following painting (Cat. 151).
The two works are close in size and style and probably were
designed as pendants.

NOTES: [1] See HdG no. 117; although the description states
that the man with the pipe is standing, the fact that the work
appeared with the same companion piece (Cat. 151) as in the
previous sale supports the identification. [2] The description
corresponds, however, with the measurements 25×25″
(61× 61 cm).

PRINT: W. Unger (H. no. 13; cf. Schlie 1891).

151. *A Woman and a Man Making Music, with Dancing
Dogs*★ (Plate 154)   After 1680
Present location unknown.

Canvas 65× 55 cm. Signed right on harpsichord: P. d.
Hoogh

PROV.: *Sale F.W. Greebe, Amsterdam, 8/12/1788, no. 14—
Foucquet, 20 fl; Sale J. Gildemeester Jansz., Amsterdam,
11/6/1800, no. 80—Josi, 30 fl; Sale J. Lauwers et al., Amsterdam, 13/12/1802, no. 74—Hulswit, 16 fl; Sale, Rotterdam,
3/8/1811, no. 21—Lebrun, 210 fl; *Sale De Coutellier, Paris,
19/3/1833, no. 34;[1] *Sale [Henry], Paris, 26–7/12/1833, no.
33—400 frs;[2] Sale Petit, Amsterdam, 19/6/1913, no. 28, ill.;
Sale, Amsterdam, 13/4/1920, no. 84—Slüter, 4000 fl; R.F.
Goreneveldt, Bussum, 1960;[3] dlr. S. Nystad, The Hague,
1961;[4] Sale R. Holst et al., Amsterdam, 22/5/1962, no. 37, ill.

EXH.: Delft (Antikbeurs) 1961.

LIT.: HdG no. 148; Lilienfeld 1924, 453; BM, 272; Val. 1927,
70; Val. xxiii, no. 174 (right), [after 1680].

In the sales in 1788 and 1800 the picture was sold as the
pendant to our Cat. 150. A gardener with a watering can,
who is mentioned in early sales catalogues, formerly appeared
at the left of the foyer.[5]

NOTES: [1] BMf. [2] ibid. [3] RKD photo. [4] Exh. [5] Compare
Val. no. 174.

152. *A Woman and a Man Making Music, with Dancing
Dogs*★ (Plate 155)   After 1680
Present location unknown.

Canvas 50× 42.5 cm. Signed right on harpsichord: Hoogh[1]

PROV.: (Prob.) Sale Amsterdam, 16/6/1828, no. 40 (w/o m.)
—Gruyter, 42 fl;[2] W. Ramsay, London;[3] Sale S. Maynard,
Von Berks, et. al., Berlin, 22/3/1910, no. 46—2730 mks; G.
von Mallmann, Berlin, 1911;[4] Sale G. von Mallmann, Berlin,
12/6/1918, no. 120, pl. 10; dlr. Goudstikker, 1918, 1919, 1922,
1926, 1936, 1938;[5] Sale Goudstikker, Berlin, 3–4/12/1940, no.
96, pl. 37.

EXH.: (a) The Hague (Goudstikker, cat. no. 9) 1918, no. 26,
ill.; (b) Amsterdam 1918, no. 29; (c) Rotterdam (Goudstikker,
cat. no. 12) 1919, no. 41; (d) Copenhagen 1922, no. 58, ill.;
(e) St. Louis (Goudstikker, cat. no. 21) 1922, no. 57; (f) The
Hague (Goudstikker) 1926, no. 73; (g) The Hague 1936, no.
564; (h) Amsterdam 1938, no. 96.

LIT.: HdG (prob.) no. 154; Lilienfeld 1924, 453; BM, 284;
Val. 1927, 70: Val. xxiii, no. 174 (left) [after 1680].

The same theme appears in Cat. 151 (Plate 154).

NOTES: [1] Facsimile in cat. of Exh. b. [2] See HdG no. 154.
[3] Sale cat. 1910. [4] HdGf. [5] Exh. a–h.

153. *A Woman Kneeling by a Fire, with Figures at a Table*★
(Plate 156)   After 1680
Present location unknown.

Canvas 67.3× 83.8 cm. Signed lower left on column: P D H

PROV.: Sale J. van der Berg, Amsterdam, 29/7/1779, no. 9—
49 fl; Humphrey Ward, London;[1] dlr. C. Sedelmeyer, cat.
(1917), no. 12; Sale Thurlow et al., London, 9/7/1904, no. 87;
dlr. Kleinberger, Paris;[2] Ludwig Mandl, Moscow, by 1907;[3]
dlr. Kleinberger, Paris, cat. (1911), no. 37; Sale Kleinberger,
New York, 23/1/1918, no. 59, ill.; dlr. Kleinberger, Paris,
1923, afterwards on the art market in Germany;[4] P.C., Berlin,
before 1929;[5] dlr. Ehrlich, New York, 1929;[6] on sale in
Gimbels, New York, 1946;[7] Hammer Collection, New York,
by 1952, until after 1957.[8]

EXH.: (a) Paris (Sedelmeyer) 1897, no. 12; (b) Paris (Kleinberger) 1911, no. 37, ill.; (c) Birmingham et al. 1952–7. (d)
Greenville 1957, no. 26, ill.

LIT.: HdG no. 190 [nearer to 1690 than to 1680]; R, 104;
BM, 285; Val. no. 160 [c. 1680].

Unaware of the date of the artist's death Hofstede de Groot
suggested that the costumes pointed to a date in the late 1680s.
Like a related composition (Cat. 154, Plate 157), the picture
probably dates from the last years of the artist's life. The white
dog in the lower right-hand corner was previously overpainted.[9]

NOTES: [1] Sedelmeyer cat. 1897. [2] HdG no. 190. [3] ibid. [4] BM,
285, no. 2. [5] Val. no. 160. [6] Witt photo. [7] *A.N.*, 45, no. 4 (1946),
adv. [8] Exh. c & d. [9] Compare Val. no. 60.

154. *A Woman Kneeling by a Fire, with a Musical
Company* (Plate 157)   After 1680
C. Mumenthaler Collection.

Canvas 68× 82.5 cm.

PROV.: *Sale J. de Kommer, Amsterdam, 15/4/1767, no. 14—
De Winter, 34 fl; (prob.) J. Oets et al., Amsterdam, 31/1/1791,
no. 14—Wubbels, 12 fl;[1] T. Hamlet, 1834[2] and possibly by
1829;[3] poss. G. Cornwall Legh,[4] by 1867?;[5] dlr. P. de Boer,
Amsterdam, 1937;[6] Private Collection, Holland, 1944;[7] Sale
R. Olaf Hambro et al. (the late P. Kraaij of Hattem), London,

24/11/1961, no. 75, ill.—Gall. St. Lucas; Gall. St. Lucas, Vienna, 1962;[8] Sale E. Beatty et al. (a.c.), London, 10/4/1970, no. 36, ill.—Holstein.

EXH.: (a) London, B.I., 1829, no. 154. (b) (poss.) London, B.I., 1867, no. 103;[9] (c) Amsterdam (De Boer) 1937, no. 20, ill.; (d) Rotterdam (De Boer) 1937, no. 24; (e) Vienna (St. Lucas) 1962, no. 18, ill.

LIT.: HdG no. 142.

Related in style and composition to Cat. 153 (Plate 156), the picture probably dates from the last four years of the artist's career.

NOTES: [1] HdG no. 142; the measurements 27× 52″ are probably a misprint for 27× 32″ (68.5× 81.3 cm). [2] According to Exh. c (without source). [3] Exh. b. [4] According to Exh. c; but the painting owned by Legh probably was our Cat. 105. Unlike the latter work, the present picture did not figure in the catalogue of High Legh Hall (*c.* 1893). [5] See Exh. b; but probably identical with our Cat. 105 (see note 4). [6] Exh. c & d. [7] Note from J.G. van Gelder on RKD photo. [8] Exh. e. [9] See note 5.

155. *A Couple Playing Music on a Terrace, with a Serving Woman* (Plate 158)   After 1680

Private Collection.

Canvas 52× 64 cm. Signed left with initials on base of column (probably false).[1]

PROV.: ★Sale J.G. Korschen, Breslau, 11/6/1838, no. 71;[2] (prob.) Sale Dunford, London, 28/4/1855, no. 90 (w/o m.)— £21; Khahil Bey;[3] bought in 1876 by Teplow from heirs of Mustapha Fazyl Pasha (Turkish Ambassador in Paris); Teplow Collection, St. Petersburg;[4] Sale J.G. Menzies et al., London, 25/2/1905, no. 71—Bailey, £141; Ludwig Mandl, Wiesbaden, 1914;[5] Sale J. Camberlyn et al. (Mandl), Amsterdam, 13/7/1926, no. 644; Private Collection, Berlin, before 1929;[6] Sale A.W. Sjöstrand, Berlin, 21–2/3/1933, no. 54, pl. II.

LIT.: HdG nos. 134 & 171a; R, 104, Lilienfeld 1924–5, 187; CB, 8 [after 1675]; BM, 276; Val. no. 171 [after 1680].

While De Hooch had depicted figures on terraces by the late 1660s (cf. Cat. 75 & 76, Plates 78, 79), this work was probably correctly dated by Valentiner 'after 1680'. The figure types may be compared to those in the two preceding works.

NOTES: [1] False according to HdGf of 1925. [2] BMf. [3] ibid. (without source). [4] According to HdG no. 134 sold in 1906; however, identical with the painting in the following sale. [5] HdGf. [6] Val. no. 171.

156. *A Musical Party of Four Figures, with a Small Boy Dancing* (Plate 159)   After 1680

Berkshire Museum, Pittsfield, Mass.

Canvas 65× 75 cm. Signed right on steps: P · d · Hooghe

PROV.: Sale Neven, Cologne, 17/3/1879, no. 98—1210 mks; ★Sale Rastoin Bremond, Nice, 10/3/1886, no. 31—1250 frs;[1] F. Linton, Brighton, 1892;[2] purchased in 1898 from dlr. Colnaghi, London, by dlr. Sedelmeyer, Paris;[3] Sedelmeyer, cat. 1899, no. 23; dlr. Kleinberger, 1907;[4] dlr. Ehrich, New York, 1908;[5] acq. by Zenos Crane, March 1916, for the Museum.[6]

EXH.: (a) Paris (Sedelmeyer) 1899, no. 23, ill. (b) Pittsfield 1942, no. 21, ill.

LIT.: HdG 1892, no. 20; Wurzbach, I, 716; HdG no. 120; R, 99; Lilienfeld 1924–5, 187; BM, 276; Val 1927, 77, no. 36; Val. no. 139 [*c.* 1675].

Although the pilastered architecture resembles the settings of works from the 1670s (cf. Cat. 119, Plate 122), the figure types suggest a later date.

NOTES: [1] BMf. [2] HdG 1892, no. 20. [3] BMf. [4] HdG no. 120. [5] HdGf. [6] BM, 276, n. 15.

157. *Two Women, and a Man in Bed*★ (Plate 160)   After 1680

Present location unknown.

Canvas 70× 82 cm. Signed lower right on footwarmer: P. d. Hoogh[1]

PROV.: Sale Brun of Geneva, Paris, 30/11/1841, no. 21—620 frs. (prob.) Sale, Paris, 28/3/1843, no. 19 (w/o m.); dlr. C. Brunner, Paris, 1922–8;[2] Sale Mrs. G.L. Eaton et al. (a.c.), New York, 23/2/1955, no. 71, ill.

LIT.: HdG no. 85; BM, 265; Val. no. 158 [*c.* 1675–80].

When the painting was authenticated by Bode in 1925 the figure of the seated woman was said to be heavily overpainted.[3] The work probably dates from the artist's last years.

NOTES: [1] BMf. According to Sale cat. of 1955: P D HOOCH. [2] BMf. [3] RKD files.

158. *Three Women and a Man Making Music in a Vestibule*★ (Plate 161)   After 1680

Present location unknown.

Canvas 50× 60 cm.

PROV.: ★(Poss.) Sale J.W. van Arp, Amsterdam, 4/9/1799 delayed to 19/6/1800, no. 58—Menzaar, 85 fl;[1] (poss.) Helsleuter (Van Eyl Sluyter ?), Paris, 25/1/1802, no. 73— Nuneville, 809 frs;[2] ★(poss.) Sale, Paris, 17/1/1809, no. 59— Constantin, 520 frs;[3] ★(poss.) Sale [Constantin], Paris, 18/3/1816, no. 43—Chariot, 300 frs;[4] Sale Edward, 1st Earl of Ellenborough, London, 3/4/1914, no. 102;[5] Sale H. Lane et al., London, 6/7/1917, no. 96;[6] Sale Jonas Lek, Amsterdam, 31/3/1925, no. 34, ill.;[7] Private Collection, Munich, 1955.[8]

LIT.: (Poss.) S no. 13 (ref. Helsleuter Sale); (poss.) Havard 1880, 123:1 (ref. Helsleuter Sale); (poss.) HdG no. 144 (ref. Helsleuter Sale); BM, 285; Val. 151 (above) [*c.* 1680].

Varying measurements in early sales catalogues suggest that the work has either been cut down or exists in more than one version. Although the composition recalls Cat. 116 (Plate 119), the figure types suggest a date toward the end of the artist's career.

NOTES: [1] The extensive description corresponds in all details, but the measurements are given as 26× 31″ (66× 78.8 cm). [2] See S no. 13 & HdG no. 144. The description and measurements reversed: 24× 20″ (61× 50.8 cm). [3] Canvas 68.6× 76.2 cm. The picture did not appear in the Langeac Sale in Paris in 1808 as stated by Brière-Misme (285, n. 1). [4] Canvas 63.5× 76.2 cm; description reversed. [5] HdG handex: 55.8× 66 cm. [6] 54.6× 72.4 cm. [7] Canvas 50× 60 cm. [8] RKD photo.

158A. Possible version or copy. Canvas approx. 66× 76 cm. See Sales 1800, 1809 & 1816, and notes 1, 3 & 4 above.

159. *Two Women and a Man Eating Oysters*★ (Plate 162)   1681

Present location unknown.

Canvas 60.3× 52 cm. Signed and dated upper right: P Hoogh 1681[1]

PROV.: Sale D. van Dijl, Amsterdam, 22/11/1813 (delayed to 10/1/1814), no. 70; Rev. H. King;[2] by descent to G. Mahon, from whom it was acquired by M. Knoedler & Co., New

York, 1920;[3] dlr. Goudstikker, Amsterdam, 1928;[4] Baron Thyssen, Schloss Rohoncz Collection, Lugano,[5] cat. (1937), no. 201; Sale F.E. Short et al. (a.c.), London, 2/11/1949, no. 148—MacGregor; Germaine Hochschild, Lausanne;[6] Sale, Lucerne, 20/11/1962, no. 2435, pl. 49; Sale, Cologne, 11/11/1964, no. 93, pl. 55; Sale The Marchioness of Downshire et al. (a.c.), London, 9/7/1975, no. 40, ill.

EXH.: (a) Malmö 1920, no. 20, ill.; (b) Amsterdam (Goudstikker) 1928-9, 8, ill.; (c) Munich 1930, no. 159.

LIT.: HdG no. 218; BM, 285; Val. xx, no. 161; R. Heinemann, *Stiftung Sammlung Schloss Rohoncz*, Lugano, 1937, I, no. 201.

A meal of oysters is also shared in the painting of 1677 in London (Cat. 134, Plate 137).

NOTES: [1] Transcribed from photograph. [2] Note from Knoedler's on photo at RKD. [3] ibid. [4] Exh. b. [5] Exh. c. [6] Sale cat. 1962.

160. *A Woman Standing before a Man Seated at a Table* (Plate 163) 1683

Present location unknown.

Canvas 43×38 cm. Signed and dated 1683 on crosspiece of table.

PROV.: Sale A. L[efevre], Paris, 15-16/4/1897, no. 247—600 frs; Sale Haemacher, Amsterdam, 30/11/1897, no. 48 [style of P.d.H.]—270 fl; dlr. Mos, Arnhem;[1] dlr. Goudstikker, 1917;[2] Sale E. Glückstadt, Copenhagen, 2/6/1924, no. 671—Goudstikker; Baron Lajos Tornyai, Budapest, c. 1929;[3] Sale Lord Carew et al. (a.c.), London, 26/6/1957, no. 71—Dent.

EXH.: (a) The Hague (Goudstikker, cat. no. 5) 1917, no. 24; (b) Rotterdam (Goudstikker, cat. no. 6) 1917, no. 21; (c) Amsterdam (Goudstikker, cat. no. 7) 1917, no. 25.

LIT.: HdG no. 175; R, 36, 96; Lilienfeld 1924, 453-4; CB, 8; Val. 1926, 58, n. 2; BM, 284; Val. xx, no. 175 (left); CB 1930, 8.

When the picture was in Baron Tornyai's collection the floor was overpainted with a tiled pattern and other minor changes were visible. The authors of the Haemacher Sale catalogue and Collins Baker doubted the attribution; however, the weakness in the design and execution are not untypical of the artist's last pictures. Brière-Misme and Valentiner assumed that the man was a public notary; a similar theme is represented in Cat. 133 (Plate 134). The curious figure behind the curtain, reminiscent of the gardener who formerly appeared in Cat. 151, is unexplained.

NOTES: [1] HdG no. 175. [2] Exh. a, b, c. [3] Photo RKD.

161. *A Sportsman and a Lady in a Landscape* (Plate 164) 1684

Private Collection.

Canvas 108×134 cm. Signed and dated 1684 on fountain.

PROV.: Sale P. Pama, Amsterdam, 30/1/1781, no. 6—L. van de Velde, 6 fl 10; (prob.) Sale J.E. Graves, Amsterdam, 5/5/1806, no. 68 (w/o m.)—L. Pakker, 2 fl;[1] Derby Collection;[2] Sale S. Maynard & R. van Berks, Berlin, 22/3/1910, no. 47, pl. 9; M. von Nemes, Budapest, 9/1910;[3] Langton R. Douglas,

London, sold by 1929;[4] Mrs. Marshall Field, Washington, by 1937;[5] Sale New York, 16-17/6/1976, no. 148, ill. (bought in).

EXH.: Indianapolis 1937, no. 34, ill.

LIT.: HdG no. 301; Val. 1910a, 9, n. 1; Val. 1926, 58, n. 2, 63, 64; BM, 284; Val. xx, no. 176; MacLaren, 184, n. 14.

The picture bears the last certain date in the artist's oeuvre.

NOTES: [1] HdG no. 301. [2] Sale cat. 1910. [3] HdGf. [4] Val. no. 176. [5] Exh.

162. *A Musical Company of Four Figures*★ (Plate 165) 1684?

Present location unknown.

Canvas 72×84 cm. Signed and dated (?)[1]

PROV.: (Poss.) Sale Comte F. de Robiano, Brussels, 1/5/1837 no. 283;[2] N.N. Collection, Paris, 15/7/1906;[3] G. Horschek, Prague, cat. (1907), no. 63; Sale E. Fischof, Paris, 14/6/1913, no. 56; dlr. Kleinberger, 1926;[4] Sale A. Preyer, Amsterdam, 8/11/1927, no. 9, ill.—De Vries, 9600 fl; A. Vorst, Amsterdam;[5] dlr. B. Houthakker, Amsterdam, 1959.[6]

LIT.: HdG no. 155; W. Martin, *Galerie G.R. Horschek von Mühlheim*, Prague, 1907, no. 63; BM, 276; Val. no. 151 (below) [with incorrect measurements; c. 1675-80].

If the picture was cut down substantially at the right and to a lesser extent along the upper edge some time after 1837 and before 1907, it could be identical with the picture with two extra figures at the right which was sold in the Robiano sale.[7] In 1907 Martin observed that the work had been heavily restored and Valentiner correctly observed that the faces appeared overpainted and modernized. Martin noted that the remnants of a date '..64' ('the 4 is very clear, the 6 not certainly read as a 6') were visible at the left beside the shoulder of the woman playing a cello. Judging from photographs and allowing for what is undoubtedly extensive overpainting, a date of 1684 would seem plausible.

NOTES: [1] According to HdGf (15/7/1906): 'the beginning of an authentic signature, right centre'; Martin 1907; remnants of a signature lower right, remnants of a date, left; Fischof Sale cat.: fully signed lower left; Preyer Sale cat.: signed. [2] See HdG no. 155: two other cavaliers are mentioned entering from a door at the right; 81×104. [3] HdGf. [4] BM, 276, no. 4. [5] RKD notes. [6] ibid. [7] See HdG no. 155 & note 2.

163. *A Musical Company of Three Figures*★ (Plate 166) 1684?

Present location unknown.

Canvas 53.3×62.8 cm. Signed and dated right above door on cartouche: P./D(E?) HOOGE / A° 1684[1]

PROV.: (Poss.) Edmund Phipps, London, 1854,[2] and perhaps by 1847;[3] Sale Miss Seymour, London, 19/1/1945, no. 50.

EXH.: (Poss.) London, B.I., 1847, no. 123.[4]

LIT.: (Poss.) Waagen 1854, II, 227; (poss.) HdG no. 160.

A signature and a date 1684 are visible in a photograph taken in 1945.

NOTES: [1] Transcribed from photograph taken at the Seymour Sale. [2] Waagen 1854 & HdG no. 160 (w/o m.). [3] See Exh. [4] Described only as an interior lent by Phipps; cf. also C 30.

CLASSIFIED SUMMARY OF THE CONTENTS OF CATALOGUE SECTIONS B–D

Hofstede de Groot's system, although admittedly flawed, has been retained for the subject matter divisions in the interest of consistency.

Paintings

  A. Interiors

    I. Occupations

      (a) Mother and child: C 1–18, D 1.

      (b) Woman and maid-servant: B 1–2, C 19–41, D 2.

      (c) Pig-killing: C 42–3.

      (d) Bedroom and toilet: C 44–8.

      (e) Women or men in various occupations: B 3, C 49–78, D 4–5.

    II. Conversation

      (a) At home

        1. Figures with a parrot: C 79–82.

        2. Music scenes: B 4, C 83–136, D 6–8.

        3. Conversations or parties at table; letters: B 5–8, C 137–227, D 9–15.

      (b) Taverns and guardrooms: B 9–11, D 16–24.

        1. Gaming scenes: C 228–31.

        2. Drinking scenes: C 232–41.

  B. Open Air Scenes: B 12–13, D 25–35.

        1. Vegetable and fish dealers: C 217.

        2. Courtyard and garden scenes: C 242–54.

        3. Landscapes: C 255–60.

  C. Portraits

      (a) Family groups: C 261–2.

      (b) Single figures: B 14–15, C 263–7, D 36–8.

      (c) Still Life: C 268.

  D. Undescribed Pictures: C 269–94.

Drawings: D 39–43.

B. Tentatively Accepted and Questionable Works

B 1. *A Woman before a Mirror, with Two Women by a Hearth** (Plate 167)

Present location unknown.

Panel 35.5×48.2 cm.

PROV.: *Sale Oosten de Bruyn, Haarlem, 8/4/1800, no. 8; Sale C. H. Schultz, Amsterdam, 10/7/1826, no. 48—Brondgeest, 79 fl; Sale R. Baird et al., (a.c.), London, 19/12/1947, no. 83; Mrs. R. A. Constantine, 1960;[1] Sale Le Duc de Brissac et. al. (Constantine), London, 14/5/1971, no. 121—De Wilt.

EXH.: Dutch Festival Exh., Municipal Art Gallery, Scarborough, 1960, no. 28.

LIT.: HdG no. 226.

The theme of a woman preparing to depart on her marketing errands recalls Cat. 104 (Plate 107) and the composition resembles designs from the mid to late 1660s (cf. Cat. 73, Plate 76). Judging from photographs, however, the execution of the figures appears unusually crude for the period. St. Jerome kneeling in prayer is represented in the picture on the wall.

NOTES: [1] Exh.

B 2. *Nocturnal Scene with a Woman Paying a Maidservant* (Plate 168)

Krannert Art Gallery, University of Illinois, Champaign, acc. no. 42-1-2. Emily H. and Merle J. Trees Collection.

Canvas 36×36.5 cm.

PROV.: Dlr. K. Erasmus, Berlin, 1930;[1] Blumenreich, Berlin, 1931.[2]

Previously unpublished, the work resembles paintings from the 1670s in design (cf. Cat. 98, Plate 100) and exhibits the exceptionally dark tonality and heavy craquelure of some of De Hooch's last works (cf. Cat. 140-1, Plates 143-4). The same theme and similar figure motifs appear in Cat. 88 (Plate 91). Despite these resemblances the attribution remains uncertain owing to the work's problematic condition. The canvas has undoubtedly been cut along the lower edge and probably also at the right. Moreover, the work has been abraded and the figures overpainted. If genuine, it probably dates from c. 1675-80.

NOTES: [1] RKD photo. [2] Witt photo.

B 3. *Dog and Cat in a Room, with a View of a Woman Seated by a Fireplace**

Present location unknown.

Canvas 49×52 cm.

PROV.: P. Delaroff, St. Petersburg.

LIT.: Val. no. 167 (rt.) [c. 1680].

While elements of the painting recall De Hooch's last works (compare the pattern of the mullions in the backlighted window in Cat. 139, Plate 142), the picture is only known through poor reproductions and the attribution cannot be verified. Valentiner's statement that the work was in the Hermitage could not be confirmed.

B 3A. Poss. version or copy. (HdG no. 99). Panel 28×35 cm. (See Cat. C 70).

B 4. *A Musical Company with Four Figures** (Plate 169)

Present location unknown.

Panel 82×103 cm. (Formerly) Signed lower left: P D HOOCH

PROV.: *(Poss.) Sale J. Clemens, Ghent, 21/6/1779, no. 134;[1] Granberg Collection, Sweden;[2] dlr. J. Goudstikker, Amsterdam, 1912;[3] Private Collection, England, 1915;[4] Sale R.A.D. Fleming, London, 20/12/1929, no. 141; dlr. Van Diemen, Berlin, 1930;[5] Sale Thun et al., (a.c.), Lucerne, 31/8/1933, no. 511, pl. 27; dlr. Barendse, The Hague, 1939;[6] Sale Paris, 7/12/1967, no. 142 [attr. to P.d.H.], ill.

EXH.: Amsterdam 1938, no. 95.

LIT.: Cust 1915, 223, ill. 222; BM, 276; Val. no. 130 [c. 1670-5]; CB 1930, 198; Würtenberger 1937, 86.

Photographs taken at different times indicate that the picture has been repeatedly overpainted. When it was illustrated by Cust in 1915 the dark squares of the tiled floor had decorations in the centre and, according to the author, the picture over the fireplace represented the Good Samaritan. A photograph taken when the picture was with the dealer Van Diemen in 1930 reveals that the head of the central figure had been altered, the floor decorations removed, and details of the figures, furnishings, and paintings within the picture changed. By the time the work was photographed for the dealer Barendse in 1939 the head of the guitar player had again been altered, the painting over the mantelpiece had become an Entombment scene, and the signature previously visible in the lower left-hand corner had disappeared. Brière-Misme noted the resemblance to Cat. 74 (Plate 77), which she incorrectly surmised might be a pendant. Aspects of the work reminded Valentiner of Van der Burch and Collins Baker doubted the attribution to De Hooch. The problematic condition prohibits judgement as to authenticity, but the work would seem to document a composition invented by De Hooch in the late 1660s. The inscription on the harpsichord reads: 'VERBUM DO....I/MANET....UM/OMNIA (M)....ET'

NOTES: [1] Panel 80×95 cm. [2] HdGf. [3] RKD photo. [4] Cust 1915. [5] RKD photo. [6] RKD photo; Exh.

B 4A. Version(s?) or copy (copies?) (known only through descriptions). PROV.: Sale Museum Belgium I, Ghent, 6/11/1797, no. 63 [Panel 80×82.5 cm]; Sale, Ghent, 23/7/1804, no. 65 [Panel 85.2×87.9 cm]; Sale T. Loridon de Ghellinck, Ghent, 3/9/1821, no. 453 [= HdG no. 152: Panel 88×88].

B 5. *A Man Reading to a Woman with Needlework* (Plate 170)

    G. Nijssen, Barcelona.

    Canvas 67×57 cm. Signed lower left: P d Hooch

    PROV.: Sale Brun of Geneva, Paris, 30/11–1/12/1841, no. 19 —910 frs; *(prob.) Sale Paris, 28/3/1843, no. 18 (w/o m.); Sale Paris, 14/11/1843, no. 17—305 frs; Sale Graf von Limburg-Stirum et al., Cologne, 6–9/5/1953, no. 47, pl. 12; dlr. H. Zuppinger, Herrliberg, 1958.[1]

    LIT.: HdG no. 234.

    The picture has been abraded and overpainted. Repaint is especially evident in the woman's head. The execution resembles that of the early paintings in Moscow and Barcelona (Cat. 15 & 16, Plates 13, 15) and the theme was treated in a work of *c.* 1670 (Cat. 97, Plate 101). Resemblances to Van der Burch's art appear in the figures, which may be compared to those in Cat. D 11 (Plate 180). The attribution to De Hooch seems doubtful.

    NOTES: [1] RKD photo.

B 6. *A Woman Pouring Wine for a Man Seated at a Table*★

    Present location unknown.

    Canvas 48.7×40 cm.

    PROV.: Sale J. Crammer Simonsz., Amsterdam, 25/11/1778, no. 20 [Vermeer]—Tersteeg, 65 fl;[1] (prob.) Sale Engelberts & Tersteeg, Amsterdam, 13/6/1808, no. 225 (w/o m.)—Allart, 51 fl;[2] dlr. Cassirer, Berlin, 1918;[3] dlr. Stenman, Stockholm, 1942.[4]

    EXH.: Stockholm (Stenman) 1942, no. 41, pl. 13.

    LIT.: HdG no. 216a; BM 52 [Ochtervelt]; Val. no. 76 [*c.* 1664]; Val. 1932, 317.

    Attributed to Vermeer in the sale of 1778 and to Ochtervelt by Brière-Misme, the ascription to De Hooch cannot be supported without personal examination. In photographs the male figure appears to be particularly crudely executed.

    NOTES: [1] HdG (Vermeer) no. 40a [2] HdG 216a. [3] HdGf. [4] Exh.

B 7A. *A Woman Receiving a Man at a Door*★ (Plate 171)

    Present location unknown.

    Canvas 71×66 cm.

    PROV.: *(Poss.) Sale J. Pompe van Meerdervoort, Souterwoude, 19/5/1780, no. 19—Delphos;[1] *Sale F. W. Greebe, Amsterdam, 8/12/1788, no. 17 [S. van Hoogstraten]—Van der Schley, 50 fl; Sale Baronne de V . . . ez, Paris, 19/9/1815, no. 38—Grandchamp, 218 frs;[2] Sale C.-L. Reynders, Brussels, 6/8/1821, no. 44—Nieuwenhuys;[3] *(poss.) Sale W. Beckford, Fonthill Abbey, 11/10/1823, no. 190 (w/o m.); *Sale Lafontaine, Crafurt et al., Paris, 30/4/1827, no. 23;[4] (prob.) Sale Hope, Paris, 13–16/5/1840, no. 12 (w/o m.)—Cousin, 1900 frs;[5] Pascha Weitsch Collection;[6] *Sale E. Postle, Leipzig, 7/5/1860, no. 14; Kunsthalle, Hamburg, until 1923;[7] E. Bolton, London, 1923;[8] Jules Bache, New York, 1927;[9] dlr. Katz, Dieren, 1937;[10] Sale Mrs. E. Andriesse, New York, 24/2/1949, no. 34, ill.

    EXH.: Dieren (Katz) 1937, no. 39.

    LIT.: HdG no. 221 and poss. 54; Mellaart 1923, 269–70, ill.; Lilienfeld 1924–5, 186, ill.; BM 269 [*c.* 1680]; Val. 1927, 77, no. 28, ill. 67; Val. xix, no. 98 [*c.* 1671–4].

    Part or all of the provenance prior to the time when the picture entered the Kunsthalle in Hamburg may refer to the version of almost identical dimensions (Cat. B 7B). As Mellaart

observed, the composition bears a close resemblance to the painting of 1670 in the Rijksmuseum (Cat. 94, Plate 96), where a similar view of the Kloveniersburgwal appears through the doorway. The attribution to De Hooch, however, is not above suspicion. The picture sold as a Van Hoogstraten in 1788 and the standing woman closely resembles the figure types employed by the Dordrecht painter after *c.* 1665. The picture of the Sacrifice of Isaac on the wall is based on A. Stock's print after Rubens.

    NOTES: [1] 69.5×56.6 cm (possibly a smaller version). [2] HdG no. 221: the linen basket, no doubt, was mistaken for a cradle by the author of the catalogue. [3] Incorrectly listed under HdG no. 182 (our Cat. 84). [4] BMf. [5] BMf. [6] Ref. following sale. [7] Val. no. 98. [8] Mellaart 1923, 269. [9] BM, 269. [10] Exh.

B 7B. *A Woman Receiving a Man at a Door*★

    Present location unknown.

    Canvas 72.4×63.5 cm.

    PROV.: Weston Collection, Wokingham, 1923;[1] Sale Berwick et al. (Mrs. I. F. Weston), London, 21/10/1949, no. 35, ill.—Smith; dlr. Duits, London, 1956.[2]

    Part or all of the provenance listed for the other version (Cat. B 7A) prior to its entry into the Kunsthalle may apply to this work. Although the dimensions of the two pictures are almost identical, small changes (the twisted chair leg visible through the doorway, the notice on the tree, the more slender faces of the figures) distinguish the two versions.

    NOTES: [1] Annotation on Witt photo of our Cat. B 7A: 'A puzzling repetition in Mr. Weston's collection, Wokingham 1923.' [2] RKD photo.

B 7C. Version or copy. Canvas 69.5×56.6 cm. Sale 1780 (see Cat. B 7A).

B 7D. Version or copy. Canvas 56.1×45.7 cm. Sale L[apeyriere], Paris, 19/4/1825, no. 115—1800 frs (S no. 28; erroneously listed under HdG no. 182 [our Cat. 84]); Sale Paris, 15/12/1828, no. 59.

B 8. *Two Men and Two Women at a Table*★ (Plate 172)

    Galleria Caretto, Turin.

    Canvas 56×68 cm. Signed on gaming board on table: P. D. Hoogh[1]

    PROV.: Private Collection, London.

    The resemblance of the figure types to those of very late paintings by the artist (cf. Cat. 146 & 163, Plates 150, 166) suggests that the work could be an addition to the artist's last years of activity (after *c.* 1680). A Rembrandtesque portrait of a bearded man, similar to that in Cat. 146 (Plate 150), hangs above the fireplace.

    NOTES: [1] Transcribed from photograph.

B 9. *Two Soldiers and a Girl with a Lute* (Plate 173)

    Private Collection.

    Panel 44.5 × 35.5 cm.

    PROV.: Frauenholz Coll., Nürnberg; [1] S. C. Michel, Mainz, by 1886;[2] Sale Michel, Berlin, 27/2/1917, no. 30, pl. 30; Dr. W. von Pannwitz, Berlin; Frau von Pannwitz, Heemstede (Hartekamp), cat. (1926), no. 52.

    EXH.: (a) Düsseldorf 1886, no. 58 [Codde]; (b) Mainz 1887, no. 46 [Codde] (c) Rotterdam 1935, no. 32, fig. 36.

    LIT.: W. Bode, in *R.f.K.*, 10 (1887), 34; H. Thode, in *R.f.K.*, 10 (1887), 412; HdG no. 270; R, 102; BM 370, 376, ill. 367;

Friedländer 1926, I, no. 52; Val. 1927, 68, n. 1; Val. no. 21 [c. 1654]; CB 1930, 198.

When the picture was in the Michel collection it was assigned to P. Codde, an attribution which both Bode and Thode rejected. The former noted the resemblance to Cat. 10 (Plate 8), which he later assigned to De Hooch. Hofstede de Groot was the first to attribute the work to De Hooch. Thinly painted, it reveals numerous pentimenti; a seated figure was painted out when the standing soldier was included. The seated couple are rather awkwardly conceived and their execution seems uncharacteristically loose for De Hooch. But the treatment of the standing soldier, who appears to dance, is not unlike that of the trumpeter in Cat. 7 (Plate 6). If genuine, the picture is probably a very early work.

NOTES: [1] Friedländer 1926, I, no. 52. [2] Exh. a & b.

B 10. *A Soldier, a Serving Woman, and a Flute Player* (Plate 175)

John G. Johnson Collection, Philadelphia, no. 498.

Panel 55.9×69.2 cm.

PROV.: Unknown.

LIT.: Jantzen 1912, 9, 10; Val. 1913, no. 498, ill. [middle of the 50s]; Lilienfeld 1924, 453; CB, 3; BM, 371; Val. 1927, 76, no. 3; Val. no. 14 [c. 1653]; Phila., J.C., cat. 1941, no. 498 [attr. to P.d.H.]; 1972, no. 498 [P.d.H.], ill. 297.

Formerly attributed to Govert Camphuysen,[1] the picture was first assigned to De Hooch by Hofstede de Groot.[2] The dark horizontal composition may be compared with those of Cat. 10 and 11 (Plates 8, 9A) and De Hooch's youthful palette is recalled in the colour scheme of white, yellow and red. But the facial features differ from those of the signed early works (cf. Cat. 7, Plate 6) and reveal points of resemblance with the types used by Van der Burch and Palamedesz. Cleaning might facilitate a firmer attribution.

NOTES: [1] Val. 1913, no. 498 (without source). [2] HdGf (dated 1908) & Val. 1913.

B 11. *Nocturnal Scene in an Inn* (Plate 176)

G. Henle, Duisburg.

Panel 51×59.5 cm. Remnants of a monogram lower right on the bag (or log?).

PROV.: Sale Kathleen, Countess of Drogheda, London, 27/11/1936, no. 66; P. & D. Colnaghi, London.[1]

EXH.: Cologne 1964, no. 19, ill. [c. 1650].

LIT.: Trautscholdt 1964; Fleischer 1978, 56, fig. 14.

Unusually thin and sketchy in execution, the work remains unfinished in passages. The dramatic lighting and colour scheme recall Cat. 10 (Plate 8). While early sales references mention nocturnal scenes by De Hooch (cf. Cat. C 230, C 281, C 284, and especially C 235), at present no night scenes can confidently be assigned to the artist's early career. A nocturnal scene with multiple artificial light sources is among Van der Burch's early signed works (Fig. 54) and employs similar figure types. Only the H of the monogram is clear in the present picture and the attribution must remain open.

NOTES: [1] Exh.

B 12. *Two Women and a Man in a Courtyard* (Plate 174)

Present location unknown.

Panel 68×56 cm. Signed lower right: P.D.H.

PROV.: J. Cremer, Dortmund, cat. 1915, no. 884; Sale Cremer, Berlin, 29/5/1929, no. 61; dlr. M. Porkay, Zurich, 1951;[1] B. Mont, New York, 1951.[2]

EXH.: Münster 1931, no. 21, pl. XXI.

LIT.: H. Voss & K. Lilienfeld, *Katalog der Sammlung Cremer*, II, Dortmund, n.d. (1915), 74, no. 884, pl. 50; BM, 64; Val. no. 26 [c. 1653–5].

The picture was reported to be badly worn in 1915;[3] this could in part explain the weaknesses which seem evident in photographs. Even allowing for condition problems, though, the attribution seems doubtful.

NOTES: [1] RKD photo. [2] Witt photo. [3] HdGf.

B 13. *The Parents at the Door of their Rich Children* (Plate 177)

Present location unknown.

Panel 60×61 cm. Signed lower left (prob. falsely): P d. hooch.[1]

PROV.: *Sale Rheinischer Schlossbesitz et al., Munich, 4/7/1922, no. 448, pl. 13 [in the style of Metsu]; dlr. A.G., Lucerne, July 1923;[2] dlr. J. Böhler, Munich, 1924;[3] dlr. Steinmeyer, Cologne, Nov. 1924;[4] dlr. Benedict, Berlin, 1928;[5] Otto Adler, Frankfurt a. M., 1929.[6]

LIT.: Val. 1927, 69; Val. no. 7 [c. 1650]; T. 9, ill.: R. Bernoulli, in *Zeitschrift für schweizerische Archäologie und Kunstgeschichte*, 10 (1948), 172, n. 2, fig. 13.

Although Valentiner accepted the signature, none was recorded when the work was sold as 'in the style of Metsu' in 1922 and that which had appeared by July 1923 was judged by Hofstede de Groot to be very doubtful. Photographs reveal the picture in different states. The garments and heads of the young couple have been changed, a figure at the far left eliminated, and the tiled foreground at the right extended.[7] Bernoulli noted that the theme and composition are based on H. Gerritsz's print after David Vinckboons.[8] This source may account for the rather exaggerated perspective. The costumes suggest a date in the mid-1660s (compare those of Cat. 60A, Plate 64) as does the interest in classicized architecture. Yet the figures seem peculiarly crude for De Hooch's works of this period.

NOTES: [1] Transcribed from photograph. [2] HdGf. [3] BMf. [4] HdGf. [5] Adv. in *P.* 3/1928. [6] Val. no. 7. [7] cf. Val. no. 7. [8] Bernoulli 1948; concerning the Vinckboons, see E. Benesch, *Master Drwgs.*, 14 (1976), 166–9; on the theme, see Cat. 46, n. 4.

B 14. *Portrait of an Officer* (Plate 178)

Private Collection.

Panel 50×32 cm.

PROV.: Sale C. Pagenstecher, Cologne, 28–29/5/1889, no. 73, ill.; V. Bloch, Amsterdam, 11/1927;[1] dlr. A.G., Lucerne, 1934;[2] Galerie Stern, Düsseldorf, 1938–9;[3] Dominion Gallery, Montreal, before 1960.

EXH.: (a) The Hague (Kleykamp) 1930, no. 14, ill.; (b) London (West's Gallery) 1938–9, no. 11.

LIT.: Val. no. 8 [c. 1650]; Juynboll 1935, 190, n. 1.

Valentiner's tentative identification of the sitter as Justus de la Grange is pure speculation. The facial type resembles that of the soldier in Cat. 2 (Plate 2), while the glancing highlights on the sleeves and feathered hat and the oddly foreshortened arm seem more characteristic of Van der Burch.

NOTES: [1] HdGf. [2] RKD photo. [3] Exh. b.

B 15. ***A Woman Holding a Dog and Smelling a Rose***
(Plate 179)
    City Art Gallery, Manchester.
    Assheton Bennett Collection, 1957.
    Canvas 35.5×28.3 cm. Signed upper right: P. D. HOO[. . .].
    EXH.: London, R.A., 1965, no. 54.
    LIT.: Grossmann 1965, no. 28.

The picture has been abraded and, as noted in the Royal Academy's exhibition catalogue, overpainted. The facial type resembles some of De Hooch's women of the later 1660s (cf. Cat. 84, Plate 87), but no other portraits of this type are known by the artist and none appeared in early sales or inventories.

C. Works Known Only Through Descriptions

C 1. *A Woman with a Child,* also 'Een Kraemvrouwtje', valued at 50 fl by Z.P. Zomer, and separately by J. Roosa and Barent Graat for the same amount.

Inventory of E. van Liebergen, widow of Henry Nieugart, merchant, Amsterdam, N.A.A., no. 5641/55, 24/4/1687. (See S.A.C. Dudok van Heel, in *Amstelodamum,* 1977, 99.)

C 2. *A Woman and Child.* (HdG no. 13a.)

Sale, Amsterdam, 11/4/1698, no. 20—20 fl (Hoet, 1, 44).

C 3. *A Woman with a Child Entering an Interior.*

Sale, Amsterdam, 15/10/1738, no. 15.

C 4 & 5. *Inside of a Room, with Woman and Child.* Its companion, *A Woman Sweeping.*

The Cabinet of M. Le Brun: (cf. Sir Joshua Reynolds, *A Journey to Flanders and Holland in the Year MDCCLXXXI,* in *Collected Works,* II, London, 1809, 368).

C 6. *An Interior with a Woman and Child.* An interior, in which a woman is sitting with her child. An open door looks on to a courtyard in which a maidservant is sweeping. (HdG no. 15.)

Sale S. Loquet et al., The Hague, 8/9/1789, no. 74—De Graaf 7 fl.

C 7. *An Interior with a Woman Seated near her Child's Cradle.*

Canvas 55.8×68.5 cm.

Sale Destouches, Paris, 21/3/1794, no. 65.

C 8. *A Woman Reading beside a Child in a Cradle.* An interior scene with a view to three rooms; in the foreground a woman reading beside a covered cradle; in the distance, a child seen from the rear beside a fireplace.

Panel 62×70 cm.

Sale Lebrun, Paris, 26/12/1797, no. 48 (BMf).

C 9. *A Woman Cleaning a Child by an Open Doorway.* In an interior of a home a woman in old Dutch costume cleans her child by an open doorway; in the distance a gentleman descends a stairway.

Canvas 63.5×53.5 cm.

Sale, Amsterdam, 23/8/1808, no. 69.

C 10. *The Dutch Wet Nurse.*

Catalogue des tableaux de sa Majesté l'Impératrice Joséphine de la galerie et appartement de son Palais de Malmaison, Paris, 1811, no. 67 (cf. Lescure 1867, 270; Grandjean 1964, 145: as in the Malmaison inventory of 1814, no. 1011: 'Interior with a woman suckling her child'). The picture did not appear in the various Malmaison Sales.

C 11. *A Woman Plucking Fowl by a Cradle* in which her child lies; two older children stand by the cradle playing with the infant.

Canvas.

Sale W.G.J. van Gendt, The Hague, 25/10/1830, no. 6.

C 12. *A Woman beside a Cradle.* A woman sits making lace; beside her lies a child in a cradle. By, or in the manner of, P. de Hooge. (HdG no. 21a.)

Sale C.H. Schultz, Amsterdam, 10/7/1826, no. 240— Gruyter, 14 fl 10.

C 13. *A Woman and Child by a Fireside.* Before the fireplace in a dimly lit room sits a woman holding a knife. A child is at her side. A young man whom she appears to be questioning stands before her. In the background, through a half-opened door, another brilliantly lit room is visible. (HdG no. 22.)

Panel, 36×32 cm.

Sale Van Rotterdam, Ghent, 6/7/1835, no. 170—Burton, 75 fl.

C 14. *The Nursery.* Interior of an apartment (without windows), on the right of which is an interesting young woman kneeling by the side of a cradle, raising the clothes preparatory to placing her babe in it, which a servant standing by holds in her arms, enveloped in a blanket. On the opposite side of the room is a cheerful fire burning in a chimney. A kettle and various objects improve the composition of this carefully finished picture. (S s no. 8; Havard 1880, 96:2; HdG no. 23).

Canvas 46×51 cm.

Bought by Mr. Woodburn from Mr. De Gruyter, Amsterdam, 1841.

C 15. *The Nurse.* (HdG no. 23a.)

Sale Paris, 20/3/1883—5000 frs. (No confirmation for the entry could be found.)

C 16. *A Woman and a Child in a Room.* In the middle of a room paved with tiles a woman stands at a table, with a child and a dog. At the open door a man is talking to a woman. (HdG no. 23b.)

Panel 38×30 cm.

Sale C. Hammer, Cologne, 5/10/1894, no. 16.

C 17. *Interior, with a Woman who is Giving a Jug to a Girl.* (HdG no. 24a.)

50.8×43.2 cm.

Sale Winchester Clowes et al., London, 4/2/1901, no. 117. (Possible copy of Cat. 31.)

C 18. *Interior with a Lady and Child.* (HdG no. 24b.)

58.5×49.5 cm.

From the collection of the Duke of York, 1827; Sale R. Orr, London, 13/6/1903, no. 101.

C 19. *A Lady with a Serving Girl.* (HdG no. 43.)

Inv. of Judith Wijntjes, widow of J. van Meurs, Amsterdam, N.A.A. no. 2000, 17/5/1678. (Valued by J. Roosa at 5 fl.) (See HdG 1906, 406, no. 343; Bredius, IV, 1249.)

C 20. *A Woman Making Pancakes.* (HdG no. 44.)

Sale Petronella de la Court (widow of A. Oortmans), Amsterdam, 19/10/1707, no. 61 (together with no. 60 [see C 143], 123 fl. (See DvH 1975, 168, no. 107.)

C 21, 22. *A Woman Baking Cakes and a Woman Cutting Cabbage.* (Two pictures? The former [= C 20?] by descent?). (HdG no. 45.) Sale Abraham du Pré and Petronella Oortmans, Amsterdam, 19/5/1729, no. 26—70 fl. (Hoet, I, 342).

C 23. *A Woman and a Serving Maid.*

Sale Zeger Hasebroek, Leiden, 26/4/1763, no. 109.

C 24. *A Woman Frying Pancakes.*

Sale Greenwood et al., London, 2–3/5/1765, no. 12.

C 25. *A Woman with a Serving Girl.* In a room a woman sits at a table with a small dog (note: not a child as stated in Hofstede de Groot) on her lap. A serving girl stands beside her with a marketing pail on her arm counting money. Beyond is a courtyard, from which the light enters the room. (HdG no. 46.)

Canvas 58.5× 49.5 cm.

*Sale, Amsterdam, 14/8/1771, no. 50—Winter, 51 fl (the measurements 33× 19″ are undoubtedly a misprint for 23× 19″); Sale D. Marsbag et al., Amsterdam, 30/10/1775, no. 41 (incorrectly listed by Hofstede de Groot as sold in Leyden in 1788; see Cat. C 43).

C 26. *Interior, with a Woman, a Child, and a Serving Woman.* In an interior a woman sits with a child at her breast. Before her a long-haired dog; beside her, a cradle. This group is in full daylight, while the serving woman kneeling to light the fire—the glimmer of which is well rendered—is in shadow. In the middle distance to the left is a second room illuminated by sunshine. (HdG no. 47.)

Canvas 81× 91.5 cm. (Measurements incorrectly reported by Hofstede de Groot as 32× 26″ instead of 32× 36″).

Sale J. Christiaanze, Amsterdam, 17/11/1779, no. 54—Yver, 152 fl.; *Sale J.W. van Arp, Amsterdam, 4/9/1799, delayed to 19/6/1800, no. 59—175 fl; Sale P. Panné, London, 26/3/1819, no. 34—Heath, £174 6 s (Incorrectly under HdG no. 62 which is smaller. The description reads: A mother suckling her infant, a spaniel at her feet, a female servant on the right making up a fire on the hearth; a rich evening sunshine on the wall of a staircase at the left. Canvas 32× 36″: 81× 91.5 cm.) (Compare Cat. 113 & C 30).

C 27. *A Servant with a Fish at the Door of a House.* A serving girl stands waiting on the steps before a house; she holds a copper pail on her right arm, and holds two fillets of salmon in her left hand. A maidservant looks through a window to see who has rung. In the foreground at the side are two dogs, one standing and another lying down; in the background is a view to a town. (HdG no. 48.) (Maes?)

Canvas 68.5× 58.5 cm.

Sale J. van de Velden, Amsterdam, 3/12/1781, no. 40—Ottens, 100 fl; Sale, Amsterdam, 14/5/1791, no. 62; *(prob.) Sale, Amsterdam, 19/8/1801, no. 38 (w/o m.).

C 28. *A Woman Sewing, with a Young Girl.* A domestic interior; near a large fireplace a woman is seated sewing; on the opposite side of the picture a young girl passes into another room; various utensils are distributed in the scene.

Canvas 46× 53 cm.

Sale Dubois, Paris, 18/12/1788, no. 38.

C 29. *A Woman with a Serving Woman with a Pail.* A woman gives orders to a serving girl standing by her with a metal fish pail on her arm. Before the woman stands a table covered with a carpet on which a mirror, paper and an ink well are set.

Canvas 90× 77 cm.

Sale, Amsterdam, 16/6/1800, no. 11—Ledantie, 96 fl.

C 30. *A Woman with a Child at her Breast, and a Serving Woman.* To the left in a room is a woman, wearing an indigo blue and scarlet dress, with a child in yellow at her breast. At her right is a cradle. To the left of it is the fireplace with a mirror above it, and farther to the left is a dog. In the middle distance a serving woman is making a fire. In the background to the right is a bed; to the left a well lighted staircase leads to an upper room with a chair by a window. (Waagen 1854, II, 227; Thoré-Bürger 1860, 319; HdG no. 62; exh. in Manchester 1857, no 945.)

Canvas 56× 66 cm.

Sale Helsleuter, Paris, 25/1/1802, no. 74—1020 frs; Sale Phipps, London, 25/6/1859, no. 52—Van Cuyk, £177. (HdG's description was enlarged from a sketch by G. Scharf made in Manchester in 1857; the Panné Sale probably refers to C 26.)

C 31. *A Woman beside a Cradle, with another Woman.* An interior with a young Dutch woman seated near her child's cradle. She appears to be speaking to a woman dressed in a fur-trimmed jacket. Strong sunlight falls on the wall, while the rest of the interior is cast in a subtle shadow. This amirable work could rival the most beautiful works of G. Metzu. (Compare Cat. 100.)

Canvas 60× 72 cm.

Sale [Sauzay], Paris, 8/1/1810, no. 105.

C 32. *A Woman with a Serving Woman.* Interior; on the right the mistress seated by a fireplace gives orders to a serving woman, who stands in the shadows. At the left an open window reveals a vestibule illuminated by sunlight.

Canvas 68.5× 78.5 cm.

Sale, Paris, 9/12/1811, no. 54—Perignon (BMf); Sale C. Spruyt & Odemaer, Ghent, 3/10/1815, no. 80.

C 33. *A Woman Peeling Fruit.* At a table with a green cloth sits a woman peeling fruit. She wears a black lawn cap and a fur-trimmed jacket. (HdG no. 49.)

Sale A.L.C.H.T. de l'Epinasse de Langeac, Comte d'Arlet, Paris, 4/1/1815, no. 216—Montfort, 84 frs.

C 34. *A Woman with a Girl in a Kitchen.* A woman seated in a kitchen is plucking a fowl. In the background a maidservant is visible by a fire. In the foreground are kitchen utensils. By P. de Hooge or in his manner. (HdG no. 50.)

Sale [J. Kobell ?], Amsterdam, 24/5/1815, no. 37—Lamme, 9 fl 10.

C 35. *A Woman Peeling Potatoes, with a Serving Woman and a Child.* Seated in the middle of a room a pretty young girl in a Dutch costume peels potatoes; at the left a serving woman carries a pail of water; at the right a child in a device designed to aid children in learning to walk. This fine painting, entirely in the style of Metzu, is charming in tone and effect.

Panel 30.5×25.5 cm.

Sale M.D. . . ., Paris, 6/11/1820, no. 104 (BMf).

C 36. *A Lady Giving Orders to a Servant.*

Exh. Royal Institution, Liverpool, 1823, no. 83, loaned by Mr. Burlani.

C 37. *The Laundry.*

2nd Annual Exh. at Peale's Baltimore Museum, 1823, no. 23, loaned by F. Cook.

C 38. *A Woman Making Pancakes.* In the left foreground a woman is making pancakes. To the right is a child. In the middle distance stands a young man with a mug in one hand and a candlestick in the other. The scene is illuminated by a fire in the hearth, by a lamp on the wall, and by the candle. (HdG no. 56).

Panel 46×38 cm.

*Sale, Amsterdam, 27/10/1760, no. 7; *Sale A. Giroux, Paris, 27–9/3/1821, no. 94 (BMf); Sale Van Rotterdam, Ghent, 6/7/1835, no. 169—Bordeau, 280 fl; Sale Hinchliffe et al. (Van Rotterdam of Ghent), London, 6/5/1836, no. 106 (w/o m.).

C 39. *A Woman with a Dish of Grapes, and a Serving Woman.* An interior in which a woman has received a dish of grapes from her serving maid, with whom she speaks.

Sale A. Griedanus et al., Alkmaar, 19/8/1834, no. 131.

C 40. *A Lady with a Child, Nurse and Dog.* In the foreground of a well furnished room a richly dressed lady sits at a table covered with a Smyrna carpet. She turns her head toward a child who, frightened by a little spaniel, takes refuge in the arms of her nurse. The back of the room is adorned with pictures and furniture. (HdG no. 57.)

Canvas 46×39 cm.

Sale Stevens, Antwerp, 9/8/1837, no. 73—310 frs.

C 41. *Interior.* A woman is warming herself, while a serving woman shows her a salmon. A map of Friesland bearing the date 1772(?) hangs on the wall. (Havard 1880, 105:1: HdG no. 63.)

62×54.5 cm.

Sale D'Aigremont, Paris, 4/3/1861, no. 71—165 frs.

C 42. *A Slaughtered Pig.*

Sale J. A. Sichterman, Groningen, 20/8/1764, no. 22.

C 43. *Pig-Killing.* In the left foreground of an interior stands a woman at a table cleaning intestines. In the centre a pig's carcass hangs on a ladder placed against a cupboard. To the right sits a boy playing with the bladder. A pointer stands beside a pail. (HdG 70.)

Canvas 51×62 cm.

Sale H. Arentz of Deventer, Amsterdam, 11/4/1770, no. 23—Delfos 150fl; * Sale 'Deux Amateurs', Leiden 26/8/1788, no. 58—Delfos, 36 fl (incorrectly under HdG no. 46; cf. Cat. C 25).

C 44. *A Bedroom* (HdG no. 78a).

Inv. of Judith Wijntjes, widow of J. van Meurs, Amsterdam, N.A.A., no. 2000, 17/5/1678 (valued by J. Roosa, at 25 fl). (See HdG 1906, 406, no. 345; Bredius, IV, 1250.)

C 45. *A Maid in her Bedroom.*

Sale, Amsterdam, 27/10/1760, no. 45.

C 46. *A Young Lady at her Toilet.* A young lady in a red silk jacket and blue satin skirt is combing her hair at her toilet table. (HdG no. 81.)

Panel 35.5×25.5 cm.

Sale J.C. Werther, Amsterdam, 25/4/1792, no. 77.

C 47. *A Lady at her Toilet.* In a room a well dressed lady sits at a mirror, which stands on a table covered with a Persian carpet. A maid is dressing her hair. Upon the table lie various trinkets and other objects. (HdG no. 83.)

Canvas 107×122 cm.

*Sale R . . ., Paris, 26/10/1818, no. 33; Sale Aubert, Brussels, 8/8/1821, no. 53.

C 48. *A Woman in Childbed.* (HdG no. 85a.)

Exh. Amsterdam 1845, no. 45, loaned by the widow J.J. Beckeringh.

C. 49. *A Barber.*

Inv. Abr. Heyblon, Prot. Not. Melanen, Dordrecht, 1685, no. 46 (see A. Bredius, *O.H.*, 1910, 12).

C 50. *Picture with a Lady.* (HdG no. 89a.)

Inv. of Dirck van Dussen, Sheriff of Delft, 1706, 14 fl.

C 51. *A Woman Stirring a Fire.* (HdG no. 89b.)

Sale Seb. Heemskerk, Amsterdam, 31/3/1749, no. 27—37 fl (Hoet, II, 225).

C 52. *A Woman Making Lace.* (HdG no. 89c.)

Sale D. Ietswaart, Amsterdam, 22/4/1749, no. 192—8 fl (Hoet, II, 251). (No such entry was found in the sale catalogue.)

C 53. *A Woman Building a Fire,* very sunny.

Canvas 58×70 cm.

Sale, Amsterdam, 23/5/1764, no. 179.

C 54. *An Interior, with a Woman Cutting Cabbage.*

Sale, Amsterdam, 23/5/1764, no. 180—Fouquet, 20 fl.

C 55. *A Library with Three Doctors.*

Panel 48×56 cm.

Sale Antwerp, 3/5/1784, no. 47.

C 56. *An Interior, a Lady with a Lap Dog.*

Sale, London, 15/4/1791, no. 10.

C 57. *A Man Writing at a Table.* An interior in which a man sits writing at a table; whereupon there is a carpet on which different books lie; very sunny. By or in the manner of P. de Hooge.

Panel.

Sale J.W. Wessel, Amsterdam, 28/9/1791, no. 107—Versteeg, 30 fl.

C 58. *A Woman Reading a Book in a Kitchen.* In a room with an open cupboard a view in a kitchen reveals a woman reading a book; the light that enters the scene has a natural effect. Ascribed to P. de Hooge.

Canvas.

Sale, Amsterdam, 14/8/1793, no. 180—Fouquet, 8 fl.

C 59. *A Lady Sitting at a Table with a Dog on her Lap.*
(HdG no. 91a.)
  Sale, Amsterdam, 13–14/4/1819, no. 36—Vinkeles, 16 fl 10.

C 60. *A Woman Seated Making Lace.* (HdG no. 92.)
  Canvas 48×33 cm.
  Sale H.A. Bauer, Amsterdam, 11/9/1820, no. 58.

C 61. *A Richly Dressed Man Explaining Writings to another Man.*
  Panel 82×66 cm.
  Sale Massen, Maastricht, 14/5/1821, no 36.

C 62. *A Woman in an Interior.* A woman is sitting in an interior; through an anteroom a garden is seen. (HdG no. 92a.)
  Sale A. van den Kieboom, Rotterdam, 14/6/1821, no. 55.

C 63. *Doctors in a Hall* seeming to be discussing matters pertaining to their art.
  Canvas.
  Sale, Paris, 10–12/12/1822, no. 25 (BMf).

C 64. *A Poulterer Skinning a Rabbit.* On the table and floor a variety of dead game.
  Sale W.G.J. van Gendt, The Hague, 25/10/1830, no. 23.

C 65. *A Woman Making Lace at a Window.* A woman sits in a room making lace near an open window. (HdG no. 93.) (Compare Cat. C 69.)
  Panel 49×35 cm.
  Sale Baron Denon, Paris, 1/5/1826, no. 81 (attr. P.d.H.; BMf); Sale Amsterdam, 3/1/1831, no. 37—Roos, 25 fl.

C 66. *A Woman Seated in a Room.* (HdG no. 93a.)
  Panel 53.5×40.5 cm. Signed: 'P.DE.H.'
  Sale, Amsterdam, 1/4/1833, no. 66.

C 67. *A Young Lady with a Wine Glass.* The lady wears a red jacket trimmed with ermine and holds a glass of wine in her left hand. The head is full of expression and well modelled. (HdG no. 97.)
  Panel 29×24 cm.
  Sale P.-F. de Noter, Ghent, 27/12/1842, no. 5—30 fl.

C 68. *A Young Woman in a Vestibule.* In a vestibule a young woman is busy at her work. A good example of the artist. (HdG no. 98.)
  Panel 38×48 cm.
  Sale A.W.C. Baron van Nagle van Ampsen, The Hague, 5/9/1851, no. 27—Schroot, 134 fl.

C 69. *A Young Girl Making Lace.* She sits in a room near the window. (HdG no. 98a.) (Compare Cat. C 65.)
  Canvas on panel.
  Sale Comte de Turenne, Paris, 17/5/1852, no. 38—141 frs.

C 70. *A Woman Making Lace.* The open door and the window of a room in shadow look into a sunlit anteroom where a woman sits making lace. In the front room is a dog. (HdG no. 99; see Cat. B 3A.)
  Panel 28×35 cm.
  Sale J.F. Sigault, Amsterdam, 3/12/1833, no. 90—De Lelie, 11 fl 25; Sale Thyssen, Paris, 20/12/1856, no. 16—590 frs.

C 71. *The Armoury.* A child with a dog enters a room in which weapons and trumpets are heaped up. (Havard 1880, 124:2; HdG 100.)
  Panel 53×41 cm.
  Sale Biehler, Paris, 5/3/1859, no. 42—450 frs.

C 72. *The Studio of a Young Painter.* Broad in treatment. (HdG no 101.)
  Canvas 68×82 cm.
  Sale, Amsterdam, 11/6/1861, no. 94.

C 73. *The Embroideress.*
  In Berlin, 1863. (Parthey, I, 623; HdG no. 101.)

C 74. *The Smithy.* To the right of the forge is a woman. In the middle distance four men stand around an anvil, raising their hammers to strike the red-hot iron. To the left, behind a wooden partition with a window, sits the bookkeeper, with his face turned towards a large window in the outer wall. According to the sale cat., 'It is a good and well composed picture, though somewhat faded.' HdG: 'It is, however, very doubtful whether it was by P. de Hooch.' (HdG no. 102.)
  Panel 50×68 cm.
  Sale J.J. von Hirsch auf Gereuth, of Wurzburg, Cologne, 23/9/1878, no. 100.

C 75. *Gentlemen at Table.* In a room a man sits with his legs crossed at a table laid for a meal. In his right hand he holds up a fish; in his left is a knife. An open door looks into a kitchen, where a maid is at work. (HdG no. 105.)
  Canvas 45×35 cm. Signed and dated 1674.
  Sale Dr. Weinhagen, Cologne, 12/11/1890, no. 150.

C 76. *A Girl Reading.* A half-length picture of a young girl in black with a white collar and hood; she is reading a book which she holds in both hands. (HdG no. 107.)
  Panel 48×43 cm.
  Sale Anrep-Elmpt, Cologne, 5/6/1893, no. 67.

C 77. *A Lady at a Table.* On the left a lady sits at a table covered with a Turkish carpet, upon which are an open book, a tea service, and a small basket. A dog lies on a chair at the left. In the background is the chimney piece with a porcelain parrot and two pictures—the one a flower piece, the other a Holy Family. (HdG no. 109.)
  Panel 41×31 cm.
  *(Poss.) Sale M. A . . ., Paris, 15/12/1837, no. 65 (w/o m.; BMf); Sale M.W. Woronzow et al., Florence, 23/4/1900, no. 485.

C 78. *A Woman Making Lace.* (HdG no. 109a.)
  Panel 27.5×25 cm.
  Sale Loire, London, 4/7/1904, no. 9.

C 79. *A Picture with a Parrot,* valued at 50 fl.
  Inv. of Elisabeth Oosterdyk, widow of Johannes van Ceulen, bookseller, Amsterdam, 23/3/1716 (see Bredius, V, 1772). (Cf. Cat. C 90.)

C 80. *A Lady with a Parrot.* In a room a lady sits at a table on which is a parrot in a cage. A gentleman stands near. (HdG no. 116.)
  Panel.
  Sale P. Oets et al., Amsterdam, 31/1/1791, no. 48—Fouquet, 14 fl (together with our Cat. C 107).

C 81. *The Parrot.* In the middle of a handsomely furnished room a young lady, at a table with a cloth, feeds a parrot. A well dressed gentleman stands beside her and opens the door of the cage to let the parrot out. The room is lighted from a

XV. Detail from Plate 111: A Music Party with Five Figures (Cat. 109). *c.* 1674. Royal Museum of Fine Arts, Copenhagen

XVI. Detail from Plate 137: A Musical Party in a Courtyard (Cat. 134). 1677. National Gallery, London

window; an open door leads to a courtyard. (HdG no. 118a.)
Sale [La Neuville], Paris, 14–16/11/1813, no. 34—601 frs.

C 82. *A Family in an Interior.* An oldfashioned interior, from the window of which on the right is a view of a stream. By the window stands a serving girl holding a basket of fruit. Near her sit a well dressed gentleman and a lady with a child on her lap. The gentleman offers the child a bunch of grapes from the basket. A dog is in the foreground and a parrot on a perch in the middle distance. The composition is pleasing; the picture is effective and painted in a masterly manner. From the best period of this clever painter. (HdG no. 119.)

Panel 66× 50 cm.

Sale J.A. van Dyck, Dordrecht, 1/6/1829, no. 58—Van Eyck, 515 fl.

C 83. *The Music Party.* (HdG no. 136a.)

Inv. of Cornelius Schaepman, tollkeeper (damhouder) of Hinderdam, Delft, no. 2287, 20/5/1684 (from A. Bredius).

C 84. *The Music Party.* (HdG no. 136b.) (See Cat. 109.)

Sale, Amsterdam, 9/4/1687, no. 19—70 fl.

C 85. *A Musical Company in an Interior.* Valued by Z.P. Zomer at 70 fl. Inv. Adolf Visscher, merchant and confectioner living on the Rokin, Amsterdam, N.A.A., no. 5335, 7/2/1702; (prob.) Sale, Amsterdam, 16/5/1703 (see adv. *Amsterdamsche Courant*, 5/5/1703; DvH 1975, no. 77).

C 86. *A Musical Company.*

Inv. Johan Boogaert of Delft, Prot. Not. W. van Ruyven, Delft, 10/8/1703 (A. Bredius's unpub. papers).

C 87. *A Music Party in an Interior.* (HdG 136c.)

Sale, Amsterdam, 18/5/1706, no. 21—40 fl (Hoet, I, 95).

C 88. *A Music Party in an Interior.* (HdG no. 136d.)

Sale, Amsterdam, 18/5/1706, no. 27 (not 42 as stated in HdG)—28 fl (Hoet, I, 45).

C 89. *A Concert in an Interior.*

Sale Anth. Daems (1638–1706), haberdasher, living on the Keizersgracht, Amsterdam, 28/4/1706, no. 21. (adv. in *Amsterdamsche Courant*, 6/4/1706; see DvH 1975, 167, no. 97.)

C 90. *A Painting with a Young Woman Playing the Viol da Gamba.* 40 fl.

Inv. of E. Oosterdijk, widow of J. van Ceulen, bookseller, Amsterdam, N.A.A., no. 7270/17, 23/3/1716. (Communication S.A.C. Dudok van Heel.) (Cf. Cat. C 79.)

C 91. *A Small Picture, with a Flute Player.* (HdG no. 136e.)

Sale, Amsterdam, 4/6/1727, no. 29—22 fl (Hoet, I, 318).

C 92. *An Interior with Men and Women Making Music.*

Sale, Amsterdam, 21/5/1737, no. 5—D. Ietswaard, 29 fl 10.

C 93. *A Musical Company.*

Sale, Amsterdam, 15/10/1738, no. 14.

C 94. *A Music Party at a Table with Fruit.* (HdG no. 136f.)

Sale, Amsterdam, 25/9/1743, no. 69—9 fl (Hoet, II, 128).

C 95. *A Musical Company.*

67× 77 cm.

Sale J. de Bruyn, Amsterdam, 17/4/1754, no. 28—70 fl.

C 96. *A Musical Company with Various Figures.*

91.5× 122 cm.

Sale H. Wolters, Amsterdam, 4/5/1757, no. 11.

C 97. *A Musical Company,* a fine picture.

103× 108 cm.

Sale M. ten Hove & J.A. Tourton, Amsterdam, 8/4/1760, no. 38—Palthe, 33 fl.

C 98. *A Woman Polishing a Glass and a Lady Playing the Guitar.* In the anteroom on the left a woman, wearing a yellow silk jacket trimmed with fur, is polishing a glass. In the middle distance a lady plays a guitar. In the background are seen two houses beyond a canal.

Canvas 66× 53.5 cm.

Sale A. Sydervelt, Amsterdam, 23/4/1766, no. 63—Van Dieman, 185 fl (Terwesten, 521).

C 99. *A Guitar Player and Two Other Figures in an Interior.*

53× 61 cm.

Sale, Leyden, 11/5/1767, no. 40.

C 100. *A Couple with Musical Instruments.* An interior with a woman in the middle foreground, dressed in a red satin jacket and white satin skirt, holding musical instruments; similarly, on the right side a man with a glass of wine in his hand, and on the other side a serving woman entering from a room with a sunny view.

Canvas 56× 46 cm.

Sale, Amsterdam, 6/7/1768, no. 30—Meusche, 71 fl.

C 101. *A Man Playing a Guitar, with Two Women.* A room with one seated and one standing woman and a man playing the guitar; it is illuminated by a doorway through which a garden is seen. The depiction of the sunlight is wonderfully and naturally executed.

Panel 66× 77 cm.

Sale, Amsterdam, 15/7/1772, no. 30—Yver, 30 fl. (Compare Cat. 105.)

C 102. *Seven Men and Women Making Music.* A picture which one could say was by Gerard Terburg; it represents seven men and women making music in a room.

Canvas 96.5× 117 cm.

Sale, Paris, 20/7/1773, no. 39—Paillet, 1721 frs. (Compare Cat. C 136.)

C 103. *A Woman Playing a Clavichord.* An interior with a woman seated playing the clavichord; a fresh view in the background.

Canvas on panel 53× 45 cm.

Sale, Amsterdam, 26/7/1775, no. 138—Fouquet, 25 fl.

C 104. *A Couple Playing Music and Figures Drinking.* An officer pours a drink for some ladies; a man and a woman make music.

Canvas 94× 114 cm.

Sale Le Prince de Conti, Paris, 8/4–6/6/1777, no. 839—Paillet, 1091 frs (BMf). (Compare Cat. C 136.)

C 105. *A Musical Company.* In a vestibule one sees a musical company with a woman sitting playing the guitar by a table, on which stands a bottle of wine and a glass; in front of the table a woman plays a flute; on the right side a view through a portico leads to a canal with houses.

Canvas 67× 80 cm.

Sale S. Stinstra, Amsterdam, 26/3/1783, no. 62—Yver, 50 fl.

C 106. *A Musical Company.* An interior in the middle of which stands a table; beside the table sits a young girl playing the guitar. She is accompanied by a man playing the violin who stands beside her and another seated man who beats time; in the background a couple descend a stair. Not inferior in handling to the preceding picture (our Cat. 149).

Panel 59×57 cm.
Sale H. Rottermondt, Amsterdam, 18/7/1786, no. 129.

C 107. *The Music Party.* A lady and two gentlemen. (HdG no. 142a.)

Panel.
Sale P. Oets et al., Amsterdam, 31/1/1791, no. 48—Fouquet, 14 fl (together with our Cat. C 80).

C 108. *A Musical Company of Three Figures.* Interior of an apartment; in the distance a view to houses bordering on a canal. Three principal figures form the composition of this picture, which has been attributed several times to Netscher: a woman in a yellow silk dress sits playing the guitar; another woman stands in a silk dress and is seen from the rear. The stuffs are rendered as well as in the most beautiful pictures of the master to whom we attribute this work.

Canvas 99×84 cm.
Sale Mme B[asan], Paris, 4/4/1791, no. 22.

C 109. *A Musical Conversation,* very highly finished.
Sale, London, 15/4/1791, no. 70.

C 110. *An Interior with Figures Conversing, Playing and Singing.*
Sale, London, 15/4/1791, no. 87.

C 111. *A Musical Company with Seven Figures.* An interior with seven figures, representing two women accompanying each other on the guitar (?) or simply playing; one stands dressed in a white satin dress, the other is seated by a table covered with a Turkish carpet; nearby are three other figures and in the background two men are seen at the door of the house which reveals a view of buildings. In the beautiful manner of G. Terburg.

Canvas 76×91.5 cm.
Sale Duclos le Jeune, Paris, 2/4/1792, no. 25.

C 112. *An Interior with a Woman Playing a Guitar.*
Inv. H. Schepper & A. Mulder, Prot. Not. J. Harmsen, Amsterdam, N.A.A., no. 16419, 29/10/1795. (Communication S.A.C. Dudok van Heel.)

C 113. *A Lady and a Flute Player.* In a well furnished room an attractive young lady in elegant clothing is seen holding a glass of wine in her hand. Behind her a gentleman holding a flute sits at a table covered with a cloth, upon which are a beer mug, a pipe and other articles. At the side is an open window; there are other accessories. (HdG no. 146.)

Canvas 46×46 cm.
Sale J.E. Grave et al., 5/5/1806, no. 57.

C 114. *A Musical Company.* In a richly furnished room a musical company of men and women is represented. Through an open door in the background an officer and a lady are seen conversing in another room; the sunlight entering the room makes a charming effect.

Canvas 90×134 cm.
Sale, Amsterdam, 28/11/1808, no. 25—Spaan, 25 fl. (Compare Cat. C 122.)

C 115. *A Music Party.* In a room two ladies are playing, one on the guitar, the other on the harpsichord, while a gentleman sings. A dog and other accessories are introduced. The light entering the room is well rendered. (HdG no. 147.)

Canvas 56×61 cm.
Sale, Amsterdam, 13/6/1809, no. 60. (Compare Cat. C 99.)

C 116. *A Woman Playing a Guitar in an Interior.*
Canvas.
Sale Lafontaine, Paris, 17/1/1810, no. 70—73 frs.

C 117. *A Music Party of Ladies and Gentlemen.* (HdG no. 149a.)
Sale, Amsterdam, 14/4/1813, no. 30—20 fl 10.

C 118. *Two Young Ladies Playing Music.* Two young ladies playing a duet to divert an older woman, who appears to be ill. (HdG no. 150.)

Canvas.
Sale A.L.C.H.T. de l'Epinasse de Langeac, Comted' Arlet, Paris, 4/1/1815, no. 78—150 frs.

C 119. *A Woman Playing the Guitar, with a Cavalier.* A young woman sits playing the guitar. Near her stands a cavalier, who seems to communicate the pleasure he feels. Vigorous in colour and beautiful in the effect of light.

46×38 cm.
Sale [Comte de] C[haptal], Paris, 23/12/1816, no. 84 (BMf).

C 120. *A Woman Playing a Guitar, with a Man Listening.* Interior; a woman sits playing the guitar; near her a man dressed in black listens.

Sale l'Epinasse de Langeac, Paris, 29/10/1818, no. 29 (BMf; not in Lugt).

C 121. *A Woman Playing the Guitar.* Interior illuminated by a window with painted glass. A young woman plays the guitar; in front of her a table covered with a Turkish carpet, music books and other accessories are seen.

Canvas 61×76 cm.
Sale J.J. de Wageneer, Brussels, 29/5/1822, no. 97.

C 122. *A Musical Company.* Interior in which two men and ladies play different instruments; through an open door leading to another room a cavalier is seen in conversation with a lady.

Sale Wouwermans, Brussels, 25/7/1823, no. 79—Collens. (Compare Cat. C 114.)

C 123. *The Music Party.* Three ladies and two gentlemen are assembled, all richly dressed in velvet and silk. Two of the ladies play the guitar. A handsome cloth covers a table. A black spaniel lies on the tiled floor. In the background are seen a street and a canal in The Hague. (HdG no. 153.)

Canvas 79×96.5 cm.
George of Dessau Collection; Sale Baron de Castell, Hamburg, 21/7/1824, no. 141.

C 124. *Ladies and Cavaliers Making Music in a Vestibule.* In a vestibule decorated with columns an assembly of ladies and cavaliers are making music.

Sale H. Ruvet, Brussels, 29/3/1825, no. 1—Nieuwenhuys, 165 frs.

C 125. *A Lady Seated at Music.* (HdG no. 153a.)
Sale J. Kamermans, Rotterdam, 3/10/1825, no. 115—Esser, 49 fl. (No works by De Hooch appeared in this sale, which, furthermore, only included 113 entries.)

C 126. **The Flute Player.** In an interior, behind a table covered with a cloth, a cavalier sits playing a flute. Beside him stands a lady with a glass in her hand. A window looks into two rooms; in one a lady appears to be watching the couple in the front room. (HdG no. 156.)

Canvas 46×48 cm.

Sale J. van der Putte, Amsterdam, 22/5/1810, no. 34—Yperen, 101 fl; with Aubert, 1821 (from an annotation in the following catalogue); Sale Comte F. de Robiano, Brussels, 1/5/1837, no. 284—850 frs. (Compare Cat. C 200.)

C 127. **The Duet.** An apartment, in which are a gentleman and a lady; the former, habited in a blue jacket and a yellow sash, is seated turning towards the lady, and at the same time pointing to a violoncello as if inviting her to join in a duet; the latter is attired in white satin, and has a guitar in her hand. A hat decked with feathers is on a chair at the side, near which is a spaniel dog. (S s no. 9; Havard 1880, 118:2; HdG no. 158.)

Canvas 95×84 cm.

Formerly in the possession of Emmerson, before 1842.

C 128. **A Music Party in an Interior.** An open door looks into an adjacent room, where a woman is engaged in her housework. Broad and masterly in execution. (HdG no. 159.)

Canvas 112×122 cm (incorrect in HdG). Signed.

Sale Amsterdam, 6/5/1845, no 58—Van der Linde of Rotterdam, or according to another catalogue, Roos, 47 fl.

C 129. **A Woman Playing a Guitar.** She sits beside a table playing. There are many accessories. The light falls through a Gothic window. On the table are a cloth and some books. (HdG no. 162.)

Canvas 60×80 cm.

Sale Comte de Robiano, Brussels, 1/5/1837, no. 281—130 fl; Sale J.J. Chapuis, Brussels, 4/12/1865, no. 201 [manner of P.d.H.]—Warneck 300 frs.

C 130. **A Concert Party of Four Persons.** In a hall with two windows, two ladies and a gentleman, all richly dressed, are playing the violin and singing. Another gentleman, seen in the shadows, is also playing. (Thoré-Bürger, in *G.B.A.*, 1866, 553, no. 24 [Vermeer]; HdG no. 163).

Canvas 122×91 cm (approximately 4×3′; without comment, Hofstede de Groot reversed the measurements, probably correctly assuming that a work by De Hooch of this size and subject would be horizontal in format).

Thoré published the work as a Vermeer, but had not seen it himself, owing his description to his friend Cremer. The latter attributed it to Vermeer and remarked: 'Excellent, well preserved; doubtless some weakness in the drawing of the hands and some faults in the shadows; but what colour! In all respects a Vermeer. The bodice is yellow, the skirt red; a glitter of light on the figure. Signed "P. d'Hoogh", old signature—but probably apocryphal.' Thoré noted that some years prior to his writing, the work had been in the possession of the Berlin dealer Kurt, who vainly offered it to the Brussels Museum in 1861. Hofstede de Groot compared the description to Cat. 109, which, however, was in the Danish Royal Collections at an early date. While the reference to a violin player prompts comparison with Cat. 110, none of the women in that work wears a costume like that mentioned by Cremer. In Cat. 108 the woman by the window is clad in a yellow bodice and red underskirt.

C 131. **The Music Party.** Two ladies are seated at a table; one plays a mandolin, the other holds a music book. Behind them stands a man playing a harpsichord. A chandelier hangs from the ceiling. On the music book in elegant letters appears the word 'Tavola'. (HdG no. 164.)

Canvas 85×67 cm.

Formerly Count Schönborn of Pommersfelden, cat. (1857), no. 424 (see also Parthey 1863, I, 623, no. I, as prob. P.d.H. but according to Heller by Metsu); Sale Schönborn of Pommersfelden, Paris, 17–18, 22–4/5/1867, no. 59—Burger, 200 frs.

C 132. **The Concert.** Two ladies and two gentlemen are making music in a room. The room lies in shadow; a terrace opening out of it looks on a sunlit canal. A young man protecting his eyes with his hand from the glare of the light, looks into the distance. (HdG no. 165.)

Canvas 67×80 cm.

Sale J. Reiset et al. (H. de Bristol), Paris, 2/2/1874, no. 30—2500 frs.

C 133. **The Dancing Dog.** Before a table, on which are placed music books, fruit, and a jug, sits a young lady wearing a satin dress and a red cap adorned with white ostrich feathers. She listens to a gentleman, standing behind the table, who sings to the accompaniment of his lute. A spaniel in the foreground dances for the tidbit which his mistress holds out to him. The group is illuminated from a window high up at the left, which is half hidden by a green curtain. An open door at the back looks on a garden terrace. A boy, with a dog looking up at him, looks in at the door. (HdG no. 167.)

Canvas 60×46 cm. Signed 'P d Hooghe'

Sale C. Triepel, Munich, 28/9/1874, no. 12; Sale Dittmar, Berlin, 17/11/1875, no. 13—161 mks.

C 134. **A Music Party.** To the right before a spinet a young girl sits with her back to the viewer. Beside her a young man in red, who is laughing, plays the guitar. In the background another girl is seen; to the left a man is playing the flute. (HdG no. 170.)

Panel 54×47 cm.

Sale Clavé-Bouhaben, Cologne, 4–5/6/1894, no. 251.

C 135. **The Minuet.** Between the pillars in the background of a large and dimly lighted hall are a lady and a gentleman. Before them is a negro boy wearing a red jacket and yellow scarf, who brings a dish of oranges. A fair young gentleman with hat in hand, who stands at the back facing the viewer, and a girl in red, who waits in the right foreground with her back to the spectator, are about to dance a minuet. Beside the couple sit a man playing a fiddle and a woman who beats time and looks at a music book. The architecture is in a rich baroque style, with statues in niches. The sunlight falls from the left; the persons on the right are more in shadow. According to Hofstede de Groot, 'This is a genuine, but not a pleasing picture, being somewhat empty and covered with a thick varnish. It is in the manner of the picture belonging to Baron Steengracht (cf. Cat. 134). Of the late period it is a comparatively good example.' (HdG nos. 123 & 250; R, 102.)

Canvas 66×82.5 cm.

★Sale C. Spruyt, Ghent, 3/10/1815, no. 81; Mr. Swaby's Collection (according to the Leeds exh. cat.); Wynn Ellis, London, who loaned it to the *National Exhibition*, Leeds, 1868, no. 702; ★Sale Wynn Ellis, London, 27/5/1876, no. 16;

Sale Vicomte du Bus de Gesignies, Brussels, 14/4/1896, no. 67; with dlr. Steinmeyer, Cologne, 1897.

C 136. *A Company of Seven Figures, with Musicians.* At a table in the foreground of a handsomely furnished room sits a lady, dressed in blue and white silk, holding up a glass of sack, which a gentleman standing by her has filled. To the left stands a lady, dressed in red and yellow silk, who is tuning a guitar and conversing with a gentleman sitting at her side. Farther to the left a doorway looks into a garden, where a lady and gentleman are conversing; beyond the garden is a house brightly illuminated by sunshine. In the right-hand corner of the room are two comely figures of musicians, a girl playing the guitar and a boy blowing the clarinet. In the foreground a dark brown dog. (S no. 6; Thoré-Bürger 1858-60, II, 252-4; HdG 1892, no. 80; HdG no. 239; P. Haverkorn van Rijsewijk, *Het Museum Boijmans*, The Hague-Amsterdam, 1909, 98-9).

    Canvas 104×125.5 cm.

    (Poss.) Sale, Leyden, 1765 (see Cat. C 161); *Sale, Amsterdam, 10/4/1769, no. 13—Van der Berg, 50 fl; *(poss.) Sale, Paris, 1773 (see Cat. C 102); *(poss.) Sale, Conti, Paris, 1777 (see Cat. C 104); Sale [Abbé de Gevigny], Paris, 1-29/12/1779, no. 339 (withdrawn); Messrs. Woodburn, 1833; sold in 1854 for £216 to Lawrie; Boymans Museum, Rotterdam, suppl. cat. (1854) no 391; cat. (1859) no. 139; cat. (1862), no. 148; destroyed by fire in 1864.

    According to J.C. Ebbinge Wubben (priv. correspondence) Hofstede de Groot was in error when he stated that the picture came from the Boymans Collection. Thoré described the work at length and noted that its condition was poor.

C 137. *A Smoker with Two Young Women.* Inv. of the widow of Pieter Thierens, Amsterdam, 1681 (Bredius, IV, 1340).

C 138. *A Picture with a Woman.* A very painstaking work. (HdG no. 199a.)
    Sale, Amsterdam, 9/4/1687, no. 110—7 fl 10 (Hoet, I, 6).

C 139. *A Party.* One of the best works. (HdG no. 199b.)
    Sale, Amsterdam, 11/4/1698, no. 19—30 fl (Hoet, I, 43).

C 140. *A Suitor and his Lady.* (HdG no. 199c.)
    Sale, Amsterdam, 11/4/1698, no. 21—31 fl (Hoet, I, 43).

C 141. *A Woman Writing,* valued by Zomer at 18 fl.
    Inv. of Nicolaes van der Perre, Amsterdam, N.A.A., no. 4249/432, 14/5/1703 (Bredius, IV, 1331; concerning the owner, see I.H. van Eeghen, *Amstelodamum*, 68 (1976), 98f.)

C 142. *A Picture with a Man and a Woman.*
    Inv. of A. Daems (cf. Cat. C 89), Amsterdam, N.A.A., no. 6604/339, 8/2/1706. (Communication S.A.C. Dudok van Heel.)

C 143. *Small Figures in a Room.* (HdG no. 199d.)
    Sale Petronella de la Court (widow of Adam Oortmans), Amsterdam, 19/10/1707, no. 60—123 fl (sold with our Cat. C 20), (Hoet, I, 107).

C 144. *Figures in a Room.* (HdG no. 199e.)
    Sale, Amsterdam, 6/3/1708, no. 18—45 fl (Hoet, I, 111; adv. in *Amsterdamsche Courant*, 18/2/1708, see DvH 1975, 169, no. 111).

C 145. *An Interior with Figures.* (HdG no. 199f.)
    Sale, Amsterdam, 13/7/1718, no. 14—18 fl (Hoet, I, 217).

C 146. *A Party.* (HdG no. 199g.)
    Sale, Amsterdam, 6/5/1729, no. 29—8 fl 5 (Hoet, I, 338).

C 147. *An Interior with Ladies and Gentlemen.* (HdG no. 199h.)
    Sale A. Deutz, Amsterdam, 1/3/1731, no. 27—27 fl (Hoet, I, 362.)

C 148. *A Small Party.* (HdG no. 199i.)
    Sale, Amsterdam, 9/3/1734—12 fl 10 (Hoet, I, 399).

C 149. *An Interior with Small Figures.*
    Sale G. van Baerlen, Amsterdam, 22/8/1736, no. 13—D. Ietswaart, 5 fl.

C 150. *A Woman Sealing a Letter.*
    Sale, Amsterdam, 15/4/1739, no. 136—3 fl 5.

C 151. *A Party in an Interior.* (HdG no. 199j.)
    Sale D. Ietswaart, Amsterdam, 22/4/1749, no. 196—De Commer, 16 fl (Hoet, II, 188).

C 152. *An Interior with Figures and Accessories.*
    Sale D. Ietswaart, Amsterdam, 22/4/1749, no. 197—P. Ietswaart, 70 fl.

C 153. *A Conversation.*
    Sale Dr. Bragge, London, 19-21/3/1751, no. 34.

C 154. *An Interior with Figures.* (HdG no. 199k.)
    Sale D. Reus, Amsterdam, 24/5/1752, no. 30—14 fl (Hoet, II, 339).

C 155. *An Interior with a Man and a Woman.*
    Sale, Amsterdam, 27/6/1752, no. 51.

C 156. *A Company in an Interior.*
    104×117 cm.
    Sale, Amsterdam, 22/11/1757, no. 43—21 fl.

C 157. *An Interior.*
    Sale C. Troost & S. Arensklauw, Amsterdam, 16/3/1750, no. 164.

C 158. *An Interior.*
    Sale, Amsterdam, 17/4/1758, no. 39—Yver, 41 fl 10.

C 159. *An Interior with Four Persons.* Interior of a large room with four figures and a fireplace.
    Canvas 67×60 cm.
    Sale [Hennin], Paris, 16/1/1764, no. 66—37 frs (BMf).

C 160. *The Inside of a House with Several Figures.* Three lights artfully introduced.
    63.5×74 cm.
    Sale J. Greenwood, London, 2/2/1765, no. 31—£2.

C 161. *Convivial Party of Ladies and Gentlemen.* (HdG no. 200.)
    102×117 cm.
    Sale N ..., Leiden, 1/6/1765, no. 11—Willer, 35 fl 10 (Terwesten, 448). (Compare Cat. C 136.)

C 162. *An Interior.* (HdG no. 201.)
    68×58 cm.
    Sale A. Leers of Rotterdam, Amsterdam, 19/5/1767, no. 130—Blinkvliet, 44 fl (Terwesten, 602).

C 163. *A Young Man Offering a Woman Necklaces.*
An interior in which a young man offers necklaces to a lady
who stands by a table caressing a dog.
Canvas 54×44 cm.
Sale, Amsterdam, 14/8/1771, no. 51—Van der Berg, 16 fl.

C 164. *A Girl Reading a Letter.* She sits in a room. On
one side of her stands a soldier; on the other a chambermaid.
By P. de Hooch or in his manner. (HdG no. 203.)
Canvas 47×39 cm.
Sale, The Hague, 25/5/1772, no. 31—6 fl.

C 165. *An Interior.*
Inv. Samuel Ximenes, alias Samuel Ximenes Pereira
(Portuguese-Jewish merchant), Prot. Not. D. Geniets,
Amsterdam, N.A.A., no. 13705, 5/25/1773. (Communication
S.A.C. Dudok van Heel.)

C 166. *A Party.* A company of many ladies and gentlemen
sitting at a table in an interior, eating and drinking. Near them
people are playing music. (HdG no. 204.)
Canvas 89×96 cm.
Sale, The Hague, 12/7/1773, no. 8—Delfos, 5 fl 10.

C 167. *A Gentleman at a Table in a Room.* Behind the
table is a woman. (HdG no. 204a.)
Canvas 62×53 cm.
Sale, Amsterdam, 27/4/1774, no. 131.

C 168. *An Interior with Men and Women.*
Sale A. Le Breton, Leiden, 31/7/1775, no. 42—De Rooy,
10 fl.

C 169. *A Woman Receiving a Letter.* An interior in which
a woman sits at a table; a young moor hands over a letter; in
the background a bed; ascribed to P. de Hoogh.
Canvas.
Sale J. van der Berg, Amsterdam, 29/7/1776, no. 114.

C 170. *A Party of Men and Women.* An interior in which
a company of men and women sit at a table eating and
drinking. In the foreground sits a woman with a child at her
breast. An open door looks into another room. (HdG no. 207.)
Canvas 60×53.5 cm.
Sale [Van Tol], Leiden, 15/6/1779, no. 21—Delfos, 48 fl.

C 171. *An Interior.*
Sale N.W. Kops, Amsterdam, 18/4/1780, no. 2—P. Kops,
600 fl (a very high price).

C 172. *Persons at a Table.* An interior with playing and
drinking persons at a table, in front of which stands a woman
with a child in her arms; in the manner of Rembrandt.
Panel 35.5×40.5 cm.
Sale Pompe van Meerdevoort, Zoeterwoude, 19/5/1780,
no. 20—Delphos, 18 fl 10.

C 173 & 174. *Two Interiors.* (HdG nos. 207a & b.)
Canvas 61×46 cm.
Sale O. van Cattenburg & P. de Waart, The Hague,
29/9/1779, no. 328—38 fl.

C 175. *A Man Reading to a Woman.* In an interior a man
dressed in a robe sits reading in a book which lies on a table
beside a burning candle; beside him a woman listens attentively; at the side is a hearth with a burning fire, over which a

kettle hangs; beside the fire sits a child eating and beside him
a maid appears to be stoking the fire. (See Cat. C 197.)
Panel 37×42 cm.
Sale P. Pama, Amsterdam, 30/1/1781, no. 5—Spaan, 41 fl.

C 176. *An Interior with Persons Playing Cards and
Drinking.* At a table, beside which stands a woman with a
child in her arms. (HdG no. 208.)
Panel 35.5×40.6 cm.
Sale W. Kinckée & L. Groskoph, Leiden, 9/4/1782, no. 42
—Heenck, 15 fl.

C 177. *A Party in a Room.* Two ladies and two gentlemen
sit at a table with a cloth. One lady offers fruit on a silver dish
to an officer who drains his glass. The other gentleman smokes
his pipe by the chimneypiece. A youth with a bottle of wine
and a dish of fruit enters the room. (HdG no. 209; possibly
also the picture mentioned by Descamps [III, 1753, 164] as in
N. van Bremen's collection: 'a mixed company: this picture
is very elegant and piquant'.)
Canvas 86×104 cm.
Sale Nicolas van Bremen, The Hague, 3/4/1769, no. 59—
20 fl 5 (Hoet, II, 487); Sale P. Locquet, Amsterdam, 22/9/1783,
no. 140—Yver, 70 fl.

C 178. *A Man and a Woman at a Table, with Other
Figures.* In an interior hung with gilt leather a man and a
woman, who is eating fruit, are seated at a table on the left; a
youth offers the woman a glass of wine; further back another
woman is teaching a child to walk; through an open door a
vestibule is seen and beyond several trees and houses.
Canvas 54.5×68.5 cm.
Sale J.F. Motte, Amsterdam, 20/8/1794, no. 53—Yver, 62 fl.

C 179. *A Woman Plucking Fowl, with a Merry Gentleman.* A pretty woman is plucking fowl in an interior. Beside
her appears a barrel on which a jug of wine, a dish of coals,
a pipe and tobacco stand; beside the barrel sits a merry gentleman with a glass of wine in his hand; against the doors rest
a rifle and a powderhorn.
Panel 75×60.5 cm.
Sale Amsterdam, 23/5/1798, no. 90—Berkenbosch, 30 fl 10.

C 180. *A Woman with a Man at a Table.* Interior
with four figures in which a seated woman is offered
cakes on a plate by a Negro, who leans down; a man seated
by the woman seems to look at a glass of wine.
Canvas 52×44.5 cm.
Sale, Paris, 29/8/1797, no. 60; Sale Paris, 26/12/1798, no. 47
(BMf).

C 181. *The Inside of a Room,* fine.
Sale, London, 16/1/1799, no. 81.

C 182. *Two Men and a Woman at a Table.* In a furnished
room a man and a woman sit at a table; behind them another
man seems to be wishing them well and holds the woman's
hand; another woman with a basket of apples stands in the
foreground. (HdG no. 211.)
Panel 58.5×48 cm.
Sale J.H. Quinkhart & J. Koller, Amsterdam, 19/12/1798,
no. 1—15 fl; *Sale A. de Lange et al., Amsterdam, 12/12/1803,
no. 42—86 fl.

C 183. *Figures at a Dutch Repast.*
Sale Bryan's Gallery, London, 7/5/1804, no. 25—£22.

C 184. *A Maidservant Sweeping the Floor of a Room.* The viewer looks through a window into an adjoining room, and sideways through a door into a farther room where a lady sits at her toilet table reading a letter. The contrast of sunlight and the ordinary daylight is finely rendered. (HdG no. 212.)

Canvas 79×63.5 cm.

Sale, Amsterdam, 7/5/1804, no. 75—Spaan, 60 fl.

(As noted by Brière-Misme [1947, 176, n. 16], possibly by Janssens.)

C 185. *An Interior, with a Lady, Gentleman and Maid servant.* In an interior a man in a Spanish costume converses with a lady who holds an open letter in her hand. By the wall at the back a maidservant is sewing. Another maidservant comes down a staircase with a basket of washing. In the centre two dogs are playing. There is a view to an adjoining room, from which the lady seems to have just come. The sunlight is naturally rendered; the figures are attractive and pleasing. (HdG no. 213.)

Canvas 61×73.5 cm.

Sale M.T. Wittebol and De Labistraeten, Antwerp, 19/6/1804, no. 69—180 frs.

C 186. *Two Ladies and Two Gentlemen in an Interior.* In a furnished room a well dressed man and woman sit at a table with a coloured cloth; a woman holds a glass of wine. Another young lady plays a bass viol. At the open door a man appears; through the doorway are seen several houses on the other side of a canal. The sunlight is rendered in a natural and pleasing way. (HdG no. 214.)

Canvas 81×68.5 cm.

Sale, Amsterdam, 8/8/1804, no. 77—Hulswit, 74 fl.

C 187. *A Gentleman with a Lady Offering a Peach to a Child.* In a well furnished room a man and a seated woman appear in elegant clothing beside a covered table on which rests a jug of wine, a glass and a silver dish with fruit. The woman has a peach in her hand which she appears to be offering to a child, who enters the room with his hat in his hand. At the side [or in front on the table] stands a dog. Through an open door several buildings [along a canal] are seen. (The entries in brackets from the 1808 sale cat.; cf. HdG no. 216.)

Canvas 84×76 cm.

*Sale P. Pama, Amsterdam, 30/1/1781, no. 4—J.T. Steeg (Tersteeg), 105 fl; Sale E.M. Engleberts & Tersteeg, Amsterdam, 13/6/1808, no. 74—Van der Hielst (or Van Drielst), 235 fl.

C 188 & 189. *Two Interiors.*

Sale Pierre de Grand-Pré, Paris, 16/6/1809, nos. 102 & 103.

C 190. *An Interior with Figures.* 'Exhibiting an illusive effect of light'. (S no. 17; HdG no. 223a.)

Collection of Lord Rendlesham 1806, valued at 120 gns. No doubt identical with the picture in the Rendlesham Sale, London, 17/5/1809, no. 44—53 gns: 'An interior, . . . The effect of light is delusion itself.'

C 191. *Vista into an Interior.* With a striking effect of light. (HdG no. 223b.)

Canvas 38×33 cm.

Sale, Amsterdam, 16/7/1819, no. 72—Boormans, 8 fl.

C 192. *Preparing for a Walk.* In a room sits a dignified lady with a child before her and another child on her lap; a dog is at her side. A man stands, dressing, before a mirror; a maidservant brushes his hat. In the anteroom are two other figures. The sunlight is well rendered (HdG no. 220).

Canvas 66×56 cm.

Sale Wessel Ryers, Amsterdam, 21/9/1814, no. 62—Moll, 150 fl.

C 193. *An Interior with Three Figures.* Around a table with a cloth before a fireplace in a room sit three persons. In the background are two or three rooms leading to a garden. (HdG no. 222.)

Canvas 70×61 cm.

Sale H. van der Heuvel & J. Hackefort, Rotterdam, 18/4/1819, no. 13—100 fl.

C 194. *An Interior.* (HdG no. 222a.)

Panel 28×23 cm.

Sale, Leiden, 2/8/1816, no. 136.

C 195. *A Woman and a Man.* An elegant lady sits on an old chair; behind her a man watches her.

Panel.

Sale H.D.G. de Maree & W. Horstink, Haarlem, 12/5/1817, no. 59.

C 196. *Two Ladies Writing.* At a table in a room sit two ladies writing. An open door looks into another room and, beyond it, through a passage into the street, from which a gentleman is coming. Excellent in the rendering of sunlight. (HdG no. 223.)

Canvas 51×61 cm.

Sale [Engelberts et al.], Amsterdam, 25/8/1817, no. 41—Woodburn, 80 fl.

C 197. *A Family in an Interior.* In a furnished room sits a gentleman with a book before him at a table, on which is a lighted candle. The wife is sewing. Beside the bright fire is a servant girl with a child. (HdG no. 215.)

Panel 35.5×40.5 cm.

*(Poss.) Sale Pama, 1781. (See Cat. C 175); Sale G.G. Baron Taets van Amerongen, Amsterdam, 3/7/1805, no. 24—Roos, 107 fl; *Sale, S . . ., Paris, 10–12/11/1817, no. 73 (BMf).

C 198. *A Company Gaming.* By de Hoog or in his manner.

Sale Paulus Potter, The Hague, 8–9/6/1820, no. 50.

C 199. *A Company of Four Persons in a Room.* (HdG no. 223c.)

Canvas 61×71 cm.

Sale H.A. Bauer et al., Amsterdam 11/9/1820, no. 56—Gruyter, 20 fl.

C 200. *A Lady and Gentleman Conversing.* An attractive young lady stands in a room, with her head turned towards a young man, who sits at a table covered with a cloth and speaks to her. A servant girl watches them through a window. There are various accessories. (HdG no. 224.)

Canvas 44.5×43 cm.

Sale Aubert, Brussels, 8/8/1821, no. 52. (Compare Cat. C 126.)

C 201. *A Lady and a Child with a Gentleman.* A lady in rich costume has a child on her lap. Beside her is a dignified gentleman. (HdG no. 225.)

Sale J.A. Brentano, Amsterdam, 13/5/1822, no. 150—Hopman, 84 fl.

C 202. *An Interior.* (HdG no. 225a.)
Exh. of Old and Modern Paintings, Pinney's, 53 Pall Mall, London, 1823, no. 131.

C 203. *An Interior with Figures.* A vista with an effect of sunlight. (HdG no. 302; incorrectly as a courtyard scene.)
Sale C.H. Schultz, Amsterdam, 10/7/1826, no. 151—Roose, 20 fl.

C 204. *A Family in an Interior.* A little girl offers a flower to a man in a dressing gown, who is seated at a table. In the background are a woman and child. (HdG no. 229.)
Canvas 56×44 cm.
Sale P.J. de Marneffe, Brussels, 24/5/1830, no. 149.

C 205. *A Lady and a Gentleman at a Table.* By or in the manner of P. de Hooch. (HdG no. 229a.)
Panel 46×35 cm.
Sale, Amsterdam, 3–5/1/1831, no. 38—Keyser, 10 fl.

C 206. *Grace before a Meal.* A peasant family is saying grace over the food which is placed on the table. By P. de Hooch or in his manner. (HdG no. 232.)
Panel 32×42 cm.
Sale Van Rotterdam, Ghent, 6/7/1835, no. 171—200 frs.

C 207. *A Young Woman Writing a Letter.* A young Dutch woman in a green morning-dress trimmed with yellow fur is writing a letter at a table with a rich cloth upon it. Beside her stands a maidservant in red, holding a basket on one arm, and motioning to her with the other to warn her of the approach of her husband, who is seen at the open door. Another open door affords a view over the country, and lets in the sunlight, which illuminates the floor. (Blanc 1857–8, II, 414; HdG nos. 205 & 233.)
Canvas 50×60 cm.
*Sale Antony Grill, Amsterdam, 10/4/1776, no. 5—Wubbels, 60 fl (HdG no. 205); *Sale James Stuart, London, 23/5/1835, no. 74; Sale Henry, Paris, 23–5/5/1836, no. 53—1150 frs; *Sale Quatre-Solz de Lahante, Paris, 8/5/1838, no. 76—Simonet, 900 frs.

C 208. *A Lady and a Gentleman at a Table.* At a table in a hall, paved with marble squares and adorned with pictures, sit a lady and a gentleman with a child beside them. A servant girl enters by a half-open door, with a chaplet of flowers in her hand. By P. de Hooch, or in his manner. (HdG no. 233a.)
Canvas.
Sale, Leiden, 21/7/1841, no. 40.

C 209. *Gallant Conversation.* (HdG no. 235a.)
Canvas.
Sale Van Barneveld & Van den Haute, Antwerp, 26/2/1844,

C 210. *An Interior.* (HdG no. 235b.)
Sale (Supplementary), Paris, 22/3/1845, no. 61—336 frs.

C 211. *An Interior with Figures.* A fine composition. (HdG no. 236b.)
Signed; panel.
Sale, Antwerp, 24/2/1851, no. 120.

C 212. *A Flemish Scene.* (HdG no. 236c.)
61×67 cm.

Sale Frank Standish, London, 27/5/1853, no. 173 (a bequest to the late King Louis Philippe).

C 213. *An Interior.* (HdG no. 236d.)
Sale, Brussels, 8/8/1853, no. 162.

C 214. *A Family in an Interior.* In a handsomely furnished room, a lady dressed in white silk sits at a table partly covered with a rich cloth, upon which is fruit. She offers a peach to her husband, who stands beside her wearing a large red silk dressing-gown. A pretty little girl sits on her lap; near her are two boys holding fruit. Ascribed to Pieter de Hooch. (HdG no. 237a.)
Canvas 66×81 cm.
*Sale De Lirry, Paris, 2–5/2/1814, no. 49 [attr. P.d.H.] (BMf); Sale Comte R. de Cornélissen, Brussels, 11/5/1857, no. 31.

C 215. *Four Women Sitting Around a Table.* (HdG no. 238a.)
Van Winterfeldt, Berlin, 1863 (see Parthey, I, 622).

C 216. *Three Gentlemen in Black in a Library.* The heads are very lifelike; the colouring is transparent and warm. In both respects the picture is related to the work of T. de Keyser. (HdG no. 238b 'It is questionable whether it is a De hooch.') Mentioned by Waagen (1864, 430) as in the Lazarev collection in St. Petersburg.

C 217. *A Lady Reading and a Cavalier.* A lady sits reading. A manservant stands at table with fruit and wine upon it. A cavalier stands at the door. (HdG no. 240a.)
Sale Sir T. Baring, London, 2/6/1848, no. 176—Theobald, £72; sold by Bryant, London, 1865, to Graves for £74 11 s (did not appear in Bryant Sale, London, 23/6/1865).

C 218. *A Lady with a Man Looking at Her.* (HdG no. 240b.)
Sale, Rotterdam, 23/6/1867, no. 31.

C 219. *An Interior with Figures Spinning and Reading.* (HdG no. 240c.)
Panel 37×43 cm.
Sale P. van Arnhem, Groningen, 24/9/1868, no. 102.

C 220. *An Interior with Figures.* (HdG no. 240d.)
Exh. at Leeds, 1868, no. 590, lent by Roger Napier.

C 221. *A Conversation.* Two ladies and two gentlemen are engaged in a conversation. In the background by the fireplace a gentleman lights his pipe. To the right, by a door looking into a garden a manservant carries a cup. A dog is in the foreground. (HdG no. 196.)
Canvas 68.5×86.5 cm. Signed: P d Hooch
Exh. in Vienna, 1873, no. 116; dlr. C. Sedelmeyer, Paris.

C 222. *An Interior.* (Havard 1880, 117:3; HdG no. 240f.)
64×56 cm.
Formerly in the collection of the Comte de Turenne; Alsace-Lorraine Exhibition, Paris, 1874, no. 249.

C 223. *Ladies and Gentlemen at Breakfast.* The play of light on the figures is well rendered. (HdG no. 240g.)
Sale Graham, New York, 23/5/1876, no. 88.

C 224. *A Servant Girl Brings Refreshments to a Person* sitting to the right. Ascribed to P. de Hooch. (HdG no. 243).
Panel 39×59 cm.
Sale P. Fontaine of Ostend, Brussels, 28/11/1882, no. 50.

C 225. **Three Figures Conversing.** At the foot of a great staircase in the entrance hall of a castle. (HdG no. 244.)

    52×67 cm.

    Sale C.H. de L . . ., Brussels, 4/3/1887, no. 53.

C 226. **Two Women in a Room.** In a homely interior are two women. One is seated before a mirror while the other stands, pointing to a piece of gold in her hand. In the background a third figure is visible. (HdG no. 248.)

    Canvas 66×61 cm.

    Sale Strakosch et al., Berlin, 23/10/1900, no. 45.

C 227. **The Fortune-Teller.** In a room a lady and a gentleman sit at a table covered with a green cloth, upon which is a dish of fruit. A gipsy woman is telling the lady's fortune from her hand, while a gipsy boy close by is in the act of stealing something from her pocket. In the background two persons look on. (HdG no. 252.)

    Canvas 40×34 cm.

    Sale J. Brade et al., Cologne, 17/12/1897, no. 224; Sale J. Metz, J. Montag, et al., Cologne, 19/12/1904, no. 29.

C 228. **A Gentleman and a Girl at Cards.** A gay little picture. (HdG no. 257a.)

    Sale, Amsterdam, 11/5/1756, no. 90—10 fl 15 (Terwesten, 143).

C 229. **An Officer Playing Cards.** In an interior a richly dressed officer is playing cards with a lady, who wears a blue velvet jacket edged with fur. Fruit and other things are placed on a table covered with a cloth. A violin lies on a stool beside the officer. (HdG no. 259.)

    Panel 47×48 cm.

    Sale [Luchtmans], Rotterdam 20/4/1816, no. 69—170 fl.

C 230. **An Officer and a Lady Playing Cards by Candlelight.** (Prob. HdG no. 260.)

    Panel 38×30 cm.

    Exh. in London by Liotard, 1773, no. 23 (cf. Graves); Sale Liotard, London, 15/4/1774, no. 40; Sale Lebrun, Paris, 22/9/1774, no. 77; Sale Constantin, Paris, 18/11/1816, no. 217 (BMf); Sale Comte F. de Robiano, Brussels, 1/5/1837, no. 282—150 frs (HdG no. 260).

C 231. **Soldiers Playing Cards.** Identical with Cat. 11 bis.

C 232. **A Guardroom.**
(HdG no. 275a.)

    Sale, Amsterdam, 9/4/1687, no. 50—48 fl (Hoet, I, 6).

C 233. **A Guardroom.**
(HdG no. 275b.)

    46×63.5 cm.

    Sale Jan van Loon, Delft, 18/7/1736, no. 43—8 fl 10 (Hoet, II, 392).

C 234. **An Officer Writing, with a Standing Trumpeter.**
By P. de Hooghe in the manner of Ter Borch.

    Sale, Amsterdam, 27/10/1760, no. 8; Sale, Amsterdam, 25/11/1761, no 63. (According to a handwritten note in the latter sale catalogue at the RKD, 'after G. Terburg'; cf. Gudlaugsson nos. 129, 141 & 143.)

C 235. **An Interior with a Man and a Maid, by Candlelight.** An interior illuminated by a candle standing on a table, at which a man sits; standing before him is a maid. In the background a burning fire is seen. (Compare Cat. B 11.)

Canvas 49×57.5 cm.

Sale, Amsterdam, 19/12/1770, no. 102.

C 236. **An Interior of an Inn.** In the foreground an old woman is spinning by a table, which stands by an open window; on the side by the hearth an old man sits smoking; in the background the hostess is being embraced by a man in the vestibule. In the manner of P. de Hoogh.

    Canvas 35.5×51 cm.

    Sale J. van Dyk, Amsterdam, 14/3/1791, no. 60—Tijdeman, 39 fl; Sale J. van der Putte, Amsterdam, 22/5/1810, no. 131—Mensart, 40 fl.

C 237. **An Officer and a Girl.** At a table with a cloth in a room sits an officer holding a glass of wine and a letter. Beside him is an attractive woman, with a mug in her hand, who listens attentively to him. (HdG no. 277.)

    Sale, Haarlem, 23/9/1811, no. 37. (Compare Cat. D 24).

C 238. **Interior of an Inn.** A cavalier dressed in red sits drinking on a bench with a table behind him; a woman near a window, with her back turned to the cavalier and holding a pipe in her right hand, counts the money she has been given; the servant of the cavalier silently leans on the table. Composed in the manner of Metsu.

    Panel 53×46 cm.

    Sale Mme Veuve de . . ., Paris, 22/2/1827, no. 18.

C 239. **Interior of an Inn.** With a very good effect of light. (HdG no. 279a.)

    Panel.

    Sale Van Barneveld & Van den Haute, et al., Antwerp, 26/2/1844, no. 18.

C 240. **The Drowsy Cavalier.** A gentleman is seated, leaning his head on a table. A young woman, standing by, disturbs his sleep by tickling his neck with a straw. On the table are a jug and a glass. An open door at the back looks out upon some adjacent buildings. (S no. 66; HdG no. 280).

    Canvas 66×51 cm.

    Sale A. Hulsen, Amsterdam, 2/5/1854, no. 45—Roos, 500 fl. (Compare Val. [H. van der Burch], no. 239.)

C 241. **A Man Smoking and a Man Asleep in a Tavern.** (HdG no. 280a.)

    70×57 cm.

    Sale P. Roelfsema, A. Backer te Oever & M.P. Grimminge, Groningen, 22/6/1863, no. 42.

C 242. **A Musical Company in a Courtyard.** (HdG no. 136g.)

    Sale D. Ietswaart, Amsterdam, 22/4/1749, no. 195—A. Klaauw, 26 fl 10 (Hoet, II, 187).

C 243. **View of a Courtyard.** The light enters the scene through a porch; in the foreground a man plays the guitar and is accompanied by a seated and a standing woman.

    Canvas 66×68.5 cm.

    Sale S. van der Stel, Amsterdam, 25/9/1781, no. 67—Yver, 5 fl 15.

C 244. **An Exterior,** painted with Gonzales (Coques).

    Exh. London, B.I., 1829, no. 155, lent by C. Baring Wall.

C 245. **A Musician in a Forecourt.** (HdG no. 161b.)

    In the possession of Wallraf, Cologne, 1863 (Parthey, I, 622).

C 246. *A Lady and a Cavalier.* With the landlord in the courtyard of an inn. (HdG no. 306a.)

44.5×38 cm.

Sale Sir H.M. Thompson et al., London, 16/3/1901, no. 82— £55; Sale Duke of Marlborough et al., London, 14/5/1904, no. 50—£27.

C 247. *A Flower Garden.* (HdG no. 309a.)

Inv. of Antonie Rinck, Amsterdam, D.B.K., no. 368, 27/8/1661 (from A. Bredius).

C 248. *A Company before a House.* (HdG no. 309b.)

Inv. of Hendrick Moller, wine merchant from Hattum, Amsterdam, D.B.K., no. 383, 25/6/1677 (from A. Bredius).

C 249. **An Old Dutch Dwelling House with Four Figures.** The light falls from above towards the background. It is an excellent, beautiful and delicately painted work. (HdG no. 311.)

Canvas 75×102 cm.

Sale Frau J. Stinstra, Amsterdam, 2/7/1829, no. 74— Brondgeest 1800 fl.

C 250. *A Hawking Party.* (HdG no. 314.)

Sale J. Harding, London, 1885—£6 2 s . .

C 251. **A Young Woman Sitting on a Balcony.** There is a view across a park. The lady wears a white silk dress and a grey bodice. She has taken an apple from a white china plate on a table beside her. According to Hofstede de Groot, 'The picture is genuine, but has been repainted.' (HdG nos. 106, 315 & 325.)

Canvas 22×17 cm. Signed on the balustrade of the balcony: P.H.

Exh. The Hague (Pulchri Studio), May 1890, no. 43; Sale Galerie A. Philips-Neven, Maastricht, 24/3/1892, no. 57—70 fl.

C 252. **A Pleasure Party with Horses and Dogs.** They halt at the entrance to a park and converse with a wayfarer. (HdG no. 315a.)

Sale George, Earl of Egremont, London, 21/5/1892, no. 59 —£12.

C 253. **The Park of a Dutch Mansion with Figures.** (HdG no. 315b.)

Sale Oxenbridge, London, 9/12/1899, no. 65.

C 254. **The Lazar House** (in Delft). (HdG no. 318.)

Sale, Amsterdam, 28/3/1708, no. 87—7 fl 10 (Hoet, I, 115).

C 255. *A Landscape,* by 'd'Hooghe', the figures by 'Deyster' (sic). (Note, W. Duyster died in 1635.)

Canvas 99×117 cm.

Sale C.J. de Schryvere, Bruges, 1/6/1763, no. 46.

C 256. *Animals of Various Types in a Landscape.* This picture, in the manner of Berghem, does honour to the talents of his esteemed student.

Canvas 58.5×79 cm.

Sale [Famas], Paris, 19/11/1772, no. 38—100 frs.

C 257. *A Hilly Italian Landscape.* The landscape is divided by a river; in the middle distance some ruins with a shepherd driving forth his flock; in the distance other small figures and animals; sunny and warm in colouration; in the manner of Jan Asselyn.

Canvas 135×170 cm.

Sale V . . ., Amsterdam, 19/5/1779, no. 85—Bisschop.

C 258. *A View in Strasburgh.*

Sale W. Rawley, London, 16/5/1806, no. 32.

C 259. *An Exterior with Cottages and Figures.*

Sale W. Beckford, Fonthill Abbey, 10/10/1823, no. 222— £19 19 s (with the annotation 'Van der Haagen').

C 260. **A Pasture in the Neighbourhood of Delft, with Cattle and Figures.** (HdG no. 320; BM, 365, n. 1.)

53.5×67 cm.

Sale Paris, 16/4/1859, no. 24; Sale, London, 20/6/1903, no. 90; Sale de Vries, Amsterdam, 26/5/1908, no. 56.

C 261. *A Family Portrait.*

Inv. of Petronella de la Court, widow of Adam Oortmans, Prot. Not. Pieter Outgens, Amsterdam, 2/5/1707; inventory completed by G. Ypelaer, Amsterdam, N.A.A. no. 5338/610, 16/8/1707. (See Chapt. IV, n. 5.)

C 262. *A Family Portrait.* (HdG no. 322.)

Canvas 102×86.5 cm.

Sale J.H. Vliet, The Hague, 25/9/1780, no. 68—Van Denemarke, 24 fl. (As Hofstede de Groot noted, it is not clear from the words of the catalogue—'buiten de lijst'—whether the picture was measured with or without its frame.)

C 263. *Portrait of a Young Lady as Juno.* The hands are visible. On the horizon are two flying swans. (HdG no. 324.)

Canvas 31.5×24.5 cm.

Sale, Leipzig, 31/3/1845, no. 219.

C 264. *Portrait of a Lady.* (HdG no. 324a.)

Exh. Leeds, 1868, no. 747, lent by Sir C.W. Dilke.

C 265. *Portrait of a Woman.* A woman in black, with a broad white satin collar and a white cap, stands at a table covered with a red cloth, on which she lays a prayer book. (HdG no. 324b.)

Panel 64×49 cm.

Sale Bergerhausen, Bonn, 11/9/1891, no. 12.

C 266. *Portrait of a Small Child.* A little girl, seen to the knees, stands with a bird in her right hand and a piece of bread in her left; a curtain is drawn back in front of her. (HdG no. 326.)

Canvas 54.5×40.5 cm.

From the collection of Queen Désirée; Chr. Hammer, Stockholm, 1872; Sale C. Hammer, Cologne, 5/10/1894, no. 115.

C 267. **The Artist with Wavy Hair.** (HdG no. 327, Van Hall, 1963, 143, no. 2.)

79×66 cm.

Sale, London, 21/12/1901, no. 91.

C 268. *A Still Life.* A glass of wine on a table, other accessories, and an interior.

Sale, Amsterdam, 21/6/1784, no. 28—Van der Waard, 1 fl 10.

C 269. *A Picture.*

Among seven works for which Jan Looten, the painter, owed Laurens Mauritsz Doucy 700 fl, Prot. Not. N.G. van Breugel, Amsterdam, 6/9/1664 (see Bredius, II, 426).

C 270. *A Picture* 'by de Hoogh' (possibly Carel, by whom there was another picture in the inventory) valued by F. Bol and G. Uylenburg at 15 fl.

Inv. of Laurens Mauritsz Douci (Doucy), Amsterdam, 18/1/1669 (Bredius, II, 426).

C 271. *A Picture.*
Inv. of Willempgen Willemsdr., widow of S. Decker, sexton of the Oude Kerk, (died May 1657), 2/7/1669, Prot. Not. A. Verkerk, Delft, no. 2203. (Communication J.M. Montias.)

C 272. *A Picture.*
Inv. of Johannes Beerestraat (Beerstraten), the painter, Amsterdam, D.B.K., no. 373, 15/4/1667, no. 24 (see Bredius, III, 815).

C 273. *A Picture.*
Inv. of Laurens Bernards, painter and art dealer, Middelburg, 3/7/1676 (Bredius, III, 1676).

C 274. *A Scene by Moonlight* (*Een maneschyn*) *by De Hoogh.*
Inv. of Jacob Loys, painter and architect, Rotterdam, 30/10/1680 (Bredius, V, 1590).

C 275. *A Picture.*
Inv. of P. Muyssart, Amsterdam, D.B.K., no. 207, 28/7/ 1694. (Communication S.A.C. Dudok van Heel.)

C 276. *Picture(s?)*
Sale Jacobus van Rijck, an artist and the doorman for the Bank van Lening, living on the Achtergracht, Amsterdam, 21/6/1702 (adv. in *Amsterdamsche Courant*, 15/6/1702, see DvH 1975, 163, no. 73).

C 277–80. *Four Pictures.*
Inv. of Petronella Block, widow of Jacobus van de Velde, med. doctor and textile merchant, living on the Gelderse Kade, Prot. Not. W.J. van Midlum, Amsterdam, no. 7157/826, 19/4/1703. (Communication S.A.C. Dudok van Heel.)

C 281. *A Scene by Lamplight.* (HdG no. 328a.)
Sale Cornelius Dusart, painter, Haarlem, 21/8/1708, no. 210.

C 282. *A Picture,* 30 fl.
Inv. of Abel Horst, city surgeon living on the Herengracht (1685), Prot. Not. G. van der Groe, Amsterdam, N.A.A., no. 6621, 4/8/1712.

C 283 *Picture(s?)*
Sale Willem van Beest, bookkeeper and broker on the Herengracht (1688), Amsterdam, 6/3/1714 (adv. in *Amsterdamsche Courant*, 17/2/1714, see S.A.C. Dudok van Heel, in *Amstelodamum*, 69 [1977], 110, no. 164).

C 284. *A Scene by Candlelight.* (HdG no. 328b.)
Sale, Amsterdam, 25/3/1728, no. 83.

C 285. *A Picture.* (HdG no. 328c.)
Sale, Amsterdam, 16/5/1730, no. 37—6 fl 15.

C 286–9. *Four Works by de Hooge.*
Sale S. van Huls, The Hague, 14/5/1736, no. 3310.

C 290. *A Picture.*
Sale Ysselsteyn, Amsterdam, 26/5/1744, no. 60.

C 291. *A Picture.*
Sale Sonne et al., Amsterdam, 5/7/1759, no. 79—1 fl 5.

C 292. *A Picture.*
Sale, Leiden, 31/7/1765, no. 45.

C 293. *A Picture.*
Sale J. Koerten (widow of A. Blok), Haarlem, 7/8/1765, no. 45.

C 294. *A Picture.* (HdG no. 328d.)
Sale Strutt Derby, London, 22/6/1889—399 £.

D. Works Wrongly Attributed to De Hooch

D 1. *Mother and Child, with a Sleeping Soldier*
Paul Frederick, Milwaukee.
Panel 34 × 42.5 cm.
PROV.: Dlr. N. Fischmann, Munich; Milton Gallery, London; Sale C.S. Tower et al., New York, 12/1/1955, no. 17, ill.; Sale Lederer et al., New York, 28/11/1962, no. 17, ill.; Dr. Bader, Milwaukee.
EXH.: Oshkosh 1968, no. 18.
LIT.: Val. no. 2 [*c.* 1647].
The painting seems to be by the same hand as the scene of *Card Players*, ascribed to Benjamin Gerritsz. Cuyp, in the Museum in Brussels, inv. no. 6253.

D 2. *A Woman Sewing, with a Standing Woman and Three Children*
Present location unknown.
Panel 62 × 71 cm.
PROV.: Sale Luchtmans, Rotterdam, 20/4/1816, no. 70—90 fl; Sale, Leiden, 2/18/1816, no. 135; *Sale Lord Northwick, Thistlestone Hse., Cheltenham, 26/7/1859, no. 1708; *Sale J.D. Ichenhauser, New York, 26/2/1903, no. 101, ill.; *Sale London, 30/6/1906, no. 127.
LIT.: HdG nos. 20 & 91.

D 3. *A Girl Making Lace*
Musée des Beaux-Arts, Nîmes. Gower Collection, no. 335.
Canvas 36 × 32 cm. Signed (falsely).
LIT.: HdG no. 89 [of doubtful authenticity]; Nîmes, Mus. cat. 1940.

D 4. *A Woman Sewing*
Niedersächsisches Landesmuseum, Hannover, no. PAM 893.
Canvas 50 × 38.5 cm.
PROV.: Sale Amsterdam, 1779, no. 105 [Vermeer];[1] Sale J. Pekstok, Amsterdam, 17/12/1792, no. 70 [Vermeer]—Yperen, 30 fl; dlr. Rothman, Berlin; acq. 1926.
LIT.: Thoré-Bürger 1866, 566, no. 43 [Vermeer]; HdG [Vermeer] no. 12; Val. no. 254 [H. van der Burch]; G. von der Osten, *Katalog der Gemälde Alter Meister*, Hannover, 1954, 72; Blankert 1975, 96, n. 10, fig. 45 [Unknown Master].
The painting was sold in the eighteenth century as a Vermeer and Valentiner incorrectly attributed it to H. van der Burch. Presently catalogued as a De Hooch, the work resembles some of the master's pictures from the late 1660s in execution, but is closer in design and figure type to Van Hoogstraten's works of these years.[2]
NOTES: [1] Thoré-Bürger 1866, 566. [2] Compare, exh. Rotterdam 1935, cat. no. 55, fig. 120.

D 5. *A Man Seated at a Desk and Reading a Book*
Present location unknown.
Panel 46 × 36 cm.
PROV.: Sale Kayser of Frankfurt, Cologne, 28/10/1879, no. 121; J. Boehler, Munich.[1]
LIT.: HdG no. 103.
NOTES: [1] Witt photo.

D 6. *A Musician with Three Figures at a Table*
Private Collection, South America.
Canvas 63.5 × 53.5 cm. Signed lower right: P de hoogh.
PROV.: Dlr. W. Abraham, London;[1] N. Forbes Robertson, London;[2] dlr. F. Kleinberger, Paris, 6/1899;[3] Sale, Berlin, 22/2/1910, no. 85, pl. 15; L. Lilienfeld, Vienna, by 1915,[4] cat. (1917), no. 35; E. Trautscholdt, Düsseldorf, 1958;[5] A. Jacobs Gallery, London, cat. 1974, II, ill.
LIT.: HdG no. 131 ['a very early work, if genuine; . . . its authenticity is not above suspicion']; G. Glück, *Katalog, Lilienfeld Collection*, Vienna, 1917, no. 35; BM, 378 [poss. G. v. d. Eeckhout]; Val. no. 25 [*c.* 1653–5; not entirely certain].
Brière-Misme's tentative attribution to Van den Eeckhout is also unacceptable.
NOTES: [1] HdG no. 131. [2] ibid. [3] ibid. [4] HdGf. [5] RKD photo.

D 7. *A Musical Company*
Present location unknown.
Canvas 53 × 63 cm. Signed and dated 1670 over doorway.
PROV.: Arthur Kay, Glasgow, 1893;[1] dlr. H.O. Mietke, Vienna;[2] dlr. Sedelmeyer, Paris,[3] (sold to) Henri Heugel, Paris, 10/1901;[4] dlr. Vallotton, Lausanne, 1964;[5] dlr. L. Koetser, London, 1967–9.[6]
EXH.: (a) Paris (Sedelmeyer) 1902, no. 22, ill.; (b) 1914, no. 21, pl. 21; (c) London (Koetser) 1967, no. 24, ill.; (d) 1969, no. 19.
LIT.: C. Hofstede de Groot, in *O.H.*, 2 (1893), 225; HdG no. 132; R, 27 36; Val. 1926, 62; BM, 276; Val. no. 96; CB 1930, 198; Welu 1975, 535, n. 34.
Collins Baker correctly doubted the attribution to De Hooch. While it may be by the same hand as Cat. D 8, the crude figure types are certainly not those of De Hooch's paintings of 1670 (e.g. Cat. 94) or of any other period.
NOTES: [1] HdG, in *O.H.*, 1893, 225. [2] HdG no. 132. [3] Exh. a. [4] F. Lugt's annotation in Sedelmeyer cat. 1902. [5] RKD photo. [6] Exh. c & d.

D 8. *A Musical Company*
Private Collection.
Canvas 54.6 × 60.3 cm. Signed left on windowsill: P.d hooch.
PROV.: Sale H. Rottermondt, Amsterdam, 18/7/1786, no. 127—Yver, 10 fl; J. Hauptmann, Paris, 4/5/1891, no. 28; dlr. Sedelmeyer, Paris, 1898;[1] Sale Baron Königswarter, Berlin, 20/11/1906, no. 44—18,500 mks; Omnes Collection, Château de Nijenrode, by *c.* 1919;[2] Sale Château de Nijenrode, Amsterdam, 10/7/1923, no. 23—8200 fl; dlr. Kleinberger,

Paris, *c.* 1924;[3] E.D. Levinson;[4] Sale M.P. Bartley et al. (a.c.), London, 29/6/1962, no. 142; Mrs. Ira S. French, New York;[5] Sale, London, 29/6/1973, no. 87, ill.

EXH.: (a) Paris (Sedelmeyer) 1898, no. 72, ill.; (b) The Hague (Goudstikker) 1920, no. 56; (c) Copenhagen 1922, no. 59; (d) St. Louis (Goudstikker) 1922, no. 58.

LIT.: Wurzbach, I, 718; HdG no. 172; BM, 277; Val. no. 97 [*c.* 1670]; CB 1930, 198; BM 1947–8, III, 176, n. 17.

Collins Baker was the first to correctly doubt the attribution. After initially accepting the work, Brière-Misme also grew to doubt it.[6] Although the design recalls works by De Hooch from the late 1660s and 70s, the execution is too laboured and the figures too doll-like for the artist. The hanging on the wall appears to represent the harbour in Amsterdam and is inscribed: AMSTELODAMUM TOTIUS EUROPAE EMPORIUM CELEBRUM HOLLAND.

NOTES: [1] Exh. a. [2] BM, 277, n. 1. [3] Val. no. 97. [4] Sale cat. 1962. [5] Sale cat. 1973. [6] BM 1947–8, 176, n. 17.

D 9. *Nocturnal Scene with a Family*

Galleria Nazionale d'Arte Antica, Rome, inv. no. 996.
Canvas 63×55 cm.

PROV.: *Sale Abbé de Gevigney, Paris, 1–29/12/1779, no. 401 —Dubois, 28 frs.

EXH.: Rome 1954–5, no. 31.

LIT.: Wurzbach, I, 717 [doubtful]; HdG no. 274; G.J. Hoogewerff, *l'Arte*, 1911, 374; R, 103; BM, 376, ill. 379; Val. no. 230 [H. van der Burch].

Although the work was sold as a De Hooch in the eighteenth century, it is certainly not by the master. Valentiner's ascription to Van der Burch, although more plausible, is also problematic. The picture is abraded and in poor condition.

D 10. *A Family Group with a Maidservant**

Present location unknown.
Canvas 57.5×65 cm. Signed: P.D.H.[1]

PROV.: Edmund Lloyd, Manchester, 1842;[2] Sale E.N.F. Lloyd, London, 30/4/1937, no. 107, ill.; dlr. Katz, Dieren, 1937;[3] Schaeffer Galleries, 1938–9.[4]

EXH.: (a) Dieren (Katz) 1937, no. 38; (b) San Francisco 1938, no. 17, ill.; (c) Los Angeles 1938, no. 17, ill.; (d) Springfield, M.F.A., Summer 1938; (e) San Francisco (Schaeffer) 1939, no. 4.

LIT.: S s no. 21; Havard 1880, 100:3; HdG no. 235; 'The Lloyd Collection of Dutch Pictures', *Country Life*, 17/4/1937; cviii, ill; Sutton (forthcoming), fig. 16.

The picture appears to be by the same hand as the painting in Philadelphia which Valentiner correctly attributed to H. van der Burch.[5] The steep perspective and the figure types are similar in both works. The stairway at the right recalls the corresponding passage in De Hooch's painting of 1663 (Cat. 52, Plate 56), but the Delftware above the door resembles that in Van der Burch's picture in the Frick Collection.[6] It should be noted that the gesture of the seated man, who according to the Lloyd Sale catalogue offers a coin to the child, resembles that of the man in Terborch's so-called *Parental Admonition* (Fig. 28).

NOTES: [1] Lloyd Sale cat. [2] S s no. 21; Smith states, however, that the person holding the child is a man (?). [3] Exh. a. [4] Exh. b–e. [5] cf. Val. no. 134. [6] Cat. 1968, I, 147–9.

D 11. *A Merry Company Group** (Plate 180)

Present location unknown.

Canvas 65×58 cm. Signed lower left on bench: P d Hoogh

PROV.: *Earl of Shrewsbury;[1] *Sale De Jong of London, Paris, 10/2/1862, no. 39—5000 frs; F. Lugt, Maartensdijk, 1928;[2] dlr. Matthiesen, Berlin & London, 1929–46.[3]

EXH.: (a) London (Slatter) 1945, no. 18; (b) London (Matthiesen) 1946, no. 32 [*c.* 1653–5].

LIT.: Val. no. 261 [*c.* 1653–5]; Val. 1930, 261, 298; Val. 1932, 318, ill. detail; *Phoenix*, 2 (1949), 35, ill.

Although aspects of the work recall De Hooch's designs of *c.* 1657–8 (compare Cat. 25 & 26, Plates 22, 23), the attribution to the artist is unacceptable. The figure types, steep perspective, and glittering highlights are more typical of H. van der Burch's works.

NOTES: [1] De Jong Sale cat. [2] RKD photo. [3] Val. no. 261; Exh. a & b.

D 12. *A Couple Playing Cards*

Metropolitan Museum of Art, New York, acc. no. 60.71.33.
Canvas 65×77 cm.

PROV.: Dr. Weil, Prague, 1922–3;[1] art market, Germany, 1927;[2] Private Collection, New York, 1929.[3]

LIT.: T. von Frimmel, 'Ein Gemälde von Pieter de Hoogh im Prager Privatbesitz,' *Der Kunstwanderer*, 9/1922–8/1923, 128–9, ill. 128; BM, 285, n. 7; Val. no. 117 [*c.* 1670–5]; Pelinck 1958, n. 6.

In 1922–3 a small dog appeared at the right of the picture and the man's head seemed to be overpainted.[4] The execution and figures resemble late works by Van Hoogstraten.

NOTES: [1] Frimmel 1922–3, 128. [2] BM, 285, n. 7. [3] Val. no. 117. [4] Ill. in Frimmel 1922–3, 128.

D 13. *A Couple Drinking Wine**

Present location unknown.
Panel 29×22.5 cm.

PROV.: Dlr. J. Boehler, Munich, 1924;[1] Sale Kodella, Lucerne, 29/8/1934, no. 1867.

LIT.: BM, 285; Val. no. 164; CB 1930, 198; Kauffmann 1930, 198.

In Valentiner's opinion the attribution was not certain and Collins Baker felt it was doubtful. The figure types call to mind those of Job Berckheyde (compare Val. no. 205; presently with dlr. Hoogsteder, The Hague).

NOTES: [1] BM, 285.

D 14. *A Visit of Condolence to the Home of the Wassenaar Family**

Present location unknown.
Canvas 53×63 cm.

PROV.: Art market, Hamburg, 3/1923;[1] Heiden Collection, Hamburg, *c.* 1929.[2]

LIT.: Val. no. 170 [after 1680].

According to Valentiner the picture was attributed to De Hooch by Hofstede de Groot, who identified the heraldry shields as those of the Wassenaar Family. The slightly stooped figure types are more typical of Job Berckheyde's art.

NOTES: [1] HdGf. [2] Val. no. 170.

D 15. *A Couple Looking out from a Vestibule**

Present location unknown.
Canvas 110×85 cm.

PROV.: *Sale London, 4/6/1923, no. 135; dlr. London, 1924 [Van Hoogstraten];[1] dlr. Bottenwieser, Berlin;[2] A. Beskow, Stockholm;[3] Demotte Collection, Paris;[4] Sale, Cologne, 11/6/1958, no. 54, pl. 11; Sale, Frankfurt, 16/3/1962, no. 9, pl. 1; Sale G. Bassege, Berlin, 7/11/1972, no. 151, ill. (bought in).

LIT.: Lilienfeld 1923-4, 187, ill.; Val. no. 168 [*c.* 1680]; CB 1930, 198; J. Pijoan, *Art in the Modern World,* Chicago, 1940, 228, ill.; *Weltkunst,* 1/3/1962, 23.

First published as a De Hooch by Lilienfeld, the picture was tentatively assigned to the artist by Valentiner, who felt that the figures resembled those of P. Janssens. Collins Baker correctly doubted the attribution. Judging from photographs, the work more closely resembles the late architectural fantasies of D. van Delen.[5]

NOTES: [1] Lilienfeld 1923-4, 187. [2] Sale cat. 1958. [3] ibid. [4] ibid. [5] Compare *Figures under a Portico,* signed and dated 1661, exh. dlr. L. Koetser, 1972, no. 24, ill.

D 16. *A Guardroom Scene*★
Present location unknown.
Panel 42.5×47.8 cm.
PROV.: Dlr. Goudstikker, Amsterdam, 10/1925;[1] K. Lilienfeld, Berlin, 1927.[2]
LIT.: Val. no. 4 [*c.* 1648].

The attribution to Simon Kick, under whose name the picture is presently filed at the RKD, is also probably incorrect.
NOTES: [1] HdGf. [2] BMf.

D 17. *Soldiers in a Stable*★
Present location unknown.
Panel 59×69.5 cm.
PROV.: English dlr., 1924;[1] Private Collection, Düsseldorf, 1926;[2] P. Bottenwieser, Berlin, 1927;[3] dlr. Rothman, Amsterdam, 1929;[4] Sale, Cologne, 5/5/1937, no. 235, pl. 60.
LIT.: Lilienfeld 1924-5, 184, ill.; BM, 340; Val. no. 10 [after 1650]; Collins Baker 1930, 198.

The figures, particularly the two at the far left, are too crudely conceived for the youthful De Hooch. The design and execution suggest that the work is by H. van der Burch (compare Fig. 4).
NOTES: [1] Lilienfeld 1924-5, 184. [2] RKD photo. [3] ibid. [4] Witt photo.

D 18. *Nocturnal Scene with Soldiers and a Serving Girl*
Groninger Museum, Groningen, inv. no. 1931-112. Bequest of Cornelis Hofstede de Groot.
Panel 50.5×38 cm.
PROV.: (Poss.) Sale [Wreesman], Amsterdam, 8/17/1818, no. 116;[1] C. Hofstede de Groot, The Hague, by 1906.[2]
EXH.: (a) Rotterdam, Boymans Museum, Autumn 1908; (b) Berlin (Schäffer) 1929, no. 37.
LIT.: Bode 1906, 57; HdG no. 267; K. Freise, 'Gemälde aus der Sammlung Dr. Hofstede de Groot im Haag,' *M.f.K.,* 2 (1909), 22, ill.; Jantzen 1912, 9; R, 18, 96; Lilienfeld 1924, 453; BM, 372, 376, ill. 372; Val. 1927, 68, n. 1; Val. xvi, no. 18.

The composition with central repoussoir (compare Fig. 54) and the glancing highlights support attribution to H. van der Burch.
NOTES: [1] Without attribution or measurements. The reference to the Ryers Sale (Amsterdam 1814) included under HdG no. 267 does not apply to this work. The description mentions only two soldiers and gives the dimensions 35.5×35.5. [2] HdG no. 267.

D 19. *Nocturnal Scene of Soldiers and a Serving Woman at a Table*★
Present location unknown.

Panel 52×62 cm.
PROV.: Dlr. Agnew, London, Sept. 1921;[1] Sale Goldstein et al. (a.c.), London, 26/7/1933, no. 55; Sale Huth et al. (a.c.), London, 29/6/1966, no. 106; Sale Van Alen Bruguire et al. (a.c.), London, 5/12/1969, no. 9.
LIT.: BM 372; Val. no. 19 [1654-7]; Kauffmann 1930, col. 805.

According to Valentiner the picture was in problematic condition in 1929. The compositional scheme and figure types are typical of H. van der Burch (compare Fig. 54).
NOTES: [1] HdGf.

D 20. *Paying the Hostess* (Plate 182)
Private Collection, New York.
Panel 66×63 cm. Signed on stool: Pr. d hooch
PROV.: Jocelyn Beauchamp, Langley Park, Norwich; Sale Beauchamp, London, 11/6/1956, no. 117 [G. van Tilburg]—W. Sabin.
EXH.: Waltham 1966, no. 19, ill.
LIT.: Fleischer 1978, 60 [L. de Jongh], fig. 20.

As late as 1956 the picture was sold as a Gillis van Tilburg and evidently bore no signature. C. Gilbert attributed it to De Hooch[1] and most recently Fleischer has persuasively argued that it should be assigned to De Jongh. The smoothly modelled forms, tonal clarity, and figure types are characteristic of the latter's art. The signature reveals evidence of overpainting and, as Fleischer observed, could easily have been altered from that of De Jongh. The panel originally was horizontal in format and of dimensions comparable to Cat. D 21 (Plate 181), which is also probably by De Jongh. At an early date a strip approximately 15 cm high was added at the upper edge. The artist himself may have made these changes to convert the picture to the upright format, which became popular in the 1650s.
NOTES: [1] Exh.

D 21. *Soldiers at Reveille* (Plate 181)
North Carolina Museum of Art, Raleigh, inv. no. 52.9.46.
Panel 48.2×63.5 cm.
PROV.: Sale J. Pompe van Meerdevoort, Soeterwoude, 19/5/1780, no. 45 [L. de Jongh]—Delphos, 42 fl; Sale J. Engelman, Haarlem, 16/7/1782, no. 12 [L. de Jongh]—58 fl; ★Eastman Johnson, New York;[1] Henry Blank, Newark, by 1926;[2] Sale H. Blank, New York, 16/11/1949, no. 34, ill.
LIT.: Val. 1926, 52, n. 1; BM, 370, ill. 366; Val. 1927, 76, no. 1 [1647-57]; Val. xv, n. 1, no. 5 [*c.* 1648; with incorrect measurements]; T, 10, ill. 8; Val. 1956, 49, no. 53, ill.; exh. cat. Waltham 1966, ref. no. 19; Fleischer 1978, 57 ff. [L. de Jongh], fig. 16.

The picture appeared in two early sale catalogues as a Ludolf de Jongh and, as Fleischer has observed, is probably the work of that master. The facial types may be compared with those in De Jongh's painting of 1658 in the Groningen Museum[3] and Fleischer has compared the modelling technique and details like the treatment of the straw to other works by the master.
NOTES: [1] Blank Sale cat. [2] Val. 1926, 52, n. 1. [3] See Val. no. 185 (below).

D 22. *Soldiers with a Serving Woman in a Stable* (Plate 183)
National Gallery, Prague, inv. no. DO-5398.
Panel 59×70 cm.

PROV.: *Sale [André of Rouen], Paris, 22/4/1798, no. 45—
Lebrun;[1] from the Cistercian Monastery at Osek, Czecho-
slovakia.

LIT.: J. Opitz, *Galerie des Stiftes Osseg*, Komotau, 1931, no.
58 [S. Kick], ill.; J. Šíp, in *Umění*, 8 (1960), 558; J. Šíp, *Výstara
přírůstků holandského malířství 17. stol.*, National Gallery
Prague, 1961, no. 79; J. Šíp, in *Výtvarné umění*, 8 (1963), 100;
J. Šíp, *Holanská figurální malbe 17. století*, National Gallery,
Prague, 1969, 27; Fleischer 1978, 64 ff. [L. de Jongh], fig. 21.

Opitz attributed the work to S. Kick and J. Šíp first
assigned it to De Hooch. The picture fits the description of a
work which was sold in 1798 as a De Hooch 'in the manner
of Weninx', but that picture seems to have been somewhat
smaller. The central soldier with slender proportions and long
nose recalls De Hooch's early figures, but the soldier at the
left and the serving woman are closer to De Jongh's types.
The slightly more refined technique also lends support to
Fleischer's attribution to De Jongh.

NOTES: [1] 53.5×63.5.

D 23. **Soldiers Playing Tric-Trac★**
Present location unknown.
Copper 58.4×83.8 cm.
PROV.: Sale, Paris, 4/6/1891, no. 23; Sale Sykora, Frankfurt,
6/6/1898, no. 70, ill.; Sale Sedelmeyer, Paris, 25/5/1907, no. 83.
EXH.: Paris (Sedelmeyer) 1905, no. 17, ill.
LIT.: HdG no. 264a.

D 24. **A Seated Officer with a Standing Serving Woman★**
Private Collection, Italy.
Canvas 55.5×43.5 cm. Signed right on fireplace: P d Hoogh
PROV.: (Poss.) Sale, Haarlem, 23/9/1811, no. 37 (w/o m.);[1]
dlr. Goedhart, Amsterdam, May 1892;[2] Private Collection,
London; dlr. Giorgio Caretto, Turin, 1970.[3]
EXH.: Turin (G. Caretto) 1970, no. 36, ill. (on cover).
LIT.: HdG nos. 265 & poss. 277.

Although the work was accepted by Hofstede de Groot
as a 'late example', its figure types are not those of the master.
NOTES: [1] HdG no. 277; cf. Cat. C 237. [2] HdG no. 265.
[3] Exh.

D 25. **A Seated Soldier with a Pipe** (Plate 184)
Galleria Nazionale d'Arte Antica, Rome, inv. no. 973.
Panel 55×47 cm.
PROV.: Torlonia Collection, Rome.
EXH.: (a) Rome 1928, no. 28, ill.; (b) London, R.A., 1929,
no. 326 [attr. to P.d.H.]; (c) Zurich 1953, no. 64 [c. 1655].
LIT.: A. Venturi, *Le Gallerie Nazionali Italiane*, 5 (1902),
358 [Palamedesz]; S. Müller, in *Z.f.b.K.*, N.F. 14 (1903),
44-45, ill. [C. Fabritius]; Bode 1906, 57 [P.d.H.]; HdG no.
273; G. J. Hoogewerff, in *l'Arte*, 1911, 359; Cust 1914, 205;
R, 34, 35, 105, ill. frontispiece; Bode 1919, 306; Hermanin
1924, no. 401; Lilienfeld 1924, 453; CB, 3; Val. 1926, 52;
BM, 379; O. Benesch, in *Belvedere*, 12 (1928), 65-6 [B.
Fabritius]; A. Bredius, *Belvedere*, 13 (1928), 14; O. Benesch,
in *Belvedere*, 13 (1928), 94 [B. Fabritius]; Bredius 1928, 65;
Val. no. 22 [1654 or 5]; anon. reviewer of Val. in *P.*, 5 (1930),
xxxiv [neither P.d.H. nor C. Fabritius].

Attributed to Palamedesz by Venturi, the picture was later
assigned to Carel Fabritius by Müller, who felt it was the
forerunner of that artist's *Sentinel* in Schwerin. Bode and
Hofstede de Groot attributed the work to De Hooch and,
like most later writers, assumed that it was executed under

the influence of C. Fabritius. The fully rounded forms differ
from De Hooch's more angular soldiers. The broad facial
type is characteristic of the figures of Carel's brother Barent,
to whom Benesch assigned the picture; compare the figures
and the arch motif in Barent's *Slaughtered Pig* (signed and
dated 1656, Gemäldegalerie, Berlin–Dahlem, no. 819 B),
which also once was attributed to De Hooch.

D 26. **A Family Group in a Garden★**
Present location unknown.
Panel 53×70 cm.
PROV.: R. Semmel, by 1929;[1] Sale R. Semmel, Berlin,
21/11/1933, no. 24, ill.; Sale P. Chavan, Geneva, 20/3/1937,
no. 7, pl. 4.
EXH.: Berlin (Schäffer) 1929, no. 31.
LIT.: Val. no. 3 [c. 1647; not entirely certain]; Wichmann
1929, 11 [circle of the Le Nains]; P.W., 'Die Gemäldesamm-
lung Semmel, Berlin,' in *P.*, 5 (1930), 278, ill. 277; Juynboll
1935, 190-2 [Peter Angillis].
First attributed to De Hooch by Plietzsch,[2] the work was
probably correctly assigned to the Franco-Flemish artist Peter
Angillis (1685-1734) by Juynboll.
NOTES: [1] Val. no. 3. [2] ibid.

D 27. **Three Figures in a Flower Garden** (Plate 185)
The Brooklyn Museum, Brooklyn, acc. no. 34.481. Michael
Friedsam Bequest.
Panel 52×41.9 cm.
PROV.: Sale C. Ploos van Amstel, Amsterdam, 3/3/1800, no.
12—Coclers, 21 fl; brought to England by Woodin, 1840;[1]
E.N. Dennys, London, 1841[2] & 1842;[3] Sale Mrs. J. Ashley,
London, 31/5/1907, no. 40—Agnew, £630; Langton Douglas,
London;[4] Humphrey Ward, London;[5] dlr. F. Wildestein,
Paris (sold to) A. de Ridder, Schönberg near Cronberg,[6] cat.
1910, no. 26; Sale A. de Ridder, Paris, 2/6/1924, no. 29—
Kleinberger, 250,000 frs; Michael Friedsam, New York, by
1927,[7] bequeathed to the Metropolitan Museum, which
presented it to the Brooklyn Museum.
EXH.: (a) London, B.I., 1841, no. 60; (b) New York
(Kleinberger) 1913, no. 36, ill.; (c) Rotterdam 1935, no. 35,
fig. 38; (d) Brooklyn 1945-6, no. 25; (e) Hartford 1950-1, no.
26 [Sch. of P.d.H.].
LIT.: S s no. 17; Havard 1880, 118: 1, 125: 1; HdG nos.
310 & 312; Bode 1910, no. 26; BM, 70-1; Val. no. 36
[c. 1656]; Val. 1932, 319.
The coarse technique, rather strident palette and simplistic
perspective suggest the work of a follower. A dog in the
foreground, a basket held by the woman, and vines on the
house proved to be later overpaintings and were removed in
c. 1935.[8]
NOTES: [1] S s no. 17. [2] Exh. a. [3] S s no. 17. [4] Bode 1910. [5] ibid.
[6] ibid. [7] BM, 71. [8] cf. Val. no. 36.

D 28. **A Woman with a Child Blowing Bubbles in a
Courtyard** (Plate 186)
D.M. Koetser, Zurich.
Panel 59×52 cm. Signed left in shadow by gate: P. de
Hooghe
PROV.: Sale H. Ker Colville, Market Drayton, n.d., no.
928—H.M. Clark; dlr. Colnaghi, London, 1925;[1] H.A.
Wernher, London, by 1929;[2] Sale Wernher, London,
27/6/1975, no. 72.
EXH.: (a) London, R.A., 1929, no. 327; (b) London (Slatter)

1945, no. 24, ill. (c) London (Wildenstein) 1946, no. 24; (d) Paris 1950–1, no. 54 [*c.* 1656].

LIT.: BM, 69, ill. 68; Val. no. 34 [*c.* 1656]; Val. 1932, 319.

While the composition resembles that of Cat. 38, the broader execution and the less subtly modulated colour scheme indicate another hand. The garden plants are treated in the same manner as in Cat. D 27 (Plate 185), suggesting that both works may be by the same follower.

NOTES: [1] BM, 69. [2] Exh. a & Val. no. 34.

D 29. *A Party Eating Oysters on a Terrace*★

Present location unknown.

Canvas 62×48 cm. Signed.[1]

PROV.: Mrs. V. Le Chesne, Leipzig, 1921;[2] Sale J.L. Crawford et al. (Private Collection, New York), New York, 20/2/1946, no. 68, ill.; Sale S. Borchard et al. (Private Collection, New York), New York, 9/1/1947, no. 34.

LIT.: Lilienfeld 1924–5, 187; BM, 285; Val. no. 172 [after 1680]; CB 1930, 198.

Valentiner felt that the attribution was uncertain and Collins Baker doubted it. While Brière-Misme likened the picture to works by Hieronymus Janssens, Gudlaugsson[3] offered the plausible suggestion that it could be a copy after a lost work by G.P. van Zijl; compare the general conception and arrangement of Van Zijl's *Letter* (monogrammed, F.C. Butot Collection).[4]

NOTES: [1] BM, 285. [2] Borchard Sale cat. [3] RKD notes. [4] Bernt, III, no. 1957.

D 30. *A Party on a Terrace*★

Present location unknown.

Panel 75×99 cm.

PROV.: Private Collection, Mannheim, 1929.[1]

LIT.: Val. no. 173 (below) [after 1680]; CB 1930, 198.

Valentiner submitted the attribution tentatively and Collins Baker doubted it. Like a similar picture in the Johnson Collection in Philadelphia,[2] which also was formerly assigned to De Hooch, the work is probably Flemish in origin.

NOTES: [1] Val. no. 173. [2] Cat. (1972), no. 502, ill.

D 31. *Figures with a Coach in a Courtyard*★

Present location unknown.

Canvas 101.5×84.5 cm.

PROV.: Dlr. Van Diemen, Berlin, 2/1924; Sale L. Jay et al, (Gen. Konsul R[oussel]), Frankfurt, 31/5–2/6/1934, no. 65, pl. 8.

LIT.: Lilienfeld 1924–5, 187, ill.; Val. no. 169 [after 1680]; CB 1930, 198.

Lilienfeld's and Valentiner's attribution to De Hooch was correctly doubted by Collins Baker. The figure types and the treatment of the architecture seem more typical of Job Berckheyde.

D 32. *Figures with a Coach in a Courtyard*★

Present location unknown.

Canvas 64×80 cm. Signed on back of carriage: P.D.H.

PROV.: J. Bell, London, 1881;[1] Sale Crews, London, 2/7/1915, no. 55 [Ochtervelt]; Sale Beith, London, 8/4/1938, no. 24, ill.—Katz; dlr. Katz, Dieren, 1938;[2] Sale Goudstikker, Berlin, 12/3/1941, no. 55, pl. 29; dlr. P. de Boer, Amsterdam, 1963[3] & 1967.[4]

EXH.: (a) Dieren (Katz) 1938, no. 45; (b) Amsterdam (De Boer) 1963, no. 19, ill. [P.d.H. & L. de Jongh]; (c) Paris, I.N., 1967, no. 51, pl. 29.

LIT.: HdG no. 307; R, 101; Lilienfeld 1924–5, 187–8, n. 8; BM, 272 [doubts attr.]; Val. no. 253 [H. van der Burch]; T, 51, ill.; Plietzsch, fig. 81 [L. de Jongh]; Wagner 1971, 44 [L. de Jongh].

Despite the putative monogram of De Hooch, Plietzsch's attribution to De Jongh is undoubtedly correct. The treatment of the courtyard space resembles the latter's painting in Detroit[5] and the figures and especially the dogs are characteristic of De Jongh's work. There seems no reason to suppose, as was suggested in the De Boer catalogue of 1963, that the work was a joint effort of the two artists.

NOTES: [1] Crews Sale cat. 1915. [2] Exh. a. [3] Exh. b. [4] Exh. c. [5] acc. no. 58.169; repr. Plietzsch, fig. 78.

D 33. *Soldiers in Camp*★

Present location unknown.

Canvas 77×100 cm.

PROV.: Dlr. P. de Boer, 1929,[1] 1930[2] and 1932.[3]

EXH.: (a) Amsterdam (De Boer) 1930, no. 47, ill.; (b) Amsterdam (De Boer) 1932, no. 66.

LIT.: Val. 1926, 51; Val. xv, no. 1 (1647–50); T, 6–8, ill. 7; Fleischer 1978, 49, n. 2, fig. 1.

Fleischer reserved judgement on the attribution to De Hooch, but noted the resemblance to an early landscape probably correctly assigned to Dirck Stoop in Dresden.[4]

NOTES: [1] Val. no. 1. [2] Exh. a. [3] Exh. b. [4] Fleischer 1978, fig. 3.

D 34. *A Couple on Horseback with a Gipsy in a Landscape* (Plate 187)

Dienst Verspreide Rijkskollekties, The Hague, no. NK 2428.

Canvas 97×130 cm.

PROV.: Sale S. Harvey et al., London, 13/12/1923, no. 100 [A. Cuyp]; dlrs. Asscher, Koetser & Welker, London, 1924;[1] P. Bottenwieser, Berlin, 1925;[2] dlr. Goudstikker, Amsterdam, 1926,[3] 1927[4] and 1935;[5] dlr. P. de Boer, Amsterdam.[6]

EXH.: (a) Berlin 1925, no. 182; (b) Enschede (Goudstikker) 1926, no. 14, ill. [attr. to P.d.H.]; (c) Rotterdam (Goudstikker) 1927, no. 35, ill.; (d) Rotterdam 1935, no. 30, fig. no. 34.

LIT.: Lilienfeld 1924, 453; Lilienfeld 1924–5, 184, ill. 185; CB, 2; H. Kauffmann, *O.H.*, 42 (1925), 286; Val. 1926, 51; BM, 362, 364 n. 3, 366, ill. 365 [*c.* 1648]; Val. 1927, 69; Bredius 1928, 67 [L. de Jongh]; Val. xv, no. 6 [*c.* 1650]; T, 6–9, ill. 5; Fleischer 1978, 49, fig. 5.

The picture was sold in 1923 as an Albert Cuyp. At that time the men walking in the distance at the left and the shepherdess and her flock at the right were not visible. Independent of one another, Hofstede de Groot and Lilienfeld first attributed the work to De Hooch.[7] Brière-Misme reported in 1927 that the artist's signature was visible near the dog; a recent examination revealed no evidence of a signature. Kauffmann first noted the resemblance to the art of Ludolf de Jongh and Bredius attributed it unequivocally to the artist. Valentiner and Van Thienen revived the attribution to De Hooch, which has recently been supported by Fleischer. When the work is compared with various hunting scenes by De Jongh,[8] Bredius's attribution to that artist seems entirely justified. The combination of a thinly painted, luminous country vista with precisely executed foliage details in the foreground is typical of the artist, as are the figure and animal types. Individual motifs, like the gun carrier who is partially obscured as he mounts the hill also reappear in De Jongh's art. Brière-Misme's theory that the work could be a companion piece to a picture by Ochtervelt (Sale Amsterdam,

3/4/1900, no. 68: Panel 91×123 cm)[9] seems unlikely despite the similarities in design and size. The resemblance does, however, provide additional evidence of De Jongh's influence on the younger painters of Rotterdam.

NOTES: [1] Lilienfeld 1924, 453. [2] Exh. a. [3] Exh. b. [4] Exh. c. [5] Exh. d. [6] RKD photo. [7] According to Lilienfeld 1924. [8] See examples: signed Rijksmuseum, Amsterdam, no. A 1858; signed, Schwagermann Coll., Schiedam, 1935, repr. exh. Rotterdam, 1935, cat. no. 61, fig. 121; Sale, London, 3/7/1925, no. 155; present location unknown, ill. Fleischer 1978, fig. 7. [9] Fleischer, 1978, fig. 6.

D 35. *The Gipsy Fortune-Teller*★ (Plate 188)
National Museum, Danzig, inv. no. MI.429.
Panel 52×42 cm. Signed lower left: P D hooch
PROV.: Sale Viscount Hampden et al. (a.c.), London, 28/11/1938, no. 139—Fenouil.
LIT.: W. Drost, *Die Danziger Gemäldegalerie. Neuerwerbungen*, Danzig, 1943, 10; Tomkiewicz 1950, no. 153, pl. 146; Danzig Mus. cat. 1969, no. 64, ill.
Old photographs reveal that the signature has been falsified. The figure types are closer to those of A. Palamedesz.

D 36. *Full-Length Portrait of a Woman*★
Present location unknown.
Panel 36×28 cm. Signed: P.v.H. 16–
PROV.: Sale Lachmann et al., Munich, 2/6/1902, no. 216, ill.
LIT.: HdG no. 328.

D 37. *Portrait of a Woman in a Landscape* (Plate 189)
Musées Royaux des Beaux-Arts, Brussels, inv. no. 3692.
Canvas 70.5× 55 cm. Signed lower right: P.D.H.
PROV.: Acq. Sale Brussels (Fievez), 7/1903.
EXH.: Brussels, 1962-3, 112.
LIT.: R, 32, 97; Brussels. Mus. cat. 1922, no. 690; BM, 57, n. 1; I.Q. van Regteren Altena, in *M.B.K.*, 7 (1930), 380.
On the advice of Bredius,[1] the work has been catalogued as a combined effort of De Hooch (the portrait) and another artist (the landscape; assigned to J. van Mosscher by Van Regteren Altena). The portrait, whose costume suggests a date of *c.* 1650-5, is perhaps by the same hand as the three-quarter length *Portrait of a Woman in a Landscape* in the Duchange Sale, Brussels, 25/6/1923, no. 92, ill. (also incorrectly as by De Hooch). The present work has also been likened to the art of H.M. Doncker.[2]
NOTES: [1] See R, 32. [2] Exh.

D 38. *Portrait of a Woman with a Fan*★
Present location unknown.
Canvas 72×61 cm. Signed (falsely): P. D. Hooghe/ A 165(?)[1]
PROV.: A. van den Heuvel, Brussels, 1935.[2]
EXH.: Rotterdam 1935, no. 54a [attr. to P.d.H.], fig. 58. H. Schneider attributed the work to L. de Jongh.[3]
NOTES: [1] RKD photo mat. [2] Exh. [3] RKD photo.

D 39. *A Woman Bending to Pick up a Teapot*★ (Plate 190)
Present location unknown.
Drwg., black chalk, 27.8× 15.2 cm.
PROV.: R.P. Roupell; J.P. Heseltine, cat. 1910, no. 12.
LIT.: *Original Drawings of the Dutch School in the Collection of J.P.H* [eseltine], London, 1910, no. 12, pl. 10.
The drawing was probably a study for the figure of the maidservant at the right of the painting of a *Gentleman Offering a Peach to a Lady at a Table* by M. van Musscher. (Sale Ingram, London, 12/3/1926, no. 44, ill.)

D 40. *A Seated Woman Sleeping*★ (Plate 192)
Present location unknown.
Drwg., red chalk, 20× 15 cm.
PROV.: Sale, Dr. Sterne, Vienna, 12/1/1886, no. 280, ill.; E. Parsons & Sons, London, cat. 46, no. 203.
Similar drawings (see Kupferstichkabinett, Berlin, no. 5912) have been attributed to Cornelis Bega.

D 41. *A Standing Woman* (Plate 191)
British Museum, London, no. 1836.8.11.43.
Drwg., black chalk, 23.2× 10.9 cm.
PROV.: Sheepshanks Collection, inv. 1836, as C. Bega.
LIT.: A.M. Hind, *Catalogue of Drawings By Dutch and Flemish Artists . . . in the British Museum*, 4 vols., London, III, 120, pl. LXIV.

D 42. *A Woman with a Basket*★ (Plate 193)
Musée des Beaux-Arts, Besançon, ref. no. 2754.
Drwg., black chalk on blue paper, heightened with white, 28× 22 cm. Inscribed lower left in pen: P de Hooge
PROV.: Jean Gigoux, 1896.

D 43. *A Soldier Playing Cards*★ (Plate 194)
Detroit Institute of Arts, Detroit, acc. no. 5704. Gift of W.R. Valentiner.
Drwg., black and brown chalk, 16.2× 14 cm.
PROV.: Sale E.C. Innes, London, 3/12/1935, no. 10.

1. Self-Portrait (?) (Cat. 1). 1648–9(?). Rijksmuseum, Amsterdam

2. A Soldier Smoking (Cat. 2). c. 1650. John G. Johnson Collection, Philadelphia

3. Liberation of St. Peter (Cat. 3). *c.* 1650–5. Ch. de Roy van Zuydewijn, Amsterdam

For Cat. 4 see Colour Plate I

4. A Soldier with an Empty Glass and a Serving Woman
(Cat. 5). *c.* 1650–5. Museum Boymans - Van Beuningen,
Rotterdam

5. A Soldier Offering a Glass of Wine to a Seated Woman
(Cat. 6). *c.* 1650–5. Hermitage, Leningrad

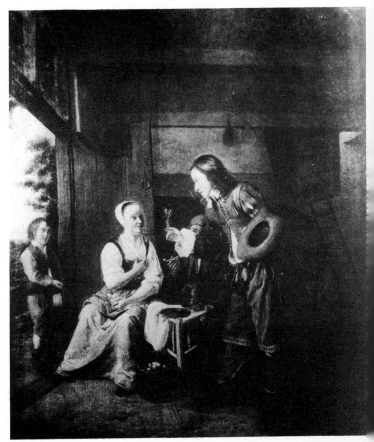

6. Two Soldiers and a Serving Woman with a Trumpeter in a Stable (Cat. 7). *c.* 1650–5. David M. Koetser, Zurich

7. Two Soldiers with a Serving Woman and a Boy in a Tavern (Cat. 8). *c.* 1650–5. Present location unknown

8. Soldiers with a Serving Woman and a Flute Player (Cat. 10). *c.* 1650–5. Borghese Gallery, Rome

9A. A Soldier and a Serving Girl with Card Players (Cat. 11). *c.* 1655. Wallraf-Richartz Museum, Cologne

9B. Soldiers Playing Cards, with a Woman and Two Children (Cat. 11 bis). *c.* 1655. P. de Boer Collection, Amsterdam

10. Two Soldiers Drinking with a Serving Woman (Cat. 9). *c.* 1650–5. Private Collection

11. Tric-Trac Players (Cat. 12). *c.* 1652–5. National Gallery of Ireland, Dublin. See also Colour Plate II

12. A Seated Soldier with a Standing Serving Woman (Cat. 13). *c.* 1652–5. Private Collection, England

13. A Soldier Dressing and a Woman Making a Bed (Cat. 15). *c.* 1655–7. Pushkin Museum of Fine Arts, Moscow

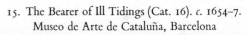

14. A Soldier with Dead Birds and Other Figures in a Stable (Cat. 14). *c.* 1655–7. National Gallery, London

15. The Bearer of Ill Tidings (Cat. 16). *c.* 1654–7. Museo de Arte de Cataluña, Barcelona

16. Mother and Child with a Serving Woman (Cat. 17). *c*. 1657. Private Collection, Switzerland

17. A Woman Preparing Vegetables, with a Child (Cat. 18). *c.* 1657. Louvre, Paris

18. A Merry Company with Two Men and Two Women (Cat. 19). *c.* 1657. Metropolitan Museum of Art, New York

For Cat. 20 and 21 see Colour Plates IV and V.

19. Drawing after Woman and Child in a Street (Cat. 22).
c. 1657–9. Formerly Lord Ashburton, The Grange; destroyed by fire

20. A Woman and Two Men in an Arbour (Cat. 23). c. 1657–60.
Metropolitan Museum of Art, New York

For Cat. 24 see Colour Plate III

21. Detail from Colour Plate III: A Family in a Courtyard (Cat. 24). c. 1657–60. Akademie der bildenden Künste, Vienna

22. Two Soldiers Playing Cards and a Girl Filling a Pipe (Cat. 25). *c.* 1657–8. Private Collection, Switzerland.

23. A Girl Drinking with Two Soldiers (Cat. 26). 1658. Louvre, Paris

24. A Soldier Paying a Hostess (Cat. 27). 1658. Marquis of Bute Collection

25. Detail from Plate 24

26. Detail from Colour Plate VI: Card Players (Cat. 28). 1658. Royal Collection. *Reproduced by gracious permission of Her Majesty Queen Elizabeth II*

27. A Woman Drinking with Two Men, and a Serving Woman (Cat. 29). *c.* 1658. National Gallery, London

28. A Woman with a Baby on her Lap, and a Small Child (Cat. 30). 1658. Private Collection, England

29. A Woman and Child in a Pantry (Cat. 31). *c.* 1658. Rijksmuseum, Amsterdam

30. Detail from Colour Plate VII: A Woman Nursing an Infant, with a Child (Cat. 32). *c.* 1658–60. M. H. de Young Memorial Museum, San Francisco

31. Detail from Colour Plate VII: A Woman Nursing an Infant, with a Child (Cat. 32). *c.* 1658–60. M. H. de Young Memorial
Museum, San Francisco

32. Detail from Colour Plate VIII: Figures Drinking in a Courtyard with an Arbour (Cat. 33). 1658. On loan to the National Gallery of Scotland, Edinburgh

33. Detail from Colour Plate IX: The Courtyard of a House in Delft, with a Woman and a Child (Cat. 34). 1658. National Gallery, London

34. Two Soldiers and a Woman Drinking in a Courtyard (Cat. 35A). *c.* 1658–60. National Gallery of Art, Washington, D.C.

35. A Man Smoking and a Woman Drinking in a Courtyard (Cat. 35B). *c.* 1658–60. Mauritshuis, The Hague

36. Detail from Plate 34

37. Detail from Plate 39

38. Detail from Plate 34

39. Two Women in a Courtyard (Cat. 36). *c.* 1657–60. Royal Collection. *Reproduced by gracious permission of Her Majesty Queen Elizabeth II*

40. A Woman Carrying a Bucket in a Courtyard (Cat. 37). *c.* 1658–60. Private Collection, England

41. A Woman with a Glass of Wine and a Child in a Garden (Cat. 38). *c.* 1658–60. Private Collection

42. A Woman and a Child in a Courtyard (Cat. 39). *c.* 1658–60. National Gallery of Art, Washington, D.C.

43. The Bedroom (Cat. 40A). *c.* 1658–60. Staatliche Kunsthalle, Karlsruhe

44. The Bedroom (Cat. 40B). *c.* 1658–60. National Gallery of Art, Washington, D.C.

45. 'Kolf' Players (Cat. 41). *c.* 1658–60. National Trust, Polesden Lacey

46. A Woman Delousing a Child's Hair (Cat. 42). *c.* 1658–60. Rijksmuseum, Amsterdam

47. A Young Couple with a Dog (Cat. 43). *c.* 1660–5. Metropolitan Museum of Art, New York

48. A Woman and a Maid in a Courtyard (Cat. 44). 1660–1 or 1663. National Gallery, London. See also Colour Plate X

49. A Girl with a Basket in a Garden (Cat. 45). 1661? Kunstmuseum, Basel

For Cat. 46 see Colour Plate XI

50. A Soldier Smoking, with a Woman by a Hearth (Cat. 47). *c.* 1660–3. Baron van der Feltz, Holland

51. A Woman Preparing Bread and Butter for a Boy (Cat. 48). *c.* 1660–3. Kunstmuseum, Düsseldorf, on loan

52. A Boy Handing a Woman a Basket in a Doorway (Cat. 49). *c.* 1660–3. Wallace Collection, London

53. A Woman Reading, with a Child (Cat. 50). *c.* 1662–6. Present location unknown

54. A Woman Lacing her Bodice beside a Cradle (Cat. 51). *c.* 1661–3. Staatliche Museen, Berlin-Dahlem

55. Detail from Plate 54

56. Two Women beside a Linen Chest, with a Child (Cat. 52). 1663. Rijksmuseum, Amsterdam

57. Detail from Colour Plate XII: Family Portrait Group Making Music (Cat. 53). 1663. The Cleveland Museum of Art, Cleveland

For Cat. 54 see Colour Plate XIII.

58. An Officer and a Woman Conversing, and a Soldier at a Window (Cat. 55). *c.* 1663–5. Germanisches Museum, Nuremberg

59. A Party of Four Figures at a Table (Cat. 56). *c.* 1663–5. Metropolitan Museum of Art, New York

60. A Party of Five Figures, with a Man Entering from a Doorway (Cat. 57). *c.* 1663–5. Museu Nacional de Arte Antiga, Lisbon

61. Card Players beside a Fireplace, with an Embracing Couple and a Serving Boy (Cat. 58), *c.* 1663–5. Louvre, Paris

62. Three Figures at a Table in a Garden (Cat. 59). *c.* 1663–5. Rijksmuseum, Amsterdam

63. Detail from Plate 62

64. Skittles Players in a Garden (Cat. 60A). *c.* 1663–6. The James A. de Rothschild Collection, Waddesdon Manor

65. A Woman Peeling Apples, with a Small Child (Cat. 61). *c.* 1663. Wallace Collection, London

66. A Woman Placing a Child in a Cradle (Cat. 62). *c.* 1663–7. Museum and Art Gallery, Birmingham

67. A Woman Reading a Letter by a Window (Cat. 63). 1664. Museum of Fine Arts, Budapest

For Cat. 64 see Colour Plate XIV

68. A Couple with Musicians in a Hall (Cat. 65). *c.* 1664–6. Royal Museum of Fine Arts, Copenhagen

69. A Musical Party in a Hall (Cat. 68). *c.* 1664–6. Museum der bildenden Künste, Leipzig

70. A Couple Walking in the Gallery of the Town Hall (Cat. 67). *c.* 1663–5. Musée des Beaux-Arts, Strasbourg

71. The Council Chamber of the Burgomasters in the Town Hall in Amsterdam, with Figures (Cat. 66). *c.* 1664–6. The Thyssen-Bornemisza Collection, Lugano-Castagnola

72. A Man with a Glass of Wine and a Woman Lacing her Bodice (Cat. 69). 1665. Lord Barnard, Raby Castle, Darlington

73. A Woman at her Toilet, with an Officer (Cat. 70), c. 1665. Wellington Museum, Apsley House, London

74. Mother and Child by a Cradle (Cat. 71). *c.* 1665–8. Rijksmuseum, Amsterdam

75. Mother and Child by a Cradle (Çat. 72). *c.* 1665–8. Nationalmuseum, Stockholm

76. A Woman Plucking a Duck, with a Woman by a Fireplace (Cat. 73). *c.* 1665–8. National Museum, Danzig

77. Mother and Child by a Window, with a Woman Sweeping (Cat. 74). *c.* 1665–8. The Wernher Collection, Luton Hoo, Bedfordshire

78. Family Portrait on a Terrace (Cat. 75). 1667(?). Present location unknown

79. A Musical Party on a Terrace (Cat. 76). *c.* 1667. Present location unknown

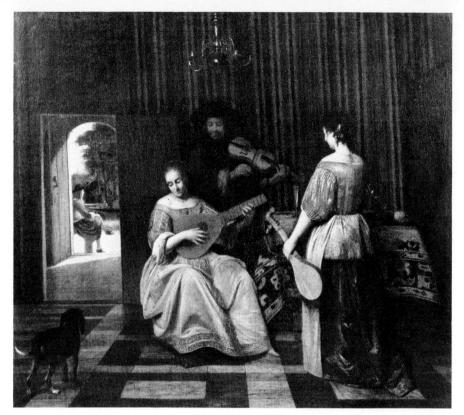

80. Two Women and a Man making Music (Cat. 77). 1667. Royal Collection, Hampton Court. *Reproduced by gracious permission of Her Majesty Queen Elizabeth II*

81. A Woman with a Mandolin and a Couple at a Table Singing (Cat. 78). *c.* 1667–70. Taft Museum,. Cincinnati

82. A Woman with a Basin and a Flagon, and a Man Dressing (Cat. 79). *c.* 1667–70. Metropolitan Museum of Art, New York

83. A Wounded Man Being Treated in a Stable (Cat. 80). *c.* 1667. Present location unknown

84. Mother and Child, with a Boy Descending a Stair (Cat. 81). 1668. H. Bischoff, Bremen

85. A Mother Sewing, with a Child (Cat. 82). *c.* 1668. The Thyssen-Bornemisza Collection, Lugano-Castagnola

86. A Woman Sewing and a Man Drinking (Cat. 83). *c.* 1668. Michaelis Collection, The Old Town House, Cape Town

87. A Woman Receiving a Letter from a Man (Cat. 84). *c.* 1668–70. Kunsthalle, Hamburg

88. A Woman Reading a Letter, and a Man at a Window (Cat. 85). *c.* 1668–70. Nationalmuseum, Stockholm

89. A Man and Two Women Conversing (Cat. 86). *c.* 1668–70. City Art Museum, Manchester

90. Two Women Teaching a Child to Walk (Cat. 87). *c.* 1668–72. Museum der bildenden Künste, Leipzig

91. A Woman Handing a Coin to a Serving Woman with a Child (Cat. 88). *c.* 1668–72. Los Angeles County Museum of Art, Los Angeles

92. **A Woman with a Child and a Serving Woman** (Cat. 89).   93. Women with a Child Feeding a Parrot (Cat. 90).
c. 1668–72. Present location unknown   *c.* 1668–72. Private Collection, England

94. Three Women and a Man with a Monkey on a Terrace (Cat. 91). 1669. Private Collection, England

95. Portrait of the Jacott-Hoppesack Family (Cat. 92). *c.* 1670. Private Collection, England

96. A Woman and a Young Man with a Letter (Cat. 94). 1670. Rijksmuseum, Amsterdam

97. A Merry Company with a Trumpeter (Cat. 93). *c.* 1670. Musées Royaux des Beaux-Arts, Brussels

98. A Man Playing the Lute and a Woman Singing (Cat. 95). Probably 1670. Present location unknown

99. Card Players at a Table (Cat. 96). *c.* 1670–4. Private Collection

100. Woman and Child, with a Serving Woman Holding Asparagus (Cat. 98). *c.* 1670–4. Present location unknown

101. A Man Reading a Letter to a Woman (Cat. 97). *c.* 1670–4. Private Collection, France

102. Two Women and a Child by a Fireplace (Cat. 99). *c.* 1670–4. North Carolina Museum of Art, Raleigh

103. A Woman Seated beside a Cradle, with an Older Woman (Cat. 100). *c.* 1670–4. Pushkin Museum of Fine Arts, Moscow

104. A Woman and a Serving Girl with a Fish (Cat. 101). *c.* 1670–4. Museum Boymans - van Beuningen, Rotterdam

105. Woman and Child with a Parrot (Cat. 102). 1673. Present
location unknown

106. A Woman Knitting, with a Serving Woman and a Child
(Cat. 103). c. 1673. Private Collection, England

107. Two Women and a Child Preparing to Depart (Cat. 104). c. 1673. Pushkin Museum of Fine Arts, Moscow

108. A Couple Playing Music at a Table, with a Serving Woman and a Couple Embracing (Cat. 105). *c.* 1673–5. Private Collection, England

109. Two Embracing Couples, with a Man Smoking and a Serving Boy (Cat. 106). *c.* 1673–5. Private Collection

110. A Musical Party with Four Figures (Cat. 108). 1674. Academy of Arts, Honolulu

111. A Music Party with Five Figures (Cat. 109). *c.* 1674. Royal Museum of Fine Arts, Copenhagen. See also Colour Plate XV

112. A Musical Company with Five Figures (Cat. 110). *c.* 1674. Deder Collection

113. A Merry Company with a Trumpeter (Cat. 107). *c.* 1673–5. Staatliche Museen, Berlin-Dahlem

114. An Officer Paying a Woman in a Stable (Cat. 111). *c.* 1674. Metropolitan Museum of Art, New York

115. Mother and Child with a Serving Girl (Cat. 112A). *c.* 1674–6. John G. Johnson Collection, Philadelphia

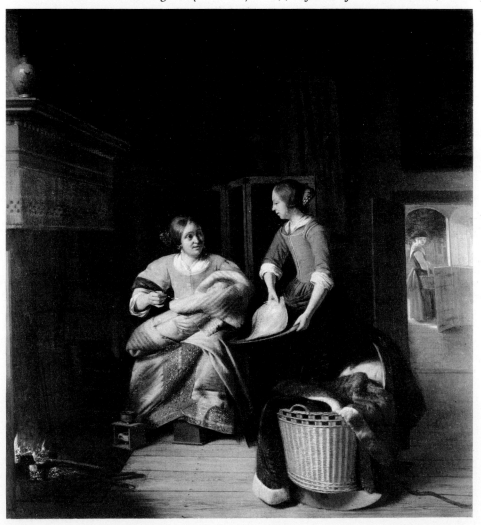

116. Mother and Child by a Cradle (Cat. 113). *c.* 1674–6. Detroit Institute of Arts, Detroit

117. A Party of Six Figures (Cat. 114). Probably 1675. Philadelphia Museum of Art, Philadelphia

118. A Standing Woman with a Woman Playing the Cello (Cat. 115). c. 1675. Private Collection, West Germany

119. A Musical Party (Cat. 116). c. 1675. Indianapolis Museum of Art, Indianapolis

120. A Musical Party with Twelve Figures (Cat. 117). *c.* 1675–7. Wellington Museum, Apsley House, London

121. Three Figures at a Table, and a Couple at a Harpsichord (Cat. 118). *c.* 1675–7. Lord Barnard, Raby Castle, Darlington

122. A Man and a Serving Woman behind a Screen, with Card Players (Cat. 119). *c.* 1675–80. Present location unknown

123. A Couple Playing Cards, with a Serving Woman (Cat. 120). *c.* 1675–80. Metropolitan Museum of Art, New York

124. A Party of Four Figures at a Table (Cat. 121). *c.* 1675–7. Corcoran Gallery of Art, Washington, D.C.

125. A Couple with a Parrot (Cat. 122). *c.* 1675–7. Wallraf-Richartz Museum, Cologne

126. An Asparagus Vendor, with Two Women and a Man (Cat. 123). *c.* 1675–80. Private Collection, Minneapolis

127. A Woman Giving Money to a Girl with a Marketing Basket, with a Woman Sweeping (Cat. 124). *c.* 1675–80. Present location unknown

128. A Mother with Two Children and a Serving Woman (Cat. 125). *c.* 1675–80. Present location unknown

129. A Serving Woman and an Officer, with Card Players (Cat. 126). *c.* 1675–80. The Saltram Collection, National Trust, Plympton

130. A Woman Seated by a Fire with Two Gaming Soldiers (Cat. 127). *c.* 1675–80. Present location unknown

131. Tavern Scene with a Smoker (Cat. 128). *c.* 1675–80. Nationalmuseum, Stockholm

132. A Woman Holding a Wineglass in a Doorway (Cat. 129). *c.* 1675–80. John C. Weber, U.S.A.

133. A Doctor and a Sick Woman (Cat. 132). *c.* 1675–80. Present location unknown

134. A Man with a Book, and Two Women (Cat. 133). 1676. Staatliche Museen, East Berlin

135. Mother and Child with a Serving Woman Holding a Duck (Cat. 130). *c.* 1675–80. Worcester Art Museum, Worcester, Mass.

136. Mother and Child by a Fireplace (Cat. 131). *c.* 1675–80. Present location unknown

137. A Musical Party in a Courtyard (Cat. 134). 1677. National Gallery, London. See also Colour Plate XVI.

138. Two Men and a Serving Woman in a Courtyard (Cat. 135). *c.* 1677–80. Royal Museum of Fine Arts, Copenhagen

139. A Woman with a Duck, and a Woman with a Cabbage (Cat. 136). After 1677. Present location unknown

140. A Musical Party with Three Figures and a Serving Woman (Cat. 137). *c.* 1677–80. Present location unknown

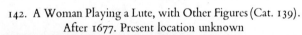

141. A Woman with a Lute and a Man with a Violin (Cat. 138). After 1677. Present location unknown

142. A Woman Playing a Lute, with Other Figures (Cat. 139). After 1677. Present location unknown

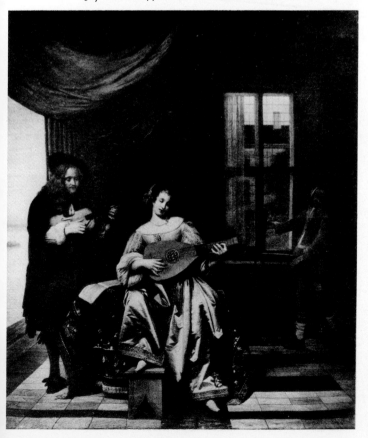

143. A Woman Kneeling by a Fire and a Woman with a Basket (Cat. 140). 168[?]. Museum of Fine Arts, Boston

144. Two Women by a Fireplace (Cat. 141), c. 1680–4. Musée Granet, Aix-en-Provence

145. A Woman Taking Butter from a Plate Held by a Little Girl (Cat. 142). *c.* 1680 or later. Present location unknown

146. A Woman with a Serving Girl (Cat. 143). 1680? Palais des Beaux-Arts, Lille

147. A Woman Seated by a Window with a Child in a Doorway (Cat. 144). *c.* 1680. Metropolitan Museum of Art, New York

148. A Woman Sewing with a Serving Girl and a Child (Cat. 145). *c.* 1680. G. Douwes, Amsterdam, and D. M. Koetser, Zurich

149. A Woman Feeding a Parrot, with a Man and a Serving Woman (Cat. 148). *c.* 1680. Present location unknown

150. A Couple Making Music at a Table, with a Serving Girl (Cat. 146). *c.* 1680. Hermitage, Leningrad

151. A Man with a Serving Woman at a Table (Cat. 147). *c.* 1680. Present location unknown

152. A Man Offering a Letter to a Lady Feeding a Parrot
(Cat. 149). After 1680. Leger Galleries, London

153. Figures with a Parrot at a Table (Cat. 150). After 1680.
Private Collection, Holland

154. A Woman and a Man Making Music, with Dancing Dogs
(Cat. 151). After 1680. Present location unknown

155. A Woman and a Man Making Music, with Dancing Dogs
(Cat. 152). After 1680. Present location inknown

156. A Woman Kneeling by a Fire, with Figures at a Table (Cat. 153). After 1680. Present location unknown

157. A Woman Kneeling by a Fire, with a Musical Company (Cat. 154). After 1680. C. Mumenthaler Collection

158. A Couple Playing Music on a Terrace, with a Serving Woman (Cat. 155). After 1680. Private Collection

159. A Musical Party of Four Figures, with a Small Boy Dancing (Cat. 156). After 1680. Berkshire Museum, Pittsfield, Mass.

160. Two Women, and a Man in Bed (Cat. 157). After 1680. Present location unknown

161. Three Women and a Man Making Music in a Vestibule (Cat. 158). After 1680. Present location unknown

162. Two Women and a Man Eating Oysters (Cat. 159). 1681.
Present location unknown

163. A Woman Standing before a Man Seated at a Table
(Cat. 160). 1683. Present location unknown

164. A Sportsman and a Lady in a Landscape (Cat. 161). 1684. Private Collection

165. A Musical Company of Four Figures (Cat. 162). 1684? Present location unknown

166. A Musical Company of Three Figures (Cat. 163). 1684? Present location unknown

Tentatively Accepted and Questionable Works

Works Wrongly Attributed to De Hooch

A SELECTION

167. A Woman before a Mirror, with Two Women by a Hearth (Cat. B 1). Present location unknown

168. Nocturnal Scene with a Woman Paying a Maidservant (Cat. B 2). Krannert Art Gallery, University of Illinois, Champaign

169. A Musical Company with Four Figures (Cat. B 4). Present location unknown

170. A Man Reading to a Woman with Needlework (Cat. B 5).
G. Nijssen, Barcelona

171. A Woman Receiving a Man at a Door (Cat. B 7A).
Present location unknown

172. Two Men and Two Women at a Table (Cat. B 8). Galleria Caretto, Turin

173. Two Soldiers and a Girl with a Lute (Cat. B 9). Private
Collection

174. Two Women and a Man in a Courtyard (Cat. B 12).
Present location unknown

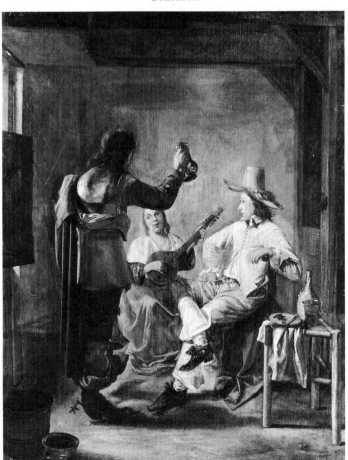

175. A Soldier, a Serving Woman and a Flute Player (Cat. B 10). John G. Johnson Collection, Philadelphia

176. Nocturnal Scene in an Inn (Cat. B 11). G. Henle, Duisburg

177. The Parents at the Door of their Rich Children (Cat. B 13). Present location unknown

178. Portrait of an Officer (Cat. B 14). Private Collection

179. A Woman Holding a Dog and Smelling a Rose (Cat. B 15). City Art Gallery, Manchester

180. Merry Company Group (Cat. D 11). Present location unknown

181. Soldiers at Reveille (Cat. D 21). North Carolina Museum of Art, Raleigh

182. Paying the Hostess (Cat. D 20). Private Collection, New York

183. Soldiers with a Serving Woman in a Stable (Cat. D 22). National Gallery, Prague

184. A Seated Soldier with a Pipe (Cat. D 25). Galleria Nazionale d'Arte Antica, Rome

185. Three Figures in a Flower Garden (Cat. D 27). The Brooklyn Museum, Brooklyn

186. A Woman with a Child Blowing Bubbles in a Courtyard (Cat. D 28). D. M. Koetser, Zurich

187. A Couple on Horseback with a Gipsy in a Landscape (Cat. D 34). Dienst Verspreide Rijkskollekties, The Hague

188. The Gipsy Fortune-Teller (Cat. D 35). Museum, Danzig

189. Portrait of a Woman in a Landscape (Cat. D 37). Musées Royaux des Beaux-Arts, Brussels

190. A Woman Bending to Pick up a Teapot (Cat. D 39). Black chalk. Present location unknown

191. A Standing Woman (Cat. D 41). Black chalk. British Museum, London

192. A Seated Woman Sleeping (Cat. D 40). Red chalk. Present location unknown

193. A Woman with a Basket (Cat. D 42). Black chalk on blue paper. Musée des Beaux-Arts, Besançon

194. A Soldier Playing Cards (Cat. D 43). Black and brown chalk. Detroit Institute of Arts, Detroit

Comparative Illustrations

Fig. 1. Nicolaes Berchem: Pastoral Landscape. 1649. Toledo Museum of Art, Toledo

Fig. 2. H. M. Sorgh: Two Smokers. Signed. With H. Schlichte Bergen, Amsterdam

Fig. 3. Ludolf de Jongh: A Man Reading a Letter. 1657. Mittelrheinisches Landesmuseum, Mainz

Fig. 4. Hendrick van der Burch: Guardroom Scene. Private Collection

Fig. 5. Gerard Terborch: 'Unwelcome News'. 1653. Maurits-huis, The Hague

Fig. 6. Gerbrand van den Eeckhout: Tric-Trac Players. 1651. Private Collection, Detroit

Fig. 7. By or after Gerrit van Honthorst: Liberation of St. Peter from Prison. Formerly J. C. E. Graaf van Lynden, Leiden

Fig. 8. Anthonie Palamedesz: A Merry Company. 1633. Rijksmuseum, Amsterdam

Fig. 9. Paulus Potter: Two Cows and a Bull. 1647. Private Collection

Fig. 10. Gerrit Houckgeest: The Interior of the Nieuwe Kerk in Delft. 1651. Mauritshuis, The Hague

Fig. 11. Delft School: The Terrace. Art Institute of Chicago, Chicago

Fig. 12. Carel Fabritius: A View in Delft. 1652. National Gallery, London

Fig. 13. Jan Vredeman de Vries: Engraving from *Scenographiae sive perspectiva*, 1560, plate 10

Fig. 14. Dirck van Delen: A Merry Company. 1629. National Gallery of Ireland, Dublin

Fig. 15. Isaak Koedijk: The Empty Beaker. 1648. Formerly
Dr. L. J. K. van Aalst, Hoevelaken

Fig. 16. Nicolaes Maes: The Idle Servant. 1655. National
Gallery, London

Fig. 17. Johannes Vermeer: A Sleeping Girl. Metropolitan
Museum of Art, New York

Fig. 18. Nicolaes Maes: A Woman Making Lace. 1655.
Private Collection

Fig. 19. Jacobus Vrel: A Woman at a Window. 1654.
Kunsthistorisches Museum, Vienna

Fig. 20. Johannes Vermeer: A Soldier with a Laughing Girl.
Frick Collection, New York

Fig. 21. Johannes Vermeer: A Girl Drinking with a Gentleman. Staatliche Museen, Berlin-Dahlem

Fig. 22. Jan Steen: Portrait of a Man with a Young Girl and Beggars (known as 'The Burgomaster of Delft and his Daughter')
1655. Private Collection

Fig. 23. Dirck van Delen: A Palace Courtyard with Figures. 1635. Herzog Anton Ulrich - Museum, Braunschweig

Fig. 24. Jan Vredeman de Vries: Engraving from *Perspective*, Part II, Antwerp 1604–5, pl. 9

Fig. 25. Samuel van Hoogstraten: Portrait of a Couple in the Garden of a Country House. 1647. Formerly art market, Berlin

Fig. 26. Gabriel Metsu: The Family of the Amsterdam Burgomaster Dr. Gilles Valckenier. Staatliche Museen, Berlin-Dahlem

Fig. 27. Gabriel Metsu: A Visit to the Nursery. 1661. Metropolitan Museum of Art, New York

Fig. 28. Gerard Terborch: 'The Parental Admonition'. Staatliche Museen, Berlin-Dahlem

Fig. 29. Emanuel de Witte: A Woman Playing the Harpsichord. Dienst Verspreide Rijkskollekties

Fig. 30. Jacob Vennekool: The North East Gallery of the Town Hall of Amsterdam. Engraving from *Afbeelding van 't Stadt Huys van Amsterdam*, 1661

Fig. 31. Barent Graat: Portrait of a Family (traditionally identified as the Deutz Family). 1658. Private Collection

Fig. 32. Johannes Vermeer: A Woman Holding Scales. National Gallery of Art, Washington, D.C.

Fig. 33. Jacob Ochtervelt: A Merry Company. 1668. Count
Natale Labia Collection, Cape Town

Fig. 34. Michiel van Musscher: Marketing Money. 1669. Sale
Weber, Hamburg, 21/2/1912, no. 330

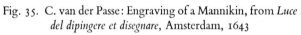

Fig. 35. C. van der Passe: Engraving of a Mannikin, from *Luce
del dipingere et disegnare*, Amsterdam, 1643

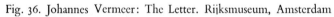

Fig. 36. Johannes Vermeer: The Letter. Rijksmuseum, Amsterdam

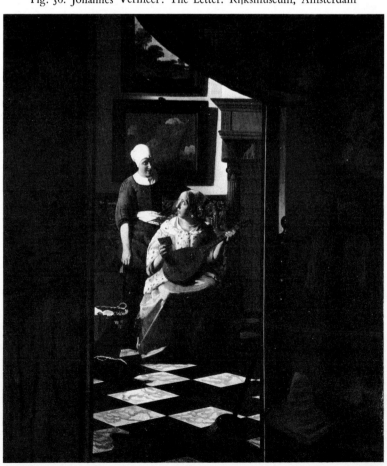

Fig. 37. Jan Sadeler after Dirck Barendsz: Mankind Awaiting the Last Judgement. Engraving

Fig. 38. Anonymous Early Seventeenth-Century Flemish Artist: The Education of the Virgin. Eszterhazy Chapel, Ering, South Bavaria

Fig. 39. Jan Saenredam after Hendrick Goltzius: Lot and his Daughters. Engraving

Fig. 40. Detail from Plate 87 (Cat. 84).

Fig. 41. C. Bloemart after Abraham Bloemart: The Nativity. 1625. Engraving

Fig. 42. Albert Haelwegh after Carel van Mander III: The
Rape of Ganymede. Engraving

Fig. 43. Jan Saenredam after Hendrick Goltzius: Morning,
from a series of Times of the Day. Engraving

Fig. 44. Geertruyt Roghman: A Woman by a Window. Engraving

Fig. 45. Jan Baptist Weenix: Mother and Child. 1647. Formerly with Van Diemen, Amsterdam

Fig. 46. Gerard Dou: An Old Woman Peeling Apples. Staatliche Museen, Berlin-Dahlem

Figs. 47–8. Adriaen van de Venne: Wife and Mother. Illustrations from Jacob Cats's *Houwelick*, second ed., The Hague, 1632

Fig. 49. A Doll's House. Centraal Museum, Utrecht

Fig. 50. 'The Coat of Arms of the Spinster'. From Jacob Cats's *Houwelick*.

Fig. 51. Emblem entitled 'Sorght voor de koele wijn niet.' From Roemer Visscher, *Sinnepoppen*, Amsterdam, 1614, I no. 32

Figs. 52–3. Two emblems from Jan Luiken, *Het Leerzaam Huisraad*, Amsterdam, 1711, no. 7

Fig. 54. Hendrick van der Burch: Nocturnal Scene with Soldiers. Monogrammed. Private Collection, Geneva

Fig. 55. Hendrick van der Burch: A Woman with a Jug in a Courtyard. Formerly monogrammed. Krannert Art Gallery, Champaign, Ill.

Fig. 56. Pieter Janssens Elinga: A Woman Reading. Alte Pinakothek, Munich

Fig. 57. Esaias Boursse: A Woman Spinning. 1661. Rijksmuseum, Amsterdam

Fig. 58. Pieter Janssens Elinga: A Woman Reading with a Maid Sweeping. Stadel Institute, Frankfurt

Fig. 59. Jacobus Vrel: A Street Scene. Marquis of Bath, Longleat

Fig. 60. Cornelis de Man: A Couple Playing Chess. Signed. Museum of Fine Arts, Budapest

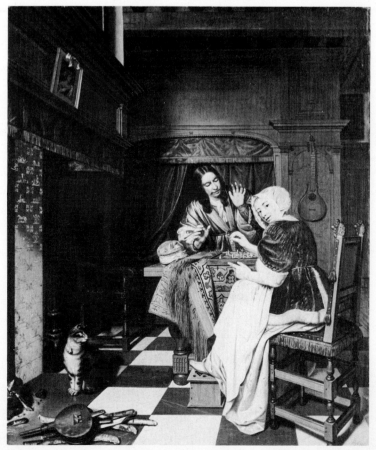

Fig. 61. Ludolf de Jongh: Women in a Garden. 1676. Count Natale Labia Collection, Cape Town

Fig. 62. Eglon van der Neer: A Dutch Interior. Museum of Fine Arts, Boston

Fig. 63. Abraham van Strij: Mother and Child in a Pantry. Dienst Verspreide Rijkskollekties

Fig. 64. Han van Meegeren: A Merry Company (forgery of De Hooch). Present location unknown

Fig. 65. Han van Meegeren: Card Players (forgery of De Hooch). Boymans - van Beuningen Museum, Rotterdam

Fig. 66. X-ray of Cat. 65 (Copenhagen)

Documents

The documents are arranged chronologically with abbreviated references (consult Bibliography) to their initial publications. For the sake of brevity, some documents, which are either published in full elsewhere or mention De Hooch only as a witness, have been partially or wholly paraphrased. Previously unpublished documents are followed by an asterisk. Some of those discovered by S. A. C. Dudok van Heel of the Municipal Archives in Amsterdam were mentioned in the catalogue of the exhibition *Art in Seventeenth Century Holland*, National Gallery, London, 1976 (designated below by the notation: 'DvH; London, 1976'). Documents without credits are the author's discoveries.

1. 31 Dec. 1628: Proclamation of the betrothal of Hendrick Hendricks de Ooge of Rotterdam to Annetgen Pieters, widow of Aernout Mote, living on the Visserdijk in Rotterdam. (Marriage Register of the Reformed Church in Rotterdam; HvR 1892).

2. 15 Jan. 1629: Marriage settlement of Hendryck Hendrijcksz. de Ooghe, bachelor, and Annetgen Pietersdr., widow of master Arnout Mota. The couple mutually promise to contract a legal marriage with the stipulation that, if one of them dies childless, the other should pay the relatives of the deceased 20 fl each. (Prot. Not. N. van der Hagen, Rotterdam, O.N.A., 107/84; communication R.A.D. Renting).*

3. 19 Jan. 1629: Marriage of the couple in the Reformed Church in Rotterdam (HvR 1892).

4. 20 Dec. 1629: Baptism of son named Pieter; father: Heindrick Heindricksen. (Baptismal Register of the Reformed Church in Rotterdam; ibid.).

5. 3 Sept. 1631: Baptism of son named Christoffel. (ibid.).

6. 23 May 1633: Baptism of son named Johannes (who apparently died soon thereafter). (ibid.).

7. 25 Feb. 1635: Baptism of second son named Johannes. (ibid.).

8. 21 Oct. 1637: Baptism of son named Hendrick; the profession of Annetge Pieters recorded as 'vroetvrou' (midwife). (ibid.).

9. 8 Nov. 1648: Burial of Annetge Pieters; her husband, Henderijck Henderijksz, recorded as living on the Visserdijk (Register of Burials, Rotterdam; ibid.).

10. 9 May 1649: Proclamation of betrothal of Heijnderick Heijndericks de Hoogh, widower living on the Visserdijk, to Adriaentge Philips de Wijmer, widow of Jan Pieters der Hoef, living on the Hoochstraet. (Marriage Register of the Reformed Church in Rotterdam; ibid.).

11. 24 May 1649: Marriage of the couple in the Reformed Church in Rotterdam (ibid.).

12. 20 July 1651: Conveyance by the heirs of the late Johannes Huijssens of a house and yard on the west side of the Lombertstraat to Hendrick de Hooge; total price: 1700 fl, of which 300 fl is paid in cash, the remainder to be mortgaged. (Schepen Archives [Conveyance Books], Rotterdam, 512/131 v; communication with R.A.D. Renting).*

13. 20 July 1651: Hendric de Hooge mortgages his house and yard on the Lombertstraat; a loan of 300 fl negotiated with the heirs of Johannes Huijssens; and a loan of 1100 fl negotiated with Jan Teunisz Leutering; both at 5% per annum and to be redeemed with at least 100 fl per annum. (Schepen Archives [Debt Books], Rotterdam, 785; communication R.A.D. Renting).*

14. 5 Aug. 1652: The will of Willem Claessen van Koxsoon (?) and Neeltgen Franssens, naming each other as universal heirs; witnesses: Pieter de Hooch and Heyndrick van der Burgh, who are both said to be residing in the city. (Prot. Not. F. Boogert, Delft, no. 1999/73).*

15. 28 May 1653: Inventory of the possessions of a servant of Monsr. Justianus de la Oranje, which have been ordered by the Sheriff (Alderman) to be sold at public auction. The servant had disappeared taking with him the coat of a second servant (dienaar), who was also a painter, called 'de Hooch, schilder'. A cloth coat and two shirts were to be reserved from the sale for the artist (Schepen Archives [Insolvente Boedels], The Hague, no. 788, 3; Bredius 1881a).

16. 11 July 1653: The Sheriff of The Hague allows Joost Laorangie and P.R. de'Hooch to take the 31 fl 6 st realized through the sale of the other servant's possessions. (Schepen Archives, Appointementen van Schepenen, The Hague, no. 547, 85v–86; Bredius 1881b).

17. 30 Nov. 1653: Baptism of son named Henricus in the Hooglandsche Kerk in Leiden; father: Barent Gast (brother-in-law of Hendrick van der Burch); witnesses: Pieter de Hooch, Jannetje van der Burgh, Maertje van der Burgh.*

18. 12 Apr. 1654: Proclamation of betrothal of Pieter de Hooch, living on the Lombertstraat in Rotterdam, and

Jannetje van der Burch, living in Delft. (Marriage Register of the Reformed Church in Rotterdam; HvR 1892).

19. 18 Apr. 1654: Proclamation of betrothal of Pieter de Hooch of Rotterdam and Jannetje van der Burch living on the Binnenwatersloot in Delft. (Marriage Register of the Reformed Church in Delft; Havard 1877).

20. 29 Apr. 1654: Maertgen Corssen van Vliet (probably Van der Burch's aunt), living in Lier, gives her brother-in-law, Joris Corsz, power of attorney, to appear before the local court on her behalf, concerning a suit raised by or against Ary Cornelisz. Keyser; witnesses: Pieter de Hooch and Heyndrick van der Burgh. (Prot. Not. F. Boogert, Delft, no 2000/40).★

21. 3 May 1654: Marriage of Pieter de Hooch and Jannetje van der Burch in the Reformed Church in Delft (Havard 1877).

22. 2 Feb. 1655: Baptism of son named Pieter; father: Pieter de Hooch; mother: Jannetje van der Burch; witnesses: Heyndrick and Jacquemyntyen van der Burch (Baptismal Register Oude Kerk, Delft; Havard 1877).

23. 28 Aug. 1655: Inventory of paintings owned by Justus de la Grange which are to be handed over to S. Pieter Persijn of Hoorn, his relative, presumably to cover a debt. The following works with their valuations were listed:

a painting by Stooter	15 fl
another by 'H. M.'	20 fl
one by Versteech	15 fl
one by the same	6 fl
one by the same	6 fl
one by Dou	6 fl
a portrait	
a picture by Blocklandt	6 fl
a landscape	12 fl
ditto	15 fl
a picture by De Hooch	20 fl
one by Pieter Paret	15 fl
one by Jan Lievens	18 fl
a painting by Van Beijeren	100 fl
one by Jan Lievens	18 fl
one by De Hooch	20 fl
a Droochsloot	26 fl
a Versteech	15 fl
a De Hooch	20 fl
a Molijn	20 fl
a portrait	
a cupid	15 fl
a small head (tronij) by Rembrandt	20 fl
a Stooter	26 fl
a Fabritius	40 fl
a small picture (stuckie)	3 fl
ditto	3 fl
a De Hooch	6 fl
a small picture	2 fl
a picture	50 fl
a Stooter	26 fl
a Droochsloot	26 fl
two small pictures by Van Goyen	3 fl
two more by the same	18 fl
a Blommaert	60 fl

a Mostaert	10 fl
an Everdingen	60 fl
a clay figure (boetseersel) by Abele	30 fl
a picture by Jan Lievens	40 fl
a drawing by Plas	15 fl
a De Hooch	20 fl
a large picture	50 fl
a clay figure by Abele	20 fl
a picture by De Bos	120 fl
six small pictures	36 fl
a picture by Versteech	18 fl
a Jan Lievens	40 fl
a De Hooch	20 fl
a Van der Stoffe	15 fl
a De Hooch	15 fl
one by 'H. M.'	15 fl
a De Hooch	12 fl
a Versteech	10 fl
a Rijkhals	10 fl
a Versteech	6 fl
a De Hooch	10 fl
ditto	20 fl
ditto	10 fl
a portrait	40 fl
a picture by Pieter Paret	50 fl
a picture by Rijkhals	6 fl

(Prot. Not. J. Spoors, Delft, no. 1676, fols. 637–9v.; Bredius 1889).

24. 6 Sept. 1655: The will of Joost Jansz. Wilmet, barge skipper from Leiden, and Pietergen Aryensdr., his wife, living on the St. Annenstr.; they name each other as heirs and state that after the survivor's death 200 fl are bequeathed to the daughters of Caspar van Stackelberg; witnesses: Pieter de Hoogh and Heynderick van der Burch (Prot. Not. F. Boogert, Delft, no. 2000, fols. 57–8).★

25. 22 Sept. 1655: De Hooch is inscribed as a member of the Guild; payment of 3 of the 12 fl required of entering members born outside the city. (Meesterboek Sint-Lucas-Gilde, Delft; Obreen, I, 1877–9 & Havard 1877).

26. 6 Dec. 1655: Baptism of son named Francois in the Nieuwe Kerk in Delft; father: Francois Bogaert; witnesses: Pieter de Hooch, Adrijana Spoors, Jacomijntje van de Burch.★

27. 1 Jan. 1656: De Hooch pays three additional guilders against his debt to the Guild (Meesterboek Sint-Lucas-Gilde, Delft; Obreen, I, 1877–8 & Havard 1877).

28. 1 Sept. 1656: Baptism of son named Cornelis in the Pieterskerk in Leiden; father: Hendrick van der Burgh; witnesses: Dirck Michiels van Rossum, Pieter d'Hooch, Aeltje Cornelis (H. van der Burch's sister-in-law).★

29. 14 Nov. 1656: Baptism of daughter named Anna in the Oude Kerk, Delft; father: Pieter de Hooch; mother: Anna van der Burch; witnesses: Hendrick de Hooch, Divertgen Jochems, Suzanna Borger (Havard 1877).

30. —— 1657: De Hooch pays 3 fl 3 st against his debt to the Guild. (Meesterboek Sint-Lucas-Gilde, Delft; Obreen, I, 1877–8 & Havard 1877).

31. 21 Dec. 1657: The will of 'Henrick de Hoge, metselaer (bricklayer)' and his wife Ariaentje Flips de Wijmer, living on the west side of the Lomberstraat near the Molewerf in Rotterdam. He names as his heirs, his wife and his son, Pieter de Hooch, painter', or [if his son predeceases him], his grandchildren who are to divide the inheritance equally. She names as her heir her husband. If he remarries, by three months after the wedding day he must pay her two brothers and sister, or in the event of the death of the latter, to her children, 100 fl (each or together?). If he does not remarry, three quarters of her wealth are to go to her husband's first son, Pieter, or his descendants, and the remaining quarter to her aforementioned relatives. [See also Doc. 34] (Prot. Not. J. Duyfhuisen, Rotterdam, O.N.A., 216/179; HvR 1892).

32. 23 Feb. 1659: Baptism of daughter Susanna of Barent Gast in Hooglandse Kerk, Leiden; witnesses: Frans Bogaert, Jannetje and Maritje van der Burgh.★

33. 4 Apr. 1660: Baptism of the son Mourus of Hendrick van der Burch and Cornelia van Rossem in the Wester Kerk in Amsterdam; witnesses: Mourus van Toeledo, Janneken de Hooch (Pieter de Hooch's wife), Aeltien van Rossem (H. van der Burch's sister-in-law). (Communication S.A.C. Dudok van Heel).★

34. 11 Nov. 1660: Ariaentje Flips de Wijmer revokes her former will (see Doc. 31) and names her husband, Hendrick de Hooch, as her sole heir, save for 50 fl to go to her siblings. (Prot. Not. B. Roose, Rotterdam, 678/846).★

35. 14 Nov. 1660: Burial of Ariaentje Flips de Wijmer in Rotterdam. (HvR 1829).

36. 15 April 1661: Baptism of daughter named Diewertje in the Wester Kerk in Amsterdam; father: Pieter de Hoogh; mother: Jannetje van der Burch; witnesses: Francoys Boghert, Marritien van der Burgh. (DvH; London, 1976).

37. 19 June 1661: Announcement of betrothal of Henrick de Hooghe, widower from Rotterdam, to Christina Langenberg, spinster from Colonia, living in Middelburg. With the consent of the Reformed Church to marry at Middelburg on 3 July 1661. (Marriage Register of the Reformed Church, Rotterdam).★

38. 5 Jan. 1663: Baptism of son named Fransois in the Oude Kerk in Amsterdam; father: Pieter de Hoogh; witnesses: Francois Boghert, Saertje Jans. (Communication S.A.C. Dudok van Heel).★

39. 20 May 1663: Gijsbrecht Corneliszn. (van) Groot and his wife Cornelia (Arentsdr.) van Sanen, living in Leiden, empower Arent van Sanen to dispose of their share of the estate of Willem Aryensz. van Linde (Cornelia's great-uncle). Witnesses: Johannes Boogert and Pieter de Hooch. (Prot. Not. F. Boogert, Delft, no. 2004/34; communication. J.M. Montias).★

40. 2 June 1663: Burial in the Leidse Kerkhof in Amsterdam of a child of Pieter de Hoogh, living on the Regulierspad. (Communication S.A.C. Dudok van Heel).★

41. 11 Dec. 1663: Conveyance by Christina Langenberg, authorized by her husband, Hendrick de Hoogh, living in Middelburg (authorization before Jacob Jansz. de Mol, notary at Middelburg, 28 Nov. 1663), of a house and yard on the west side of the Lombertstraat to Vincent Symonsz. de Ruijt; total price: 1600 fl, paid in cash. (Schepen Archives [Conveyance Books], Rotterdam, 518/158; communication R.A.D. Renting).★

42. 1 Oct. 1664: Baptism of a daughter named Dieuwertien in the Zuider Kerk, Amsterdam; father: Pieter de Hoogh; witnesses: Francoys Boogaert, Saertje Jans. (Communication S.A.C. Dudok van Heel).★

43. 27 March 1665: Burial in the Leidse Kerkhof in Amsterdam of a child of Pieter de Hoogh, living on the Engelspad. (Communication S.A.C. Dudok van Heel).★

44. 27 June 1666: Baptism of a daughter named Anna in the Ooster Kerk in Amsterdam; father: Pieter de Hoogh; witnesses: Henricus de Hoogh, Marritje Simons. (Communication S.A.C. Dudok van Heel).★

45. 22 Nov. 1668: Pieter de Hoogh testifies that he has been living on the Konijnenstraat since May (1668), and complains about unruly neighbours. (According to Bredius [1889] the document appeared among the notarial records of J. de Vos, Amsterdam; however, no such document has been found).

46. 8 Oct. 1669: Last will of Gabriel van de Kemp, tailor, living on the Konijnenstraat; witnesses: Andries van Apen and Pieter de Hoogh, also living on the Konijnenstraat. (Prot. Not. J. Hellerus, Amsterdam, N.A.A., no. 2495 B, fol. 444, damaged by fire; from Bredius's unpub. papers at the RKD).★

47. 13 Nov. 1670: The artist offers testimony in the law suit brought by Adriana van Heusden against the painter Emanuel de Witte (for a full discussion of the case in point, see Manke, 4–5, 69). Recorded as being about 40 years old and living on the Konijnenstraat, De Hoogh testifies that three years earlier he had seen the painting in question sold by the son of Laurens Mauritsz. Doucy to the painter Johannes Collaert in the latter's house in Amsterdam. He goes on to say that S. Wijbrant van Portengen had seen the picture in Collaert's house about two years earlier. (Prot. Not. J. Hellerus, Amsterdam, N.A.A., no. 2496, fol. 996; Bredius 1889).

48. 15 & 18 Nov. 1670: Pieter de Hoogh and the painter Hieronymous Pickaart testify that they had seen the painting by De Witte in the house of Joris de Wijs in Amsterdam. (This would have occurred sometime after 1658 when De Witte came to live in the house and before Sept. 1663 when he left, taking the picture with him). (Prot. Not. C. de Grijp, Amsterdam, N.A.A., no. 2594, fol. 373–4; Bredius 1889).

49. 4 May 1672: Baptism of a son named Francoys in the Wester Kerk in Amsterdam; father: Pieter de Hoogh; witnesses: Franssoijs Boogaert, Jacomina van der Burgh (communication S.A.C. Dudok van Heel).★

50. 24 March 1684: Burial of Pieter de Hooch at the Sint Anthonis Kerkhof in Amsterdam, coming from the 'Dolhuys' (bedlam). (DvH; London, 1976).

Bibliography

Armstrong 1904 — Walter Armstrong, *The Peel Collection and the Dutch School of Painting*, London 1904.

Balkema 1844 — C. H. Balkema, *Biographie des peintres Flamands et Hollandais qui ont existé depuis Jean et Hubert van Eyck jusqu'à nos jours*, Ghent, 1844.

Bernt — *The Netherlandish Painters of the Seventeenth Century*, 3 vols., London, 1970. (German eds. 1948, 1960, 1969.)

Bille 1961 — C. Bille, *De Tempel der Kunst of het kabinet van den heer Braamkamp*, 2 vols., Amsterdam, 1961.

Blanc 1857 — Charles Blanc, *Les Trésors de l'Art à Manchester*, Paris, 1857.

Blanc 1857–8 — Charles Blanc, *Le Trésor de la curiosité*, 2 vols., Paris, 1857–8.

Blanc 1863 — Charles Blanc, *Histoire des peintres de toutes les écoles*, vol. X *École hollandaise*, Paris, 1863.

Blanc 1869 — Charles Blanc, 'Galerie Delessert', *Gazette des Beaux-Arts*, 2e per., I (1869), 201 ff.

Blankert 1975 — Albert Blankert, *Johannes Vermeer van Delft 1632–75*, Utrecht-Antwerp, 1975 (with the collaboration of Rob Ruurs & W. L. van de Watering) (revised English ed., *Vermeer of Delft*, Oxford, 1978).

Bode 1895 — W. von Bode, 'Alte Kunstwerke in den Sammlungen der Vereinigten Staaten', *Zeitschrift für bildende Kunst*, N.F., 6 (1895), 70–6.

Bode 1906 — W. von Bode, *Rembrandt und seine Zeitgenossen*, Leipzig, 1906.

Bode 1910 — W. von Bode, *Die Gemäldegalerie des Herrn A. de Ridder in seiner Villa zu Schönberg bei Cronberg im Taunus*, Berlin, 1910.

Bode 1911 — W. von Bode, 'Jan Vermeer und Pieter de Hooch als Konkurrenten', *Jahrbuch der preussischen Kunstsammlungen*, 32 (1911), 1–2.

Bode 1913 — W. Bode, *The Collection of Pictures of the late Herr A. de Ridder in his Villa at Schönberg near Cronberg in the Taunus*, (trans. H. Virgin), Berlin, 1913.

Bode 1919 — W. Bode, 'Ein neu aufgefundenes Jugendwerk von Pieter de Hooch', *Zeitschrift für bildende Kunst*, N.F., 30 (1919), 305–8.

Breckenridge 1955 — J. D. Breckenridge, *Dutch and Flemish Paintings in the William Andrews Clark Collection*, The Corcoran Gallery of Art, Washington, 1955.

Bredius 1881 — A. Bredius, 'Iets over de Hooch', *Nederlandsche Kunstbode, Beeldende Kunst, Oudheidkunde, Kunstnijverheid*, 3 (1881), 126.

Bredius 1881b — A. Bredius, 'Nog eens de Hooch', *Nederlandsche Kunstbode, Beeldende Kunst, Oudheidkunde Kunstnijverheid*, 3 (1881), 172.

Bredius 1889 — A. Bredius, 'Bijdragen tot de biographie van Pieter de Hooch', *Oud-Holland*, 7 (1889), 161–8.

Bredius — A. Bredius, *Künstler-Inventare: Urkunden zur Geschichte der Holländischen Kunst des XVIten, XVIIten und XVIIIten Jahrhunderts*, 8 vols., The Hague, 1915–22.

Bredius 1928 — A. Bredius, 'Pieter de Hooch und Ludolph de Jongh', *Kunstchronik und Kunstliteratur, Beilage zur Zeitschrift für bildende Kunst*, 62, no. 6 (Sept. 1928), 65–6.

Bredius 1939 — A. Bredius, 'Een Prachtige Pieter de Hoogh', *Oud-Holland*, 56 (1939), 126–7.

Brieger 1922 — Lothar Brieger, *Das Genrebild; die Entwicklung der bürgerlichen Malerei*, Munich, 1922.

BM 1921 — Clotilde [Brière-] Misme, 'Un Pieter de Hoogh inconnu au Musée de Lisbonne', *Gazette des Beaux-Arts*, 5e per, 4 (1921), 340–4.

BM — Clotilde Brière-Misme, 'Tableaux inédits ou peu connus de Pieter de Hooch',

Parts I–III, *Gazette des Beaux-Arts*, 5e per., 15 (Ju. 1927), 361–80; 16 (July–Aug., Nov. 1927), 51–79, 258–86.

BM 1935   C. Brière-Misme, 'Un "Intimiste" hollandais, Jacob Vrel', Part I and II, *Revue de l'art ancien et moderne*, 67–8 (1935), 97–114, 157–72.

BM 1935b   C. Brière-Misme, 'Un émule de Vermeer et de Pieter de Hooch, Cornélis de Man', Parts I and II, *Oud-Holland*, 52 (1935), 1–26, 97–120.

BM 1947–8   C. Brière-Misme, 'A Dutch Intimist, Pieter Janssens Elinga', Part I–IV, *Gazette des Beaux-Arts*, 6e per, 31 (1947), 89–102; 151–64; 32 (1948), 159–76; 347–66.

BM 1954   C. Brière-Misme, 'Un "Intimiste" hollandais Esaias Boursse, 1631–1672', Parts I–IV, *Oud-Holland*, 69 (1954), 18–30, 72–91, 150–66, 213–21.

CB   C. H. Collins Baker, *Masters of Painting. Pieter de Hooch*, London, 1925.

CB 1930   C. H. Collins Baker, 'De Hooch or not De Hooch', *The Burlington Magazine*, 57 (1930), 189–99. (Review of Valentiner).

Coremans 1949   P. B. Coremans, *Van Meegeren's Faked Vermeers and De Hooghs*, Amsterdam, 1949.

Cust 1914   Lionel Cust, 'Notes on Pictures in the Royal Collection—XXVIII', *The Burlington Magazine*, 25 (1914), 205–7.

Cust 1915   Lionel Cust, 'A Music Party by Pieter de Hooch', *The Burlington Magazine*, 26 (1914–15), 222–3.

Cust 1931   Lionel Cust, *The King's Pictures from Buckingham Palace, Windsor Castle, and Hampton Court*, London, 1931.

Dayot   A. Dayot, *Grands & Petits Maîtres Hollandais*, Paris, 1911.

Descamps   J. B. Descamps, *La vie des peintres flamands, allemands et hollandais*, 4 vols., Paris, 1753–63.

Demonts 1922   Louis Demonts, *Catalogue des peintures exposées dans les galeries*, III. *Écoles Flamande, Hollandaise, Allemande et Anglaise*, Paris, 1922.

DvH 1975   S. A. C. Dudok van Heel, 'Honderdvijftig advertenties van kunstverkopingen uit veertig jaargangen van de Amsterdamsche Courant 1672–1711', *Jaarboek Genootschap Amstelodamum*, 67 (1975), 149–73.

Ebbinge-Wubben 1969   *The Thyssen-Bornemisza Collection*, Castagnola, 2 vols., 1969 (cat. of Dutch and Flemish masters by J. C. Ebbinge Wubben).

Eisler 1923   Max Eisler, *Alt-Delft Kultur und Kunst*, Amsterdam–Vienna, 1923.

Eisler 1977   Colin Eisler, *Paintings from the Samuel H. Kress Collection*, Oxford, 1977.

Fleischer 1976   Roland E. Fleischer, 'An Altered Painting by Pieter de Hooch', *Oud-Holland*, 90 (1976), 108–14.

Fleischer 1978   Roland E. Fleischer, 'Ludolf de Jongh and the Early Work of Pieter de Hooch', *Oud-Holland*, 92 (1978), 49–67.

Foucart 1976   J. Foucart, 'Un troisième Pieter de Hooch au Louvre', *La revue du Louvre*, 26 (1972), 30–4

Freise 1909   K. Freise, 'Gemälde aus der Sammlung Dr. Hofstede de Groot im Haag'. *Monatshefte für Kunstwissenschaft*, 1909.

Friedländer 1926   Max J. Friedländer, *Die Kunstsammlung von Pannwitz*, 2 vols., Munich, n.d. (1926).

Friedländer 1947   Max J. Friedländer, *Essays über die Landschaftmalerei und andere Bildgattungen*, The Hague, 1947 (Engl. ed., trans. R. F. C. Hull, 1963).

Fritz 1932   R. Fritz, *Das Stadt- und Strassenbild in der holländischen Malerei des 17. Jahrhunderts*, Stuttgart, 1932.

Fromentin   Eugène Fromentin, *Les maîtres d'autrefois*, Paris, 1882 (first pub. in *Revue des Deux-Mondes*, 1876).

Geffroy 1908   Gustave Geffroy, *Les Musées d'Europe: La Hollande*, Paris, 1908.

Gerson 1942   H. Gerson, *Ausbreitung und Nachwirkung der holländischen Malerei des 17. Jahrhunderts*, Haarlem, 1942.

Gerson 1952   H. Gerson, *De Nederlandse Schilderkunst*, Vol. II, 'Het tijdperk van Rembrandt en Vermeer', Amsterdam, 1952.

Gerson 1966   H. Gerson, 'Pieter de Hooch', in *Kindlers Malerei-Lexikon*, III, Zurich, 1966, 308–12.

Glück 1907   G. Glück, *Niederländische Gemälde aus der Sammlung des Herrn Alexander Tritsch in Wien*, Vienna, 1907.

Goldscheider 1964   L. Goldscheider, 'Vermeers Lehrer', *Pantheon*, 22 (1964), 35–8.
Gower 1875   Ronald Gower, *Art Galleries: Belgium and Holland*, London, 1875.
Gower 1880   Ronald Gower, *The Figure Painters of Holland*, London, 1880.
Gowing 1952   L. Gowing, *Vermeer*, London, 1952.
Grandjean 1964   S. Grandjean, *Inventaire après décès de l'impératrice Joséphine à Malmaison (1814)*, Paris, 1964.

Graves   Algernon Graves, *Art Sales from Early in the 18th Century to Early in the 20th Century*, 3 vols., London, 1918–21.

Grossmann 1965   F. G. Grossmann, *Catalogue of Paintings and Drawings from the Assheton Bennett Collection*, City Art Gallery, Manchester, 1965.

Gudlaugsson   S. J. Gudlaugsson, *Gerard Ter Borch*, 2 vols., The Hague, 1959–60.
Van Hall 1963   H. van Hall, *Portretten van Nederlandse beeldende Kunstenaars*, Amsterdam, 1963.

Hannema 1949   D. Hannema, *Catalogue of the D. G. van Beuningen Collection*, 1949.
Havard 1877   H. Havard, 'L'État civil des maîtres hollandais, Pieter de Hooch', *Gazette des Beaux-Arts*, 2e per, 15 (1877), 519–24.

Havard 1879   H. Havard, *L'Art et les artistes hollandais*, Paris, 1879.
Havard 1880   H. Havard, 'Pieter de Hooch', Chap. I, in *L'Art et les artistes hollandais*, III, Paris, 1880, 61–138.

Havard 1881   H. Havard, *Histoire de la peinture hollandaise*, Paris, n.d. (1881).
Havard 1888   H. Havard, *Les artistes célèbres, Van de Meer de Delft*, Paris, 1888.
Havelaar 1919   J. Havelaar, *Oud-Hollandsche figuurschilders*, Haarlem, 1919 (2nd ed.).
HvR 1880   P. Haverkorn van Rijsewijk, 'Pieter de Hooch', *Nederlandsch Kunstbode, Beeldende Kunst, Oudheidkunde, Kunstnijverheid*, 2 (1880), 163–5.

HvR 1892   P. Haverkorn van Rijsewijk, 'Pieter de Hooch of De Hoogh', *Oud-Holland*, 10 (1892), 172–7.

Hermanin 1924   F. Hermanin, *Catalogo della R. Galleria d'Arte Antica nel Palazzo Corsini–Roma*, Bologna, 1924.

Hoet 1752   G. Hoet, *Catalogus of naamlyst van schilderyen, met derzelver pryzen, zedert een langen reeks von jaaren [. . .] verkopt*, 2 vols., The Hague, 1752.

HdG 1892   C. Hofstede de Groot, 'Proeve kritische beschrijving van het werk van Pieter de Hooch', *Oud-Holland*, 10 (1892), 178–91.

HdG c. 1895   C. Hofstede de Groot, *Hollandsche Kunst in Engelsche Verzamelingen* (etchings by P. J. Arendzen), Amsterdam, n.d. (c. 1895).

HdG 1906   C. Hofstede de Groot, *Die Urkunden über Rembrandt*, The Hague, 1906.
HdG   C. Hofstede de Groot, *Beschreibendes und kritisches Verzeichnis der Werke der hervorragendsten holländischen Maler des XVII. Jahrhunderts*, 'Pieter de Hooch', in vol. I (with the collaboration of W. R. Valentiner), Esslingen–Paris, 1907. Eng. ed., trans. by E. G. Hawke, 1907.

HdG & Val. 1913   C. Hofstede de Groot & W. R. Valentiner, *Pictures in the Collection of P. A. B. Widener*, Philadelphia, 1913.

HdG 1921   C. Hofstede de Groot, 'Hendrick van der Burgh, een voorganger van Pieter de Hoogh', *Oud-Holland*, 39 (1921), 121–8.

H   F. W. H. Hollstein, *Dutch and Flemish Etchings, Engravings and Woodcuts*, vol. 9, Amsterdam, n.d., 117.

Houbraken   Arnold Houbraken, *De groote schouburg der nederlandsche konstschilders en schilderessen*, 3 vols., Amsterdam, 1718–21; The Hague, 1753. (Modern reprint ed. P. T. A. Swillens, 3 vols. Maastricht, 1943–53).

Houssaye 1848   Arsène Houssaye, *Histoire de la peinture flamande et hollandaise*, 2 vols, II, Paris, 1848.

Immerzeel 1842   J. Immerzeel, *De levens en werken der hollandsche en vlaamsche kunstschilders, beeldhouwers, graveurs en bouwmeesters, van het begin der vijftiende eeuw tot heden*, Amsterdam, (3 vols.) vol. II, 1842, 51–2.

Jameson 1844   Mrs. Jameson, *Companion to the most Celebrated Private Galleries of Art in London*, London, 1844.

Jantzen 1912   H. Jantzen, *Farbenwahl und Farbengebung in der holländischen Malerei des XVII. Jahrhunderts*, Parchim i. M., n.d. [1912].

De Jongh 1974   E. de Jongh, 'Grape Symbolism in paintings of the 16th and 17th centuries', *Simiolus*, 7 (1974), 166–91.

Juynboll 1935   W. R. Juynboll, 'Pieter de Hoogh of Peter Angillis', *Oud-Holland*, 52 (1935), 190–2.

Kauffmann 1930   Hans Kauffmann, (review of Valentiner) in *Deutsche Literaturzeitung*, 17 (26/4/1930), cols. 801–5.

Kauffmann 1931   Hans Kauffmann (review of Valentiner) in *Oud-Holland*, 48 (1931), 236–7.

Van der Kellen 1876   D. van der Kellen, 'Pieter de Hooge', *Eigen Haard*, 1876, no. 18, 151–2.

Keyszelitz 1956   R. Keyszelitz, 'Der "clavis interpretandi" in der holländischen Malerei des 17. Jahrhunderts', diss., Munich, 1956.

Kramm 1859   Christiaan Kramm, *De Levens en Werken der Hollandsche en Vlaamsche Kunstschilders, Beeldhouwers, Graveurs en Bouwmeesters van den vroegsten tot op onzen tijd*, vol. III, Amsterdam, 1859.

Kugler 1847   D. Franz Kugler, *Handbuch der Geschichte der Malerei seit Constantin dem Grossen*, 2 vols., Berlin, 1847.

Lafenestre-Richtenberger 1896   Lafenestre-Richtenberger, *Les Musées d'Europe: La Belgique*, Paris, 1896.

Lauts 1960   J. Lauts, ed., *Holländische Meister aus der Staatlichen Kunsthalle Karlsruhe*, Karlsruhe, 1960.

Lauts 1966   J. Lauts, *Katalog alter Meister bis 1800*, Staatliche Kunsthalle, 2 vols., Karlsruhe, 1966.

Lebrun 1792   J. B. P. Lebrun, *Galerie des peintres flamands, hollandais et allemands*, I, Paris–Amsterdam, 1792.

Lemcke 1878   C. Lemcke, 'Pieter de Hooch. Jan Van der Meer van Delft. Adrian van der Werff', in 'Kunst und Künstler Deutschlands und der Niederlande', in *Kunst und Künstler des Mittelalters und der Neuzeit* (ed. R. Dohme), Part I, vol. II, nrs. 29–31, Leipzig, 1878.

Lescure 1867   M. de Lescure, *Le Château de la Malmaison*, Paris, 1867.

Lilienfeld 1924   Karl Lilienfeld, 'Pieter de Hooch', in Thieme & Becker, *Allgemeines Lexikon der bildenden Künste*, 17, Leipzig, 1924, 452–4.

Lilienfeld 1924–5   Karl Lilienfeld, 'Wiedergefundene Gemälde des Pieter de Hooch', *Zeitschrift für bildende Kunst*, 58 (1924–5), 183–8.

Maccoll 1916   D. S. Maccoll, 'The New De Hooch at the National Gallery', *The Burlington Magazine*, 29 (1916), 25–6.

MacLaren   N. MacLaren, *National Gallery Catalogues. The Dutch School*, The National Gallery, London, 1960.

Martin 1935–6   W. Martin, *De hollandsche schilderkunst in de 17e eeuw*. I, *Frans Hals en zijn tijd*, Amsterdam, 1935, II, *Rembrandt en zijn tijd*, 1936.

Mellaart 1923   J. H. J. Mellaart, 'An Unpublished Pieter de Hoogh', *The Burlington Magazine*, 43 (1923), 269–70.

Nagler 1838   G. K. Nagler, *Neues allgemeines Künstler-Lexikon von dem Leben und den Werken der Maler, . . .*, vol. 6, Munich, 1838.

Neoustroieff 1904   A. Neoustroieff, 'Galerie des tableaux de S. A. le duc G. N. de Leuchtenberg...' in *Trésors d'art en Russie*, IV, St. Petersburg, 1904.

Nieuwenhuys 1834   C. J. Nieuwenhuys, *A Review of the Lives and Works of Some of the Most Eminent Painters: with Remarks on the Opinions and Statements of Former Writers*, London, 1834.

Obreen   F. D. O. Obreen, *Archief voor Nederlandsche Kunstgeschiedenis*, 7 vols., Rotterdam, 1877–90.

Oosterloo 1948   J. H. Oosterloo, *De Meesters van Delft. Leven en werken van de Delftse schilders der zeventiende eeuw*, Amsterdam, 1948.

Von der Osten 1966   G. von der Osten, *Wallraf-Richartz Museum Köln*, 2, Cologne, 1966.

Parthey 1863–4   G. Parthey, *Deutscher Bildersaal, Verzeichnis der in Deutschland vorhandenen Oelbilder verstorbener Maler aller Schulen*, 2 vols., Berlin, 1863–4.

Pelinck 1958   E. Pelinck, 'Een portretgroep van de familie Jacott-Hoppesack', *De Nederlandsche Leeuw*, 75 (1958), cols. 308–11.

Della Pergola 1959   Paola della Pergola, *La Galleria Borghese*, 2 vols., Rome, 1959.

Petrovics 1924   Alexius Petrovics, 'Pieter de Hooch im Budapester Museum der bildenden Künste', *Belvedere*, 5 (1924), 62–4.

Pigler 1968   A. Pigler, *Katalog der Galerie alter Meister*, Museum der bildenden Künste, 2 vols., Budapest, 1968.

Plasschaert 1924   Albert Plasschaert, *Johannes Vermeer en Pieter de Hooch*, Amsterdam, 1924.

Plietzsch 1956   E. Plietzsch, 'Randbemerkungen zur holländischen Interieurmalerei am Beginn des 17. Jahrhunderts', *Wallraf-Richartz-Jahrbuch*, 18 (1956), 174–96.

Plietzsch 1960   E. Plietzsch, *Holländische und Flämische Maler des XVII. Jahrhunderts*, Leipzig, n.d. (1960).

Van Regteren Altena 1930   I.Q. van Regteren Altena (review of Valentiner), *Maandblad voor Beeldende Kunsten*, 7 (1930), 379–80.

Reuterswürtt 1956   P. Reuterswürttt, 'Tavelförhänget. Kring ett motiv holländskt 1600-talsmålerei', *Konsthistorisk Tidskrift*, 25, nos. 3–4 (1956), 97–113.

Reynolds 1781   Joshua Reynolds, 'A Journey to Flanders and Holland in the year MDCCLXXXI', *Collected Works*, vol. II, 1809.

Roberts 1897   W. Roberts, *Memorials of Christie's*, 2 vols., London, 1897.

Robinson 1974   F. W. Robinson, *Gabriel Metsu (1629–1667)*, New York, 1974.

Rooses 1894   Max Rooses, 'De Hollandsche Meesters in den Louvre. Pieter de Hoogh of de Hooch', *Elsevier's Geillustreerd Maandschrift*, 8 (July–Dec. 1894), 179–83.

Rosenberg 1932   Jakob Rosenberg (review of Valentiner), *Zeitschrift für Kunstgeschichte*, 1 (1932), 85–6.

Rosenberg–Slive–TerKuile   Jakob Rosenberg, Seymour Slive, & E. H. TerKuile, *Dutch Art and Architecture 1600–1800*, Harmondsworth and Baltimore, 1966.

Rothes 1921   W. Rothes, 'Pieter de Hooch', in 'Terborch und das holländische Gesellschaftsbild', *Die Kunst dem Volke*, 41–2 (1921), 38–56.

R   A. de Rudder, *Pieter de Hooch*, Brussels, 1913 (reviewed by C. Veth, *Elsevier*, 47 [1914], 451–2; C. M., *Chron. d. Arts*, 1914–16, 85; *Connoisseur*, 39 [1914], 144; *Arte*, 12 [1914], 477; A. Potez, *Revue du Nord*, 5 [1914–19], 275–7).

Rudolph 1938   H. Rudolph, '"Vanitas", Die Bedeutung mittelalterlicher und humanistischer Bildinhalte in der niederländischen Malerei des 17. Jahrhunderts', in *Festschrift für Wilhelm Pinder*, Leipzig, 1938.

Sánchez Cantón 1955   F. J. Sánchez Cantón, *La Colección Cambó*, Barcelona, 1955.

Slive 1974   Seymour Slive, 'Dutch School', in *European Paintings in the Collection of the Worcester Art Museum*, Worcester, Mass., 1974.

S   John Smith, *A Catalogue Raisonné of the works of the most eminent Dutch, Flemish and French Painters*, vol. IV, London, 1833.

S s   John Smith, *Supplement to the Catalogue Raisonné of the works of the most eminent Dutch, Flemish and French Painters*, London, 1842.

Staring 1956   A. Staring, *De Hollanders thuis, Gezelschapstukken uit drie eeuwen*, The Hague, 1956.

Stechow 1966   Wolfgang Stechow, *Dutch Landscape Painting of the Seventeenth Century*, London, 1966.

Steenhoff 1920   W. J. Steenhoff, 'Pieter de Hoogh', *Van Onzen Tijd*, 20 (3/7/1920), 164–7, 169–70.

Suida 1955   W. E. Suida, *The Samuel H. Kress Collection*, M. H. de Young Memorial Museum, San Francisco, 1955.

Sutton 1979   P. C. Sutton, 'A Newly Discovered Work by Pieter de Hooch', *The Burlington Magazine*, 121 (1979), 32–5.

Sutton   P. C. Sutton, 'Hendrick van der Burch', *The Burlington Magazine* (forthcoming).

Terwesten 1770   P. Terwesten, *Catalogus of naamlyst van schilderyen, met derzelver pryzen, zedert den 22. Aug. 1752 tot den 21, Nov. 1768 [. . .] verkopt.*, The Hague, 1770 (vol. 3 of Hoet, see above).

T   F. van Thienen, *Pieter de Hooch*, Palet Series, Amsterdam, n.d. (c. 1945).

Thoré-Bürger 1858–60   W. Bürger, *Musées de la Hollande*, I. *Amsterdam et La Haye*, Paris, 1858; II. *Musée van der Hoop à Amsterdam et Musée de Rotterdam*, 1860.

Thoré-Bürger 1860   W. Bürger, *Trésors d'Art exposés à Manchester en 1857*, Brussels, 1860.

Thoré-Bürger 1866   W. Bürger, 'Van der Meer de Delft', in *Gazette des Beaux-Arts*, 21 (1866), 279–330, 458–70, 542–75.

Tietze-Conrat 1922   E. Tietze-Conrat, *Die Delfter Malerschule. Carel Fabritius, Pieter de Hooch, Jan Vermeer*, Leipzig, 1922.

Tomkiewicz 1950	W. Tomkiewicz, *Catalogue of Paintings Removed from Poland by the German Occupation Authorities during the Years 1939–1945*, I. *Foreign Paintings*, Warsaw, 1950.
Trautscholdt 1964	E. Trautscholdt, 'Bemerkungen zum Zeitstil in der holländischen Figurenmalerei zwischen 1615 und 1680', *Pantheon*, 22 (1964).
Valdivieso 1973	Enrique Valdivieso, *Pintura Holandesa del Siglo XVII en España*, Valladolid, 1973.
Val. 1910	W. R. Valentiner, *Catalogue of Paintings by Old Masters*, The Metropolitan Museum of Art, New York, 1910.
Val. 1910a	W. R. Valentiner, 'Die Ausstellung holländischer Gemälde in New York', *Monatshefte für Kunstwissenschaft*, 3 (1910), 5–12.
Val. 1913	W. R. Valentiner, *Catalogue of a Collection of Paintings and Some Art Objects* (J. G. Johnson Collection), II. *Flemish and Dutch Paintings*, Philadelphia, 1913.
Val. 1926	W. R. Valentiner, 'Pieter de Hooch. Part One', *Art in America*, 15 (12/1926), 45–64.
Val. 1927	W. R. Valentiner, 'Pieter de Hooch. Part Two', *Art in America*, 15 (2/1927), 67–77.
Val. 1927–9	W. R. Valentiner, 'Dutch Painters of the School of Pieter de Hooch', Parts I and II, *Art in America*, 16 (1927–8), 168–80, 17 (1928–9), 87–92.
Val.	W. R. Valentiner, *Pieter de Hooch. Des Meisters Gemälde in 180 Abbildungen mit einem Anhang über die Genremaler um Pieter de Hooch und die Kunst Hendrick van der Burchs*, Klassiker der Kunst, vol. 35, Berlin–Leipzig, 1929. (Engl. ed., trans. Alice M. Sharkey and E. Schwandt, London, n.d. [1930]).
Val. 1932	W. R. Valentiner, 'Zum 300. Geburtstag Jan Vermeers, Oktober 1932. Vermeer und die Meister der holländischen Genremalerei', *Pantheon*, 10 (1932), 305–24.
Val. 1956	W. R. Valentiner, *Catalogue of Paintings*, North Carolina Museum of Art, Raleigh, 1956.
Van Vloten 1874	J. van Vloten, *Nederlands Schilderkunst van de 14e tot de 18e eeuw*, Amsterdam, 1874.
Vey-Kesting 1967	Horst Vey & Annamaria Kesting, *Katalog der niederländischen Gemälde von 1550 bis 1800 im Wallraf-Richartz-Museum und im öffentlichen Besitz der Stadt Köln*, Cologne, 1967.
Villot 1865	F. Villot, *Notice des tableaux exposés dans les galeries du Musée Impérial du Louvre*, 3 vols., Paris, 1865.
Vosmaer 1874	C. Vosmaer, 'La famille delftoise par Pieter de Hooch', *Gazette des Beaux-Arts* 2e per., 10 (1874), 145–6.
Waagen 1837–8	G. F. Waagen, *Kunstwerke und Künstler in England*, 2 vols., Berlin, 1837–8.
Waagen 1839	G. F. Waagen, *Kunstwerke und Künstler in Paris*, Berlin, 1839 (vol. III of Waagen 1837–8).
Waagen 1843–5	G. F. Waagen, *Kunstwerke und Künstler in Deutschland*, 2 vols., Leipzig, 1843–5.
Waagen 1854	G. F. Waagen, *Treasures of Art in Great Britain*, 3 vols., London, 1854.
Waagen 1857	G. F. Waagen, *Galleries and Cabinets of Art in Great Britain*, London, 1857 (Suppl. to Waagen 1854).
Waagen 1862	G. F. Waagen, *Handbuch der deutschen und holländischen Malerschulen*, Stuttgart, 1862.
Waagen 1864	G. F. Waagen, *Die Gemäldesammlung in der Kaiserlichen Ermitage zu St. Petersburg nebst Bemerkungen über andere dortige Kunstsammlungen*, Munich, 1864.
Wagner 1971	H. Wagner, *Jan van der Heyden*, Amsterdam–Haarlem, 1971.
Walker 1976	John Walker, *National Gallery of Art, Washington, D.C.*, New York, n.d. (1976).
Waterhouse 1967	Ellis Waterhouse, *The James A. de Rothschild Collection at Waddesdon Manor. Paintings*, London, 1967.
Wedmore 1880	Frederick Wedmore, *The Masters of Genre Painting*, London, 1880
Von Weiher 1937	L. von Weiher, *Der Innenraum in der holländischen Malerei des 17. Jahrhunderts*, Würzburg, 1937.
Welu 1975	James A. Welu, 'Vermeer: His Cartographic Sources', *The Art Bulletin*, 57 (1975), 529–47.
Weyerman	J. C. Weyerman, *De levens beschryvingen der nederlandsche konstschilders en konstschilderessen*, 4 vols., The Hague, 1729–69.

L

Wichmann 1929 — H. Wichmann, 'Die Meister des holländischen Interieurs, Ausstellung, 1929, in der Galerie Dr. Schäffer—Berlin', *Kunstchronik*, 2 (5/1929), 9–11.

Würtenberger 1937 — F. Würtenberger, *Das holländische Gesellschaftsbild*, Schramberg, 1937.

Wurzbach — A. von Wurzbach, *Niederländisches Künstler-Lexikon*, 2 vols., Vienna, 1906–11.

Yerkes Collection cat. 1893 — *Catalogue from the Collection of Charles T. Yerkes, Chicago, U.S.A.*, Chicago, 1893.

Yerkes Collection cat. 1904 — *Catalogue of Paintings and Sculpture in the Collection of Charles T. Yerkes, Esq.*, 2 vols., New York, 1904.

Catalogues of Public Collections

Aix-en-Provence, M.G., cat. 1900 — *Musée d'Aix*, II, *Le Musée Granet*, Aix-en-Provence, 1900.

Amsterdam, V.d.H., Mus. cat. 1872 — *Beschrijving der Schilderijen in het Museum van der Hoop*, Amsterdam, 1872.

Amsterdam, R., cat. 1976 — *All the Paintings of the Rijksmuseum in Amsterdam*, Rijksmuseum, Amsterdam–Maarsen, 1976.

Basel, Kunstm., cat. 1966 — *Die Kunst bis 1800*, Kunstmuseum, Basel, 1966.

Berlin–Dahlem, St.M., cat. 1975 — *Katalog der Ausgestellten Gemälde des 13.–18. Jahrhunderts*, Gemäldegalerie, Staatliche Museen preussischer Kulturbesitz, Berlin–Dahlem, 1975.

Boston, M.F.A., cat. 1921 — *Catalogue of Paintings*, Museum of Fine Arts, Boston, 1921.

Brussels, M.R.B.A., cat. 1973 — *Art Ancien*, Musées Royaux des Beaux-Arts, Brussels, 1973.

Cincinnati, A.M., *Handbook*, 1975 — *Cincinnati Art Museum Handbook*, Cincinnati, 1975.

Cincinnati, Taft Mus., cat. — *Taft Museum Catalogue*, Cincinnati Institute of Fine Arts, Cincinnati, n.d.

Copenhagen, R.M., cat. 1951 — *Catalogue of Old Foreign Paintings*, Royal Museum of Fine Arts, Copenhagen, 1951.

Danzig, Mus., cat. 1969 — *Muzeum Pomorskie w Gdańska zbiory sztuki*, Danzig, 1969.

Detroit, I.A., cat. 1930 — *Catalogue of the Paintings in the Permanent Collection of the Detroit Institute of Arts*, Detroit, 1930.

Dublin, N.G., cat. 1971 — *Catalogue of the Paintings*, National Gallery of Ireland, Dublin, 1971.

The Hague, M., cat. 1977 — *Catalogue of Paintings*, Mauritshuis, The Hague, 1977.

Hamburg, Kunsthalle, cat. 1956 — *Katalog: Die alten Meister der Hamburger Kunsthalle*, Hamburg, 1956.

Indianapolis, I.M.A., cat. 1970 — *Catalogue of European Paintings*, Indianapolis Museum of Art, 1970.

Leipzig, Mus., cat. 1967 — *Katalog der Gemälde*, Museum der bildenden Künste zu Leipzig, Leipzig, 1967.

Leningrad, Hermitage, cat. 1958 — *Catalogue of Paintings*, Hermitage, Leningrad, 1958 (in Russian).

Lisbon, Mus. cat. 1956 — *Roteiro das Pinturas*, Museu Nacional de Arte Antiga, Lisbon, 1956.

London, Apsley Hse., cat. 1901 — Evelyn Wellington, *A Descriptive and Historical Catalogue of Pictures and Sculpture at Apsley House*, London, 1901.

London, B.P., cat. 1920 — *Catalogue Raisonné of the Pictures in the possession of King George V in the Picture Gallery and the Royal Closet and on the Chapel Stairs at Buckingham Palace*, London, 1920.

London, N.G., pls. 1958 — *National Gallery Catalogues. Dutch School. Plates*, I, London, 1958.

London, Wallace Coll., cat. 1968 — *Pictures and Drawings*, Wallace Collection Catalogues, London, 1968.

Los Angeles, C.M.A., cat. 1954 — *A Catalogue of Flemish, German, Dutch and English Paintings, XV–XVIII Century*, Los Angeles County Museum of Art, 1954.

Moscow, P.M., cat. 1961 — *Catalogue of the Pushkin Museum of Fine Arts*, Moscow, 1961 (in Russian).

New York, M.M.A., 1931 — *Catalogue of Paintings*, Metropolitan Museum of Art, New York, 1931.

Nuremberg, G.M., cat. 1909 — *Katalog der Gemälde-Sammlung des Germanischen Nationalmuseums in Nürnberg*, Nuremberg, 1909.

Phila., J.C., cat. 1972 — *John G. Johnson Collection. Catalogue of Flemish and Dutch Paintings*, Philadelphia, 1972.

Phila., Mus., cat. 1965 — *Checklist of Paintings*, Philadelphia Museum of Art, Philadelphia, 1965.

Poznan, N.M., cat. 1958 — *Malarstwo Holenderskie XVII–XVIIIw.*, National Museum, Poznan, 1958.

Rotterdam, B.M., cat. 1962   *Catalogus Schilderijen tot 1800*, Museum Boymans-van Beuningen, Rotterdam, 1962.

San Francisco, D.Y. Mus, cat. 1966   *European Works of Art in the M. H. de Young Memorial Museum*, Berkeley, 1966.

Stockholm, N.M., cat. 1958   *Äldre utlandska Målningar och Skulpturer*, National Museum, Stockholm, 1958.

Strasbourg, Mus., cat. 1938   *Catalogue des peintures anciennes*, Musée des Beaux-Arts, Strasbourg, 1938.

Toledo, M.A., cat. 1976   *European Paintings*, The Toledo Museum of Art, Toledo, 1976.

Vienna, A.d.b.K., cat. 1972   *Katalog der Gemälde Galerie*, Akademie der bildenden Künste, Vienna, 1972.

Washington, N.G., cat. 1975   *European Paintings: an Illustrated Summary Catalogue*, Washington, 1975.

Exhibitions Catalogue

All exhibitions in public institutions and loan exhibitions held in dealers' galleries are abbreviated and listed below. The full titles of dealers' exhibitions of their own holdings have been omitted.

Aix-en-Provence 1970   *Hommage à Rembrandt*, Musée Granet, Aix-en-Provence, 1970.

Amsterdam 1872   *Tentoonstelling van zeldzame en belangrijke schilderijen van oude Meesters*, Arti et Amicitiae, Amsterdam, 1872.

Amsterdam 1900   *Catalogus der verzameling schilderijen en familie-portretten van de heeren Jhr. Six van Vromade, Jhr. Dr. Six en Jhr. W. Six wegens verbouwing in het Stedelijk Museum van Amsterdam tentoongesteld*, Amsterdam, 1900

Amsterdam 1906   *Catalogue de l'Éxposition de Maîtres Hollandais du XVIIe siècle*, F. Muller & Co., Amsterdam, 10/7–15/9/1906.

Amsterdam 1918   *Catalogus van de Collectie Goudstikker*, Arti et Amicitiae, Amsterdam, 11–12/1918.

Amsterdam 1925   *Catalogus der Historische Tentoonstelling der Stad Amsterdam*, 2 vols., Rijksmuseum, Amsterdam, 3/7–15/9/1925.

Amsterdam (Goudstikker) 1928   *De Gedekte Tafel*, Goudstikker, Amsterdam, Dec. 1928.

Amsterdam 1929   *Catalogus van de Tentoonstelling van Oude Kunst*, Vereeniging van handelaren in Oude Kunst in Nederlanden, Rijksmuseum, Amsterdam, 7–8/1929.

Amsterdam 1935   *Vermeer Tentoonstelling*, Rijksmuseum, Amsterdam, 21/10–3/11/1935.

Amsterdam 1936   *Tentoonstelling Oude Kunst uit het bezit van den internationalen handel*, Rijksmuseum, Amsterdam, 7–91936.

Amsterdam (Waaggebouw) 1937   *Oude Raadhuizen*, Waaggebouw, Amsterdam, 1937.

Amsterdam 1938   *Gedenck-Clanck, Muziektentoonstelling*, Stedelijk Museum, Amsterdam, May 1938.

Amsterdam 1947   *Kunstschatten uit Wenen*, Rijksmuseum, Amsterdam, 10/7–12/10/1947.

Amsterdam 1950   *120 Beroemde schilderyen uit het Kaiser-Friedrich Museum te Berlijn*, Amsterdam, Rijksmuseum, 17/6–17/9/1950.

Amsterdam 1971   *Hollandse schilderijen uit Franse musea*, Rijksmuseum, Amsterdam, 6/3–23/5/1971.

Amsterdam 1975   *Kunst als regeringszaak in Amsterdam in de 17e eeuw. Rondom schilderijen Ferdinand Bol*, (cat. by A. Blankert), Koninklijk Paleis, Amsterdam, 7/6–31/8/1975.

Amsterdam 1976   *'tot Lering en Vermaak'*, Rijksmuseum, Amsterdam, 16/9–5/12/1976.

Antwerp 1975   *Henri de Braekeleer*, Koninklijk Museum voor Schone Kunsten, Antwerp, 24/3–3/6/1956.

Arnhem 1934   *Tentoonstelling van Schilderijen van 17e eeuwsche Nederlandsche Meesters*, Gemeente-Museum, Arnhem, 31/3–22/4/1934.

Arnhem 1960–1   *Collectie B. de Geus van den Heuvel te Nieuwersluis*, Gemeente-Museum, Arnhem, 11/12/1960–26/2/1961.

Atlanta 1950   *Paintings and Sculpture, Gothic to Surrealism*, The High Museum of Art, Atlanta, Ga., 8/1–5/2/1950.

Baltimore 1943   *Living Masters of the Past*, Baltimore Museum of Art, Baltimore, 10/10–21/11/1943.

Basel 1947   *Kunstschätze aus den Strassburger Museen*, Kunstmuseum, Basel, 1947.

Berlin 1890   *Katalog der Ausstellung von Werken der Niederländischen Kunst des 17. Jahrh. im Berliner Privatbesitz*, Königl. Akademie, Berlin, 1/4–15/5/1890.

Berlin 1906   *Ausstellung von Werken alter Kunst aus dem Privatbesitz der Mitglieder des Kaiser Friedrich-Museums-Vereins*, Kaiser Friedrich Museum, Berlin, 27/1–4/3/1906.

Berlin 1914   *Ausstellung von Werken alter Kunst aus dem Privatbesitz von Mitgliedern des Kaiser-Friedrich-Museums-Vereins*, Berlin, May 1914.

Berlin 1925   *Gemälde alter Meister aus Berliner Besitz*, Kaiser-Friedrich-Museum-Verein, Akademie der Künste, Berlin, 7–8/1925.

Berlin (Schäffer) 1929   *Die Meister der holländischen Interieurs*, Galerie Dr. Schäffer, Berlin, 4–5/1929.

Berlin 1964   *Meisterwerke aus dem Museum in Lille*, Schloss Charlottenburg, Berlin, 1964.

Bethnal Green 1872–5   *Catalogue of Paintings [. . .] lent for exhibition in the Bethnal Green Branch of the South Kensington Museum by Sir Richard Wallace, Bart., M.P.*, London, 1872 & 1874.

Bielefeld 1973   *Aus Hollands grosser Malerei. Kunstmuseum Düsseldorf*, Museum für Kulturgeschichte, Bielefeld, 4/2–25/3/1973.

Birmingham 1950   *Some Dutch Cabinet Pictures of the 17th Century*, Museum and Art Gallery, Birmingham, 26/8–8/10/1950.

Birmingham et al. 1952–7   (See Greenville 1957.)

Birmingham et al. 1957–8   *An Exhibition of Dutch, Flemish and German Paintings from the Collection of Walter P. Chrysler, Jr.*, The Birmingham Museum of Art, Birmingham, Ala., 14/1–6/1957, and 10 other institutions through May 1958. (For details see *Arts*, 3/1957, 43.)

Bordeaux 1959   *La découverte de la lumière des Primitifs aux Impressionnistes*, Galerie des Beaux-Arts, Bordeaux, 20/5–31/7/1959.

Bordeaux 1972   *Trésors du Musée de Budapest*, Galerie des Beaux-Arts, Bordeaux, 26/5–1/9/1972.

Brighton 1956   *Paintings and Furniture from the Collection of Mrs. Geoffrey Hart*, Art Gallery, Brighton, 1956.

Bristol 1946   *Exhibition of Dutch Old Masters*, Red Lodge, Bristol, 14/3–6/4/1946.

Brussels 1946   *La Peinture hollandaise de Jérôme Bosch à Rembrandt*, Palais des Beaux-Arts, Brussels, 2/3–28/4/1946.

Brussels 1947   *Chefs d'oeuvre des Musées de Vienne*, Palais des Beaux-Arts, Brussels, 4–6/1947.

Brussels 1962–3   *Peintures et dessins hollandais dans les collections des Musées royaux*, Musées Royaux des Beaux-Arts, Brussels, 1962–3.

Brussels 1971   *Rembrandt en zijn tijd*, Palais des Beaux-Arts, Brussels, 23/9–21/11/1971.

Brussels 1977–8   *Mens en Landschap in de 17de Eeuwse Hollandse Schilderkunst*, Musées Royaux des Beaux-Arts, Brussels, 17/11/1977–15/1/1978.

Budapest 1967   *Dutch Masters of the Seventeenth Century*, Szepmüveszeti Museum, Budapest, 1967 (catalogue in Hungarian).

Cape Town 1952   *Exhibition of XVII Century Dutch Painting*, National Gallery of South Africa, Cape Town, 1952.

Cape Town 1959   *Catalogue of the Exhibition of the Joseph Robinson Collection. Lent by Princess Labia*, National Gallery of South Africa, Cape Town, 1959.

Caracas 1967   *Grandes Maestros, Siglos XV, XVI, XVII, y XVIII*, Museo de Bellas Artes de Caracas, 5/11–17/12/1967.

Chicago 1933   *Century of Progress Exhibit*, Art Institute of Chicago, Chicago, 1/6–1/11/1933.

Chicago 1942   *Paintings by the Great Dutch Masters of the 17th Century*, Art Institute of Chicago, Chicago, 18/11–16/12/1942.

Cincinnati 1941   *Masterpieces of Art*, Cincinnati Art Museum, Cincinnati, 15/1–9/2/1941.

Cincinnati 1959   *The Lehman Collection*, Cincinnati Art Museum, Cincinnati, 8/5–5/7/1959.

Cleveland 1936   *Twentieth Anniversary Exhibition*, Cleveland Museum of Art, Cleveland, 26/6–4/10/1936.

Cleveland 1958   *In Memorian Leonard C. Hanna, Jr.*, The Cleveland Museum of Art, Cleveland, 1958.

Cologne 1937   *Der holländische Nationaldichter Joost van den Vondel und seine Welt*, Wallraf-Richartz-Museum, Cologne, 1937.

Cologne 1964   *Die Sammlung Henle. Aus dem grossen Jahrhundert der niederländischen Malerei*, Wallraf-Richartz-Museum, Cologne, 22/2–5/4/1964.

Colorado Springs 1951–2   *Paintings and Bronzes from the Collection of Mr. Robert Lehman*, Colorado Springs Fine Arts Center, Colorado Springs, 1951–2.

Columbus 1967   *Gordian Knot: Design and Content*, Biennial Beaux-Arts Exhibition, Gallery of Fine Arts, Columbus, 30/4–7/1967.

Copenhagen 1922   *Udstilling af aeldre og nyere hollandsk malerkunst*, Statens Museum, Copenhagen, 1922.

Delft 1950-1   *Vermeer Thuis*, Het Prinsenhof, Delft, 11/1950–4/1951.

Delft 1962   *Meesterwerken uit Delft*, Stedelijk Museum het Prinsenhof, Delft, 2/6–15/8/1962.

Detroit 1925   *Loan Exhibition of Dutch Paintings of the Seventeenth Century*, Detroit Institute of Arts, Detroit, 9–25/1/1925.

Detroit 1929   *Loan Exhibition of Dutch Genre and Landscape Painting*, Detroit Institute of Arts, Detroit, 16/10–10/11/1929.

Detroit 1939   *Masterpieces of Art from Foreign Collections*, Detroit Institute of Arts, Detroit, 10/11–10/12/1939.

Detroit 1941   *Masterpieces of Art from European and American Collections*, Detroit Institute of Art, Detroit, 15/4–31/5/1941.

Dublin 1964   *1864-1964. Centenary Exhibition*, National Gallery of Ireland, Dublin, 10–12/1964.

Düsseldorf 1886   *Bilder von älteren Meistern*, Kunsthalle, Düsseldorf, 1886.

Düsseldorf 1904   *Kunsthistorische Ausstellung*, Kunsthalle, Düsseldorf, Aug. 1904.

Edinburgh 1949   *Dutch & Flemish Paintings from the Collection of the Marquess of Bute*, National Gallery of Scotland, Edinburgh, 6/8–25/9/1949.

Frankfurt 1925   *Verzeichnis der Ausstellung von Meisterwerken alter Malerei aus Privatbesitz*, Städelsches Kunstinstitut, Frankfurt a.M., 1925.

Grand Rapids 1940   *Masterpieces of Dutch Art*, Grand Rapids Art Gallery, Grand Rapids, 7–30/5/1940.

Greenville 1957   *The Hammer Collection* (cat. by W. R. Valentiner & P. Wescher), Bob Jones U., S.C., 15/3–15/4/1957. (Previously exhibited at Birmingham Mus. of Art, Birmingham, Ala., 1952, and five other institutions, 1953-7.)

Haarlem 1934   *Oudhollandsche Meesters uit de Coll. Katz te Dieren*, Frans Hals Museum, Haarlem, 1934.

The Hague 1948   *Masterpieces of the Dutch School From the Collection of H.M. the King of England*, Mauritshuis, The Hague, 6/8–26/9/1948.

The Hague–Paris 1966   *Five Centuries of Painting. In the Light of Vermeer*, Mauritshuis, The Hague, 25/6–5/9/1966; Orangerie des Tuileries, Paris, 24/9–28/11/1966.

Hartford 1934   *Avery Memorial Opening Loan Exhibition*, Wadsworth Atheneum, Hartford, 1934.

Hartford 1947   *Fifty Painters of Architecture*, Wadsworth Atheneum, Hartford, 30/10–7/12/1947.

Hartford 1950-1   *Life in Seventeenth Century Holland*, Wadsworth Atheneum, Hartford, 21/11/1950–14/1/1951.

Hull 1961   *Dutch Paintings of the Seventeenth Century*, Ferens Art Gallery, Kingston-on-Hull, 6/6–2/7/1961.

IJzendijke 1955   *Hollands leven in de Gouden Eeuw*, Raadhuis, IJzendijke, 1955.

Indianapolis 1937   *Dutch Paintings, Etchings, Drawings, Delftware of the Seventeenth Century*, John Herron Art Museum, Indianapolis, 27/2–11/4/1937.

Kansas City 1940-1   *Seventh Anniversary Exhibition of German, Flemish and Dutch Painting*, Nelson Gallery of Art, Kansas City, 12/1940–1/1941.

Kansas City 1967-8   *Paintings of 17th Century Dutch Interiors*, The Nelson Gallery of Art and Atkins Museum, Kansas City, 1/12/1967–7/1/1968.

Kingston, *see* Hull

Laren 1958   *Kunstbezit rondom Laren*, Singer Museum, Laren, N.H., 1958.

Laren 1969   *Het Kind in de noord-nederland Kunst*, Singer Museum, Laren, 29/3–2/6/1969.

Leeds 1936   *Masterpieces from the Collections of Yorkshire and Durham City Art Gallery*, Leeds, 6–31/7/1936.

Leiden 1906   *Catalogus der Tentoonstelling van Schilderijen en Teekeningen van Rembrandt en Schilderijen van andere Leidsche Meesters der zeventiende eeuw*, De Lakenhal, Leiden, 15/7–15/9/1906.

Leipzig 1889   *Einundzwanzigste Sonderausstellung älterer Meister aus sächsischem Privatbesitz*, Leipziger Kunstverein, Leipzig, 1889.

Leipzig 1914   *Ausstellung alter Meister aus Leipziger Privatbesitz*, Leipziger Kunstverein, Leipzig, 11–12/1914.

Leipzig 1937   *Alte Meister aus mitteldeutschem Besitz*, Leipziger Kunstverein, Museum der bildenden Künste, Leipzig, 13/5–15/8/1937.

Little Rock 1963   *Five Centuries of European Art*, Arkansas Art Center, Little Rock, 16/5–26/10/1963.

Liverpool 1944   *Exhibition of Works of Dutch Masters of the 17th Century*, City School of Art, Liverpool, 22–29/9/1944.

London 1891   *Catalogue of Pictures of Dutch and Flemish Schools lent to the South Kensington Museum by Lord Francis Pelham Clinton-Hope*, Victoria and Albert Museum, London, 1891.

London, Guildhall, 1894   *Descriptive Catalogue of the Loan Collection of Pictures*, Corporation of London Art Gallery, Guildhall, London, 1894.

London, B.F.A.C., 1900   *Exhibition of Pictures by Dutch Masters of the Seventeenth Century*, Burlington Fine Arts Club, London, 1900.

London, G.G., 1913–14   *Catalogue of the Second National Loan Exhibition. Woman and Child in Art*, Grosvenor Gallery, London, 1913–14.

London, R.A., 1929   *Exhibition of Dutch Art 1450–1900*, Royal Academy of Arts, London, 4/1–9/3/1929.

London, R.A., 1938   *Exhibition of 17th Century Art in Europe*, Royal Academy of Arts, London, 3/1–12/3/1938.

London, A.C., 1945   *Dutch Paintings of the 17th Century*, Arts Council of Great Britain, London (also Worthing, Wakefield, Derby, Cardiff, and Norwich), 1945.

London (Slatter) 1945   *Masterpieces of Dutch Painting in the Seventeenth Century*, Anglo-Netherlands Society, Eugene Slatter Gallery, London 27/6–28/7/1945.

London (Wildenstein) 1946   *Loan Exhibition of the Collection of Sir Harold Wernher*, Wildenstein & Co., London, 3/10–9/11/1946.

London, R.A., 1946–7   *Catalogue of the Exhibition of the King's Pictures*, Royal Academy of Arts, London, 1946–7.

London (Whitechapel) 1948   *5 Centuries of European Painting*, Whitechapel Art Gallery, London, 3/2–14/3/1948.

London 1949   *Art Treasures from Vienna*, The Arts Council of Great Britain, Tate Gallery, London, 11/5–3/9/1949.

London (Slatter) 1949   *Masterpieces of Dutch and Flemish Painting*, Loan Exhibition in Memory of Ralph Warner, Eugene Slatter Gallery, London, 16/2–16/3/1949.

London, R.A., 1952–3   *Dutch Pictures 1450–1750*, Royal Academy of Arts, London, 1952–3.

London, A.C., 1956   *Children Painted by Dutch Artists*, The Arts Council of Great Britain, London, 1956.

London 1958   *Exhibition of 17th Century Dutch Pictures*, King's Lynn, and London, 26/7–9/8/1958.

London, R.A., 1958   *The Robinson Collection*, Royal Academy of Arts, London, 2/7–14/9/1958.

London et al., A.C., 1960   *Portrait Groups from National Trust Collections*, Arts Council of Great Britain, London and five other cities, 1960.

London, Q.G., 1971   *Dutch Pictures from The Royal Collection*, The Queen's Gallery, Buckingham Palace, London, 1971.

London 1976   *Art in Seventeenth Century Holland*, The National Gallery, London, 30/9–12/12/1976.

London (Agnew) 1978   *Dutch and Flemish Pictures from Scottish Collections*, T. Agnew & Sons, Ltd., London, 1978.

Los Angeles 1933   *Five Centuries of European Painting* (loaned by Wildenstein & Co., New York), Los Angeles, 25/11–31/12/1933.

Los Angeles 1938   *Exhibition of Paintings by Old Masters Lent by Schaeffer Galleries, Inc.*, Los Angeles Museum, Los Angeles, Apr. 1938.

Mainz 1887   *Bilder aus Mainzer Privatbesitz*, Stadttheater, Mainz, 15/5–6/6/1887.

Malmö 1926   *Utställning av en Samling Gamla Mälningar*, Museum, Malmö, Feb. 1926.

Montreal 1942   *Loan Exhibition of Masterpieces of Painting*, Museum of Fine Arts, Montreal, 5/2–8/3/1942.

Montreal 1944   *Five Centuries of Dutch Art*, Museum of Fine Arts, Montreal, 9/3–9/4/1944.

Montreal 1967	*Man and his World. Fine Arts Exhibition Expo 67*, Montreal, 28/4–27/10/1967.
Munich 1930	*Sammlung Schloss Rohoncz*, Neue Pinakothek, Munich, 1930.
Münster 1939	*Meisterwerke holländischer und flämischer Malerei aus westfälischem Privatbesitz*, Landesmuseum der Provinz Westfalen für Kunst und Kulturgeschichte, Münster, 6/8–22/10/1939.
Münster 1975	*Gemälde des 17. Jahrhunderts*, Westfälisches Landesmuseum für Kunst und Kulturgeschichte, Münster, 1975.
Nancy 1875	*L'Exposition rétrospective de Nancy*, Nancy, 1875.
New Haven 1960	*Paintings and Drawings and Sculpture Collected by Yale Alumni*, Yale University Art Gallery, New Haven, 19/5–26/6/1960.
New York 1909	*The Hudson–Fulton Celebration. Catalogue of an Exhibition held in the Metropolitan Museum of Art*, New York, 9–11/1909.
New York (Kleinberger) 1913	*Catalogue of the A. de Ridder Collection Exhibited at the F. Kleinberger Galleries*, New York, 24/11–15/12/1913.
New York (Knoedler) 1915	*Loan Exhibition of Masterpieces by Old and Modern Masters*, Knoedler & Co., New York, 16–24/4/1915.
New York (Knoedler) 1925	*Loan Exhibition of Dutch Masters of the 17th Century*, Knoedler & Co., New York, 16–28/11/1925.
New York (Reinhardt) 1928	*Loan Exhibition of Paintings from Memling and Holbein to Renoir and Picasso*, Reinhardt Galleries, New York, 27/2–17/3/1928.
New York 1930	*The H. O. Havemeyer Collection. A Catalogue of the Temporary Exhibition*, Metropolitan Museum of Art, New York, 10/3–2/11/1930.
New York (Anderson) 1931	*Old and Modern Masters in the New York Market*, American Art Assoc., Anderson Galleries, New York, 15/3–4/4/1931.
New York (Kleinberger) 1931	*Exhibition of Dutch Paintings of the Seventeenth Century* (assembled by College Art Assoc. & W. R. Valentiner), Kleinberger Gallery, New York, 24/10–5/11/1931.
New York 1939	*Masterpieces of Art. Catalogue of European Paintings and Sculpture from 1300–1800*, World's Fair, New York, 5–10/1939.
New York (Schaeffer) 1939	*17 Masterpieces of the 17th Century*, Schaeffer Galleries, New York, 3/2–15/3/1939.
New York 1940	*Catalogue of European & American Paintings 1500–1900*, World's Fair, New York, 5–10/1940.
New York (Duveen) 1942	*Paintings by the Great Dutch Masters of the 17th Century*, Duveen Bros. Galleries, New York, 8/10–7/11/1942.
New York (Knoedler) 1945	*Dutch Masters of the 17th Century*, Knoedler's Gallery, 5–24/2/1945.
New York et al., 1948–9	*Paintings from the Berlin Museum*, The Metropolitan Museum of Art, New York, 17/5–12/6/1948; and 11 other institutions in the U.S.A.
New York–Toledo–Toronto 1954–5	*Dutch Painting. The Golden Age*. The Metropolitan Museum of Art, New York, 28/10–19/12/1954; Toledo Museum of Art, Toledo, 2/1–13/2/1955; The Art Gallery of Toronto, Toronto, 18/2–25/3/1955.
New York (Wildenstein) 1958	*Fifty Masterpieces from The City Art Museum of St. Louis*, Wildenstein Gallery, New York, 6/11–13/12/1958.
New York 1971	*The Painter's Light*, The Metropolitan Museum of Art, New York, 5/10–10/11/1971.
Newark 1940	*Masterpieces of Art. European Paintings from the New York and San Francisco World's Fairs 1939*, Newark Museum, Newark, 1–27/10/1940.
Newcastle 1951	*Pictures from Collections in Northumberland*, The Hatton Gallery, King's College, Newcastle-upon-Tyne, 8/5–15/6/1951.
Oshkosh 1968	*Dutch Art of the 1660's*. The Paine Art Center and Arboretum, Oshkosh, 24/9–30/10/1968.
Oslo 1952	*Kunstskatter fra Wien*, Nasjonalgalleriet, Oslo, 5–7/1952.
Oslo 1959	*Fra Rembrandt ti Vermeer*, Nasjonalgalleriet, Oslo, 9/10–9/12/1959.
Paris 1866	*Tableaux anciens empruntés aux galeries particulières*, Palais des Champs-Elysées, Paris, May 1866.
Paris (Sedelmeyer) 1898	*Illustrated Catalogue of 300 Paintings by Old Masters which have at various times formed part of the Sedelmeyer Gallery*, Sedelmeyer Gallery, Paris, 1898.

Paris 1911   *Éxposition rétrospective des grands et des petits maîtres hollandais*, Jeu de Paume, Tuileries, Paris, 1911.

Paris 1921   *Éxposition hollandaise*, Jeu de Paume, Tuileries, Paris, 4–5/1921.

Paris 1946   *Les chefs-d'oeuvre des collections françaises retrouvés en Allemagne par la commission de récuperation artistique et les services alliés*, Orangerie des Tuileries, Paris, 1946.

Paris 1950–1   *Le Paysage hollandais au XVIIIe siècle*, Orangerie des Tuileries, Paris, 25/11/1950–18/2/1951.

Paris 1951   *Chefs-d'oeuvre des Musées de Berlin*, Petit Palais, Paris, 1951.

Paris 1952   *Chefs-d'oeuvre de la collection D. G. van Beuningen* (cat. by D. Hannema), Petit Palais, Paris, 1952.

Paris 1957   *Éxposition de la collection Lehman de New York*, Orangerie des Tuileries, Paris, 1957.

Paris, I.N., 1965   *Le décor de la vie privée en Hollande au XVIIe siècle*, Institut Néerlandais, Paris, 1/2–7/3/1965.

Paris, I.N., 1967   *La vie en Hollande au XVIIe siècle* (organized by Institut Néerlandais), Musée des Arts Décoratifs, Paris, 11/1–20/3/1967.

Paris 1970   *Choix de la collection Bentinck*, Institut Néerlandais, Paris, 20/5–28/6/1970.

Paris 1970–1   *Le siècle de Rembrandt. Tableaux hollandais des collections publiques françaises.* Musée du Petit Palais, Paris, 17/11/1970–15/2/1971.

Philadelphia 1950–1   *Diamond Jubilee Exhibition*, Philadelphia Museum of Art, Philadelphia, 4/11/1950–11/2/1951.

Pittsburgh 1930   *Loan Exhibition of Old Masters*, Carnegie Institute, Pittsburgh, 1930.

Pittsburgh and St. Louis 1940   *Masterpieces of Art, European Paintings from the New York World's Fair and the Golden Gate International Exhibition*, Carnegie Institute, Pittsburgh, 15/3–14/4/1940; City Art Museum, St. Louis, 21/4–19/5/1940.

Pittsburgh 1954   *Pictures of Everyday Life: Genre Paintings in Europe, 1500–1900* (intro. by G.B. Washburn), Carnegie Institute, Pittsburgh, 14/10–12/12/1954.

Pittsfield 1942   *Music in Art*, Berkshire Museum, Pittsfield, Mass. 11/8–6/9/1942.

Providence 1938   *Dutch Painting in the Seventeenth Century* (cat. by W. Stechow), Rhode Island Museum, Providence, 1938.

Raleigh 1943   *Living Masters of the Past*, North Carolina State Art Gallery, Raleigh, 1943.

Rome 1928   *Mostra di Capolavori della Pittura Olandese*, Galleria Borghese, Rome, 1928.

Rome 1954   *Mostra di pittura olandese del seicento*, Palazzo delle Esposizioni, Rome, 4/1–14/2/1954.

Rome 1954–5   *Pitture Fiamminghe e Olandesi del 1600*, Galleria Nazionale, Palazzo Barberini, Rome, 12/1954–1/1955.

Rome 1956–7   *Le XVIIe siècle européen, Réalisme, Classicisme, Baroque*, Palais des Expositions, Rome, 12/1956–1/1957.

Rotterdam 1935   *Vermeer: oorsprong en invloed: Fabritius, De Hooch, De Witte*, Boymans Museum, Rotterdam, 9/7–9/10/1935.

Rotterdam 1938   *Meesterwerken uit vier eeuwen, 1400–1800*, Boymans Museum, Rotterdam, 25/6–15/10/1938.

Rotterdam 1955   *Kunstschatten uit Nederlandse verzamelingen*, Boymans Museum, Rotterdam, 19/6–25/9/1955.

St. Louis 1947   *40 Masterpieces: A Loan Exhibition of Paintings from American Museums*, City Art Museum, St. Louis, 6/10–10/11/1947.

St. Petersburg 1909   *Les anciennes écoles de peinture dans les palais et collections privés russes* (organized by *Starye Gody*), St. Petersburg, 1909. (French cat. pub. Brussels, 1910).

St. Petersburg–Atlanta 1975   *Dutch Life in the Golden Century. An Exhibition of Seventeenth Century Dutch Paintings of Daily Life* (essay and notes by F. Robinson), Museum of Fine Arts, St. Petersburg, 21/1–2/3/1975; High Museum of Art, Atlanta, 4/4–4/5/1975.

San Francisco 1938   *Exhibition of Paintings by Old Masters lent by Schaeffer Galleries*, San Francisco Museum, San Francisco, March 1938.

San Francisco 1939   *Masterworks of Five Centuries. Golden Gate Exposition*, San Francisco, 1939.

San Francisco–Toledo–Boston 1966–7   *The Age of Rembrandt. An Exhibition of Dutch Paintings of the Seventeenth Century.* Palace of the Legion of Honor, San Francisco; The Toledo Museum of Art; Museum of Fine Arts, Boston, 1966–7.

Schaffhausen 1949 — *Rembrandt und seine Zeit*, Museum zu Allerheiligen, Schaffhausen, 10/4–2/10/1949.

Seattle 1962 — *Masterpieces of Art*, Seattle World's Fair, 21/4–4/10/1962.

Stockholm 1956 — *Fest och verdag i 1600—talets Nederländera*, Nationalmuseum, Stockholm, 1956.

Stockholm 1959 — *Konstskatter från Hollands Guldålder*, Nationalmuseum, Stockholm, 24/1–5/4/1959.

Stockholm 1967 — *Holländska Mästare i Svensk Ägo*, Nationalmuseum, Stockholm, 3/3–30/4/1967.

Tokyo–Kyoto 1968/9 — *The Age of Rembrandt. Dutch Paintings and Drawings of the 17th Century*, The National Museum of Western Art, Tokyo, 19/10–22/12/1969; Municipal Museum, Kyoto, 11/1–2/3/1969.

Tokyo 1969 — *Masterpieces from Britain*, Marubeni Art Gallery, Tokyo, 26/9–5/10/1969.

Toronto 1937 — *Trends in European Painting from the XIIIth to the XXth Century*, The Art Gallery of Toronto, Toronto, 15/10–15/11/1937.

Toronto 1950 — *Fifty Paintings by Old Masters*, The Art Gallery of Toronto, Toronto, 12/4–21/5/1950.

Valenciennes 1918 — *Geborgene Kunstwerke aus dem besetzten Nordfrankreich*, Museum, Valenciennes, 1918.

Vancouver 1957 — *Rembrandt to Van Gogh*, Art Gallery, Vancouver, 17/9–13/10/1957.

Vienna 1953 — *Oesterreichs Amerika-Ausstellung 'Kunstschätze aus Wien'*, Kunsthistorisches Museum, Vienna, 1953.

Waltham 1966 — *17th Century Paintings from the Low Countries* (cat. by C. Gilbert), Rose Art Museum, Brandeis U., Waltham, Mass., 27/2–27/3/1968.

Washington 1948 — *Paintings from the Berlin Museums*, National Gallery, Washington, D.C., 17/3–25/4/1948.

Washington–New York–San Francisco–Chicago 1949–50 — *Art Treasures from the Vienna Collections*, National Gallery of Art, Washington; Metropolitan Museum of Art, New York; M. H. de Young Memorial Museum, San Francisco; The Art Institute of Chicago, Chicago, 1949–50.

Washington 1961–2 — *Exhibition of Art Treasures for America from the Samuel H. Kress Collection*, National Gallery of Art, Washington, D.C., 10/12/1961–4/2/1962.

Wilmington 1951 — *Paintings by 17th Century Dutch Masters*, Wilmington Society of Fine Arts, Wilmington, Del., 1951.

Worthing 1952 — *Dutch and Flemish Paintings from the Collection of Mrs. Geoffrey Hart*, Art Gallery, Worthing, 19/7–30/8/1952.

Zurich 1946–7 — *Meisterwerke aus Oesterreich, Abteilung freie Kunst*, Kunsthaus, Zurich, 11/1946–3/1947.

Zurich 1953 — *Holländer des 17. Jahrhunderts*, Kunsthaus, Zurich, 4/11–20/12/1953.

Zurich 1958 — *Sammlung Emil G. Bührle*, Kunsthaus, Zurich, 7/6–30/9/1958.

Zurich 1962 — *Sammlung Sir Joseph Robinson 1840–1929. Werke europäischer Malerei vom 15. bis 19. Jahrhundert*, Kunsthaus, Zurich, 17/8–16/9/1962.

List of Collections

Concordance

In order to find paintings in the present catalogue which were mentioned by C. Hofstede de Groot (*Catalogue Raisonné*, 1907), look up his catalogue number in the left hand column; its number in the present catalogue will be found on the same line in the column headed 'HdG'. To find the catalogue numbers of paintings mentioned by W. R. Valentiner (*Pieter de Hooch*, 1929), follow the same procedure using the page number of his illustration and the new number will be found under the column headed 'Val'. Annotations are provided for works which do not appear in the present catalogue.

	HdG	Val		HdG	Val
Frontis.	—	I	28	112A and B	D. Vosmaer, Johnson Collection, Phila., no. 500
I	31	D33			
2	71	D1	29	143	—
3	51	D26	30	88	—
4	82	D16	31	88	24
5	50	D21	32	145	25
6	30	D34	33	61	26
7	71a	B13	34	49	D28
8	62	B14	35	87	38
9	H. van der Burch, see Val no. 211	2	36	18	D27
			37	J. Ochtervelt, formerly Van Horne Coll., Montreal; see BM52; S. Donahue Kuretsky, *Ochtervelt*, no. 67, fig. 137	23
10	48	D17			
11	32	8			
12	100	11			
13	72	4			
13a	C2	—			
13b	possibly 62	—			
14	31	B10	38	89	44
15	C6	7a	39	144	39
16	S. van Hoogstraten, Private Collection, Spain (photo RKD)	5	40	140	20
			41	46	21
			42	125	18
17	71	12	43	C19	35B
18	possibly 50	D18	44	C20	35A
19	131	D19	45	C21	36
20	D2	10	45a	C22	—
21	50B	B9	46	C25	45
21a	C12	—	47	C26	46
22	C13	D25	48	C27	27
23	C14	16	49	C33	30
23a	C15	—	50	C34	31
23b	C16	—	51	88	28
24	131	15	52	130	29
24a	C17	—	53	136	S. van Hoogstraten, Louvre, Paris, inv. no. RF 3722
24b	C18	—			
24c	31d	—			
25	52	D6	54	possibly B7A	33
26	124	B12	55	probably 144	34
27	73	14	56	C38	51

HdG	Val	HdG	Val	HdG	Val
57	C40	41	92a	C62	—	134	155	121
58	E. de Witte, Museum of Fine Arts, Boston, acc. n. 47.1314; see Manke cat. no. 243	40A	93	C65	84	135	110	78
			93a	C66	—	136	76	77
			94	129	85	136a	C83	—
59	L. de Jongh, Metropolitan Museum, New York, acc. no. 20.155.5	40B	95	79	95	136b	C84 or possibly 109	—
			96	64	D7	136c	C87	—
			96a	C. Bisschop, formerly dlr. L. Koetser, London; see Val no. 246, incorrectly as H. van der Burch		136d	C88	—
60	99	42				136e	C91	—
61	101	43				136f	C94	—
62	C30	19				136g	C242	—
63	C41	49	97	C67	D8	137	C98	138
64	98	10	98	C68	B7A	138	possibly 108 or 109	114
65	142	82	98a	C69	—	139	117	156
66	54	50	99	C70 or B3A	—	140	probably 115	143
67	141a	—	100	C71	—	141	68	144
68	145	—	101	C72	109	142	154	83
69	B. Fabritius, Gemäldegalerie, Berlin–Dahlem, no. 819B	52	101a	C73	—	142a	C107	—
			102	C74	110	143	139	117
			103	D5	108	144	possibly 158	133
			104	133	119	145	118	123
			105	C75	111	146	C113	132
70	C43	61	106	C251	80	147	C115	134
71	42	32	107	C76	107	147a	possibly 137	—
72	40A	55	108	S. van Hoogstraten, Louvre, Paris, inv. no. RF 3722	102	148	151	76
73	70	70				149	137	75
74	43	63				149a	C117	—
75	15	64	109	C77	103	150	C118	—
76	104	B6	109a	C78	—	150 above	—	105
77	132	58	110	149	145	150 below	—	106
78	40B	56	111	150	90	151	118	
78a	C44	—	112	103	104	151a	Probably Rijksmuseum, Amsterdam, cat. no. C151, as 'Manner of C. de Man'	—
79	probably 15	57	113	90	113			
80	79	59	114	102	112B			
81	C46	60a	115	148	131	151 above	—	158
82	J. Siberechts; see BM, 52	60B	116	C80 or possibly 149	130	151 below	—	162
			117	150	D12	152	B4A	116
83	C47	68	118	122	54	153	C123	137
84	40C	65	118a	C81 or possibly 122	—	153a	C125	—
85	157	66	119	C82	98	154	probably 152	136
85a	C48	—	119a	Not by P.d.H., Hessisches Landesmuseum, Darmstadt, no. 272 (incorrectly as H. van der Burch); see Val no. 241	—	155	162	124
86	40F	67				156	C126	100
87	74	81				157	53	125
88	Follower of I. Koedijk, (add. prov.) Sale Leinster et al. (H. Pritchard-Gorden), London, 14/5/1926, no. 96, as P.d.H. (photo Witt)	89				158	C127	157
			120	156	101	159	C128	69
			121	95	141	160	possibly 163	153
			122	134	140	161	H. van der Burch, (add. prov.) Sale C. O'Neil, London, 2/5/1838, no. 80, as P.d.H.; Sale Willys, New York, 25/10/1945, no. 18, as P.d.H. or H.v.d. Burch; see Val no. 249	159
89	D3	62	123	C135	99			
89a	C50	—	124	65	71			
89b	C51	—	125	109	71a			
89c	C52	—	126	68	72			
89d	Not by P.d.H.; see BM, 52, as C. de Man	—	127	115	79			
			128	117	73			
			129	77	74	161a	108	—
90	63	87	130	108	B4	161b	C245	—
91	D2	88	131	D6	120	162	C129	147
91a	C59	—	132	D7	118	163	C130	135
92	C60	94	133	146	93	164	C131	D13

HdG		Val	HdG		Val		HdG		Val
165	C132	146	194	55	—	226	B1		—
166	116	—	195	26	—	227	83		—
166 left	—	148	196	C221	—	228	probably 123		—
166 right	—	150	197	114	—	229	C204		—
167	C133	—	198	85	—	229a	C205		—
167 left	—	139	199	67	—	230	L. de Jongh, National	—
167 right	—	B3	199a	C138	—		Trust, Ascott House	
168	139	D15	199b	C139	—	231	P. Janssens Elinga;	
169	E. de Witte, Museum	D31	199c	C140	—		see BM 1947–8,	
	of Fine Arts, Montreal,		199d	C143	—		IV, 176, n. 15	
	cat. (1960), no. 41;		199e	C144	—	232	C206		
	see Manke cat. no.		199f	C145	—	233	C207		—
	241a		199g	C146	—	233a	C208		—
170	C134	D14	199h	C147	—	234	B5		—
171	138	155	199i	C148	—	235	D10		—
171a	155	—	199j	C151	—	235a	C209		—
172	D8	D29	199k	C154	—	235b	C210		—
172a	141	—	200	C161	—	236	H. van der Burch,	
173	94	D30	201	C162	—		Frick Collection,	
174	Unknown Flemish	—	202	Probably P. Janssens	—		New York, cat. (1968),	
	Artist, Johnson			Elinga; see BM			I, 147–8	
	Collection, Phila.,			1947–8, III, 162, n. 3		236a	102		—
	no. 502		203	C164	—	236b	C211		—
174 left	—	152	204	C166	—	236c	C212		—
174 right	—	151	204a	C167	—	236d	C213		—
175	160	—	205	C207	—	237	Not by P.d.H.; see	—
175 left	—	160	206	C. de Man, Musée	—		BM 1954, 85, n. 47,	
175 right	—	149		des Beaux-Arts,			fig. 14 as 'L. de	
176	107	161		Marseille			Jongh?'	
177	63	—	207	C170	—	237a	C214		—
178	118	—	207a	C173	—	238	P. Janssens Elinga;	—
179	69	—	207b	C174	—		no. 8 under HdG's	
180	66	—	208	C176	—		list of works wrongly	
181	Replica of N. Maes's	—	209	C177	—		attributed to De	
	Eavesdropper (Dienst		210	Probably P. Janssens	—		Hooch; see BM	
	Verspreide			Elinga; see BM			1947–8, III, 172, n. 10	
	Rijkskollekties); see			1947–8, III, 162, n. 3		238a	C215		—
	C. Brière-Misme, in		211	C182	—	238b	C216		—
	O–H, 45 (1950),		212	C184	—	239	C136		—
	237, n. 3		213	C185	—	240	97		—
182	84	—	214	C186	—	240a	C217		—
183	29	—	215	C197	—	240b	C218		—
184	106	—	216	C187	—	240c	C219		—
185	H. van der Burch,	—	216a	B6	—	240d	C220		—
	Frick Collection,		217	H. van der Burch;	—	240e	H. van der Burch,	—
	New York, cat.			see Val no. 250			(add. prov.) Sale	
	(1968), I, 147–8		218	159	—		C. O'Neil, London,	
186	83	—	219	possibly 133	—		2/5/1838, no. 80, as	
187	56	—	220	C192	—		P.d.H.; Sale Willys,	
188	Not by P.d.H.; see	—	221	B7A	—		New York, 25/10/1945,	
	Val no. 237, as H. van		222	C193	—		no. 18, as P.d.H. or	
	der Burch		222a	C194	—		H.v.d. Burch; see Val	
189	Delft School, National	—	223	C196	—		no. 249	
	Gallery, London,		223a	C190	—	240f	C222		—
	no. 2552		223b	C191	—	240g	C223		—
190	153	—	223c	C199	—	241	possibly 43		—
191	121	—	224	C200	—	242	75		—
192	19	—	225	C201	—	243	C224		—
193	147	—	225a	C202	—	243a	75		—

HdG		Val		HdG		Val		HdG		Val
244	C225	—	268	27	—	302	C203	—
245	H. van der Burch, Dienst Verspreide Rijkskollekties, no. NK2422	—	269	14	—	303	37	—
			270	B9	—	304	L. de Jongh, Metropolitan Museum, New York, acc. no. 20.155.5	—
			271	6	—			
			272	10	—			
246	Not by P.d.H.; see Val no. 195 (right), as Follower of P.d.H.	—	273	D25	—			
			274	D9	—	305	41	—
			275	128	—	306	23	—
246a	16	—	275a	C232	—	306a	C246	—
247	Circle of L. de Jongh, (add. prov.) Sale Pelletier, Paris 28/4/1870, no. 16, as P.d.H. (= HdG no. 285); Sale Jhr. van P. et al., Amsterdam, 31/10/1916, no. 29, as Sch. of P.d.H.; see Pleitzsch 1960, fig. 83, as L. de Jongh	—	275b	C233	—	307	D32	—
			276	111	—	308	60A	—
			277	C237, possibly D24	—	309	38	—
			278	7	—	309a	C247	—
			279	126	—	309b	C248	—
			279a	C239	—	310	D27	—
			280	C240	—	311	C249	—
			280a	C241	—	312	D27	—
			281	111	—	313	60B	—
			282	2	—	314	C250	—
			283	J. Ochtervelt, Museum Mayer van den Bergh, Antwerp, no. 895	—	315	C251	—
248	C226	—				315a	C252	—
249	H. van der Burch, Frick Collection, New York, cat. (1968), I, 147–8	—				315b	C253	—
			284	E. de Witte, National Gallery, London, no. 3682; see Manke cat. no. 22a	—	316	L. de Jongh, Natalie Labia Collection, Fig. 61	—
250	C135	—	285	Circle of L. de Jongh, (add. prov.) Sale Pelletier, Paris, 28/4/1870, no. 16, as P.d.H. (= HdG no. 285); Sale Jhr. van P. et al., Amsterdam, 31/10/1916, no. 29, as Sch. of P.d.H.; see Plietzsch 1960, fig. 83, as L. de Jongh	—	317	D. Vosmaer, Johnson Collection, Phila., no. 500	—
251	47a	—						
252	C227	—				318	C254	—
253	22	—				319	J. Vrel, Johnson Collection Phila., no. 542	—
254	28	—						
255	58	—						
256	H. van der Burch; see Val no. 242	—				320	C260	—
						321	24	—
257	H. van der Burch, (add. prov.) Sale, London, 30/11/1973, no. 83, as H. van der Burch; see Val no. 223	—				322	C262	—
						322a	92	—
			286	59	—	323	L. de Jongh, signed and dated 1661, Virginia Museum of Fine Arts, Richmond, cat. (1966), no. 90	—
			287	20	—			
257a	C228	—	288	135	—			
258	96	—	289	E. Bourse; see BM 1954, 54	—			
259	C229	—				324	C263	—
260	C230	—	290	44	—	324a	C264	—
261	11	D11	291	34	—	324b	C265	—
262	120	18a	292	36	—	325	C251	—
262a	L. de Jongh, Frölich Coll., Vienna, 1938; see Val no. 186	—	293	22	—	326	C266	—
			294	39	—	327	C267	—
			295	35A	—	328	D36	—
263	11 bis	128	296	37	—	328a	C279	—
264	25	—	297	35B	—	328b	C282	—
264a	D23	—	298	21	—	328c	C283	—
265	D24	—	299	33	—	328d	C291	—
266	119	—	300	probably 18a	—	329	By or after Jan Steen; see BM, 52	—
267	D18	—	301	161	—			

Index of Names